Professional SQL Server 2000 Data Warehousing with Analysis Services

Tony Bain

Mike Benkovich

Robin Dewson

Sam Ferguson

Christopher Graves

Terrence J. Joubert

Denny Lee

Mark Scott

Robert Skoglund

Paul Turley

Sakhr Youness

Wrox Press Ltd. ®

Professional SQL Server 2000 Data Warehousing with Analysis Services

Published by Wrox Press Ltd,
Arden House, 1102 Warwick Road, Acocks Green,
Birmingham, B27 6BH, UK
Printed in Canada
ISBN 1-861005-40-7

Trademark Acknowledgements

Wrox has endeavored to provide trademark information about all the companies and products mentioned in this book by the appropriate use of capitals. However, Wrox cannot guarantee the accuracy of this information.

Credits

Authors
Tony Bain
Mike Benkovich
Robin Dewson
Sam Ferguson
Christopher Graves
Terrence J. Joubert
Denny Lee
Mark Scott
Robert Skoglund
Paul Turley
Sakhr Youness

Technical Architect
Catherine Alexander

Technical Editors
Alessandro Ansa
Victoria Blackburn
Allan Jones
Gareth Oakley
Douglas Paterson

Author Agent
Avril Corbin

Project Administrator
Chandima Nethisinghe

Category Manager
Sarah Drew

Illustrations
Natalie O'Donnell

Cover
Dawn Chellingworth

Proof Reader
Chris Smith

Index
Fiona Murray

Technical Reviewers
Christine Adeline
Sheldon Barry
Michael Boerner
Jim W. Brzowski
James R. De Carli
Michael Cohen
Paul Churchill
Chris Crane
Edgar D'Andrea
John Fletcher
Damien Foggon
Hope Hatfield
Ian Herbert
Brian Hickey
Terrence J. Joubert
Brian Knight
Don Lee
Dianna Leech
Gary Nicholson
J. Boyd Nolan, PE
Sumit Pal
Ryan Payet
Tony Proudfoot
Dan Read
Trevor Scott
Charles Snell Jr.
John Stallings
Chris Thibodeaux
Maria Zhang

Production Manager
Liz Toy

Production Coordinator
Emma Eato

About the Authors

Tony Bain

Tony Bain (MCSE, MCSD, MCDBA) is a senior database consultant for SQL Services in Wellington, New Zealand. While Tony has experience with various database platforms, such as RDB and Oracle, for over four years SQL Server has been the focus of his attention. During this time he has been responsible for the design, development and administration of numerous SQL Server-based solutions for clients in such industries as utilities, property, government, technology, and insurance.

Tony is passionate about database technologies especially when they relate to enterprise availability and scalability. Tony spends a lot of his time talking and writing about various database topics and in the few moments he has spare Tony hosts a SQL Server resource site (www.sqlserver.co.nz).

Dedication

I must thank Linda for her continued support while I work on projects such as this, and also our beautiful girls Laura and Stephanie who are my motivation. Also a big thank-you to Wrox for the opportunity to participate in the interesting projects that have been thrown my way, with special thanks in particular to Doug, Avril, and Chandy.

Mike Benkovich

Mike Benkovich is a partner in the Minneapolis-based consulting firm Applied Technology Group. Despite his degree in Aerospace Engineering, he has found that developing software is far more interesting and rewarding. His interests include integration of relational databases within corporate models, application security and encryption, and large-scale data replication systems.

Mike is a proud father, inspired husband, annoying brother, and dedicated son who thanks his lucky stars for having a family that gives freely their support during this project. Mike can be reached at mbenko@atgmn.com.

Robin Dewson

Robin started out on the Sinclair ZX80 but soon progressed and built the basis of a set of programs for his father's post office business on later Sinclair computers. He ended up studying computers at the Scottish College of Textiles where he was instilled with the belief that mainframes were the future. After many sorry years, he eventually saw the error of his ways, and started to use Clipper, FoxPro, and then Visual Basic. Robin is currently working on a system called "Vertigo", replacing the old trading system called "Kojak", and is glad to be able to give up sucking lollipops and looking forward to allowing his hair to grow back on his head. He has been with a large US Investment bank in the City of London for over five years and he owes a massive debt to Annette "They wouldn't put me in charge if I didn't know what I was doing" Kelly, Daniel "Dream Sequence" Tarbotton, Andy "I don't really know, I've only been here for a week", and finally, Jack "You will never work in the City again" Mason.

Thanks to everyone at Wrox, but especially Cath Alexander, Cilmara Lion, Sarah Drew, Douglas Paterson, Claire Brittle, Ben Egan, Avril Corbin, Rob Hesketh, and Chandy Nethisinghe for different reasons throughout the time, but probably most importantly for introducing me to Tequila slammers (!). Also thanks to my mum and dad for finding and sending me to the two best colleges ever and pointing me on the right road, my father-in-law who until he passed away was a brilliant inspiration to my children, my mother-in-law for once again helping Julie with the children. Also a quick thank-you from my wife, to Charlie and Debbie at Sea Palling for selling the pinball machine!!! But my biggest thanks as ever go to Julie, the most perfect mother the kids could have, and to Scott, Cameron, and Ellen for not falling off the jet-ski when I go too fast.

'Up the Blues'

Sam Ferguson

Sam Ferguson is an IT Consultant with API Software, a growing IT Solutions company based in Glasgow, Scotland. Sam works in various fields but specializes in Visual Basic, SQL Server, XML, and all things .Net.

Sam has been married to the beautiful Jacqueline for two months and happily lives next door to sister-in-law Susie and future brother-in-law Martin.

Dedication
I would like to dedicate my contribution to this book to Susie and Martin, two wonderful people who will have a long and happy life together.

Christopher Graves

Chris Graves is President of RapidCF, a ColdFusion development company in Canton Connecticut (www.rapidcf.com). Chris leads projects with Oracle 8i and SQL Server 2000 typically coupled to web-based solutions. Chris earned an honors Bachelor of Science degree from the US Naval Academy (class of 93, the greatest class ever), and was a VGEP graduate scholar. After graduating, Chris served as a US Marine Corps Officer in 2nd Light Armored Reconnaissance Battalion, and 2nd ANGLICO where he was a jumpmaster. In addition to a passion for efficient CFML, Chris enjoys skydiving and motorcycling, and he continues to lead Marines in the Reserves. His favorite pastime, however, is spending time with his two daughters Courtney and Claire, and his lovely wife Greta.

Terrence J. Joubert

Terrence is a Software Engineer working with Victoria Computer Services (VCS), a Seychelles-based IT solutions provider. He also works as a freelance Technical Reviewer for several publishing companies. As a developer and aspiring author, Terrence enjoys reading about and experimenting with new technologies, especially the Microsoft .Net products. He is currently doing a Bachelor of Science degree by correspondence and hopes that his IT career spans development, research, and writing. When he is not around computers he can be found relaxing on one of the pure, white, sandy beaches of the Seychelles or hiking along the green slopes of its mountains.

He describes himself as a Libertarian – he believes that humans should mind their own business and just leave their fellow brothers alone in a culture of Liberty.

Denny Lee

Denny Lee is the Lead OLAP Architect at digiMine, Inc. (Bellevue, WA), a leading analytic services company specializing in data warehousing, data mining, and business intelligence. His primary focus is delivering powerful, scalable, enterprise-level OLAP solutions that provide customers with the business intelligence insights needed to act on their data. Before joining digiMine, Lee was as a Lead Developer at the Microsoft Corporation where he built corporate reporting solutions utilizing OLAP services against corporate data warehouses, and took part in developing one of the first OLAP solutions. Interestingly, he is a graduate of McGill University in Physiology and prior to Microsoft, was a Statistical Analyst at the Fred Hutchison Cancer Research Center in one of the largest HIV/AIDS research projects.

Mark Scott

Mark Scott serves as a consultant for RDA, a provider of advanced technology consulting services. He develops multi-tier, data-centric web applications. He implements a wide variety of Microsoft-based technologies, with special emphasis on SQL Server and Analysis Services. He is a Microsoft Certified System Engineer + Internet, Solution Developer, Database Administrator, and Trainer. He holds A+, Network+ and CTT+ certifications from COMPTIA.

Robert Skoglund

Robert is President and Managing Director of RcS Consulting Services, Inc., a Business Intelligence, Database Consulting, and Training Company based in Tampa, Florida, USA. Robert has over 10 years experience developing and implementing a variety of business applications using Microsoft SQL Server (version 1.0 through version 2000), and is currently developing data warehouses using Microsoft's SQL Server and Analysis Services. Robert's certifications include Microsoft's Certified Systems Engineer (1997), Solution Developer (1995), and Trainer (1994). He is also an associate member of The Data Warehousing Institute. Additionally, Robert provides certified training services to Microsoft Certified Technical Education Centers nationwide and internationally. Robert also develops customized NT and SQL courses and presentations for both technical and managerial audiences.

Robert is proud to be an Eagle Scout and an avid chess player. He can be reached at rskoglund@rcs-consulting-inc.com or by visiting www.rcs-consulting-inc.com.

Paul Turley

Paul is a Senior Instructor and Consultant for SQL Soft+ Training and Consulting in Beaverton, Oregon and Bellevue, Washington. He specializes in database solution development, software design, programming, and project management frameworks. He has been working with Microsoft development tools including Visual Basic, SQL Server and Access since 1994. He was a contributing author for the Wrox Press book, *Professional Access 2000 Programming* and has authored several technical courseware publications.

A Microsoft Certified Solution Developer (MCSD) since 1996, Paul has worked on a number of large-scale consulting projects for prominent clients including HP, Nike, and Microsoft. He has worked closely with Microsoft Consulting Services and is one of few instructors certified to teach the Microsoft Solution Framework for solution design and project management.

Paul lives in Vancouver, Washington with his wife, Sherri, and four children – Krista, 4; Sara, 5; Rachael, 10; and Josh, 12; a dog, two cats, and a bird. Somehow, he finds time to write technical publications. He and his family enjoy camping, cycling and hiking in the beautiful Pacific Northwest. He and his son also design and build competition robotics.

Dedication

Thanks most of all to my wife, Sherri and my kids for their patience and understanding.

To the staff and instructors at SQL Soft, a truly unique group of people (I mean that in the best possible way). It's good to be part of the team. Thanks to Douglas Laudenschlager at Microsoft for going above and beyond the call of duty.

Sakhr Youness

Sakhr Youness is a Professional Engineer (PE) and a Microsoft Certified Solution Developer (MCSD) and Product Specialist (MCPS) who has extensive experience in data modeling, client-server, database, and enterprise application development. Mr. Youness is a senior software architect at Commerce One, a leader in the business-to-business (B2B) area. He is working in one of the largest projects for Commerce One involving building an online exchange for the auto industry. He designed and developed or participated in developing a number of client-server applications related to the automotive, banking, healthcare, and engineering industries. Some of the tools used in these projects include: Visual Basic, Microsoft Office products, Active Server Pages (ASP), Microsoft Transaction Server (MTS), SQL Server, Java, and Oracle.

Mr. Youness is a co-author of *SQL Server 7.0 Programming Unleashed* which was published by Sams in June 1999. He also wrote the first edition of this book, *Professional Data Warehousing with SQL Server 7.0 and OLAP Services*. He is also proud to say that, in this edition, he had help from many brilliant authors who helped write numerous chapters of this book, adding to it a great deal of value and benefit, stemming from their experiences and knowledge. Many of these authors have other publications and, in some cases, wrote books about SQL Server.

Mr. Youness also provided development and technical reviews of many books for MacMillan Technical Publishing and Wrox Press. These books mostly involved SQL Server, Oracle, Visual Basic, and Visual Basic for Applications (VBA).

Mr. Youness loves learning new technologies and is currently focused on using the latest innovations in his projects.

Mr. Youness enjoys his free time with his lovely wife, Nada, and beautiful daughter, Maya. He also enjoys long-distance swimming and watching sporting events.

Data Warehouse

Table of Contents

Table of Contents

Table of Contents

Table of Contents

Table of Contents

Table of Contents

Table of Contents

xiii

Table of Contents

Table of Contents

Data Warehouse

Introduction

It has only been roughly 20 months since the first edition of this book was released. That edition covered Microsoft data warehousing and OLAP Services as it related to the revolutionary Microsoft SQL Server 7.0. Approximately seven months after that, Microsoft released its new version of SQL Server, SQL Server 2000. This version included many enhancements on an already great product. Many of these came in the area of data warehousing and OLAP Services, which was renamed as "Analysis Services". Therefore, it was important to produce an updated book, covering these new areas, as well as present the original material in a new, more mature, way. We hope that as you read this book, you will find the answers to most of the questions you may have regarding Analysis Services and Microsoft data warehousing technologies.

So, what are the new areas in Microsoft OLAP and data warehousing that made it worth creating this new edition? We are not going to mention the enhancements to the main SQL Server product; rather, we will focus on enhancements in the areas of Data Transformation and Analysis Services. These can be summarized as:

❑ **Cube enhancements**: new cube types have been introduced, such as distributed partitioned cubes, real-time cubes, and linked cubes. Improved cube processing, drillthrough, properties selections, etc. are also among the great enhancements in the area of OLAP cubes.

❑ **Dimension enhancements**: new dimension and hierarchy types, such as changing dimensions, write-enabled dimensions, dependent dimensions, and ragged dimensions have been added. Many enhancements have also been introduced to virtual dimensions, custom members, and rollup formulae.

❑ **Data mining models** are introduced for the first time, allowing the transition from the collection of information with OLAP to the extraction of knowledge from this information by studying patterns, relations, and trends. Two mining models are introduced: the decision tree and the clustering model. These data mining enhancements extend to the areas of Multidimensional Expressions language (MDX) and Data Transformation Services (DTS). New MDX functions that relate to data mining have been added, as well as the inclusion of a new data mining task, adding to the already rich library of out-of-the-box DTS tasks.

- ❑ Other enhancements include improvements in the security area, allowing for cell-level security, and additional authentication methods, such as HTTP authentication.

- ❑ OLAP clients can now connect to Analysis servers through HTTP or HTTPS protocols via the Internet Information Services (IIS) web server. Allocated write-backs have also been introduced in this area, as well as the introduction of data mining clients.

- ❑ The long-awaited MDX builder has also been introduced in this version, allowing developers to easily write MDX queries without having to worry about syntactical errors, thus enabling them to focus on getting the job done.

- ❑ The introduction of XML for Analysis Services.

- ❑ Enhancements of the programming APIs that come with Analysis Services, such as ADO-MD and DSO objects.

- ❑ Microsoft has added many new tasks to DTS, making it a great tool for transformations – not only for data being imported into a SQL Server database, but also for any RDBMS. For instance:

  - ❑ DTS packages can now be saved as Visual Basic files
  - ❑ Packages can run asynchronously
  - ❑ Packages can send messages to each other
  - ❑ Packages can be executed jointly in one atomic transaction
  - ❑ Parameterized queries can now be used in DTS packages
  - ❑ Global variables can now be used to pass values among packages
  - ❑ There are new logging capabilities
  - ❑ We can use a customizable multi-phase data pump

This is only a partial list of the enhancements to Analysis Services and DTS. Many enhancements in SQL Server itself have led to a further increase in the support for data warehousing and data marts. These include the enhanced management and administration (new improved tools like SQL Server Manager, Query Analyzer, and Profiler), and the support for bigger hardware and storage space.

Is This Book For You?

If you have already used SQL Server 7.0 OLAP Services, or are familiar with it, you will see that this book adds a great value to your knowledge with the discussion of the enhancements to these services and tools.

If you are a database administrator or developer who is anxious to learn about the new OLAP and data warehousing support in SQL Server 2000, then this book is for you. It does not really matter if you have had previous experience with SQL Server, or not. However, this book is not about teaching you how to use SQL Server. Many books are available on the market that would be more appropriate for this purpose, such as *Professional SQL Server 2000 Programming* (Wrox Press, IBSN 1-861004-48-6) and *Beginning SQL Server 2000 Programming* (Wrox Press, ISBN 1-861005-23-7). This book specifically handles OLAP, data warehousing, and data mining support in SQL Server, giving you all you need to know to learn these concepts, and become able to use SQL Server to build such solutions.

If you have experience in data warehousing and OLAP using non-Microsoft tools, but would like to learn about the added support for these kinds of applications in SQL Server, then this book is also for you.

If you are an IS professional who does not have experience in data warehousing and OLAP services, then this book will help you understand these concepts. It will also provide you with the knowledge of one of the easiest tools to accomplish these tasks nowadays, so that you can instantly start working in the field.

If you are a client-server application developer or designer who has worked on developing many online transaction processing (OLTP) systems, then this book will show you the differences between such systems and OLAP systems. It will also teach you how to leverage your skills in developing highly normalized databases for your OLTP systems to develop dimensional databases used as backends for OLAP systems.

What Does the Book Cover?

This book covers a wide array of topics, and includes many examples to enrich the content and facilitate your understanding of key topics.

The book starts with an introduction to the world of data modeling, with emphasis on dimensional data analysis, and also covers, at length, the different aspects of the Microsoft Analysis Services: OLAP database storage (MOLAP, ROLAP, HOLAP), OLAP cubes, dimensions and measures, and how they are built from within Analysis Services's front end, Analysis Manager.

There are two chapters that discuss Microsoft Data Transformation Services (DTS), and how it can be used in the Microsoft data warehousing scheme (Chapters 7 and 8). The new Multidimensional Expressions (MDX) language that was introduced with the first release of Microsoft OLAP is discussed in Chapters 10 and 11.

Client tools are also discussed, in particular, the PivotTable Service (introduced in Chapter 12) and its integration with Microsoft OLAP and other Microsoft tools, such as Microsoft Excel, and development languages such as Visual Basic and ASP.

The book also covers the new data mining features added to SQL Server Analysis Services. It describes the new mining models, the client applications, related MDX functions, DTS package, and other programmable APIs related to data mining. Data mining is covered in Chapters 16 and 17.

Other topics covered in the book include an introduction to data marts and how these concepts fit with the overall Microsoft data warehousing strategy; web housing and the BIA initiative, and using English Query with Analysis Services. Security, optimization, and administration issues are examined in the last three chapters of the book.

Please note that a range of appendices covering installation; MDX functions and statements; ADO MD; and XML and SOAP are also available from our web site: www.wrox.com.

We hope that by reading this book you will get a very good handle on the Microsoft data warehousing framework and strategy, and will be able to apply most of this to your specific projects.

What Do You Need to Use to Use This Book?

All you need to use this book is to have basic understanding of data management. Some background in data warehousing would help too, but is not essential. You need to have SQL Server 2000 and Microsoft Analysis Services installed. Chapters 12 to 15 that center around the use of client tools require Microsoft Office XP and access to Visual Studio 6. Most of all, you need to have the desire to learn this technology that is new to the Microsoft world.

Conventions

We've used a number of different styles of text and layout in this book to help differentiate between the different kinds of information. Here are examples of the styles we used and an explanation of what they mean.

Code has several fonts. If it's a word that we're talking about in the text – for example, when discussing a for (...) loop, it's in this font. If it's a block of code that can be typed as a program and run, then it's also in a gray box:

```
for (int i = 0; i < 10; i++)
{
    Console.WriteLine(i);
}
```

Sometimes we'll see code in a mixture of styles, like this:

```
for (int i = 0; i < 10; i++)
{
    Console.Write("The next number is: ");
    Console.WriteLine(i);
}
```

In cases like this, the code with a white background is code we are already familiar with; the line highlighted in gray is a new addition to the code since we last looked at it.

Advice, hints, and background information comes in this type of font.

> **Important pieces of information come in boxes like this.**

Bullets appear indented, with each new bullet marked as follows:

❑ **Important Words** are in a bold type font

❑ Words that appear on the screen, or in menus like the File or Window, are in a similar font to the one you would see on a Windows desktop

❑ Keys that you press on the keyboard like *Ctrl* and *Enter*, are in italics

Customer Support

We always value hearing from our readers, and we want to know what you think about this book: what you liked, what you didn't like, and what you think we can do better next time. You can send us your comments, either by returning the reply card in the back of the book, or by e-mail to feedback@wrox.com. Please be sure to mention the book title in your message.

How to Download the Sample Code for the Book

When you visit the Wrox site, http://www.wrox.com/, simply locate the title through our Search facility or by using one of the title lists. Click on Download in the Code column, or on Download Code on the book's detail page.

The files that are available for download from our site have been archived using WinZip. When you have saved the attachments to a folder on your hard-drive, you need to extract the files using a decompression program such as WinZip or PKUnzip. When you extract the files, the code is usually extracted into chapter folders. When you start the extraction process, ensure your software (WinZip, PKUnzip, etc.) is set to Use Folder Names.

Errata

We've made every effort to make sure that there are no errors in the text or in the code. However, no one is perfect and mistakes do occur. If you find an error in one of our books, like a spelling mistake or a faulty piece of code, we would be very grateful for feedback. By sending in errata you may save another reader hours of frustration, and of course, you will be helping us provide even higher quality information. Simply e-mail the information to support@wrox.com; your information will be checked and if correct, posted to the errata page for that title, or used in subsequent editions of the book.

To find errata on the web site, go to http://www.wrox.com/, and simply locate the title through our Advanced Search or title list. Click on the Book Errata link, which is below the cover graphic on the book's detail page.

E-mail Support

If you wish to directly query a problem in the book with an expert who knows the book in detail then e-mail support@wrox.com, with the title of the book and the last four numbers of the ISBN in the subject field of the e-mail. A typical e-mail should include the following things:

❑ The **title of the book**, the **last four digits of the ISBN**, and the **page number** of the problem in the Subject field.

❑ Your **name**, **contact information**, and the **problem** in the body of the message.

We **won't** send you junk mail. We need the details to save your time and ours. When you send an e-mail message, it will go through the following chain of support:

❑ Customer Support – Your message is delivered to our customer support staff, who are the first people to read it. They have files on most frequently asked questions and will answer anything general about the book or the web site immediately.

❑ Editorial – Deeper queries are forwarded to the technical editor responsible for that book. They have experience with the programming language or particular product, and are able to answer detailed technical questions on the subject. Once an issue has been resolved, the editor can post the errata to the web site.

❑ The Authors – Finally, in the unlikely event that the editor cannot answer your problem, he or she will forward the request to the author. We do try to protect the author from any distractions to their writing; however, we are quite happy to forward specific requests to them. All Wrox authors help with the support on their books. They will e-mail the customer and the editor with their response, and again all readers should benefit.

The Wrox Support process can only offer support on issues that are directly pertinent to the content of our published title. Support for questions that fall outside the scope of normal book support is provided via the community lists of our http://p2p.wrox.com/ forum.

p2p.wrox.com

For author and peer discussion join the P2P mailing lists. Our unique system provides **programmer to programmer**™ contact on mailing lists, forums, and newsgroups, all in addition to our one-to-one e-mail support system. If you post a query to P2P, you can be confident that it is being examined by the many Wrox authors and other industry experts who are present on our mailing lists. At p2p.wrox.com you will find a number of different lists that will help you, not only while you read this book, but also as you develop your own applications.

Particularly appropriate to this book are the sql_language, sql_server and sql_server_dts lists.

To subscribe to a mailing list just follow these steps:

1. Go to http://p2p.wrox.com/

2. Choose the appropriate category from the left menu bar

3. Click on the mailing list you wish to join

4. Follow the instructions to subscribe and fill in your e-mail address and password

5. Reply to the confirmation e-mail you receive

6. Use the subscription manager to join more lists and set your e-mail preferences

Data Warehouse

Analysis Services in SQL Server 2000 – An Overview

Data warehousing is an expanding subject area with more and more companies realizing the potential of a well set up OLAP system. Such a system provides a corporation with the means to analyze data in order to aid tasks such as targeting sales, projecting growth in specific areas, or even calculating general trends, all of which can give it an edge over its competition. Analysis Services provides the tools that you as a developer can master, with the aid of this book, so that you become a key player in your corporation's future.

Before we delve into Analysis Services, this chapter will introduce you to general OLAP and data-warehousing concepts, with a particular focus on the Microsoft contribution to this field. To this end we will consider the following:

❑ What is Online Analytical Processing (OLAP), what are its benefits, and who will benefit from it most?

❑ What is data warehousing, and how does it differ from OLAP and operational databases?

❑ What are Online transactional processing (OLTP) Systems?

❑ Challenges rising from the flood of data generated at the corporate and departmental levels resulting in need for decision support and OLAP Systems

❑ What is data mining and how does it relate to decision support systems and business intelligence?

❑ How SQL Server 2000 promises to play a big role in meeting these challenges, through the introduction of new features to support data transformation, OLAP systems, data warehouses and data marts, and data mining

What is OLAP?

Let's answer the first question you have in mind about On-Line Analytical Processing (OLAP), which is simply, "What is OLAP?"

Transaction-handling (operational) databases such as those handling order processing or share dealing, have gained great popularity since the mid 1980s. Many corporations adopted these databases for their mission-critical data needs. Almost all of these operational databases are relational. Many database vendors supported relational databases and produced state-of-the-art products that made using such databases easy, efficient, and practical.

As a result, many corporations migrated their data to relational databases, which were mainly used in areas where transactions are needed, such as operation and control activities. An example would be a bank using a relational database to control the daily operations of customers transferring, withdrawing, or depositing funds in their accounts. The unique properties of relational databases, with referential integrity, good fault recovery, support for a large number of small transactions, etc. contributed to their widespread use.

The concept of data warehouses began to arise as organizations found it necessary to use the data they collected through their operational systems for future planning and decision-making. Assuming that they used the operational systems, they needed to build queries that summarized the data and fed management reports. Such queries, however, would be extremely slow because they usually summarize large amounts of data, while sharing the database engine with every day operations, which in turn adversely affected the performance of operational systems. The solution was, therefore, to separate the data used for reporting and decision making from the operational systems. Hence, data warehouses were designed and built to house this kind of data so that it can be used later in the strategic planning of the enterprise.

Relational database vendors, such as Microsoft, Oracle, Sybase, and IBM, now market their databases as tools for building data warehouses, and include capabilities to do so with their packages. Note that many other smaller database vendors also include warehousing within their products as data warehousing has become more accepted as an integral part of a database, rather than an addition. Data accumulated in a data warehouse is used to produce informational reports that answer questions such as "who?" or "what?" about the original data. As an illustration of this, if we return to the bank example above, a data warehouse can be used to answer a question like "which branch yielded the maximum profits for the third quarter of this fiscal year?" Or it could be used to answer a question like "what was the net profit for the third quarter of this fiscal year per region?"

While data warehouses are usually based on relational technology, OLAP enables analysts, managers, and executives to gain insight into data through fast, consistent, interactive access to a wide variety of possible views of information. OLAP transforms raw data to useful information so that it reflects the real factors affecting or enhancing the line of business of the enterprise.

A basic advantage of OLAP systems is that they can be used to study different scenarios by asking the question "What if?" An example of such a scenario in the bank example would be, "What if the bank charges an extra $1.00 for every automatic teller machine (ATM) transaction performed by a user who is not a current bank customer? How would that affect the bank revenue?" This unique feature makes OLAP a great decision making tool that could help determine the best courses of action for the company's business. OLAP and data warehouses complement each other. As you will see later in the book, the data warehouse stores and manages the data, while OLAP converts the stored data into useful information. OLAP techniques may range from simple navigation and browsing of the data (often referred to as '**slicing and dicing**'), to more serious analyses, such as time-series and complex modeling.

Raw data is collected, reorganized, stored, and managed into a data warehouse that follows a special schema, whereupon OLAP converts this data to information that helps make good use of it. Advanced OLAP analyses and other tools, such as data mining (explained in detail in Chapters 16 and 17), can further convert the information into powerful knowledge that allows us to generate predictions of the future performance of an entity, based on data gathered in the past.

E.F. Codd, the inventor of relational databases and one of the greatest database researchers, first coined the term OLAP in a white paper entitled *"Providing OLAP to User Analysis: An IT Mandate"*, published in 1993. The white paper defined 12 rules for OLAP applications. Nigel Pendse and Richard Creeth of the OLAP Report (http://www.olapreport.com/DatabaseExplosion.htm) simplified the definition of OLAP applications as those that should deliver fast analysis of shared multidimensional information (FASMI). This statement means:

- ❑ **Fast**: the user of these applications is an interactive user who expects the delivery of the information they need at a fairly constant rate. Most queries should be delivered to the user in five seconds or less, and many of these queries will be *ad hoc* queries as opposed to rigidly predefined reports. For instance, the end user will have the flexibility of combining several attributes in order to generate a report based on the data in the data warehouse.

- ❑ **Analysis**: OLAP applications should perform basic numerical and statistical analysis of the data. These calculations could be pre-defined by the application developer, or defined by the user as *ad hoc* queries. It is the ability to conduct such calculations that makes OLAP so powerful, allowing the addition of hundreds, thousands, or even millions of records to come up with the hidden information within the piles of raw data.

- ❑ **Shared**: the data delivered by OLAP applications should be shared across a large user population, as seen in the current trend to web-enable OLAP applications allowing the generation of OLAP reports over the Internet.

- ❑ **Multidimensional**: OLAP applications are based on data warehouses or data marts built on multi-dimensional database schemas, which is an essential characteristic of OLAP.

- ❑ **Information**: OLAP applications should be able to access all the data and information necessary and relevant for the application. To give an example, in a banking scenario, an OLAP application working with annual interest, or statement reprints, would be required to access historical transactions in order to calculate and process the correct information. Not only is the data likely to be located in different sources, but its volume is liable to be large.

What are the Benefits of OLAP?

OLAP tools can improve the productivity of the whole organization by focusing on what is essential for its growth, and by transferring the responsibility for the analysis to the operational parts of the organization.

In February 1998, *ComputerWorld* magazine reported that Office Depot, one of the largest office equipment suppliers in the US, significantly improved its sales due to the improved on-line analytical processing (OLAP) tools it used directly in its different stores. This result came at a time when the financial markets expected Office Depot's sales to drop after a failed merger with one of its competitors, Staples. *ComputerWorld* reported that the improved OLAP tools used by Office Depot helped increase sales a respectable 4% for the second half of 1997. For example, Office Depot found that it was carrying too much fringe stock in the wrong stores. Therefore, the retail stores narrowed their assortment of PCs from 22 to 12 products. That helped the company eliminate unnecessary inventory and avoid costly markdowns on equipment that was only gathering dust.

*It seems that the 80/20 rule applies to many aspects in life. One of these aspects has to do with retailers. Retailers usually make most of their profits (around 80%) from the sales of around 20% of the goods they stock. Goods that fall into the 80% with least sale and profit potential are usually referred to as **fringe stock**.*

The Office Depot example is a strong indication of the benefits that can be gained by using OLAP tools. By moving the analyses to the store level, the company empowered the store managers to make decisions that made each of these stores profitable. The inherent flexibility of OLAP systems allowed the individual stores to become self-sufficient. Store managers no longer rely on corporate information systems (IS) department to model their business for them.

Developers also benefit from using the right OLAP software. Although it is possible to build an OLAP system using software designed for transaction processing or data collection, it is certainly not a very efficient use of developer time. By using software specifically designed for OLAP, developers can deliver applications to business users faster, providing better service, which in turn allows the developers to build more applications.

Another advantage of using OLAP systems is that if such systems are separate from the On-Line Transaction Processing (OLTP) systems that feed the data warehouse, the OLTP systems' performance will improve due to the reduced network traffic and elimination of long queries to the OLTP database.

In a nutshell, OLAP enables the organization as a whole to respond more quickly to market demands. This is possible because it provides the ability to model real business problems, make better-informed decisions for the conduct of the organization, and use human resources more efficiently. Market responsiveness, in turn, often yields improved revenue and profitability.

Who Will Benefit from OLAP?

OLAP tools and applications can be used by a variety of organizational divisions, such as sales, marketing, finance, and manufacturing, to name a few.

The finance and accounting department in an organization can use OLAP tools for budgeting applications, financial performance analyses, and financial modeling. With such analyses, the finance department can determine the next year's budget to accurately reflect the expenses of the organization and avoid budget deficits. The department can also use its analyses to reveal weakness points in the business that should be eliminated, and points of strength that should be given more focus.

The sales department, on the other hand, can use OLAP tools to build sales analysis and forecasting applications. These applications help the sales department to realize the best sales techniques and the products that will sell more than others.

The marketing department may use OLAP tools for market research analysis, sales forecasting, promotions analysis, customer analysis, and market/customer segmentation. Such applications will reveal the best markets and the markets that don't yield good returns. They will also help decide where a given product can be marketed versus another product. For instance, it is wise to market products used by a certain segment of society in areas where people belonging to this segment are located.

Typical manufacturing OLAP applications include production planning and defect analysis. These applications will help determine the effectiveness of quality assurance and quality control (QA/QC), as well as determining the best way to build a certain product, and the source for its raw materials. Information delivered by an OLAP system in this case may lead to the discovery of problem areas for a company, that are hidden behind numbers that may be misleadingly indicating good performance.

For all the types of OLAP users above, OLAP will deliver the information they need to make effective decisions about their organization's line of business and future directions. The information delivered by the OLAP tools is delivered fast, and just-in-time when needed. This fast delivery of information is the key to successful OLAP applications. Time is the critical piece to make really effective decisions.

The information delivered by OLAP applications usually reflects complex relationships and is often calculated on the fly. Analyzing and modeling complex relationships is practical only if response times are consistently short. In addition, because the nature of data relationships may not be known in advance, the data model must be flexible, so that it can be changed according to new findings. A truly flexible data model ensures that OLAP systems can respond to changing business requirements as needed for effective decision-making.

What are the Features of OLAP?

As we saw in the previous section, OLAP applications are found in a wide variety of functional areas of an organization. However, no matter what functions are served by an OLAP application, it must always have the following elements:

- ❑ Multidimensional views of data (data cubes)
- ❑ Calculation-intensive capabilities
- ❑ Time intelligence

Multidimensional Views

Business models are multidimensional in nature. Take the Office Depot example: several dimensions can be identified for the business of that company; time, location, product, people, and so on. Since sales, for example, can differ in time from quarter to quarter, or from year to year, the time dimension, therefore, has several levels within it. The location, or geography dimension, can also have multiple levels such as city, state, country, and so on. The product dimension is no different from the previous two dimensions. It can have several levels, such as categories (computers, printers, etc.), and more refined levels (printer cartridge, printer paper, etc.).

This aspect of OLAP applications provides the foundation to 'slice and dice' the data, as well as providing flexible access to information buried in the database. Using OLAP applications, managers should be able to analyze data across any dimension, at any level of aggregation, with equal functionality and ease. For instance, profits for a particular month (or fiscal quarter), for a certain product subcategory (or maybe brand name) in a particular country (or even city) can be obtained easily using such applications. OLAP software should support these views of data in a natural and responsive fashion, insulating users of the information from complex query syntax. After all, managers should not have to write structured query language (SQL) code, understand complex table layouts, or elaborate table joins.

The multidimensional data views are usually referred to as **data cubes**. Since we typically think of a cube as having three dimensions, this may be a bit of a misnomer. In reality data cubes can have as many dimensions as the business model allows. Data cubes, as they pertain to Microsoft SQL Server 2000 Analysis services, will be discussed in detail in Chapter 2.

Calculation-Intensive

While most OLAP applications do simple data aggregation along a hierarchy like a cube or a dimension, some of them may conduct more complex calculations, such as percentages of totals, and allocations that use the hierarchies from the top down. It is important that an OLAP application is designed in a way that allows for such complex calculations. It is these calculations that add great benefits to the ultimate solution.

Trend analysis is another example of complex calculations that can be carried out with OLAP applications. Such analyses involve algebraic equations and complex algorithms, such as moving averages and percent growth.

OLTP (On-Line Transaction Processing) systems are used to collect and manage data, while OLAP systems are used to create information from the collected data that may lead to new knowledge. It is the ability to conduct complex calculations by the OLAP applications that allows successful transfer of the raw data to information, and later to knowledge.

Time Intelligence

Time is a universal dimension for almost all OLAP applications. It is very difficult to find a business model where time is not considered an integral part. Time is used to compare and judge performance of a business process. As an example, performance of the eastern region this month may be compared to its performance last month. Or, the profits of a company in the last quarter may be judged against its profits in the same quarter of the previous year.

The time dimension is not always used in a similar way to other dimensions. For example, a manager may ask about the sales totals for the first two months of the year, but is not likely to ask about the sales of the first two computers in the product line. An OLAP system should be built to easily allow for concepts like "year to date" and "period over period comparisons" to be defined.

When time is considered in OLAP applications, another interesting concept is that of **balance**. A balance of the computers built in a quarter will be the sum of the computers built in the individual months of the quarter. So, if the company built 20 computers in January, 10 in February, and 25 in March, the balance of computers built for the first quarter will be $20 + 10 + 25 = 55$ computers. On the other hand, the balance of cash flow for a quarter will usually be the ending balance at the end of the quarter regardless of the cash flow balance of the individual months in the quarter. So, if the balance at the end of January is $20,000, at the end of February is $15,000, and at the end of March is $25,000, the balance for the end of the quarter will be $25,000. Lastly, the balance of employees in a quarter will usually be the *average* balance of the number of employees in the company in the individual months. So, if the number of employees in January is 10, in February 8, and in March 15, the balance of employees for the first quarter will be $(10 + 8 + 15)/3$ or 11.

Month/Quarter Balance	Number of Employees	Number of Computers Built	Cash Flow at the End of the Month
January, 1999	10	20	$20,000
February, 1999	8	10	$15,000
March, 1999	15	25	$25,000
First Quarter, 1999	**11 (Average)**	**55 (Summation)**	**$25,000 (End Value)**

What is a Data Warehouse?

As you have already seen in the previous sections about OLAP, a data warehouse is a central repository that stores the data collected in the enterprise's business operations. Originally, a data warehouse was located on a mainframe server, although nowadays, you can see data warehouses built on PC-based servers. Data from various OLTP applications and other sources is selectively extracted and organized into the data warehouse. The data is used by OLAP systems and user queries to aid in decision-making.

A data warehouse may integrate data from several diverse, heterogeneous sources. It consolidates such data and stores it in a step-by-step fashion. The data warehouse organizes and stores the data needed for informative analytical processing over a long historical time perspective. The data is thus stored as snapshots of the corporate business in time, and once stored, it does not change.

Not only does the data warehouse store data collected from the corporate OLTP applications, but it may also store data generated by the OLAP reports. Such data is canned as snapshots at a certain point in time and stored in the data warehouse to facilitate quick retrieval.

Data Warehouse vs. Traditional Operational Data Stores

The data warehouse differs from operational database systems in many ways. One of the main differences between these two types of systems is the data collected in each of them. In operational systems (OLTP systems), the data is called **operational data** and is constantly in a state of flux, while in the data warehouse, the data is usually referred to as **decision support data** and remains relatively static. The table below summarizes the main differences between operational data found in OLTP systems and decision support data found in a data warehouse.

Operational Data	Decision Support Data
Application-oriented: data serves a particular business process or functionality. For example a fully normalized banking system with separate tables for each business process.	Subject-oriented: data serves a certain subject of the business, such as customer account, customer information, etc. De-normalized data where one record may cover the whole business process.
Detailed data where, for example, you could see every bank transaction carried out.	Summarized or refined data with complex calculations at times. Perhaps a summary of the day's, week's or month's banking transactions summing up the total amounts in and out.
Structure is usually static.	Structure is dynamic where new data cubes can be created as needed. Existing cubes can also be extended, by adding either new dimensions or dimension levels.
Targets data-entry people. The data is structured so that data entry is fast and accurate giving the data entry person as much help as possible.	Targets decision makers at all levels. Data structures are designed so that analysis can be made at different levels and different areas within a business.
Volatile (can be changed).	Non-volatile (is not changed after it is inserted).
Requirements are usually known before the design of the system.	Requirements are not totally understood prior to the design of the system.
Follows the classical development life cycle where an iteration of the design is completed through data normalization, and user requirement checking	Completely different life cycle, where you take an existing application's data structures and make the design ready for analysis. Less cycles are involved since the user definition of the system has been done.
Performance is important because of the large number of concurrent users that may access the data.	Performance issues are more relaxed, since a far smaller number of people are expected to access the data simultaneously, thus there are no serious concurrency issues to worry about
Transaction-driven.	Analysis-driven.

Table continued on following page

15

Operational Data	Decision Support Data
Must be highly available for the end users (back-up and recovery plans are very well planned).	Does not have the same degree of high availability requirement and plans for back-up and recovery are more relaxed.
Usually retrieved in units or records at any given time. This leads to processing only a small amount of data in any given process (transaction)	Usually retrieved in sets of records. This leads to processing large amounts of data in one single process (such as finding out a particular trend based on data collected over several years).
Reflects current situation.	Reflects values over time (historical).
When managed (administered), it is usually managed as a whole.	Usually managed in pieces, or smaller sets.

We will now discuss the major differences between data-warehouse data and operational OLTP data.

Purpose and Nature

The data warehouse is subject-oriented, which means it is designed around the major subjects of the enterprise business. Traditional operational databases, on the other hand are usually process-oriented based on the functionality provided by the applications accessing them. For example, an operational system may be designed around processes like bank savings, loans, and other transactions, while a data warehouse may be organized around subjects like customer data, vendor data, activity data, etc.

The subject-orientation of the data warehouse makes its design different from the design of an operational database. As a result, the data warehouse design involves data modeling and database design. The business processes, which are the heart of the operational database design, do not affect the design process of the data warehouse.

The data warehouse may exclude data that is not directly relevant to the decision support process. This data may be essential for the daily activities taking place in operational databases and is therefore included in them. For example, a banking OLTP database may include a lookup table about available statuses of a customer account. This table may be linked to other tables lending them its primary key as a foreign key, which makes maintaining status information easy by maintaining only the lookup table. Thefollowing figure shows a sample of the data that may be contained in the status lookup table. The figure shows different fields that are important for the OLTP system, such as the description of the status and the last two fields that keep track of who last updated the table, and when. In the data warehouse, data is not expected to change, and the different fields in the status table may not be needed. Instead, the StatusName field may be stored in the fact table

The fact table is the table that holds the facts of the business that need to be analysed, such as sales, profits, amount of storage at hand, etc. For more explanation of what a fact table is, refer to Chapter 2.

	StatusID	StatusName	Description	LastUpdateID	LastUpdateDate
	1	New	New account queued for processing	1023	1/30/1999
	2	Pending	Account request is being processed and pending approval	1025	2/1/1999
	3	Active	Account is currently active	1023	1/30/1999
	4	Suspended	Account is temporarily inactive. Justification required when	1025	2/1/1999
▶	5	Closed	Account is closed	1025	2/2/1999
*					

Data Structure and Content

Operational databases also differ from the data warehouse in their structure. Operational systems are usually designed to allow a large number of small transactions (OLTP systems). This requirement makes it necessary to optimise the database for data inserts, updates, and deletions. The most efficient way to do so is by normalizing the database tables according to E.F. Codd's rules. Further details on these rules can be found in Chapter 5.

The data warehouse, on the other hand, is not expected to be subject to updates and deletions; however, inserts may happen periodically when data is added to it. Improving the query performance against the data warehouse may require that its tables be de-normalized so as to less strictly adhere to Codd's Rules.

Another aspect of the data structure in a data warehouse stems from the very nature of OLAP systems. Specifically, OLAP's multi-dimensional database that stores data represented by multi-dimensional views, and the complex calculations that take place in such systems, mean that the data structures built may take the database down to a design where it is possible to move in different directions for investigation. This is in stark contrast to OLTP which is very flat in its design.

Most OLAP applications are intended for interactive use, and users of these applications expect to get a fast response to queries (ideally, not more than a few seconds). This is simple to achieve if queries only have to retrieve information from a database, reformat it, and present it to a user, but gets slower and more complicated if a significant amount of calculation work has to be done to service the query. This might include hierarchical consolidation, calculations of variances, analyzing trends, deriving computed measures, and so on. As the amount of calculations performed on the data increases, so does the time it takes to get the query results. This becomes more apparent as calculations involve a larger number of items retrieved from the database.

In order to get a fast response, all large multidimensional applications need to pre-calculate at least some of the information that will be needed for analysis. This might, for example, include high-level consolidations needed for reports or *ad hoc* analyses, and which involve too much data to be calculated on the fly. In multi-dimensional databases, the storage of pre-calculated data is usually automatic and transparent. OLAP systems typically store such aggregations in what are called **OLAP cubes** (explained in detail in the next chapter).There are some OLAP systems that store the data in the same ways OLTP system, usually referred to as **relational OLAP** (**ROLAP**) systems, normally using summary tables. The summary tables store similar pre-calculated and pre-aggregated information to that stored by a multi-dimensional database. Again, although the details of the implementation differ, there is no difference in principle between multi-dimensional databases and ROLAP products in this regard.

The next figure shows a sample of customer transaction data as it makes its way from an OLTP system to a data warehouse, and finally to an OLAP system where a report may be generated.

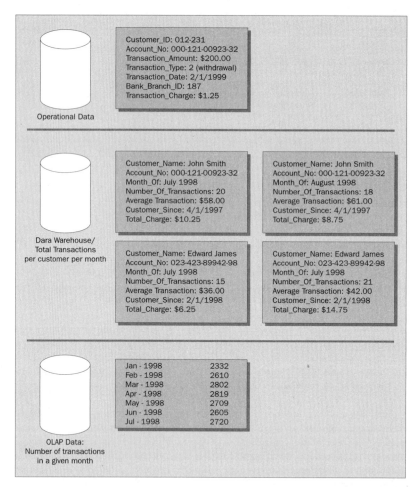

The figure above shows that the OLTP system holds detailed information about the transaction. What we are not able to see is that the transaction table is linked to many other tables according to certain relationships. The data warehouse stores the collective transactions over time after selecting the important pieces of data to store, and performing some transformation on it. In the figure, we see that the data warehouse stores each customer with the date when they opened an account, the total number of transactions, and the total bank charges as a result of these transactions. The data in the data warehouse is used to generate the OLAP data, which shows the number of transactions for the bank customers for each month. For a bank manager, the information drawn from this analysis concerns whether their bank is serving more transactions, or not, over time.

Data Volume

OLTP systems are designed to be small in size to allow for efficient updates, inserts, and deletions. Once some data is recognized to have become static and not likely to change, the data is archived from such systems or moved into the data warehouses after some transformation. The archived data can then be deleted from the OLTP system leaving room for new data to be collected.

The data warehouse is designed to hold large amounts of data. While an OLTP system can rarely exceed the 100 GB limit, a data warehouse is likely to be measured in the TB ranges. The data stored in the data warehouse is organized in a way that optimizes query performance.

This rule is not always the case. You may find that a corporation is using its OLTP system as the backend for its analysis tools. In this case, the data warehouse and the OLTP have the same size. This practice is not recommended, because optimizing the database for transaction processing will degrade its performance in analytical processing, and vice versa. Performance tuning will be discussed in Chapter 20.

Data storage volume is not the only difference between operational OLTP systems and data warehouses. The volume of data processed when retrieval occurs is also extremely different. With OLTP systems, a small amount of data is retrieved for every performed transaction. In data warehouses and OLAP systems, a large set of data may have to be processed when queries are issued against the data store. The data is retrieved in sets, rather than in small units as is the case with OLTP systems.

Timeline

OLTP systems depict the current state of the business. For example, a banking OLTP system will hold records that show the current customer accounts, and the daily transactions that take place around them. The data warehouse for the same bank, on the other hand, will store historical information about bank customers, accounts, and activities over a long period of time. Data is retrieved from the data warehouse as snapshots in time.

How Data Warehouses Relate to OLAP

In the OLAP section you read that the OLAP services and tools are usually used to convert the enterprise raw data stored in the data warehouse into information and knowledge within the OLAP service. The data warehouse is the storage area that OLAP may tap into to do its analyses. Data is fed into the data warehouse over time from operational systems using many techniques. In the process, the data is said to be scrubbed and transformed. This transformation and scrubbing is done because the raw data in the operational system may not be in the format and shape that can lead to efficient storage in the data warehouse, or efficient analyses by the OLAP tools. Furthermore, if the data was collected from several sources before storing it into the data warehouse, inconstancies in the data have to be resolved. An example is one of the sources storing states by their abbreviation (CA for California), and other sources using the full state name.

The data warehouse, thus, still holds raw data. OLAP systems aggregate and summarize such data making good use of it as we saw earlier in the chapter, by organizing it in OLAP cubes or other forms of special storage that allow for fast retrieval of the "information" expected from a query or report.

Data Warehouses and Data Marts

Today's corporations strive to conduct their business on a national and global basis. We see companies that originated in the US expanding their business across the oceans to Europe, Asia, and Africa. Business expansion creates the need to access corporate data from different geographical locations in a timely manner. For example, a salesperson who is working in Texas for a company based in California may need instant access to the enterprise database to identify names of potential customers in Texas, or to retrieve certain information that would help in selling the product to an existing Texan customer when meeting with them.

The solution to this problem is to create smaller versions of the data warehouse based on certain criteria, called **data marts**. The data marts in this salesperson's case could hold corporate data for customers in Texas. Being of a manageable size, the data mart can fit on a mobile PC, such as a laptop, that the salesperson may carry with them. Data marts create a new way of thinking when designing corporate data repositories:

❑   Some corporations completely replace the concept of having a data warehouse with that of having smaller data marts that can be fed with the data they need from the operational systems.

❑   Other companies use data marts to complement their data warehouses by moving data into them from the data warehouse allowing for more efficient analysis based on criteria such as department, geographical area, time period, etc.

❑   Finally, some corporations use their data marts as the first stage of storing operational data. The data is then replicated from all of the corporate data marts into a central "enterprise" data warehouse. Such a data warehouse then evolves over time as the data marts continue to be built to cover as many aspects of the company business as needed.

The figure below shows a typical data warehouse/OLAP system architecture. The following three figures show how this architecture changes to accommodate the introduction of data marts according to the strategies discussed above. First, we have a diagram depicting a typical data warehouse/OLAP system architecture with no data marts.

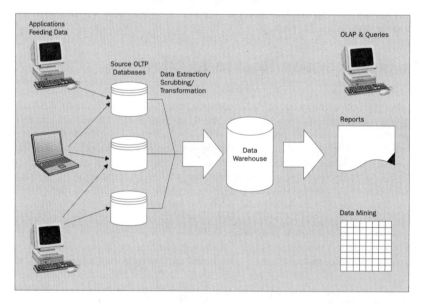

The next diagram shows a typical data mart/OLAP system architecture in which the data marts replace the data warehouse:

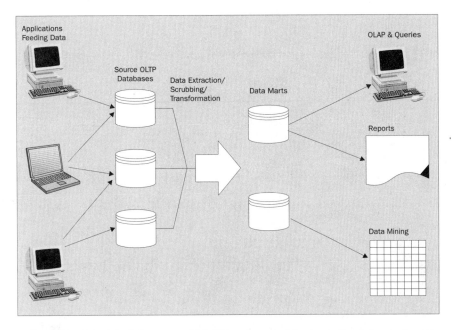

In the next diagram of a typical data mart/OLAP system architecture, the data marts are populated with data from the data warehouse:

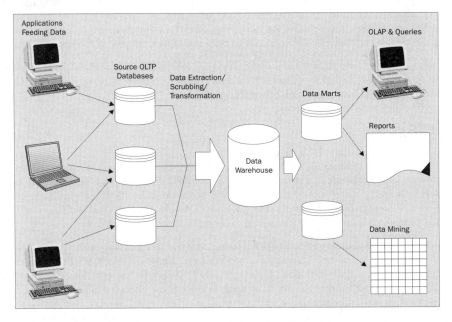

Finally, we have a diagram that illustrates a typical data mart/OLAP system architecture, with the data mart data being used to populate the data warehouse:

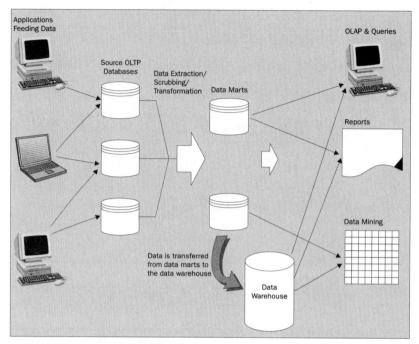

Each one of these solutions has its relevant advantages and disadvantages to the companies that adopted it. No matter what the solution is, data marts usually have similar characteristics to those of the data warehouse, except for the data volume. Actually, due to the smaller data volume and focus in the subject matter, queries are usually faster to run in data marts as opposed to the data warehouse.

However, where you will see data warehouses have the greatest advantage is being able to analyze areas of information and allow that analysis to be seen from different viewpoints, where in the OLTP system, this may not be possible due to the lack of summary data.

Data Mining

Many corporations accumulate the data they collect in the process of their daily operations in a data warehouse and data marts for analysis reasons. The analyses they conduct on the stored data help the managers in the decision making process. One relatively new, but powerful, concept that has started to gain popularity in the business intelligence (BI) world is **data mining**. With data mining, managers find out aspects and facts about their business that may not be evident otherwise. Data mining establishes relationships between business elements that may seem completely unrelated.

As an example, managers of a grocery store decided to distribute free coupon cards. When a customer pays for groceries, the cashier scans their card to see if any coupons apply to the customer's groceries. This actually makes the customer happy since they don't have to manually search for the coupons, clip them and argue with the cashier about their validity. At the same time, as the cashier scans the customer's card, the database is updated with whatever has been bought from the store, and may even be associated with a zip code or a phone area code (geographical location). The data collected for all the customers can then help the managers decide which products are selling the most in which geographic locations, or which ones that are to be found near the cashiers really get the most attention among "impulsive" buyers. This is possible because managers have access to a wide range of data about the customers and their purchases. They also know if a product is to be found near the cashier from its serial number. Linking these pieces of information will help them design their product displays at the checkout stations better.

In general data mining leads to the following results:

❑ Discovering unknown associations. Such associations can be found when one event can be correlated to another event that **seems** completely unrelated (for example, beer buyers are likely to purchase peanuts).

❑ Sequences, where one event leads to another later event (for example, customers who purchase curtains are likely to come back to purchase rugs from the same store).

❑ Recognizing patterns that lead to classification, or new organization of data (for example, certain profiles are established for customers based on what they purchase).

❑ Finding groups of facts not previously known. This process is known as event clustering.

❑ Forecasting, or simply discovering patterns in the data that can lead to predictions about the future.

Data mining is the topic of Chapters 16 and 17.

Overview of Microsoft Analysis Services in SQL Server 2000

One of the biggest problems for OLAP tools in the early 1990s was that these tools were not too easy or intuitive for the end users to use. The end-user is usually the person who will make the decisions based on analyzing the historical data collected in the data warehouse. Previously, developers had to build costly applications around these tools to make them easier to use and to cut down on the learning curve for the end users.

Microsoft recognized the importance of providing a better database system that can be used for data warehousing. Microsoft also recognized the importance of providing tools that would make the data analysis an easy and enjoyable process. With the release of Microsoft SQL Server 7 and the tools that accompanied it, Microsoft was able to deliver a viable solution to the problem. Microsoft enhanced its solution tremendously with the new release of SQL Server 2000, included a new version of OLAP Services adding to it data mining capabilities and labeling them as Analysis Services. This section briefly introduces these tools and their effectiveness. A detailed description of each of these tools, and their use, is presented in this book.

The figure overleaf shows a schematic of the architecture of the Microsoft SQL Server Analysis Services. In the figure, several tools are shown, and each of these tools has its unique function. The tools can be divided into several major parts: data source, data transformation and export, data storage, data analysis, and data presentation. We will dedicate the remainder of this chapter to presenting an overview of the different parts shown in this schematic.

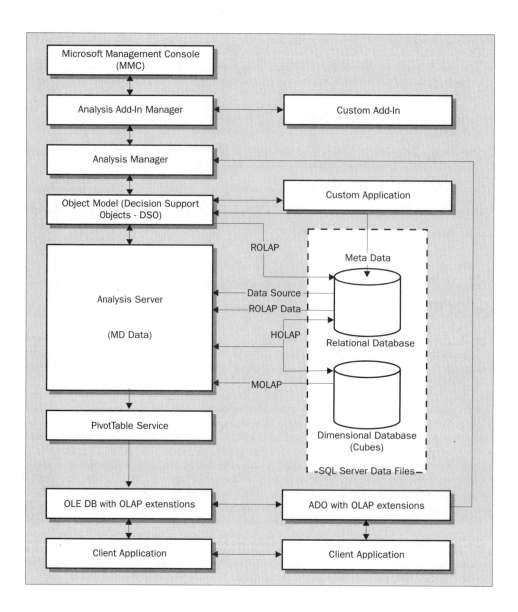

Features of Microsoft Analysis Services

Microsoft Analysis Services comes with some good features that address the complexity of the OLTP systems. These features are:

❑ **Ease of use** – Many wizards, editors, and help materials are available to help the user at every step of the way. The Analysis Manager user interface not only gives you access to metadata views and cube data, among other things, but also provides you with wizards to create and edit cubes, dimensions, and levels. Other wizards include a usage analysis wizard and a usage-based optimization wizard.

If, like me, you are not an advocate of using wizards, then you will find several editors that allow you to perform the tasks that the wizards are able to do, and more. However, you can always use the wizard to make a start and then use the editors to expand the specific area you are dealing with.

❑ **Flexibility** – Several storage modes are available through the Microsoft OLAP Server. These include storing cube data into multidimensional cube files (MOLAP), relational databases (ROLAP), or a hybrid of the two (HOLAP). Cubes can also be partitioned, with each partition stored in a different storage mode. Cube partitioning and storage modes will be covered in more detail in Chapter 3.

❑ **Scalability** – Microsoft Analysis services support both the Intel-based servers and existing DEC Alpha servers (future DEC Alpha servers will not support Windows NT). The OLAP client can run on Windows 9x, Windows NT, and Windows 2000. Analysis Services has also been designed to address a variety of data warehousing scenarios, such as customized aggregation options, usage-based optimization, data compression, and distributed calculations, among other things. All these features make the Microsoft Analysis services highly scalable.

❑ **Integration** - Analysis Services are integrated with the Microsoft Management Console (MMC). You can add Analysis Manager as a snap-in to the MMC. Security in Analysis Services is integrated with SQL Server and Windows NT security. This integration allows for powerful usage of OLE DB data sources as a result of having an OLE DB provider for OLAP services, and client- and server- side cache. Finally, many third-party vendors are developing integration adaptors between their products and Microsoft Analysis Services as part of the Microsoft Data Warehousing Alliance.

❑ **Widely supported APIs and functions** – The OLAP Server and Microsoft PivotTable service support OLE DB, ADO, user-defined function, and decision support objects (DSO).

These are only a few of the features that make Microsoft Analysis Services a powerful contender in the data warehousing world. Although this book covers Analysis Services and you will come across many of the tools and technologies within this book, if you wish to learn more concerning the specifics of requirements that you need to run these technologies, such as the hardware and software necessities, then more information can be found within Books Online.

New Features to Support Data Warehouses and Data Mining

There are a large number of new features or enhancements to Analysis Services since SQL Server 7.0. The following list gives an idea of some of the major additions/improvements which will be discussed throughout this book:

❑ The ability to distribute data used by cubes over more than one server, (including remote servers), allowing analysis processing to take place without the need to pull data onto a single server.

❑ The ability for users or processes to continue to update cube data while Analysis Services is still processing that cube data. This allows real-time OLAP solutions to be available so that at any point in time, it is possible to see exactly what the current information within a system is defining. This removes the (sometimes) large delay when processing OLAP data to getting results, which benefits businesses such as, for example, trading houses, that need up-to-the-minute analysis of trades, prices, volumes, and trading trends. Any delay in getting that data out of the OLAP system could cost thousands of pounds as the trading moment would have been lost.

❑ It is also possible when processing cubes to allow processing of the cubes to continue when errors occur, and to have any errors found logged for future analysis.

❑ Indexed views, introduced with SQL Server 2000, have also helped relational OLAP. If you have an OLAP built for a web based solution, there is a new aggregate function that you can use to check the number of unique hits your web site has had, as opposed to just the number of page refreshes that have taken place. By using the `DistinctCount` aggregate function it is possible to check the number of unique occurrences of a value.

❑ From a security perspective, the ability to hide cube and dimension information from direct access via tools such as ISQL, just as you can with tables, allows your OLAP data to become more secure.

❑ Moving to data mining, the largest and most effective changes surround the user interface, which has been greatly enhanced in order to speed up development of data mining solutions. Further details on data mining can be found in Chapters 16 and 17.

The Foundation: Microsoft SQL Server 2000

SQL Server 2000 is the foundation of the Microsoft data warehousing and Analysis Services. It provides many advantages to decision makers, many of which you will be aware of already having dealt with SQL Server within your current development environment. Specific advantages include:

❑ SQL Server is compatible with many other software components and tools used in the deployment of data warehouses.

❑ Data replication is built into the SQL Server engine, which cuts down on the cost of using third-party tools, or additional tools to conduct the replication.

❑ Scalability is another important feature of SQL Server. SQL Server 2000 scales up from the Windows 9x platforms to the Windows 2000 advanced server, and a system built on a local machine can be scaled up with little or no extra work involved to multiple servers which could also be working as replication servers.

Data Transformation Services (DTS)

SQL Server relational databases serve as the main data source for the Analysis and data warehousing Services. Naturally, the data source could be any other database, such as Oracle, or any others that have an OLE DB Provider written for them. However, in this book, we will be assuming that the whole data warehousing architecture is based on Microsoft technologies.

Microsoft introduced data transformation services (DTS) into SQL Server 7 to facilitate the collection and transfer of data from its OLTP sources to the OLAP system. DTS was further enhanced in SQL Server 2000, with additional functionalities and refinements that make it an essential tool to use in data transformation and migration. DTS provides a means of moving the data from the source to the destination data warehouse. In the process, DTS performs data validation, cleanup, consolidation, and transformation of the data when needed.

Data Validation

Data validation is purely the art of looking at the data and deciding if what is being checked is valid or not. It is an essential task that has to be conducted during or after extracting the data from the source OLTP databases and transferring it to the destination data warehouse. If the data is not valid, the integrity of any business analysis based on it will be in question. For example, in the case of a currency field, where the OLAP system may exist in different countries, one has to make sure that the data in this currency field is always converted appropriately according to the currency of the destination data warehouse.

A further point you need to pay close attention to when validating the data is information related to geographical regions. You need to make sure that the referenced cities are in the right countries as the country field states. A further example of validating data is to make sure that products are represented in a consistent manner across all data sources.

In transferring data to a data warehouse it may be necessary for the data to be scrubbed. Note however that is not always necessary for validation to take place prior to data scrubbing. Let's now take a look a brief look at how data scrubbing fits in.

Data Scrubbing

Data reconciliation has to take place between multiple sources feeding the same data warehouse. The reconciliation process is referred to as **data scrubbing**. For example, if a product is classified as beverage in one OLTP system, and soft drink in another system, the two different classifications must be reconciled during the data transformation process before the data related to them can be aggregated and stored in the data warehouse. Both of these values are valid, and therefore would pass the validation phase, but of course, it is necessary to determine which is the accurate value in relation to the other data. Failing to deal with the difference in values, will yield inaccurate results in the final reports that are generated based on the data warehouse.

Data scrubbing can be achieved in different ways, as summarized here:

❑ Using DTS import and export wizards to modify data as it is copied from the source to the destination data store.

❑ By writing a Microsoft ActiveX script or program. This kind of script or program may use the DTS API to connect to the data source and scrub the data. This is not the easiest method to perform data scrubbing, but it provides a great deal of flexibility since it uses the power of the scripting or programming language to access the data, which often can provide a tremendous amount of control and manipulation across heterogeneous data sources.

❑ DTS Lookup provides the ability to perform queries using one or more named, parameterized query strings. This allows for building custom transformation schemes to retrieve data from locations other than the immediate source or destination row being transformed.

Data Migration

Ideally, when migrating data from OLTP data sources to a data warehouse, data is copied to an intermediate database before it is finally copied to the data warehouse. This intermediate process is necessary to allow for data scrubbing and validation to occur.

Special care should be taken when performing the data migration. The migration process should be performed during periods of low activities at the operational OLTP systems to minimize the impact on the performance of these systems. If the data migration is done from multiple data sources that are replicas, or share in replication processes, the migration must happen when all these sources are synchronized to ensure that consistent data is copied from these sources.

A commonly deployed strategy is to execute data migration procedures after the nightly database backups occur. This ensures that if a migration procedure crashes the system, the backup was just performed.

Data Transformation

When you move the data from the source OLTP databases to the destination data warehouse, you may find yourself performing many transformations of existing data to make it more operational and practical when used in the destination store. Below are examples of data transformations you may want to consider when moving data from the OLTP databases to the data warehouse:

❑ Break a column into multiple columns, such as dividing a date or timestamp field into its date components, day, month, quarter, and year.

❑ Calculate new fields based on the values in source fields, such as creating a total price field in the destination database, which is a result of multiplying the unit price by the quantity sold fields in the source database.

❑ Merge separate fields into one field, such as merging the first name and last name fields in the source database into one name column in the destination data warehouse.

❑ Map data from one representation to another, such as translation of code to literal values and converting values from decimal numerical values (1, 2, 3, etc.) to Roman numerals (I, II, III, etc.).

DTS Components

DTS comprises the following components:

❑ An import/export wizard that steps the user into the necessary functions needed to import data from other systems into SQL Server and export data from SQL Server to other systems or formats

❑ A graphical designer that helps the user in creating DTS packages and maintaining them, called DTS Designer

❑ A graphical tool to help build DTS queries, called DTS Query Designer

❑ COM programming interfaces that allow for the creation of custom import/export and transformation applications

A detailed discussion of these topics is presented in Chapters 7 and 8 of this book.

Meta Data and the Repository

Meta data is, by definition, data about data. In other words, the information about the way storage is structured in the data warehouse, OLAP, data mining, and DTS services are all kept as meta data, which is stored in the Microsoft Repository. The Repository is built to maintain such technical information about the data sources involved with the services mentioned above.

SQL Server stores repository information in its msdb database, which is a relational database. As you will see in Chapter 7, four storage types are available for DTS packages:

- ❏ Repository through Meta Data Services, which stores the information in the `msdb`
- ❏ SQL Server as a local package, which does not provide as much information about the packages as one stored in the Repository
- ❏ SQL Server structure files, which are external to SQL Server but hold the total information about a package and are a means of passing packages between computers
- ❏ External files such as a Visual Basic file

The repository is the preferred means of storing DTS packages in a data-warehousing scenario because it is the only method of providing data lineage (information such as which version of a package created which particular row within a database), for packages. DTS packages are discussed in more detail in Chapter 7.

Access to the repository is possible through the interfaces exposed by the Analysis Manager's graphical user interface (GUI). Analysis Manager is discussed in detail in Chapter 3 and Chapter 9. Meta data can also be accessed through the decision support objects (DSO), and through programs that use interfaces to the Repository. Microsoft recommends only using DSO or Analysis Manager's GUI to access the meta data because the Repository is subject to change in future releases of SQL Server.

Decision Support Systems (DSS)

Microsoft Decision Support Systems (DSS) consist of the DSS Analysis server, also referred to as the OLAP server, and the PivotTable Service. Below is an overview of these components. A detailed discussion of them is provided in later chapters.

Analysis Server

The Analysis server is the heart of Microsoft Analysis Services, extracting data from heterogeneous sources across the organization for analysis and querying, as well as storing aggregated and processed data in the multi-dimensional database for quick access when needed. It can also utilize data stored in summary tables in the OLTP database as well. Decision support objects (DSO) can be used to access the Analysis server and create custom applications that provide custom reports to the end-user. In SQL Server 2000, the Analysis Server is also responsible for creating and using the mining models to extract trends and predictions from OLAP data.

PivotTable Service

PivotTable Service was first added to SQL Server 7.0 after being tested for quite a long time in Microsoft Excel and Access. This service allows the user to create cross-tab tables on the fly by specifying the columns and rows on which aggregations should be made. Improvements have been made to this service to cater for the advances in data mining and analysis within SQL Server 2000 as well as enhancements to the communication between the Analysis server and areas such as cube data.

By using T-SQL statements within an application it is possible through the PivotTable Service to build a local data mine.

Analysis Server can work with several tools on the OLAP client side, such as English Query, and Microsoft Office (especially, MS Excel and MS Access) allowing these tools to access its cube data through the pivot table service. This gives the user a great advantage, because they are most likely familiar with these tools, and can use them efficiently for the data analysis.

PivotTable service is a client-side processing tool, a standalone and distributable component.

Analysis Manager

Analysis Manager is a graphical user interface (GUI) that allows the user to build an OLAP solution based on existing data sources. The screenshot below shows the main screen of Analysis Manager when you first open it from the Windows Start menu.

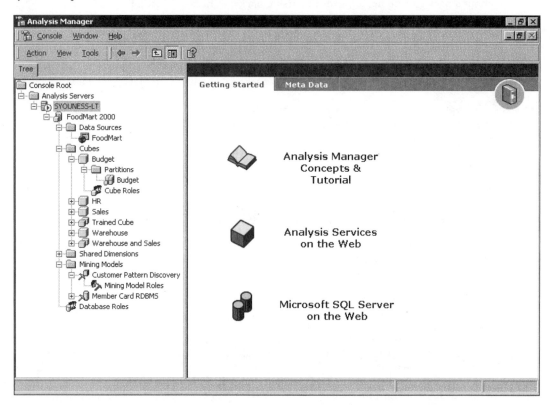

Analysis Manager is opened as a snap-in into the Microsoft Management Console (MMC). MMC is a graphical tool that allows you to access several Microsoft (and non-Microsoft) services in the Windows NT environment. These services are added as snap-ins using the add-in manager. This actually allows you to open the Microsoft Analysis Manager if you are working with other tools that are opened as MMC snap-ins as well.

Analysis Manager allows you to easily manage your OLAP databases. It provides you with wizards to add new data cubes, and to change the structure of existing cubes by adding or changing dimensions and their levels of complexity.

Analysis Manager also allows you to manage the security of your cubes so that you can guarantee only authorized access to their data.

Analysis Manager enables you to use the new data mining features in SQL Server 2000 Analysis Services by allowing you to create your mining models and use them to make predictions based on historical data collected during the business operations.

Finally, Analysis Manager allows you to access the meta data of your cubes and their components. As you select an element that has representation in the meta data from the left-hand pane of the Analysis Manager Screen (for example, a cube), you are able to click the **Meta Data** menu on the top of the right-hand pane to access the meta data for the selected cube (see the screenshot below).

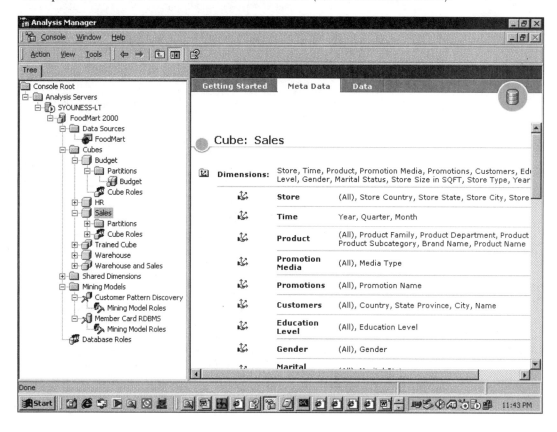

You will find more details regarding the Analysis Manager in Chapter 3.

Client Architecture

The figure overleaf shows a schematic of the client architecture of Microsoft Analysis Services, which is based on the PivotTable Service. Data access abstraction technologies, such as OLE DB (version 2.5 or higher with OLAP and data mining support) and ActiveX Data Objects (ADO 2.0 or higher with OLAP extensions) may be used in combination with the PivotTable Service to build custom client applications. These applications are responsible for presenting the information extracted from the data warehouse to the end user. The Analysis server will be used to extract the cube or mining model data for the PivotTable Service. Standard tools can also be used instead of custom applications. These tools include the powerful Microsoft Excel spreadsheet program and Microsoft Access.

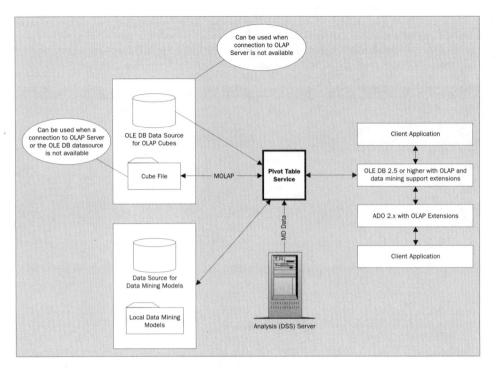

One unique feature of the Microsoft OLAP client architecture is that the user can work with the information off line. If a connection is not available to the OLAP server, the user can access the operational database, which includes summary tables that mimic the OLAP database. These summary tables can then be used by the client applications to generate the needed reports. If a connection to the OLE DB source is not available, the user can still use stored cube files to do their analyses. These cube files can be saved locally when the cubes are created and viewed in the Analysis Manager screen against the OLAP database when the source is not available.

Summary

Data warehousing and OLAP is gaining great attention among information technology professionals, companies, and clients. It is a natural step in the evolution of data management, where large amounts of data are being collected by the organization every day. The data can yield tremendous benefits when analyzed. Microsoft recognized this trend and as a result embarked on enhancing its enterprise database management system, SQL Server, to handle data warehousing needs. It augmented the database management system with its OLAP services, which make data warehousing easier and more cost-effective.

The following chapter will show you how to install Microsoft Analysis Services and start using them for your data warehousing needs. The next chapters will go into more detail about the architecture of these services and exactly how they can be utilized to build optimal data warehousing solutions.

Data Warehouse

2

Microsoft Analysis Services Architecture

The previous chapter presented a quick overview of Microsoft data warehousing and Analysis Services, and also introduced you to the architecture behind this technology. In this chapter, we will take an in-depth look at the architecture of Microsoft Analysis Services presenting a detailed description of its components and how they work together. The two main components of Analysis Services to discuss are the server components and the client components.

The topics covered in this chapter include:

- ❑ OLAP cube architecture including cube dimensions and dimension levels
- ❑ The meta data that stores information about the cubes and their components
- ❑ Relational OLAP (ROLAP) versus Multi dimensional OLAP (MOLAP) and Hybrid OLAP (HOLAP)
- ❑ Star and snowflake schemas used in the multi dimensional database are introduced. More details about these are included in Chapter 6, *Designing the Data Warehouse and OLAP Solution.*
- ❑ Decision Support Objects
- ❑ The PivotTable Service

Overview

Although you have already read a brief overview of the Microsoft Analysis Services' architecture in Chapter 1, it is necessary to repeat some of the general concepts before diving into the details of the architecture.

The figure below presents a high-level view of Analysis Services, system architecture. In the figure, three main levels can be identified, the operational data source, Analysis Services and its tools, and client applications that offer reporting and other business intelligence services. The middle component, Analysis Services, is also comprised of different high-level components, including data transformations, data storage, Analysis Server, and the PivotTable Service. Data storage includes the data warehouse or data marts, the OLAP databases, and the mining models. It could also include any relational databases used to store summary tables used by Analysis Services to build the OLAP cubes (these cubes will be discussed later in the chapter).

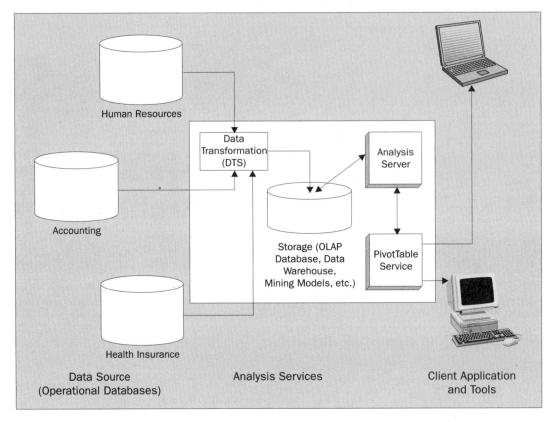

In the figure opposite we zoom in on Analysis Services for a more detailed view. In this figure we can see the underlying components of Analysis Services and the interactions that occur between them.

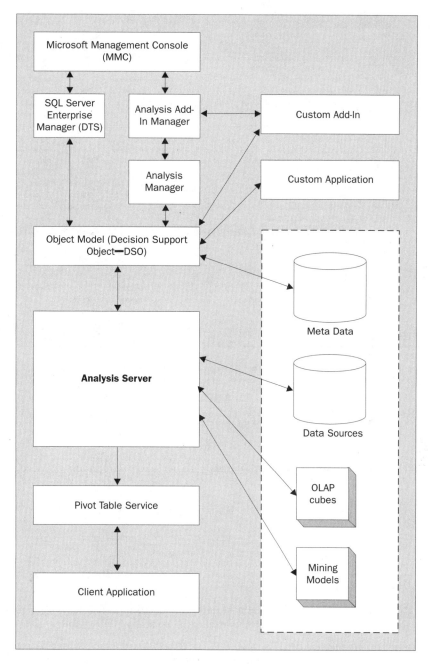

The heart of the architecture diagram above is the Analysis server component. It is the service that is installed when you install Analysis Services and shows up in the Services applet as MSSQLServerOLAPService. This service controls the creation and management of all OLAP data including mining OLAP cubes and mining models. To see this service in Windows 2000, select Administrative Tools from the Start menu, and click on the Services applet. In Windows NT, you can find the Services applet in the Windows Control Panel. This is what you expect to see when you open the Services applet in Windows 2000:

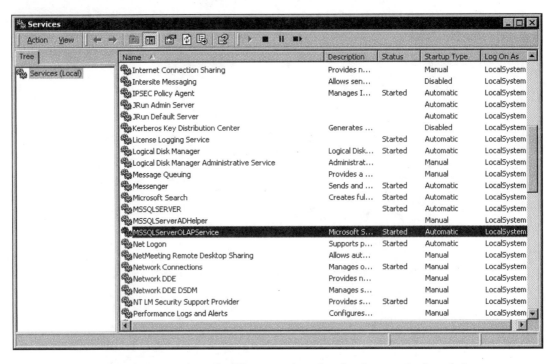

Analysis server is exposed to users through different tools and technologies, which include:

❑   Analysis Manager, the console for administering the Analysis server and data repository, and Analysis Manager Add-in

❑   SQL Server Enterprise Manager, which allows the Analysis server to interact with the Data Transformation Services (DTS) of SQL Server

❑   The Decision Support Objects (DSO) library, which allows programmatic access to Analysis Server

Another major component of Analysis Services is the data repository. This component holds different types of data:

❑   Data that describes other data, referred to as meta data

❑   Data obtained from operational systems after performing transformation and stored in what is called a data warehouse or data mart

❑   Data including OLAP cubes, or multi dimensional data that is managed by the Analysis server and used to create the information that builds the business intelligence reports

❑   Data mining models used to generate predictions and trend analyses based on other types of data, such as operational databases, the data warehouse, or even OLAP cubes

The source data for the OLAP system, specifically for the multidimensional cubes, is usually a relational database. The data structure in such databases is usually transformed into a star or snowflake schema typically used in OLAP data warehouse systems (star and snowflake schemas are explained in the *Dimensional Databases* section later in the chapter). Data can be fed into the data warehouse database from multiple sources, such as legacy databases, OLTP systems, etc. Which should support connection via ODBC or OLE DB. The Data Transformation Services (DTS) of SQL Server provide a means to manage the data warehouse by importing data into it from these heterogeneous sources. The Analysis server then uses the data in the data warehouse to create the data cubes.

Cube definition and specification is called cube meta data. The OLAP server stores cube meta data in a Repository. As you already saw in Chapter 1, data cubes can be stored in a variety of storage modes, such as multidimensional database files (MOLAP) located in a multidimensional database. The cubes can also be stored as tables in a relational database (ROLAP), or as a hybrid of multidimensional database files and relational tables (HOLAP).

The Analysis Manager graphical user interface (GUI) provides control over Analysis Services. Custom applications can be developed using the Decision Support Objects (DSO) object model to control the OLAP server as well. DSO applications may control the creation and management of data cubes by the server, and also may be designed to manage the cube meta data in the repository. The Analysis Manager program is an application based on the DSO object model to provide the necessary control over the Analysis server and the cube meta data. The Analysis Manager is used as a snap-in to Microsoft Management Console (MMC). Popular programming languages, like Microsoft Visual Basic, can utilize the DSO object model to provide custom programmatic control of the Analysis server. DSO can also help developers build custom applications that interact with the Analysis Manager user interface. You can find more details on DSO in Chapter 14.

The Microsoft Repository

We start by briefly defining and describing the Microsoft Repository, and discussing how it relates to the Analysis Services architecture.

The Microsoft Repository is a place to store and share objects between software tools, such as development tool add-ins, services, system descriptions (tool information models, or TIMs), instances of system objects, and custom reusable components. SQL Server is one such Repository client and uses it to store information about the different objects presented by the SQL Server services and tools. As an example, the following two figures show Analysis Services manager displaying the meta data stored in the repository for an OLAP cube.

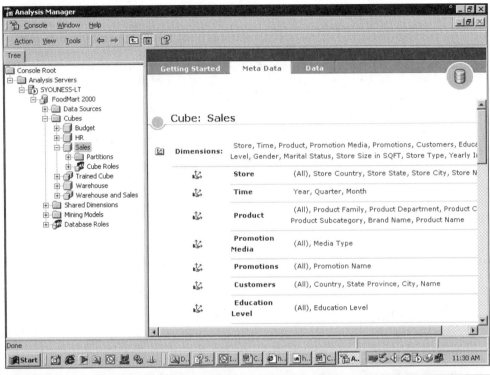

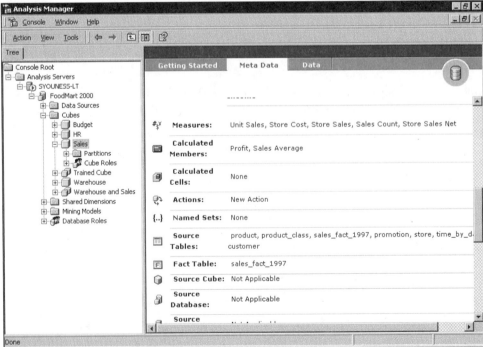

The meta data for the Sales cube, in the two figures above, shows different components and attributes of the cube. Some of these components and attributes are the dimensions, measures, calculated members, and fact table, which we will discuss later in the chapter and also learn more about as we progress through the book. As an analogy, think of a regular SQL Server database; meta data associated with such a database includes such things as its size, the data file locations, the log files, the increment, etc.

Almost all of the new releases of Microsoft development and data management tools support and allow access to the Repository. Some of the benefits achieved by using a central location to store information about the different objects and tools are:

❑ Reusability: With the storage of such information in the Repository, the information can be organized in a way that allows for its reuse if needed

❑ Dependency tracking: The Repository does not only store information about the different objects used by the software tools, but also facilitates establishing and querying relationships between stored objects

❑ Tool interoperability: This facilitates the use of these tools in different systems.

❑ Data resource management: The Repository stores global meta data for an enterprise data warehouse, and a resource library of available services and components, which makes managing such data easier and more efficient

❑ Team development: The Repository can store meta data about a development project's source control, which facilitates the management of concurrent activities on different versions and configurations of project design and development

The heart of the Repository is an engine, which is a set of Component Object Model (COM) and OLE Automation interfaces. These interfaces provide access to the Repository allowing browsing 08 its data and writing 08 data to it. The Repository data is stored in a relational database; in the case of SQL Server this is msdb (by default). With other development tools, this database can be a SQL Server database, or a Microsoft Access database.

Architecture of the Microsoft Repository

The figure overleaf shows the different parts that constitute the Microsoft Repository (or what is referred to sometimes as the "Meta Data Services") in general. In the figure, notice that there are different tiers in the Repository architecture: the Repository database, the Repository engine, the Repository APIs, and tools and applications.

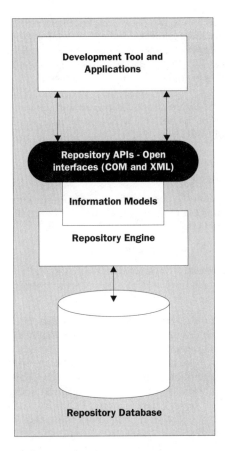

The following is a description of these tiers and how they relate to each other.

- ❑ The Repository database: A relational database, this is a Microsoft Access database by default with Analysis Services, but can be migrated to SQL Server. Queries can be issued directly against this database. It is not recommended that you write directly to the database, as the Repository engine carries out the necessary validation of the data before it is stored, which would be bypassed by direct updates and could lead to corruption. However, several tools can be used to do any such writing, and these tools interact with the Repository engine, which makes the necessary updates.

- ❑ The Repository engine: a COM-based tool that manages data in the Repository. The engine provides basic functions to store and retrieve Repository objects and the relationships among them. An elaborate object model is provided for the Repository engine. This object model allows developers to create their own applications that provide custom access to the Repository.

- ❑ Information models: These are object models that specify the types of information of interest to one or more tools. For example, The Data Transformation Services Information Model (DTS IM) specifies the types of data of interest to data transformation services users, such as package structure and objects. This information model allows database administrators and developers to create custom Repository-aware tools to analyze the structure of the DTS packages. DTS architecture is discussed later in this chapter.

Also included under information models is what is called the data type information model. This specifies the types of information of interest to information model creators. Who usually use this to describe their application-specific model to the Repository.

❑ Open interfaces that allow for programmatic access to the Repository engine. These interfaces are based on the Component Object Model (COM) technology as well as open standards, such as Extensible Markup Language (XML). These interfaces are referred to as the Repository Applications Programming Interfaces (APIs).

❑ Application development tools and other tools: Software application development tools manage the process of developing, deploying, and maintaining software applications. The "other tools" refers to services and tools used by SQL Server developers and administrators to build custom solutions for specific issues. As an example, such a developer would use DTS to perform data transformation and conversions.

Microsoft Repository in Data Warehousing

The Microsoft Repository can be used as a framework within which the different tools used to design and build a data warehouse can be assembled into a single data warehousing application system. Different vendors can create these tools, allowing software designers and developers to produce data warehousing solutions combining the strengths of these various tools.

The tools introduced by SQL Server that are readily incorporated in this framework include the operational database system; data extraction and transformation services (DTS); Analysis Services, which allows for dimensional analyses of the aggregate of the historical data; data mining models; and end-user tools, such as English Query and PivotTable.

The repository provides a shared facility that can be accessed by all of those who are developing any of the parts of the data warehousing application. This facility also expresses the inter-relationships among the various parts of the data warehousing application.

The Data Source

The data sources in Microsoft Analysis Services and data warehousing (including data marts) are comprised of the heterogeneous operational sources that provide the data to the data warehouse, and the services that transform data from these sources to a form that can be stored in a data warehouse, a data mart, a normal relational database, and finally in OLAP data cubes.

This section discusses these elements in some detail, starting with the operational data sources and ending with the data warehouse and data cubes.

Operational Data Sources

With Microsoft Analysis Services, an operational data source is usually a relational database. However, any data source that can provide connection to its data through Open DataBase Connectivity (ODBC), or through OLE DB, can be used as a source for Microsoft Analysis Services. Microsoft Data Transformation Services (DTS) can be used to transfer the data from these sources to the Analysis Services.

Some of the commonly required OLE DB and ODBC providers are included as part of the data access components installed with SQL Server. However, if you need a provider that is not installed by default, it may be available with the Microsoft Host Integration Server product, or from a third-party vendor.

Actually, even if a system does not have the ability to connect through OLE DB or ODBC (such as some mainframe systems), it can still be used as a source for the OLAP system if data is extracted in batch mode from it and fed into the OLAP system.

For example, consider a department store with stores in many different cities around the country. These stores may use relational databases for their everyday activities. Such databases will hold information about the customer, especially if the customer has a credit card that they obtained through the department store. The database will also store inventory information, as well as information about the employees. Financial information may also be stored in these databases. When a customer purchases an item from a store, the inventory tables will be updated, as well as the transactions tables, and the customer tables may also be updated.

> Note the intentional use of the plural for "tables" in the previous paragraph, because in operational systems, the database is usually highly normalized and the data is spread across many tables. Customer data, for instance, may span several tables: a central customer table that is linked to tables such as customer type, a location table, a locale table, a transaction history table, etc. However, for the purposes of our discussion here, a simplified data model for such systems will be used.

Business rules may be put in place to enable some actions or prevent others. For instance, when a new transaction is processed, the inventory table will be updated by subtracting the number of purchased items from the available inventory. The inventory of the purchased items will then be evaluated against the order threshold limits to decide whether new items should be ordered to replenish the stock.

Operational systems are designed to handle the daily operations of the online transaction processing system. They inherently have business rules and conduct a large number of small transactions. A typical simple database schema for these systems is shown in the figure opposite.

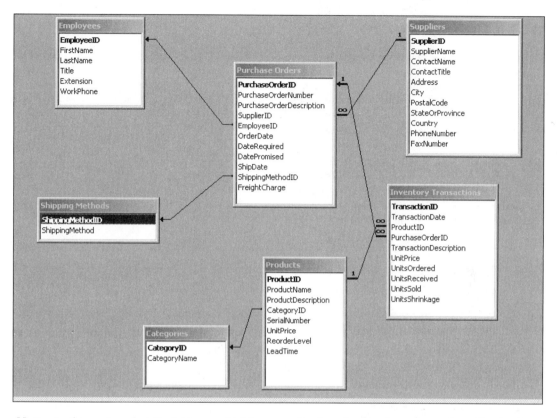

Notice in this system that the tables are highly normalized, and related to one another. This leads to fragmentation of the data. A purchase order, for example, is stored over four different tables (Purchase Orders, Employees, Shipping Methods and Suppliers).

As the number of small transactions increases, the data volume increases to a level that could affect query performance in these systems. Therefore, the data volume should be periodically reduced to maintain the desired system performance. The data reduction is usually done through backing up and then deleting the old data, or by exporting historical data to the data warehouse and then deleting it from the local database.

Data export to the data warehouse is not simply moving the old records to their new home; rather, the data is consolidated, scrubbed, and transformed in the process. This is all accomplished with the Microsoft Data Transformation Services (DTS). The reason for this transformation is that the data structure in the data warehouse is different from that in the operational system. The data warehouse data structure is optimized for query performance, rather than for transaction processing, as is the case in the operational systems.

As an example of transforming data from the operational system to the data warehouse, think of timestamp fields in the operational systems. These fields are better if transformed into regular datetime data types as we may never need the fine resolution of the time values when we build reports based on the data warehouse data. Chances are the smallest increment we would go to is the day level. Also, if you are extracting data from more than one source, you may find one source saves the data for one field as a short date, and yet another source saves it as a long date, requiring consolidation of the data between the various sources. By transforming the data, all these differences will be leveled and the data will be stored in the data warehouse in a consistent manner.

Data Transformation Services

Microsoft SQL Server's Data Transformation Services are designed to allow for import, export, and transformation of data. A basic object, called a **package**, stores information on these tasks and the order in which they need to be launched. A package can include one or more connections to different data sources, and different tasks and transformations that are executed as steps that define a workflow process. This section outlines the architecture of the DTS package and shows the types of objects, tasks, and steps that can be included in it. It also outlines the informational model of DTS and how it interacts with the meta data.

DTS Package Tasks

Microsoft enriched the default DTS package task list that can be used out-of-the-box to include many new tasks in SQL Server 2000. Here is a list of the tasks you can readily use to build your DTS package right after installing SQL Server 2000.

❏ Copy files from a remote source to a local destination using the File Transfer Protocol task

❏ Transform data using Microsoft ActiveX scripting technologies using the ActiveX Script task

❏ Execute SQL statements at the database server using the Execute SQL task

❏ Run an external program that performs certain data manipulation and transformation using the Execute Process task

❏ Transfer database objects from one machine to another, given that the machines are running SQL Server, using the Copy SQL Server Objects task

❏ Transform data as you move it from one data source to another using the Transform Data task

❏ Send notifications using the Send Mail task

❏ Bulk-insert data from text files into database tables using the Bulk Insert task

❏ Execute other DTS packages from your own using the Execute Package task

❏ Subscribe to Microsoft Message Queuing Service (MSMQ) queues, giving the ability to send and receive messages from these queues using the Message Queue task

❏ Transfer databases using the Transfer Database task

❏ Process OLAP cubes using the Analysis Services Processing task

❏ Transfer stored procedures between different databases using the Transfer Master Stored Procedures task

❏ Transfer SQL Agent jobs between different databases using the Transfer Jobs task

❏ Transfer logins between two databases using the Transfer Logins task

Four kinds of objects can be found in a DTS package: a Connection Object, a Task object, a Step object, and a Transformation object.

❏ Connection Object: The Connection object defines an OLE DB data source that connects to a source or a destination data store.

❏ Task Object: The Task object includes the details of the tasks that constitute the workflow process, such as copying data, running certain SQL statements, or running certain programs.

❏ Step Object: A Step object is assigned to a single Task object and they control the flow of execution throughout a package. Each Step object my have precedence constrains assigned that specify what other tasks must have executed, and what the outcomes of those task executions must be, before the step object can execute theTask object that it is assigned to.

❏ Transformation Object: Transformation objects allow you to do custom transformation of data between two data sources using T-SQL or ActiveX script. Constraints are associated with these objects that allow enforcing precedence rules on task executions. For example, an On-Success constraint for task 1 will prevent task 2 from executing, unless task 1 has been finished successfully.

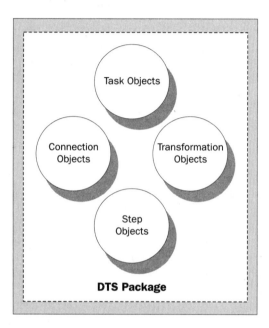

Defining DTS Package Components

You can define the components in a DTS package using several tools. These tools are installed with SQL Server, but support OLAP and building a data warehouse. The main tools used to define DTS packages are:

❏ DTS Designer: This tool is a graphical user interface that can be accessed from the SQL Server Enterprise Manager to create and modify DTS packages. To use the DTS Designer, right-click the **Data Transformation Services** node in Enterprise Manager and select **New Package**. The figure overleaf shows the DTS Designer screen with two connections, the two arrows representing Transform Data tasks and the third arrow indicating the sequence of the two steps. DTS designer will be discussed in great detail in Chapters 7 and 8.

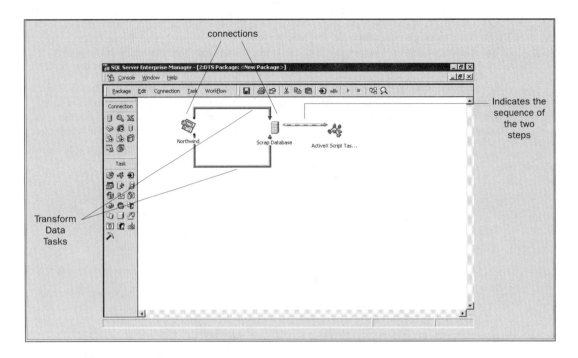

❑ DTS Import/Export Wizards: These are sequences of screens that lead the user into creating and running DTS packages to export and import data between two OLE DB-compliant data sources. The wizards allow for performing data transformation during the import/export process. These wizards can be accessed through the SQL Server Enterprise Manager Select Wizard dialog, or can be run from the command line using the dtswiz utility.

❑ DTS programming interface: DTS services expose a set of COM (Component Object Model) interfaces, and provide a set of OLE automation-compliant interfaces that allow developers to create custom export/import and data transformation programs. The DTS object model includes objects, properties, methods, and collections used to write programs that copy or transform data from an OLE DB source to an OLE DB destination. DTS programs using these interfaces can range from simple Microsoft Visual Basic or Microsoft JScript scripts to complex C++ applications.

This last feature is especially important in data warehouse projects. In such projects, data transformation can become rather complex because the data has to be transformed to fit a different schema from the original operational database schema. Also, data imported into the data warehouse has to undergo aggregation and validation. With the flexibility provided by the COM interfaces, all of these requirements can be achieved.

OLE Automation and the Component Object Model (COM) are technologies that allow developers to write encapsulated reusable code according to object-oriented programming principles. With these technologies, developers don't have to deal with the internal complexities and data of such objects; instead, they only deal with the interfaces they exhibit. These interfaces are a set of properties, methods, and sometimes events exposed to the outside world to allow interaction and use of the objects. Numerous books available from Wrox Press deal with these subjects covering the theories behind and practical application of these technologies.

The Data Warehouse and OLAP Database – The Object Architecture in Analysis Services

The Analysis server is the engine that drives the data analysis and management in the OLAP database. As we have seen in Chapter 1, operational databases may not be feasibly used to generate reports based on historical data in general. This led to the new concepts of "flattening" the operational databases, eliminating some of the relationships among its tables, and creating databases with dimensional schemas.

This section discusses the structure of dimensional databases and the object architecture of Analysis Services, starting with the OLAP cubes.

Dimensional Databases

Although the relational database schema model allows for great flexibility in defining ways to look at and process the data in the database, in a business situation, we often find that the way data is processed is different, especially by decision makers. Decision makers are not interested in the details of every single transaction recorded in the database, instead, they are interested in looking at the "big" picture. For instance, instead of looking at individual customer records in the operational database, which may include data about the customer's phone, address, etc., they are interested in knowing the number of customers per quarter or at the end of each month. As an example, let's take a look at the transaction table in an operational banking database shown below.

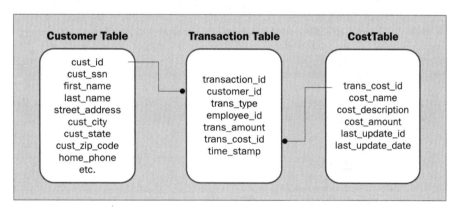

Notice how the Transaction table is linked to many other tables through relationships. In the diagram, we show only the links to the Customer and Cost tables. However, all but two fields in the Transaction table are foreign keys, linking to other tables. The three non-foreign key fields are trans_amount, trans_type and time-stamp.

As the OLTP system is used over time, the table grows in size and becomes full of transaction data, sometimes for the same customers, conducting similar transactions with different amounts and at different costs. Because of the large amount of data it holds and the versatility of the types of activities stored, the table becomes a good candidate for business analysis.

The business analyst may be interested in finding out the effect the transaction cost of ATM withdrawals had on the revenue. In this case, they would be looking for the results in a table or even graph format similar to the chart overleaf:

Cost	Number of Transactions	Revenue
$1.50	7,000	$10,500
$1.00	3,500	$3,500
$2.00	2,500	$5,000
$2.50	2,000	$5000

To get such results, the business analyst may ask a SQL developer to write a, possibly complex, query for them that would extract the data from the OLTP system and put it in the format they want. An example query may look like the code presented below.

```
SELECT    cost_amount AS Cost,
          COUNT (transaction_id) AS [Number of Transactions],
          cost_amount * COUNT (transaction_id) AS Revenue
FROM      Transaction, Cost
WHERE     Cost.trans_cost_id = Transaction.trans_cost_id
AND       Transaction.trans_type = 'ATM'
GROUP BY  cost_amount
```

It is needless to say how time- and resource-consuming it is to follow this path whenever the business analyst wants to get some summaries and aggregations of data. This is a simplified version of what could happen in the real world. In production OLTP systems, such a query may be much larger, involving many table joins that would affect the speed at which the results will return and affect the performance of people using the operational database for everyday important business transactions.

To solve this problem, a separate database would be built to represent the business facts more accurately. This database will be fed from the operational database, but after the data has been transformed to fit the new structure. This is because the schema of this database will not be relational; instead, it will be dimensional. Such database can have what is called a **star** or a **snowflake schema**, or a combination of both.

In these schemas, a fact table is usually joined to a number of "dimension" tables. For our example, we may build a `Transaction` table to record daily transactions of products offered by a given store. This table is referred to as the **fact table**. The `Transaction` table includes the facts of the business activities identified by dimensions. The facts are measures of activities. In our example, the transaction amount, `trans_amount`, is the only measure of facts in the `Transaction` table, just as it usually is in a typical relational database. Dimensions help put the facts in context and represent such things as, time, service, customer, and location. In our example, these dimensions include time, branch, customer, and service. The next figure shows a representation of the star database schema. More details about dimensional analysis, including star and snowflake schemas, are included in Chapter 6, *Designing the Data Warehouse and OLAP Solution.*

In the diagram opposite, you can see that the sales fact table, called `Transaction` in the diagram, captures transactions on a daily level for each branch, for all customers, and for all services. This table, therefore, will grow to be very large. To improve the efficiency with which data is retrieved from the database, aggregates are pre-computed at different levels and stored in the database or in an optimized format, as we will see in later chapters.

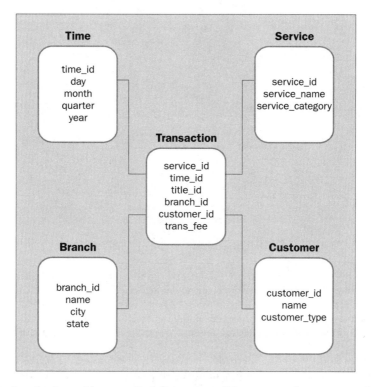

The tables linked to the fact table are called dimensions. They are used to generate the aggregations from the fact table. For instance, you can find the total monthly transaction fees of all services to all customers by all branches when you query the `Transaction` table grouping by month of the year. Or, you can find the total transaction fees by state at all times, for all customers, and for all services when you query the sales table grouping on state. You can have aggregations on a combination of the dimensions in the sales fact table. For example, you can find the total fees for a particular service by state on a monthly bases for a certain type of customers by grouping on state and month and adding the appropriate criteria in the `WHERE` clause for the customer and book category.

OLAP Cubes

The previous section introduced us to the concepts of dimensional databases and dimensional analysis. Let's get back to the Analysis server architecture now. The most important part of the Analysis server architecture is the OLAP cubes. These cubes usually represent the data. The dimensions of the cube represent the dimensions of the fact table. Each cell in the cube represents a fact corresponding to a level of detail for the different dimensions of the cube. Although the graphical representation of the cube can only show three dimensions, a data cube can have up to 128 dimensions when using SQL Server's Analysis Services (up from 64 in SQL Server 7 OLAP Services). The figure overleaf shows a representation of a data cube for the transaction table with the branch, service, and time dimensions shown.

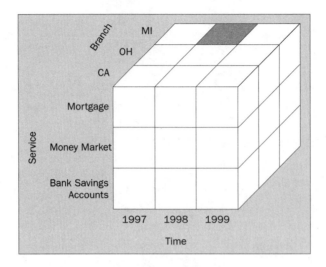

If you want to use this cube to find out the total mortgage transaction fees collected for branches in Michigan (MI) during 1998 for the mortgage service category, you need to look at the shaded cell in the figure above, which is the resulting cell from the intersection of the three mentioned dimensions. That cell should contain the total fees for mortgages collected in 1998 in the state of Michigan. In other words, this value is the sum of the mortgage fee fact along these dimensions in the fact table.

The Analysis server works with the Microsoft Decision Support Services (DSS) to allow you to build your cube from any source of data that has an OLE DB provider. This source can be a relational database in any database management system that has an ODBC driver, such as Oracle or Sybase SQL Server, or has a native OLE DB provider, such as SQL Server, or Microsoft Access. The data source for the cube can also be a dimensional database, text files, or even a directory service that is accessible with an LDAP data source such as the Active Directory.

Cube Partitions

Partitions represent logical divisions of cube data broken down by the values of a particular dimension or the data source. For example, you can have a partition on the transaction cube based on the state values creating partitions for regions like Midwest or Northeast. Alternatively, you may want to create a partition that stores transaction data based on a three-year basis. Note that a cube will always contain at least one partition.

A partition can be saved separately on a different disk drive from the original cube. This allows you to place data that is not used or queried frequently on slower storage media, or alternatively place frequently queried data on higher speed storage media. A description of partitions is presented in Chapter 9.

Partitions can also be distributed and stored on different Analysis servers, providing a clustered approach to cube storage and distributing workload across Analysis servers. The partitions stored on other Analysis servers than the one that stores the meta data for them are called remote partitions.

Linked Cubes

OLAP data cubes are comprised of dimensions and measures. A measure is a set of values based on a column in the cube's fact table, which are usually numeric. Measures are also the central values of a cube that are analyzed, that is the numeric data that is of primary interest to those querying the cube.

One feature of the Analysis server is that it allows linking two or more OLAP cubes that share common dimensions. This process creates linked cubes. An example of a shared dimension is time. The time dimension can be used, as we saw in the previous example, for the transaction cube. Time dimensions can also be used for an employee cube, and so on.

Linked cubes take advantage of the shared dimensions to create links among data sets that seem unrelated. Linked cubes require no additional storage, and can link cubes based on different storage types. For instance, you can create a linked cube that links the employee and transaction cubes, even if the employee cube is stored in the relational database and the transaction cube in the multidimensional database.

With the linked cubes proposed above, bank managers and decision makers can establish the relationship between the average number of bank tellers or mortgage officers in a branch, and the total revenue of the branch related to their services, for a particular time period. Such information will give these managers an insight into this complex relationship and help them decide the optimal average number of employees for a particular service per branch. It is worth warning that going overboard with these relationships may be counterproductive. Many of the relationships established may make no sense and have no value, such as the number of ATM transactions and the number of checkbooks ordered.

> **The validity of these relationships is closely associated with the quality of the raw data that supports them.**

OLAP Storage Architecture

The Analysis server and the Decision Support Services that ship with SQL Server 2000 support three options of storage, based on the data cube storage method. These options are multidimensional OLAP (MOLAP), relational OLAP (ROLAP), and a hybrid of the previous two options (HOLAP). Each of these options provides certain benefits, depending on the size of your database and how the data will be used. These options are discussed in the following sections below.

MOLAP

MOLAP is a high performance, multidimensional data storage format.The data supporting the cubes is stored with this option on the OLAP server as a multidimensional database. MOLAP gives the best query performance, because it is specifically optimized for multidimensional data queries.

Since MOLAP requires copying all the data and converting its format appropriately to fit the multidimensional data store, MOLAP is appropriate for small to medium-sized data sets. Copying all of the data for such data sets would not require significant loading time or utilize large amounts of disk space.

ROLAP

Relational OLAP storage keeps the data that feeds the cubes in the original relational tables. A separate set of relational tables is used to store and reference aggregation data in this OLTP system. These tables are not downloaded to the DSS server. The tables that hold the aggregations of the data are called materialized views. These tables store data aggregations as defined by the dimensions when the cube is created.

With this option, aggregation tables have fields for each dimension and measure. Each dimension column is indexed. A composite index is also created for all of the dimension fields. Due to its nature, ROLAP is ideal for large databases or legacy data that is infrequently queried. The only drawback to these systems is that generating reports from them or processing the cube data may affect users of the operational database reducing me performance of their transaction processing.

HOLAP

The DSS server also supports a combination of MOLAP and ROLAP. This combination is referred to as HOLAP. With HOLAP, the original data is kept in its relational database tables similar to ROLAP. Aggregations of the data are performed and stored in a multidimensional format. An advantage of this system is that HOLAP provides connectivity to large data sets in relational tables while taking advantage of the faster performance of the multidimensional aggregation storage. A disadvantage of this option is that the amount of processing between the ROLAP and MOLAP systems may affect its efficiency.

OLAP Client Architecture

The figure below shows a schematic of the client architecture of the Microsoft Analysis Services.

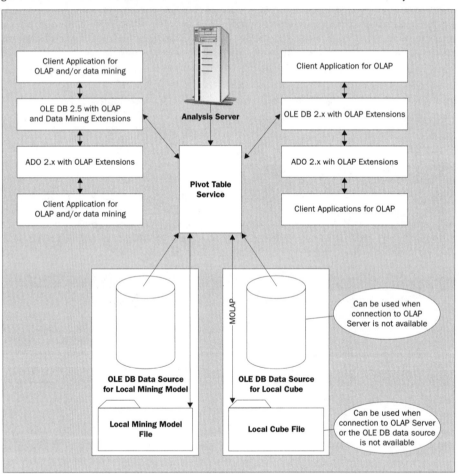

The heart of the client architecture is the PivotTable Service. The PivotTable Service interacts with the Analysis server and provides COM-based interfaces for use by client applications accessing OLAP data on the server. Depending on the language the client applications are written in, these applications connect to the PivotTable Service using OLE DB 2.0 with the optional OLAP support extensions, or Microsoft ActiveX Data Objects (ADO 2.x) also using the OLAP extensions. If the applications are to access data mining models, the version of OLE DB has to be 2.5 or later with support for data mining.

The PivotTable Service is an in-process desktop version of the Analysis server. This service is designed to provide online and offline data analysis and online access to OLAP data. The PivotTable Service functions as a client of the Analysis server. In other words, this allows the PivotTable Service to access OLAP data and data mining models online, perform analyses and predictions on the data, including building data cubes, perform some cache management for offline analyses, and conduct offline analyses of cached data on the client. In addition to this functionality, the PivotTable Service provides COM interfaces to other client applications to access the Analysis server, the OLAP data, and the client cache.

In a nutshell, the PivotTable Service provides the following functionality:

❑ Serves as a shared connection point to the OLAP server for all of the client applications, for both online and offline analyses.

❑ Allows for building data cubes using relational data by functioning as a service provider to implement multidimensional functionality and expose the OLE DB interfaces with OLAP extensions.

❑ Serves as a tabular data provider by supporting a subset of SQL. This allows the presentation of the data returned from the SQL statement as a pivot table.

❑ Supports multidimensional expressions (MDX), which makes it a multidimensional data provider. MDX is the structured query language used for the definition and handling of multidimensional data and objects. It allows access to data cubes, and their dimensions from SQL statements. MDX will be discussed in detail in Chapters 10 and 11.

❑ Enables client applications to create a local cube directly from a relational data source.

❑ Enables client applications to create local data-mining models from those stored in the Analysis servers.

❑ Allows users to download data from data sources and store the data in a multidimensional structure on a local computer for offline analysis.

You can build your own applications that use the PivotTable Service to access OLAP data, or you can use Microsoft or third-party applications that already support this service for access to multidimensional OLAP data. Microsoft Excel and Microsoft Access (Office 2000) support the PivotTable service and can use it to connect to an OLAP server to retrieve and analyze data, and to create and use local cube files. The PivotTable Service will be discussed in more detail in Chapter 12.

Summary

In this chapter, you have read about the Microsoft Analysis Services architecture. This architecture is divided into three main parts, source data, Analysis server, and the client architecture. The Analysis server is the main mechanism for analyzing multidimensional data, creating data cubes, building data aggregations, and connecting to the client and data sources. The PivotTable Service is the essential part of the client architecture having the unique and important feature of allowing both online and offline analyses of the OLAP data and mining model predictions. Offline analyses are possible thanks to this service's cache management that allows users to download data from the multidimensional or relational data sources and use it offline in local cubes and mining models that can be used to conduct the analysis locally.

In the next chapter, you will read about the different SQL Server tools that can be used to facilitate the use of the powerful features and capabilities of Analysis Services.

Professional SQL Server 2000 Data WareHousing
Data Warehouse

3

Analysis Services Tools

This chapter introduces the main tools that ship with SQL Server 2000 and Analysis Services to help developers, database administrators, and to some extent end users, build sound solutions based on this technology. We will focus on the tools that help us use Analysis Services, such as the Analysis Manager, and SQL Server Data Transformation Services (DTS) Designer. We will also briefly discuss other tools that help with administration and performance tuning of SQL Server databases in general. These tools include SQL Server Enterprise Manager, Query Analyzer, and DTS Package Designer. Based on this, this chapter will cover with the following:

❑ Analysis Manager, an overview of the different parts that constitute this tool and the different "sub-tools" and wizards associated with it, such as the Cube Editor,and the Dimension Editor.

❑ SQL Server Enterprise Manager, a brief description of this tool

❑ SQL Server DTS Designer, an overview that shows you how this tool can be used to migrate data between different data sources

❑ SQL Server Query Analyzer, a brief description of this tool that can be used to issue SQL queries against SQL Server database

Analysis Manager

Analysis Manager is the main graphical tool that allows users to interact with Analysis Services. With this tool, you can create new OLAP databases, or data-mining models, and you can create cubes and dimensions. You can also import OLAP databases or cubes, and edit them, among many other things. The main screen of Analysis Manager is shown overleaf:

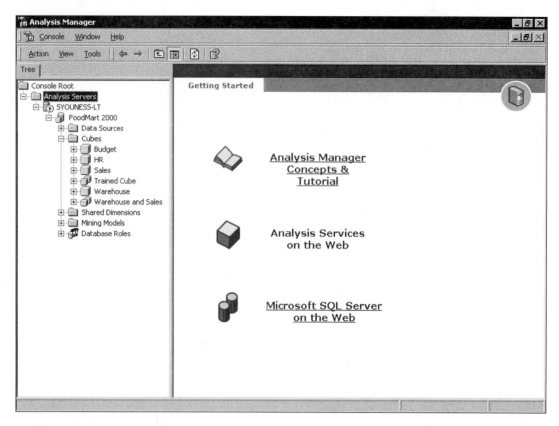

If you are familiar with the Microsoft Management Console (MMC), this screen will look familiar to you. This is because Analysis Manager is a snap-in into MMC and the very top menu bar is the MMC menu bar with its Console, Window, and Help menus. As you may already know, other tools that plug into MMC as snap-ins include SQL Server Enterprise Manager, Windows Component Services, and Internet Services Manager.

Like other MMC snap-ins, the Analysis Manager screen has two major panes: a tree-structure pane on the left that includes a hierarchy of the items in Analysis Services, and a web page pane on the right that includes details of the selected item from the left pane.

The hierarchy under Analysis Services in the left pane starts with the Analysis server name. Under the server name, you can see the OLAP databases hosted on the server. You can register as many servers as you like into Analysis Manager allowing you to have a central place to manage these servers. To do so, you need to right-click on the Analysis Services option in the tree structure and select the Register Server option from the context-sensitive menu. This will open a dialog box into which you fill in the name of the server you are registering, assuming you have network connectivity to it from your machine. A message indicating that Analysis Manager is connecting to the server appears, and then the server name will show up in the left pane under Analysis Services.

As an example on using this tool, you can create a new OLAP database. To do so, expand the tree branches by clicking on the "plus" signs next to the items on the tree structure. Expand your server and create a new database by right-clicking the server name and selecting "New Database" as shown opposite.

Following this, a new dialog will show up into which you can enter a database name and description:

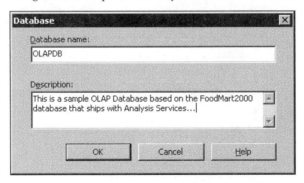

The new database shows up the in tree structure under the server name with five items below it: Data Sources, Cubes, Shared Dimensions, Mining Models, and Database Roles.

Data Sources

The first item, data sources, helps you connect to a data source for your OLAP database. Right-click **Data Sources** under the OLAPDB database and select **New Data Source**. A dialog will appear asking you to select an OLE DB provider; select "Microsoft Jet 4.0 OLE DB Provider" to connect to the FoodMart 2000 database, which is a sample MS Access database that ships with Analysis Services, and click the **Next** button.

The default location of the FoodMart 2000 database is at **c:\program files\Microsoft Analysis Services\Samples\FoodMart 2000.mdb.**

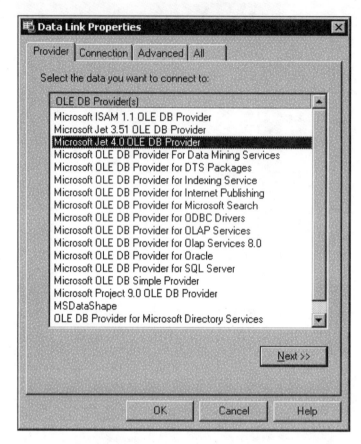

You find the Access database using the browse button (with the ellipsis). Test the connection to make sure that you can actually connect to the Access database by clicking the Test Connection button:

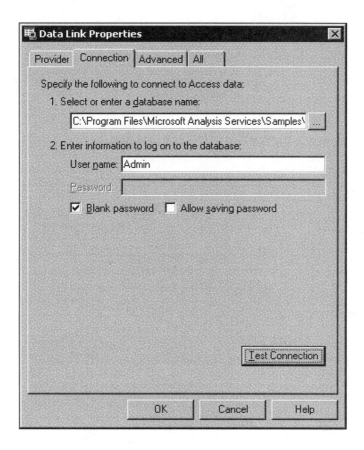

Cubes

The Cubes item in the tree structure allows you to view and perform some operations on OLAP cubes that are in your database. In Chapter 9 we will learn how to actually build cubes, here our goal is to familiarize ourselves with the tool. You can expand the Cubes item under the FoodMart 2000 database to expose a number of OLAP cubes underneath in the database as shown overleaf:

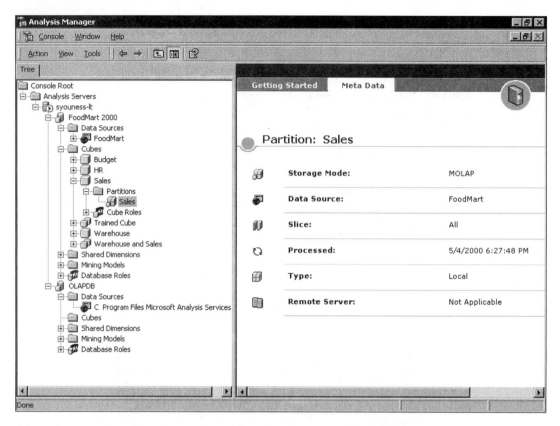

The right pane shows data that corresponds to the selection in the hierarchy in the left pane's tree structure. In many cases, data is presented in different tabs on that pane. For instance, the figure above shows the Meta Data tab for a particular partition of a cube. More tabs may also become visible as the selection on the left pane changes. For instance, if a cube were to be selected, a new tab, called "Data", would appear allowing the user to browse the cube data as shown in the figure below:

> *Do not worry if you do not know what some of the items of the tree structure of Analysis Manager or the right-hand page (such as meta data and partitions) mean. They will all be explained in later chapters in great detail. These references are descriptions of the screens you see.*

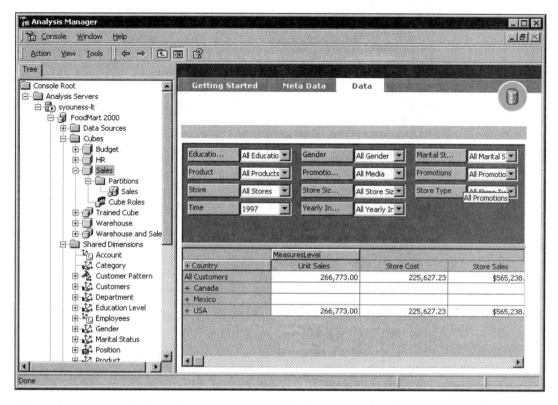

The right pane is basically a client application to OLAP services. This allows the user to "slice" and "dice" the data across any dimension and for any fact they are after. Chapter 9 and Chapter 12 will have explanations of these terms as they discuss building OLAP cubes (Chapter 9), and using Analysis Services clients through the discussion of the PivotTable service (Chapter 12).

> We will be seeing more on OLAP, OLAP cubes and how they are built and stored in Microsoft Analysis Services in Chapter 6 about planning the data warehouse and the OLAP solution.

Shared Dimensions

Shared dimensions are dimensions that can be shared by multiple cubes. Examples include the time, product, and customer dimensions.

Mining Models

Mining models are algorithms used to conduct advanced analysis of the data that could lead to predictions of certain behaviors based on existing data. For instance, a model could predict the buying trend of a line of products based on statistical analysis of historical data. This item in Analysis Manager allows you to manage such mining models.

Database Roles

This item allows you to manage custom and built-in roles in the Analysis database.

Analysis Manager Wizards

Many wizards are included with Analysis Manager to make it easier to perform various tasks. For example, there are wizards that guide you through connecting to an OLAP data source, others that help you build a cube, or dimensions within a cube, and so on.

One of the wizards provided by the Analysis Manager is the Cube wizard that can be launched by right-clicking the Cubes item in the tree-structure pane, selecting New Cube, and then the Wizard option. This brings up the Cube wizard's welcome screen. The subsequent screens guide you step by step through building your cube by identifying the cube measures, dimensions, partitions, and so on.

Other wizards can be launched from the Cube wizard, such as the Dimension wizard. This wizard will in turn guide you through creating a new dimension and adding it to your cube. The Dimension wizard can also be launched by right-clicking the Shared Dimensions item in the hierarchy and selecting New Dimension and the Wizard option from the context-sensitive menu.

Another wizard we will encounter later in the book is the Virtual Cube wizard. Virtual cubes work in a similar way to views in a relational database. They are created by joining cubes together, creating a "super cube" so that you can make a large view on your OLAP data without consuming disk space. For more information on virtual cubes, read Chapter 6, *Designing the Data Warehousing and OLAP Solution*.

Even though wizards can be a great help in building cubes quickly, they can sometimes impose constraints on what one can do when creating these cubes, especially for advanced users who know the ins and outs of building OLAP cubes. For instance, the wizard may not be able to join some of the dimension tables to the fact table leaving you to do this yourself in the Cube Editor, which we will take a look at now.

Cube Editor

The Cube Editor is another important tool that comes with Analysis Manager. This tool is a full application that allows you to create, edit, and manage OLAP cubes. The main screen of the Cube Editor consists of two panes, with the left-hand pane containing several hierarchies for dimensions, measures, actions, calculated members, and named sets. The right-hand pane contains two tabs, the Schema tab and the Data tab. The Schema tab is a page in which you can view or build an entity-relation diagram representing the data warehouse or data mart schema. This schema is dimensional and follows what is called a star or snowflake paradigm. To learn more about star and snowflake schemas, you may want to read Chapters 2, 4, and 6.

You can launch the Cube Editor by right-clicking on a cube and selecting Edit from the context-sensitive menu, or by right-clicking on the Cubes item in the tree structure and selecting New Cube, and then Editor from the context-sensitive menu:

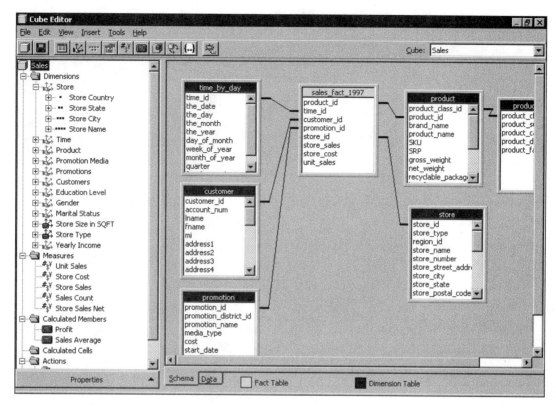

The Data tab shows you a page in which you can view the cube data in a fashion similar to the one we saw earlier in the Analysis Manager screen's right-hand pane. Another element that is worth mentioning here is that in the left pane, a button at the bottom labeled "Properties" can be used to view or hide the a mini pane that shows detailed properties of items selected in the main left-hand pane. For instance, in the figure overleaf, the properties mini pane shows basic and advanced attributes (notice the tabs within the mini pane) of the Store Country level in the Store dimension of the Sales cube. The figure also shows the data tab in the right pane:

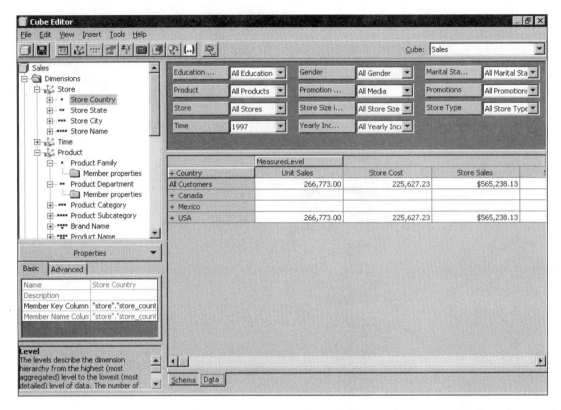

Other functionality provided by the Cube Editor includes validating cube structure, drilling down and rolling up data, designing the cube storage, optimizing the schema, and processing the cube. You can find these functions under the Tools menu of the Cube Editor.

We will be seeing more of this tool in Chapter 9.

Let's now take a look at how we can use the Analysis Manager to build and edit dimensions.

Dimension Editor

Similar to the Cube Editor, you can use the Dimension Editor to build new dimensions or edit and process existing ones. You can only launch the Dimension Editor from the main Analysis Manager screens. To do so, right-click on one of the existing dimensions and select Edit from the context-sensitive menu. Or, right-click the Shared Dimensions item in the tree structure and select New Dimension, then Editor from the context-sensitive menu.

The screen you will be presented with should look similar to the one opposite. The Dimension Editor looks similar to the Cube Editor; it also has the mini Properties pane within the left-hand pane that serves a similar purpose to the one in the Cube Editor. The differences are that in the tree structure in the left pane, you only see the selected dimension, in the screenshot opposite we selected Store, and you can expand it to see its levels and member properties for each level:

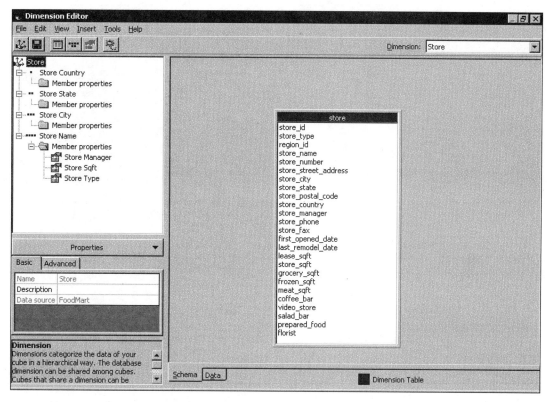

In the right-hand pane of the Dimension Editor, you can see a representation of the table structure that holds the data for the dimension in the data warehouse in the Schema tab. The data tab in this pane holds a three-part page showing the dimension data (members) in the form of a hierarchy that you can expand to the level you want as seen in the figure overleaf. Another part shows the member property attributes of the selected member in the dimension. The third part is a work pad that allows you to manipulate custom members in a particular level:

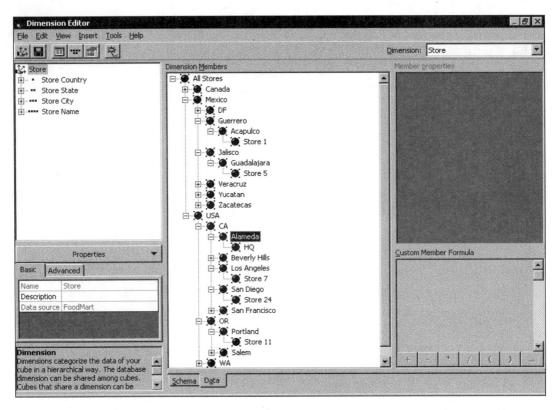

Again, the Dimension Editor is another great graphical tool that allows you to build and edit your dimensions with ease and a great deal of flexibility not provided by the Dimension wizard. Other functionality provided by this tool includes validating dimension structure, counting dimension members, and processing the dimension.

Enterprise Manager

The main graphical tool that ships with SQL Server is Enterprise Manager (EM). This tool is used by database administrators and developers to maintain all aspects of the SQL Server databases, but in this book we will focus only on areas that relate directly to data warehousing and Analysis Services.

> *Many books discuss Enterprise Manager in great detail including* Professional SQL Server 2000 Programming *(Wrox Press, ISBN 1-861004-48-6) and* Beginning SQL Server 2000 Programming *(Wrox Press, ISBN 1-861005-23-7).*

Of course, this does not mean that other areas in this tool are not essential for the data warehousing development and construction. After all, the data warehouse is a SQL Server database and EM is the tool to maintain it. Also, EM is the tool you can use to maintain all operational databases, called On Line Transaction Processing (OLTP) systems, which are the source of the data that gets fed into the data warehouse.

The screen shot below shows the main screen of EM with the Data Transformation Services item highlighted in the left-hand pane:

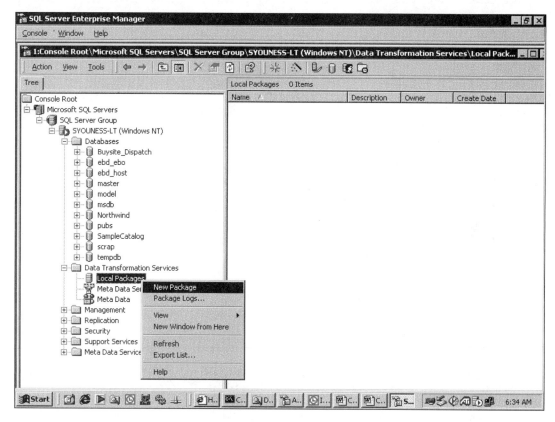

Data Transformation Services (DTS) is the main service in EM that relates directly to Analysis Services and data warehousing. It is the service you will use to transfer and transform data between the OLTP system and the data warehouse or data mart. The main tool that comes with this service is the DTS Package designer or editor. This tool allows you to build what are called DTS packages. These packages, as you will see in Chapters 7 and 8, are collections of tasks that are related to some data sources and organized in a workflow fashion to allow the safe and efficient transfer of data between different data sources.

DTS Package Designer

As you can see in the figure above, you can launch the DTS package designer by right-clicking the Local Packages item underneath the Data Transformation Services section in the EM screen and selecting New Package to create a new package. Or, if you already have a package, you can double-click it to open it, which will open the DTS package designer. This figure overleaf shows the main package screen. The screen consists of many sections, a tool bar, a menu bar, and two tool boxes, the connection and the task tool boxes. These tool boxes are actually tool bars that are located on the left-hand side of the screen by default.

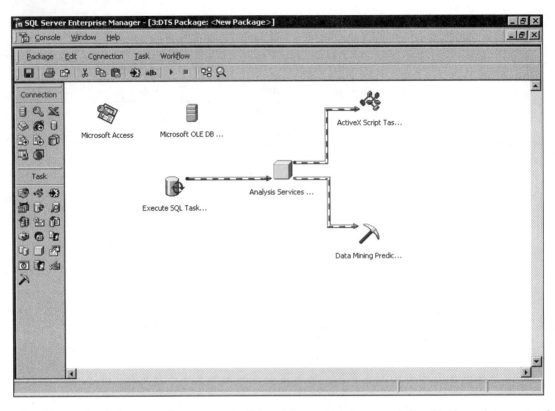

The DTS package designer allows you to build transformations from predefined tasks or from script that you write in a special kind of task called an **ActiveX Script Task**. The scripting languages that can be used are VB Script, JScript, or PerlScript, however, you can call external code that is written in any programming language that supports object linking and embedding (OLE) automation, such as Visual Basic, Visual C++, Delphi, and other languages.

In the diagram above, you can see two connections, one to a SQL Server database and the other to an Access database. You also see several tasks:

❑   An Execute SQL Task that allows you to execute any T-SQL code whether it is a stored procedure or a query you build and run from this task.

❑   An Analysis Services Processing task that allows you to link to OLAP cubes and process them.

❑   An Data Mining Prediction task that allows you to construct a data-mining model and perform some prediction for your data based on it.

❑   An ActiveX Script task that allows you the flexibility to do almost anything you want in terms of transformations using VB Script. Also, as was mentioned before, it is this kind of task that allows you to call external code you wrote as COM objects to handle especially complex situations.

You can also see in the diagram above some lines linking the tasks together. These lines represent a **workflow process** with one task executing first and the other next. The Execute SQL task is the first task to be executed followed by the Analysis Services Processing task. If the latter task executes successfully, the Data Mining Prediction task is executed; otherwise the ActiveX script task is executed. This is a situation where depending on the success of one task either one of two tasks can be executed. For instance, you could have error handling code in the ActiveX script task that allows you to handle errors according to the way you like and even call some error objects that your company standardizes making your error handling in the DTS package consistent with other error handling code in your projects.

Another powerful aspect of the DTS package is allowing you to perform transformations on the data using a transformation task. This functionality allows you to map certain fields from one table to fields in another table performing some processing as well, such as data time format conversion. You can also use ActiveX scripting to perform the transformations you choose within the transformation task.

This is a brief description of what you can do with the DTS package designer and DTS in general, you can read more details about this powerful technology in Chapters 7 and 8. Let's now take a look another important tool, the Query Analyzer.

Query Analyzer

Query Analyzer is an important tool that is useful in OLTP systems. It is a tool that comes with SQL Server Enterprise Manager to allow the user to issue SQL queries against tables in the database. You can launch this tool from the SQL Server Program Group in under the Start | Programs menu on your desktop, or from EM by selecting Tools | Query Analyzer from the EM menu bar. Query Analyzer also allows the user to write stored procedures, views, and triggers. In short, this is a SQL editor with many powerful features. The scripting language used in this editor is Transact SQL, the SQL Server flavor of SQL. It comes with a user interface that makes it easy to use and powerful. The user interface is seen below:

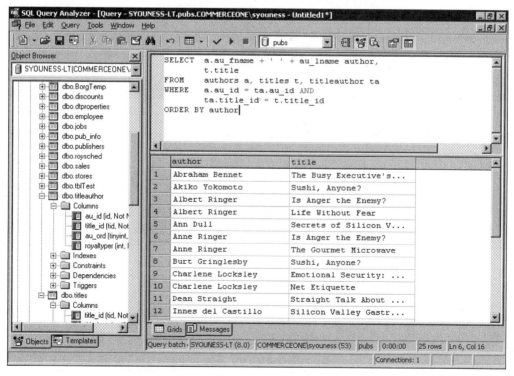

As you can see the user interface of the Query Analyzer consists of two main parts:

- ❑ The left-hand pane that includes a hierarchy of the databases on the server and allows you to drill down to the individual fields in the tables, or even indexes on the table and its fields.

- ❑ The right-hand pane, which is the editor in which you enter your SQL code and view the results. In the figure above, you can see a query that returns the authors in the pubs database, which ships with SQL Server, and the books they wrote. The results of the query are shown in the lower section of this pane a tabular format.

You can also display the execution plan of the query allowing you to fine-tune it for optimal performance. We will not go into any more depth in explaining this tool, but you can see detailed coverage of it in *Beginning SQL Server 2000 Programming* (Wrox Press, ISBN 1-861005-23-7) or *Professional SQL Server 2000 Programming* (Wrox Press, ISBN 1-86190094-48-6).

SQL Server Profiler

SQL Server Profiler is a tool that ships with SQL Server to allow you to monitor the performance of SQL Server. This tool allows you to create monitors for certain events in SQL Server, such as execution of SQL queries, stored procedures, etc. or for events, like starting the service and logging in, etc. The Tool can be launched from the Start | Programs | Microsoft SQL Server program group on the desktop, or from the Tools menu in EM. The main screen looks like the figure below:

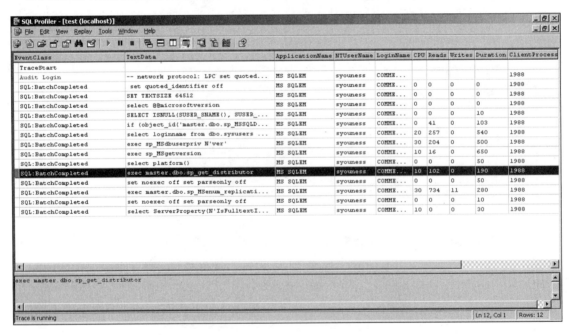

The opposite shows a sample of the output of a trace event by the SQL Server Profiler. The traces can be defined to many levels within the database from the database itself to the smallest element, such as an index, field, etc. The following screenshot shows the dialog that allows for this to happen:

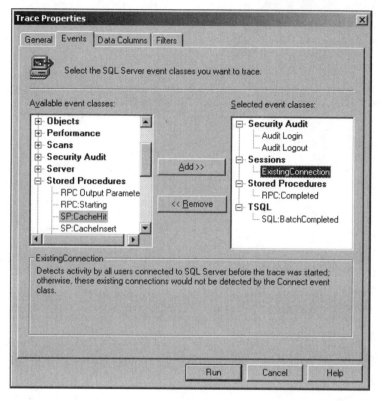

This tool is very helpful in debugging database applications in general, allowing you to find performance bottlenecks and the best places you may tackle to get optimal performance. I am not going to explain this tool in much detail, because this is out of the scope of this book. However, you can find detailed explanation of this tool in other SQL Server books, such as the Wrox book: *Professional SQL Server 2000 Programming* by Rob Vieira.

Summary

In this chapter we familiarized ourselves with some important tools that we will be using later on in the book to build solutions with this technology. We looked at many tools in this chapter, including the Analysis Manager with many of its functions and capabilities. We also looked at the wizards and editors that come with Analysis Manager that allow you to create and manipulate OLAP cubes and their dimensions. Finally, we briefly covered SQL Server Enterprise Manager focusing on the DTS package designer and the Query Analyzer.

Data Warehouse

Data Marts

This chapter presents an overview of the data mart concept and how it differs from a data warehouse from business-process and structural-design perspectives. In the chapter, you will read about the development of data marts, with the most widely adopted theories, the top-down, and the bottom-up approaches, in addition to other approaches. Managing the data mart is another topic that is covered from a high level leaving the details of such management to the data warehouse management chapter in the book.In this chapter we will cover:

- ❑ What a data mart is and how it fits in the business processes

- ❑ How a data mart differ from an enterprise data warehouse, and who should implement a data mart solution

- ❑ How a data mart developed:

- ❑ The top-down approach

- ❑ The bottom-up approach

- ❑ The federated approach

- ❑ Managing the data mart: planning, construction, pilot, data loading, roll-out, and maintenance

What is a Data Mart?

Data warehousing has grown into a full-blown architecture separate from the operational or transactional systems. Today, data warehousing has different components that serve different purposes and communities. The architecture that has grown from the origins of data warehousing is today something that can be called the enterprise information architecture as you can see in the figure below. In this architecture, the operational systems are usually On-Line Transaction Processing (OLTP) systems that serve end-user applications. Such an application could be a point-of-sale application allowing customers to buy goods from your enterprise, or a purchasing application allowing you to buy goods from your suppliers. These applications could simply be time reporting applications for your employees to enter their time, or they could be specialized in specific functionality called upon by other applications, such as a credit check.

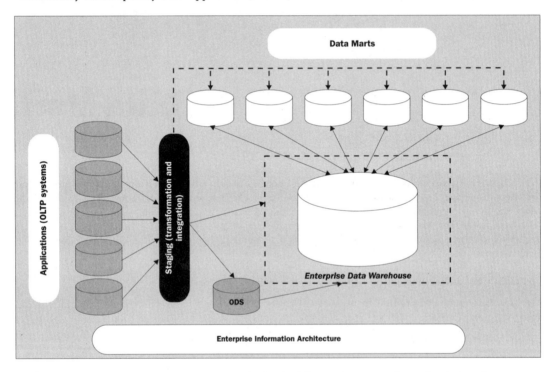

The transaction data that is collected through the OLTP systems passes through a layer of programs whose purpose is to integrate and transform the data to make it fit to enter the data warehouse. The layer of programs can be called a **staging layer** or "integration and transformation" programs or ETL – Extract/Transform/Load programs. These programs can be written manually or in an automated manner by program generators specifically designed to suit the needs of this interface.

Once the transactional data passes through the staging layer, the data is fundamentally changed to meet the informational needs of the enterprise according to the data warehouse design. Keys are altered so that there is one corporate understanding of data, structures are changed, and encoding algorithms are unified. The data enters the layer of integration and transformation programs in an "unintegrated" state and passes out of the layer of programs in an integrated state. The data then passes into the enterprise data warehouse in a very granular form. Once in the enterprise data warehouse, the data is ready to serve as a basis for all sorts of **decision support systems** (DSS) processing.

The data warehouse is also fed by the **operational data store** (ODS). ODS is a hybrid of the transactional system and the decision support system with functionality straddling the needs of both systems. The ODS provides standard transaction response time (two to three seconds) as well as serving as a place where data can be aggregated.

On the other side of the picture you see emanating from the enterprise data warehouse a collection of data marts. To the end user, the data marts seem to be the data warehouse, because it is here that the end user has direct interaction with the data warehouse environment. The data marts are oriented to the needs and specific requirements, such as serving the data needs of a particular department, or maybe serving as a subset of the data warehouse for a particular period of time, etc. The data marts are either fed granular data from the enterprise data warehouse that is then reshaped to meet the specific requirements around which the data mart was designed; or, they are fed directly from the integration and transformation layer, in which case this layer tailors the data to the specific requirements of the data mart. The data marts, in the later case, feed the data warehouse with data that is then kept in the central repository of all enterprise data, the enterprise data warehouse.

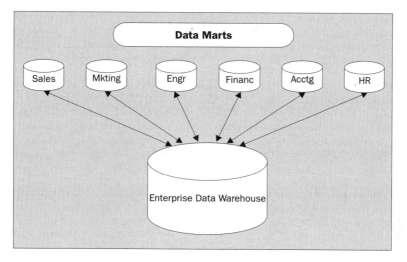

From the above, we can say that a data mart is a data structure that resembles the data warehouse and is designed to help with decision support, but holds a subset of the data warehouse data in a way that meets specific requirements.

One of the advantages of a data mart is its mobility, for instance, a salesperson can load the data mart onto a laptop computer and take it with them on to one of their sales trips. The data mart can in this case be tailored to give them information that would help them with this particular sales endeavor. For instance, if the sales trip is to Japan, the data mart can be holding data about sales in Japan for the last few years with information about the key customers and statistics about the transactions they have saved in the data mart. With this, the salesperson can do their job and use the data in the data mart for their advantage without having to be connected to the enterprise data warehouse.

How Does a Data Mart Differ from a Data Warehouse?

There are two main differences between the data mart and the data warehouse. I have already mentioned the first difference, which is that the data mart contains a subset of the data in the data warehouse. The data in the data mart is requirement-driven and is designed to satisfy a particular requirement, such as departmental data, customer group data, data for a specific period, etc. The data warehouse, on the other hand, serves as a repository of the enterprise data regardless of specific requirements.

The data warehouse is designed as part of the strategic approach towards the enterprise planning, whereas, a data mart is designed as part of the tactical planning to satisfy a particular requirement. This does not mean, of course, that an enterprise can go about designing data marts randomly without looking at the overall strategy. If this happens, the resulting data marts will be disconnected and will be very difficult to integrate into the enterprise data warehouse later on. Therefore, the design of the data warehousing strategy should include coming up with certain standards and criteria with which data mart designs should conform in a way that does not hinder their assimilation into the data warehouse later on.

As a result of this fact, the fact that a data mart includes only a subset of the data warehouse, implementation of the data warehouse is more time-consuming and costs much more (on the order of several million US dollars to tens of millions in some cases). The implementation of the data mart is much faster and costs much less (on the order of several hundred thousands of US dollars to a few millions).

Many decision support systems (DSS) vendors came up with "out-of-the-box" data mart solutions that they claim can be implemented in a very short period of time. You have to be extra cautious when you deal with such solutions because they are usually designed to meet the mundane requirements of the area they tackle. Once you have specific requirements that are not covered by these systems, it takes just as much effort to customize them as to build the data mart from scratch in most cases. Also, with such solutions, chances are the design will not conform to whatever guidelines you set for your data mart design as part of the overall enterprise data warehousing strategy for your enterprise.

The other main difference of the data mart from the data warehouse is that the data in the data mart can be more granular than the data warehouse. Since the requirements of the data mart are more defined than those of the data warehouse, you can afford to pre-aggregate the data along the requirements you are aware of and store the results of the queries you expect will be run against the data mart to make the extraction of the data faster and more efficient.

Who Should Implement a Data Mart Solution?

There are three options for implementing the data mart:

❑ The enterprise information technology department can do it using whatever expertise it may have in this area from the point of gathering requirements and planning to the roll-out stage.

❑ A vendor can be hired to implement the data mart. In this case, the vendor is assumed to have the expertise to do such implementations quickly and efficiently.

❑ The enterprise information technology department can work together with a vendor to implement the data mart.

Each one of the approaches above has its benefits and disadvantages. For instance, the first option seems to keep the cost of the implementation within the organization, but, it involves a great deal of risk of the enterprise not having the sufficient experience in building such data structures, which may end up with a collection of data marts that serve several departments without the overall vision and design of the enterprise data warehouse. This could result in huge problems down the road when data from the data marts needs to be aggregated into the data warehouse.

With the second approach, you guarantee yourself a professional solution implemented by experts. However, there is risk that these experts may miss some of the crucial requirements of the business due to the lack of the domain knowledge needed to build a perfect solution.

With the last approach, both the enterprise and the vendor win. A good solution that satisfies most of the requirements can be achieved at a lower cost in the long term.

Development Approaches

Data warehouse and data mart experts developed three major approaches towards building data marts. Each of these approaches has its advantages and disadvantages. Some advocate having an enterprise data warehouse that feeds the data to a set of dependent data marts according to their specific requirements. Some advocate building data marts first and then aggregating them into the enterprise data warehouse, or even into a "distributed" data warehouse. Finally, some experts take a hybrid solution where independent data marts can be built side by side to dependent data marts that take their feeds from the enterprise data warehouse.

Top-Down Approach

As mentioned in the paragraph above and depicted in the figure overleaf, this approach involves building a data warehouse and having it feed the data to a set of dependent data marts. For instance, data related to the human resources (HR) department can be extracted from the data warehouse into one of the data marts, and data belonging to customers in Eastern Europe can be extracted into another data mart. So, according to this approach, data flows from the operational systems (OLTP systems) into the staging area where transformations and aggregations are conducted. The data comes out of the staging areas into the data warehouse, which then feeds it to the dependent data marts. Some of the benefits of this approach include:

❑ It employs a rigorous and familiar methodology for gathering, modeling, and implementing end-user decision processing requirements. This methodology comes from the implementaion of the data warehouse, where it is passed to the design and implementation of these data marts.

❑ It creates a data warehousing system that gives end users the ability to have an enterprise-wide perspective of business operations, issues, and potential opportunities for business development.

❑ It is based on a subject-oriented data model that minimizes integration problems between data warehouse projects. This is also mainly due to the fact that all the data marts will follow the same design and implementation processes, thus integrating them later on using DSS tools will be a relatively easy task.

❑ It permits underlying dependent data marts to be constructed from enterprise data warehouse information, thus providing a managed approach to using data mart technology.

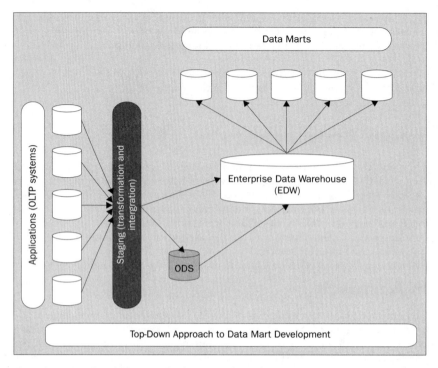

Top-Down Approach to Data Mart Development

However, these benefits should be weighed against the following disadvantages before deciding on following this approach:

❑ Top-down data mart projects often lead to long delivery schedules, high capitalization, cost overruns, and poor end-user functionality, even when adequate cost justification is done prior to the project. This is because the data mart project is dependent on the data warehouse, which may still be evolving. Also, the budget of the data mart development is, in most cases, dependent on that of the data warehouse and on other data mart development efforts.

❑ Enterprise data warehouse approaches with their long delivery cycles cannot deliver solutions fast enough to satisfy the demand of organizations for solutions that enable them to respond rapidly to changing business conditions and quickly exploit new business opportunities.

Bottom-Up Approach

This approach involves building the data marts first, then aggregating their data in an enterprise data warehouse. Actually, some of the proponents of this approach go as far as declaring that there is no need for a central enterprise data warehouse, instead, they call for having a distributed data warehouse that is composed of the independent data marts connected via integration software, middleware, or decision support tools that make a consistent view of all of these data marts. This glues the independent data marts creating the distributed data warehouse environment, and may also provide other important services, such as business views of the data warehouse information, enhanced security, monitoring facilities, and better control over end-user access to the data.

So, according to this approach, data flows directly from the operational systems into the staging area, and from there, it flows directly into the independent data marts. These data marts may eventually feed the enterprise data warehouse as you can see in the next diagram.

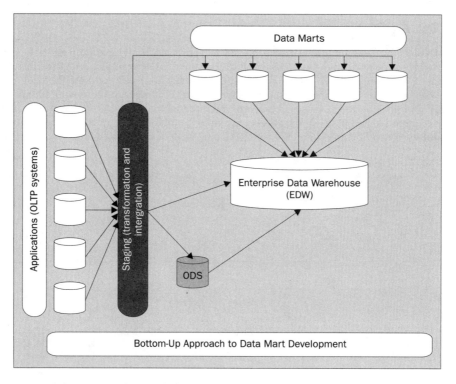

Bottom-Up Approach to Data Mart Development

Disadvantages of this approach include:

❑ An uncontrolled construction and proliferation of independent data marts may result in integration problems between these data marts and a future enterprise data warehouse. Actually, the development of the enterprise data warehouse may not be possible without major changes to the design of the existing data marts. Most of these integration issues are due, however, to differences in business terminology, data formats, and representations between data mart designs. These problems can be solved by the use of a common warehouse information model (either a business model or a data model) for documenting decision processing requirements when developing independent data marts.

❑ As data marts proliferate, business users will want to access data marts belonging to other departments for cross-business unit analysis. Seamless access to data marts is difficult without appropriate database middleware, which is unlikely to provide complete transparency, is complex to manage, and can lead to poor performance when queries access multiple data marts.

❑ The need to develop independent data marts as rapidly as possible frequently leads to data mart design being driven by the data that exists in operational systems, rather than by business user information requirements. It is important to point out, however, that this criticism can also be leveled at many enterprise data warehouse implementations. Actually, I have seen in some hastily implemented designs a data mart with the same structure as the OLTP system feeding it. This defeats the purpose of having a data mart, which should follow the design principles of a dimensional database just like a data warehouse.

Federated Approach

As you have already seen, the previous approaches to data mart implementation have their own strengths and weaknesses. A middle-ground solution was sought after to guarantee the low cost and rapid return on investment (ROI) advantages of the data mart approach, without the problems of data integration in the future. To achieve this, the design and development of independent data marts must be managed and must be based on a common shared information model of data warehouse decision processing requirements, that is organizations must apply the development disciplines of the enterprise data warehouse environment to data mart development.

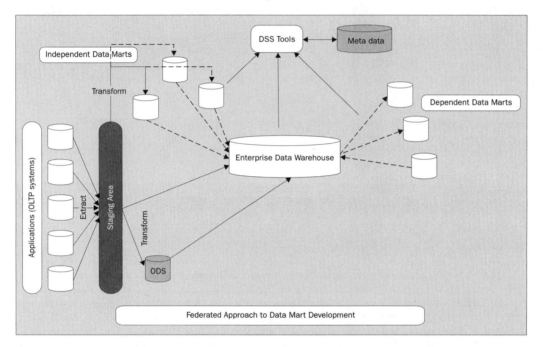

Federated Approach to Data Mart Development

With the federated approach, the development of the data warehousing system becomes an iterative process. The data warehouse system in this case contains independent data marts that get their data feed directly from the staging area. The system may also include an enterprise data warehouse with underlying dependent data marts that get their data feed from the enterprise data warehouse as you can see in the figure above.

The key to data integration in a federated data warehouse is a common information model of the information stored and managed by the warehousing system. This information model is updated as new independent data marts are built, or when new dependent data marts (subject areas) are added to an enterprise data warehouse. The information model represents the single source of the information in a warehousing system, and is the source from which all of the data warehouse meta data is created.

Data warehouses or data marts can be driven by one of two factors: operational data needs, and business decision support requirements. The common information model should be flexible so that when the data warehouse or data mart is driven by the transactional data, the model takes the form of a data warehouse data model (still following the star schema or snowflake schema). On the other hand, if the driving force behind the data warehouse is business-user decision process requirements, then the data warehouse data model documents a business model from which one or more data marts can be created as part of this model.

As you see in the figure opposite, data in the operational systems is extracted to be loaded into the independent data marts or the enterprise data warehouse. With new independent data marts added, or new subject areas (dependent data marts) added to the data warehouse, a considerable amount of work needs to be done to support the extraction and transformation for the new addition. With the federated model, this concern has been reduced by the use of the staging area, into which operational data is first extracted. The data is then transformed in a way that suits the data mart or the enterprise data warehouse before it is loaded into it. With the use of a common information model, at least the extraction of the data can be standardized in a way that, from this perspective, makes any new requirements minor enhancements to the extraction process.

Managing the Data Mart

Since a data mart is considered a special case of a data warehouse, its management follows the same lines as that of the data warehouse. Data warehouse management and administration is discussed in detail in the chapters of the last section of this book. For the purposes of this discussion, however, I will list the most important steps that need to be followed to achieve a successful data mart. These steps are shown below. They start with the team selection, followed by the planning phase, the construction of the pilot release (QA), the data loading, the final release (rollout), operation and maintenance, and possibly back to the planning board.

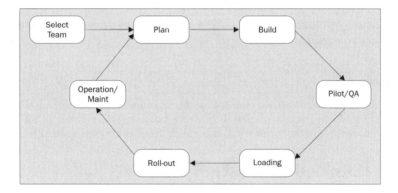

Selecting the Project Team

Due to the nature of the data mart development project, the team conducting this development must be versatile. It needs to have people who understand the business. After all, the data mart is business-driven and is, for the most part, built to satisfy a particular business requirement. It is beneficial to include someone from the decision makers on the team. Such an inclusion, even if marginal, could speed up needed approvals that might be behind many of the project delays.

The team members should be able to commit time to the project, especially during the design phase. The team should have business analysts, a database designer and programmer, a number of developers as needed, data transformation experts, and quality assurance (QA) testers.

Data Mart Planning

The planning sessions result in a blueprint of the data mart. This blueprint will serve as the specification document of the data mart. Therefore, special attention should be given to this stage because it is the corner stone for all the stages that follow. In the planning of your data mart, avoid what is called "analysis paralysis". In other words, make sure you make decisions when they are warranted without having to reconsider the solution and waste additional time only to come up with a simple change to your spec that would not matter.

Also avoid as you plan your data mart the temptation to try to build the ultimate data mart. Understand the scope of the project and make sure you create your plan accordingly. After all, the data mart is supposed to solve a specific business requirement.

In the planning, identify your facts and dimensions for the data mart according to the general guidelines you put in place as part of the overall data warehouse strategy. This is very important if you want to reduce the effort needed to integrate your data marts into the data warehouse later on, or even to create views across the different data marts you build.

Planning includes identification of the business requirements. Without these requirements you will not be able to establish your facts and dimensions and build your database schema. Planning also involves acquainting yourself with the data in the operational system, evaluation of hardware and software requirements to build and rollout the system, establishment of the security plan as well as producing a project plan document that spells out the roles and responsibilities of the team members and the client personnel, and spells out the scope very clearly.

Construction

Using the blueprint from the planning session, you can start the construction phase. Make sure you follow the overall guidelines for your data warehousing data model every step of the way. Also make sure you document the progress of your work and check it against the milestones in your project plan.

Pilot Phase (Limited Rollout)

After the data mart is built and the initial testing is done, consider a limited pilot phase. In this pilot, you may load the data mart with some historical data and let the project team see the results of the planning decisions. As defined, does the data mart provide what's needed? Should changes be made at this time? If necessary, make adjustments to the data mart based on the project team's review.

Initial Loading

Based on user requirements, begin loading the historical data into the data mart. Understand the strengths (and weaknesses) of the vendor's application. Does historical data need to be loaded before net changes can be applied? What are the typical load times for large volumes? Do all aggregation levels need to be defined before loading? Does adding an aggregation level require a reload or does the application allow aggregations to be built over existing data?

Rollout

The main concern in this stage is to make sure you train the end users to use the system you built for them. Make sure the training is well planned to get the maximum benefit. Your training should cover all kinds of users, from the power users to those who do not know the basics about using PCs.

With the rollout, make sure all locale issues, such as language, time zone, and currency, had been taken care of if needed. Also monitor the systems and their performance and be ready with your team to intervene in case of emergency.

Operations and Maintenance

This is an on-going stage that may eventually result in a re-evaluation of the whole data mart solution leading to enhancements, or even replacements in some cases. You may also want to consider some software packages that help make the operations and maintenance easier.

Data Mart Design

As mentioned earlier, the data mart follows the same design principles as the data warehouse. The data mart database usually has a dimensional structure as opposed to operational databases that have relational structures. In this section, I will explain quickly the basic principle of the data mart design by explaining the basic principles of dimensional analysis as well as things to watch for when dealing with data marts.

Design Considerations – Things to Watch For...

When building data marts as part of the enterprise-wide decision support system, you need to take special consideration of some issues. These issues are related to the fact that data marts should work together in tandem allowing querying across while still representing separate functional business units. The following are some of the issues you need to be aware of when building your data warehousing solution.

Minimize Duplicate Measure Data

In the data mart models described above, the top-down and the bottom-up models try to minimize any duplication of measure data by making the data marts very specific to individual subject areas. It is the measure data that makes up most of the size of the data mart. The descriptive, textural, and dimension data surrounding the measures is very small in size compared to the measure data, hence we can afford to have such dimension data duplicated across data marts.

Allow for Drilling Across and Down

With the two models described in the previous paragraph, the data marts usually add up to the whole data warehouse. In this case, these data marts must function together so we can drill across data marts to assemble integrated views of the enterprise. Drilling across, similar to drilling down, has a very specific technical interpretation. For example, if we were to line up some measures across a line in a report that spans several of these data marts, we need to make sure the dimensions in these different marts correspond to the same entities and concepts. Hence, when one data mart defines a geographic region as the northeastern region, this region should exist in the other data marts participating in the query, and should mean the same thing too. These issues have to be addressed before the data marts are built and outlined in an enterprise DSS strategy that results in a unified meta data that can be used for all of these data marts.

Build Your Data Marts with Compatible Tools and Technologies

The data marts that eventually compose the enterprise data warehouse and the building blocks of the organization's decision support strategies should be implemented with the same or compatible technologies. You cannot afford to have these small units built with diverse incompatible technologies such as different hardware and software. Allowing this to happen will make it a nightmare to integrate data and reports from these various data marts.

Take into Account Locale Issues

Many design issues arise from spreading the geographic reach of the data warehousing solution across time zones and international boundaries. These issues include currency rates, time issues, and language.

To synchronize multiple time zones, it seems tempting to store each underlying transaction with an absolute timestamp and leave it up to the application to sort out issues of local times. Although this is a somewhat conservative and safe approach, it does not solve the problem of time zone synchronization; instead, it just transfers it to the application programmer. You need to come up with a really good design that uses the capabilities of the database engine to take care of the majority of the problem, rather than delegating it with all the complexities associated with it to the application developer.

As an example of solving multiple time zone issues, you can represent the time in the database as absolute time, such as Eastern Standard Time (EST). Given that the geographical location is also known, you can have an additional field in the geographical dimension table (or the geographical lookup table in case of operational relational databases). This column can hold the offset from the standard time for all locations. When you build your queries, you can use these two date/time columns to present the result with sufficient accuracy according to any time you want.

Another issue arises when considering multiple national calendars with different holidays for different cultures. Your design should take this into consideration when building the time dimension and the fact table.

Multiple currencies may create one of the biggest challenges to you in the process of your design. This is because exchange rates are so dynamic and fluctuate almost constantly. Usually, operational systems provide the data in local currencies. The data has to be transformed to a standard currency when saved in the data warehouse or data mart because reporting will be in the standard currency. The easiest way to handle this is by storing the values in two fields, local currency and standard currency while using a daily agreed-upon exchange rate that also gets stored if needed. The solution will mean more storage space requirement, but will alleviate many issues when time comes to report profits and sales across branches of the organization in multiple countries.

Another important issue that arises with multi-national data marts is harmonizing the character data sets in SQL Server. By making sure that every national system uses the same character set all sorts of problems can be avoided. For instance, it is not possible to do a straightforward data dump from one SQL server database to another if they have different character sets specified. It is also not possible to change the character set of an SQL server installation at a later date without a complete re-install.

Finally, another issue that arises from extending the data warehousing solution across international boundaries is multinational names and addresses. Address standards are different from one country to another, and your design should find a way to incorporate the different standards while minimizing storage and empty cells in the fact table.

Data Modeling Techniques

Data modeling is an essential step in building any database application. The data model is the blueprint that is used to build and create the database. The model usually describes the business process and the relationships among the different entities that interact in the business world.

Entity Relation (ER) Models

The Entity Relation (ER) model is an abstraction tool because it can be used to understand and simplify the ambiguous data relationships in the business world and complex systems environments. ER modeling is based on two basic concepts: entities and the relationships between those entities. ER models are used to produce a data model for the specific area of interest. The figure below shows a representation of a typical ER diagram:

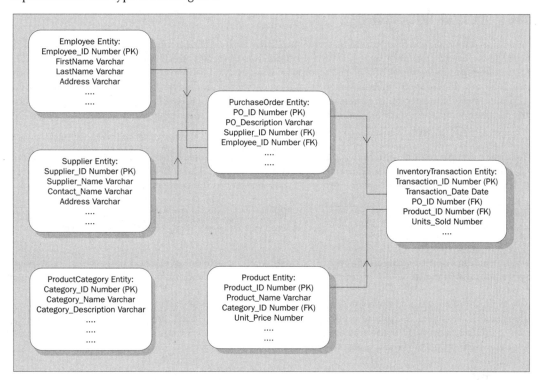

Entities represent real-world objects that can be observed and classified by their properties and characteristics. An entity has its own business definition and a clear boundary definition that is required to describe what is included and what is not. In the detailed ER model, it is critical to find out the unique identifier of an entity. These unique identifiers are called candidate keys. Candidate keys are used to select the key that is most commonly used to identify the entity. This key is usually referred to as the primary key.

Attributes are defined as part of the entities and relations. Attributes describe the characteristics of properties of the entities. An attribute name should be unique in an entity and should be self-explanatory. For example, simply saying field1 or field2 is not allowed, we must clearly define each attribute by a descriptive name. Simply speaking, an entity in the logical model maps to a database table in the physical model of the database, and an attribute maps to a table column.

Another important concept in ER models is the concept of a domain. A domain consists of all the possible acceptable values and categories that are allowed for an attribute. Simply, a domain is just the whole set of the real possible occurrences. As an example, the data type, such as integer, date, and character, provides a clear definition of domain.

An attribute is said to be a primary key if it uniquely identifies the record in the table and cannot be NULL. A primary key can be composed of one attribute, or multiple attributes. In the later case, it is called a composite primary key.

A foreign key in a table identifies the relationship between the entity represented by the table and the entity that has the same attribute as its primary key. Foreign keys allow the storage of information in related tables eliminating the need for repeating groups of columns in the main table.

Dimensional Modeling

Dimensional modeling is a technique for conceptualizing and visualizing data models as a set of measures that are described by common aspects of the business. It is especially useful for summarizing and rearranging the data and presenting views of the data to support data analysis. Dimensional modeling focuses on numeric data, such as values, counts, weights, balances, and occurrences. In data warehousing, dimensional modeling is simpler, more expressive, and easier to understand than ER modeling. ER modeling, however, has been around much longer and is more established. More research is still needed in the area of dimensional modeling, which has only been around for a decade or so.

The basic concepts of dimensional modeling are facts and dimensions. These concepts serve in the Microsoft Analysis Services as the basic components of the cube structures. Data cubes and dimensional modeling are powerful in representing the requirements of the business user in the context of database tables.

The following are definitions of the main concepts in dimensional data modeling.

Fact

A fact is a collection of related data items, consisting of measures and context data. Each fact typically represents a business item, a business transaction, or an event that can be used in analyzing the business or business processes. When you want to view the sales of the company by store by quarter, you usually look at the total revenue and net profits. These are the facts you are interested in. In the Microsoft OLAP services, facts are implemented in the core tables of the OLAP database in which all of the numeric data is stored. These tables are referred to as the fact tables, and are usually derived from the raw data in the operational database systems.

Dimension

A dimension is a collection of properties along which we conduct our analysis of the facts. Dimensions allow us to view the fact in different contexts. For instance, the total sales can be viewed in terms of store, city, or region. These three levels are members of the geographical dimension of the sales process. In a dimensional model, every data point in the fact table is associated with one and only one member from each of the multiple dimensions. This becomes clear if you look at the following figure, where the cell that has a measure value of 400 corresponds to a unique set of dimensions: Q3 (3rd quarter), Pitta Bread, and Detroit. Many analytical processes are used to quantify the impact of dimensions on the facts. To clarify the relationship between the facts and the dimensions, think of a record in the fact table. The record has many links to the dimension tables. These links identify the record to be unique. Keep this in mind and don't worry if you cannot visualize it yet. This will all make sense as you read on about the OLAP cubes later in the chapter.

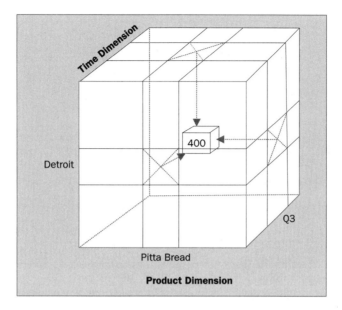

Common dimensions used in sales-related data marts include:

- Time
- Geography
- Customer
- Salesperson
- Scenarios such as actual, budgeted, or estimated numbers

Dimension Members: Take the time dimension as an example. The dimension consists of several levels, such as, day, week, month, quarter, and year. Each one of these levels consists of members. For example, the members of the day level would be Monday, Tuesday, etc., or Day1, Day2, ... Day7. As for the month dimension, the members would be January, February, etc. or Month1, Month2, ... Month12. Therefore, you may assume that a dimension contains many dimension members organized in levels inside the dimension. When you combine these concepts with the fact table records, you find that the dimension member determines the position in the dimension with which a certain record in the fact table is associated.

Dimension Hierarchies: We can arrange the members of a dimension into one or more hierarchies. Each hierarchy can also have multiple hierarchy levels. A member of a dimension may be located on more than one hierarchy structure. An example to consider is the time dimension hierarchy as shown in the figure overleaf:

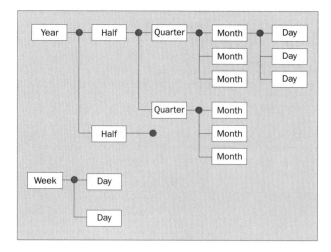

Two hierarchies are defined in the figure for the time dimension because the week member does not follow the first hierarchy. If data is to be aggregated on a weekly basis, the second hierarchy has to be used. This is because a week can span two months. Thus, the time dimension is a good example of multiple hierarchies of a dimension.

Data Cubes

One effective way to visualize the data model and the dimensional hierarchies and facts is to build a cube. The dimensions of the cube will be the dimensions of the fact table. We can represent a three-dimensional model using a cube. Usually a dimensional model consists of more than three dimensions and is referred to as a **hypercube**. However, a hypercube is impossible to visualize, so a cube is the more commonly used term. In the figure opposite, the measurement is the volume of sales in hundreds of units for a chain of auto dealerships. This measurement is determined by the combination of three dimensions: geography, product, and time. The geography dimension and product dimension have their own two levels of hierarchy. For example, the geography dimension has the region level and state, while the product has the levels of make and model.

The time dimension shows the time levels down to the quarter level. Assuming that the data presented is for 1999, the cube will help us read that this chain of dealership sold 1700 Taurus vehicles in Wisconsin in the first quarter, and 1200 Mercury Sable vehicles in New Jersey for the same quarter. In other words, the cube is a great tool to visualize the data summaries and aggregations in a most useful way.

> *If you are thinking to yourself that this is not an ideal way to represent data to end users, don't worry. The cube representation in the figure is only meant for visualization purposes. It is the simplest form possible, with only three dimensions. If we had more than three dimensions, we probably would be in trouble trying to represent the cube in that figure. Actually, cube data is represented in tabular forms with multiple column and row headings that correspond to the cube dimensions as you will see later.*

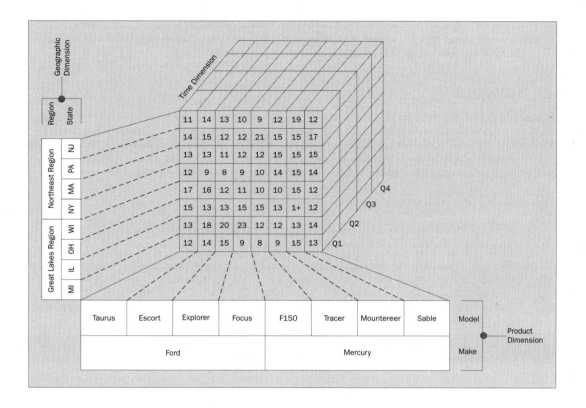

Data Mart Schema

Data marts are very similar in structure and nature to data warehouses. The essential difference between data warehouses and data marts is that data marts are more focused on one aspect of the business. For instance, a data mart can store departmental data, or data for certain periods of time or certain products, etc.

Data marts are usually much less complex and easier to deal with than data warehouses. The amount of data is smaller and the data model is smaller with fewer tables to worry about in some cases. However, data marts still have to be designed properly with their database structure established after extensive data modeling.

Modeling for the data mart has to be more end-user focused than modeling for a data warehouse. End users must be involved in the data mart modeling process, as they are the ones who will use the data mart. Because you should expect that end users are not at all familiar with complex data models, the modeling techniques and the modeling process as a whole should be organized such that complexity is transparent to end users.

Data mart developers recommend dimensional modeling for data mart development. Dimensional modeling, as a powerful data modeling technique, is suitable for developing data marts that support dimensional data analysis for a business problem. Such analysis could include using an OLAP tool to analyse the data, organize it in cubes, and slice and dice it to come up with the data aggregations necessary. The dimensional modeling techniques presented in this chapter therefore are also suitable for those who are primarily interested in a narrower scope of the work of data warehouse modeling, that is, those who are interested in developing data models for data marts.

Generally speaking, data marts, like data warehouses, follow specific types of schemas in their structure. The two most famous types of schemas are what are called the star schema and the snowflake schema. The following sections explain these data structures in some detail.

Star Schema

Looking at the model we have discussed earlier, the dealership chain model, we see that we mainly have three dimensions of the data in the model. These dimensions are geographic location, time, and automobile. The fact table, which includes the measures, such as sales, inventory, number of customers, etc., also includes foreign keys that point to the dimensions in the dimension table. The collection of the fact table and the dimensions linked to it are usually referred to as the star schema.

The classic star schema is characterized by the following:

❑   A single fact table containing a compound primary key, with one segment for each dimension, and additional columns of additive, numeric facts.

❑   A single dimension table for each dimension with a generated key, and a level indicator that describes the attribute level of each record. For example, if the dimension is VEHICLE, records in the dimension table might refer to MAKE (Ford, Mercury), MODEL (Taurus, Crown Victoria), MODEL YEAR (1999, 2000), etc. We might assign a level number to these (such as 1=make, 2=model, 3=model_year) and put that value in the "level" column.

❑   The single fact table will contain detail (or "atomic") data, such as sales dollars, for a given dealership, for a given model in a given time period.

❑   The fact table may also contain partially consolidated data, such as sales dollars for a region, for a given make/model for a given time period.

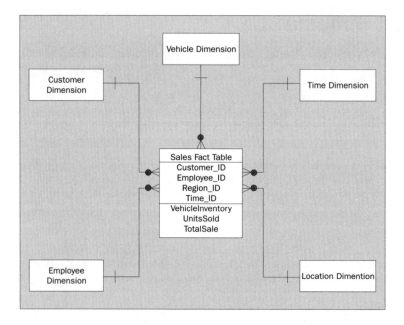

Snowflake Schema

The star schema is the simplest representation of the business entities and their relationships in the dimensional model. However, sometimes one or more of the dimension tables could grow in size to become a very big table, which prompted database modelers and developers to create the snowflake schema.

The snowflake model is the result of decomposing one or more of the dimensions, which sometimes have hierarchies themselves. We can define the many-to-one relationships among members within a dimension table as a separate dimension table with a hierarchy. Let's take for example the automobile dealership sample we have been discussing so far. The customer dimension may be composed of two sub-dimensions, customer type, and customer region. Other sub-dimensions could also be included in the analysis, such as customer education level and customer income (see figure below):

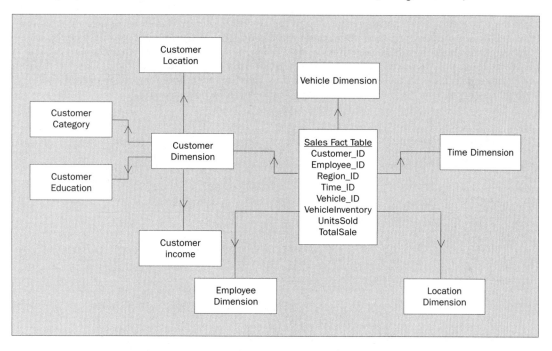

The decomposition of the customer dimension makes the model look like a snowflake; hence came the name for this kind of data model.

Microsoft Data Warehousing Framework and Data Marts

Microsoft Data Warehousing Framework (DWF) supports both data warehouses and data marts. To add to this, Microsoft SQL Server, the database engine, has been well tested and proven to work very well with small and medium sized databases, which would be a good fit for data marts. With the latest release, SQL Server can handle very large databases (on the order of terabytes) very smoothly. Other technologies that accompanied SQL Server, such as Data Transformation Services help make this happen.

Analysis Services supports dealing with data marts and data warehouse. Analysis Services is able to query data within the data warehouse at any level of detail possible. It can also drill down in a data mart just like it does in a data warehouse. Some features, such as virtual cubes, make Analysis Services able to drill across several data marts if needed making it easy to query decision support systems designed with multiple data marts that add up to the enterprise data warehouse.

Many case studies that handle situations where the clients opted to having data marts as the building block of their DSS systems can be found on the Microsoft Web site at http://www.microsoft.com/SQL/techinfo/bi/casestudies.asp.

Summary

Data marts are considered an important step in the evolution of data warehousing technologies and data analysis. In this chapter, you read about these important data structures and how and when to use them. You also read about the design principles of data marts, as well as how to manage them in general. You also read about the Microsoft support for data marts in Analysis Services. Although many of the design principles apply to data warehouses in general, they were included here for your reference and to highlight some specific points about data marts that need to be considered.

Data Warehouse

5

The Transactional System

Since E.F. Codd first publicly discussed relational theory in 1970 as a means of storing and retrieving structured data very little change to the original theory has occurred. Certainly the relational language, SQL, has been updated to include new features, but the underlying architecture has remained largely unchanged in its 30-year history.

With technology this old we would expect it to be nearing the end of its useful lifecycle: a technology that does away with the need for relational databases must be on the horizon? Fortunately for us who work exclusively with RDBMS almost all new technologies only serve to increase the use of relational database in some way; in fact they are more popular today than in any point in their history and the momentum doesn't look like it will be decreasing anytime soon. The relational model is one of the few technologies that have stood the test of time and fundamentally influenced the way we use information technology.

Before we dive into data warehousing we should understand where the data that populates our warehouse comes from and why it is necessary to extract this information from its source. We should understand the limiting factors of traditional transaction processing databases and how these limitations are addressed by technologies such as OLAP.

The Relational Theory

While vendors tend to implement their own unique features into their relational database products as a point of difference, the underlying data structure model is usually very similar between products as they are all based on the relational theory.

In this section we will take a look at the most important concepts of a Relational Database. Bear in mind we are just scratching the surface of what is known as relational theory, for a much more in-depth description I recommend you read *Professional SQL Server 2000 Database Design* (Wrox Press, ISBN 1-861004-76-1).

Database

A database is a loose term that simply means a collection of data, whether this is a filing cabinet, this book, or just about anything you can think of that contains information. However as this is a book about data warehousing we will throw caution to the wind and just assume we are talking about a Relational Database and give a more defined description. We consider a relational database a collection of tables, views, indexes and other objects that are used for storing information generated by an organization's business processes.

Table

A table is the most important object within a database and very few databases will exist without at least one table. A table is a two-dimensional object that contains columns and rows that we use to store our data.

Tables have well-defined structures that make them ideal for storing well-defined data. The data types and validation rules are part of the table definition, so a clear understanding of the information a database is going to store is essential when designing table structures. The diagram below shows an example of an Orders table. You can see that each column has a name, data type and length defined.

Orders			
Column Name	Data Type	Length	
♀ OrderID	int	4	
CustomerID	nchar	5	
EmployeeID	int	4	
OrderDate	datetime	8	
RequiredDate	datetime	8	
ShippedDate	datetime	8	
ShipVia	int	4	
Freight	money	8	
ShipName	nvarchar	40	
ShipAddress	nvarchar	60	
ShipCity	nvarchar	15	
ShipRegion	nvarchar	15	
ShipPostalCode	nvarchar	10	
ShipCountry	nvarchar	15	

Relational databases are optimized for the storage and retrieval of structured data contained in these tables. We are also able to store unstructured data within binary columns as part of a table. The storage of this unstructured data, sometimes referred to as BLOB data, is not done for performance reasons. This is more commonly stored in a table for manageability and security reasons as relational databases are not very efficient in dealing with information of this type, such as binary files, documents, and images.

Indexes

An index is created on columns in a table to assist us with locating specific rows in a table. The library analogy is a common way of explaining how indexes improve query performance and, while it has been done to death in almost every book on database design, it is probably the best explanation of how indexes are useful so no apologies are offered for using one it more time.

When visiting the public library it is more efficient to find a book by using the catalogue, rather than walking around the library looking at every book to see if it is the one you want. It doesn't matter if the library has one thousand books or one million books because the way the catalogue is organized means that finding the book you are looking for doesn't take much longer. If you were unable to use the catalogue for some reason, then finding your book in the thousand book library, while slow, will probably be a lot quicker than finding it in the million book library.

The same concepts are true when we describe SQL Server tables. Finding a row without using an index will get slower as more rows are added. However, locating the row using an index will not suffer substantial performance loss when the number of rows within the table increases.

The reverse analogy is also true. If you are locating a book in a very small library, maybe a home library, that only has a couple of shelves of books it would be quicker to simply scan the books to find the one you want. Once again SQL Server works in the same way, if it determines that it can locate a row more efficiently by taking a look at every row, then is chooses this method rather than unnecessarily using an index.

SQL Server uses a B-Tree structure for storing indexes. A discussion of how indexes work internally is outside the scope of this book, however you should bear in mind that retrieving rows using an index is usually orders of magnitude faster than retrieving rows by looking at every row in the table. When the rows of a table are changed, due to new rows being created or existing rows being modified (or deleted), the indexes on the table are automatically updated to reflect these changes. The time it takes to modify rows within a table will get longer the more indexes that are created, as each of the indexes will also require updating as part of a data modification.

Views

A view can be thought of as a virtual table. Like a table, it consists of columns and rows and can be used in place of a table within queries. However, unlike a table, a view does not store any data. The view definition itself is a query that selects data from tables, or even other views. The rows we retrieve from a view are the result set generated by the query that is part of the view's definition.

Views can be used to hide complex query logic from users or developers of the database. For example, suppose we regularly needed to query product information within our database code. As the database is highly normalized the product information is split into 4 different tables. However, we often wish to return all the information for a given product, throughout our application. We could copy the query that joins all the product related tables throughout our application code, but this would make it difficult to change the structure of our product tables in the future as all these queries embedded in our applications would require updating. Alternatively we could define a view using a query that joins all the product-related tables, and then reference only this product view from our application code. If at any stage we modify the underlying structure of the underlying product tables, we would only need to change this view definition for our application to continue working after the change.

A new feature in the SQL Server 2000 relational database engine is the ability to create indexes on views. Creating an index on a view causes the results of the view definition to be persisted within the database. When changes are made to the data of tables that are used by the view, the persisted data is automatically updated to reflect the base table change. Indexed views can improve query performance, especially when the view contains aggregated functions. When you select from an indexed-view the aggregations have already been performed and stored by SQL Server, so the results can be returned immediately. Non-indexed views on the other hand require the aggregations to be carried out every time a query is made on the view.

As indexed views impact an the performance of changes to the underlying base tables, they are usually not used in OLTP databases. However, than can offer substantial improvements in performance for certain query types in reporting or analytical databases.

Transactions

Transactions are a core component of relational databases. A transaction is a logical unit of work that may be made up of modifications to many different tables within the same database or even a database located on different server. **ACID** is an acronym that is used to define transactional behavior and this acronym has the following meaning:

- ❑ **Atomicity:** A transaction is a single unit of work. All changes made in the transaction must complete successfully, otherwise none of the changes can be carried out.

- ❑ **Consistency:** Once a transaction has completed due to being committed or rolled back, it must leave all database structures including tables and indexes in a consistent state. Put more clearly, a transaction cannot break anything, even if it fails.

- ❑ **Isolation:** When a transaction is in progress, it cannot be affected by other transactions that are also in progress on the database. Locking rows of a table for use by a single transaction is how isolation is enforced.

- ❑ **Durability:** Once a transaction commits it stays committed even if, for example, the server fails a millisecond after the transaction has been committed.

Long running transactions hold locks on the rows they touch for the duration of the transaction. This can degrade concurrency, as other users may have to wait until the transaction has completed before they can take out their own locks on the table rows. Databases that are designed to support a high number of transactions always keep transactions very short by optimizing the operations that are participating in the transaction.

Relationships

Normalization requires tables to be dependent on each other. A relationship is a link between two tables. There are a number of relationship types, but the two most common are *one-to-many* and *many-to-many*, and these are both created using primary and foreign key constraints.

- ❑ **Primary Key** – A primary key, which is defined by one or more columns in the table, is used to uniquely identify a row in the table. Only one primary key can exist per table.

- ❑ **Foreign Key** – A foreign key is defined by one or more columns in a table, and links to the primary key of another table. Once a foreign key has been defined, only primary key values of the linked table can be inserted into the foreign key columns.

One-to-Many Relationships

A one-to-many relationship between two tables, A and B, means that a row in table A can be referenced by many rows in table B. A primary key is used in table A as the unique identifier that is referenced by a foreign key constraint in table B. Our example below shows the relationship between an employee and a department. An employee can work for one department and one department can have many employees. In this diagram, the key symbol on the left-hand side of our relationship line indicates that the department table contains rows that are unique for this relationship (the one in one-to-many). The infinity symbol on the employee end of the relationship line indicates that any number of rows in the employee table can reference a row in the department table (the many in one-to-many):

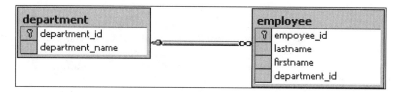

Many-to-Many Relationships

A many-to-many relationship between two tables, A and B, means that one or more rows in table A can be referenced by one or more rows in table B. It is not possible to create a many-to-many relationship directly between two tables in SQL Server. To create this type of relationship an intermediate table is required along with two one-to-many relationships. This intermediate table need only contain the columns that make up the foreign keys of the tables that are participating in the many-to-many relationship.

A classic example is the authors of a book. An author can write many books, and a book can have many authors. This would be implemented using an intermediate table that defines the relationship between an author and a book:

Normalization

The concept of **Normal Forms** was defined by E.F. Codd, as part of the relational theory of databases, and it is still core to modern database design. A level of normalization known as **Third Normal Form** is commonly used for databases that have many users inserting and updating data regularly, however, it is rare to find a database that does not violate relational theory at some level in the database design. Sometimes this is for perfectly valid reasons, such as improving data retrieval performance, and other times it is simply due to rushed database development. However, most databases will be normalized in some shape or form.

Normalization is a complex subject that database designers spend years becoming skilled at. The purpose of this section is not to train you in the proficiencies of data normalization, but to give you an overview of how transactional databases are modeled, which will assist your understanding of the structure when you come to pull information into a data warehouse.

First Normal Form (1NF)

The rules of First Normal Form are quite straightforward, and a table is considered to be in First Normal Form if it satisfies the following rules:

- ❑ All columns must only contain a single value

- ❑ All rows must have the same number of attribute instances

- ❑ Every row must be different

For example, you may have a table that records employee information, containing a column called PHONE that is used for storing the employee's phone number. You are finding that a number of employees have more than a single phone number. You really want to record all these numbers so they are all being entered in the PHONE column separated by commas, such as **555-4433, 555-4422, 555-4411**. Such practices violate the first rule of the First Normal Form, as multiple values stored within a single table column are not allowed.

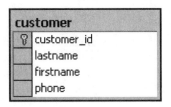

customer

customer_id	lastname	firstname	phone
1	Smith	John	555-1234, 555-9678
2	Glucina	Linda	555-1234, 555-9989, 555-6667
3	Doe	Joe	555-2341

So, we violated the first rule of First Normal Form by putting all our phone numbers into one column. Ok, instead we will add 5 PHONE columns to our table that are named phone_1 through to phone_5. Great, now our table design will satisfy the first rule by only storing a single value per column.

customer

customer
- customer_id
- lastname
- firstname
- phone_1
- phone_2
- phone_3
- phone_4
- phone_5

customer

customer_id	lastname	firstname	phone_1	phone_2	phone_3	phone_4	phone_5
1	Smith	John	555-1234	555-9678			
2	Glucina	Linda	555-1234	555-9989	555-6667		
3	Doe	Joe	555-2341				

Unfortunately this design violates the second rule of the First Normal Form. This rule states that if one instance of our entity, in this case a customer, has 5 phone numbers then all instances of our entities, or all customers, must also have 5 phone numbers, which clearly isn't the case.

To solve this rule violation, we require another table. A simplistic solution would be to create a table that contains both the `customer_id` and a `phone_number` column as part of the primary key. In this solution, a customer could have any number of unique phone numbers defined for them simply by creating a new row for each `customer_id` and `phone_number` combination in the `customer_phone` table:

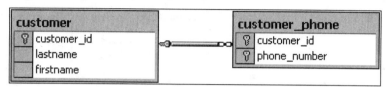

To see this relationship more clearly, we will once again look at the data contained within these tables.

customer

customer_id (PK)	lastname	firstname
1	Smith	John
2	Glucina	Linda
3	Dow	Joe

customer_phone

customer_id (PK)(FK)	phone_number (PK)
1	555-1234
1	555-9678
2	555-1234
2	555-9989
2	555-6667
3	555-2341

The last rule of First Normal Form simply states that you cannot duplicate rows within a table. In other words you cannot have a row where all the column values are the same as another row. To enforce this rule a primary key is created on columns that make the row unique, such as `customer_id`.

Second Normal Form (2NF)

Second Normal Form is only slightly more difficult to understand than First Normal Form. The rules of Second Normal Form are:

- ❑ All the rules from First Normal Form
- ❑ Every column that is not part of the key must depend upon the **whole** key

Second Normal Form only applies when your primary key contains more than one column. This rule states that all the columns within a table must be relevant to the combination of the columns in the key, not just individual key columns.

For example, in a delivery database we may have the table structure shown below. The `truck` table contains details of the trucks owned by the delivery company and the `driver` table stores the personal information of drivers employed by the delivery company:

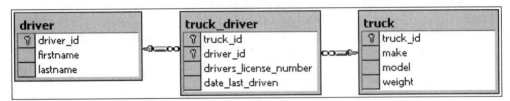

The `truck_driver` table stores information on which trucks the drivers can operate. The `drivers_license_number` column causes a violation of Second Normal Form, as this is dependent only on part of the primary key, namely the `driver_id` column. However, the `date_last_driven` column does not violate Second Normal Form, as this depends on both the driver and the truck. To resolve the violation the `drivers_license_number` column should be moved to the `driver` table:

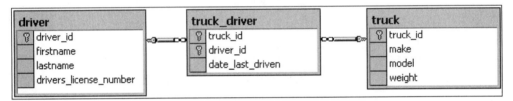

Third Normal Form (3NF)

As mentioned earlier, most relational databases that support concurrent user transactions are designed using Third Normal Form. There are Fourth and Fifth Normal Forms but implementing databases with such designs often becomes impractical. There is always a trade off between the pure theory and the practical implementation, and Third Normal Form seems to be where the line is most often drawn. The rules of Third Normal Form are:

❏   Everything in the First and Second Normal Form

❏   All non-key columns must depend only upon the key of the table not another non-key column

This is probably the most difficult of the Normal Forms to grasp. Put simply it means that all columns that do not make up the primary key of a table have to be a fact or description of the table in some way. For example if we take this table out of a customer application:

customer

customer_id	lastname	firstname	city	state	country
1	Smith	John	Sydney	New South Wales	Australia
2	Glucina	Linda	Los Angeles	California	USA
3	Doe	Joe	Sydney	NSW	OZ

The `customer` table records information about the location of customers. The Third Normal Form dictates that all columns have to be a fact about the primary key, not another column. The `lastname`, `firstname`, and `city` columns are all dependent on the `customer_id`. However the `state` column is dependent on the `city` column, not the `customer_id`, and in addition the `country` column is dependent on the `state` column also not the `customer_id` so both these cause a violation of Third Normal Form. To correct this, we would create additional tables that store information about the Cities States and Countries, which we will reference from the `customer` table.

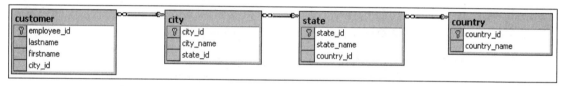

customer

customer_id	lastname	firstname	city_id
1	Smith	John	1
2	Glucina	Linda	2
3	Doe	Joe	1

city

city_id	city_name	state_id
1	Sydney	1
2	Los Angeles	2

state

state_id	state_name	country_id
1	New South Wales	1
2	California	2

country

country_id	country_name
1	Australia
2	United States of America

Structured Query Language (SQL)

The language of the relational database is the Structured Query Language, or SQL. This is a powerful batch language used to maintain database objects as well as select, insert, update, and delete rows from database tables.

SQL is referred to as a batch language as opposed to the most common type of development language which is a procedural language. While modern implementations have added procedural constructs to the SQL language to allow run-time application logic to be written in SQL, the way the SQL queries table data is considered a batch process.

To describe this more clearly, consider an application written in VB for a moment. The developer creates a program by creating a list of steps that are followed when the application is run. For example:

1. Begin executing code

2. Ask us if the user is Male or Female

3. If user enters Male then ouput Hello Sir

4. If user enters Female then out Hello Madam

5. End executing code

While this is an elementary application, it does show how the developer writes steps to be performed in order when executed to reach a desired result. As we have said, SQL is a batch language and the difference between this and a procedural language may seem subtle at first; when writing SQL, we are actually defining the outcome we want, and then instructing the relational database to carry out our instructions and inform us when it has completed.

1. Define request as "I wish you to show me customers who have purchased more than 3 products in the last month who live in New York and have an income of greater than $50,000"

2. Execute request

3. Return query results

Data Definition Language (DDL)

Two forms of SQL exist; the first is called **Data Definition Language**. DDL is used for defining the database objects such tables, views, and indexes. An example of a DDL statement is the CREATE TABLE command; in this example we create a table named Customers, which contains three columns.

```
CREATE TABLE Customers
(
    Customer_ID int         PRIMARY KEY,
    LastName    varchar(50) NOT NULL,
    FirstName   varchar(50) NOT NULL
)
```

Data Manipulation Language (DML)

The second form of SQL is called **Data Manipulation Language**. This is used to query and modify the data stored in our tables. There are four DML commands in SQL, which are SELECT, INSERT, UPDATE, and DELETE.

```
INSERT into Customers([CustomerId],[FirstName],[LastName])
values(1,'Linda' , 'Glucina')

UPDATE Customers
set [LastName]='Bain'
where [CustomerID] = 1

SELECT [FirstName], [LastName]
from Customers
where [CustomerID] = 1

DELETE from Customers
where [CustomerID] =1
```

Contained within the square parentheses are the column names of our tables, and From and Where are clauses of the DML statements which control what tables and rows within those tables are affected. In this example we create a new customer, update the last name column for that customer, retrieve the customer information and finally, we delete this customer.

Data Analysis Support in SQL

SQL is a language for retrieving and modifying data that matches given criteria. While it does provide a low level of mathematical aggregate functions, it does not provide a rich set of analytic functions that are available in data analysis languages such as MDX.

You can find more details regarding MDX in Chapters 10 and 11.

SQL allows you to order the results of a query, but there is no concept of row navigation available to functions within the query while it is executing. For example it is not possible for a row of a result set to contain a value from a column in the previous row divided by a column in the current row. This makes reporting using advanced functions such as a moving aggregate not possible.

Online Transaction Processing (OLTP)

Online Transaction Processing (OLTP) databases contain the information organizations use everyday to run the business. An OLTP database usually contains data specific to a business process and in many organizations you will find numerous OLTP systems running on a mixture of operating systems0 and database platforms. While the platforms that various OLTP databases use may be different, they often share the same goal of optimally allowing users to record and change real-time data.

We have already discussed that relational databases aren't a new concept, as they have been around for a long time vendors have spent many years tuning their query optimizers, the component of the relational database that resolves a query, to work extremely efficiently with OLTP workloads. As the amount of CPU processing power available is doubling every 18 months, so the number of transactions modern OLTP databases can support is growing at an astronomical rate. The Transaction Processing Council is a vendor, neutral organization that defines a standard database benchmarking process. A vendor can submit the results it achieve which after independent auditing is added to a list of results that the TPC maintains. As this benchmark process is common between vendors, it provides a non-biased comparison of performance that has been achieved on various platforms. As all vendors want to say their database is the most scalable, getting the highest TPC result has become very competitive between the various software companies.

At the time of writing the top TPC-C benchmark (the benchmark that measures OLTP performance) for clustered database systems was 668,220 tpm-C (new order transactions per minute). This particular result is achieved using SQL Server 2000 as the database platform. For more information I suggest you visit http://www.tpc.org.

This is an extremely high number of transactions that is well above the level required by most OLTP databases. While the platforms have demonstrated their ability to support astronomical workloads, unless an OLTP database is designed using appropriate techniques it is unlikely to perform adequately with many users generating transactions concurrently.

OLTP Design

Databases designed for OLTP need to process high numbers of insert, update, and delete operations while also retrieving small result sets used to display information to the application users. For this to be possible the database has to be designed to be extremely efficient in the way in manages the data it contains.

The following characteristics of OLTP databases are the most important when considering our design:

- ❑ High number of users. Depending on the nature of the database application there may be a requirement for the database to support hundreds or even thousands of concurrent users.

- ❑ High rate of transactions. All those users connected to the database are not going to be sitting still. They will be generating select, insert, update, and delete transactions that the OLTP database must be able to support.

- ❑ Data integrity. With such a high number of users generating a high number of transactions any errors that occur in the data would be very costly to an organization. Therefore, protecting the integrity of the data contained in the OLTP database is of utmost priority.

Normalization

OLTP databases should be highly normalized so they can achieve good transactional throughput. A normalized design removes redundant data from the tables, which in turn improves the performance of updating rows. Reducing the amount of unnecessary data also optimizes the use of the data cache.

With a de-normalized structure redundant data is common throughout a table. For example, a successful online retail store has many thousands of products that are organized by categories. One of the top-level categories that is used is "Videos". Due to the recent growth in DVD sales the online store wishes to change the name of this category to "Videos/DVDs". Let's look at how this would be done in a de-normalized table structure.

For this example the `Level1_Category` column must be updated to "Videos/DVDs" for every row where the existing `Level1_Category` is "Videos". If we have only a few hundred products this isn't too much of a problem, however, our online retailer has over 10,000 thousands products available in its online store. 3,000 of these are videos. To locate and update 3,000 out of our 10,000 products is going to take a long time, and other users of our database who may also need product information will be blocked for the duration of our transaction. For our update to be more efficient we may create an index on the `Level1_Category` so we more easily locate the 3000 video records. However this index would cause additional overhead, as the index would be updated once all the `Level1_Category` rows had changed from "Videos" to "Videos/DVDs".

Let's take a look at the same example using a normalized database. We have the same information, 10,000 products of which 3000 are in the "Videos" category but this time the category information is maintained in a separate table to the product information.

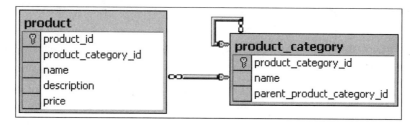

To change the category for all 3,000 records we only need to change a single record in the category table. As we only have 25 categories in total an index is not even required on the category table to assist with locating the "Videos" record. This update will happen in a sub-second timeframe and other users of the system will experience no impact.

Normalized tables are much thinner than their de-normalized counterpart, which allows the RDBMS to update and maintain these tables more efficiently. By separating a table into a normalized structure we also improve concurrency of transactions as locks become more granular by only locking the specific table that contains the data being modified.

> **OLTP database are highly normalized, which improves the speed of inserts, updates and deletes.**

Transactions

When we were talking about relational concepts earlier we mentioned that transactions must be isolated from other transactions while they are modifying data. Locks are held on the rows that are being modified by the current transaction to prevent other transactions from viewing or modifying the data until the first transaction that is blocking their access has completed. If a transaction takes too long to complete then other transactions can form queues waiting for the original transaction to finish before they can access the rows they need. The more users who access the database the worse the waiting time can be, as long queues will start to form. This is commonly the problem users experience when they phone the helpdesk and complain, "The database is running slow."

Data Integrity

Getting data entered from users is all well and good, but there is little point if the data is not valid. Data integrity is another important requirement of an OLTP database. These databases are used for everything from entering customer orders, right through to collecting critical data from nuclear power stations. Data that violates the rules that are set up is simply not allowed and I am sure any vendor who released a RDBMS product that did not provide facilities to enforce data integrity would find its product an instant flop.

Indexing

OLTP databases are optimized for the specific, predictable queries generated by the front-end applications that access the database. When data in a column that is indexed is modified SQL Server must update the index structure to reflect the change as part of the transaction. Creating indexes on unnecessary columns adds additional overhead to our data modifications reducing the transactional throughput, as even though these indexes are rarely used they must still be updated when changes to the base table occur. Transaction-processing databases are accessed by specific predictable queries that are generated from our database applications. These queries are predictable as they are built into the application and are not normally modifiable by users. The transaction-processing database can therefore be optimized for the specific application queries removing any uncertainly on what indexes are needed.

As OLTP operations predominately deal with individual rows most queries request data by specifying the unique key for the row they require. These types of queries do not require indexes on any other columns in the table. It is common for tables in an OLTP database to have only one or two indexes.

Because of this OLTP databases do not respond at all well to ad hoc querying, as often the indexes needed to support the ad hoc query do not exist. In fact the impact of ad hoc requests for data can be so great that a single query without supporting indexes can bring a large OLTP database to its knees. Often organizations that allow the ad hoc querying of their OLTP database only allow such queries to be schedule to run during periods of low system activity.

> **Indexes are created in OLTP databases only to improve the performance of predicted queries.**

Data Archiving

Removing unnecessary data from tables is an important part of OLTP house cleaning. Historical data that is not used as part of the day-to-day transaction processing applications is just dead weight sitting in you data structures. This redundant data will slow inserts, updates, index creations, and backup procedures so it should be regularly archived. While deleting historical data from existence is one approach to tiding up your OLTP database it is likely that this information could be used elsewhere. You may wish to retain your historical information for reporting purposes. Moving this information into a data warehouse will improve the performance of your OLTP database and also facilitate reporting and analysis of the information from the warehouse.

OLTP Reporting

We have covered why OLTP databases are good for processing high numbers of transactions. However getting information into the database is only one piece of the puzzle. Organizations have realized that the information they have locked up in these databases can be extremely valuable in making better business strategy decisions.

Before we launch off in the next chapter with discussions on planning a data warehouse solution we should discuss why a data warehouse is required at all, and why we cannot simply perform the reporting and analysis functions directly from our OLTP database.

Firstly, while normalized designs are brilliant for making changes to data, they can make retrieving the information contained with the database a real pain. OLTP databases support queries that satisfactorily return small result sets from a small number of tables. If this didn't happen, we would have unhappy application users if our database allowed them to update records in sub-second time, but took several seconds to show the record in the first place. Where OLTP databases start to suffer is when we wish to look at the big picture, such as when we wish to look at the information contained within our OLTP database as a whole, to see what has changed over time.

Joining large numbers of tables to retrieve a single result set requires a lot of CPU-and-disk intensive processing. This will reduce the amount of system resources available to other users of the database, potentially slowing their transactions. If our reports require a large number of rows, which may be returned to the report as is, aggregated to produce totals, or looked through for specific information, this will cause additional degradation to the performance of online transactions. This is due to the fact that while we are retrieving the rows for our reporting tool, no other users can modify the rows we have requested. Once we start using arbitrary criteria that can't be assisted by indexes to locate rows within our OLTP database, we will really kill the performance for our already unhappy users. As we have already discussed, indexes in an OLTP database are kept to an absolute minimum and are only created to support predicted queries. Returning data using non-indexed columns will cause table scans within our OLTP database to occur. Depending on the number of rows within our tables, which could potentially be millions of rows, users could be blocked from performing any sort of data updates for periods of seconds, minutes, or even hours. Obviously, this simply is not going to be a practical solution.

If your organization is of the 9-to-5 variety, a possible solution could be allowing users to schedule reports to run after normal business hours. If you only require reporting that can be satisfied in a timely manner using the existing database structure, this approach may be ideal. If you are trying to assist your users in making better business decisions this approach simply won't be successful. When analyzing information, the results of one report may generate more questions that can only be answered by another report. If these can only run every night it can end up taking days for users to discover information useful in improving the decision-making process. For this information to be of value to an organization it has to be available when and where the users need it.

Another attempt at a solution is to have offline copies of the OLTP databases located on different servers for the purpose of reporting. This provides more timely access to the information but does not improve on the poor performance caused by the highly normalized structures. This approach may be suitable if you only need to produce a set of standard reports from information that can be obtained from a relatively small number of tables.

Another issue confronted when attempting to report from OLTP systems is that not all the data necessary to generate the desired reports is available within a single OLTP database. Sometimes this information can be located in numerous separate OLTP database and reporting requires accessing data from various different locations. This is not always easy, as different databases can store the same type of information in very different ways, such as different units of measure for example.

What database designers have found is that to provide the response times needed for ad hoc querying and to facilitate reporting across multiple disparate systems it is often necessary to pull the data from the various sources into a common denormalized database structure. This is more commonly referred to as a data warehouse.

> **Reporting from OLTP databases is difficult due to their normalized structures, their minimal indexes, and their high number of users making online data changes.**

Online Analytical Processing (OLAP)

Unlike databases designed to support OLTP workloads, databases designed for OLAP, such as a data warehouse, are not required to support high volumes of users modifying, entering, and retrieving small sets of data. Instead, databases designed for OLAP workloads need to support ad hoc querying and reporting over potentially large volumes of data.

Online users rarely modify the data contained in a database used for OLAP. Instead, these databases are populated by batch updates that may occur on a nightly or weekly basis. These batch updates often import data from a number of OLTP databases and sometimes other data sources such as spreadsheets, text files, or web site log files. During the import it may be necessary to scrub the data from these various sources to convert it into a consistent format for loading into the data warehouse.

Instead of using highly normalized structures, data warehouses are designed to minimize the joins required to query the data. This is commonly achieved by either using a denormalized structure, where as much related data as possible is stored within the same table, or by using a star or snowflake schema. This will be discussed in more detail later when we begin designing our data warehouse.

OLTP vs. OLAP

Do you use a hammer to put in a screw, or a screwdriver to put in a nail? No, because in real life people recognize the value of using the appropriate tool for the job. It is hopefully apparent that there are fundamental differences between databases designed for OLTP and OLAP purposes. To this end, we can compare fundamental database characteristics to discover the differences between these database systems:

Characteristic	OLTP databases	OLAP databases
Purpose	To support business processes.	To assist with making better business decisions.
Where the data comes from	Online entry, point of sale devices, data loggers etc.	OLTP databases, flat files.
Criticality	Generally considered mission-critical. Regularly back up to protect from data loss.	Important to decision support; however; organizations can continue to operate without it. Back up less often than OLTP databases.
Database Size	Relatively small database size if the history information is regularly archived. Can quickly bloat if history is not removed.	OLAP database can be very large. Contains historical information generated by various OLTP databases within an organization.
Concurrent Users	Potentially very high numbers of users. Some OLTP databases support thousands of concurrent users.	OLAP databases support a much lower number of users than their OLTP counterparts.
Response Time	All application queries should complete in less than a second.	Queries commonly take seconds, minutes, and hours.
Data Changes	High number of insert, update, and delete operations are generate by user transactions.	Very low number of data changes generated by users. Data is updated by bulk import batches.
Ad hoc querying	Poor ad hoc query performance. Indexes are only created to support defined application queries.	Very good ad hoc query performance. Indexes are created to support queries possible queries.
Querying complexity	Data is highly normalized requiring many joins to retrieve information.	Data is denormalized requiring few joins to retrieve information.

When planning to develop and implement a new database application it is not always a case of selecting one of the two database design types. Databases designed for both OLTP and OLAP workloads are sometimes needed to support a business requirement. However, if you currently do not have any OLTP databases then you are unlikely to require an OLAP database unless you intend to populate this from information contained in flat files.

FoodMart 2000

Now that we have discussed the fundamental differences between OLTP and OLAP style databases, and why we require denormalized databases, it is an appropriate time to introduce the sample database that we will be using throughout this book.

`FoodMart 2000` is installed by default with Analysis Services and is a Microsoft Access database. This is already in a denormalized structure that is optimized for data retrieval. Unlike an OLTP database this denormalized structure contains much redundant data, as well as pre-aggregated summary information.

If the `FoodMart 2000` database were used by a real organization it would likely be populated from one or more OLTP data sources but unfortunately an example of an OLTP data source is not included with SQL Server Analysis Services. To assist our understanding of how our denormalized database may have come into existence I have created a fictional overview of the FoodMart company, along with a description of an OLTP database that could have been used as the data source of our sample analysis database.

FoodMart – An Overview

FoodMart is a fictional grocery store chain that employees 1,155 people and operates 24 stores throughout the United States. These stores receive goods from a number of warehouses in the USA, Canada, and Mexico that are also operated by FoodMart. FoodMart has over 10,000 customers recorded in its loyalty database.

The FoodMart OLTP Database

FoodMart operates an online transactional database for recording information about customer sales and inventory control. It records all the transactions that are processed, including not only the ordering and delivery of stock items from the various warehouses to the supermarkets, but also the recording of inventory changes as the barcode reader scans each item at the checkout. A database server is located in each store, as well as each distribution warehouse, and the data is replicated over high-speed WAN connections to the Headquarters.

The OLTP database model is too large to display in its entirety; however, this diagram shows the main tables and the relationships that exist between them:

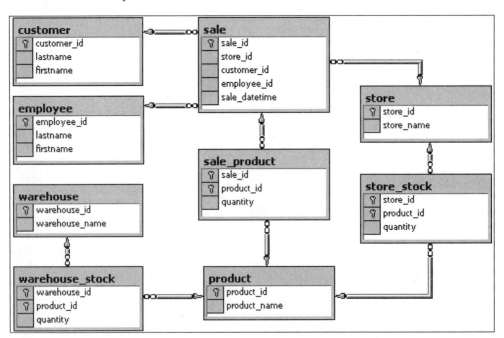

The database is designed to be in Third Normal Form and is optimized for a high number of transactional updates. Each store processes over 1800 transactions a minute during opening hours of 7am to 11pm. Each warehouse processes over 1500 requests for stock each day from the supermarkets. Each night the orders from the previous day are organized into efficient delivery schedules that will be used the following day.

The Need for the Data Warehouse

As competition in the foodstuffs sector is increasing, FoodMart is under increasing pressure to deliver more effective marketing campaigns as well as more efficient product purchasing. The information stored in the OLTP database is viewed as valuable to the organization and a project team has been formed to develop a method of leveraging the information to assist in making better business decisions.

FoodMart's marketing department has been requesting online access to near real-time sales information for the last two years to help with targeting their advertising campaigns to high value customers. Retrieving this information from the OLTP database has been difficult, as complex queries are required to return the information the marketing team needs. The impact of the marketing reports has been so great that the CIO has banned these reports from running during the day, so the marketing people must schedule these to run overnight. This has been less than ideal as often the results of one report generate questions that require another report to answer, which has to be scheduled for the following evening. The marketing people are unhappy with the current environment as they are finding it takes too long to gain access to the critical information they need.

The FoodMart Sample

If we took the requirements described above and created a de-normalized database structure that contains information extracted from our OLTP database, we may very well end up with a similar database to `FoodMart 2000`, which is installed with Analysis Services.

This is a Microsoft Access .MDB database and you can find this in the `\Program Files\Microsoft Analysis Services\Samples` directory on the drive on which you installed Analysis Services. An important point demonstrated here is that SQL Server 2000 Analysis Services does not require data to be located within a SQL Server 2000 database, any OLEDB-compliant source can be used. However, if this were a real implementation we would generally choose to store the data within SQL Server 2000, as this is a much more scalable and powerful database.

Upgrading to SQL Server 2000

To improve our ability to query and transform the data contained within the `FoodMart 2000` database we need to upgrade it from Microsoft Access to Microsoft SQL Server 2000. The easiest way to do this is using the Data Transformation Wizard to copy the table structure and the data contained within our tables.

To begin with we need to create an empty database within SQL Server to store our `FoodMart` tables. We do this in SQL Server Enterprise Manager by connecting to our SQL Server, right-clicking the database node, and selecting **New Database**. The following window will appear for us to enter information about the database we wish to create:

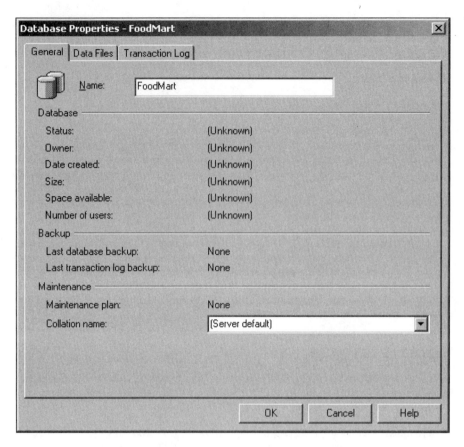

Enter FoodMart as the database name and if you wish to locate the data and log files in a location other than the default file locations click the Data Files and Transaction Log tags and enter the necessary path information. Once finished clicking OK will create our database.

Next we can use the DTS Import Export wizard to populate our database. This can be started in a number of ways, either by selecting Import and Export Data from the Microsoft SQL Server program group on the Start menu, from Tools | Data Transformation Services | Import Data from within SQL Server Enterprise Manager or by running DTSWIZ.EXE from the command line.

Once the DTS Wizard is started, click Next to select our data source. This specifies where we want the data to come from; in this case we want the Access FoodMart 2000.mdb database. To do this first select Microsoft Access as the data source, then enter the path of the FoodMart 2000.mdb file in the File name field. This Access database is not secured therefore we do not need to specify a username or password.

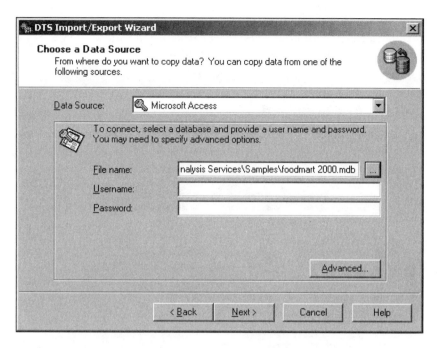

Click Next to choose a destination. On this screen we select where we want the data from the Access database to be copied to. Select the SQL Server where we created our empty database earlier, and choose FoodMart from the database drop-down list.

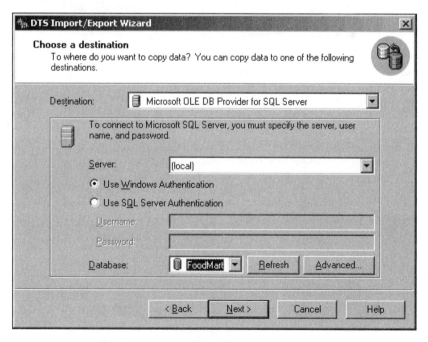

Click Next and leave the default option, to copy the tables and views from the source database, selected.

Click Next again to move to the screen that allows you to choose what tables we wish to import. As we wish to bring all the tables and data from the Access database into SQL Server you can simply click Select All and a tick should appear by all the tables in the list:

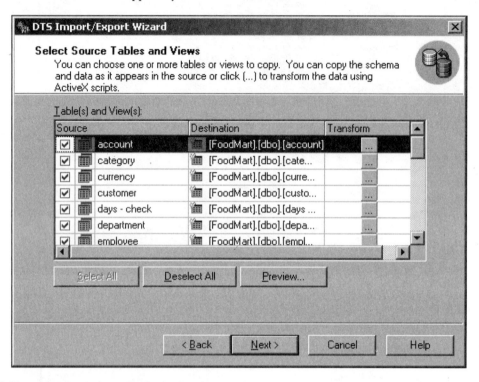

Click Next again and you will asked when you wish to run this import; we wish to run it immediately so leave the default selected and click Next again.

Finally clicking on Finish will start the import process and this should complete within a couple of minutes.

Keys and Indexes

Unfortunately the Data Transformation Wizard does not copy the primary keys, relationships, or indexes from the Access database into SQL Server so we must recreate these manually.

The remaining steps in our upgrade process require the use of the Query Analyzer tool to run SQL Scripts against our newly created database. Query Analyzer can be started from the SQL Server Program group off the Start Menu. Once running you will be asked which server you wish to connect to. Select the server on which you previously created the FoodMart database and select OK. You should be presented with a window similar to that shown opposite:

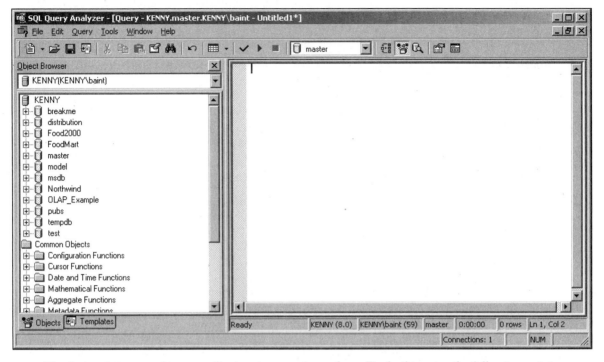

The first script we need to run will recreate our primary keys. To do this enter the following script within Query Analyzer and hit the execute query button ('Play' button in the toolbar).

```
USE FoodMart
ALTER TABLE account ADD PRIMARY KEY(account_id)
ALTER TABLE category ADD PRIMARY KEY(category_id)
ALTER TABLE currency ADD PRIMARY KEY(currency_id,date)
ALTER TABLE customer ADD PRIMARY KEY(customer_id)
ALTER TABLE department ADD PRIMARY KEY(department_id)
ALTER TABLE employee ADD PRIMARY KEY(employee_id)
ALTER TABLE expense_fact ADD PRIMARY KEY(store_id,account_id,exp_date)
ALTER TABLE position ADD PRIMARY KEY(position_id)
ALTER TABLE product ADD PRIMARY KEY(product_id)
ALTER TABLE product_class ADD PRIMARY KEY(product_class_id)
ALTER TABLE promotion ADD PRIMARY KEY(promotion_id)
ALTER TABLE region ADD PRIMARY KEY(region_id)
ALTER TABLE reserve_employee ALTER column employee_id int NOT NULL
ALTER TABLE reserve_employee ADD PRIMARY KEY(employee_id)
ALTER TABLE salary ADD PRIMARY KEY(pay_date, employee_id)
ALTER TABLE store ADD PRIMARY KEY(store_id)
ALTER TABLE time_by_day ADD PRIMARY KEY(time_id)
ALTER TABLE warehouse ADD PRIMARY KEY(warehouse_id)
ALTER TABLE warehouse_class ADD PRIMARY KEY(warehouse_class_id)
```

Next we must re-establish the relationships between the tables within our database. Running the following script in Query Analyzer will do this.

```
USE FoodMart
ALTER TABLE employee ADD FOREIGN KEY(position_id) references position(position_id)
ALTER TABLE employee ADD FOREIGN KEY(department_id) references
department(department_id)
ALTER TABLE inventory_fact_1998 ADD FOREIGN KEY(product_id) references
product(product_id)
ALTER TABLE inventory_fact_1998 ADD FOREIGN KEY(warehouse_id) references
warehoUSE(warehouse_id)
ALTER TABLE inventory_fact_1998 ADD FOREIGN KEY(store_id) references
store(store_id)
ALTER TABLE product ADD FOREIGN KEY(product_class_id) references
product_class(product_class_id)
ALTER TABLE product ADD FOREIGN KEY(product_id) references product(product_id)
ALTER TABLE sales_fact_1997 ADD FOREIGN KEY(promotion_id) references
promotion(promotion_id)
ALTER TABLE sales_fact_1997 ADD FOREIGN KEY(store_id) references store(store_id)
ALTER TABLE sales_fact_dec_1998 ADD FOREIGN KEY(product_id) references
product(product_id)
ALTER TABLE sales_fact_dec_1998 ADD FOREIGN KEY(promotion_id) references
promotion(promotion_id)
ALTER TABLE sales_fact_dec_1998 ADD FOREIGN KEY(store_id) references
store(store_id)
ALTER TABLE store ADD FOREIGN KEY(region_id) references region(region_id)
ALTER TABLE warehouse ADD FOREIGN KEY(warehouse_class_id) references
warehouse_class(warehouse_class_id)
```

Finally we must recreate the indexes that are needed to optimize queries on the FoodMart database. Running the following script will do this for us:

```
USE FoodMart
CREATE INDEX ix_cust_accnum ON customer(account_num)
CREATE INDEX ix_cust_lname ON customer(lname)
CREATE INDEX ix_cust_fname ON customer(fname)
CREATE INDEX ix_cust_postal_code ON customer(postal_code)
CREATE INDEX ix_cust_customer_region_id ON customer(customer_region_id)
CREATE INDEX ix_cust_num_children_at_home ON customer(num_children_at_home)
CREATE INDEX ix_cust_num_cars_owned ON customer(num_cars_owned)
CREATE INDEX ix_emp_position_id ON employee(employee_id)
CREATE INDEX ix_emp_store_id ON employee(store_id)
CREATE INDEX ix_emp_department_id ON employee(department_id)
CREATE INDEX ix_emp_supervisor_id ON employee(supervisor_id)
CREATE INDEX ix_expfact_time_id ON expense_fact(time_id)
CREATE INDEX ix_expfact_currency_id ON expense_fact(currency_id)
CREATE INDEX ix_invfact1997_product_id ON inventory_fact_1997(product_id)
CREATE INDEX ix_invfact1997_time_id ON inventory_fact_1997(time_id)
CREATE INDEX ix_invfact1997_warehouse_id ON inventory_fact_1997(warehouse_id)
CREATE INDEX ix_invfact1997_store_id ON inventory_fact_1997(store_id)
CREATE INDEX ix_invfact1998_product_id ON inventory_fact_1998(product_id)
CREATE INDEX ix_invfact1998_time_id ON inventory_fact_1998(time_id)
CREATE INDEX ix_invfact1998_warehouse_id ON inventory_fact_1998(warehouse_id)
CREATE INDEX ix_invfact1998_store_id ON inventory_fact_1998(store_id)
CREATE INDEX ix_prod_brand_name ON product(brand_name)
CREATE INDEX ix_prod_product_name ON product(product_name)
CREATE INDEX ix_prod_sku ON product(sku)
CREATE INDEX ix_prodcls_product_subcategory ON product_class(product_subcategory)
CREATE INDEX ix_prodcls_product_category ON product_class(product_category)
CREATE INDEX ix_prodcls_product_department ON product_class(product_department)
```

```
CREATE INDEX ix_prm_promotion_district_id ON promotiON(promotion_district_id)
CREATE INDEX ix_rgn_sales_district_id ON regiON(sales_district_id)
CREATE INDEX ix_resemp_position_id ON reserve_employee(position_id)
CREATE INDEX ix_resemp_store_id ON reserve_employee(store_id)
CREATE INDEX ix_resemp_department_id ON reserve_employee(department_id)
CREATE INDEX ix_resemp_supervisor_id ON reserve_employee(supervisor_id)
CREATE INDEX ix_sal_department_id ON salary(department_id)
CREATE INDEX ix_sal_currency_id ON salary(currency_id)
CREATE INDEX ix_sal_salary_paid ON salary(salary_paid)
CREATE INDEX ix_sal_overtime_paid ON salary(overtime_paid)
CREATE INDEX ix_salefact1997_product_id ON sales_fact_1997(product_id)
CREATE INDEX ix_salefact1997_time_id ON sales_fact_1997(time_id)
CREATE INDEX ix_salefact1997_customer_id ON sales_fact_1997(customer_id)
CREATE INDEX ix_salefact1997_promotion_id ON sales_fact_1997(promotion_id)
CREATE INDEX ix_salefact1997_store_id ON sales_fact_1997(store_id)
CREATE INDEX ix_salefact1998_product_id ON sales_fact_1998(product_id)
CREATE INDEX ix_salefact1998_time_id ON sales_fact_1998(time_id)
CREATE INDEX ix_salefact1998_customer_id ON sales_fact_1998(customer_id)
CREATE INDEX ix_salefact1998_promotion_id ON sales_fact_1998(promotion_id)
CREATE INDEX ix_salefact1998_store_id ON sales_fact_1998(store_id)
CREATE INDEX ix_salefactd1998_product_id ON sales_fact_dec_1998(product_id)
CREATE INDEX ix_salefactd1998_time_id ON sales_fact_dec_1998(time_id)
CREATE INDEX ix_salefactd1998_customer_id ON sales_fact_dec_1998(customer_id)
CREATE INDEX ix_salefactd1998_promotion_id ON sales_fact_dec_1998(promotion_id)
CREATE INDEX ix_salefactd1998_store_id ON sales_fact_dec_1998(store_id)
CREATE INDEX ix_str_store_type ON store(store_type)
CREATE INDEX ix_str_region_id ON store(region_id)
CREATE INDEX ix_str_store_postal_code ON store(store_postal_code)
CREATE INDEX ix_wrh_warehouse_class_id ON warehouse(warehouse_class_id)
CREATE INDEX ix_wrh_stores_id ON warehouse(stores_id)
CREATE INDEX ix_wrh_warehouse_state_province ON warehouse(warehouse_state_province)
CREATE INDEX ix_wrh_warehouse_postal_code ON warehouse(warehouse_postal_code)
```

Once all these scripts have been successfully run our database upgrade is complete. Throughout the remainder of this book we will utilize the upgraded SQL Server version of the FoodMart 2000 database as a data source for various examples of Analysis Services functionality.

Summary

In this chapter we looked at how relational databases are designed and how normalization is used to create efficient data structures for storing information. We took a look at the most important objects within a database and got a feel for how they are used.

Next, we looked specifically at how OLTP databases are designed. We discussed how normalization, transactions, and indexing all have an effect on the number of users our OLTP database can support. Then we looked at the key differences between OLTP and OLAP databases and why we cannot use our existing OLTP database for reporting purposes.

We introduced the FoodMart 2000 database that comes as part of Analysis Services and described a hypothetical example of where the information in this database may have been generated. Finally we upgraded the FoodMart 2000 database from Microsoft Access to Microsoft SQL Server 2000 so it is ready for use as our sample database for later chapters.

Data Warehouse

6

Designing the Data Warehouse and OLAP Solution

In the previous chapters, we looked at the general background to data warehousing and Analysis Services plus OLAP versus OLTP databases. This background is essential if you are a newcomer to the world of data warehousing, since you need to understand these concepts before you can proceed with the next steps of building the data warehouse. The background is also useful if you are a seasoned data warehousing professional, but have not yet gained experience using Microsoft enterprise data management tools and technologies.

This chapter deals with the design of the data warehouse and OLAP solution. It discusses the pre-requisites for a successful design and, the tools needed, ending up with the detailed design ready for implementation. In the process of presenting these issues, we look at how to build a data warehouse and OLAP application for a typical sale and inventory system. This example is similar in many areas to the FoodMart 2000 sample that is installed with the Microsoft Analysis Services.

Several issues will be covered throughout the chapter, including:

- ❑ Pre-requisites for a successful design: data, people, and tools
- ❑ Understanding the business model and its importance in the design process
- ❑ The importance of meta data
- ❑ The star schema design and its variants
- ❑ The need and strategies for data extraction and migration
- ❑ Production and delivery issues

Pre-requisites for a Successful Design

As an engineer, the design phase of any project is the most important phase, in my opinion. This is true in any project and applies to any discipline. When you design a software project, it is essential to start it in the right way, even if it means spending more time and resources than you would think are necessary. The better your design, the better your product will be. Because a good design minimizes the number of iterations that a project will go through during its life cycle, you will end up saving time and precious resources.

A data warehousing project has its own life cycle. The first step in this cycle, which is illustrated in the diagram below, is defining and gathering requirements. Once the requirements for the project at hand have been defined, prototypes can be developed to select the most satisfactory design, then the data analysis and design stages can begin, along with the development, testing, and documentation. After these steps, the application can be tested by the client (which also forms part of the construction phase). Once testing is complete, and bugs ironed out, the project is ready for rollout and to be used by the client. At this stage, the project isn't yet completely finished. Once the project has been released, issues will be raised either through maintenance, or through the needs of the clients, that may require modifying the project. This may lead to additional analysis and development of the new desired functionality, or fixing issues raised during the first few days of real-time operation:

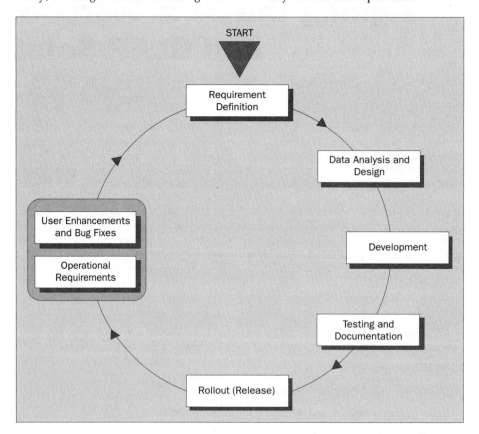

A good data warehouse design will cut down on the number of iterations the project may be subjected to in its life cycle. It will anticipate the added requirements as much as possible and be flexible enough to accommodate them beforehand, or at least make adding them later less expensive. As users start using the data warehouse, they might come up with what are called "operational requirements" which were not thought of during the requirement gathering stage. It is therefore important to gather details about all possible operational requirements and arrangements, such as user interface changes that might affect the data structure, who will be using the data warehouse, and where it is to be deployed, etc. in the design stage.

So, if the design phase of the data warehousing project is so important, how do we make sure the design is really good? The answer to this question lies in the following sections.

Customer Management

Customer management (end user and client) simply means collecting the data you need from the customer in an adequate manner. When you gather the data required for your design, you need to make sure you talk to the right people. Knowing the audience who will use your application and talking to them directly will help you obtain accurate information about what functionality is really needed.

Your first step is to talk to the executives, and convey to them of the importance of a data warehousing project. Then speak to these executives about how they use the system. You will probably find that these executives know the system best via the reports that they receive that help with every-day decision making and planning.

The next logical step is to talk to the people who produce these reports. These users are not necessarily members of the IT department, or computer wizards; they could be (in addition to the business analysts) secretaries who prepare current reports by compiling data given to them by analysts in a spreadsheet format, or clerks who feed data to the analysts. These users are the ones who usually give you the best information about the business, and what data is being collected. These people are the future intelligent users of the data warehouse and the OLAP solution.

You also need to communicate with the information technology (IT) people in the client's organization. This will allow you to gather information about the client's systems, their infrastructure, tools, etc. This knowledge is essential in the selection of the technologies to be used for the data warehouse project.

Other people you need to interact with on the client side are people using the current production systems. These systems will feed the data warehouse, and it is essential to know their data structure, size, and even samples of the data stored in them. This is important for the successful design of your data transformation system that will scrub, transform, and transfer data from their data stores to the data warehouse.

In your investigation of current production systems, you need to investigate all possible sources that may feed the data warehouse in the future and plan to include them in the design. Frequently, the customer will come back to you with a fifth request after you fulfill the four they asked for during the requirement gathering. Knowing all possible sources of data that might feed the data warehouse may make meeting these additional requirements easier and less costly in the future.

The Project Team

Building a successful data-warehousing project requires the right people who are dedicated and enjoy doing what they do. You need to have experts on your team, even if they are outside consultants, including "domain experts" who have worked on projects handling similar situations before. The expertise these people will bring may make a big difference in the design specifications and throughout the different stages of the project. Because of their experience, they know what should be included and what to avoid. This would probably become apparent at the later stage of the projects, but then it may be too late to take care of. Also, their experience will help in project scoping, phasing and execution.

> *Project scoping* – setting the functionalities that need to be covered or handled by the project, and also setting the functions that will not be handled to avoid raising undue expectations.
>
> *Phasing the project* – dividing the tasks into groups that will be carried out in phases.
>
> *Execution of the project* – designing and building the data warehouse based on the scope, and phases of the project.

However, in building your project team, you should try **not** to rely solely on outside consultants as it is very difficult for outside sources to understand the business requirements well enough to code the project alone. Also, if you do, you may quickly find that supporting the project after its release will be a big problem, since these people may not be available quickly enough to help with the support. Ideally you need to have a balanced team of in-house professionals and outside experts who will work together and share their knowledge and experiences to ensure adequate support of the application at all times.

Once the team is assembled, try to make sure it stays intact for the duration of the project. You don't want to use the revolving door policy with people joining the team late and others leaving it for other projects at will. Doing so is a recipe for failure because each phase of the project requires special expertise in different areas. Losing someone who has already acquired the knowledge and has been working on the project for some time is a big loss to the project. Replacements of such people will need to be trained and brought up to speed before they can contribute to the project, which may adversely affect the timetable of the deliverables during the different phases of the project.

The skills required by different team members needed during the life-cycle of the data warehousing project include:

❑ **Project Management**: a team member who will be responsible for managing the project and communicating with the client regarding progress and day-to-day issues.

❑ **Technical Leadership**: this is someone who knows the technical aspects of the project and has leadership skills that enable them to lead other team members to do their work the best way possible.

❑ **Senior Analysis Skills**: this is someone who will communicate with the customer, gather information about their business and their systems, and learn about all potential sources of data that may end up in the data warehouse. This team member's role is crucial in the design phase, and in phases where changes to the project scope are considered.

❑ **Database Design**: a team member who will be responsible for the data modeling and database design for the data warehouse. This person should have experience in data warehouse database design, due to the unique nature of these databases, which you have already seen in the previous chapters.

❑ **Data Transformation**: this person will be responsible for the transfer and transformation of the data from its sources to the destination warehouse, and possibly to the query processing system, which contains the tables of pre-calculated and pre-aggregated data.

❑ **Database Administration**: a team member who can perform database administration duties for the development databases. This person will be helpful in identifying operational needs for the data warehouse database that can be planned for in the design phase.

❑ **Development**: these are team members who will develop the different parts of the data warehousing solution. They are the ones who will design the cubes and build them. They are the ones who will also design the strategies and tools for data transformation and loading into the warehouse.

❑ **Quality Assurance/Testing**: this person is responsible for testing the project to ensure that it meets the specific quality requirements of the business every step of the way.

❑ **Technical Writing**: this team member will work closely with other team members to document the data warehouse solution throughout its stages.

❑ **Other**: these include system administrators, secretaries, and intern personnel who help with testing and data population of the development environment. The role of these people is essential for the success of the testing and debugging processes.

Although all the skills and positions mentioned above are important, they don't mean that you have to have separate people with each one fulfilling only one need; rather, you can have one person who covers more than one needed skill, just like you may need several people performing the same task which requires more than one person to fulfill.

The Tools

The last element for a successful data warehouse solution is the tools used to build and operate the data warehouse. The tools include everything you use in terms of hardware and software to build your warehouse. The hardware should be adequate to store immense amounts of data collected and transferred to the data warehouse, and the software should be adequate for running the data warehouse in the most efficient and fault-free fashion possible.

Hardware

Hardware spans a long list of elements used in the building and operation of the data warehouse system. First, the computers that house the data warehouse should have great processing power and vast disk storage. Fault-tolerance should be planned for by having redundancy and backup servers. The data in the warehouse should be backed up to other media that can be kept and protected off-site, for use when database recovery is needed.

The Analysis server should also be powerful with a great amount of RAM and CPU power to allow for fast processing of the queries issued against the data warehouse data, and generated the desired reports in a timely fashion. Performance Tuning is discussed in more detail in Chapter 20.

The network elements, routers, cables, switches, hubs, etc. should allow for broad bandwidth to facilitate fast transfer of the data from its origins to its destinations. The network is one of the most important pieces that can ensure successful delivery of the solution to the end user. With robust networks, data will be transferred quickly from operational databases and other sources to the data warehouse, and data will also be transferred quickly after its processing at the OLAP server.

When you set the hardware budget for your project, you need to look at real-life situations in which Microsoft Analysis Services and SQL Server 2000 were used to build a data warehousing solution, then compare these situations with the one you are dealing with. You also need to do some prototyping that will allow you to scale up what you really need in production environments. The basic requirements as stated by Microsoft should only be seen as guidelines.

Software

Software also spans a wide range of components starting with the operational database systems, to the data warehouse database management system (DBMS), to the Analysis Services used and the data transformation tools, and finally the reporting tools used at the client machines.

The operational database should allow for fast access and querying of its data when feeding the data warehouse. The data warehouse DBMS should be optimized for data retrieval, and should be powerful and capable of handling potentially huge amounts of data. The data transformation tools should be efficient to allow for smooth transformation of the data from the sources to the destination data warehouse. The Analysis Service should be powerful and capable of performing aggregations and summary tables quickly. Finally, the presentation tools should be user-friendly and allow powerful tables and graphs of the data to be built in response to the user's ad hoc queries. This is important to accurately reflect the nature and findings of the data summaries in a robust fashion.

For details on how to improve performance see Chapter 20 on Performance Tuning.

Given that you have the right hardware in place, Microsoft software and tools present an integrated set of software tools for building a successful data warehouse. The Microsoft Windows NT/2000 Server operating system serves as the networking software and the software on which the databases will be based. Microsoft SQL Server is a proven relational database that can be used efficiently for operational systems, and certainly Microsoft SQL Server 2000 is an excellent candidate for very large databases (VLDB), which are usually needed for data warehousing solutions. Microsoft SQL Server 2000 also includes an integrated set of tools for data transformation between the origins and the destination data warehouse. These tools utilize other Microsoft technologies that are designed specifically for the Windows environment, such as ActiveX technologies, and Active Directory support.

Microsoft Analysis Services serves as a good solution for conducting OLAP operations, because it is tightly integrated with other Microsoft tools and with SQL Server. OLAP client tools, such as the PivotTable Service, are also a great choice for data presentation because they are also integrated with other popular tools, such as Microsoft Office, and can utilize the ActiveX technologies.

In short, the Microsoft solution for data warehousing not only includes Analysis Services, but also the operating system, the database management system, the networking system, the presentation tools, and the technologies that bind these components, such as ActiveX and Component Object Model (COM).

Designing the Data Warehouse

After meeting the pre-requisites for the data warehousing project, and as a first step in the design of the data warehousing and OLAP solution, a strategy has to be laid out for the data warehouse project design and construction. The core components of this strategy include:

❑   **Policy**: rules that will determine how the data warehouse will be managed and used after its construction. These policies include the goal and scope of the data warehouse, rules that govern operational issues like loading and maintenance frequency, and organizational issues, such as security determination.

❑   **Transformation**: The data stored in the data warehouse is not likely to be the same raw data generated by OLTP systems. Instead the data has to be scrubbed, cleansed, transformed, and migrated, then the data may need to be summarized, filtered, refined, etc. Chapters 7 and 8 discuss in more detail how these operations can be conducted.

❑   **Meta data**: this is a repository of information about the data structures, applications, objects, and business rules in the data warehouse. This data is constructed once and centrally located for potential reuse in the future.

❏ **Storage**: After transformation the raw data is moved to its final destination – the data warehouse database. Data storage in the warehouse has to be optimized for easy accessibility, manageability, and flexibility.

The strategy mentioned above should be the guidance throughout the different phases of the project. We will now move on to discuss the different steps involved in the design process of our data warehousing solution for a typical sale and inventory system.

In the following sections, we will discuss the design steps for the data warehousing application in general without using the Microsoft Analysis Manager. The steps in the following sections of this chapter include:

❏ Analyzing the business, user, and technical requirements

❏ Designing the data warehouse database

❏ Designing the meta data

❏ Designing the data transformation strategy

❏ Designing the data warehouse policy and long-term maintenance and operation

❏ Designing the user interface tools

Analyzing the Requirements

Let's assume that a client representative contacted your company to perform an analysis and feasibility study for building a sale and inventory data warehouse solution, that would allow them to generate reports to assist them in the decision making and planning for future products, marketing, and sales strategies.

As a result, you establish a plan for gathering the requirements from the client. The plan includes interviewing the top managers at the client company, to find out about their specific vision and expectations from the data warehouse. The plan also includes identifying and meeting with all people who can provide valuable input to the design process.

It is important to ask the right questions when gathering the requirements; questions that increase your knowledge of the data and enhance your familiarity with the business issues and rules involved. Knowing the data will allow you to find the measures you need to represent in your OLAP solution. It will also allow you to identify the dimensions that you need to use to assess these measures. Finding the right measures and dimensions and identifying their relationships from the start will save you a great deal of time and effort later on after you have built your solution. Let's say that, after building your warehouse and OLAP application, you found out that a measure relates to some dimensions in a different way from the way represented in the design. This will mean modifying your design, and probably modifying your data transformation schemes, and re-importing the data into the data warehouse. Identifying the right relationships at design time will spare you from doing all of that.

We have already looked at the schema of the OLAP database earlier in the book. We are using the term OLAP database here as a reference to the repository of the OLAP cube data. This schema includes a fact table with multiple dimension tables linked to it. The fact table has the measures that represent the issues of interest that you want to identify. Designing the OLAP solution starts by identifying these measures, and the dimensions related to them.

To identify the measures used in your OLAP solution, you need to ask the business analysts the kind of questions that will lead you to the purpose they want to use the data for. For instance, the client management and/or business analysts will tell you that they are interested in knowing about total sales by region, data, salesman, customer, etc. They may also tell you that they are interested in knowing their inventory and its relationship to the number of orders at any given time.

Gathering requirements for your data warehouse design involves identifying several types of requirements. These types include:

❑ Business requirements: owner requirements

❑ Architect requirements

❑ Developer requirements

❑ End-user requirements

Business Requirements

Identifying the business requirements can be a complex and tricky task. This task includes identifying the objectives of the data warehouse or the data mart, determining the scope of the solution and any special requirements by the customer among other things. Therefore, when you set out gathering business requirements, you need to look into the following areas:

Business objectives

In our example, these objectives may include broad objectives like organizing the corporate data that is collected through the production OLTP systems in a way that may produce meaningful information that can be used for the decision making and planning for company's future. The objectives also include more specific needs like knowing the sales by region, time, and customer. Examples of broad objectives would be something like improving vendor assortments, or improving customer service, etc. A more specific goal would be to determine the average weekly rate of sales for each family of products per region over last quarter.

Solution scope and objectives, customers, and stakeholders

In our example the scope will include the sales and inventory areas of the company business. Other areas, such as accounting, human resources, etc. will not be handled by this solution at this time. The door will, however, be open for expanding the solution to cover the other areas in the future, if needed. The customer of this solution will be the company's decision makers and business analysts. This includes the management, some of the IT department personnel, and the owners of the company. The owners and shareholders, if the company is traded publicly, will be stakeholders as well because they will benefit from the solution in learning about the performance of the company and the status of their business.

Sources of data

One of the important business and customer requirements is identifying the data sources that can contribute to the data warehouse and establishing the optimal plans for collecting the data, sorting out what is beneficial and should be stored in the data warehouse, and moving it into the data warehouse database.

For instance, a company may be migrating from legacy systems to the more modern PC-based systems. In the process, the company wants to salvage the data it collected over the years with the old system, and probably will continue to collect through the same system in place for some time in the transitional phase of the migration process. A basic requirement is to transform and transfer the data to the new system with a high degree of accuracy and efficiency.

Another concern customers have is when their data is hosted by different sources. Customers want their data to be well consolidated and transferred to the data warehouse. For instance, a company may have the payroll system based on a Unix-based Oracle database, the production and inventory data in a DB2 database on the mainframe, and the sales data in a SQL Server database, or possibly one branch only uses spreadsheets to keep track of timesheet information. The processes used to transfer the data and transform it should be well defined and polished. In cases like these, you need to identify all possible sources that can contribute to the data warehouse, study the data structure of these sources, and decide on what to keep and what to ignore. All this can be done by asking the customer and their agents the right questions.

Planning, budgeting, scheduling, and allocating resources

Another concern the customers will have has to do with the planing and implementation of the data warehouse, the budget they need to allocate for it, and the schedule and resources necessary for building it. All these are requirements that have to be identified early in the planning process. Failing to assess these elements with some degree of accuracy will eventually lead to difficulties that would probably fail the whole project.

As a result of identifying good business requirements, specifications for the data warehouse can be defined in terms of the following:

- ❏ Subject Areas: topics of interest to various business functions. As an example, the marketing department may have interest in one or more of the following topics: market research, competitive analysis, buyer behavior, market segmentation, product (market matching), pricing and budgeting decisions, product decisions, promotion decisions, channel decisions, and forecasting trends.

- ❏ Prototyping: this is an important step that will yield specific subject areas for the marketing department, such as orders, promotions, markets, sales, and time cycle.

- ❏ Granularity: the higher the granularity, the more the amount of detail increases. This is defined by increasing the number of levels in the dimensions.

- ❏ Dimensions: Based on the analysis of the requirements, the following dimensions could be recognized:

  - ❏ Time with a calendar hierarchy (day, week, month, quarter, year)
  - ❏ Customer groups (customer, market segment, market, industry)
  - ❏ Product families (product, product family, product line)
  - ❏ Geography and location (sales rep, territory, district, country region, country, international region, corporate)
  - ❏ Organization structure (department, business unit, division, strategic business unit, subsidiary, corporation)

Architect's Requirements

Besides business and customer requirements, you need to identify architect requirements. In many cases, corporations use specific tools offered by certain vendors. The architect should be aware of the options that can be explored and the tools available. Also, the architect should be able to look at previous project catalogs, which would provide a great deal of information on how things were done. The architect, however, may still find that they need to use some tools that have not been used in previous projects, or that are not offered by the company's vendors. In this case the architect has to build a good case to present to the management for approval to obtain the required tools when they are not provided by the conventional vendors.

Developer's Requirements

Developer requirements should also be taken into consideration when gathering the requirements for the data warehousing solution. These requirements include specific applications, interfaces, computers, databases, communications, and user-interface screens. They also include technology requirements, deployment requirements, data warehouse production readiness requirements, security requirements, and other requirements for development and deployment such as personnel, their skills, and availability.

End-user Requirements

It is extremely important to collect the requirements of the end users because they are the ones who will be working with the system on a daily basis. These users will be mostly concerned with workflow. In other words, how does the functionality offered by the data warehouse fit into the end user's daily workflow? Other end-user requirements include query and reporting requirements, data analysis requirements, and types of activities including slicing and dicing separate data items in various ways, drilling down progressively exposing more details about the data, data mining to look for hidden patterns, and data surfing to browse the data warehouse data in an undirected manner. End users also want to be able to download and make local modifications, build business models, for example, using spreadsheets, data viewing in the form of two-dimensional views like spreadsheets, relational and relational tables, multi-dimensional views, reports and charts, and sample databases. Finally, it is very important to build a user-friendly GUI that the user approves of and finds easy to use.

Design the Database

Microsoft Analysis Services requires an OLE DB data source. The data source contains one or more fact tables from which cubes can be built. The database also requires defining numeric measures based on certain fields in the fact table (such as unit price). Dimension tables should also exist to be used for analysis of the fact table measure data. These dimensions include things like, customer, time, product, store, etc. Dimension tables contain a minimum of two columns, one of which should be a key column. Other columns describe and define individual attributes of the dimension, such as product brand category and sub-category. Dimension tables could also include keys to other dimension tables, for instance the product dimension may include the product category key, which is the key of the product category dimension table. The relationships between the fact table and dimension tables, specified by the joins of these tables, follow the star or snowflake schema.

In this section, we will look more closely at the design of a sales and inventory database as the basis for our data warehouse. The schema of this database is presented in the following diagram. Looking at the schema, we notice that there are two facts to analyze: sales and inventory. Each one of these facts has a fact table of its own. The fact tables are joined by dimension tables forming a star schema in each case.

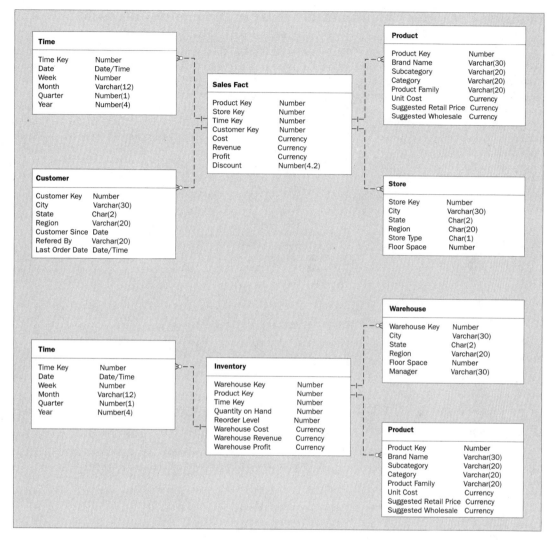

When designing an OLAP solution with the Microsoft Analysis Services, you need to make sure that the logical and physical design of the database takes into account the following important design considerations:

Be Aware of Pre-Calculations

Another thing you need to be aware of is that sometimes you need to do some calculations before you do the aggregation. For example, if you have in your fact table the cost, unit price, and sale amount, you can calculate the profit by subtracting the cost from the product of the unit price and sales amount. This new value has to be calculated before you do any aggregation on it, in order for the aggregation to be accurate. The new value can be saved as a calculated measure, or in some cases a calculated member.

Dimension Data Must Appropriately Exist in Dimension Tables

Dimension tables in Microsoft Analysis Services should have columns representing level members as member key, name, and properties. With this, each level in the hierarchy is represented in its own table. This is not the only way hierarchical data is represented in relational databases. Sometimes you may find hierarchies represented in one table with self-joins of a key field to a parent key field. These tables provide great benefits in that they allow for unbalanced hierarchies to be represented where the leaf levels can be located at different distances from the root. Another benefit these tables provide is that they allow you to move subtrees easily in the hierarchy by changing the parent key for the root of these subtrees. However, these tables will not work with Microsoft Analysis Services and have to be converted to a series of tables using a snowflake schema and must represent a balanced hierarchy before using them. The following diagram shows the difference of the two representations:

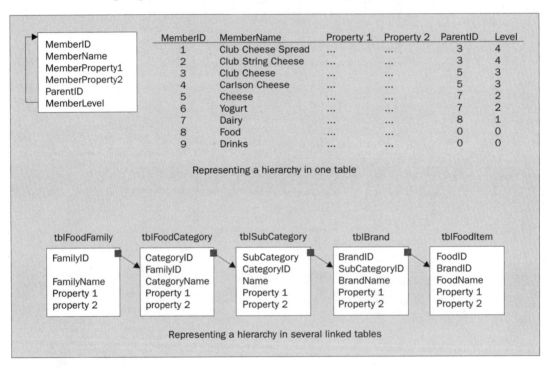

Representing a hierarchy in one table

Representing a hierarchy in several linked tables

tblFoodFamily			
FamilyID	FamilyName	Property1	Property2
1	Food	...	...
2	Drinks	...	...

tblFoodCategory			
CategoryID	CategoryName	Property1	Property2
1	Dairy	...	...
2	Meat	...	...

tblSubCategory				
	SubCategoryID	Name	Property1	Property2
	1	Cheese	...	...
	2	Milk	...	...
tblBrand				
	BrandID	BrandName	Property1	Property2
	1	Club	...	...
	2	Carlson	...	...
tblFoodItem				
	FoodID	FoodName	Property1	Property2
	1	Cheese Spread	...	...
	2	String Cheese	...	...

Indexed Views

One of the new features of SQL Server 2000 is Indexed Views. It is worth noting here that an indexed view can greatly increase performance of some types of queries. Indexed views are best used when querying data that is unlikely to change very often. In cases where the data does change frequently, the maintenance cost can far outweigh the performance gained in using the indexed view. Some of the query types that an indexed view are generally used for are:

❑ Joins and aggregations that involve a great number of records

❑ Joins and aggregations that are involved in a number of different queries

❑ Decision Support Workloads

In some cases when the query we are using does not fall into the above categories, we should look at using indexed views on components of the query that do. An example of this is if we were using a query to pull together aggregations from disparate tables and then unioning the results. We cannot use a union in an indexed view, but we can create indexed views on the individual aggregations.

Use Star or Snowflake Schema

Microsoft Analysis Services can create dimensions from one or more columns in a table. This table can be the fact table, or could be a separate dimension table linked to the fact table through a key column. It is recommended, however, that you use separate linked dimension tables, rather than the fact table to create your dimensions. This choice usually results in a star or snowflake schema. Using these kinds of schemas enhances visibility of the dimension data, while optimizing its storage according to the basic principle of relational database models. It is easier to see the relationships between the different dimensions and the fact table with this representation. Storage need is optimized due to the possibility of using smaller key columns in the fact table that join to the dimension table, which includes the descriptive name column of the dimension and its levels. This is because name columns are usually of the character data type, which requires more storage than the numeric data type of the key columns. Indexes related to the dimension member keys in the fact table will also be smaller in this case, which not only improves the storage situation, but also improves the speed at which data is retrieved from the table in queries.

To get a better grasp on this concept, assume that the fact table includes 3 million records. Assuming that the table has three dimensions, let's see the difference in storage needed for each case: either including the dimensions in the fact table, or separating them out in their own tables. In the first case, let's assume that the dimension name field is a character field of length 30 characters. That means the storage needed for the three dimension columns in the fact table, not considering the indexes related to them is calculated according to the following formula:

Needed Storage = `3,000,000 x 3 x 30/(1,024 x 1,024) = 257.5MB`

> **The formula above simply multiplies the number of columns in the fact table corresponding to the dimensions by the size of the columns, and the result is multiplied by the number of rows in the table. The division by (1024 x 1024) converts the result from Bytes to MB.**

In the second case, the storage needed for the same dimensions if they are separated out in their own tables and joining them to the fact table through a 4-byte numeric key column is calculated according to the formula:

Needed Storage = `3,000,000 x 3 x 4/(1,024 x 1,024) = 34.3MB`

The benefit becomes even more obvious when you add the storage needed for the indexes on the fact table in both cases. The added storage needed to accommodate the separate dimension tables is usually minimal and negligible compared to the space savings in the fact table. This is because these dimension tables are usually small in size and include only a few records to several hundred records in extreme situations.

Another benefit of using the star or snowflake schema is that maintaining the dimensions becomes much easier. Dimensions are processed by Analysis Services by performing SELECT DISTINCT on the dimension column in the fact table. If this column is a long character field, it will take much longer to process this query than if it is a numeric value. This leads to even better performance.

Finally, by separating dimension tables out from the fact table, you ensure that all members at the different levels of the dimension exist even if they are not represented in the fact table. For example, if the fact table for December 1998 sales does not include brand XYZ of food, this brand will still exist as a member of the brand level of the product dimension table.

How About Dimension Members?

When it comes to dimension members, several rules have to be fulfilled in your design for the Microsoft Analysis Services database. These rules are described below.

Member Names

Member names need not be unique within a level. However, within the hierarchy the member names should be unique. In other words, you may have the member name Jackson for a city in the state of Mississippi and for a city in Michigan at the same time. The member name here is not unique to the overall city level. However, for the hierarchy it is unique because there is only one Jackson in Mississippi and only one Jackson in Michigan.

One thing you may want to consider in the design stages of your dimension members is when converting numbers to textual types, add insignificant zeros because if you do not do this, Analysis Services will. This is because Analysis Services can only sort text values. For instance, if you perform the transformation, 1 becomes "01" and 2 becomes "02". If Analysis Services does the conversion on its own, you will have difficulties sorting the numbers correctly. When Analysis Services converts the numbers to text types the 1 becomes "1" and the 2 becomes "2". Sorting the numbers from 1 to 20 will then yield something like: 1, 10, 11, 12, 13, 14, 15, 16, 17, 18, 19, 2, 20, 3, 4, 5, 6, 7, 8, 9; which probably isn't the way you want the sort to happen.

Members and Aggregate Levels

Microsoft Analysis Services requires that hierarchies be fully connected. In other words, any member at a non-leaf level should have at least one child member in the next lower level. If this next level is a leaf level, then the child will be at that leaf level and this child will not have any more children. What this means is that dimension members should exist at all aggregate levels, and you cannot have a level that is void of members. If a hierarchy is irregular and not fully connected, members have to be filled in at the leaf and other missing levels. These members could be empty, as long as the hierarchy is transformed into a fully connected hierarchy. One way to accomplish this practically is to use outer joins to create views on tables in a snowflake schema defining the dimension to return all members of the dimension. The dimension would then be based on the view, rather than the original snowflake tables.

Let's present an example to make this clearer. Look at the following figure. It represents a simple irregular hierarchy representing different monthly expenses: insurance, payroll, and utility bills. The insurance shows payments for life, health, and auto insurance. The leaf level is supposed to be the types of insurance. However, this level is missing for the payroll and utilities categories. In order to make this hierarchy work in Microsoft Analysis Services, we need to construct a view based on the tables of the hierarchy using outer joins. Assuming we have an `Expense Category` table and an `Expense` table with the structures shown in the following figure, we can write the SQL (as shown after the diagram) to create the view:

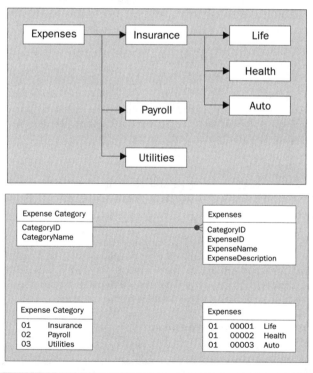

```
CREATE VIEW vwExpenses AS
SELECT   [Expense Category].CategoryID,
         [Expense Category].CategoryName,
         Expenses.ExpenseID, Expenses.ExpenseDescription
FROM     [Expense Category] LEFT JOIN Expenses ON
         [Expense Category].CategoryID = Expenses.CategoryID;
```

As a result the view will have the values in the table below:

CategoryID	CategoryName	ExpenseID	ExpenseDescription
01	Insurance	0001	Life
01	Insurance	0002	Health
01	Insurance	0003	Auto
02	payroll	NULL	NULL
03	Utilities	NULL	NULL

You notice that the view will have empty cells for the missing leaf levels for the payroll and utilities categories.

One more thing to consider when designing dimensions and hierarchies in Microsoft Analysis Services is that each fact should relate to a single member in the lowest level used by each dimension in the cube. For instance, in our sales and inventory example, the `sales` fact should relate to the lowest member in the dimensions involved: `time`, `product`, `store`, and `customer`. In other words, the facts should be at the levels: `day`, `product name`, `store`, and `customer name` of these dimensions respectively. You cannot have a fact at the `day`, `product name`, `state`, and `customer name` levels of these dimensions because the `state` level of the `store` dimension is not the lowest level in that dimension.

Designing OLAP Dimensions and Cubes

The most important step in designing the multidimensional database for the OLAP solution is designing the cubes and dimensions. Microsoft OLAP solutions provide a wide variety of options when it comes to these designs. You can design shared, private, or virtual dimensions, or you can also choose to make your cube either a stored cube or a virtual one. So let's look at how we design cubes and dimensions in a way that utilizes the many powerful aspects of Analysis Services.

Naming Dimensions and Cubes

Once a dimension or cube is saved, its name cannot be changed. Therefore, pay special attention when naming these objects, especially when you want to define multiple hierarchies, which can only be done through dimension names.

Naming a cube or dimension follows the general naming conventions in Analysis Services. That is, the name can have only letters and digits in addition to some characters, such as, "@" and "#", in addition to spaces and underscores. Cube and dimension names must start with a letter. Any leading or trailing spaces to the name are truncated by Analysis Services. Dimension names allow a maximum of one period, which is used to represent multiple hierarchies in the dimension.

Choosing Between Shared and Private Dimensions

Private dimensions are used exclusively by the cube they are created in. Shared dimensions, on the other hand, can be used by multiple cubes in the database. Private dimensions require that the cube be processed if they or their data ever change. With this, private dimensions do not allow for incremental update processing. Also, virtual dimensions cannot be formed from member properties of private dimensions. However, private dimensions can participate in multiple hierarchies with other private or shared dimensions in the cube, as long as the names of these dimensions are unique.

Unless it is absolutely necessary to use a dimension exclusively with a cube, it is recommended that you build your dimensions to be shared. Private dimensions don't really offer any benefits over shared dimensions.

Parent-Child Dimensions

With Microsoft Analysis Services we can also define Parent-Child dimensions. These dimensions enable us to design dimensions in a way that relates to the real-world hierarchical structure. In this case we define a member key column that identifies each member, and a parent key column that relates the member to its parent. Below is an example `Staff` table showing this structure where the `StaffID` column is the member column and the `ManagerID` is the parent column:

Name	StaffID	ManagerID
Glen Harding	1	2
Jacquie Ferguson	2	2
Joe McDermott	3	5
Martin Findlay	4	5
Susan Fordyce	5	5

Both the member column and the parent column must be of the same type and both must occur in the same table.

Multiple Hierarchies

Microsoft Analysis Services defines multiple hierarchies in terms of the name of the dimension that they are part of, by introducing a period in the name that separates the name of the dimension from that of the hierarchy. For example, to create two hierarchies for the `Time` dimension, `fiscal` and `calendar`, you can create two dimensions and give them the names: `Time.Fiscal` and `Time.Calendar` respectively. Therefore, as you see, multiple hierarchies are treated as separate dimensions in Analysis Services. One undesirable side effect of this is that Analysis Services will create aggregates between the two dimensions representing the hierarchies. These aggregates are usually meaningless and only consume disk space and processing time for the cube.

If you want to design multiple hierarchies in your OLAP solution, make sure the naming of the dimensions participating in the hierarchy is correctly established and make sure you set the properties of the dimensions and their members appropriately because these properties don't have to be the same between the two dimensions forming the multiple hierarchy.

Member Properties

Microsoft Analysis Services allows you to create member properties for members of a certain level of a dimension. These member properties are defined by any field in any of the tables that make up the dimension. This feature provides you with the flexibility and ability to build virtual dimensions and filter MDX query results.

Member properties are not automatically aggregated in the same way measures are. Analysis Services do not group query results based on member property values. Such grouping has to be done in a view. Member property values are treated as text values by Analysis Services regardless of the type behind these values. Therefore numbers, string values, and dates are all considered text values. If you use member properties in SQL queries and you want to express them in the result set in terms of their true type, you need to use SQL conversion functions, such as `CAST` and `CONVERT` to explicitly convert them to the type they are supposed to have. This conversion allows the client that is issuing the query to format the values in the proper way. For instance, dates can be formatted to show day/month/year instead of month/day/year, and currency values can be formatted to show a currency sign, separating comas, and decimals.

In your design, you need to highlight all these points so that when the development of the client queries and reports takes place, these issues can be accounted for.

Virtual Dimensions and Virtual Cubes

Virtual dimensions have greatly improved in SQL Server 2000 as compared with those in SQL Server 7.0. Some of the more important enhancements include the fact that there is now no limit to the number of members a virtual dimension can have. Also virtual dimensions can now have multiple levels and need not be based on member properties. The interested reader is pointed to the section on "Virtual Dimensions" in SQL Server Books Online.

As we discussed in the previous chapter, member properties can be used to create virtual dimensions. The next chapter will illustrate how this can be done with the Analysis Manager. Virtual dimensions act like views. They add valuable analysis capabilities, as well as security among other benefits, but they increase query processing time compared to regular dimensions. Virtual dimensions have only two levels, the ALL level and a base level, and can be used to break a dimension on multiple display axes. For example, for the Time dimension, if you create a virtual dimension that includes only the month level together with the ALL level, you can use the *virtual* Time dimension with the *regular* Time dimension to display a matrix in which the column headings are years and the row headings are months as shown in the table below.

Sales in $1,000	1997	1998	1999
Jan	20	19	23
Feb	18	17.6	22.2
Mar	19.5	22	17
Apr	21	22.1	20.5
...	...	...	...

When you design virtual dimensions, you need to weigh the benefits of saving storage space against the disadvantage of increased query processing time. If the benefits outweigh the losses, then virtual dimensions become a good option to include in the design of your data warehouse.

Virtual cubes are another feature offered by Microsoft Analysis Services, to allow for better dimensional analysis and reporting. They allow you to view data from multiple cubes across any dimensions, shared or private that are part of these cubes, and they may contain calculated members and other definitions. Virtual cubes can also offer a viable solution for analysis of a situation that is much more difficult to analyze with a single regular cube.

Designing Partitions

In the previous chapter we discovered that multiple partitions are allowed on a single cube in Analysis Services with SQL Server 2000 Enterprise Edition. Partitions are considered a great feature because they physically implement logical segments of data, and therefore can be used for optimization and maintenance purposes of the system. Designing partitions has to be done with extensive care to avoid duplicating data or eliminating data in some cases.

In chapter 9 we will see how to use partitions in the Analysis Manager, the GUI tool provided with Microsoft Analysis Services to design, manage, and maintain the system. However, things to be careful about when dealing with partitions include overlapping partitions and incomplete partitions. These concepts are discussed in some detail below.

Microsoft Analysis Services does not track overlapping partitions, which may lead to duplicating data in the partitions resulting in incorrect aggregations. To illustrate how this can take place, let's consider the sales and inventory database example we have been using so far. If we design our partitions so that each will include data for one quarter of the year and still have a partition for the whole year, then if the year partition uses the same fact tables as the quarter partitions, your values will be counted twice. The solution to this problem is merging the quarter partitions to form a year partition instead.

Incomplete coverage of the cube with the partitions will yield empty cells. Therefore, when you suspect that empty cells are encountered where they shouldn't be, examine your partitions to see if they are incomplete and don't cover the whole cube. Just like overlapping partitions, incomplete partitions lead to erroneous aggregation results.

Meta Data and the Microsoft Repository

In the first two chapters, we met the Microsoft Repository, and discovered how it is used to store the meta data describing the different aspects of the data warehouse and Analysis Services. In this section, we will re-iterate the ideas discussed previously, and add more explanation to them in light of the new information introduced in this chapter.

When you create any object in Analysis Services, data about the object is called meta data and is stored in the Microsoft Repository. Meta data describes the object, its properties, and all aspects related to it. You can view some of the meta data in the Analysis Manager by selecting the meta data tab (where available) in the detail pane. The screenshot on the following page shows an example of the meta data display in the Analysis Manager. The following is a meta data summary for different components and objects of the Analysis Services.

Data Source

The data source used for the OLAP database and for the individual cube has its own meta data that describes it. As you will see in Chapter 9, as we define a data source for a cube, when you prepare your design for the OLAP database, you need to specify the name of the data source, the source data store (a SQL Server database for example), the location of the data store (server name), and the name of the OLE DB Provider that facilitates the connection to the data source. When you create the data source, you will see these items listed as part of the meta data for it in addition to the status, which indicates whether the connection to the source is established or not.

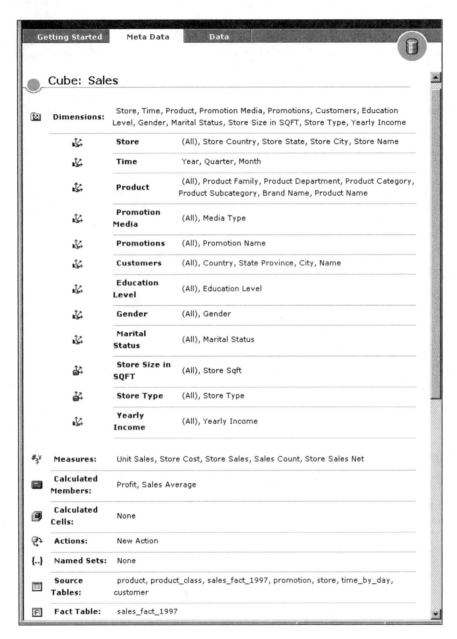

OLAP Cubes

In the process of designing your data warehouse and OLAP solution, you need to define the meta data for OLAP cubes. This includes specification of the dimensions, measures, calculated members, source tables, storage type (MOLAP, ROLAP, or HOLAP), and data source. You also need to identify the security of this cube and possibly create separate roles to limit access to it. Each of these items has to be identified in detail with great care. You also need to estimate the aggregation sizes and storage need for the cube so that the customer takes necessary measures to have the needed resources to support them.

Dimensions

When it comes to dimensions, you need to specify the number of dimensions you will be using in your solution, the names of these dimensions, the number of levels in each one, and the type of each dimension – whether it is a standard or a time dimension. You also need to specify for each dimension whether it is a private dimension or a shared one. Finally, you need to specify when you need to have each of the dimensions processed, whether before the cube processing (for shared dimensions) or during the cube processing.

Individual Dimensions

Meta data for individual dimensions includes information about the levels included in the dimension, the source table for the dimension, the source columns for the levels of the dimension, and the member count. You may find it difficult to predict the member count for each level of the cube dimension, but a rough estimate will help determine the degree of aggregation and size of the aggregates that you can get away with. Also defined as part of the dimension meta data are the cubes it is used in.

Cube Partitions

As you have already seen, cube partitions are only available in the SQL Server 2000 Enterprise Edition of Analysis Services. The Standard edition allows for only one partition for the cube, which includes the whole cube. Meta data for the partition defines its name, data source, storage type (MOLAP/ROLAP/HOLAP), and the slices for the partitions.

SQL Server stores repository information in its `msdb` database, which is a system relational database that ships with SQL Server.

Sample Model Meta Data

The following is an example of a specification of meta data for a data warehouse design for a typical sales and inventory data warehouse system we looked at earlier in the chapter. The specification shows the kind of information you should keep track of in the meta data.

Defining the model goals (inventory and sales)

Inventory	
Name:	Inventory
Definition:	This model contains inventory data for each product model in each warehouse, on a daily basis
Purpose:	The purpose of this model is to facilitate the analysis of inventory levels and warehouse profits
Contact Person:	Warehouse Manager
Dimensions:	Warehouse, Product, and Time
Facts:	Inventory
Measures:	Quantity on hand, reorder level, cost, revenue, profit
Calculated Members:	Floor space in sq ft, profit

Sales	
Name:	Sales
Definition:	This model contains sales data for each product model, on each order, on a daily basis
Purpose:	The purpose of this model is to facilitate the analysis of product sales
Contact Person:	Regional Sales Manager
Dimensions:	Customer, Product, Store, and Time
Facts:	Sales
Measures:	Cost, revenue, profit, amount sold, and discount amount
Calculated Members:	Floor space in sq ft, and store type

Fact Meta Data

Inventory	
Name:	Inventory
Definition:	This fact table contains inventory data for each product model in each warehouse, on a daily basis as well as cost and profit data for the warehouse
Load Frequency:	Daily
Load Statistics:	Last load date: N/A
	Number of rows loaded: N/A
Usage Statistics:	Average number of queries/day: N/A
	Average rows returned/query: N/A
	Average query runtime: N/A
	Maximum number of queries/day: N/A
	Maximum rows returned/query: N/A
	Maximum query runtime: N/A
Archive Rules:	Data will be archived after 24 months, on a monthly basis
Archive Statistics:	Last archive date: N/A
	Date archived to: N/A
Purge Rules:	Data will be purged after 48 months, on a monthly basis
Purge Statistics:	Last purge date: N/A
	Date purged to: N/A

Inventory	
Data Quality:	Inventory levels may fluctuate throughout the day as more stock is received into inventory from production and stock is shipped out to retail stores and customers. The measures for this fact table are collected once per day and thus reflect the state of inventory at that point in time, which is the end of the working day for a plant.
Data Accuracy:	The measures of this fact are "some value%" (preferably as close to 100% as possible) accurate at the point in time they represent. This is based on the results of physical inventories matched to recorded inventory levels. No inference can be made from these measures as to values at points in time not recorded.
Time Granularity:	The measures of this fact represent inventory levels on a daily basis.
Key:	The key to an inventory fact is the combination of the keys of its dimensions: Warehouse, Product, and Time.

Sales	
Name:	Sale.
Definition:	This fact table contains sale data for each transaction that has been recorded in the sales systems at each retail store.
Load Frequency:	Daily.
Load Statistics:	Last load date: N/A.
	Number of rows loaded: N/A.
Usage Statistics:	Average number of queries/day: N/A.
	Average rows returned/query: N/A.
	Average query runtime: N/A.
	Maximum number of queries/day: N/A.
	Maximum rows returned/query: N/A.
	Maximum query runtime: N/A.
Archive Rules:	Data will be archived after 24 months, on a monthly basis.
Archive Statistics:	Last archive date: N/A.
	Date archived to: N/A.
Purge Rules:	Data will be purged after 48 months, on a monthly basis.
Purge Statistics:	Last purge date: N/A.
	Date purged to: N/A.
Data Quality:	It is possible for errors to be made by staff completing a transaction. However, the numbers recorded represent what is actually contracted with the customer and must be honored.

Table continued on following page

Sales	
Data Accuracy:	The measures of this fact should be 100% accurate in that they represent what was actually sold.
Time Granularity:	The measures of this fact represent sales of a given product on a given transaction.
Key:	The key to a sale fact is the combination of the keys of its dimensions: `Customer`, `Stores`, `Product`, and `Time`.
Key Generation Method:	The time portion of the key is simply the date the sale takes place. The `product` key is retrieved from the product tables in the operational system. The `store` key is retrieved from the store tables in the operational system using the `region ID` and `store ID`. The seller key is retrieved from the seller translation table using the `region ID`, `outlet ID`, and `salesperson ID`. The `customer` key is retrieved from the customer translation table using the `customer ID` and `customer location ID`. The `order ID` from the original order is used as the `order` key for the sale fact.
Source:	`Order` table in operational system database.
	Conversion Rules: Rows in each order table are copied into the sale fact on a daily basis. You may add some scrubbing and cleansing conversion rules for the copy process.
Selection Logic:	Only rows for the current transaction date are selected.

Dimension Meta Data

Customer	
Definition:	A customer is any person or organization who purchases goods from the client company or any of its subsidiaries. A customer may be associated with many business locations (hence the geography aspect or hierarchy of the dimension).
Hierarchy:	Data can be summarized at three levels for a customer. The lowest level of summarization is the customer city appearing in the ship-to address. Data from each location (ship-to address) can be further rolled up to be summarized by state, then by region.
Change Rules:	New customer locations are inserted as new rows into the dimension. Changes to existing locations are updated in place.
Load Frequency:	Daily.
Load Statistics:	Last load date: N/A.
	Number of rows loaded: N/A.
Usage Statistics:	Average number of queries/day: N/A.
	Average rows returned/query: N/A.
	Average query runtime: N/A.
	Maximum number of queries/day: N/A.

Customer	
	Maximum rows returned/query: N/A.
	Maximum query runtime: N/A.
Archive Rules:	Customer data is not archived.
Archive Statistics:	Last archive date: N/A.
	Date archived to: N/A.
Purge Rules:	Customers who have not purchased any goods from the client or any of its subsidiaries in the past 48 months will be purged on a monthly basis.
Purge Statistics:	Last purge date: N/A.
	Date purged to: N/A.
Data Quality:	When a new customer is added, a search is done to determine if we already do business with them at another location. In rare cases separate branches of a customer are recorded as separate customers because this check fails. Until such time as the customer notices separate locations dealing with us, these occurrences remain as originally recorded. The region attribute was not originally in the operational system. It is added based on a matrix that shows the regions based on zip codes in the ship-to-address attribute.
Data Accuracy:	Incorrect association of locations of a common customer occurs in less than "x%" of our customer data. The value of "x" will be based on some research of the operational data.
Key:	The key to the customer dimension consists of a system-generated number.
Key Generation Method:	When a customer is copied from the operational system, the translation table is checked to determine if the customer already exists in the warehouse. If not, a new key is generated and the key along with the `customer ID` and `location ID` are added to the translation table. If the customer and location already exist, the key from the translation table is used to determine which customer in the warehouse to update.
Source:	
Name:	`Customer` table.
Conversion Rules:	Rows in each `customer` table are copied on a daily basis. For existing customers, the name is updated. For new customers, once a location is determined, the key is generated and a row inserted. Before the update/insert takes place a check is performed for a duplicate customer name. If a duplicate is detected, a sequence number is appended to the name. This check is repeated until the name and sequence number combination are determined to be unique. Once uniqueness has been confirmed, the update/insert takes place.
Selection Logic:	Only new or changed rows are selected.
Name:	`Customer Location` table.

Table continued on following page

Customer	
Conversion Rules:	Rows in each customer location table are copied on a daily basis. For existing customer locations, the ship-to address is updated. For new customer locations, the key is generated and a row inserted.
Selection Logic:	Only new or changed rows are selected.

Customer Attributes	
Attribute 1:	**Customer key**
Definition:	This is an arbitrary value assigned to guarantee uniqueness for each customer and location
Change Rules:	Once assigned, the values of this attribute never change
Data Type:	Numeric
Domain:	1 – 999,999,999
Derivation Rules:	A system-generated key of the highest used customer key +1 is assigned when creating a new customer and location entry
Source:	System-generated
Attribute 2:	**Name**
Definition:	This is the name by which a customer is known to the client
Change Rules:	When a customer name changes it is updated in place in this dimension
Data Type:	Char(30)
Domain:	Derivation rules: To ensure the separation of data for customers who have the same name but are not part of the same organization, a number will be appended to names where duplicates exist
Source:	Name in Customer table
Derivation Rule	Name is derived by concatenating first name, middle initial, and last name of the retail customer, or by copying the company name for business customers

Customer Attributes:	
Attribute 3:	**City**
Definition:	This is the city part of an address where the client ships goods to a corporate customer. It is possible for a corporate customer to have multiple ship-to locations, hence multiple `City` member values. For retail customers no `City` is kept because no ship-to-address is kept in the source table. Therefore, there can only be one entry in the customer dimension for a retail customer.
Change Rules:	When a `City` changes it is updated in place in this dimension.
Data Type:	Char(60).
Domain:	All valid cities within the client's service area.
Derivation Rules:	The ship-to (City) is derived from the ship-to-address in the operational table.
Source:	Ship-to address in the `Customer Location` table.
Facts:	Sale.
Measures:	Cost, revenue, quantity sold, and discount amount.
Attribute 4:	**State**
Definition:	This is the state part of an address where the client ships goods to a corporate customer. It is possible for a corporate customer to have multiple ship-to locations, hence multiple `State` member values. For retail customers no `State` is kept because no ship-to-address is kept in the source table. Therefore, there can only be one entry in the customer dimension for a retail customer.
Change Rules:	When a `State` changes it is updated in place in this dimension.
Data Type:	Char(60).
Domain:	All valid states within the client's service area.
Derivation Rules:	The ship-to (State) is derived from the ship-to-address in the operational table.
Source:	Ship-to address in `Customer Location` table.
Facts:	Sale.
Measures:	Cost, revenue, quantity sold, and discount amount.

Table continued on following page

Customer Attributes:	
Attribute 5:	**Region**
Definition:	This is the region in which an address where the client ships goods to a corporate customer is located. It is possible for a corporate customer to have multiple ship-to locations, hence multiple `Region` member values. For retail customers no `Region` is kept because no ship-to-address is kept in the source table. Therefore, there can only be one entry in the customer dimension for a retail customer.
Change Rules:	When a `Region` changes it is updated in place in this dimension.
Data Type:	Char(60).
Domain:	All valid regions within the client's service area.
Derivation Rules:	The ship-to (Region) is derived from the ship-to-address' zip code based on a matrix the client establishes to define regions.
Source:	Ship-to address's zip code and client's region/zip code matrix.
Facts:	Sale.
Measures:	Cost, revenue, quantity sold, and discount amount.

You can actually continue with this specification adding to it the remaining dimensions, measures, member properties, virtual dimensions, etc. This specification will eventually serve as the blueprint for the design and policy of your OLAP solution.

Data Loading and Transformation Strategy

Part of the design of the data warehouse is the design of the data loading and transformation strategy. SQL Server 2000 includes Data Transformation Services (DTS), which make this task much easier than it would have been.

Loading the data into the data warehouse goes through several stages. These stages are: data capture, data transformation, and data application. The designer has to focus on all three stages determining the techniques to use for each one and the physical storage for the data during each stage.

Capturing the Data

The data warehouse receives data captured from the operational systems and other external sources. Capturing the data means collecting it from these sources, which include various file formats and both relational and non-relational database management systems. The data can be captured from many types of files, including extract files or tables, image copies, changed data files or tables, DBMS logs or journals, message files, and event logs. The technique used for capturing the data varies with the type of the data being captured, as you will see below. Data capturing techniques include source data extraction, DBMS log capture, triggered capture, application-assisted capture, timestamp-based capture, and file comparison capture. Let's discuss the application and use of each of these techniques.

Source Data Extraction

Source data extraction provides a static snapshot of source data at a specific point in time. This technique is suitable for a static temporal data model that doesn't require a continuous history. Source data extraction works best when files, tables, or image copies are sought from the capture process. This technique may be best used when a whole block of data is to be loaded into the data warehouse, maybe replacing some data in the warehouse that is related to the same source, but at a different snapshot in time. As an example of using this method, a school might usually update its data warehouse with the year data at the end of the year, while archiving the data of the last year.

DBMS Log Capture

Log capture enables the data to be captured from the DBMS logging system. It has minimal impact on the database or the operational systems that are accessing the database. This technique requires that DBMS logging is supported and turned on, as well as a clear understanding of the format of the log records and fairly sophisticated programming to extract only the data of interest based on what is logged in the log files. This method is not directly possible with SQL Server since the format of the log files generated by the SQL Profiler is internal to SQL Server, and cannot be easily read outside the SQL Profiler. A workaround for this is to have the SQL Profiler log the traces to a table in the database, and then you can use Triggered Capture (see below) to extract data from it.

Triggered Capture

Many database management systems, such as SQL Server and other SQL92-compliant systems, support triggers and stored procedures. Triggers are procedures that provide for the execution of SQL or complex applications when specific events in the database take place, such as inserting new records, updating or deleting existing ones. These triggers can enable any type of capture. The trigger itself simply recognizes the event and invokes the procedure. It is up to the user to actually develop, test, and maintain the procedure. This technique must be used with care because it is controlled more by the people writing the procedures rather than by the database management system. Therefore, it is open to easy access and changes as well as interference by other triggering mechanisms.

Application-assisted capture

Application-assisted capture involves writing programs that include the logic to capture the data from almost any operational source. This implies total control by the application programmer along with all the responsibilities for testing and maintenance. Microsoft data abstraction technologies, such as OLE DB and ADO, allow for writing such applications to access a wide variety of data sources using the programming language of your choice. Although a valid technique, it is considered better to have application-assisted capture performed by products developed specifically for this purpose, rather than to develop your own customized application unless you sufficiently test and verify that your application will do what it is intended to do without unwanted side effects.

One benefit of DBMS log capture, triggered capture, and application-assisted capture is that each of these techniques can produce an incremental record of source changes, to enable use of a continuous history model. Each of these techniques typically requires some other facility for the initial load of data.

Timestamp-based Capture

Timestamp-based capture is a simple technique that involves checking a `timestamp` value to determine whether the record has changed since the last capture. If a record has changed, or a new record has been added, it is captured to a file or table for subsequent processing. This technique may require structural changes to existing operational systems to ensure that `timestamp` fields exist in each table participating in the capture process of such systems.

File Comparison

A technique that has been used for many years is file comparison. Although it may not be as efficient, it is an easy technique to understand and implement. This technique involves saving a file that includes a snapshot of the data source at a specific point in time of data capture. Then, at a later point in time, the current file is compared with the previous snapshot file. Any changes and additions that are detected are captured to a separate file for subsequent processing and adding to the data warehouse databases. As an example, an auto manufacturer wanted to create a Web-based application that allows potential customers to search all dealer inventories and factory inventories on the Web to find the car they like, and possibly buy it online. The database supporting the search engine is a SQL Server 2000 data warehouse. Data is extracted from thousands of individual dealer's databases and consolidated in an ASCII format file. The data is compared to factory data, with new built cars that are not in dealer inventory being added as well. The resulting file is then uploaded into the database every week. However, every night, the file is compared to the previous night's upload to check for differences. These differences are then loaded appropriately when found.

It seems at first that timestamp-based capture and file comparison capture, with their comparison technique, produce a record of the incremental changes that enables support of a continuous history model. However, this may or may not be accurate. Care must be exercised because more than one change of a record may occur between capture points resulting in not recording all changes to the operational system, which may lead to losing some of these changes that took place between capture points. Therefore, the history captured would be more accurately described as a history based on points in time, rather than a record of the continuous change history.

As a data warehouse designer, you need to take all these techniques into consideration when planning your data capture based on the sources you are capturing data from, the kind of data you need to capture from these sources, and the nature of capture history, continuous versus based on points in time. It is possible, for instance, to use a mixture of these extraction techniques for example you may use 'Application, assisted Capture' to produce records in an intermediate database which is then 'Source Data Extracted'. This can be especially useful for remote data sources or where the security and integrity of the raw data is an issue. The table below will help you to quickly find the proper techniques you want to consider for a specific situation.

	Best Use Scenario		
Data Capture Technique	Initial Load	Incremental Load with Continuous Change History	Incremental Load with Periodic Change History
Source data extraction	X		
DBMS Log Capture		X	
Triggered Capture		X	
Application-assisted Capture		X	
Timestamp-based Capture			X
File Comparison Capture			X

Transforming the Data

Transforming the data to the data warehouse involves several processes. These processes should be designed to ensure validity and integrity, adequacy and usefulness, and in some cases aggregation and calculation of new values based on data source values. These functions are usually classified as data validation, data scrubbing, and data transformation. The following paragraphs briefly describe these functions. A detailed discussion of these issues is available in Chapter 7, which introduces Microsoft Data Transformation Services.

Data validation involves ensuring data integrity and validity. For example, it ensures that the cities mentioned are in the right states, or countries. It also ensures that when working with currency fields, the data is transformed to the right currency for the country in which the data mart or data warehouse will be used. Validation also ensures referential integrity in terms of primary and foreign keys in the database.

Data scrubbing reconciles data coming from different sources to feed the same destination table in the target data warehouse database. It eliminates discrepancies or conflicts between the different data sources. For example, if a product is classified as a beverage in one source and spirit in another, one of these two classifications will be accepted and the other dropped to ensure that the product will always fall under the same classification in the data warehouse. Microsoft SQL Server allows you to use several techniques to perform data scrubbing. These techniques include: the Data Transformation Services import/export wizard, writing custom ActiveX-based scripts or programs to do the scrubbing, or using DTS lookup. These techniques are discussed in greater detail in Chapter 7.

The data transformation process converts the captured source data into a format and structure suitable for loading into the data warehouse. Meta data is usually used to store the mapping characteristics used to transform the source data in the Microsoft Repository. Meta data defines any changes that are required prior to loading the data into the data warehouse. The data transformation process will help to resolve the anomalies in the source data and produce a high quality data source for the target data warehouse. Transformation of data can occur at the record level or at the attribute level. Three basic techniques are used for the transformation in general: structural transformation, content transformation, and functional transformation.

Structural transformation changes the structure of the source records to be similar to that of the target database. This technique transforms data at the record level. Which means that the whole record is transformed to match the structure of the record in the target database.

Content transformation changes data values in the records. This technique transforms data at the attribute level. Content transformation converts values by use of algorithms or by use of data transformation tables.

Functional transformation creates new data values in the target records based on data in the source records. This technique transforms data at the attribute level. These transformations occur either through data aggregation or enrichment. Aggregation is the calculation of derived values such as totals and averages based on multiple attributes in different records. Enrichment combines two or more data values and creates one or more new attributes from a single source record or multiple source records that can be from the same or different sources.

The transformation process may require processing through the captured data several times because the data may be used to populate various records during the application process. Data values may be used in a fact table as a measure and they may also be used to calculate aggregations. This may require going through the source records more than once. The first pass would be to create records for the fact table and the second to create records for the aggregations. Finally, update interval is closely related to the time it takes to perform data transformations. Some transformations involve complex processes and huge amounts of data, not to mention having to go through the data more than once. Therefore, processing these transformations can take long hours, which will affect the frequency of their occurrence.

Populating the Data Warehouse

When the data warehouse model is being created, consideration must be given to the plan for populating the data warehouse. Limitations in the operational system data and processes can affect the data availability and quality. In addition, the populating process requires that the data model be examined because it is the blueprint for the data warehouse. The modeling process and the populating process affect each other.

The data warehouse model determines what source data will be needed, the format of the data, and the time interval of data capture activity. If the data required is not available in the operational system, it will have to be created. For example, sources of existing data may have to be processed to create a required new data element. In the case study, the Sale fact may require Total Cost and Total Revenue. However, these values do not reside in the source data model, therefore they must be calculated. In this case, Total Cost is calculated by adding the cost of each component, and Total Revenue is calculated by adding all of the Order Line's Negotiated Unit Selling Price times Quantity Ordered. The model may also affect the transform process. For example, the data may need to be processed more than once to create all the necessary records for the data warehouse.

The populating process may also influence the data warehouse model. When data is not available or is costly to retrieve, it may have to be removed from the model. Or, the timeliness of the data may have to change because of physical constraints of the operational system, which will affect the time dimension in the model.

OLAP Policy and Long-Term Maintenance and Security Strategy

OK, now you have completed the database design for the data warehouse, and you have even designed the data loading strategy for it. Now you have to take care of important issues that will have a great impact on the success of the data warehouse. Some of these issues, such as security and maintenance, are discussed in this section. Other issues, such as user interface design and choosing reporting tools are discussed in the following section.

What is the OLAP Policy, After All?

Designing the data warehouse does not stop at designing the database, data loading strategies, and meta data for the OLAP solution. It is important that the design take into account on-going maintenance and security issues while the data warehouse is in use. Establishing what I call the "OLAP Policy" is actually meant to help make this task as easy and smooth as possible. The OLAP Policy means creating rules and policies regarding the use of the data warehouse, maintaining it, and establishing the security strategy.

When you wrote the requirements and specifications documents for your data warehouse, you probably included sections about how the data warehouse will be used, how the use will be monitored and what kind of statistics will be generated to help refine it in the future. Hopefully you also remembered to document the frequency at which the data is loaded into the data warehouse, and the frequency and rules of archiving data out of the data warehouse. You probably also added rules for backing up the data warehouse's database, and rules for handling customer requests, in case the customer still wanted to add feedback after they started using the thing, and maybe rules for what actions to take in cases of emergency, when the data warehouse is down or has suffered major disaster and recovery efforts need to be underway to recover the data up to the latest backup. If you have done all these tasks, then you have already written your OLAP policy rules.

What Rules Does the OLAP Policy Contain?

The OLAP policy includes rules that should be incorporated in the OLAP and data warehouse meta data. These rules are designed to handle the following situations:

Security Plan

A very important component of the policy is the security plan for the data warehouse. Security in SQL Server data warehousing spans over several levels, the OLAP cubes, the SQL Server data warehouse database, and the operating system level. Analysis Services provides security through roles that can be defined at the cube level. These roles are tightly integrated with Windows NT users and groups. The purpose of a security plan is to identify which users can see what data and perform what activities in the database. To develop your security plan, you need to list all the items and activities in the database that must be controlled through security, identify the individuals and groups in the company, and cross-reference the two lists to identify which users can see what data and perform what activities in the database.

SQL Server provides a sophisticated security model that, if used well, prevents unwanted access to the data and the database objects. Although sophisticated, the security model in SQL Server is easy to understand and manage. SQL Server Enterprise manager provides the tools to establish and manage security. You can also perform the same tasks, and more by using security-related system and extended stored procedures, or SQL Server's database management objects (SQL DMO). The security model allows for two modes of authentication, NT authentication only, and mixed (SQL Server and NT) authentication. After the user is authenticated, the security mechanism is the same for both modes.

The security model allows for implementation of security at the Windows NT domain level, Windows NT computer level for the computer hosting the SQL Server, the SQL Server level through login accounts, and database and application level through the use of roles and permissions and assigning them to the database object level.

Database Backup and Recovery

As you probably know, a common practice in the database administration world is backing up the databases. Backups allow for recovery of the data in disaster cases. Backup and recovery plans should be an important part of the OLAP Policy and the OLAP and data warehouse solution meta data. SQL Server provides tools for to perform backups, which, in turn, provide safeguard for protecting critical data stored in the data warehouse databases. Backing up and restoring a database allows for the complete restoration of data over a wide range of potential system problems. These problems include:

❑ Media failure: If one or more of the disk drives holding a database fail, you are faced with a complete loss of data unless you can restore an earlier copy of the data.

❑ User errors: If a user or application, unintentionally or maliciously, causes invalid modifications to a large number of records of data, maybe deleting many records or changing the value of a table field with an erroneous UPDATE SQL statement to one value for all records. In these cases, the best way to deal with the problem may be to restore the data to a point in time before the modifications were made.

❑ Permanent loss of a server: If a server is disabled permanently, or a computer is lost to a fire or flooding, you may need to activate a warm standby server or restore a copy of a database to another server.

Additionally, backing up and restoring databases is useful for other problems, such as moving or copying a database from one server to another. Backing up a database from one computer, and restoring the database to another can make a copy of a database quickly and easily on the target computer.

Backing up a database makes a copy of a database, which can be used to restore the database if it is lost. Backing up a database copies everything in the database, including any needed portions of the transaction log. The transaction log is used during recovery operations to commit completed transactions, and roll back uncompleted transactions. Backing up a transaction log backs up only the changes that have occurred in the transaction log since the transaction log was last backed up.

Restoring a database backup returns the database to the same state it was in when the backup was created. Any incomplete transactions in the database backup, (transactions that were not complete when the backup operation completed originally), are rolled back to ensure the database remains consistent.

Backup, recovery, and replication (when needed) are some of the administrative tasks that will be discussed in later chapters.

Auditing

Auditing allows you to recognize all activities that happened in the database and who did these actions. This is an important requirement, since if, for any reason, unwanted events happen, auditing can tell you when the event took place, and can probably tell you who conducted the activity. Auditing is implemented in SQL Server as part of security.

Statistics Gathering

It is important to monitor how the users are using the data warehouse and OLAP tools. Knowing the number of queries and type of these queries issued against a particular fact cube, for example, will allow you to make modifications accordingly to either make such queries more efficient, or maybe change them to be more attractive if they are hardly ever used. Therefore, your initial design should plan to add monitoring of such statistics to the meta data of the project. Some examples of these statistics may include:

❑   Average and maximum number of queries against a certain fact

❑   Average and maximum rows returned per query

❑   Average and maximum query run time

❑   Last archive data

❑   Last backup date

❑   Last load data

❑   Number of rows loaded in number of rows returned

❑   Date archived to

❑   And other stats as needed

Archiving and Data Distribution Plans

As the data warehouse receives more and more data from operational sources, its size grows and queries against it become slower. To maintain high query performance, you will need to separate the data in the fact tables according to the data field (dimension) to multiple fact tables (for example sales fact table for 1999 and sales fact table for 1998, etc.). Hence the cut-off point at which you start separating the data has to be estimated as part of your design. Also, at some point, when you notice that some of the fact tables that relate to a few years in the past are sparsely used, you may want to consider archiving them out of the database into a different location to recover the space they occupy for newly added data. The design should estimate the point at which the data is archived, with plans to retrieve it quickly when needed.

Data distribution is encountered when the operational data goes directly into small data marts. Data mart data is then replicated into the data warehouse. This is another issue that has to be taken into account in the design stages of the data warehousing solution. If the data marts are fed from the data warehouse, then you need to determine the frequency at which you load data into the data marts from the data warehouse.

User Interface and Querying Tools

Data presentation and query tools are some of the most important parts of the data warehousing solution, mainly because they are accessed directly by the end users and are designed to meet their display requirements. Microsoft SQL Server Analysis Services is integrated with the PivotTable Service, which acts as the engine that transfers the data requested by the queries from the cubes and aggregate tables to the user interface elements. These elements could be custom made using any programming language, or a well-established reporting or spreadsheet application, like Microsoft Excel.

PivotTable Service and user interface tools are discussed in great detail in Chapter 12.

Summary

In summary, this chapter dealt with the design of the data warehouse and OLAP solution. It discussed the pre-requisites for a successful design and the tools needed, ending up with the detailed design plan ready for implementation. In the process of presenting these issues, we discussed the issues involved with the design of a data warehousing solution beginning with the pre-requisites for a successful design, to analyzing the requirements, and ending with establishing a policy for long term maintenance.

Professional SQL Server 2000 Data WareHousing
Data Warehouse

7

Introducing Data Transformation Services (DTS)

One of the most challenging issues with building a data warehouse is populating it with data after its construction. The warehouse is usually expected to accommodate data from multiple heterogeneous sources. The data has to go through several stages of extraction, validation, scrubbing, transformation, and transfer.

In SQL Server 7.0, a new set of utilities, **Data Transformation Services (DTS)**, were formed and grouped together to enable a developer to import data in an ordered and controlled fashion. In previous versions of SQL Server, the only way to move data in to a SQL Server database or extract data from a SQL Server database to an outside file, was to use a utility called bcp (bulk copy program), or through using programs such as Visual Basic with ODBC and RDO/ADO. Although bcp still exists, it is a command-line utility that is restricted in what tasks it can perform and which data it can work with.

We begin with a detailed overview of DTS, which takes a closer look at how DTS has grown from SQL Server 7.0 to SQL Server 2000, and we will move on to demonstrate that DTS is not just a method of moving data in and out of a SQL Server database, and how it can aid you in your development of your Analysis Services. This chapter and the next will concentrate on DTS from an Analysis viewpoint only; however, the general power of DTS will begin to reveal itself to you.

When dealing with data import through to analysis manipulation, DTS can handle all the stages involved with data transformations such as validation, and scrubbing, because it is integrated with the Microsoft Universal Data Access technologies and the Microsoft ActiveX technologies. It is not a requirement that you have Analysis Services installed to use DTS, but this chapter and the next will concentrate on DTS within a data warehouse scenario. As you will see in this chapter, DTS packages can be used to extract data from **OLE DB** and **ODBC**-compliant data sources. They can also be used to run scripts and programs written in other languages to perform the needed tasks of data handling before storage into the data warehouse.

To investigate DTS further, take a look at "Professional SQL Server 2000 DTS " (Wrox Press, ISBN 1-861004-41-9). We will look at DTS purely in SQL Server, although you can use DTS in any language that can implement and work with COM interfaces.

We discussed Microsoft DTS to some extent in the earlier chapters of this book, and by now you probably have an idea of what it is, and what it is used for. Let's start with a detailed overview of DTS.

DTS Overview

In the process of creating your OLAP and data warehouse solution, you will design the data warehouse, even build it and create the database and the tables that will host the data to be kept in the warehouse. You may then ask yourself a question: "Did my design take into account the population plan of the data warehouse?" You may be in a situation where you need to get data from at least several different incompatible sources. For example, imagine a scenario where some of the data is in an accounting system, which resides in an old proprietary system developed by IBM for the mainframe computer twenty years ago. Other information is available in an Oracle database that holds the information about all of the products produced by the company, and keeps track of a transaction and sales record. Other sources may include daily dumps from remote servers to an FTP directory.

Even if your solution does not cover a large number of different systems, hardware, or technologies, you may be looking at simply importing data from a simple Access database that has outgrown its life-span. You still face the same problem of getting the data in to a SQL Server 2000 database without having to re-key every item of data, and validating the keying to ensure that every item is 100% accurate. To further complicate matters, as each moment passes, new data or alterations to existing data could be occurring.

The next question you will probably ask is: "What technology can I use to perform all these daunting data transfer tasks, and can this technology perform some transformations to the data before populating the data warehouse? Does SQL Server offer this service?" The answer to these questions is yes; you can use SQL Server 2000's data transformation services (DTS) to do the job. DTS is a technology introduced in SQL Server 7.0 to consolidate many tools that already existed in previous versions and added new tools and functionality that was not available before. DTS will answer such questions, allowing you to do the transfers and transformations necessary for a successful population of the data warehouse.

How Will DTS Help Me?

Without a doubt, DTS is the best technology you can use to interactively, or automatically on a regularly scheduled basis, populate the data warehouse and data marts with the data coming from multiple heterogeneous sources, as the diagram opposite illustrates. No other technology at this present point in time can perform as well, or be as flexible as DTS, with importing or manipulating data into SQL Server.

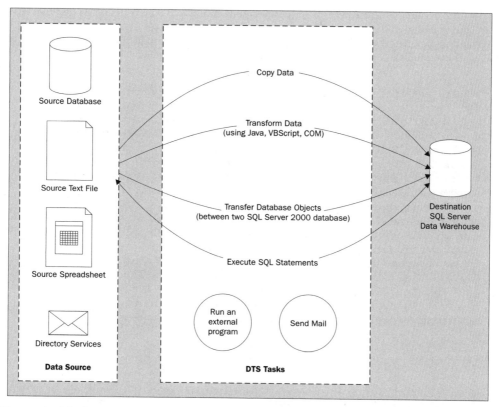

DTS can schedule these import or manipulation jobs for you because it is integrated with SQL Server 2000, which allows it to use the **SQL Agent service** to do the scheduling. Of course, it is not mandatory to use SQL Agent service and it is possible to run any DTS tasks ad hoc. DTS can be used to perform data validation before populating the data warehouse. It can also be used to create custom transformation objects that can be integrated into third-party products, for example when using DTS to upgrade an Access system to one that will now run within SQL Server. Finally, DTS can be used to access applications using third-party OLE DB providers. This allows applications for which an OLE DB provider exists, to be used as sources and destinations of data. To clarify, DTS can do more than move and transform data between SQL Server databases. For example, DTS can be used to transform data from a source such as Microsoft Excel, and move it into an Access database, using SQL Server's powerful DTS to make the whole process easier and smoother.

DTS facilitates access to native OLE DB providers such as SQL Server, Microsoft Excel, Microsoft Access, and Oracle, as well as IBM's DB2 that commonly runs on an IBM mainframe. DTS also facilitates access to ODBC data sources for which no native OLE DB providers are available yet. This is done using the Microsoft OLE DB Provider for ODBC. This provider still uses an ODBC driver to access the ODBC data source, with an OLE DB wrapper around it.

OLE DB is the Universal Data Access (UDA) technology adopted by Microsoft, and is the data abstraction technology of choice for Microsoft. OLE DB allows access to virtually any data source (such as relational databases, text files, directory services, mail data stores), and Microsoft is putting a great deal of support behind it. It is also useful to note that using native OLE DB providers will provide you with faster access to data sources than using ODBC.

DTS also allows you to access ASCII fixed-field length text files and ASCII delimited text files using the built-in DTS Data Pump flat file OLE DB provider. This provider makes it easier to access ASCII files and retrieve information from them by assuming that the data follows a certain pattern (fixed length fields, or delimited fields, such as would be produced by exporting an Excel spreadsheet to a comma-delimited file).

What is an OLE DB provider, by the way? OLE DB providers are pieces of data abstraction software that give you access to a variety of data sources, such as databases, e-mail and Lightweight Directory Access Protocol (LDAP) directories, which is used by Active Directory services, file system objects, etc. Hence, OLE DB providers can be used to define the source and destination for the DTS job. Some OLE DB providers are created by Microsoft, and others by third-party software companies or even rival database vendors who want to use OLE DB technology to allow access to their products. OLE DB providers are an essential part of the OLE DB technology, which is the core of the Universal Data Access technologies (UDA) adopted by Microsoft as the data access method of the future. Many database vendors and third-party companies produce native OLE DB drivers, which will only strengthen OLE DB as the technology of choice to define the sources and destinations of data. OLE DB is based on the component object model (COM). The following figure illustrates the UDA architecture, and where OLE DB fits in it. The figure clearly shows that OLE DB is the core component of this architecture, facilitating connection between the application and the data sources.

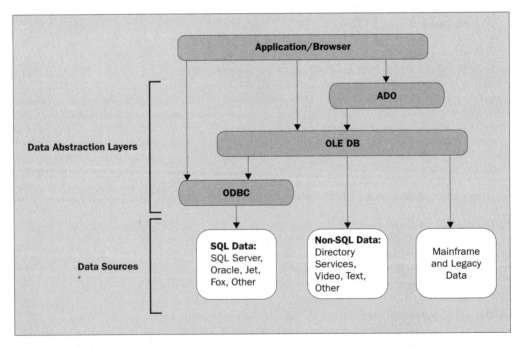

The following points highlight the importance of DTS as the data transfer and transformation technology for use with SQL Server data warehousing:

❑ DTS supports high-speed non-logged bulk copy program (BCP) inserts into the SQL Server database. This is so far the fastest method to move large amounts of data into SQL Server tables. BCP is explained in more detail later in the chapter.

❑ DTS supports the creation of customized transformations with script, such as VBScript, or JavaScript. It also allows the creation of such customized components with full programming languages, such as Visual Basic or Visual C++, by accessing and running programs written in these languages, and can also be used within the .NET technologies such as VB.Net and C#.

❑ DTS also supports the transfer of complete database objects between source and destination data sources, as long as these sources are on SQL Server 2000. You can also transfer objects between SQL Server 7.0 and SQL Server 2000. A DTS task, **Transfer SQL Server Objects**, can be used to transfer all of the meta data and data for some or all of the objects in one SQL Server database to another SQL Server database. For example, the Transfer SQL Server Objects task can be used to move a table with all of its associated indexes, constraints, rules, defaults, and trigger definitions, along with the existing rows in the table. The Transfer SQL Server Objects task can also be used to transfer the definitions of objects such as views and stored procedures between the SQL Server data sources. This feature makes it easy to transfer a database in the development environment to a developer's laptop so that they can continue to work against a real database when they are disconnected from the team development environment.

In other words, the main tasks that are performed by DTS can be classified in one or more of these categories:

❑ Data import and export

❑ Data transformation (including validation, scrubbing, and cleansing)

❑ Transferring database objects

The following sections discuss these categories in more detail explaining what is involved in each of them.

Data Import and Export

Importing and exporting data is the process of exchanging data between applications by reading and writing data in a common format. For example, DTS can import data from an ASCII text file or Access database into SQL Server. Alternatively, data can be exported from SQL Server to an OLE DB data destination, such as an Excel spreadsheet. In other words, data import and export involves a source and destination and the data in between. DTS provides easy-to-use wizards that guide you through the process of importing and exporting data, as you will see later in the chapter.

The following DTS features make DTS a great tool to perform imports and exports through a DTS package:

❑ **Ability to use an OLE DB provider's advanced properties:** this is especially true when using native OLE DB providers. These providers will allow you to use features and functions specific to the data source you are trying to access, which add a great deal of flexibility and power when extracting the data for import from the source, or preparing it for export to the destination. For instance, using the OLE DB provider for Oracle will allow you to use some of the Oracle features such as Unicode, that the OLE DB provider for ODBC, or simply ODBC, cannot provide.

❑ **Column mappings:** DTS import/export wizards allow you to map database table field names to the names of the fields in the destination database. You no longer have to live with naming conventions that don't conform to your standard naming conventions.

❑ **Data transformation script:** as part of the import/export package, you can define scripts to perform data transformations.

❑ **Advanced transformation properties**: these allow for complex data scrubbing and cleansing before dumping it into the destination database.

❑ **Transferring data and database objects** between computers running Microsoft SQL Server 7.0/2000: These objects include tables, fields, constraints, referential integrity and relationships, indexes, stored procedures, views, etc.

❑ **Saving the DTS package:** The DTS package can be prepared and saved as part of the database, allowing it to be re-used as a template in the future.

❑ **DTS package scheduling:** With this feature, you don't always have to perform the DTS import or export tasks immediately after creating the DTS package. The package can be prepared, and executed repeatedly later interactively or on a scheduled basis.

Data Transformation

A data transformation is the set of operations applied to source data before it is stored in the destination database. Examples of data transformation are:

❑ DTS allows calculating new values from one or more source fields, such as calculating the profit based on the sales and cost fields.

❑ DTS allows for breaking a single field into multiple values to be stored in separate destination fields, such as breaking the CustomerName field into a FirstName, MiddleInitial, and LastName fields.

❑ DTS may also be used to combine several fields into one value and store the result of the combination in a separate field in the database, such as combining the area code and phone number fields to produce a long phone number.

❑ DTS also allows for data validation, such as making sure the city of London belongs to the correct country, England, or that Mr. Jones, the human resources manager, belongs to the human resources department. You may use a lookup table to perform this process, and DTS transformations cater for this eventuality.

Because of the importance of such transformations in building a successful data warehouse, these features make DTS an ideal fit for Microsoft Analysis Services and data warehousing. Transformations make it easy to implement simple and complex data validation, scrubbing, and enhancement of information, such as returning the US state from the given address, during data import and export. We will discuss different aspects of this process in more detail in the next chapter.

Database Object Transfer

DTS can transfer database objects between heterogeneous data sources, such as transferring objects between an Oracle database and a SQL Server database. Obviously, DTS can also transfer database objects between SQL Server databases. When using heterogeneous data sources, the built-in facilities of DTS only move table definitions and data. There are restrictions with this area of DTS; you can only copy database objects between two SQL Servers of the same version, and it is not possible to transfer database objects between SQL Server 7.0 and SQL Server 2000. Many of the other DTS tasks don't have this restriction. To transfer other objects such as indexes, constraints, and views you must use methods such as specifying tasks that execute the SQL statements needed to create these objects on the destination data source. As an example, if you want to transfer the UNIQUE constraint on the CustomerName and CustomerPhoneNumber fields from an Oracle database to a SQL Server database table, you need to write a statement similar to the one below after transferring the table.

```
ALTER TABLE customer
CONSTRAINT u_customer_unique  NONCLUSTERED (CustomerName, CustomerPhoneNumber)
```

The code above ensures that the combination of customer name and phone number is unique in the customer table. The NONCLUSTERED keyword is not absolutely necessary since this is the default value that SQL Server uses. However, because the source is an Oracle database, where the concept of clustered indexes has a completely different meaning from that in SQL Server, we need to ensure that as a result of the constraint, the index created is non-clustered.

The tasks and steps of DTS transfers are explained in detail later in the chapter. However, if both the source and destination are SQL Server 7.0/2000 data sources, you can define a Transfer SQL Server Objects task to transfer indexes, views, logins, stored procedures, triggers, rules, defaults, constraints, and user-defined data types in addition to transferring the data. Now that you know what a package can do for you, it is necessary to know what is contained within a package.

DTS Packages

DTS packages exist within SQL Server to allow you to develop a DTS solution, and save it as a template for other DTS packages, storing it to run at a later date or on an infrequent basis, or finally, to schedule a DTS package to run at specific dates and times.

There are two different types of DTS packages that can be created, a **local package** and a **meta data package**. A local package, which we shall concentrate on within this chapter and the next, is used for most DTS tasks that are stored as packages. The second type of package that can be stored in SQL Server is a meta data package, which would be used if you want to keep track of the changes made to the meta data, in other words, the structure or content, held within the SQL Server package. Each time a change is made to the meta data package, a new package is stored within meta data services and can therefore be used to refer back to changes completed in previous versions. This is excellent for change control and could be seen as SourceSafe for SQL Server DTS packages. When a package is first created and saved, an identifier known as a **GUID**, or Globally Unique Identifier is created along with a version number, also a GUID, for the package. Each time a modification is made and saved for the package, a new version GUID is created, while the package GUID will obviously remain the same.

Package Contents

Many packages will contain one or more connections to a data source. Not every package will contain a specific data connection, as there are tasks that can perform without any data connection. There are up to 11 different data source connection types that are built into SQL Server DTS, although 10 are specifically created for defined data sources and have specialized settings available. The last data source, defined as **Other Connections**, can be used for any of the 10 data sources already set up, or for any other ODBC source available to you as a developer. This could be a Visual FoxPro database through to DB2. As you will see later in the chapter, within the package itself you can have many different connections to data sources by adding these from the Connections menu, or a single connection to a single data source. The only limit is the number of connections your installation can support.

What every package will contain though, is at least one task to perform. Within DTS there are 19 specific tasks to choose from, but there is also the ability to register or use a **custom task**. This is a new feature of SQL Server 2000 that gives you the ability to use a COM-based program to perform additional processing that perhaps existing tasks do not provide.

If you build a DTS package that contains one or more tasks, you may wish these tasks to be linked so that one task doesn't start until a previous task succeeds, fails, or completes. To implement this you would use **steps** within your package using a **workflow** item within your package. A workflow item will allow a task only to perform when a linked task succeeds, fails, or completes. For one task you can have as many workflow items as required, so one task could start many other tasks, but what you tend to find are three workflow items. There would be the workflow item into the task from a previous task, then we would use another workflow item if the task succeeds, but if the task were to fail, you would normally set up a third workflow item to record the failure, whether this was to send a mail, or to fire off some other exception task.

Although there are only 3 areas to a DTS package, they can very easily and very quickly become powerful and useful additions to a developer's bag of tools.

This chapter will look at packages and how they are built up using these components, and we will look at importing an Access database example that is supplied with SQL Server 2000, through DTS. This example will look at two different data sources, so let's now cover the use of multiple data sources within DTS.

Support for Multiple Data Sources

DTS supports multiple data sources as its source and destination. You don't always have to use DTS to import data to a SQL Server database, nor do you always have to use it to export data from such a database. DTS source and destination can be any valid OLE DB or ODBC-compliant data source, including Relational Database Management Systems (RDBMS), text files, spreadsheets, and directory services such as LDAP.

Sources and destinations are defined in the DTS package or from wizards by specifying a connection. In the case of a SQL Server connection, the following screenshot taken from the DTS Import wizard within SQL Server 2000, shows the information needed to establish such a connection. You need to specify the OLE DB provider, which in this case is the Microsoft OLE DB Provider for SQL Server. You also need to specify the server on which the database you need to link to is located, in addition to the security authentication mode to use. You can specify using NT authentication, or SQL Server authentication using a login name and password. Of course, don't forget to specify the database you want to link to as well.

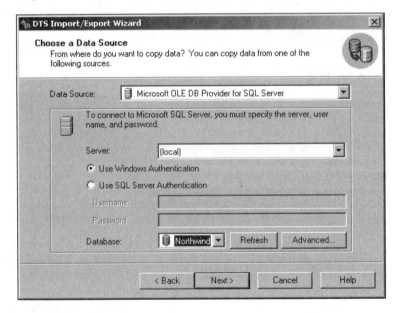

If you click on the **Advanced…** button found near the bottom right of the Data Source figure, the following screenshot demonstrates the additional settings that could be set for the required data source exposed by the OLE DB driver. Not every driver will expose the same properties. Compare the screenshot on the left showing the **Advanced Connection Properties** for a SQL Server connection, with the screenshot on the right taken from an Access 2000 connection.

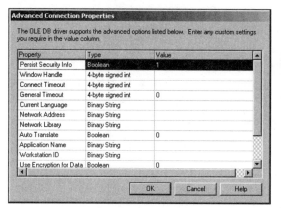 

Generally, these settings will remain unaltered. However, if you find that you are using different ANSI code pages between the import or export data source and the server you are running in when using two SQL Server databases, then setting **Auto Translate** to 1 will ensure that the correct code page translation occurs. If you know that you are using the same ANSI code page settings, leave this option as 0 to avoid any unnecessary extra processing.

The information required to connect to a different data source can be a little different, depending on the connection mechanism. For instance, connecting to the same SQL Server database using the OLE DB Provider for ODBC with the Microsoft ODBC driver for SQL Server may require providing an ODBC data source name (DSN), which is not required when using the native OLE DB provider for SQL Server. Also, connecting to a file data source, such as an Access database, will require different information from that provided for the connection to a SQL Server, as shown in the screenshot overleaf, which shows a Microsoft Access connection placed in a DTS package.

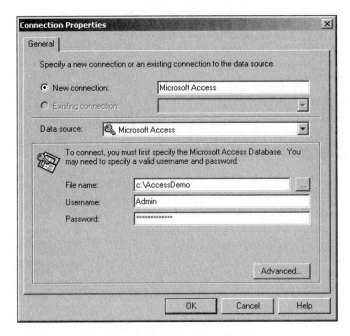

In the above example, notice that you can specify the source to be Microsoft Access, and the file path and name. If you have security set up for the file, you also need to provide the Username and Password.

The following is a list of the different data sources that can be connected to through native OLE DB providers provided by Microsoft:

❑   Microsoft OLE DB Provider for Data Mining Services

❑   Microsoft OLE DB Provider for Internet Publishing

❑   Microsoft OLE DB Provider for OLAP Services

❑   Microsoft OLE DB Provider for OLAP Services 8.0

❑   Microsoft OLE DB Provider for Oracle

❑   Microsoft OLE DB Provider for SQL Server

❑   Microsoft OLE DB Provider for Visual FoxPro

Some of these providers are installed with SQL Server, while others are installed when you install Analysis Services. You will also find that providers such as SQL Server and Visual FoxPro may exist on your system from an ADO installation, so therefore don't be surprised if your list differs slightly from that above. However, if you complete a standard installation of SQL Server and Analysis Services then the above list should be complete.

Data Transformations

Although mentioned in the overview section above, data transformation is a big reason why DTS is an important (even integral) part of the Microsoft data warehousing strategy. Therefore, we will expand on the discussion of data transformation in this section with detailed definitions and some examples on data validation, scrubbing, transformation, and migration.

Data Validation

Before data is entered into the data warehouse, it has to be validated. Data validation ensures the consistency of the information in the data warehouse. After all, your data warehouse is only as good as the data stored in it. Validating the data also increases the integrity of the data warehouse and the confidence in the information extracted out of it later. The validation process can be time-consuming and difficult, but is still necessary. Microsoft SQL Server 2000 helps you automate some of the validation tasks by implementing constraints in the **data definition language** (DDL). DDL is the part of the SQL language used to create database objects, such as tables, views, etc. SQL Server also allows you to implement your own complex validation algorithms in the form of scripts, stored procedures, or extended stored procedures. The following sections explain how simple and complex validation can be achieved using SQL Server's features.

Simple Validation

As mentioned in the previous section, SQL Server provides several features that allow for simple validation of the data. Such validation includes ensuring integrity through constraints on database object creation and data insertion. Simple validation is usually done through data definition, which includes table, column, and constraint definitions. Triggers can sometimes be used for simple validation. Examples of simple validation include:

Constraints

```
ALTER TABLE customer ADD CONSTRAINT
u_customer_unique   NONCLUSTERED (CustomerName, CustomerPhoneNumber)
```

The uniqueness constraint on the customer table presented in the code sample above ensures that each record in the table is unique. No two records in the table will have the same values of customer name and phone number. When a user tries to insert a record that violates the constraint, an error is generated and the record will not be inserted.

```
ALTER TABLE customer
ADD CONSTRAINT state_check
CHECK (state IN ('MI', 'OH', 'IL', 'IN', 'MN', 'WI'))
```

The **check constraint** above ensures the state field can only have states in the Midwest. This check constraint can be used when a table is partitioned based on the state field. The resulting partitions can be used in separate data marts each holding their partition information. Therefore, you may have three customer tables, one for the Midwest, one for the Eastern Seaboard and another for the Pacific Seaboard.

NULL and NOT NULL

```
ALTER TABLE customer
customer_name VARCHAR(30) NOT NULL
```

The NOT NULL condition ensures that the customer name field cannot be left blank, and will always have a value. The DEFAULT keyword can also be used to ensure having a default non-NULL value for a column. If a user tries to insert a NULL value in a field that does not accept NULLs, an error will be generated and the record will not be inserted.

Data Types

Data types also dictate the kinds of data accepted for the fields in the database. Hence, you cannot store simple numbers or string values in a date/time field.

Complex Validation

DTS allows you to take validation beyond the simple validations mentioned in the previous section. DTS allows you to reference database scripts, **stored procedures**, or even external programs in the DTS package that perform complex validation and return the results that determine whether to accept, modify and correct, or reject the data.

As an example of a trigger used in data validation, the following trigger ensures that the inserted record in the sales fact table of a sales and inventory data warehouse solution has a product associated with it in the product dimension table. If no product is found, the record is written to a log file with an error message. A different stored procedure is called to perform the error logging to centralize this process, which could be accessed by more than one trigger in the database.

```
USE OLAP_EXAMPLE

/**********************************
* Check if trigger already exists *
**********************************/

IF EXISTS (SELECT name FROM sysobjects
        WHERE name = 'verifyProductCost' AND type = 'TR')
        DROP TRIGGER verifyProductCost
GO
CREATE TRIGGER verifyProductCost
ON sales_fact_2001
FOR INSERT, UPDATE
AS
DECLARE   @product_id int,
          @sales_id int
SELECT    @product_id = product_id,
          @sales_id =sales_id
FROM      sales_fact_2001 s
INNER JOIN inserted i
   ON s.sales_id = i.sales_id
JOIN products p
   ON p.product_id = i.product_id
IF (@product_id IS NULL)
BEGIN
logError('product does not exist in the product table for transaction: '
+ @sales_id)
        ROLLBACK TRANSACTION
END
```

Of course, stored procedures give you a great flexibility, through raising exceptions, in what to do when your validation fails. For instance, you can raise an exception that causes another step in the package to log the failure in a log file or the Windows event log. You can also mail exceptions that occur to any e-mail address providing that there is an e-mail system installed on the server.

Data transformation is just one area within DTS that aids importing data in to a database for use with Analysis Services. Another area that is just as crucial is data scrubbing.

Data Scrubbing

Data coming from different sources may not be consistent even if it points to the same entity. For example, a national grocery store chain company is building a data warehouse. Data about inventory of the individual stores around the country is gathered and consolidated before it is transferred to the data warehouse to allow for searching on a national level. However, the stores don't all use the same system to keep track of their inventories, especially since the company acquires new stores almost every month. These new stores take some time before they can really start using the tools and applications provided by the corporate offices. As a result, the same data could be represented differently in the different databases of the individual stores. You may see some refer to the item "Italian salad dressing" as "Italian Dressing", or just "Italian" knowing that the category they belong to is salad dressing. Some stores may refer to reduced fat milk as:

- Milk (reduced fat)
- Reduced fat milk
- Redc'd fat milk
- 2% fat milk
- 98% fat-free milk

All of these representations point to the same item and have to be consistently represented in the data warehouse, and this is where data scrubbing comes into play. When the data is received from various sources, it is examined for such inconsistencies in representing the same thing. The examination can be by building queries that separate these items in separate result sets, then examining these result sets to collect all the different forms of something. If the values were not made consistent, any queries using the data would probably evaluate the values as different products. If the detail data in the data warehouse is to produce consistent information, the product name must be made consistent for all values.

Data scrubbing can be achieved in several ways:

- Using the DTS Import and DTS Export wizard to modify data as it is copied from the source to the destination. This wizard is discussed later in the chapter.
- Writing a Microsoft ActiveX script, executed by a program that uses the DTS API, to connect to the data source and scrub the data.
- Using a DTS Lookup.
- Using an Execute SQL Task within the package.

As an example on using DTS Lookup, the data in the system should be scrubbed; for example the values for the State field should always be a two-character value, such as "MI" instead of "Michigan", "Mich", or even "mi". DTS lookup allows for searching for the right values based on a named parameterized query that you provide. The query can retrieve data from sources that are not immediately involved in the transformation process. DTS Lookup is explained in more detail in the next chapter.

Data Transformation

Let's say we made our data look consistent. Are we ready yet to move it into the data warehouse? Not yet. You may still find some columns needing some change or transformation, examples:

- Calculating new values based on existing data, including data aggregation and summarization.
- Changing all alphabetic characters to uppercase or vice versa.

❑ Breaking up a single value into multiple values, such as a product code in nnnn-description format into separate code and description values, or a date value in MMDDYY format into separate month, day, and year values

❑ Merging separate data values into a single value, such as concatenating a first name value with a last name value

❑ Mapping data from one representation to another, such as converting data values (1, 2, 3, 4) to (A, B, C, D)

❑ Data transformation also involves formatting and modifying extracted data from operational systems into merged or derived values that are more useful in the data warehouse

❑ Another example is converting numeric representations for decimals from European to US or vice versa (123.45 in US is written as 123,45 in some parts of Europe)

The transformation process usually takes place during the migration process: when data is copied either directly from the operational sources or from an intermediate database, because the data has been scrubbed.

In addition to performing insert-based transformations of data, DTS provides data-driven-queries, in which data is read from the source and transformed, and a parameterized query is executed at the destination, using the transformed values in the destination row. Data-driven queries are explained with examples in the next chapter.

Note that when using DTS to create fact tables for use with Microsoft SQL Server Analysis Services, you don't really need to create any aggregations while migrating the data. Analysis Services is specifically designed to create the optimal aggregations after the data warehouse has been populated with DTS. Also, you don't really need to segment a date into individual time levels, such as week, month, quarter, or year columns in the Time *dimension table. The Analysis Services Dimension Wizard provides an automated facility for this type of time transformations (see Chapter 5).*

Planning Your Transformations

Before starting to build your package, if your process involves doing any sort of transformation of data, it may be necessary to work out the transformations that will take place. Of course, there will be occasions when this is not required, such as a first name, middle name, surname scenario, when you wish to move these into one column and store the initials and surname in your data ware house. Although even at this point, you would need to plan for NULL values when no middle name exists.

The data warehouse you are going to build will have been designed and the tables and the columns that it will contain should have been defined. From this, you can start organizing what transformations are required to populate your OLAP database with data from your source destination. Columns may merge, split, or acquire data from several columns to form the basis of a calculation. Each transformation should be analyzed by inspecting the existing data, determining the range of possible values or values that may not already exist, checking to see if the source column could contain NULL values, and ensuring that the destination column will be large enough to cope with the largest possible value.

These are just some of the considerations to be taken into account when planning the task in hand.

Data Migration

As like the name suggests, this process copies large amounts of scrubbed, transformed, and validated data from the source to the destination data warehouse. Of course, it is also possible to scrub or transform data from a source in to an intermediate table, residing within the warehouse, and use this as the source for another task to copy the data to the warehouse. This is the last step of the data transformation, and takes place after the validating and scrubbing has been done. Data migration can either be conducted through the Import/Export wizard, or through the Bulk Copy Program (BCP). In either case, since the set of data processed is usually large, you can choose to do full or incremental updates. These updates must be conducted when there is little activity on the server to minimize the impact on the users.

As a rule of thumb, use BCP when you don't have validations and transformations taking place during the migration process. BCP will give you the fastest migration you can possibly have. This is because BCP is just a data dump utility, optimized for dumping data with little, if any, logical processing.

> **If you are conducting some logic or processing during this last migration process, don't use BCP; instead, use the Import/Export wizards, or ActiveX scripting.**

Using the DTS Package

The most prominent feature that DTS offers to interact with is the DTS package. Interaction with DTS packages can be accomplished through the Microsoft SQL Server Enterprise Manager, or through applications using the DTS API such as Visual Basic .NET or C#. The DTS package includes all the information needed to connect to the data store, both the source and destination, and perform the necessary transformations. The DTS package not only houses this information, but also controls how and when the connections, validations, and transformations are conducted. We will cover this within this section. As part of the definition of the DTS package, you can choose to do one or more of the following:

❑ Define connections to the data sources representing the source and destination for your transformation

❑ Define task objects that define certain actions within the package

❑ Define step objects to define the sequence of execution of the task objects

Once the DTS package has been defined, you can:

❑ Run the package immediately

❑ Create a DTS package for replication

❑ Schedule the package to be executed at specific times

❑ Schedule certain tasks of the package to be executed at different times

A DTS package can be stored in one of the following forms:

❑ In DTS COM-structures storage files

❑ In the msdb database of Microsoft SQL Server.

❏ In the Microsoft Repository (see Chapters 1 and 2 for explanations of the Microsoft Repository)

❏ As an external Visual Basic file

You can create packages in the DTS Designer, which is a part of SQL Server Enterprise Manager, as described later in the chapter, or in fact through programming languages such as Visual Basic, Visual FoxPro, Visual Basic .NET, C#, or any language that can utilize a COM interface.

Anatomy of the DTS Package

The DTS package is primarily composed of three types of objects (see figure below), the connection object, the task object, and the workflow, or step, object. SQL Server uses step and workflow interchangeably within Enterprise Manager, so you may see that also within this book. While the connection object defines the connection properties and conditions to the source and destination data source, the DTS task object defines a particular course of action to be taken as part of the transformation. The DTS workflow determines the order of execution of the DTS tasks. In a moment we will give a description of each of these objects.

First of all, it is important to understand that the relationship between the components of the DTS package is functional and not hierarchical, as the following figure demonstrates. There are three tasks represented in the figure that use either one or both of the two connections. Task 1 uses connections 1 and 2, task 2 uses only connection 1, while task 3 uses only connection 2. The tasks represent a situation similar to executing an ActiveX component, dumping data into the database, or sending e-mail. The connections may be to two SQL Server databases. Task 1 has only one step, Step 1, while task 2 has both Steps 1 and 2, and task 3 has Step 2 only. The task objects use the connection objects to establish connection to the data sources. The workflow objects, defined and demonstrated by the arrows within the diagram, determine what order the task objects will be executed, and what order actions within the task should be carried out.

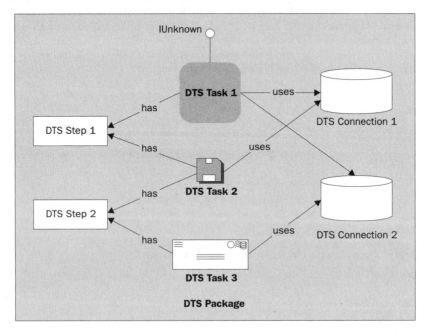

DTS Connection

Each DTS task may have zero or more connection objects. These connection objects store the information needed to connect to the respective data source when the package is executed. There are three types of connection objects available: data source connections, file connections, and Microsoft Data Link connections.

Data source connections specify information about the source and destination OLE DB or ODBC data sources as we have already seen earlier in the chapter. The way the information is requested in the DTS wizards and screens varies based on the data source. However, the connection object stores the following information for most data sources:

❑ Server name

❑ Data format and location, including database name (catalog) and table name if applicable

❑ User name and password

❑ ODBC data source (DSN) if the OLE DB provider for ODBC is used

File connections specify information about source and destination files, data format, file names and locations. Microsoft file connection settings are stored in the data link file (extension .udl). This occurs when you set up the connection through OLE DB. Once saved in the data link file, the connection can be established by loading this file.

DTS Task

The most prominent object within the DTS package is the task, which defines a work item to be performed as part of the transformation process. SQL Server 2000 includes several built-in tasks. Each performs a different type of work item, from sending mail, to working with Analysis Services. SQL Server also provides the DTS object model with which you can create custom tasks. Creating custom tasks is beyond the scope of this book. For more information about this topic, *see "Professional SQL Server 2000 DTS"* (Wrox Press, ISBN 1-861004-41-9).

Tasks, whether they are custom or SQL Server tasks, must be installed and registered on the machine on which you want to use them. The nineteen built-in tasks included with SQL Server 2000 are registered automatically during installation; however, if you do find that a registry has become corrupt, or there is some other problem, rather than re-installing SQL Server, you may find it easier to re-register the tasks using regsvr32. Custom tasks are installed and registered separately. All created and registered tasks are available for addition to any DTS package by using the DTS Designer.

The nineteen original built-in tasks that come with SQL Server 2000 DTS services are listed below:

Task	Description
File Transfer Protocol	Used to transfer files or complete directories using FTP either from an internet site, or a directory on a local or network machine, in to a directory on a local or network machine. You can use UNC naming to map on to a server to retrieve or store the information and if you have DNS installed, then you can also FTP to and from a Unix box within your organization. DNS also does allow direct connection to a web site. FTP can be tricky especially when firewalls are involved. Enabling the right ports can be crucial.

Table continued on following page

Task	Description
ActiveX Script	This task executes scripts written in scripting languages, such as VBScript or JScript allowing you to use the full capabilities of the scripting language. ActiveX scripts can access data using ActiveX Data Objects (ADO) or invoke any object that supports COM. VBScript and JScript are installed with SQL Server 2000. If you wish to use another scripting language, such as Perl Script, then you must install the product's language library.
Transform Data	The most basic task, but also very powerful. The task can insert data from a source file, database, text, or elsewhere, into a destination file, which can be one of a myriad of data repositories. This process can also take data and apply transformations to the data to the source data repository where required.
Execute Process	Enables you to launch a separate batch file or executable program.
Execute SQL	Allows you to write one or more SQL statements to be executed. The SQL task is associated with a DTS `Connection` object. The SQL statement(s) must use valid syntax for the OLE DB provider of the `Connection` object it's associated with.
Data-Driven Query	Implements advanced data transformation functionality. This is often used as a tool to update information in a data warehouse by scanning rows in the source data and by executing a query based on the value of the rows.
Copy SQL Server Objects	Any object within a SQL Server database can be copied to another SQL Server database.
Send Mail	Allows you to send e-mail including e-mail attachments in the form of attached data files. You can also execute the tasks of sending mail using the generic Execute Process task. MAPI must be installed on the machine that has SQL Server running on it and have a valid log in.
Bulk Insert	Provides a way to transfer large amounts of data into the data warehouse. Its flexibility is limited, but this task is the best choice when you need to load data into the warehouse very fast.
Execute Package	Allows the current DTS package to execute another DTS package within the server as part of the DTS solution.
Message Queue	If you want to send messages between DTS packages, then you can do this using the Message Queue task.
Transfer Error Messages	Allows transfer of user error messages between two SQL Servers.
Transfer Databases	Allows the transfer of databases between servers, and also allows specification of the location of those databases.
Analysis Services Processing	Any object defined within Analysis Services can be processed using this task. More on this in the next chapter.

Task	Description
Transfer Master Stored Procedures	Used to transfer stored procedures found in the master database from one server to another. Used mainly to restore a corrupt master database where a stored procedure has been inadvertently removed, and a full rebuild is not desired.
Transfer Jobs	Transfer SQL Server jobs between one server and another.
Transfer Logins	Used to transfer SQL Server logins from one server to another. Take care with this as you may be exposing production security on a non-production machine, or vice versa, giving too much access to logins by transferring development logins to a production server.
Dynamic Properties	Each package and tasks within a package have properties. This task will allow the setting of these values to occur at run time, from a file external to the DTS package. This should be found in most packages as it allows a package to be built with an external file determining crucial information such as whether the package is being executed in a production environment or a development environment.
Data Mining Prediction	Creates a prediction query from a data mining model within SQL Server.

DTS Data Pump

The DTS data pump is the engine behind DTS functionality. It is an OLE DB service provider that moves data at a high speed between heterogeneous data sources and the destination data source. Any task that performs data movements is actually an instance of this in-process COM-based server. At least two connections (source and destination) are needed for the data pump to do its work. More than two connections are needed if more than one data source is involved.

Being an OLE DB provider, the data pump is extensible and allows for complex transformations and validations of the data as it transfers it. The data pump instance or DTS task requires the following three elements to be defined:

❑ Source rowset, which is usually a table or the result of a SELECT query returning records from one or more tables in the source databases.

❑ Destination, which is usually a table in the destination data warehouse.

❑ Transformation mappings, which are usually mappings of columns from the source rowset to the destination table. The mapping can be one to one, one to many, many to one, or many to many. In other words, you can have three columns in your source rowset that represent a customer name, with each one of them coming from a different connection. The three customer name fields, in the source, are mapped to one such field in the destination table.

With the data pump, you can simply copy the data as it is, from the source rowset to its destination, implement ActiveX scripting driven transformations, or even implement highly complex custom transformations using programming languages such as C#, C++, Visual Basic .Net.

There are different types of tasks that can be created with the data pump. Therefore, whether you create an Execute SQL task or a Data-Driven Query task, you will be using the data pump behind the scenes, because all of these tasks are basically instances of the data pump.

DTS Object Transfer

This component uses the SQL Distributed Management Objects (SQL-DMO) interfaces to move database objects between one SQL Server database and another. Almost all objects you can think of can be transferred with this task:

- ❑ Tables, views, and stored procedures
- ❑ Defaults and rules
- ❑ User-defined data types
- ❑ Logins, users, and roles
- ❑ Indexes and constraints

When transferring tables, you can choose to transfer only the definitions of the tables, the data only, or both the definitions and data. The data pump as described above can perform each of these three possibilities.

DTS Step/Workflow

The last component of the DTS package we will discuss is the DTS step. Steps, or workflows, control the processing of the tasks in the DTS package. Most tasks are associated with at least one workflow. However, some tasks, such as the FTP task, can run standalone and in this case no workflow would exist. However, this tends to be the exception rather than the rule, and therefore you will find most packages will contain a number of tasks that need to be organized into a semblance of order. Since workflows define the sequence of execution of the tasks in the DTS package, these sequences are usually logical. For example, you may have to perform the task of creating a table within the destination database before you can query the data source for a source rowset. The link between these two actions would be the step or workflow.

Workflows contain constraints that help determine precedence of actions. What this means is that you can use a constraint to prevent one task from starting until another task has already completed, or to execute a task only when a preceding task has completed successfully, or has failed, or just completed no matter how. It is these constraints that control the flow of execution of the package tasks in the end. There are three types of precedence constraints that can be defined on a workflow:

- ❑ **Completion** – The step will execute as soon as the prior step is complete, regardless of its success or failure
- ❑ **Success** – The step will execute only if the prior step has completed execution successfully
- ❑ **Failure** – The step will execute only if the prior step has failed; if the prior step completes execution successfully, the step will not be executed

As an example on precedence constraints, let's assume that you are loading data from a text file into a table. The first task is creating the table in the destination database. The second task is loading the data into the table. The second task will not execute until the table has been created successfully. Therefore, a success workflow constraint is placed on the second task. Assuming that the table is created and the data is loading, if a failure happens, you want to cancel the loading, deleting the rows that have already been loaded and sending an e-mail message to the database administrator informing them of the problem. This third task will not execute unless the table loading (task 2) fails.

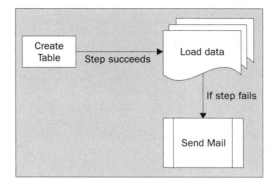

Later in the chapter, you will see examples on building a DTS package and creating tasks within the package. You will then see how these workflows are applied.

The final area we are going to look at is the storage of DTS packages. This will complete the basics of a DTS package and allow us to begin developing packages for Analysis Services.

Storing the DTS Package

The DTS package can be stored in one of four forms, the Meta Data Services Repository which is found as **Meta Data Services Packages** in Enterprise Manager, in the msdb database found as **Local Packages** within Enterprise Manager, as Visual Basic files, or in external COM-structure files. It is worth noting that database storage of the DTS package puts it in the msdb database. This database is also used for storing the meta data. However, packages stored in the database and those stored in the Repository are placed in separate sets of system tables.

> When SQL Server is installed, several system databases get installed, including: **master, msdb, model,** and **tempdb.** All of these databases, except for **tempdb,** need to exist when the server is restarted. The **msdb** database stores meta data information and information about DTS packages.

How DTS Packages are Stored in SQL Server

Packages stored in SQL Server are stored in the msdb database as binary large objects (BLOBs). These packages are stored in the sysdtspackages table, and are displayed in Enterprise Manager's DTS subtree. The following figure shows two local DTS packages in the **Detail** pane with the **Local Packages** folder selected in the tree pane of the SQL Server Enterprise Manager. Those with sufficient security privileges can view the packages. These packages, however, must have unique names. If your server is set with non case-sensitive sort order, the case of the name is stored, and a package named as mypackage is the same as MYPackage.

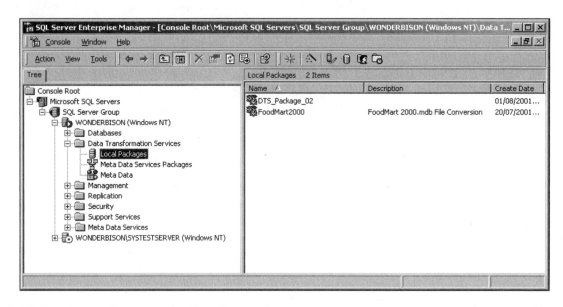

DTS Package Storage in the Repository

DTS packages can be stored in the Repository, which is stored in the msdb database. This is the preferred way to stored DTS packages in data warehousing because it is the only storage method that provides data lineage for the packages. Data lineage allows us to store where the data came from, how it was calculated, and when it was stored, among other things. This falls in line with the Microsoft data warehousing strategy of providing a meaningful way to integrate multiple products through shared meta data.

Given that multiple repositories can exist on a SQL Server, DTS only supports one repository, the one stored in msdb. Just like packages stored in the SQL Server msdb, repository DTS packages must have unique names.

> It is recommended that no changes are made to the msdb directly, so although there are system tables mentioned, it is with a strong warning. Alter them directly at your peril!

DTS Packages Storage in Visual Basic Files

One method of saving packages outside of SQL Server for distribution is to save the package as a Visual Basic .bas file. Saving this package as such will allow any Visual Basic developer to use the package as a basis for expanding a package's functionality, in other words, using a saved package as a template, or to see what processes occur within the COM-based package components. Not only will the .bas file be able to be loaded in to VB.Net, but also any preceding versions of Visual Basic that support COM-based processing. Developers using other languages that support COM, should also be able to see the COM structure exposed by DTS and use this as a basis of building their own packages within their specific language.

Once a package is stored as a Visual Basic file, the only method of re-applying the package to SQL Server is to run the .bas file generated. There is no other method of importing the package into SQL Server in this situation.

The .bas file generated is rather complex, and those not familiar with Visual Basic or the intricacies of DTS, should not attempt to modify this file as an erroneous change could have very serious effects on your package.

Saving to a Visual Basic file is a simple and straightforward process. However, the flip side to this is that you do not get any aid with versioning the package; therefore, you need to take care of this yourself and the use of a repository to store the code is strongly recommend, for example Visual SourceSafe.

DTS Packages Storage in COM-Structured Files

If you want to save your packages outside the database and make them mobile so that you can install them on other servers any time you want, you can use this type of storage. DTS packages can be saved in COM-structured files. Each one of these files can contain one or more packages. It can even hold different versions of the same package. The files can be located on the SQL Server box, on the client, or simply on a file server. These files cannot be viewed automatically in the SQL Server Enterprise Manager. To view them and their packages, right-click the **Data Transformation Services** folder in the SQL Server Enterprise Manager, then select **Open Package**. This will open a dialog box that allows you to browse the directory and network to find the DTS package file.

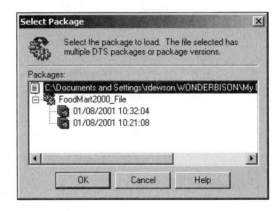

Packages stored in COM-structured files do not have to have unique names. You can use the same name for more than one DTS package, however they will have to be stored in different locations.

DTS packages are uniquely identified by the combination of package ID assigned when the package is first created, and version IDs re-assigned every time the package is saved. Both the package ID and version IDs are Globally Unique Identifiers (GUID). When a package is saved to a COM-structured storage file, each package version is saved in a separate area of substorage under the package ID. In essence, this works like Visual SourceSafe, where every version of a file checked in to SourceSafe can be retrieved, and the same is true for structured storage files for DTS.

Each package version contains substorage for the package components: tasks, steps, connections, and global variable collections (collection of variables available to all tasks within the package). The COM interface IStorage is used to accomplish this. The following figure illustrates how packages and their components are stored in COM-structured files.

> The Component Object Models (COM) IStorage interface supports the creation and management of structured storage objects, allowing hierarchical storage of information within a file. IStorage interface is often referred to as "a file system within a file".

Elements of objects following a structured storage scheme are divided into storages and streams. Storages are analogous to directories, and streams are analogous to files in a file system. Within a structured storage there will be a primary storage object that may contain substorages (which may be nested), and streams. Storages provide the structure of the object, and streams contain the data, which is manipulated through another COM interface called the IStream interface.

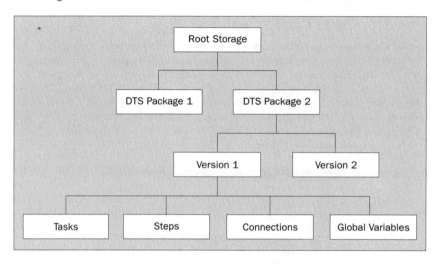

Now that we have covered how DTS packages work and are stored, it is time to move on to creating our own package within SQL Server for Analysis Services.

Creating a DTS package

SQL Server 2000 Analysis Services examples provide an Access database, called FoodMart 2000, which will be the basis of the database structure and data to be used to import to SQL Server via DTS. The FoodMart 2000.mdb database can be found in the C:\Program Files\Microsoft Analysis Services\Samples directory. The package required to achieve full persistence of FoodMart 2000 is quite large, although far from complex. It is simply a case of making a connection to the Access database, creating the necessary tables within SQL Server, and then transforming the data from Access to SQL Server. Even the data transformations are very straightforward with no concatenation or calculation processes to take place. However, this whole process is useful for getting FoodMart 2000 ready for further DTS tasks within the next chapter.

This package will allow several DTS steps and tasks to run asynchronously and therefore there will be sections that are self-contained units of work. The whole DTS package though, is too large to fit within one figure, but opposite is a screenshot of part of the package demonstrating two aspects, the small standalone areas, as well as part of the largest combination of tasks, seen on the left-hand side. The screenshot opposite shows part of the completely built package within the DTS package designer. Although this section will be building part of the package, the whole package is available for download from the Wrox web site, www.wrox.com.

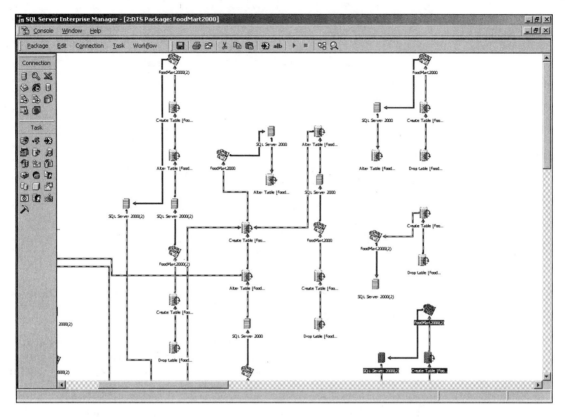

If you take a look at the package created, you will notice that there are a large number of SQL Server 2000 connections as well as Access 2000 connections. A package does not need to have just one connection per data source or destination, and having multiple sources and destinations, allows processes to run independently. Having one source and one destination leads to many transformations being bundled together, making it very hard to read or understand, and each task would run synchronously and therefore not utilize the performance available to its best advantage. Therefore, where possible, do use multiple connections.

Assuming that you have created an empty FoodMart 2000 database within SQL Server, we will start to create the SQL Server DTS package. Expand the nodes on your server until you get to Local Packages found under Data Transformation Services. Right-click on Local Packages and select New Package.

Package Settings

Now that you have an empty package window, the first priority is to define the package properties. To do this, right-click on any white space within the package designer, and select Package Properties. This will bring up the screen overleaf. Enter any meaningful Description, but mentioning FoodMart somewhere would definitely be worthwhile. Notice that there are two GUIDs created for the package. Both IDs are exactly the same, which is what you see when you are on the first version of the package design. Whenever the package design is modified and saved, the package GUID remains constant, while the Version GUID increments.

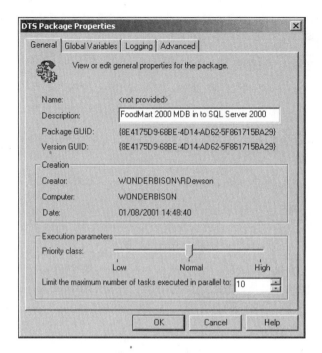

At the base of the screen you can see two **Execution parameters**. First of all, you can determine the priority of processing that the package will expect to receive within Windows. Normally this priority is left as it is, but important or long running tasks may benefit from a higher priority. Don't forget that this will have a detrimental effect on any other processes running on Windows at that time.

Another performance gain, or hit, surrounds the number of tasks that can run concurrently. As mentioned above, having several connections, or for that matter, several tasks, as their own unit of work, allows multiple processes to run concurrently. The more processes that can run concurrently, the more process threads that are taken up. Also, you will find that the more processes that can run, the more processing power will be taken up on the computer running the package. This might be what you want, as there could be spare capacity. The ideal situation is to monitor the package, and monitor the computer and ensure that resources are not stretched. Depending on the server you are building this package on, alter this second parameter as you wish. You can either leave the value at the default, or modify it to any other value, as I have done; you can keep a check on the processes by simply using Task Manager or any installed system monitoring software you have.

Moving to the **Logging** tab, the **Log package execution to SQL Server** option has been selected, although the default is for this is not to be selected, indicating that every item of the package execution will be stored in the msdb database. This should only be selected during development, or in production when a package has errors that you cannot track down through normal debugging methods. When executed, each step of the package will have details of the success or failure of that step logged. Obviously, this leads to a performance degradation, albeit a minor degradation, but unless required, then leave this option off. As we will be building a large package, during development this will be switched on. You can view the package logs from within Enterprise Manager by right-clicking on **Local Packages** and then selecting **Package Logs**. Of course, to log the package to SQL Server a connection will be required. This is separate from any connections within the package, as it could be a connection within the package that is failing, but that aside, you may have created a package that does not use SQL Server data itself. Finally, this also keeps the connection for logging separate from any other process.

If there is a problem in logging the execution of the package to the msdb, then selecting the **Fail package on error** will stop the package from running any further. This could occur when the package logging in to SQL server fails, for example. Only use this option if it is crucial for package execution to be logged. For our example, we will not select this option.

It is possible for errors to be placed in to a file. Moving down to Error handling allows us to control this. Finally you can place the completion status of the package into the Windows Application Log

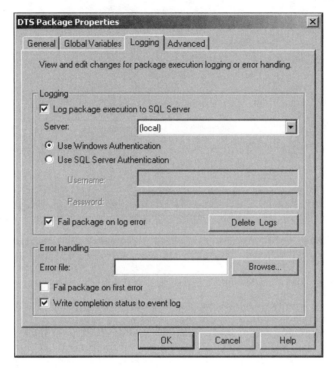

The final tab that we will look at here is the **Advanced** tab. The main area of concern will undoubtedly arise from the use of transactions. If any T-SQL commands are used within the package that we will be building, then each step with the commands will either be committed if successful, or rolled back if there is an error. This will avoid having partially filled tables, or partially completed units of work when a calculation, or a transformation fails.

Now that the package has been set up, we can add the necessary components to it.

Building Tasks

This package will be able to run as many times as required; therefore, it is necessary to clear out the information placed within the database from a previous run. To do this, the package will drop every table from the FoodMart 2000 SQL Server database that the package will be building. Therefore, if you do add any of your own tables, they will remain within the database. There are a number of tables to bring in from the Access databases as the screenshot below, from Access, demonstrates. The first table that we will look at is the customer table.

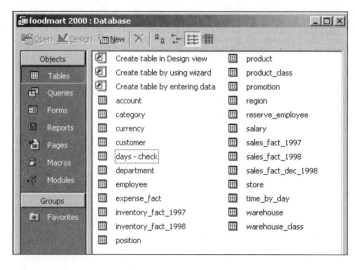

To deal with this table, it is necessary to drop any existing instance of the table within SQL Server. This is completed through an **Execute SQL Task** where the DROP TABLE command will be used. But before this task can be placed within the package, it is necessary for a SQL Server connection to exist. If there is no connection, then the task cannot be placed within the package, as one of the criteria of the task is to use an existing connection. Therefore, it is necessary to place a connection to SQL Server 2000 into the package. As mentioned at the top of this section, there should be an instance of a SQL Server database to place the FoodMart 2000 tables into. If there is not, then from the connection that is about to be built, it is possible to build the database by selecting <new> from the list of databases that are detailed at the foot of the connection tab.

From the **Connection** menu, create a connection using the **Microsoft OLE DB Provider for SQL Server**, and enter the necessary connection information. In the screenshot below, you will see how the setup would look like if you were using a local non-networked connection, using Windows Authentication. Once you have placed in the necessary information that is pertinent to your installation and security to connect to SQL Server, clicking **OK** will place the connection in to the package.

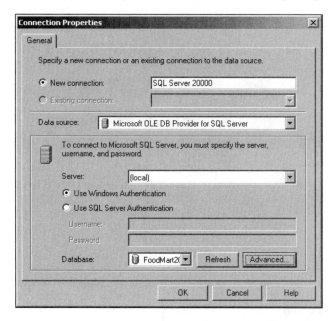

Now that a SQL Server connection exists, it is possible to place the **Execute SQL Task** within the package. Quite simply, this can perform any T-SQL command on a SQL Server database, or if you are connected to another data source, can perform any SQL command that the data source and connection object support. When this task is executed, the SQL command is passed to the connection source and passed through the relevant data provider for that connection. This is an important point to keep in mind as not all data providers support every SQL command.

Select **Execute SQL Task** from the **Task** menu; enter the DROP TABLE T-SQL command as you can see overleaf. As this is a simple statement, just click **OK**.

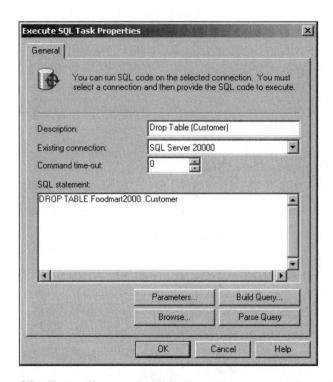

The second **Execute SQL Task** will create the table. It is of course, possible to place these two actions (dropping the table and then creating the table) into one task. However, if the table did not exist, the first statement of dropping the table would generate a failure and so the second statement might not execute, or might in fact generate a failure to pass on to the next stage. By using two tasks, the second task of creating the table would succeed. So, unless you are 100% certain you wish the two tasks to be linked tightly together, use two separate tasks.

By getting the structure of the existing table within Access, and making any necessary modifications to the data types that exist in Access but do not exist within SQL Server, the table creation command can be built up. There are a number of transformations that need to take place. Also notice that the Unicode definitions for column data types are used as it is not known whether this will be required for our solution.

Place the following code within the second **Execute SQL Task**, which we will call **Create Table (Customer)**, and to ensure that there are no problems, before pressing OK, check the T-SQL code by clicking on the **Parse Query** button found on the bottom right of the dialog. No checks are completed that columns exist, but it will check that the syntax of the query is correct. There will not be a 100% copy of every column within the Access **customer** table to that in SQL Server; there are in fact 3 missing columns. More on this when we get to the data transformation.

```
CREATE TABLE FoodMart2000.dbo.customer (
customer_id int NOT NULL DEFAULT 0,
account_num float NULL DEFAULT 0,
lname nvarchar (100) NULL,
fname nvarchar (50) NULL,
mi nvarchar (20) NULL,
address1 nvarchar (100) NULL,
address2 nvarchar (100) NULL,
```

```
address3 nvarchar (100) NULL,
address4 nvarchar (100) NULL,
city nvarchar (50) NULL,
state_province nvarchar (50) NULL,
postal_code nvarchar (50) NULL,
country nvarchar (50) NULL,
customer_region_id int NULL DEFAULT 0,
phone1 nvarchar (50) NULL,
phone2 nvarchar (50) NULL,
birthdate smalldatetime NULL,
marital_status nvarchar (1) NULL,
yearly_income nvarchar (50) NULL,
gender nvarchar (1) NULL,
total_children smallint NULL DEFAULT 0,
num_children_at_home smallint NULL DEFAULT 0,
education nvarchar (30) NULL,
date_accnt_opened smalldatetime NULL,
member_card nvarchar (50) NULL)
```

The final object to place within the package, for the moment, is the last connection that enables the whole process to work. We are missing the Access 2000 connection from which to retrieve the Access data and to build the data transformation that will exist between Access and SQL Server. This time the connection object will take the Microsoft Access connection and we will now set this up as required.

From the Connection menu, create a Microsoft Access connection, and enter the filename of the FoodMart 2000 Access database (C:\Program Files\Microsoft Analysis Services\Samples\FoodMart 2000.mdb). With the samples that come with SQL Server, there is no security on the database so you could leave the Password blank. Once everything is set up, click OK to add the connection to your package.

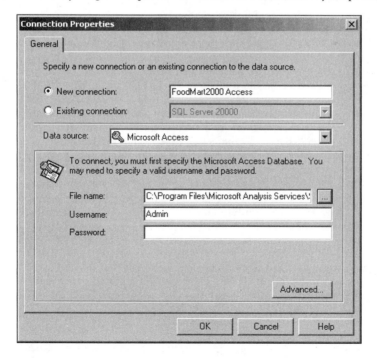

There are now four objects in the package waiting to be used, the two connections and the two Execute SQL Tasks. However, you cannot yet execute the package as there is nothing linking these objects together. Without linking these objects together, at the moment, all that would happen is the DROP TABLE (Customer) and CREATE TABLE (Customer) Execute SQL Tasks would run simultaneously, producing an error. Therefore, the package needs to have some workflow information placed within it, as well as the transformation of data from Access to SQL Server 2000. This will ensure that each step will run synchronously.

Within the diagram, place the four objects in a layout that you are comfortable with. It really doesn't matter how they are laid out at this stage, and to demonstrate that fact, the figure below quite deliberately has the process working from right to left. The crucial factor is how each step is linked together.

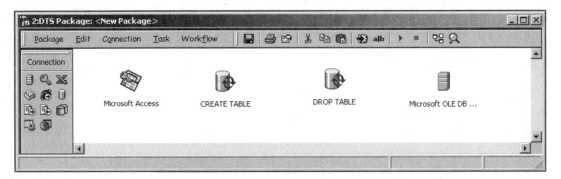

The first task to perform in the sequence will be to drop any existing instance of the customer table within SQL Server. Be careful here, as there may be no instance of this table within the FoodMart 2000 database if this is the first time of running the package. Therefore a success workflow is not suitable, as the DROP command would fail. Also a failure workflow would not be suitable, as this may be a subsequent run of the package. It would not make sense to have both workflows within the package emanating from the DROP TABLE command; therefore, it would be prudent to use the On Completion workflow. Then, it doesn't matter if this step works or not. The workflow will move the package execution on to the next step no matter what the outcome. To add a workflow item, choose the two items to link, selecting the source task item first, then select On Completion from the Workflow menu.

However, the table creation task is much more important and is crucial to the success of the process. Without the table, no data transformation could take place. Placing an On Success workflow from the CREATE TABLE to the Access 2000 data connection used in the last process ensures that the data transformation will only happen if the table creation is successful. It is also possible to set up a workflow item from the Create Table Execute SQL Task, allowing a step to run if the task fails. This could for example, mail a support team member so they can act on the problem. Don't forget that this package execution is being logged and the monitoring of the package should take place from that point. This will save having several Send Mail Tasks within the package, when all that is required, is a second package to be created that will complete this process for you.

> **By creating a second package, it would be possible to use that to execute this package, and on the package completion, check for any failures and mail any support team member at that point. This saves a great deal of time entering tasks that could result in several mails, when one mail would be sufficient.**

At this point, it is worth executing the package. This will allow the two Execute SQL Tasks to run and create the customer table within SQL Server. The reason behind this will be explained in a moment.

If you try to place the On Success workflow in to the package at this time from the CREATE TABLE (Customer) Execute SQL Task to the Microsoft Access connection, you will receive an error message. It is not possible to point a workflow purely to a connection. Therefore, it is first necessary to place the Transform Data Task between the two connections in the package.

To add a Transform Data Task to a package, it is mandatory to select the source connection first, followed by the destination connection. SQL Server prompts you to do this when you select this task from the Task menu. Once the Transform Data Task is in place, right-click on it and select Properties. For our example, select the Microsoft Access connection, then the Microsoft SQL Server connection, and then from the Task menu, select a Transform Data Task.

Earlier it was mentioned that not every column is to be brought across from the Access database; this leaves us with two choices on how to transform the data. The first method is to use a T-SQL command to bring the data in from the source connection, which is demonstrated in the screenshot below. This will simply read the data from the defined table in the FROM clause, and build up the records as required. The OLE DB provider, using the information contained within the Options tab, will then use this statement to bring back a set of records at a time for processing. The second method is to select the customer table, and then use the Transformations tab to remove the necessary columns. This is probably going to be the more common option, however, by using a SELECT command, if the order of columns in the two tables differs, it is possible to build the correct order from the Access table to fit the SQL Server table. This will save a great deal of problems and confusion if you use the Transformations tab.

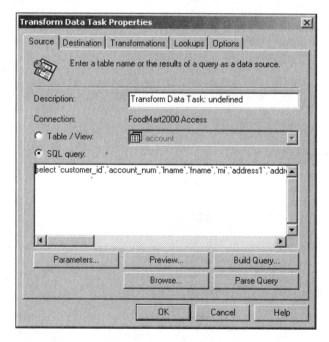

The T-SQL code for the select statement is detailed below, however, it is your choice if you wish to use this method or not. You can select the customer table.

```
SELECT customer_id, account_num, lname, fname, mi, address1, address2, address3,
address4, city, state_province, postal_code, country, customer_region_id, phone1,
phone2, birthdate, marital_status, yearly_income, gender, total_children,
num_children_at_home, education, date_accnt_opened, member_card FROM CUSTOMER
```

Moving to the Destination tab, it is quite simply a process of selecting the customer table as the destination for the data. However, this would only work if the customer table already existed, which of course it doesn't. This is where a bit of forethought could be used to aid and speed development. If you create the first stage of the package, which creates every table that you need within the package, save it, and then execute it, when you then come to build further tasks, as you see here, then you will have the ability to use the full feature set of DTS by using options like this. This is why earlier, after building the two Execute SQL Tasks, it was suggested that you should run the package at that point.

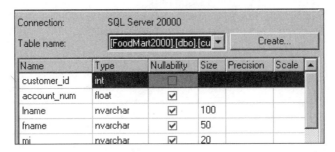

Now comes the real work-horse of this process, the Transformations tab. When you first enter this tab, you will see that there already exists a one-to-one mapping between each of the columns. This is ideal and has come about from the use of similar column details. If you have chosen to use the table name as the source to this transformation, rather than using the T-SQL code, then you will find that SQL Server has even left off the last columns, because there are more columns in the source than the destination. Don't think that in this way every transformation will be defined for you, as this only allows one source and one destination column to be transformed. If you pressed the OK button now, the task will be saved but only the customer_id column will be transformed. It would have been better if Microsoft had left the transformation arrows off the graphic. To achieve the column transformation that we require, it is necessary to first of all remove each of these transformations defined, and this is achieved by clicking the Delete All button seen near the foot of the figure.

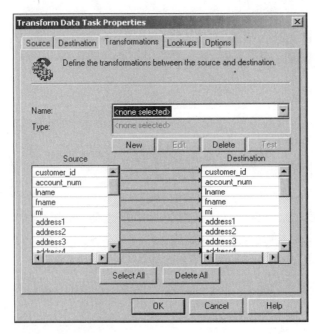

To define the new transformations, press the New button, which brings up the following intermediate dialog. There are nine different types of transformations that can be achieved, with the top two options probably going to be the most common transformations you will use. It is possible to use an ActiveX Script to work with data and perform some of the more complex transformations and it would be this option that is used if you wished to perform data scrubbing, or other tasks such as calculations, before allowing the data in to the destination data source.

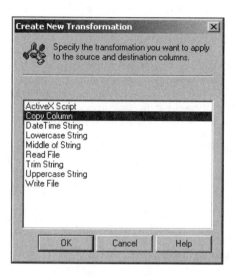

The second option, Copy Column, purely allows the straight transformation of one column to another column, which is ideal for our purpose, and so select this option and click OK, which brings us to the Transformation Options dialog.

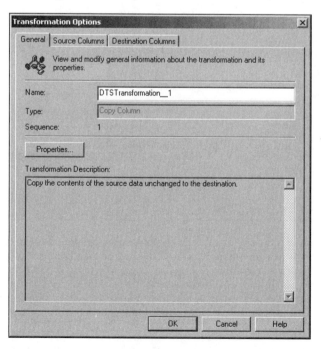

The first tab is purely to name the transformation that you want to perform, however, by clicking on Properties, it is possible to alter the column order, which makes the mapping process that is about to be performed easier. This again would remove the necessity to have a SELECT statement as the source method of bringing the data in. It is just a different method of getting the same results giving you, the developer, greater flexibility.

The second tab is the Source Columns tab where you will find all the columns listed from the Access database. If we had instead chosen to use a SELECT statement within the Source of the task, then only those columns named within the T-SQL statement would be listed here. By selecting all the columns it is a simple process of removing the last three columns from the list, which won't exist within SQL Server, which are occupation, houseowner, and num_cars_owned. These three columns are surplus to requirements within our data warehouse, and are therefore not selected. A similar process will be performed on the Destination Columns tab where all the columns will be selected. The column information is derived from querying the data structures of the tables through the data connection. By clicking OK, you will move back in to the Transform Data Task.

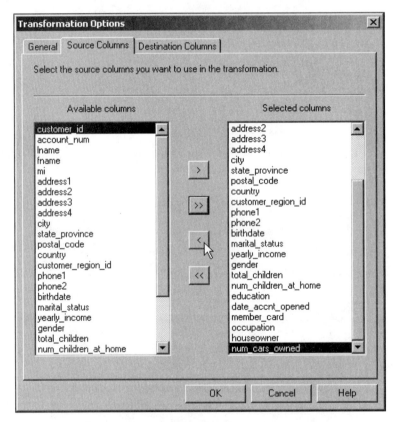

The layout has now altered to demonstrate the column mappings that have occurred. The main area that should interest you is how the mappings from the source data connection all merge in to one line and then emerge to the destination source. It is this single line in the middle that determines how the Transformation tabs works. If you recall from earlier, there were many lines in the middle of the screen. This task can only deal with one transformation line and therefore by following the steps we have just undertaken, this goal is achieved, hence all of the columns chosen will be dealt with.

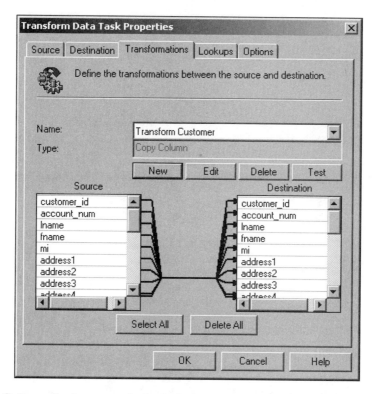

Moving to the Options tab, shown overleaf, which allows you to define how this task will perform. From a performance viewpoint, the main areas to look at deal with the SQL Server section at the foot of the tab. By selecting Use Fast Load, you are instructing the task to use a high-speed bulk copy transfer. This option, which is only available if you are performing a Transform Data Task with a connection that is using the Microsoft OLE DB Provider for SQL Server, instructs the data pump that it can accept batches of transformed data, rather than processing a record at a time. Batch sizes are controlled by the Insert batch size option. Passing a batch of records to the data pump allows the process to work with that batch of data while the next batch of data is being prepared. When working with large batch sizes for SQL Server, this option can have a large impact on your processing. It is very difficult to advise on an acceptable value, as there are a number of factors to take in to consideration. For example, you may have to consider your acceptable failure level within a batch with data insertion, or what sort of connection you have. If it is a fast connection, the batch size might be larger than that for a slow connection. If in doubt, leave it as it is.

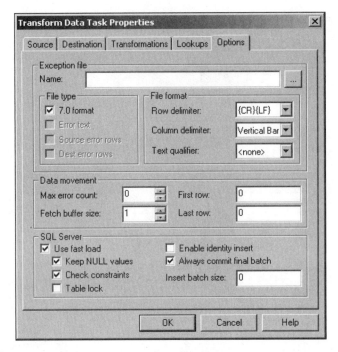

The final piece in the jigsaw is for you to place the **On Success** workflow from the **Create Table Execute SQL Task** to the Access 2000 data connection. This is now possible because of the **Transform Data Task**. This has to be a success workflow as there is no point in trying to transform data in to a table that has not been created. It is at this point that the first major error could occur through a problem with the table creation, and since we earlier set up the package to log errors, an error will be logged in this case.

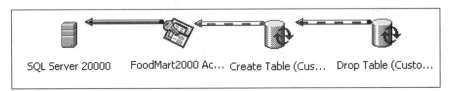

We are now ready to save and execute the package.

Saving the Package

In order to track the versions of the package and roll back to a previous version, if required, the package will be stored within SQL Server Meta Data Services. We could also achieve this by saving the package to a structured storage file, but storing the file within SQL server ensures that the package will be backed up when the rest of the SQL Server is backed up on a routine basis. Saving to a structured storage file could mean the file is placed in a directory that is excluded from a server back-up, or on a client machine which is never backed up.

Saving a package is a very straightforward process. Clicking on the floppy disk icon, or selecting the **Save** option from the **Package** menu, prompts you with a screen for the package details. Notice that the package will be saved to **Meta Data Services** which is selected from the **Location:** combobox.

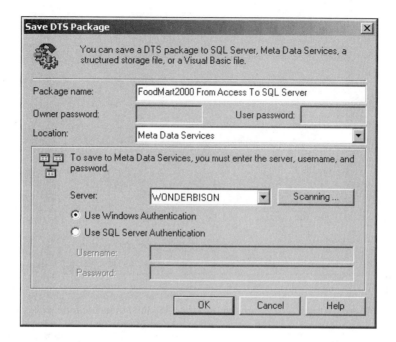

It is not necessary to save the package before executing it, but it is something that is recommended. Although SQL Server is a stable product, as you build more complex packages, if something were to go wrong and the package became corrupt, you would need to start from scratch. Once you have saved the package, we can move on to executing it.

Executing the package

It is possible to run packages on an adhoc basis within the DTS Designer itself, or you can schedule them through a SQL Server Job. Either way, the same logging of the package execution within the **Package Log** takes place. Every time a package executes, a note of the execution is placed within a specific logging area of the msdb, exclusive to DTS package execution information. However, placing the package within a job does give extra functionality that allows extra notification of job failure, success or completion, or running this package along with a series of other steps. We won't go in to setting up the package as a job, as there is no major difference from running any other object. The important point to note when you schedule a package through the sub-context menu within Enterprise Manager, is that the amount of exposed functionality for a scheduled job set up is limited, compared to the functionality exposed when setting up a job through SQL Server Agent

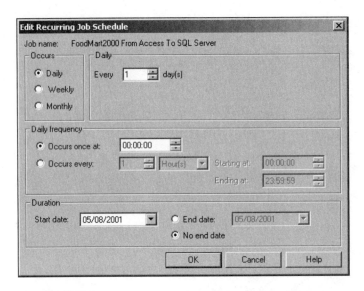

If your package produces a SQL Server error message, you can also use Alerts as a way of notifying of errors, or even the completion of tasks. This is moving the error handling outside of the package, but it does give a central place to cater for exceptions from potentially a myriad of areas within a large set of packages.

Other methods of executing a package include using any language that supports COM, for example Visual Basic .NET, or from a command prompt using a SQL Server utility called dtsrun. Using dtsrun will allow a package that has been stored as a structured storage file to be run within SQL Server as a local package, or as a Meta Data Services package. With the aid of dtsrun, we have the possibility of executing DTS packages from any language that can execute a command-line statement, and therefore does not need to be COM-compliant. Once a package is created, the ways to run the built package are almost endless.

The simplest method though, is to execute the package standalone. It is simply a case of finding the package you wish to execute, right-clicking on the package, and then selecting the Execute Package option.

The screenshot opposite shows a snapshot of the execution of the simple DTS package we have created. If you execute the package that we have created, you will see a similar graphic. A simple progress bar is displayed as the package executes and each step within the package is detailed. With the conclusion of a successful step, a green tick is placed against the step, or if the step fails, a white cross in a red circle is shown. You will also see as the step executes, if records are being manipulated, an incrementing number in the status column indicating the number of records processed. This does not update after each record, but after a batch of 1000 records or when the step completes.

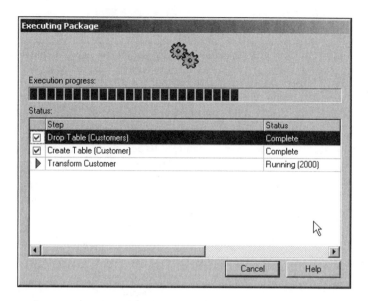

When there are asynchronous batches running, you may see several large green arrows at the same time in the Executing Package screen. Each arrow denotes a currently executing process and you should be able to correlate these with the number of concurrent steps allowed to execute as detailed within the package properties. However, do keep in mind that if there are fewer steps available to run simultaneously, or if the server is under heavy utilization, you may not see that number of processes running.

Even in this day and age of GUI interfaces, there is still a place for executing a package through DTS using the dtsrun utility.

Using the dtsrun Utility

Packages run using this command-prompt utility will run in the context of the command-prompt window. This utility can be useful when executing batch files, or simply when we wish to use a command-line utility to execute DTS packages. The syntax for this command is:

```
dtsrun [/?] | [ [ /[~]S server_name[\instance_name] { {/[~]U user_name
[/[~]P password]} | /E } ] { {/[~]N package_name } |
{/[~]G package_guid_string} | {/[~] V package_version_guid_string}}
[/[~]M package_password] [/[~]F filename] [/[~]R repository_database_name]
[/A global_variable_name:typeid=value] [/L log_file_name]
[/W NT_event_log_completion_status] [/Z] [/!X] [/!D] [/!Y] [/!C]
```

Arguments available to this command are listed below:

Argument	Description
/?	Similar to help utility for this command. When issued, it displays the command prompt options listed in this table.

Table continued on following page

199

Argument	Description
~	Specifies that the parameter to follow is encrypted and its value is represented in a hexadecimal text format. Can be used with the /S, /U, /P, /F, /R, /N, /M, /G, and /V options. Using encrypted values increases the security of the command used to execute the DTS package because the server name, password, and so on, are not visible.
/S server_name	Server name/SQL Server instance, or SQL Server name found on the hosting server that DTS is executing on.
/U user_name	SQL Server-defined login ID used to connect to the machine hosting the SQL Server that you are connecting to.
/P password	Password for the user_name login account.
/E	Specifies that a trusted connection is used where no password is required.
/N package_name	The name of the DTS package to execute.
/G package_guid_string	The GUID representing the package ID.
/V package_version_guid_string	The GUID representing the version ID assigned to the DTS package when it was first saved or executed. A new version ID is assigned to the DTS package each time it is modified or executed.
/M package_password	Used if an optional password was assigned to the DTS package when it was created.
/F	The name of the file containing the DTS package.
/R repository_database_name	The name of the repository database containing DTS packages. If no name is specified, the default database name is used.
/A	Used for a global variable. You need one /A for each global variable
/L	The name of the log file for the package
/W	Used for the NT log completion status. When the package completes, an entry in to the Windows Application log denotes whether the package has succeeded or failed.
/Z	Not used although it is listed as an available option.
/!X	Retrieves the DTS package from SQL Server, and overwrites the contents of the DTS file specified by the filename argument, without executing the package. If this option is not specified, then the DTS package is executed immediately.
/!D	Deletes the DTS package from SQL Server and the package is not executed in this case. It is not possible to delete a specific DTS package from a structured storage file. If you want to delete a DTS package from such file, the entire file needs to be overwritten using the combination of the /F and /S options.

Argument	Description
/!Y	This argument is used when the ~ argument is used. It displays the encrypted command to be used to execute the DTS package without executing it.
/!C	Copies the command line to the Windows clipboard.

As an example, if you want to execute a package called DTSPackage0001, which is stored in the SQL Server's msdb database, you can issue the command:

```
dtsrun /myServerName /U sa /P saPWD /N DTSPackage0001 /M packagePWD
```

For those options with a tilde (~) preceding them, if the tilde is in place, it will inform DTS that the value that follows is encrypted and that the hexadecimal value will follow.

Completing the FoodMart package

The remainder of the package transforming data from the FoodMart 2000 database within Access will not be covered within this book as the remainder of the package is very similar to that we have covered already.

It is therefore not instructive to continuing covering the package in this chapter, but the complete package is available for download from the Wrox web site as a structure file. To import this file for your own use, from within Enterprise Manager, just right-click on the Data Transformations Services node and select Open Package.... Doing this will allow you to search for the relevant dts file.

Summary

Data Transformation Services is a great technology that makes transforming and loading data into data warehouses an easier and more flexible task. DTS is another feature of Microsoft SQL Server and a example of the integration of the different tools and technologies that come with it to work in tandem to produce the best possible results.

Working with DTS to scrub data, transform, and migrate it from one data source to another that will be used for analysis can become a complex task and a great deal of planning should take place before embarking on processes with any major area of complexity. With the greater number of pre-built tasks available for use, then you can build your DTS packages with more power and with greater ease than with previous versions of SQL Server.

Although we have looked in depth at how DTS works and can be used in Analysis Services, we have only scratched the surface of actually using the power of this area of SQL Server for areas within OLAP. The next chapter will look at how the specific OLAP tasks can be used to work within Analysis Services.

Data Warehouse

8

Advanced DTS Topics

You have begun to see how DTS is an extremely powerful tool that you can use to satisfy your data transformation needs in a very flexible way. In the previous chapter, we discussed the theory behind some of the aspects that make DTS such a powerful tool from a data warehousing perspective. However, we have only scratched the surface of DTS, and in this chapter we will now look at how to include a Data Driven Query (DDQ), which allows you to update data from one connection source within your package to another connection source, and a DTS Lookup, which can form part of a DDQ task and allow you to perform a lookup on another table which is outside those chosen for the DDQ. We will also cover the viewing of package meta data, among other things, and touch on performance with DTS. You will find that lookups are a great advantage when building packages, but can have a detrimental effect on package performance, and you will see how it is possible to retrieve some of that performance loss.

There are two specific tasks that cater for Analysis Services; the Analysis Services Processing task, which is design specifically for working with cubes, dimensions, and data mining tasks, and also the Data Mining Prediction task, which looks at mining prediction models; we will look at these tasks in detail, and how they can help you within your data mart. We will also look at a second example where we take an OLTP system and load the data from it in to a star schema database.

To summarize, this chapter will demonstrate:

- ❑ Data Driven Query
- ❑ Using DTS Lookups to incorporate the inclusion of missing items of information, and we will also consider performance issues concerning this area of DTS
- ❑ The Analysis Services Processing task
- ❑ The Data Mining Prediction task

❑   Working with an OLTP system to populate a star schema

❑   Dealing with multiple or single connections within a package

❑   Transactions within packages

❑   Overall DTS Performance issues and what to look out for

❑   DTS Security

First of all, let's look at how to build queries that are driven by data.

Data Driven Query (DDQ)

Often, you would like to be able to select data from a source, transform it, and dump it in a destination table. However, real life situations usually require more flexibility in the way you design and run your queries. Data Driven Query (DDQ) is one of the tasks that you can select in the DTS Designer that provides you with greater flexibility than regular SQL queries used in SQL tasks.

A Data Driven Query is row-based. The query engine loops through the result set of a query and takes action as determined by conditions defined in an ActiveX Script, using VB Script as the language. This action makes these queries perform their inserts row by row as opposed to the bulk inserts of regular queries, just as you would see a cursor used within a stored procedure. The script determines which one of the four different types of queries is to be executed on each row. These four types are **insert**, **update**, **delete**, and **user-defined** queries.

A DDQ is used when extensive business logic is to be implemented while transforming the data; for example, it can be implemented to populate data marts on an incremental basis. DDQ allows you to log errors arising from the processing of the rows, skip certain rows from the insert process, or quit the whole process if a certain error took place.

As a quick example of using the DDQ in a data warehouse situation, let's say that a task of updating the Customer dimension is required to run every night. The complexity of this task comes from the fact that in the operational OLTP system feeding the data warehouse, the Customer region field is not available or is not populated. Also, when updating the Customer dimension table, you need to loop through the rows and find out if the row already exists within the data warehouse. If it does, you need to skip it; if it does not exist, you need to insert the new row. However, before you insert the new row, you need to look-up the value for the region of the customer based on the state and city values; this done by using DTS Lookup, which is explained in the next section after we have gone through the beginnings of the implementation.

To implement this example, create a new DTS package, place a DTS Microsoft OLE DB SQL Server Provider connection to the FoodMart database in SQL Server that we successfully created in the last chapter, and add another connection, this time the DTS Microsoft Access connection, to the Access FoodMart, database, as it will be from the Access tables the updates will be derived from simulating that the Access database is the OLTP system. Select the Data Driven Query task from the Task menu in the DTS designer of your DTS package, select SQL query and enter the following query as the source for the transformation.

```
SELECT customer_id,customer_region_id,city,state_province,
       fname, lname, country, address1, address2
FROM customer
```

The DDQ Task screen looks similar to the SQL Query task dialog in that it has a Source, destination or Bindings tab, and Transformations tabs. These tabs function in a similar fashion to those in the SQL Query task, which you saw before in the previous chapter.

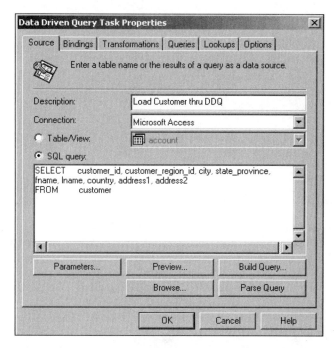

The **Lookups** tab can be used to create the two lookups that we will need for our DDQ example. The next figure shows the two lookups that have been created. In this screen it is necessary to populate the **Name** and **Connection** columns before you can create the **Query** of the lookup. Enter any name; it doesn't have to be as you see it within the screenshot, but choose a name that describes what each of these lookups does. The first lookup will be used to populate the **region** field when that detail is missing. The second lookup will be used to determine if the customer already exists within the SQL Server `FoodMart` database or not.

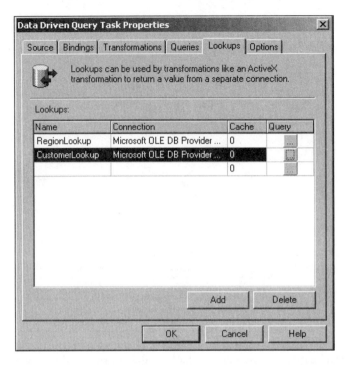

The contents of the two lookups follow next. You can get to these screens by clicking on the ... under the Query column, which will take you in to the Query Designer. The left-hand screenshot is the lookup to find the region for the customer, while the right-hand screenshot shows the lookup that will search to see if the customer record already exists.

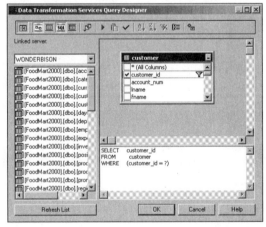

The Queries tab of the Data Driven Query Properties dialog is where you can specify the queries to use as the basis for your Data Driven Query task. For example, let's specify an insert query with several parameters corresponding to the fields in the destination table. For this example, we will only insert a handful of columns. The following screenshot shows this query.

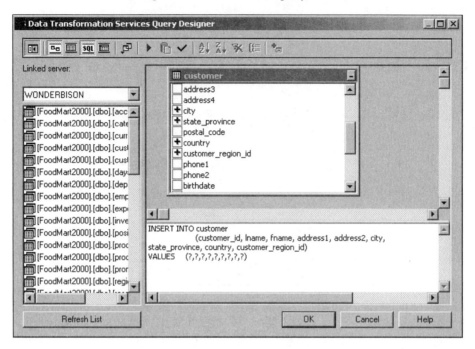

You can add other queries, such as a delete query and an update query depending on your circumstances and requirements. The final area of the Data Driven Query Properties dialog that needs dealing with is the Transformations tab. From here you can change each of the mappings to a script passing back the desired value of DTSTransform_Stat_xxxx for each condition. It is from an ActiveX script rather than from specific mappings as demonstrated in the previous chapter that the transformations will take place. The script will also decide, based on the business logic contained within the script, whether to delete a row, update it, or insert it using any of the queries you defined in the Queries tab.

From the Transformations tab, delete the automatic mappings SQL Server has generated, and then click the New button to create a new transformation, and from the ensuing dialog, select ActiveX script.

Give the script a meaningful name, and then if you press the Properties button, you will be taken to an ActiveX Script entry screen. You can save a bit of time when building the script by using the Source Columns and the Binding Columns tabs to create mappings. The following screenshot shows the ActiveX dialog:

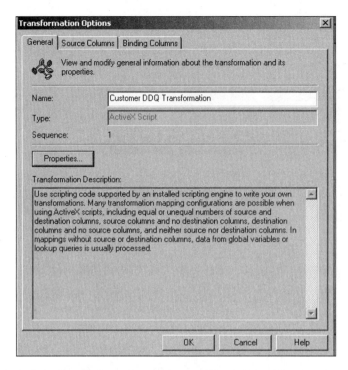

Once you have clicked the **Properties…** button, you will find yourself within the scripting editor, where you can enter any Visual Basic scripting commands. Notice how the look ups are used with the parameters required placed inside brackets. The syntax for the lookup is as follows:

```
Return Value = DTSLookups("QueryName").Execute(Parameter Values)
```

Where:

- ❏ Return Value is the value that the lookup returns. This could be tested for empty, true, or false, or can be used to place the specific value in to a defined local or global variable

- ❏ Query Name is the name of the query defined as the lookup within the **Lookups** tab

- ❏ Parameter Values is the parameter values used to populate the query.

The sample script to perform the transformations we required looks like:

```
'*******************************************************************
'  Visual Basic Transformation Script
'*******************************************************************

'  Copy each source column to the destination column
Function Main()
    If Not IsEmpty(DTSLookups("CustomerLookup")._
            Execute(DTSSource("customer_id"))) Then
        Main=DTSTransformStat_SkipRow
    Else
        DTSDestination("address2") = DTSSource("address2")
```

```
        DTSDestination("address1") = DTSSource("address1")
        DTSDestination("country") = DTSSource("country")
        DTSDestination("lname") = DTSSource("lname")
        DTSDestination("fname") = DTSSource("fname")
        DTSDestination("state_province") = DTSSource("state_province")
        DTSDestination("city") = DTSSource("city")
        DTSDestination("customer_region_id") = _
            DTSLookups("RegionLookup").Execute(DTSDestination("city"),_
            DTSDestination("state_province"))
        DTSDestination("customer_id") = DTSSource("customer_id")
        Main = DTSTransformStat_InsertQuery
    End If
End Function
```

This completes the building of the package. By clicking **OK** under the editor window, then on the **Transformations** dialog, and finally the task itself, you should find yourself back in the package.

When, the package you execute, which you can do by removing and altering some of the records brought in by the FoodMart package in the previous chapter, you will see how this package works. Let's take a more in depth look at DTS Lookups.

DTS Lookup

We have already seen how DTS Lookups can be used in combination with DDQ. DTS Lookups allow a custom transformation to retrieve data from locations other than the immediate source or destination row being transformed. The main advantage of using DTS Lookups, as opposed to COM objects or other programs, is that DTS Lookups use a connection that is already open in the DTS Designer. A COM object or other program would need to open a connection to the data source before they could perform the work, which adds a performance hit when such a connection is created. Therefore, using DTS Lookups will give you an edge in performance. A DTS Lookup, as the name suggests, basically looks-up a specific column of information, which your DDQ can then act on. The table does not need to be one of those within the DDQ and in fact, nearly every time, the lookup source will be another table within the database.

However, if you do use COM objects, you will find that DTS Lookups are objects grouped in one collection, the DTSLookups collection, which is available in DataPumpTask and DataDrivenQueryTask objects in the DTS Designer. You can also use DataPumpTask2 or DataDrivenQueryTask2 objects that extend the functionality, while retaining backward compatibility. We won't look at these here, since they are more advanced techniques, and covered in "PROFESSIONAL SQL SERVER 2000 DTS" *(Wrox Press, ISBN 1- 861004-41-9).*

> *The DataPumpTask and DataDrivenQueryTask are two objects that represent the data pump and data driven query respectively. These objects allow for programmatic control of the data pump and the DDQ.*

A DTS Lookup is defined by several attributes:

❑ Name – this should be unique per collection. For instance, a DTS Lookup object can have the same name in each of the DTSLookups collections associated with the DataPump task and the DDQ task.

❑ Parameterized query – as we saw in the previous section where you created a lookup query using a question mark, ?, to define where the parameter value will be inserted.

❑ Connection ID – related to any connection defined within the package. It is not necessary for this connection to be one of those used within the task.

❑   Maximum number of rows to be cached – such caching is designed to improve performance of the lookup actions.

When using a DTS Lookup, only the first row of a multiple row resultset returned from a lookup is used, and the remaining rows are discarded. Therefore, if you are defining a lookup that can return more than one row, you may be required to use an ORDER BY statement within your lookup query.

DTS Lookups can be slower when using an internal value, which is any value specified within the query such as other columns, as the parameter to the lookup. Where possible use an external value to the lookup, such as a **global variable**, a variable defined at the package level. You may actually find that lookups perform better when an internal value is moved to a global variable defined within the package, and the global value is used as part of that lookup.

Moving back to our query, the following code snippet demonstrates how a global variable could be used to make our lookup faster. A global variable has been set up within the package, which is then set from the source table. This is then used as the parameter to the lookup. For small queries such as ours, the extra coding won't make much difference.

```
Function Main()
    DTSGlobalVariables("gvCustomerId").Value = DTSSource("customer_id")
    If NOT IsEmpty(DTSLookups("CustomerLookup").Execute _
        (DTSGlobalVariables("gvCustomerId").Value)) Then
       Main=DTSTransformStat_SkipRow
    Else
    ...
```

Keep in mind though, that DTS Lookups are not the fastest of processes within SQL Server, and performance-critical applications should try to avoid using them. However, avoiding lookups is not easy, as they do give the advantage of single record processing, when other methods such as the Transform Data task do not. Useful, but potentially painful!

With our example, the number of rows being processed will probably be small. The theoretical process that we were dealing with covered new customers or updates to existing customers. We are therefore applying a small number of updates to a large number of records. However, our first lookup is processing records against our region table, which has a very small number of records, 109 to be precise. Therefore, a speed advantage would be gained by caching the results returned from this lookup so that for two or more records coming from the source table with the same search criteria, the region_id information will be stored within the cache. This is a faster method for retrieving the information than physically retrieving the data from disk. Although earlier the cache size was set to 0, if you were processing a larger number of records than perhaps you set up for testing, setting this cache size to a larger number might be advantageous. There is no hard and fast rule for calculating this figure; based on your configuration or set up, it is simply a case of trying out different settings with the workloads that are being seen at the time. If a large number of updates were to be processed, then set the cache size to the maximum number of records in the table, with perhaps a few spare for any expansion of the table.

Finally, keep in mind DTS Lookups can fail just like any other DTS function. When this happens, the current source row within the query is discarded, processing of that row is stopped, and an error is recorded against the step's maximum error count count, and therefore could fail the step if the maximum number of errors is exceeded, which could lead on to failing the package.

Our DTS Lookups so far have only used SELECT statements, but it is possible to use lookups to perform INSERT, UPDATE, or DELETE T-SQL commands, or in fact to call a stored procedure. If you do wish to use these functions then they are included within any transaction processing within the parent task or package. Therefore, if you don't wish them to be included in any transaction processing, and wish the command to commit even if other areas fail, then wrap the necessary T-SQL statements within their own transaction. There will be more on transactions later in the chapter.

Now that we have exhausted DTS lookups, let's take a look at a specific OLAP task, the Analysis Services Processing task.

The Analysis Services Processing Task

There are specific processing tasks that are unique to Analysis Services that either cannot be completed at all, or not easily with the other tasks within DTS, and this is when it comes to processing for example cubes, dimensions, and so on. An ActiveX script could be used to get some of the way there, however, this would not be a straightforward and quick task. The Analysis Services Processing task allows the creation of processes to update the data content of cubes, and dimensions to be created quickly and simply from one screen.

How Can You Use It?

Select the Analysis Services Processing Task from the Task menu in the DTS Designer. The task is used to process one or more objects in Analysis Services from within the DTS Designer. Once you had built your cubes and dimensions within your OLAP system, you would place this task within a package to enable frequent updates or a refresh of any of these objects. In this main dialog, you can specify a name for the task and provide a description for it:

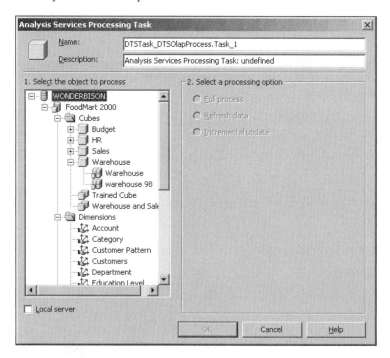

You can then select an OLAP object from the tree view. The objects you can select include:

Object	Graphic	Description
Database		If selected, all cubes, partitions, virtual cubes, and dimensions in the database will be processed
Cubes folder		If selected, all cubes and virtual cubes in the folder will be processed
Cube		You can choose to process the cube, refresh its data, or conduct an incremental update
Partition		You can either process the partition, or conduct incremental updating of it
Remote Partition		Process a partition found on a remote computer
Linked cube		Same as processing a cube but this cube is based on another cube that is defined and stored on another computer
Virtual cube		Same processing as the cube
Dimensions folder		All dimensions in the folder will be processed
Shared dimension		Dimension will be processed or incrementally updated
Virtual dimension		Same processing as the shared dimension
Relational mining model		Process relational mining models: Incremental updates option is disabled
OLAP mining model		As with Relational mining models, the incremental update option is disabled

When selecting the incremental update processing option for a cube, the dialog shows five additional fields, as the followings screenshot shows : Incrementally Update Dimension, Cube settings..., Data Source, Fact Table, and Filter:

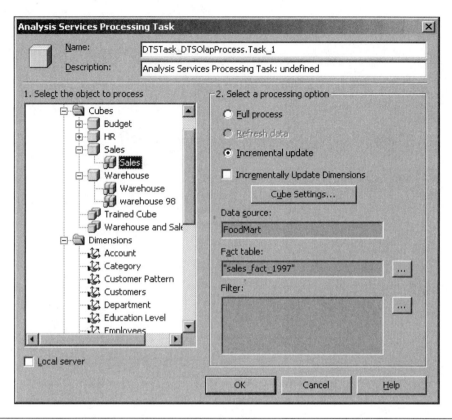

Field	Description
Incrementally Update Dimensions	Allow incremental updates of the structure of the cube being processed.
Cube Settings...	Allows the setting of processing options. These settings are primarily concerned with error handling. See below.
Data source	This textbox displays the data source for an incremental update of a cube or partition. You can change the data source by clicking the ellipsis (...) button next to the Fact table box, launching the Choose Fact Table dialog box.
Fact table	This textbox displays the fact table for an incremental update of a cube or partition. You can change the fact table by clicking the ellipsis (...) button as above.
Filter	This textbox displays the filter for an incremental update of a cube or partition. A filter limits the fact table records used in the incremental update. You can add or change a filter by clicking the ellipsis (...) button next to it, launching the Filter Expression dialog box.

Clicking the Cube Settings... button reveals options that can be set for processing. These mainly concern error handling, however the Processing Optimization Mode does allow for data to be available for processing by other tasks or connections at two different points in the processing. Unless there is a good reason for the data to be available before the aggregation calculations have been processed, then leave this option at its default, as shown in the figure below. Although the data will be available immediately after loading by using the second option, the Analysis Services task will utilize the majority of the processing resources of the Analysis server and therefore other connections or tasks will be slow or unresponsive.

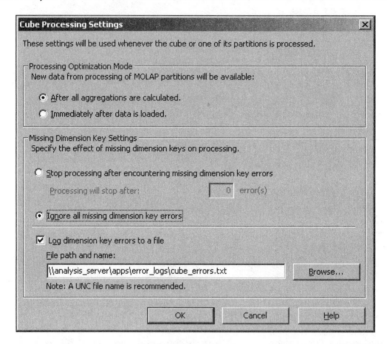

Benefits of Using the Analysis Services Processing Task

This tools offers the seamless integration of data transfer and processing of the OLAP objects. You can also benefit from the DTS Designer's features when processing OLAP data by imposing some precedence constraints, such as preventing a dimension from processing until data transfer to its table has completed successfully.

Data Mining Prediction Task

Data mining is a form of knowledge discovery in which an exhaustive search of data is done, looking for patterns and trends, and is the subject of Chapters 16 and 17. If you wish to create a data mining prediction within your DTS solution, then a specific task is available to you for use, and we shall cover that now. This is a simple, self-contained task that allows the creation of a prediction query, and specification of a location for the output of the query. All of the connections required do not come from connections within the package but from the task itself. This does mean that this process will use extra resources as every time the task is run new connections will be made, and then dropped at the end.

Prior to setting up the Data Mining Prediction task, it is necessary for the database you will be using to have at least one mining model already in place. You cannot create a mining model within the DTS package and then allow this task to pick up that model. If this is required, then you will need to look at creating the package through Visual Basic or another language that supports COM. For details on creating a data mining model within SQL Server Analysis Manager, see Chapter 17.

The object of this task is to build a data mine within a table within a database, or any other form of output such as a text file, building up a set of information from the input data. In this case specifically, we are trying to find out for each customer their gender, their marital status, and their education directly from the source table, and then, using an existing data mining model, what type of membership card they own.

Once the relevant model has been selected, along with a suitable name and description for the task, it is possible to move on to the Query tab and create the necessary T-SQL commands for the task.

One anomaly with the Data Mining Prediction task is that for those who are on standalone machines, it does not accept a server name of (local) *within the* Mining Model *tab, and you will have to insert the physical local server name of your machine. When you move on to the* Query *and* Output *tabs, you are allowed to use* (local) *as the server name.*

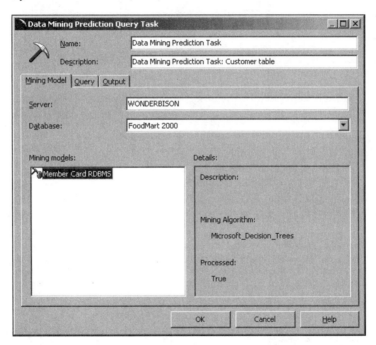

From the Query tab, it is necessary to create an input data source for the incoming information. The first action required within this tab is to select a **Microsoft Data Link** connection, or **UDL**, to make the connection to the incoming data. Once a valid connection has been made, it is then possible to create the prediction query. Clicking the New Query... button within this tab allows you to graphically select the required columns; this means that you don't have to know the physical T-SQL commands of the prediction query. In the screenshot overleaf, you can see how the Case table has been chosen and that the columns to be used for the input, which will then become the columns stored within the results of the query, have been selected. Any selected column will form part of the output, and a mapping from the input data stream to a source column is required. Where possible, this dialog will attempt to find a match but will only do this on an exact match basis. If there is even the slightest difference in names between the two sets of data, then no automatic matching takes place.

215

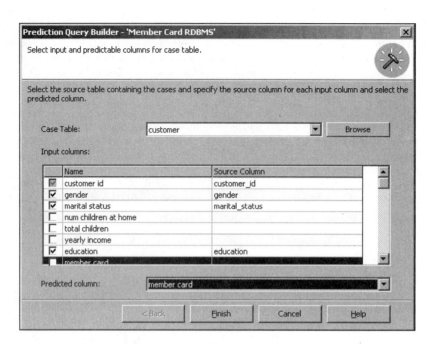

Once you have created the columns, you will be brought back to the **Query** tab with the necessary T-SQL syntax, automatically generated by the task. For our example, the T-SQL syntax generated is detailed below.

```
SELECT FLATTENED
    [T1].[customer id], [T1].[gender], [T1].[marital status], [T1].[education],
[Member Card RDBMS].[member card]
FROM
    [Member Card RDBMS]
    PREDICTION JOIN
        OPENROWSET
        (
            'SQLOLEDB.1',
            'Provider=SQLOLEDB.1;Integrated Security=SSPI;Persist Security
Info=False;Initial Catalog=FoodMart2000;Data Source=(local)',
            'SELECT "customer_id" AS "customer id", "gender", "marital_status" AS
"marital status", "education" FROM "customer" ORDER BY "customer_id"'
        )
    AS [T1]
    ON
        [Member Card RDBMS].[customer id] = [T1].[customer id] AND
        [Member Card RDBMS].[gender] = [T1].[gender] AND
        [Member Card RDBMS].[marital status] = [T1].[marital status] AND
        [Member Card RDBMS].[education] = [T1].[education]
```

All that remains is for the output destination to be defined by selecting the repository through another UDL, the name of the file or table for the information to be stored in to, and the task is complete. If the table or file does not exist then a new repository is created, however, if the file or table does exist then the task will fail. It is therefore advisable to place a preceding step of deleting the file prior to this task.

OLTP to Star Schema through DTS

Microsoft has provided another DTS example that can be used for analysis processing; this example concerns the processing of information from an OLTP system through to a star schema, as would be seen in an OLAP database. This example can be found and loaded from the `[Drive installation]:\[SQL Server installation]\ 80\Tools\DevTools\Misc\packages` folder; it is the batch file named oltpstar.bat. First of all, execute this batch file. Doing this will populate your server with two new databases called quite simply `OLTP` and `Star`. Star schemas have been covered prior to this point in Chapter 4, and so the theory surrounding this should be familiar to you.

Microsoft included this example as a way to demonstrate how you would populate an OLAP system such as the star schema from the more realistic scenario of an OLTP system, as opposed to the FoodMart example, which involves a straightforward move from Access to SQL Server.

The OLTP database is highly normalized to optimize the entry of orders by multiple salespersons. This database consists of thirteen tables; the most important being the orders and order details tables. The remaining tables basically link to these two tables to achieve the high degree of normalization. The Star database, on the other hand, consists of five tables: one fact table called the Sales table and four dimension tables, called Customers, Product, Time, and Geography.

The OLTP database scheme is in the screenshot below.

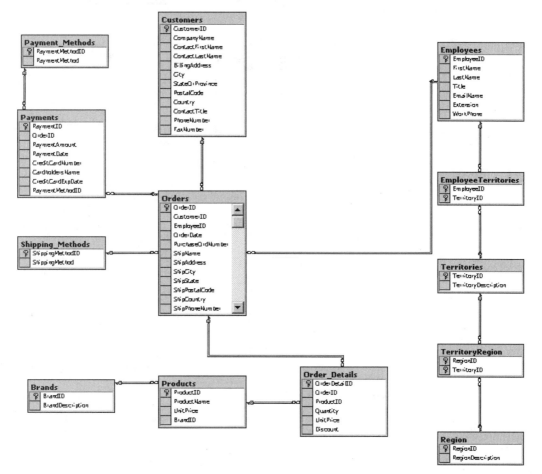

The star database schema is diagrammed in the figure below. Both of these figures come from database diagrams built and stored within SQL Server:

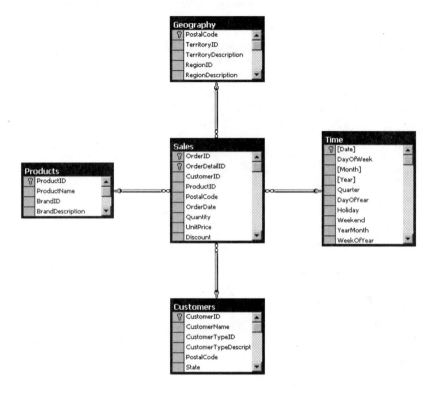

OLTP/Star Package Design

Next, we need to design a DTS package that can perform the transformation from the source OLTP database to the destination Star data mart. The following figure shows the design of the DTS package. The design includes five connections to the OLTP database, and two connections to the Star database.

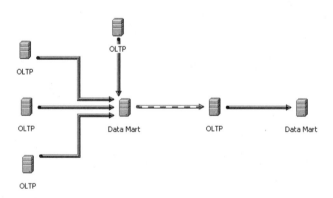

The On Success Workflow has to be completed last, just as it was within the FoodMart example, but in this instance, the workflow has four steps of execution to take into account. This is to ensure that the last step does not commence until all four preceding steps complete successfully. If any of the defined tasks do not complete successfully, then the remaining steps of the package will not proceed.

Notice as well, if you check back to the task layout diagram, that the OLTP connections all have the same name, as do the two Data Mart connections. This is similar to the FoodMart database where one connection dealt with more than one task. One connection of each database, the OLTP and Access connections put in the package earlier, is a New Connection within the Microsoft OLE DB provider for SQL Server, and the remaining connections will use the created connections as an Existing Connection instead.

Multiple Connections and Single Connections

It is totally feasible to share connections between tasks within DTS, rather than each task having its own connection. However, there are package execution restrictions when using multiple connections. Database connections are single threaded and therefore can only process one task at a time. This can therefore turn what was a multi-threaded DTS package running several simultaneous tasks using multiple connections, into a single threaded package, where you have altered the package to reduce and free up the number of connections and by doing so, only one task will run with the one connection. This will have an adverse affect on performance and may result in a package not utilizing the full resources of the server.

However, by having a single connection, if you are moving the package from a development server to a production server, this is one method of quickly altering the connection information, because any alteration to the original connection will be reflected through to the other connections derived from that connection. This can save you time, since you have one place to alter, rather than many.

The number of concurrent connections could be an issue within your installation, and so multiple tasks from one connection may be a productive and cost-effective solution. However, from a performance viewpoint, using multiple connections does give a better performance for packages.

There is another area of DTS packages that you have to be aware of when dealing with moving connections, and that deals with package transactions.

Package Transactions

Each step within a package can be contained within a transaction or not. If you wish a step to form a transaction, select the Workflow Properties option once the step is placed within the package, and then move to the Advanced tab. From here, it is possible to select the Join transaction if present option. Therefore, if the package is defined within its properties to Use transactions, the defined steps will be included within the package transaction.

Transactions within DTS packages differ to those found within T-SQL statements. Normally BEGIN TRANSACTION, COMMIT TRANSACTION and ROLLBACK TRANSACTION statements are found within T-SQL code to denote the start and end of a specific transaction. Within DTS, transactions are implicit, unless of course you are running a set of T-SQL code that specifically deals with transactions, and no transaction will actually be in progress until a DTS step is commenced that deals with any data or data structure manipulation. Once the step starts, it is not the specific step that has the transaction assigned but it is the package itself that has a transaction created; thus a package transaction can consist of several steps from within the package.

A DTS package only has one transaction within it. Although that transaction may start and end several times by differing steps running, there will only be that single transaction of work dealing with data or data structure updates. By having a single connection with several instances of that connection within your package, you will find that steps will run serially and therefore each step will start and end a transaction. Having multiple unique connections could mean steps running in parallel. Any step that commences when another step is in progress, and has a transaction in progress, will join the currently running transaction and therefore also form part of that transaction.

Loading the Customer Dimension Data

Moving back to building the package, let's now see how we can configure loading the customer dimension data from the OLTP system into the Star database. Select a Transform Data Task linking any of the OLTP and one of the Data Mart connections. Double-click to launch the Data Transformation Properties dialog box (see the next figure). In the dialog, set the description textbox to Loading Customer Dimension Data. Then, in the SQL box, type the following SQL code:

```
SELECT CustomerID = CustomerID, CustomerName=CompanyName,
    CustomerTypeID = (CustomerID % 4),
    CustomerTypeDescription = CASE (CustomerID % 4) WHEN 0
        THEN 'Excellent' WHEN 1 THEN 'Good' WHEN 2 then 'Average'
        WHEN 3 THEN 'Poor' ELSE 'Average' END,
    PostalCode=PostalCode, State=StateOrProvince
FROM Customers
```

The % operator is the modulus operator, and returns the remainder of dividing the second number into the first. Thus, 10%6 = 4

In the Destination page of the Data Transformation dialog, select the Star database and the Customer table as the destination. Make sure the mappings of the columns from the source SQL statement to the destination Customer table are accurate and close the dialog by pressing OK.

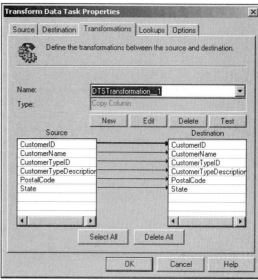

Building the Time Dimension

Building (or loading) the `Time` dimension in the data mart is similar to loading the `Customer` dimension. Create a second Transform Data Task linking any of the free OLTP connections to the same Data Mart connection as we did in the previous step. In the source page of the **Data Transformation Properties** dialog, set the description to **Loading Time Dimension Data**, and in the **SQL Query** box, type the following SQL code:

```
SELECT DISTINCT DATE=O.OrderDate, DayOfWeek=DATENAME(dw,O.OrderDate),
     Month = DatePart(mm,O.OrderDate), Year = DatePart(yy,O.OrderDate),
     Quarter =DatePart(qq,O.OrderDate),
     DayOfYear= DatePart(dy,O.OrderDate), Holiday='N',
     Weekend = CASE DATEPART(dw,O.OrderDate)

WHEN (1) THEN 'Y'
        WHEN (7) THEN 'Y' ELSE 'N'
     END,
     YearMonth = DATENAME(month, O.OrderDate) + '_' + DATENAME(year,O.OrderDate),
     WEEKOFYEAR=DATEPART(wk,O.OrderDate)
     FROM Orders O
```

Notice in the code above, the use of date functions to create the values needed for the additional fields in the `Time` table in the `Star` database that do not originally exist in the `Orders` table in the OLTP database. For example, to get a quarter field value, the function: `DatePart(qq,o.OrderDate)` was used.

In the **Destination** page of the indicated dialog, set the destination table to be the `Time` table of the `Star` database. Verify the column mappings in the **Transformations** page of the dialog box, and verify the query syntax and validity by pressing the **Parse Query** button in the **Source** page.

Building the Geography Dimension

Building the Geography dimension in the data mart is similar to loading the Customer dimension, except for the source and destination. Create a third Transform Data Task that links a free OLTP connection to the same Data Mart connection as used in the preceding steps. In the source page of the Data Transformation Properties dialog, set the description to Loading Geography Dimension Data, and in the SQL Query box, type the following SQL code:

```
SELECT PostalCode = T.TerritoryID, TerritoryID= T.TerritoryID,
       TerritoryDescription = T.TerritoryDescription,
       RegionID = R.RegionID, RegionDescription = R.RegionDescription
FROM   Territories T, Region R, TerritoryRegion TR
WHERE  T.TerritoryID = TR.TerritoryID AND TR.RegionID = R.RegionID
```

In the Destination page of the indicated dialog, set the destination table to be the Geography table of the Star database. Verify the column mappings in the Transformations page of the dialog box, and verify the query syntax and validity by pressing the Parse Query button in the Source page.

Building the Product Dimension

Building the Product dimension in the data mart is similar to building the Customer dimension, except for the source and destination. The final Transform Data Task of the first stage of the package linking a fourth free OLTP connection and the Data Mart connection from the preceding three steps is required. In the source page of the Data Transformation Properties dialog, set the description to Loading Product Dimension Data, and in the SQL Query box, type the following SQL code:

```
SELECT ProductID = P.ProductID, ProductName = P.ProductName,
       BrandID = B.BrandID, BrandDescription = B.BrandDescription
FROM   Brands B, Products P
WHERE  B.BrandID = P. BrandID
```

In the Destination page, select the Products table from the Star database as the destination table for this Transform Data task. In the Transformations page, click ActiveX Script, and then select all columns in the source and destination tables by holding the *Shift* key while you select them. Make sure ActiveX Script is selected in the New Transformation drop-down list. Then unmap and remap the columns using the Delete and New buttons respectively, just as we did for the FoodMart example in the previous chapter. The ActiveX Script Transformation Properties dialog appears. Set the language to VB Script and modify the script in the script area, changing the case of ProductName and BrandDescription columns to uppercase using the UCASE() function. The ActiveX script should then look like:

```
Function Main()
DTSDestination("ProductID")=DTSSource("ProductID")
    DTSDestination("ProductName")=UCase(DTSSource("ProductName"))
    DTSDestination("BrandID")=DTSSource("BrandID")
    DTSDestination("BrandDescription")=
    UCase(DTSSource("BrandDescription"))
    DTSDestination("ProductID")=DTSSource("ProductID")
    Main = DTSTransformStat_OK
End Function
```

On the Transformations tab, notice the many-to-many relationship indicated by the mapping diagram. Click OK to save the transformations and exit the Transform Data task.

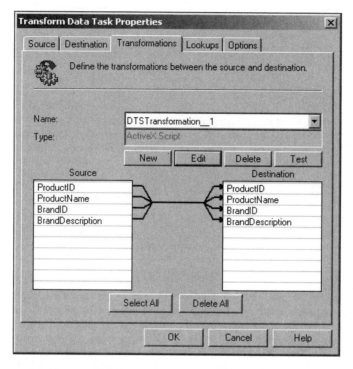

Building the Sales Fact Data

Building the sales fact data in the data mart is similar to building the Customer dimension, except for the source and destination. A Transform Data task linking the final free OLTP connection and the second Data Mart connection will be used for this purpose. In the source page of the Data Transformation Properties dialog, set the description to Loading Sales Fact Table Data, and in the SQL Query box, type the following SQL code:

```
SELECT OrderID = O.OrderID, OrderDetailID = D.OrderDetailID,
    CustomerID = C.CustomerID, ProductID = D.ProductID,
    PostalCode = C.PostalCode, OrderDate = O.OrderDate,
    Quantity = D.Quantity, UnitPrice = D.UnitPrice, Discount = D.Discount
FROM Orders O, Order_Details D, Customers C
WHERE O.OrderID = D.OrderID AND O.CustomerID = C.CustomerID
ORDER BY OrderID, OrderDetailID
```

In the Destination page of the indicated dialog, set the destination table to be the Sales table of the Star database. Verify the column mappings in the Transformations page of the dialog box, and verify the query syntax and validity by pressing the Parse Query button in the Source page.

Finally, place the On Success workflow that we discussed at the top of this section, into the package.

With this, the package has been designed and is ready to run. This will then populate the OLAP database using information from the OLTP system.

DTS Performance Issues

DTS transformation performance can be improved by using several techniques. These techniques are outlined below.

Using ActiveX Scripts

Using scripting language may slow down data transformations and data pump operations by up to four times, due to several factors such as having to interpret the language at run time. The choice of the language to use for scripting is also important for performance. VB Script is found to be faster than JScript, and JScript is found to be faster than Perl Script.

Using Ordinal Values when Referencing Columns

Using ordinal values when referencing a column is faster than using the column name. Hence, it is faster to use DTSSource(1), rather than DTSSource("CustomerID"), because this will save the database engine the step of transforming the names into ordinal values.

Using Data Pump and Data Transformations

Although the Data Pump task is designed for speed and its performance competes with the command prompt BCP (Bulk Copy Program) when copying data, this task can be slowed considerably with custom transformations. To minimize this effect, it is recommended that you avoid mapping a separate transformation function for each column involved in a data pump operation. Also, consider mapping as many similar transformations into a single script and function as possible, rather than allowing each column to have its own transformation invocation method. Again this is a speed issue due to compilation on demand

Using Data Driven Queries versus Transformations

If no transformations are used, and only direct one-to-one mapping of columns is done with the data pump task, this task will be much faster than DDQ. However, if transformations are involved, DDQ proves to be faster due to the COM interface it is using behind the scenes to transform the data, which is faster than that used for data pump transformations.

Using Bulk Inserts and BCP

The T-SQL BULK INSERT command is supported by the OLE DB provider for SQL Server. The use of BULK INSERT is faster than BCP when it is used to import files, as BCP uses an older technology, and is run through an ODBC data provider. Therefore, if no transformations are involved, consider using this command. If you want to learn more about the use of BULK INSERTS, they are covered in PROFESSIONAL SQL SERVER 2000 DTS (Wrox Press, ISBN 1- 861004-41-9).

Using DTS Lookups

As you saw earlier, DTS Lookups can be invoked from within the data transformation of a DDQ, allowing for use of the same connections to the source and/or destination. This gives DTS Lookups an edge over global variables and COM objects. However, if the transformation can use a direct SQL statement as opposed to DTS Lookup, performance will improve significantly. We have also covered earlier some other performance issues with lookups where using values for parameters within lookups can be improved by using non-internal values.

Other SQL Server Techniques

When moving data between SQL Server sources without the need for complex transformations, the fastest way to do so is by SQL statements. Also, try to use the SQL Server performance tuning and monitoring tools, such as SQL Server Profiler as much as possible when building your queries. For more details on these tools and further information on performance tuning, see Chapter 20.

DTS Security

DTS packages can be run from within SQL Server, from outside SQL Server, or from another package executing at the time. Packages contain connections to current and remote servers, possibly exposing server security log-ins to people whom you may not wish to have this information. Packages can be set up with two different levels of security, one for editing the package as well as execution, and one level purely for execution.

> **Once a password has been set for a package, there is no method to alter this setting or to recover from a lost password. Therefore, keep your password to a memorable item, and if required, store it within a secure environment in case it may be forgotten.**

Owner password

An owner password will allow both editing and execution of packages upon completion of a valid password entry. By setting this password, the data within the package is encrypted. If you are saving to anything other than SQL Server or a Structured Storage File, then this option is not available.

User Password

If you wish to secure the package but only wish to expose the package for execution, then set the user password. You can issue this password as necessary knowing that it is impossible for that person to be able to edit or corrupt the package. To set a user password, the package must have an owner password as well. If you are saving to anything other than SQL Server or a Structured Storage File, then this option is not available.

Viewing Package Meta Data

It is possible to view the meta data of a package when it is stored in Meta Data Services. Every time a package is modified and stored within the Repository, the previous version of the package remains within the Repository, and a new **version** is stored, with more recent dates and times. This allows full audit tracking of what has altered within a package and allows you to return to a previous version if required, just as you can do with Visual SourceSafe and any objects stored within that system.

As we discussed in the last chapter, when a new package is created, it is stored with a global unique identifier within the msdb repository. Each time the package is versioned, the package GUID remains static, and a new version GUID is created.

To view the meta data of a package, select the Meta Data option under Data Transformation Services

This will open up a new MMC within SQL Server. However, it is possible to run Meta Data as a separate MMC outside SQL Server. There are differences when running Meta Data from within SQL Server and without, such as the running MMC outside of SQL Server gives you the ability to work with several repository databases, and not the specific SQL Server repository database that has been built for the SQL Server instance when running Meta Data within SQL Server itself.

From within SQL Server, clicking the **Meta Data** icon takes you to the Meta Data browser, and by clicking on the **Package** tab, a list of packages that have been built within your system is displayed. By expanding these you will be able to see the versioning that has gone on:

Any lineage information that was recorded with any package would be shown, but in our example, we have not gone down this route so we only have the ability to view the versions built. To view details about the versions, clicking on the required item will display several items of information for you to peruse:

From looking at the screenshot above, you can see that a great deal of information can be viewed. From this information, if a problem were to occur within your package, you might be able to track down the origin of the problem. Maybe it was through a version change to the package, and by seeing the User who last modified it, and the dates and times, you should be able to track the user down. If you work in an installation where more than one user uses a generic login for database structure maintenance, you will have no way of finding out exactly who the user was, therefore it is essential that you avoid well known generic log ins.

Viewing the package meta data can be very useful for tracking changes and also gives you the ability to move back to a previous version of a package.

Summary

Using DTS within SQL Server can provide a highly flexible and secure method of loading data, and working with data warehouses. There is a vast amount to DTS and these last two chapters have specifically homed in on areas that are of interest to those working with OLAP databases. In this chapter we have looked at the two Analysis Services-specific tasks, the Analysis Services Processing task, which is design specifically for working with cubes, dimensions and data mining tasks, and the Data Mining Prediction task, which looks at mining prediction models.

Also in this chapter, we saw that transactions and security are areas just as important to get right, as building the package itself. These, along with connections can alter the performance of a package and so altering a package in these areas has also to be backed up with cross checking resource utilization, accomplished through viewing the package meta data.

Data Warehouse

9

Building OLAP Cubes with Analysis Manager

In this chapter we will explore building OLAP cubes with SQL Server Analysis Manager. From earlier chapters, we know that a cube is a multi-dimensional structure that contains aggregations of detail data from your relational data source. Analysis Manager offers several tools to create and edit OLAP cubes, dimensions, data sources, mining models, and roles, and it is these tools that we will cover in this chapter.

This chapter is split into two: Basic Topics *and* Advanced Topics. *To fully exploit and understand the features described in the* Advanced Topics *section, an understanding of MDX is required, and if you are a novice to MDX, you are encouraged to revisit parts of this section once you have familiarized yourself with MDX, which is the subject of the next two chapters. MDX is a language used to query an OLAP database, similar to the T-SQL that is used to query a SQL Server database.*

In the *Basic Topics* section, which introduces the key tools of Analysis Manager for manipulating the objects within an OLAP database, we cover the following:

❑ Creating a new OLAP database and its data source

❑ Using the Dimension Wizard

❑ Processing a cube, viewing dimension meta data, and browsing a dimension

❑ Using the Cube Wizard

❑ Using the Storage Design Wizard

In the *Advanced Topics* section, we cover the following features of Analysis Manager:

❑ Using the Dimension Editor including custom member formulas

❑ Using the Cube Editor including calculated cells, calculated members, and actions

❑ Creating virtual cubes

❑ Creating cube partitions

Basic Topics

The purpose of this section is to provide the reader with the basic concept of building an OLAP database and all of its objects using the Analysis Manager. More advanced topics such as building parent-child dimensions or linked cubes will be reviewed in the Advanced Topics section of this chapter. This section will focus on familiarizing you with the foundation for OLAP cube building within Analysis Manager. Note, though the Foodmart 2000 OLAP database exists for OLAP tutorials, we will be creating our own OLAP database using the existing FoodMart 2000 Access database.

> It is important to note that when creating OLAP objects within the Analysis Manager, you must be careful about the naming of the objects. Once the objects have been named, they cannot be changed. To change the name of any OLAP object, it would require you to create a new version of this object (with the new name) and to delete the old one. Performing this task may be difficult at times.

Create a New OLAP Database

An OLAP database is similar to its counterpart SQL database in that it is a repository that contains objects. While a SQL database contains relational tables, an OLAP database contains multi-dimensional cubes. In order to create an OLAP database:

❑ Open up Analysis Manager.

❑ Right-click on the server and you will be given various menu options; click on the New Database... option.

❑ You will be given the dialog box below. Type in the name of your OLAP database (for example MyOLAPDB) and, if desired, the description of the OLAP database.

❑ Click on OK and you will have created the OLAP database MyOLAPDB.

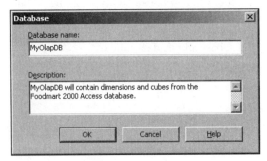

Now you have created the OLAP database MyOLAPDB.

Data Sources

An important thing to remember when dealing with Analysis Services is that its purpose is to perform aggregations (calculate summary statistics) against an existing data source. Analysis Services does contain OLAP databases, but it does not contain the detail data by which the aggregations are derived. Instead, it contains indexes and/or aggregates of the detail data based on the detail data below it.

Having said this, all OLAP databases have their own data sources – specifically for Analysis Server, it supports OLE DB-compliant providers such as SQL Server, Access, and Oracle.

Within Analysis Manager, from the MyOLAPDB, expand the tree and you will see Data Sources, Cubes, Shared Dimensions, Mining Models, and Database Roles.

Right-Click on Data Sources and select New Data source... The Data Link Properties dialog will appear. You will be given various options that you may connect to. For our example, please choose "Microsoft OLE DB Provider for ODBC Drivers" and click on Next >>.

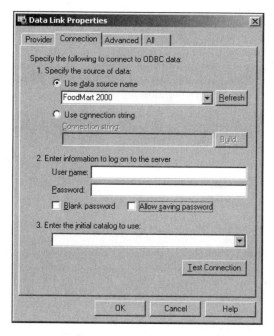

You will now have access to the Connection tab, which will allow you to connect to the ODBC data source of your choice. For our purposes, we will use the FoodMart 2000 Access database as our data source. Click on the Test Connection button to check the connection to the FoodMart 2000 database is valid.

At this point, you can click on OK and you have created your data source. However, there are additional options by which you can modify the connection under the Advanced and All tabs.

Remember, once you create a data source, any of the objects such as dimensions, or cubes, will be dependent upon it. If you want to remove the connection, then you'll have to delete these dependent objects first.

Naming the data source within Analysis Manager automatically takes the name of your server and data source (SQL Server) or the data source name (ODBC). Thus, if you are creating an OLAP database and then archiving/restoring it to another server, it may still have the name of your development environment data source. You can change it to point at the production data source, but it will still have the *name* of the development data source.

Although you have many options to work with as your data source, typically you are only dealing with the following:

❑   Microsoft OLE DB Provider for ODBC Drivers for Access databases

❑   Microsoft OLE DB Provider for SQL Server for SQL Server databases

❑   Microsoft OLE DB-compliant provides for other relational databases such as Oracle, Sybase, or DB2

Other options may prove to have issues at times. For example, when working with Microsoft OLE DB Provider for ODBC Drivers, you could theoretically attach this particular driver to any ODBC driver and make your OLAP data source a text file. However, when attempting to connect, you will notice the fact that while you can see the data, you cannot actually create a valid data source. Not all ODBC drivers will actually work to allow you to create your OLAP data source.

Building Dimensions

Dimensions are analogous to a SQL GROUP BY statement; in fact, the data of an OLAP cube is organized or grouped by the information within a dimension. For example, people will often want to see data over time, or organized by a particular hierarchy. Time or this hierarchy are actually dimensions within an OLAP cube. Therefore, before building the actual cube, you will need to build the dimensions by which you will organize the data.

Regular Dimensions

Regular dimensions can be shared or private dimensions within Analysis Services.

Shared Dimensions

A shared dimension is one that can be used by multiple cubes; such dimensions include a Time dimension. Instead of building multiple dimensions for the same type of information, you can use one dimension, saving both processing and development time. These dimensions can be found under the Shared Dimensions branch within the Analysis Manager and are processed there. Shared dimensions are automatically loaded into memory once Analysis Services has started. This is done in order to help with both processing and querying. Therefore, it is important to design shared dimensions so that the memory on the server is not overutilized.

Private Dimensions

Private dimensions are specific to the cube that contains them and are not shared with other cubes. These dimensions are only found within the cube that they were created for and are processed when the cube is processed. Private dimensions are constructed and edited via the Cube Editor (instead of the Dimension Wizard or Dimension Editor) and are automatically processed when the cube is processed. Furthermore, these dimensions are not automatically loaded into memory, hence are not a major concern (in terms of memory) when planning the design of OLAP cubes.

Regular dimensions are your standard dimensions and a majority of your dimension data will be organized within them.

Virtual Dimensions

Virtual dimensions depend on the member properties of a created regular dimension. For example, in a Store dimension, possible dimension members include the type of store, such as a grocery store, supermarket, or retail chain. By building a virtual dimension on top of these member properties, it is possible for end users to group not only by dimensions, but also by the attributes of those dimensions. In this example, they can now organize data by both the Store and the store type itself.

Parent-Child Dimensions

A parent-child dimension is a new dimension type introduced with SQL Server 2000 Analysis Services. It is a dimension type that is extremely flexible for building dimensions of various hierarchical structures. Using the Foodmart 2000 OLAP Employee dimension, you will notice the ragged hierarchy below.

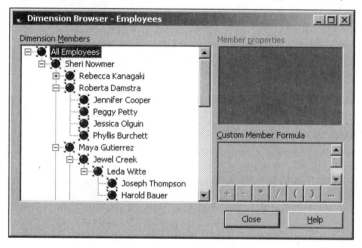

This is a common occurrence within an organizational hierarchy where some people like Roberta Damstra will have people working under them (Jennifer Cooper, Peggy Petty, etc.) while others like Maya Gutierrez will have a larger organization and a deeper hierarchy (Jewel Creek > Leda Witte > Joseph Thomson).

Building a hierarchy like this within a regular dimension is possible, but regular dimensions have their own set of restrictions that, in most cases, would require the user to manipulate the dimension to ensure that a balanced hierarchy could somehow be built. Instead, one can organize the data with a parent-child relationship so that a self-join can occur in order to build the hierarchy.

The table below is the portion of the Employee table within the FoodMart 2000 Access database, used to create the Employee OLAP dimension that can be seen within the Dimension Browser above.

Supervisor_ID (Manager)	Employee_ID (Employee)	Full_Name (Employee Name)
0	1	Sheri Nowmer
1	7	Rebecca Kanagaki
1	6	Roberta Damstra

Table continued on following page

Supervisor_ID (Manager)	Employee_ID (Employee)	Full_Name (Employee Name)
1	5	Maya Gutierrez
6	37	Jennifer Cooper
6	38	Peggy Petty
5	12	Jewel Creek
12	882	Leda Witte
882	884	Joseph Thomson
882	883	Harold Bauer
…	…	…

For example, look at the employee Leda Witte; her ID is 882 while her Supervisor_ID is 12. Going up the hierarchy, her supervisor (with an ID of 12) is Jewel Creek, and *her* supervisor has an ID of 5. Again, going up we find out that her supervisor is Maya Gutierrez, whose supervisor in turn is Sheri Nowmer (Supervisor_ID of 1). By organizing the data within this structure, one can perform a SELF JOIN between the supervisor_id and the employee_id in order to build this hierarchy. Analysis Services saves you the trouble of actually needing to perform the SELF JOIN, you only need to set up the data in this fashion.

Dimension Wizard

From the Analysis Manager, right-click on **Shared Dimensions** and then select **New Dimension…** From there, you will have the option to build a dimension using the Dimension Wizard by the Editor. Note that we begin with the Dimension Wizard because it is extremely good at setting up the base set of properties for your OLAP dimensions. It is very powerful, being able to handle most standard situations, with more exceptional situations handled by the Dimension Editor (more about this later in this chapter). For our purposes, we will begin with the Dimension Wizard:

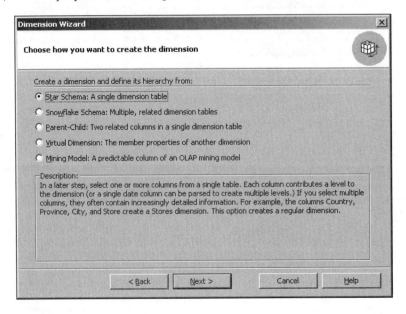

The types of dimension you can create are listed in the dimension wizard screen, and we shall discuss them now.

Dimension	Description
Star Schema: A single dimension table	This is a common dimension design by which the overall schema of a cube follows a star-schema design. As noted in earlier chapters of this book, a star-schema requires that in your database schema design, you have one central fact table and dimension tables that join directly to this one central fact table. If the dimension you are about to create is of that particular design, that is the dimension is one table that joins directly to a central fact table through a key, then this is the appropriate avenue to take. By default, this will create a regular shared dimension.
Snowflake Schema : Multiple, related dimension tables	Snowflake schemas are also relatively common. Similar to the previous option, this one allows you to build a dimension based on the idea that your cube/database schema is a snowflake schema. This means that the dimension table that you are creating depends on more than one table. If you have to build a dimension based on multiple tables, this particular option will allow you to build the dimension. By default, this will create a regular shared dimension
Parent-Child : Two related columns in a single dimension table	Introduced in Analysis Services 2000, a parent-child dimension depends on the idea that you have one dimension table that represents this dimension. It is a table that contains a parent column and a member column. The member column describes the dimension member itself while the relationship between the parent column and the member column describe the structure or hierarchy of that dimension. This dimension is very useful in describing dimension hierarchies.
Virtual dimension: The member properties of another dimension	A member property of a dimension is an attribute of a dimension member itself. It provides additional information about the dimension member. For example, in a Store dimension, possible dimension members include the type of store. By building a virtual dimension on top of these member properties, it is possible for end users to group not only by dimensions but also by the attributes of those dimensions. In this example, they can now organize data by both the Store and the store type itself.
Mining Model: A predictable column of an OLAP mining model	More information concerning mining models can be found in later chapters specific to the data mining. Introduced in Analysis Services 2000, this option will allow users to develop a predictable column that stores predicted output from a mining model as well as the input columns that are used by the mining model.

For our purposes, we will first build a star-schema dimension so that we can build a time dimension. Almost every conceivable cube a user will build will contain a time dimension. Ranging from trend analysis to deciphering daily activity, date-time information is a requirement in order to understand the data that you see within an OLAP cube. Saying this, the dimension wizard has specific options to build a Time dimension.

After clicking on the Next button from above you will be presented with the dialog below:

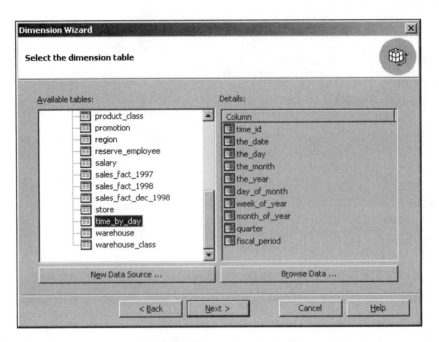

The left-hand pane provides you with the available tables based on the available data sources. In this case, the dialog is providing you with all of the available tables from the Foodmart 2000 data source recently made. The right-hand pane provides the user with the available columns when building this dimension. Click on the time_by_day table so it will be possible for us to build our time dimension, and then click on Next.

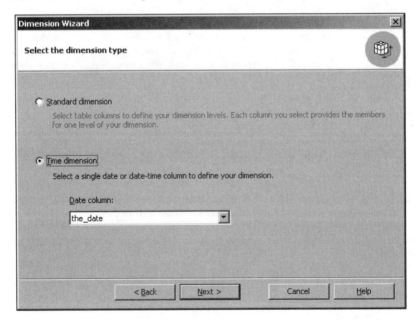

As noted previously, the Dimension Wizard specifically handles the case of time. In most cases, you will click on the Standard dimension option, but because we're creating a time dimension, click on the Time dimension option. Once you have chosen this option, you will need to define the single date or date-time column that contains the date-time information. In the case of the Foodmart 2000 database, the time_by_day table has a column called the_date that contains the time-date information. Once chosen, click on Next.

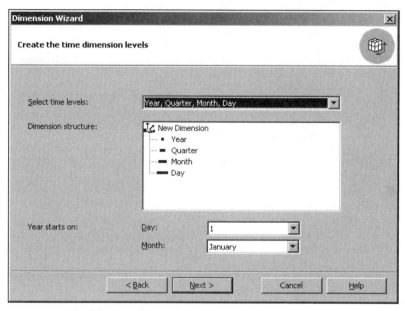

Finally, the Dimension Wizard will give you options to structure your time dimension. In many cases, you are dealing with a time dimension that will contain year, quarter, month, and day. There are other structures that may be better suited for your data warehouse such as (year, month, day) or (year, week). By clicking the Select time levels drop-down box, you will be provided an array of choices to build the structure of your time dimension.

For our purposes, leave it on the default selection of (year, quarter, month, day) and click on Next. In the Select Advanced Options dialog, click Next (we will review the significance of these Advanced Options later in the chapter). Finally, you will be able to name your dimension (for example Time) and click Finish. The Dimension Wizard will switch to the Dimension Editor, which will allow the user to manipulate the dimension on a more detailed level.

At this point, click on Save and you will have completed building a time dimension.

Build Another Time Dimension (Hierarchy)

When creating your first time dimension above, you selected Create a hierarchy of a dimension. Within Analysis Manager, you'll notice that the dimension name is now Time.yqmd. The reason this was created was because we were creating a time dimension that had a hierarchy of Year, Quarter, Month, and Day. If you wanted a time hierarchy based on year, week, and day as well, instead of creating a new dimension, you can create a new dimension hierarchy:

❏   Follow all of the steps to build the above time dimension, except at the point of the Select time levels drop-down box, choose the option Year, Week, Day. Continue with the remaining steps.

❏   For the name of the dimension, still use Time, but for the hierarchy name, use ywd for Year, Week, and Day.

In Analysis Manager, you will now see the dimensions Time.yqmd and Time.ywd. Organizing your time dimension to include multiple hierarchies allows end users to have alternative views of the same dimension, such as YQMD, YWD, or fiscal. A dimension with multiple hierarchies within SQL Server 2000 Analysis Services actually consists of separate dimensions that share the same dimension table. Since they share the same dimension table, they may be able to share the same aggregations, which optimizes the building of aggregations within Analysis Services overall.

Regular Dimension with Member Properties

The dimension we will build to encompass member properties will be the Store dimension. It will contain the store name under a geographical hierarchy (country, state, city). We will build this dimension with the Dimension Wizard:

- ❑ Right-click on Shared Dimensions, select New Dimension, and choose Wizard
- ❑ Choose Star Schema: A single dimension table and click Next
- ❑ Choose the fact table Store and click on Next
- ❑ For the Select the dimension type dialog, keep it on Standard and click Next
- ❑ Choose store_country and click on the > button. You are building the first level of your Store dimension; this will be the country where the store is located.
- ❑ Now we will choose the next level within the geographical hierarchy; this will be the state in which the store exists. Click on store_state and then click on the > button.
- ❑ The next level of the geographical hierarchy is the city in which the store is located. Click on store_city and then click the > button.

Finally, add the store name (store_name) to complete the creation of the dimension. In the screenshot below, you will note how the different levels (country to store name) are represented in the Dimension Wizard by the relevant number of little dots.

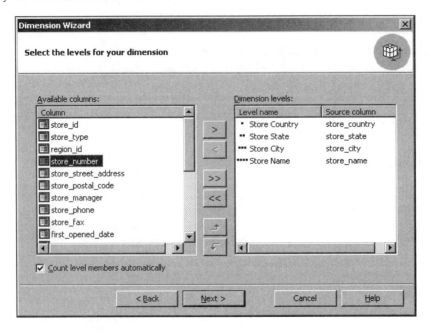

❏ Click on Next to continue creating the dimension; click on Next to pass the Select advanced options dialog

❏ Enter Store as the dimension name, and then click Finish. Now you will enter into the Dimension Editor:

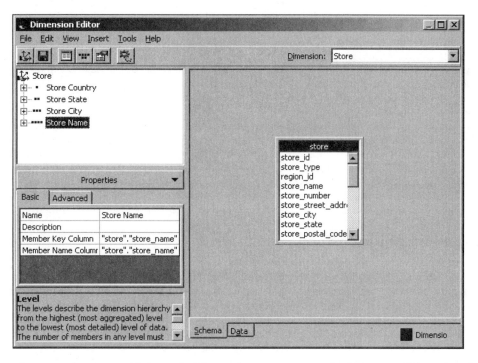

As stated previously, you could always build your dimensions using the Dimension Editor directly and not use the Dimension Wizard, it is just of a matter of taste. In the majority of cases, the Dimension Wizard is able to build a dimension in the optimal manner. However, in some cases, the Dimension Wizard will not be able to perform all the necessary tasks. For example, we will now be building member properties for the dimension using the Dimension Editor, something that cannot be done by the wizard.

❏ From the Dimension Editor, expand the Store Name level so you can see the Member Properties option

❏ Right-click the Member Properties option and click on New Property Member...

❏ The Insert Member Property dialog will appear and it will allow you to choose a source column within the table that is used to build the store dimension. For our purposes, we will create a member property on the store type.

❏ Click on store_type within the Insert Member Property dialog and click OK

❏ As you can see from the tree diagram overleaf, you will now see the Store Type member property connected to the Member properties tree under Store Name

Now you have completed building your Store dimension. Click on Tools|Process Dimension to complete the building and processing of this dimension.

The purpose of a member property is to build virtual dimension against it and also to build some set of information that you may need data aggregated against, but still want displayed. Another example of building member properties is to construct x and y coordinates that represent the latitude and longitude for the central location of a geographical hierarchy of country, state, and city, such as the latitude and longitude of the center of the country, center of the state, and center of the city. By building member properties that contain these coordinates, it is possible for you to query a cube and obtain the geographical dimension information and its coordinates without looking up the SQL table. As inferred by the above statement, you can build member properties against any level of the dimension.

Building a Virtual Dimension

Similar to the above member properties, the purpose of building a virtual dimension is to build a dimension whose aggregations are based on another dimension; this has less processing requirements. More importantly, a virtual dimension is a changing dimension allowing you to change the underlying data without the requirement of fully reprocessing the cubes.

The virtual dimension we are going to build is based on the above member properties of the Store dimension about the store type. This way, it will be possible to view your fact data by store, and also separate it out by store type. To build this dimension:

❑ Right-click on Shared Dimensions, select New Dimension, and choose Wizard.

❑ Choose Virtual Dimension: The member properties of another dimension and click Next.

❑ As opposed to your previous two dimensions, you will see a list of dimensions that actually have member properties. In this case, the one you have built so far is the Store dimension. Choose the Store dimension and click on Next

❑ At Select the levels for the virtual dimension, choose Store Name.Store Type, click the > button, and click Next. If you decided to make other member properties for the Store dimension, those member properties would be seen in this dialog.

❑ In the Select advanced options dialog, click on Next.

❑ For the dimension name, use Store Type and then click Finish. You will now enter into the Dimension Editor.

Now you have completed building your Store Type virtual dimension. Click on Tools|Process Dimension to complete the building and processing of this dimension. You will be given the option to Rebuild the dimension structure; select it, and then click Finish.

Building a Parent-Child dimension

As noted previously, a parent-child dimension is quite useful when building hierarchies. Regular dimensions can build hierarchies as well, but they are required to be balanced and not changing. This means that every node within the hierarchy is populated, all the nodes within the hierarchy go down to the same level, and there are no missing nodes within the hierarchy. The benefit of a parent-child dimension is that its structure allows for unbalanced or ragged hierarchy dimensions and it is a changing dimension, hence this type of dimension is optimized for frequent changes to the underlying data.

The main drawback of a parent-child dimension is that it has slightly slower performance when querying, but in many cases, this is negligible. Another drawback is that it requires that the hierarchy source data to be organized in a particular manner. More information can be found in the earlier *Parent-Child Dimensions* section. For now, we will construct a parent-child dimension:

- ❑   Right-click on Shared Dimensions, select New Dimension, and choose Wizard.

- ❑   Choose Parent-Child: Two related columns in a single dimension table and click Next.

- ❑   Choose the fact table Account and click on Next.

- ❑   You will now be on the Select the columns that define the parent-child data hierarchy dialog. Here you will describe the child (member) key, parent key, and the child (member) name. For the member key, choose account_id. For the parent key, choose account_parent, and for the member name, choose account_description. Click Next.

- ❑   In the Select advanced options dialog, click on Next.

- ❑   For the dimension name, use Account and then click Finish. You will now enter into the Dimension Editor.

Now you have completed building your Account parent-child dimension. Click on Tools|Process Dimension to complete the building and processing of this dimension. You will be given the option to Rebuild the dimension structure; select it, and click Finish.

Viewing Dimension Meta Data

It is possible to view the properties and structure of our dimensions, the dimension meta data.

Expand the Analysis Manager pane, expand MyOlapDB, expand Shared Dimensions, and click on the Store dimension. In the main body pane, click on the Meta Data tab located next to Getting Started.

Overleaf is a figure of the main body pane that contains the meta data relevant for the Store dimension. This pane informs the user of the properties and attributes of the Store dimension including its storage mode, structure, status, and the levels it contains.

Browsing a Dimension

It is also possible to take a look at the data in your dimension, without necessarily editing it.

From the Analysis Manager pane, expand Shared Dimensions, and click on the Account dimension. Right-click Account and you will be given the option to Browse Dimension Data. Click on this option, and you will be given the **Dimension Browser** dialog below that will allow you to browse your dimension data.

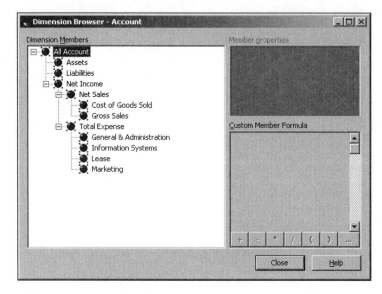

Processing Dimensions

Once you have completed building your dimension, you will need to process it before it actually becomes active. In other words, the dimension data needs to be processed before it can be queried.

There are two options to process dimensions.

❑ **Incremental Update:** This processing option performs the task of incrementally updating the OLAP dimension based on new rows added to the source dimension table. If you have a changing dimension, it can take into account restricted additions, deletions, movements, and updates of dimension members. There is more information on the restrictions of changing dimensions in SQL Server Books Online. The Incremental Update option does not require full reprocessing of dependent cubes, hence is the most common method of processing. Upon completion, the incremental update will kick off an automatic refresh on all cubes that depend on those dimensions. However, this option is not able to take into account any structural changes made to the dimension if any exist.

❑ **Rebuild Dimension Structure:** This option rebuilds the entire dimension and reprocesses all of the data. This is required any time you make any structural changes to a dimension, which unfortunately includes name changes. Once a dimension is rebuilt, any dependent cubes will also require having everything rebuilt as well.

Processing

To process dimensions, you can perform this task from the Analysis Manager menu or perform it from the Dimension Editor. From the Analysis Manager menu, right-click the dimension and choose Process. From the Dimension Editor, select Tools|Process Dimension. Both ways provide you with the same dialog to Process a dimension.

Choose your option of Incremental update or Rebuild the dimension structure, and click on OK. Upon completion of processing, you will get the dialog shown overleaf.

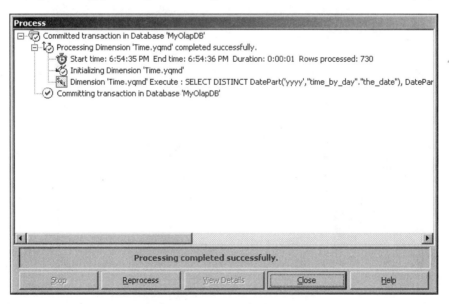

In general, you will need to process the dimension before you process the cube. The principle is that you cannot update the aggregations based on a fact table unless you have take into account of all possible dimension members that can exist.

If there are dimension members that exist within the fact data but not within the dimension, this will usually lead to the following:

❑   There is a lack of referential integrity between your fact and dimension data.

❑   Processing the cube will result in an error during processing. Through the Analysis Manager, you will usually get hints that you will need to process the dimension before processing the cube.

A common solution is to right-click on the **Shared Dimensions** option within Analysis Manager, and process all of the dimensions at once instead of processing each of them individually. Although this is a timesaving feature where you do not need to reprocess each dimension manually, there is the possibility that the processing of the dimensions in this manner will fail. Basically, having too many dimensions will occasionally result in the transaction protection surrounding all of the dimensions failing to write to all of the dimensions, resulting in the failure. This is not a catastrophic failure, and you simply have to process the dimensions individually.

Building a Cube

Now that you have built your dimensions, you can build your cube. Recall, a cube is a multidimensional structure that contains aggregations of detail data from your relational data source. Therefore, the cube schema is based on the underlying data.

We will build a cube based on budget information, and the dimensions we have just built will be added, and will group this data. In other words, the budget information can be sliced by time, category, account, store, and store type.

❑   Right-click on **Cubes,** choose **New Cube,** and choose **Wizard.**

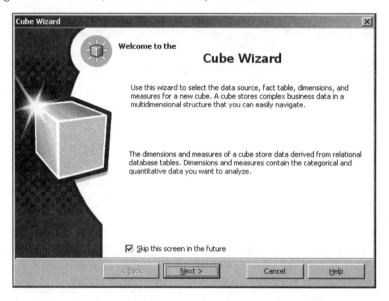

❏ From the Select a fact table from a data source, choose the fact table expense_fact and click Next.

❏ Within the Cube Wizard, you will be given the option to Select the numeric columns that define your measures. This dialog allows you to determine the measures, which are the columns on which you wish to perform your aggregations. For example, you will often want to count the number of users that have visited your web site. In this case, the userid or username is the column on which you wish to perform the aggregation, hence it is the measure. In the case of our expense_fact table (which we will use to create a Budget cube), we will perform a SUM on the amount of money, hence Amount is the measure. Click on amount and then the > arrow. You will see the dialog box below:

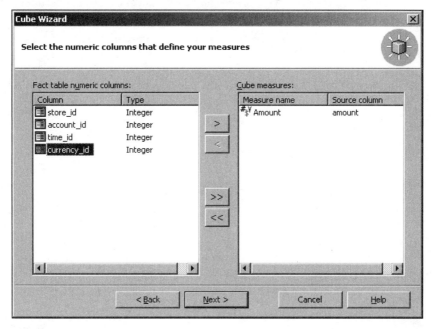

❏ Click Next and then you will see the list of dimensions that you can include within your cube. Since all of the dimensions we have built are for budget purposes, click on the >> to include all of the dimensions; then click Next.

❏ The next dialog is a Fact Table Row Count dialog that asks the question whether you want to count the number of rows within the fact table. This value is the Count value within the Dimension Editor (more on this subject later), which allows Analysis Services to build more efficient aggregations based on the amount of data within the fact table. In many cases, you will want to click Yes, but in the odd situation where you have too much data to count, you may want to click No and manually fill in this field later.

❏ For the cube name, use Budget and then click Finish. Now you will enter into the Cube Editor. For our purposes, we will review the Cube Editor later in this chapter. Select File|Save, and then close the Cube Editor.

Design Storage and Processing

By definition, OLAP cubes are a storage mechanism for pre-calculated aggregates by which to obtain faster query performance. Design Storage is the setting of these pre-calculated aggregations within the OLAP cube; processing these cubes will build these aggregations so that it will be possible to query the cubes.

❑   In the Analysis Manager, expand **Cubes**, and right-click the **Budget** cube you recently made. Select the **Design Storage...** option.

❑   Within the Storage Design Wizard, you will be offered the different types of data storage: MOLAP, ROLAP, and HOLAP. For our purposes, we will choose the default mode of MOLAP. Click **Next**.

❑   Within the **Set aggregations options**, click on the **Performance gain reaches** option, and set this value to 90. Click on **Start**.

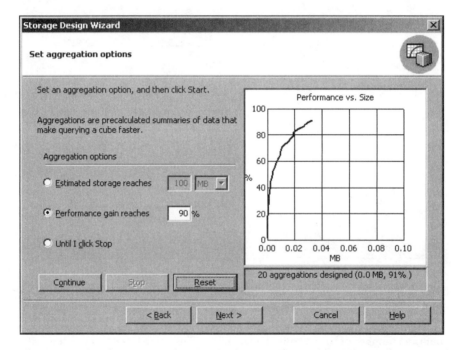

As you will notice in the above screenshot for the Storage Design Wizard, it will perform the task of building aggregations as efficiently as possible to get the performance gain desired. The graph to the right describes the performance (as a percentage) and how much space is required (in MB). In this particular case, a 91% performance gain will result in 20 aggregations designed with approximately 0.032 MB of space utilized.

Once the aggregations have been designed, click on **Next**. The final dialog of the Storage Design Wizard will give you the option to process the cube. Choose the default setting of **Process now** and click on **Finish**.

The screenshot below shows how the cube is processed.

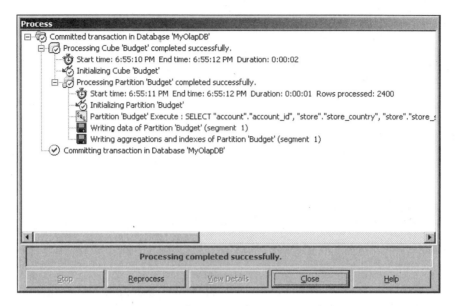

Click on Close and you will have completed processing your cube.

More on Processing Cubes

You can also process a cube by expanding the Analysis Services pane, expanding the server, expanding Cubes, and right-clicking on the cube (Budget, for our example). Select Process..., and you will see the dialog box below.

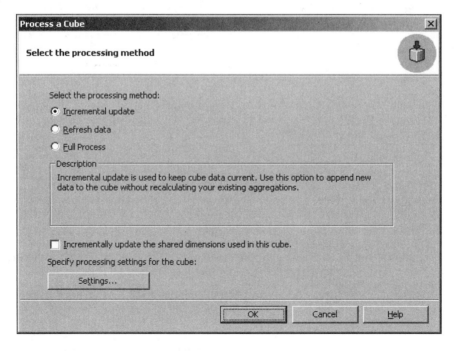

This dialog describes the three different processing options that are available for processing a cube.

❑ **Incremental Update:** Similar to the incremental update of dimensions for dimensional processing, you can process new data that was recently added to your fact table. The important difference, though, is that you will need to specify the criteria by which new data was added.

For example, if you had just added new data for the year 1999 to the fact table **expense_fact** within the `Foodmart 2000` Access database, by clicking on the **Incremental Update** in the above dialog, and clicking **Next**, you will be able to specify a `WHERE` clause statement by which to filter the set of data to process only the newly added data.

```
"Time_by_day"."the_date" >= '01/01/1999'
```

Note that if you perform this update without specifying a filter, it will incrementally update the entire fact table and add to already existing aggregates, which will duplicate your values.

❑ **Refresh Data:** If you have not made any structural changes to your cube and simply need to repopulate it with existing data, you can use this option to reprocess your cube. This option is handy if you are reprocessing a small cube and are not sure what new data has been added to the cube. From the above dialog, click on **Refresh Data** and then click **OK**. It will then proceed to refresh the data of the cube without causing any issues with users querying the cube at the same time.

❑ **Full Process:** This option is required if you changed the structure of the OLAP cube. This option will completely rebuild your cube from its underlying schema to populating the cube with data. To use this option from the above dialog, click on **Full Process** and then click **OK**. Users will still be able to query the cube when this occurs but will need to reconnect to the cube once the cube has completed processing in order to take into account of new data or structural changes.

An additional option included in the **Process a cube** dialog is to **Incrementally update the shared dimensions used in this cube**. This is important because it reflects the importance of processing your dimensions before processing your cube. Before it is possible for the cube to take into account any new data that could belong to new dimension members, we need to be certain that the dimensions are up to date, so that it is possible to build the aggregations against them. Choosing the **Incrementally update the shared dimensions used in this cube** option will have Analysis Manager automatically incrementally update the dimensions used by this cube, so that there will be no errors generated when processing the cube, based on incorrect dimension information.

Viewing your Cube Meta Data

Similar to viewing your dimension meta data, viewing the cube meta data provides the user with the properties and structure of a cube without going through the Cube Editor.

Expand the Analysis Manager pane, expand your server, expand **MyOLAPDB**, expand **Cubes**, and click on **Budget**, the cube you have recently created. In the main body pane, click on the **Meta Data** tab, next to the **Getting Started** tab.

Below is a screenshot of the main body pane that contains the meta data relevant for the **Budget** cube. This pane informs the user of the properties and attributes of the **Budget** cube, including its dimensions, measures, and calculated members:

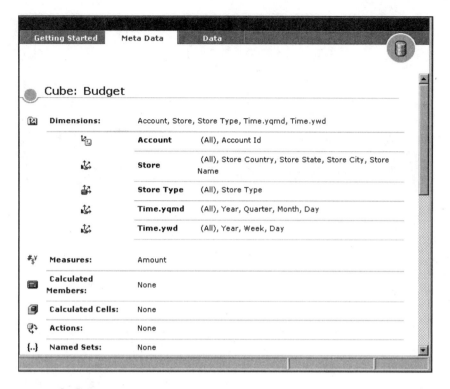

Browsing your Cubes

In order to browser your cube data, without editing the cube, click on the Data tab located next to the Meta Data tab. You can drag and drop the dimensions (category, store, store type, time) into the data pane in order to pivot around your data. If you click on the Store Type dimension and drag it on top of the Account dimension (make sure it is above All Account, Assets, Liabilities, and + Net Income and not +Level 02), you will get the screenshot below.

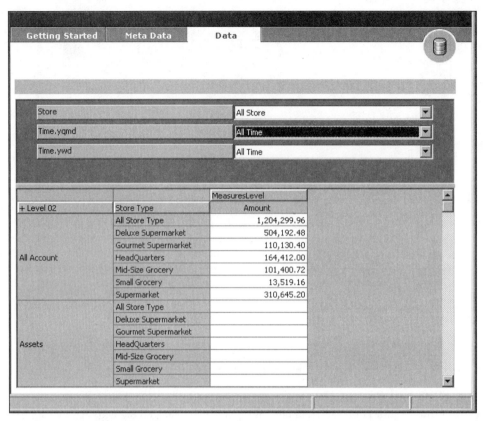

The Data browser is similar to that of Microsoft Excel or Office Web Components' PivotTable list object, allowing you to drag-and-drop dimensions in order to get different views of the data. Furthermore, you can slice by altering the drop-down boxes of the dimensions to some specific member. For example, click on the highlighted All Time box and you can slice the data by years for 1997 or 1998.

Advanced Topics

Now that you have created your basic set of dimensions and cubes, we will review more advanced concepts within the Analysis Manager. It is assumed that the reader has reviewed the past sections and/or has good knowledge of the Analysis Manager. We will be reviewing the following:

❏   Using the Dimension Editor including custom member formulas

❏   Using the Cube Editor including calculated cells, calculated members, and actions

❑ Creating virtual and linked cubes

❑ Creating cube partitions

Note that there are various sections of this chapter that are best understood with a knowledge of MDX statements. If you do not understand MDX statements, it is advisable that you refer to Chapters 10 and 11 of this book. MDX is a language used to query an OLAP database, similar to the T-SQL that is used to query a SQL Server database. It shares the same basic structure and format as T-SQL, but has its own complexities due to the fact that we are dealing with a multidimensional system.

Dimension Editor

Though we have been using the Dimension Wizard to build all of our dimensions, notice that whenever we have completed building the dimension, the Dimension Editor appears. This is because the Dimension Editor is the main interface by which to manipulate and edit a dimension. The Dimension Wizard only pre-populates default property values based on the data that exists. In doing so, it protects the user from the complexities of the Dimension Editor. Often, the developer will need to set the properties for optimum design of the dimension for their environment. The Dimension Editor allows a user to manipulate the various dimension and dimension level properties that are attributed to a dimension.

Below is a screenshot of the Dimension Editor viewing the Store dimension within the MyOLAPDB OLAP database we created within the previous section.

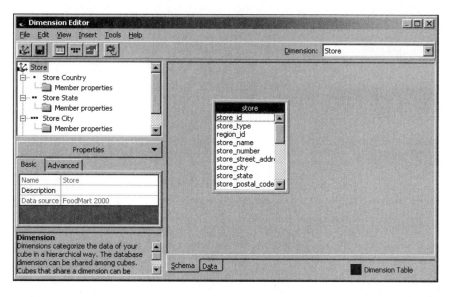

Dimension Tree Pane

The Dimension tree pane contains the dimension, its levels, and its member properties. In the above screenshot, the tree pane, in the top left section, show a tree of Store, Store Country, Store State, and Store City. You use this pane to perform the tasks of deleting a level, adding a new level, renaming a level, or adding member properties. The selection of the dimension or dimension level will activate the appropriate properties. For example, clicking on Store will activate its dimension properties, and clicking on Store Country will activate its dimension level properties in the Properties pane underneath.

In order to delete a member property or level, simply right-click the member property or level in question and click Delete.

To rename a level, you can click on the dimension level, not the dimension itself, and click Rename. Altering the Name property for that dimension level will also rename the level.

To build a member property, refer to the earlier sections in this chapter that concern the building of a regular dimension with member properties. For example, the member property Store Type was created under Store Name within the Store dimension.

The following illustrates the building of a new level:

❑ In Analysis Manager, right-click the Store dimension from under Shared Dimensions, and choose Edit.... This opens the Dimension Editor.

❑ On Store, right-click and select the New Level... option.

❑ The Insert Level dialog will appear. Click on the column region_id, and click OK.

This brings you to the Move Level dialog, informing you that the dimension level region_id has less members than the dimension level store_name. Click Yes, and the Dimension Editor will attempt to determine the correct location in the hierarchy for this level. It will perform this task by using the logic that, within the hierarchy, the levels above it have fewer members and the levels below it have a greater number of members. If for some reason, this logic is incorrect, you will need to drag-and-drop this level to the appropriate level within the hierarchy.

If you click on the Data tab and expand Mexico > Zacatecas > Hidalgo > 25 (for Region 25), you will see the two stores that belong to Region 25, namely Store 12 and Store 18.

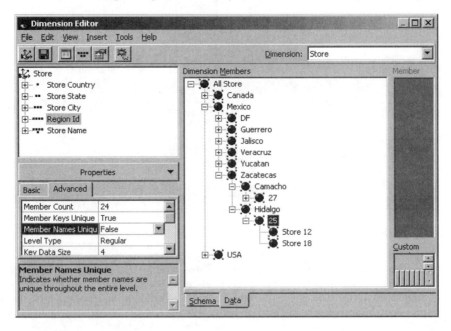

An extensive list of dimension and dimension level properties may be found at the end of this chapter.

Schema

The Dimension Editor Schema tab contains the schema of the dimension; it allows you to see the tables, views, and joins from the underlying relational database that are used in order to create the dimension. It is particularly handy for snow-flake schemas or parent-child dimensions where you will need to relate the various dimension tables or create a self-join, respectively.

The screenshot below shows the schema of the parent-child Account dimension from the Foodmart 2000 database.

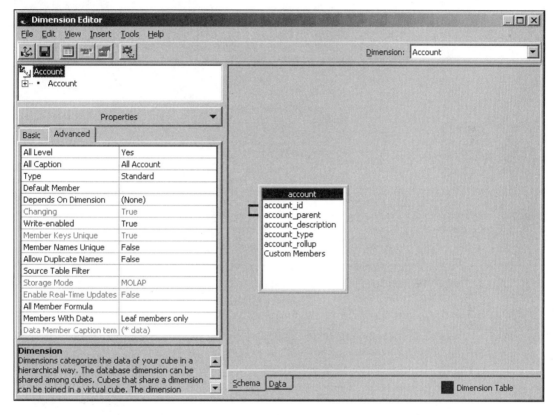

From the above screenshot, you can see the following:

❑ The source of the dimension is the account table

❑ The child node is account_id and the parent node is account_parent for this parent-child dimension

Data

From looking at the schema of the above parent-child Account dimension within the Foodmart 2000 OLAP database, click on the Data tab on the center bottom of the Dimension Editor. We can find more interesting information about this dimension from this pane.

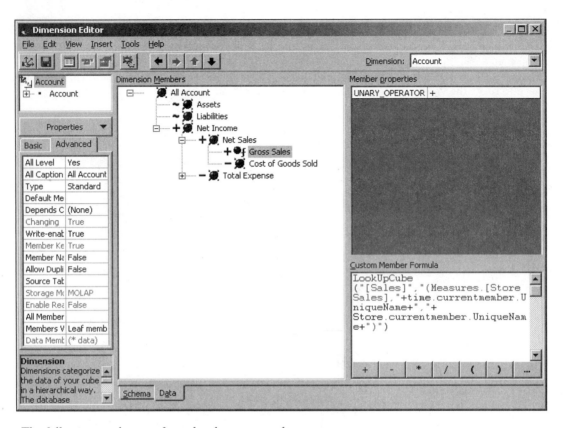

The following can be seen from the above screenshot:

❏ You can browse the hierarchy of the dimension.

❏ The Gross Sales member under Net Sales is a custom member formula, as indicated in the Custom Member Formula pane and the f symbol next to the member.

❏ The Member Properties pane indicates that this particular member formula uses unary operators. This pane can also indicate other member properties including custom members and the values of the member properties within the dimension member. For example, the Store Type member property is Deluxe Supermarket for Store 19 in Vancouver, BC, and Canada within the Store dimension.

Calculations at the Member Level

If you refer to the bottom-right corner of the Data tab, there is the Custom Member Formula pane. This pane allows you to create a calculation at the member level. These types of calculation are quite useful in that they allow you to create members that are based on other dimension members.

Consider a finance example, where you want to calculate the current year's budget based on the current year's actual expenses. If we want the budget to be 20% greater than the actual expenses, we can create a calculation at the member level so that the Current Year's Budget member is 1.2 times the Current Year's Actual member.

> **Note that calculations at the member level require that you are using SQL Server 2000 Analysis Services Enterprise Edition and that writeback to the dimension is enabled.**

Performing the following steps allows you to create a member level calculation. We will first create a Scenario dimension. It is a parent-child dimension due to the structure of the Access relational table below it; it contains `category_id`, `category_parent`, and `category_description` columns. The dimension contains the different types of budget scenarios, including Current Year's Actuals and Current Year's Budget. It is conceivable to build this dimension as a regular dimension, but because we are building a calculation at the member level, we need writeback capability. While this is the default mode for a parent-child dimension, a regular dimension would require this to be a ROLAP dimension in order to write back.

- ❑ To create the Scenario dimension, first expand the Analysis Manager pane, expand your server, expand MyOLAPDB, and finally expand Shared Dimensions. Right-click Shared Dimensions and choose New Dimension and Wizard. Though we are going to be using the Dimension Editor, laying the foundation using the Dimension Wizard is a lot easier than going to the Dimension Editor directly.

- ❑ Click on Parent-Child dimension: Two related columns in a single dimension table and click Next.

- ❑ Choose Category as your dimension table and then click Next.

- ❑ The member key is category_id, the parent key is category_parent, and the member name is category_description.

The Select advanced options dialog provides developers with advanced options that can also be found within the Dimension Editor under dimension or dimension level properties. We will detail these at the end of this section.

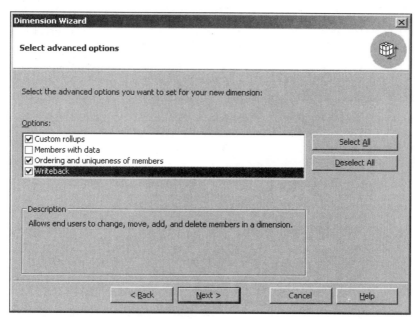

In order to build our custom member formula, we need to ensure that the Writeback and the Custom rollups checkbox options are checked. The Ordering and uniqueness of members box is checked as well in order to make it easier to set up the dimension, but is not mandatory. Click Next.

❑   In the Set custom rollups dialog, check the Enable custom rollups checkbox and click on the MDX-defined custom formula so that we can create our calculations at the member level using MDX definitions.

❑   When the Define Custom Member Column dialog appears, click on Create a new column and create the Custom_Member column. If the column already exists, check Use an existing column and choose the Custom_Member column from the drop-down box. Click OK and then click Next to continue.

❑   For the Specify ordering and uniqueness dialog, for the Order members by: choose <Name> and for the Names are unique among: option, choose Dimension members. Click Next.

❑   In the Set dimension writeback capability dialog, click the checkbox to enable writeback in this dimension and click Next.

❑   Finally, for the Dimension Name, type in Scenario and click Finish. Within the Dimension Editor, you can see how the choice of your options within the Dimension Wizard affects the properties within the Dimension Editor.

❑   Click on the Data pane to get a view of the Dimension Members. You will see the members Adjustment for Budget input, Current Year's Actuals, Current Year's Budget, and Forecast.

You will also see that when you click on any of the members, the Custom Member Formula pane to the right is not active. Furthermore, you will notice the message with the yellow background as below, indicating that you will first need to place this dimension into a cube and process it *before* you are able to modify it and create your calculation at the member level.

> Dimension writeback is unavailable until this dimension is included unmodified in a processed cube.

❑   Select Tools|Process Dimension, and choose Rebuild the dimension structure. Click on OK and the dimension should process quickly. Click Close.

❑   Close the Dimension Editor and open the Cube Editor for the Budget cube by right-clicking the Budget cube and choosing Edit... The Cube Editor will appear with the schema of the Budget cube. Within the cube tree pane, in the top left-hand corner, choose Existing Dimensions...

❑   The Dimension Manager dialog will appear, click on the Scenario dimension created, and click the > arrow to add this dimension into the cube. Click OK.

You should get the cube schema similar to that below.

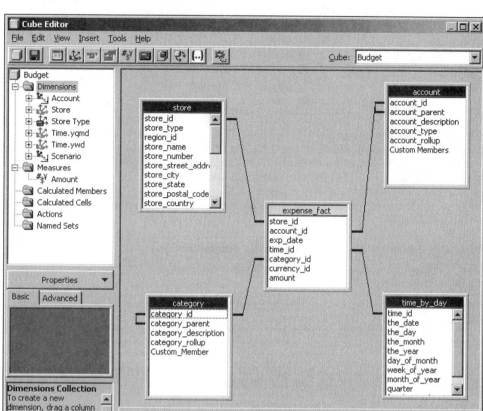

❑ Select Tools|Design Storage. Select MOLAP, click on Next, click on Performance gain reaches, and set the value to 90. Click Start and watch the Storage Design Wizard create around 39 aggregations taking approximately 0.1 MB of space with a performance gain of 91%.

❑ Click Next, and then click Finish to process the cube.

The cube will process; then click on Close to close the Cube Editor. If you look at the cube browser and you drag the Scenario dimension into the pivot, you will notice that the Current Year's Budget member is blank and has no values.

❑ To build our Current Year's Budget calculation (a calculation at the member level), go back to the Scenario dimension via the Dimension Editor. Click on Data, expand the Scenario dimension, and click the member Current Year's Budget. On the right, you will notice the Custom Member Formula is now active. Click the ... option to open up the MDX Builder dialog. Under the Data dialog, expand Level 02 and you will see the Current Year's Actuals member. Double-click this member and you will see the MDX statement appear in the MDX Expression dialog. To calculate the Current Year's Budget to be 120% of the Current Year's Actuals, simply alter the MDX statement so that it looks like below. Then click OK.

```
[Scenario].[Current Year's Actuals]*1.2
```

❑ Within the Data tab, you will notice an f next to the Current Year's Budget node representing formula, as you can see below.

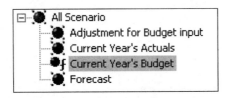

Select Tools|Process Dimension, and incrementally update the Scenario dimension so that it will now include the calculation for the Current Year's Budget. If you view the Budget cube and drag-and-drop the Scenario dimension, you will now see both the Current Year's Actuals and the Current Year's Budget; it is 20% higher than the Current Year's Actuals.

We conclude this section by detailing the options available on the Select advanced options dialog of a parent-child dimension.

Select Advanced Options Dialog of a Parent-Child Dimension

Note that these options are provided for parent-child dimensions, and regular dimensions have a slightly different set of options.

Option	Description
Custom rollups	This is a wizard form of the custom member and the custom members options dimension level properties. This will allow you to aggregate dimension members based on mathematical (unary) operators or MDX functions.
Members with data	This is the Members with Data dimension property. It allows you to associate data with non-leaf members of your parent-child dimension. For more information, please refer to "Data Members" within the SQL Server books on-line.
Ordering and uniqueness of members	This is a combination of the member keys unique, member names unique, allow duplicate names, and order by dimension level properties. These properties allow you to define the uniqueness of your data. This information will help Analysis Services build more efficient aggregates for the dimensions.
Writeback	This is the write-enabled dimension property that allows the user to write back any dimension member modifications directly to the source dimension table. This option is required if one wants to create calculations at the member or cell level.

Grouping Levels

Grouping levels is required in situations where you have a dimension that contains more than 64,000 members. In a MOLAP storage mode, Analysis Services can handle up to 10 million members (before switching to ROLAP mode), but it has a limit of 64,000 children members per parent node. This issue is often avoided by creating an artificial hierarchy; a level is placed above these members to create an artificial parent-to-child hierarchy. For example, with a customer's name, an artificial hierarchy could be that of:

```
Level 1:    A                B               Z
Level 2:    Adams,Atkins     Baker, Benson   Zolkov
```

where the bottom level is the customer name, but the level above it is the first letter of the person's last name. Building an artificial hierarchy such as this will allow you to control the children to parent ratio thus avoiding this problem.

Introduced in SQL Server 2000 Analysis Services, one can automatically have Analysis Services create this artificial hierarchy instead of creating it yourself. To illustrate Analysis Services building this hierarchy, let's continue with the example of a customer dimension.

❑ To create a shared dimension (so that you will be able to share this dimension with other cubes), open the Dimension Wizard, choose Star-schema: A single dimension table, click Next, and choose the Customer table. Click Next and then click Next again.

❑ For the available columns, choose lname (last name) and click the > arrow to bring the column over. Click Next and click Next again.

You will now see the Select advanced options dialog for regular dimensions, which we shall describe in more detail at the end of this section. For our purposes, simply check the Storage mode and member groups check box and click Next.

❑ Choose the Store as multidimensional OLAP (MOLAP), option and click the Create member groups for the lowest level, and click Next.

❑ For the dimension name, use Customer and click Finish. Now you are in the Dimension Editor again.

❑ Within the dimension tree pane, click on the lname level. In the dimension properties pane shown below, click on the Name property and change this to name.

❑ For the member key column and the member name column properties, change the properties to:

```
"customer"."fname" + ' ' + "customer"."mi" + ' ' + "customer"."lname"
```

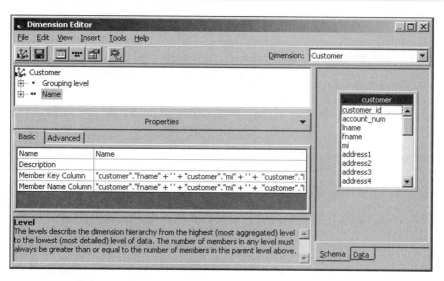

❑   Click on the dimension level grouping level and find the Visible property. Change this to False.

If you check out other dimension level properties, you will notice the Member Count property for the Name level is <6000 and the Member Count for the Grouping Level is 77. These numbers are small enough that a grouping level is not necessary. We are simply building this grouping level dimension in order to illustrate how to build a grouping level once you have dimensions with > 64,000 members.

❑   Save this dimension and process it.

Normally, you are able to see the dimension, but with the way a grouping level is built, you can only see the dimension after you process it within a cube. To do this, close the Dimension Editor, and create a new cube via the Cube Wizard.

❑   Choose Sales_fact_1998 as your fact table, click Next, choose store_sales, store_cost, and unit_sales as your measures, click Next, and finally include the dimensions Customer, Time.yqmd, Time.ywd, Store, and Store Type.

❑   For the cube name, use Sales 1998 and click on Finish. From the Cube Editor, click on Tools and click on Design Storage. Select MOLAP, click on Next, click on Performance gain reaches and set the value to 90. Click Start and watch the Storage Design Wizard create around 24 aggregations taking approximately 2.5 MB of space with a performance gain of 90%

❑   Click Next and click Finish to process the cube.

❑   You will now be able to browse your Sales 1998 cube and determine the sales made in 1998 per customer.

Note that this example was designed to allow the reader to understand how to work with grouping levels. In this particular case, there was <6000 customers and thus did not require the use of a grouping level. In many OLAP data warehouse scenarios, you will have millions of customers and you may not want to place all of these customers within one dimension.

Extremely large dimensions, regardless of ROLAP or grouping levels, can take a long time to process and may be too large to query against.

Remember that the purpose of OLAP is to provide end users with summary aggregations, in order to gain a high-level understanding of their data. For situations where you want to go down to the detail data, such as account names within bank, you may want use the drillthrough option within Analysis Services (discussed in *Drillthrough* section later in the chapter). This will allow you to view summary data within an OLAP cube and then drillthrough to the raw detail data of the relational data source making up these summary aggregations.

We conclude this section by detailing the options available on the Select advanced options dialog for regular dimensions.

Advanced Options of a Regular Dimension

Option	Description
Changing Dimension	This is a wizard form of the changing dimension properties – it optimizes a dimension for frequent changes to its data within the relational data source. Regular dimensions that are changing are required to be ROLAP; parent-child and virtual dimensions are changing in nature.

Option	Description
Ordering and uniqueness of members	This is a combination of the member keys unique, member names unique, allow duplicate names, and order by dimension level properties. These properties allow you to define the uniqueness of your data – this information will help Analysis Services build more efficient aggregates for the dimensions.
Storage mode and member groups	This property is a combination of the storage mode dimension property and the grouping dimension level property. If your dimension has greater than 10 million members, this dialog will allow you to set the storage mode to ROLAP. Meanwhile, if there are less than 10 million but greater than 64,000 members, this will tell Analysis Services to automatically create a grouping level above the lowest level.

Cube Editor

The Cube Editor's relationship to the cubes is analogous to that of the Dimension Editor's relationship to the dimensions. The Cube Editor allows you to manipulate, at a detail level, the properties that affect the structure of a cube. Below is a screenshot of the Cube Editor viewing the Sales 1998 cube recently created:

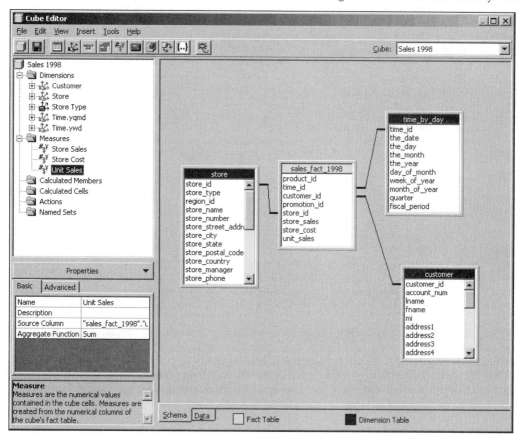

Schema Tab

The Schema tab of the Cube Editor provides the user with the view of the underlying tables used to create the OLAP cube. It allows you to insert, remove, and rename tables, change their alias, and/or browse their underlying data; you only need to right-click the objects in order to manipulate them. This pane allows you to control the schema of the relational tables that make up your OLAP cube.

Looking at the Sales 1998 cube, the schema is derived from the fact table sales_fact_1998 (which is in yellow) and the dimension tables customer (customer), time_by_day (time.yqmd, time.ywd), and store (store, store type) for their respective dimensions. Similar to dimensions, the fact tables do not need to be tables, they can also be SQL views. The advantage of views is that you will be able to control what data goes into the cube from the relational data source. A disadvantage of using this methodology, though, is the need to manipulate the relational data source every time before processing. For example, if your view is only looking at one day of data, you will need to modify the view before you are about to process a different day of data.

As you may note, the black lines between the tables represent the inner join between the dimension table and the fact table, such as:

```
"customer"."customer_id" = "sales_fact_1998"."customer_id",
"store"."store_id" = "sales_fact_1998"."store_id"
"time_by_day"."time_id" = "sales_fact_1998"."time_id"
```

As can be inferred from this design, within an OLAP cube, the relationship between its dimension tables and its fact table, or for that matter any table with any other table, is through an INNER JOIN statement. If you want to have a different relationship between your tables, such as LEFT OUTER JOIN or RIGHT OUTER JOIN, which may occur often within a SQL environment, you will need to:

❏ Go to your relational database and create a view between these two tables with their relationship, such as a LEFT OUTER JOIN.

❏ Go back to your OLAP database and refresh the data source (expand Analysis Manager, expand your server, expand Data Sources, right-click your data source MyOLAPDB, and click on Refresh). This will tell the Analysis Manager to update its own cache with any new objects recently added to the data source.

❏ Open up the Cube Editor of your cube (for example Sales 1998) and right-click the fact table (in this case sales_fact_1998) and use the replace method. This will allow you to replace your fact table with your fact view.

INNER JOIN statements can represent many relationships within an OLAP cube. For dimension members that are empty or NULL, choose some specific key value that will represent empty or NULL within the dimension table. Therefore, facts associated with an empty or NULL member can still have their foreign key columns populated with some key value. By ensuring referential integrity between the tables and utilizing key values so that the tables are joined by non-NULL values, all the rows within the fact table will be utilized when creating its aggregations.

As well, this cube has a star-schema design; there is one hop between the fact and dimension tables. But, you can build OLAP cubes using a snowflake design (refer to the HR cube within the Foodmart 2000 OLAP database) as well. With SQL Server 2000 Analysis Services, processing of snow flake designed OLAP cubes is more efficient than its predecessor (SQL Server 7.0 OLAP Services). Choosing a star-schema vs. snow-flake design is more of a matter for the database developer than of OLAP cube processing efficiencies.

Data Tab

The Data tab is also known as the Cube Browser. It provides users with the ability to pivot through the data within an OLAP cube. In addition, it provides users with the ability to perform actions and drillthrough to the detail data (more on this later in this section). In addition, if you right-click various cells or dimensions within the browser you will be able to view cell properties or dimension member properties (depending on what you click). It has drag-and-drop functionality that will allow you to drag and drop dimensions within the pivot providing users with multiple views and slices of the data. As well, it provides drill-up and drill-down functionality so you can go up and down a dimension hierarchy when viewing your data.

Cube Pane

The Cube pane contains the various structures that can be stored within a cube:

❑   Dimensions

❑   Measures

❑   Calculated Members

❑   Calculated Cells

❑   Actions

❑   Named Sets

Clicking on each structure will activate its own Properties pane underneath and provide the user with access to the various properties for the chosen structure.

Dimension

By clicking on a dimension within the Cube pane, you will be able to:

❑   Create a new dimension – this will open up the Dimension Wizard, allowing you to create a new dimension

❑   Add an existing dimension – this will open up the Dimension Manager, allowing you to add an existing dimension to this cube

By clicking on the dimension itself, you will be able to also perform the following tasks:

❑   Remove a dimension – this will activate a dialog confirming that you want to remove the selected dimension from the cube

❑   Browse a dimension – this will open up the Dimension Browser and allow you to browse the dimension data and hierarchy

Note that you will need to reprocess the cube completely if you have created, added, or removed a dimension within the cube. You have to do this because you have altered the structure of the OLAP cube, and any alteration to an OLAP cube requires the full reprocessing of the cube.

If you click on the dimension, such as the Store dimension in the Sales 1998 cube through the Cube Editor, you will notice that you have some additional options provided to you as seen in the screenshot overleaf:

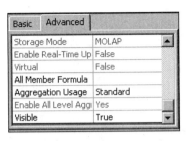

Option	Description
All Member Formula	Similar to the **All Member Formula** dimension property listed in the table of dimension properties in the previous section, this property allows you to specify an MDX formula to replace the rollup of dimension member's value.
Aggregation Usage	This property defines how the dimension is treated when aggregations are being built during the **Design Storage** stage. You have the choice of Analysis Services performing this task by default (standard) or specifying top level, bottom level, top and bottom level, and custom. Switching this property to custom will activate the **Enable All Level Aggregations** property (you can set this to **Yes** or **No**). During the **Design Storage** stage, Analysis Services will try to take into account all dimensions and their members when building the aggregations that eventually will be processed. Altering these properties will tell Analysis Services whether to include only a specific set of members when building these aggregations. For example, if you choose **Top Level only** for the **Store** dimension, Analysis Services will only build aggregations for the **Store Country** level. If you know that some levels of a dimension are not going to be accessed often, then modifying this property will help Analysis Services build more efficient aggregations for the dimensions and members.
Visible	This property sets the visibility of the dimension to the end user within the cube. If this property is set to false, the dimension can still be used in other MDX statements and in calculated members.

Measures

Using the Cube Wizard for both the **Budget** and **Sales 1998** cubes, you had created measures by simply specifying the columns by which you wanted to perform the measurement against. By default, Analysis Services applies the **Aggregate Function** of **SUM** against that column – in other words, a sum is calculated based on the rows within the table grouped by the dimensions included within the cube.

There are other measures that you can specify:

Measure	Description
SUM	The default aggregate function. This sums all of the rows for the specified column grouped by the dimensions specified within the cube.

Measure	Description
COUNT	Performs a count of all of the rows for the specified column grouped by the dimensions specified within the cube.
MIN	Calculates the minimum of all of the rows for the specified column grouped by the dimensions specified within the cube.
MAX	Calculates the maximum of all of the rows for the specified column grouped by the dimensions specified within the cube.
DISTINCT COUNT	Introduced in SQL Server 2000 Analysis Services, this aggregate function will perform a distinct count of a particular column. This measure is extremely handy, but Analysis Services stores its aggregates for this measure differently. It must store all of the distinct values of the column in order to ensure integrity. Only one distinct count measure can be stored within a cube, and it is recommended that you place a distinct count measure within its own cube due to the way the aggregates are stored.

Click on any measure (for example, Store Sales) within any cube (Sales 1998), and you will be able to access the following properties:

Basic Properties

To access these, click on the Basic tab of the Properties pane within the Cube Editor.

Option	Description
Name	Name of the measure
Description	Description of the measure
Source Column	The source column of the measure; for the Store Sales measure, the source column is sales_fact_1998.store_sales
Aggregate Function	One of the above five listed aggregate functions; in the case of Store Sales, this property is set to SUM

Advanced Properties

To access these, click on the Advanced tab of the Properties pane within the Cube Editor.

Option	Description
Data Type	This is the data type of the actual column itself. For example, the data type of the sales_fact_1998.store_sales column is double.
Display Format	Similar to that of data type, except this is the data type by which to display the data. For example, you can alter this property from is current setting of Standard to Currency for all three Sales 1998 measures so that the cube is now displaying its measure in dollar values. This type of alteration does not require you to reprocess the cube.
Visible	This measure can be either visible or non-visible. They can still be used in other MDX statements and/or calculated members.

A measure that may be interesting to users is the count of products sold during 1998. The Sales 1998 cube, and its counterpart Access fact table contains distinct product_id values of the products sold. Therefore it is possible to determine the number of products sold by each store, store type, or to each customer. To build this measure, do the following:

❑ From the Sales 1998 cube editor, right-click the Measures structure and click New Measure...

❑ The Insert Measure dialog will appear and provide you with a choice of columns that exist in the Sales_fact_1998 fact table. Click on product_id and click OK.

❑ Ensure that Product ID is still highlighted, and click on the Basic tab within the Properties Pane.

❑ Change the name to Product Count and change the Aggregate Function to Count.

❑ Click on Save. Adding a new measure to a cube changes the structure of a cube, therefore you will be required to fully re-process the cube.

❑ From the Cube Editor, select Tool|Design Storage. Select MOLAP, click on Next, click on Performance gain reaches and set the value to 90. Click Start and watch the Storage Design Wizard create around 24 aggregations taking approximately 3.0 MB of space with a performance gain of 90%.

Click Close and now you will be able to view the cube and its data when you click on the data tab. Dragging the Store type virtual dimension into the rows section of the pivot will result in the view below.

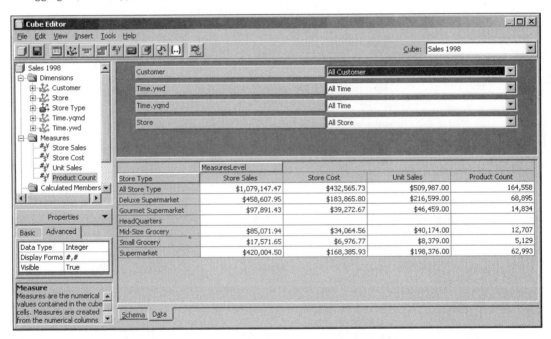

As you can see from the above view, the new Product Count measure has been added to the data view and, if you performed the display format property change indicated earlier, the $ symbols will have been automatically added on to the other three measure indicating their dollar values.

Calculated Members

Calculated members are similar to members within an MDX statement. They are member statements created by MDX that are stored directly within the cube. Only the statement is stored within the cube, with the values being calculated at query time. The actual value is not actually stored within the OLAP cube. This is similar to the idea of building a view within a relational database, where the table actually stores the facts, but the view is simply a stored SQL statement that queries the tables underneath it. If there are various calculations that you are consistently performing, instead of creating an MDX statement each time, you can create a calculated member based on the cube's measures and/or dimensions so that it is now accessible by all of your OLAP querying mechanisms.

Continuing with the Sales 1998 example, it currently contains measures for the Store Sales and the Store Cost. Suppose we wanted to calculate the Store Profit by simply subtracting the Store Cost from the Store Sales. This can be done by creating a Store Profit calculated member, which we shall now do.

❑ Within the Sales 1998 Cube Editor, right-click Calculated Members and click New Calculated Member...

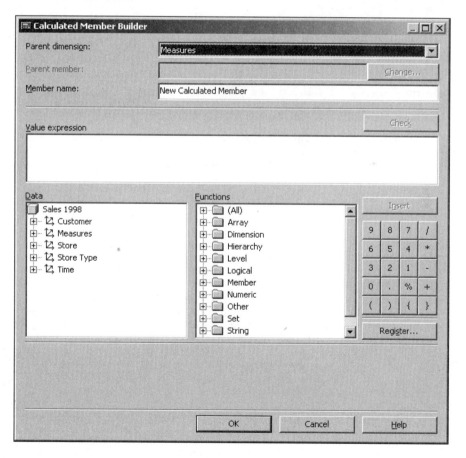

❑ The **Calculated Member Builder** dialog will appear. It allows you to define the parent dimension, provides you with functions and the cube's dimensions, and allows you to register external function libraries for the purpose of building the MDX required for a calculated member Place the MDX statement, below, into the **Value Expression** dialog. Its default parent dimension of **Measures** is correct.

```
[Measures].[Store Sales]-[Measures].[Store Cost]
```

❑ For the **Member Name**, type in **Store Profit** and click **OK**.

You have now created the calculated member **Store Profit**. If you click the **Data** tab within the Cube Editor, you will see the calculated member added to the data pivot:

	MeasuresLevel	
Store Type	Product Count	Store Profit
All Store Type	164,558	$646,581.74
Deluxe Supermarket	68,895	$274,742.15
Gourmet Supermarket	14,834	$58,618.76
HeadQuarters		
Mid-Size Grocery	12,707	$51,007.38
Small Grocery	5,129	$10,594.88
Supermarket	62,993	$251,618.57

You have access to the following properties.

Basic Property	Description
Name	The name of the calculated member, in this case **Store Profit**.
Parent Dimensions	This calculated member is based on the **Measures** dimension; hence the parent of the calculated member is **Measures**. Note, you can build calculated members based on any dimension within the cube.
Parent Member	In some cases, the calculated member may be based on a specific member. If so, the **Parent Member** value will be specified with this property. This property is typically populated when your calculated member is based on a dimension and you want the calculated member to fit within the hierarchy of the dimension.
Non Empty Behavior	In the case of a non-empty MDX statement (where only non-empty rows are shown the final output), this property allows you to specify the value of the calculated member if it is empty. In our case of the **Store Profit** calculated member, you will be given the choices of the other existing measures. This option is not provided in the case of the parent dimension being a dimension, as opposed to a measure.
Value	This is the MDX expression used to calculate **Store Profit**. It is the same MDX statement specified within the above Calculated Member Builder.

Advanced Options	Description
Visible	A Boolean value set to `True` or `False`. This value determines whether the calculated member is visible within the cube.

Advanced Options	Description
Solve Order	When Analysis Services is calculating the values of the calculated members at query time, the **Solve Order** property indicates the order in which these members need to be calculated. This is because we can include one or more calculated members in another, therefore the order of calculation is crucial.
Format String	This is the display format of the calculated member, similar to the **display format** property for measures, this property allows you to choose the format of your calculated member.
Other display formats	The additional properties are **ForeColor**, **BackColor**, **FontName**, **FontSize**, and **FontFlags**. These properties allow you to preset the visual display of any calculated members.

As noted above, calculated members do not actually take any space within the cube, as the only thing stored is the MDX expression and its values are calculated at query time. Therefore, you may add calculated members to a cube without the worry of reprocessing the cube, though there may be some minor query performance degradation.

Calculated Cells

Calculated cells are similar to calculated members in that they are MDX expressions that are calculated at query time. Calculated cells are different in that you can specify this MDX expression to be valid only for a specific subset of cells or a single cell.

Continuing with our **Sales 1998** example, click on the **Data** tab of this cube within the Cube Editor. Drag and drop the dimensions **Store** and **Store Type** so that you get the view below:

		MeasuresLevel	
+ Store Country	Store Type	Store Sales	Store Cost
	All Store Type	$1,079,147.47	$432,565.73
	Deluxe Supermarket	$458,607.95	$183,865.80
	Gourmet Supermarket	$97,891.43	$39,272.67
All Store	HeadQuarters		
	Mid-Size Grocery	$85,071.94	$34,064.56
	Small Grocery	$17,571.65	$6,976.77
	Supermarket	$420,004.50	$168,385.93
	All Store Type	$98,045.46	$39,332.57
	Deluxe Supermarket	$77,931.17	$31,264.38
	Gourmet Supermarket		
+ Canada	HeadQuarters		
	Mid-Size Grocery	$20,114.29	$8,068.20
	Small Grocery		
	Supermarket		

Suppose we want to state that the store cost for the Deluxe Supermarket is also the store cost for the Headquarters located in Canada; we will use the business example of a headquarters that was established in 1998 within Canada, but has not been added to the SQL database. Therefore, this scenario would specifically affect the following within the cube:

❏   Store Country of Canada

❏   Store Type of Headquarters

❏   time of 1998 (regardless of hierarchy)

❏   the measure Store Cost

To create the above calculated cell:

❏   Right-click Calculated Cells and click on New Calculated Cells... The Calculated Cells Wizard will appear.

❏   We will define our calculation subcube (an MDX statement that defines a set of cells within the OLAP cube to be used for calculated cells calculation) based on the above requirements:

❏   Measures: click the option a single measure, and click on Store Cost

❏   Customer: click the option a single member, and click on All Customer

❏   Store: click the option a single member, and click Canada

❏   Store Type: click the option a single member, and click Headquarters

❏   Time.yqmd: click the option a single member, and click 1998

❏   Time.ywd: click the option a single member, and click 1998

❏   Click Next and you will be given the option to define the calculation condition (optional). This option allows you to apply this calculation to all members within the subcube specified above, or you may enter a MDX statement here to further filter the subcube. Click Next.

❏   For the MDX Expression, simply enter [Store Type].[Deluxe Supermarket]. This is a rather simplistic MDX statement and, frankly, you can place some pretty complex MDX statements here to apply to a subcube. For the purposes of our scenario, all you want to do is to have the Store Type Headquarters (for Canada) equal to the Store Type Deluxe Supermarket (for Canada). Click Next.

❏   For the name, use Canada HQ 1998 Store Cost and click Finish.

If you view the data by clicking on the Data tab within the Cube Editor, you will now see the value $31,264.38 at row Canada, Headquarters, under the measure Store Cost. You will notice also the properties accessible by the Properties pane.

Basic	Advanced	
Name	Canada HQ 1998 Store Cost	
Description		
Calculation Subcube	{[Measures].[Store Cost]}, {[Customer].[All Customer]}, {[Store].[Store Country].&[Ca	
Calculation Condition		
Calculation Value	20000	

The following properties are accessible:

Basic Options

❏   Name: This is the name Canada HQ 1998 Store Cost recently specified.

❏   Description: If you would like to describe this particular calculated cell, you can place this description within this property.

❑ Calculation Subcube: Above, we used the Calculated Cells Wizard to specify the requirements for our subcube. This property field contains the equivalent MDX statement used to create this subcube.

```
{[Measures].[Store Cost]}, {[Customer].[All Customer]}, {[Store].[Store
Country].&[Canada]}, {[Store Type].[Store Type].&[HeadQuarters]},
{[Time].[yqmd].[Year].&[1998]}, {[Time].[ywd].[Year].&[1998]}
```

❑ **Calculation Condition:** This is the above specified calculation condition dialog within the Calculated Cells Wizard. Instead of necessarily specifying the MDX statement within the wizard, you can specify a statement to further slice the subcube.

❑ **Calculation Value**: This is the MDX statement used to calculate the values for the subcube specified above. Because our requirements are so stringent that it affects only one cell, we need only to place the value [Store Type].[Deluxe Supermarket].

Advanced Options

Basic	Advanced	
Disabled	False
Visible	True
Solve Order	0
Format String	$##,###.00
ForeColor	
BackColor	
FontName	
FontSize	
FontFlags	
Calculation Pass Number	1
Calculation Pass Depth	1

❑ Disabled: A Boolean value to specify whether this subcube and calculated cell are disabled.

❑ Visible: A Boolean value to specify whether this subcube and calculated cell are visible.

❑ Solve Order: Allows you to specify the order by which this calculated cell is solved when Analysis Services attempts to resolve this calculated cell during query time.

❑ Format String: This is the FORMAT_STRING MDX statement – for example, in order to have the value 20000 look like $20,000.00, specify the format string of $##,###.00 within this property. For our purposes, you need not populate this property.

❑ Other display formats: The additional properties are ForeColor, BackColor, FontName, FontSize, and FontFlags. These properties allow you to preset the visual display of this calculated cells

After creating your calculated cell and specifying the above format string property, you will have the view overleaf. If you compare the previous screenshot with the screenshot overleaf, you will notice in the highlighted section of the screenshot that the value $31,264.38 has been added to your data output.

This is an application of a calculated cell specific to a single cell. However, calculated cells can be a lot more generic; you need only to create a more generic subcube and possibly use additional MDX statements so that you may apply the usage of this advanced calculation to your environment.

| + Store Country | Store Type | MeasuresLevel | |
		Store Sales	Store Cost
All Store	All Store Type	$1,079,147.47	$463,830.10
	Deluxe Supermarket	$458,607.95	$183,865.80
	Gourmet Supermarket	$97,891.43	$39,272.67
	HeadQuarters		$31,264.38
	Mid-Size Grocery	$85,071.94	$34,064.56
	Small Grocery	$17,571.65	$6,976.77
	Supermarket	$420,004.50	$168,385.93
+ Canada	All Store Type	$98,045.46	$70,596.95
	Deluxe Supermarket	$77,931.17	$31,264.38
	Gourmet Supermarket		
	HeadQuarters		$31,264.38
	Mid-Size Grocery	$20,114.29	$8,068.20
	Small Grocery		
	Supermarket		

Since these calculations are determined at query time, there is no structural change within the OLAP cube that requires a full reprocessing of the cube.

Actions

Actions are properties of an OLAP cube that allow the end user viewing the data to act on their data analysis. For these actions to be accessible, the client that is connected to the OLAP cube must also support actions, such as the Cube Browser, or applications that use the COM interfaces of the SQL Server 2000 Analysis Services libraries.

Actions that are supported include:

- A URL that can be launched by a web browser
- An HTML script that can be viewed by a web browser
- A dataset that can be returned by an MDX statement
- A rowset that can be returned by an MDX DRILLTHROUGH statement
- A command line execution
- Some proprietary action

A typical scenario that can utilize an OLAP cube action involves the user drilling down the Store dimension from Store Country to the Store State. The user realizes that they want to do a quick search on that particular state or province. To provide the user with this functionality, we simply have to:

- Right-click Actions within the Cube Editor and click on New Action...
- Leave the target as A level in this cube, because we are providing the user with an action from the dimension level Store State. Change the dimension to Store and change the levels option to Store State. Define the target of this action as the members of the selected level. Click Next.
- Leave the type of action as a URL. Click Next.
- Within the syntax dialog, type the following statement, and click Next. Note that %20 represents a space within a querystring.

```
"http://search.msn.com/results.asp?q=" + [Store].CurrentMember.Name + "%20" +
[Store].CurrentMember.Parent.Name
```

❏ For the **Action Name**, type **Search MSN on** and click Finish.

Going back to the Cube Browser (**Data** tab within the Cube Editor), ensure that you have the **Store** dimension displayed within the pivot. Double-click the member **Canada** so that it expands to include the **Store State** level. If you right-click the member **BC**, in addition to the usual properties of **Drill down**, **Drill up**, and **Member Properties...**, you also have the option to **Search MSN on**.

		All Store Type	$98,045.46
		Deluxe Supermarket	$77,931.17
		Gourmet Supermarket	
	Canada Total	HeadQuarters	
		Mid-Size Grocery	$20,114.29
		Small Grocery	
- Canada		Supermarket	
		All Store Type	$98,045.46
		Deluxe Supermarket	$77,931.17
	+ BC	**Drill Down**	
		Drill Up	
		Member Properties...	
			$20,114.29
		Search MSN on	

Click this option and a browser window will appear, and you will be searching MSN for the keywords **BC** and **Canada**.

This is just a small example of the type of actions you can provide for your end users so that they can expand their data analysis. Other examples include giving the users the ability to drillthrough to the raw SQL data or giving them an additional data set to analyze based on the cell chosen.

Named Sets

A named set is a set of dimension members that can be stored and repeatedly used. It is a MDX statement that can contain measures, dimensions, and levels as well as mathematical calculations, numbers, and functions. It will be enclosed by braces – {}.

For example, if you wanted to create a named set that contained only the stores located in the states within the Pacific Northwest region of the United States and Western provinces of Canada, you could create a named set called **PacificNW Stores**. To do this:

❏ Right-click **Named Sets** within the Cube Editor of the **Sales 1998** cube and click **New Named Set...**

❏ You will see the **Named Set Builder** dialog; for the set name, type in **PacificNW Stores**. For the **Set Expression**, expand the Store dimension within the data dialog, and expand **Store State**.

❏ Within the **Set Expression** dialog, type in a {. Double-click the Store State member **BC**. The statement {[Store].[Store State].&[BC] will appear in the **Set Expression** dialog. Continue with this until you have included BC, OR, and WA, and then add the closing }.

```
{[Store].[Store State].&[BC], [Store].[Store State].&[OR], [Store].[Store
State].&[WA]}
```

❑   Click OK. As you can see within the cube pane, under **Named Sets**, you will see:

{..} PacificNW Stores

❑   Click on **Save** to ensure that the named set has been saved to the cube.

Note that the named set **PacificNW Stores** is only accessible through a client application that queries OLAP cubes using MDX statements. This particular form of a named set can be utilized by any client accessing the cube. A named set is simply an MDX statement set that can be repeatedly used and edited. It retains no structure, other than the statement itself, that allows client applications like the Cube Browser to connect.

To access a named set, you can use the **MDX Sample Application** (underneath the Analysis Manager within the **Start** menu). Connect it to your **Sales 1998** cube and type the MDX statement below.

```
select { [Measures].members, [Measures].[Store Profit] } on columns,
   { [PacificNW Stores] } on rows from [Sales 1998]
```

You will get the output below from the MDX Sample Application:

	Store Sales	Store Cost	Unit Sales	Product Cou	Store Profit
BC	$98,045.46	$39,332.57	$46,157.00	14,632	$58,712.89
OR	$128,598.5(	$51,512.78	$60,612.00	19,315	$77,085.72
WA	$267,696.4:	$107,196.0(	$126,287.0(	41,318	$160,500.4:

As you can see, by using the named set [PacificNW Stores], you will now get the stores within BC, OR, and WA. This type of named set is particular handy if you have a large number of members and you do not want to repeatedly recreate the MDX statement. Instead, the MDX statement can simply reference the named set.

Drillthrough

As end users are viewing data within a cube, there are times when they will want to know the raw data that makes up these aggregations. In other words, they want to see the detail data that makes up the aggregations that they are viewing within the OLAP cube. Of course, this is subject to the user being granted permission to this information; refer to Chapter 19 for more information on securing OLAP cubes.

Introduced with SQL Server 2000 Analysis Services, you can now provide end-users with drillthrough capacity provided that the detail data exists. Note that OLAP cubes built in MOLAP mode can operate without the underlying SQL data once the cube has been processed. In many enterprise level data warehouses, it may make sense to remove the detail data once the cubes have been processed. In order for drillthrough to work, you will need to ensure that the detail data used to process the cube is available.

Furthermore, for drillthrough to work, you need to have a client that can support drillthrough. Similar to **Actions**, clients such as the Cube Browser, or applications that use COM interfaces of SQL Server 2000 Analysis Services libraries will be able to drillthrough to the raw data from the OLAP cube to which they are connected.

In the screenshot from the *Named Sets* section above, we were able to see that the stores in the province of British Columbia (BC) had sales of $98,045.56. In order to provide users with the detail data information that lies behind this information, perform the following:

❑ Open the Sales 1998 with the Cube Editor, click on Tools, and click DrillThrough Options...

❑ Click the Enable drillthrough checkbox.

❑ For our purposes, click the following checkboxes: store_sales, store_cost, unit_sales, account_num, lname, fname, region_id, store_name, store_city, store_state, store_country, and the_date. As you can see, the drillthrough allows you to specify all four tables that have been used to make your cube. Click OK to get a Drillthrough Settings dialog box, which will inform you that these options are only effective after the cube is saved. Click OK. Click Save.

By performing these actions, you have now provided the user with the ability to drill through to the underlying detail data used to create the OLAP cube.

To view the data, simply activate the Cube Browser (the Data tab within the Cube Editor). For the purpose of the screenshot below, ensure that the customer dimension is on the rows and the measures are on the columns within the pivot. Right-click on the cell intersecting Store Cost and Aaron S. Young ($21.66) and click Drillthrough...

Drillthrough Data (first 1000 rows)

	store_sales	store_cost	unit_sales	account_num	lname	fname	region_id	store_name
1	4.59	1.836	3	77672170996	Young	Aaron	6	Store 20
2	1.92	0.96	3	77672170996	Young	Aaron	6	Store 20
3	11.58	3.5898	3	77672170996	Young	Aaron	6	Store 20
4	4.26	1.4484	3	77672170996	Young	Aaron	6	Store 20
5	1.92	0.8256	3	77672170996	Young	Aaron	6	Store 20
6	14.52	4.7916	4	77672170996	Young	Aaron	6	Store 20
7	3.88	1.9012	4	77672170996	Young	Aaron	6	Store 20
8	7.23	3.4704	3	77672170996	Young	Aaron	6	Store 20
9	7.68	2.8416	3	77672170996	Young	Aaron	6	Store 20

Virtual Cubes

A virtual cube allows you to bring specific measures and dimensions of other regular cubes into a logical cube. It is analogous to the idea of having a SQL view that includes multiple tables or views. If there is information that is located in multiple cubes, by building a virtual cube you can query this one cube instead of querying each cube individually.

When creating virtual cubes, it is important to note that you should only bring in the measures and dimensions of cubes that share the same set of dimensions. The aggregates between the different cubes are related by the shared dimension. If you attempt to bring in data from cubes that do not share some set of dimensions, you can still view the data from the two cubes, but there is no cohesion or relationship with the data viewed. A good example of creating a virtual cube using two different cubes can be seen in the FoodMart 2000 OLAP database Sales & Warehouse virtual cube.

Another method for building virtual cubes is to join similar cubes where one of them has a distinct count measure. As indicated previously, a distinct count measure performs the task of calculating the distinct count of a column and it is recommended that you place this measure in its own cube. For the example of the Sales 1998 cube, this would be used if you wanted to know the number of different customers that visited each store.

Build a Distinct Count Cube

First you will need to build a distinct count cube. Here are the steps.

- ❑ In the main hierarchy of the Analysis Manager, expand **MyOLAPDB**, expand **Cubes**, right-click the **Sales 1998** cube, and click on **Copy**.

- ❑ Right-click **Cubes** and click on **Paste**. It will provide you with a pop-up dialog to change the name of this new cube. Type in **Sales 1998 Distinct Customer** and click **OK**. Note, copy and pasting an OLAP cube does not bring across its data, it only copies and pastes the schema of the cube. If you are to look at the **Sales 1998** and **Sales 1998 Distinct Customer** cubes, they will have the same schema, but the latter will lack any design storage or data.

- ❑ Edit the **Sales 1998 Distinct Customer** cube using the Cube Editor. Within the **Cube** pane, delete all of the measures and create a new measure, **Customer Distinct Count**, based on the customer_id column. Remember to change the **Aggregation Type** of this measure to **Distinct Count**. You will also want to delete the **Canada HQ 1998 Store Cost** calculated cell and the **Store Profit** calculated member since they are no longer applicable. Click on **Save**.

- ❑ Click on **Tools** and click on **Design Storage**. Select **MOLAP**, click on **Next**, click on **Performance gain reaches** and set the value to 90. Click **Start** and watch the **Storage Design Wizard** create around 24 aggregations taking approximately 1.4 MB of space with a performance gain of 90%.

- ❑ Click **Next** and click **Finish** to process the cube.

Build a Virtual Cube with the Virtual Cube Wizard

Now that we have built the two sets of cubes, let's build the virtual cube joining them. Note, as with building a cube, you will first create the base structure of your virtual cube using the Virtual Cube Wizard. Having completed the base structure, you will then have access to the Virtual Cube Editor.

- ❑ In the main hierarchy of the Analysis Manager, expand **MyOLAPDB**, right-click on **Cubes**, and click **New Virtual cube...** In the main hierarchy of the Analysis Manager, expand **MyOLAPDB**, expand **Cubes**, right-click the **Sales 1998** cube, and click on **Copy**.

- ❑ Within the Virtual Cube Wizard, include the **Sales 1998** and **Sales 1998 Distinct Customer** cubes by clicking on > for those cubes and clicking **Next**

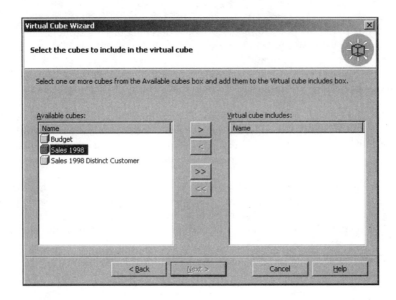

❑ Click on >> to include all of the measures existing in both cubes. Click Next.

❑ Click on >> to include all of the dimensions existing in both cubes. Click Next.

❑ For the name of the virtual cube, type in Sales and click on Finish to process. Note that, processing a virtual cube is different from processing a regular cube, as there is no design storage and virtually no space is occupied by the virtual cube. Processing a virtual cube is for the purpose of saving and indexing the schema.

❑ Click on Close for the processing window and you will see the Virtual Cube Editor.

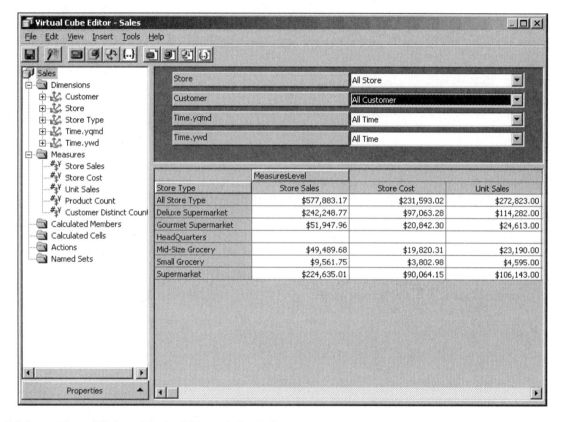

Editing a Virtual Cube with the Virtual Cube Editor

The Virtual Cube Editor is similar to its Cube Editor counterpart. It contains a Virtual Cube Browser and the Cube and Properties pane. It does not have a schema pane because the cubes, measures, and dimensions that are included in it define the schema of a virtual cube.

When you create a virtual cube, calculated members, calculated cells, actions, and named sets are not brought over from the regular cubes. In order to do this you can either create a new calculated member (calculated cell, action, or named set) or import it from your cube. To build a new one simply follow the instructions for each option as in the previous sections. To import the Store Profit calculated member:

❑ Right-click Calculated Member within the Virtual Cube Editor of the Sales virtual cube and click Import Calculated Member...

❑ The Import Calculated Member dialog will appear with the Store Profit calculated member. Check its checkbox and click OK. The calculated member is now included within the Sales virtual cube and you can see the addition of it into the Virtual Cube Browser.

❑ For the other advanced options (calculated cells, actions, and named sets), you need only to follow the same instructions as above.

You have now created the Sales virtual cube, which will allow you to relate multiple cubes into one logical cube thus requiring only one pivot or one query to view the data.

Partitions

Partitions allow you to organize the source and aggregate data of the cube Each cube automatically has one partition when it is first created, but creating partitions of data, similar to creating multiple tables by date for one fact within a relational database, allows you more control over each partition of data. This includes the ability to distribute the partitions to other servers.

If you expand the Sales 1998 cube and expand Partitions, you will see the primary partition, the Sales 1998 partition. In this particular case, there is only one partition that is used to hold the aggregations within the cube.

If your underlying relational database is quite large, it is to your advantage to partition your cube so that you will be able to process each partition instead of processing a cube against a large amount of data. If you find that you need to process a particular segment of data more times than others, instead of processing the entire cube, you can just design the aggregation level and process that particular partition. Partitions can be defined by any dimension that exists within the cube; commonly, partitions are created within a date range, using a time dimension.

To edit the primary partition:

❑ Expand the Analysis Manager pane, expand your server, expand MyOLAPDB, expand the Sales 1998 cube, and expand Partition.

❑ Right-click the partition Sales 1998 and click Edit.

❑ Within the Partition Wizard, click Next, and then select the dimension Time.yqmd. Within the Members pane, expand All Time, expand 1998, and click on Quarter 1. You will see within the Dimension pane the data slice All Time.1998.Quarter 1. Click Next.

Within this dialog, you can specify the partition type: local or remote. This feature allows you to specify whether this partition is to be located on the local server or on another OLAP server. Choosing remote allows you to distribute memory and CPU utilization to the remote server but does complicate administration. Archiving and restoration of an OLAP database does not include the remote partitions hence these partitions will require reprocessing after a restoration occurs. In this case, the option for remote has been disabled (only the local option is active). This is because the choice of local or remote partition can only be made when creating new partitions. Click Next

❑ Leave the option to Use the current set of aggregations. This tells Analysis Services to utilize the aggregations already built for this cube, instead of activating the Storage Design Wizard to create new aggregations. Check the Process the partition when finished checkbox and click Finish.

If you view the data within the Cube Browser, you will note that only data for 1998 Quarter 1 exists, as per your partition modifications above. To create a new partition to encompass more data:

- ❏ Expand the Analysis Manager pane, expand your server, expand MyOLAPDB, expand the Sales 1998 cube, and expand Partition. Right-click Partitions and click on New Partition...

- ❏ Follow the middle three steps from above, except choosing 1998, Quarter 2.

- ❏ For the partition Name, type Sales 1998Q2 and click the radio button Copy the aggregations design from an existing partition. This will activate the drop-down list that will allow you to choose the partition from which to copy the aggregations. Keep the Sales 1998 partition, click on the Process the partition when finished checkbox and click Finish.

By creating this partition, you will include data from 1998 Quarter 2 when viewing through the Cube Browser. As you can see from the tasks performed, you can manipulate the design storage and processing of each partition, therefore allowing you to have more control on the how the data is stored within each partition of your cube.

A few notes about partitions – it is advantageous to not have too many partitions.

When Analysis Services is attempting to render a query, it will take a longer time if it has to go across too many partitions. Therefore, when building your partition strategy, you will need to balance your processing needs against your query performance.

Furthermore, although you can physically delete the primary partition of the cube, namely the partition that has the same name as the cube itself, it is advised that you do not do this. Past experience has indicated schema and calculation issues when this is done.

Because you have built partitions now, when you attempt to process a cube, you can no longer perform this task for the overall cube. You will have to perform the task of storage design and processing for each partition individually.

Dimension Properties

Here is a list of the basic dimension properties. Note that for both the dimension and dimension properties, the property type is indicated below the property name. The different property types are:

- ❏ **Text:** The property value is a text field, which ranges from a description to a SQL statement.

- ❏ **Boolean:** The property value is a Boolean value (TRUE/FALSE).

- ❏ **Multi:** The property value is a drop-down box.

- ❏ **Values Listed:** Sometimes, the possible values are actually listed such as MOLAP/ROLAP or Automatic/None.

- ❏ **Integer:** The property value is an integer value.

- ❏ **Selection:** The property value requires that some selection (as opposed to a drop-down box) be made.

- ❏ **/Task:** This is indicated after some property value above such as Boolean/Task. This notes the fact that if you alter the first value (Boolean), there will be some task that will need to be performed.

Property	Description
Name *Text*	This is the name of the dimension and this property is determined at the creation of the dimension using the Dimension Editor or the Dimension Wizard (after which it becomes a read-only property). As noted previously, the names of OLAP objects are set once they are created. If you want to change the name of an OLAP object, it will require you to delete and recreate it, which often is not a viable option. For example, if you had created an OLAP cube that already contains a dimension, to rename that dimension you would have to delete the dimension from the cube, delete the dimension, recreate the dimension with the new name, place the dimension back into the cube, and then perform a full reprocess of the cube.
Description *Text*	Allows the user to specify a description for the dimension. This property is readily available for reading from the Analysis Manager meta data or from DSO if requested.
Data Source *Text*	As noted previously, all OLAP objects are dependent on some data source. The data source within the Dimension Editor is a read-only property that is also first created when using the Dimension Editor or the Dimension Wizard. To change this typically requires a deletion and recreation of the dimension as well.

The advanced properties are as follows:

Property	Description
All Level *Boolean*	This option indicates whether there is an All-Level member that is an aggregate of all the dimension members below it. Using the time dimension, its All-Level member is an aggregate of all of dates within the time dimension table. In the case of Foodmart 2000, this encompasses 1997-1998.
All Caption *Text*	When you create the above All-Level property, the name of this dimension member can be specified via the All Caption property, directly below the All-Level property. By default, Analysis Services will use the name All DimensionName; using the time example, it would be All Time.
Type *Multi*	This property provides client applications with the type of information contained within the dimension. Dimension types include standard (which is default), time, geography, and range to scenario, currency, and promotion. The Dimension Wizard will choose the appropriate dimension type when a user is building a dimension, but by default the value is Standard. For the purpose of our time dimension, the dimension type is Time.
Default Member *Text*	If a user queries an OLAP cube specifying the dimension but does not specify any specific member, this property will allow Analysis Services to specify a default member by which to query.
Depends on Dimension *Text*	This is a property that allows the user to specify that a particular dimension depends on another dimension. This property is useful for most dimensions in that it helps Analysis Services optimize aggregation design when processing cubes and dimensions. This is a required property for virtual dimensions. Recall, virtual dimensions are built on top of member properties from another dimension. For example, for the Store Type virtual dimension recently built, this dimension was built on top of the member properties from the Store dimension. Hence, the Store Type virtual dimension Depends on Dimension property is the Store dimension.

Property	Description
Changing *Boolean*	This property specifies that a particular dimension should be optimized for frequent changes. By definition, parent-child and virtual dimensions are changing dimensions; regular ROLAP dimensions can be changing dimensions as well. Although this property allows for more flexibility, queries against these types of dimensions are slower.
Write-Enabled *Boolean*	This property allows you to specify whether a dimension is write-enabled. A requirement of write-enabled dimensions is that they are a changing dimensions as well. By activating this property, writebacks to write-enabled dimension are recorded directly against the source dimension table. Note, this feature is only available if you installed Analysis Services 2000 Enterprise Edition.
Member Keys Unique *Boolean*	Also known as the AreMemberKeysUnique property within DSO, this property indicates whether the dimension member key is unique throughout the entire dimension. This property helps Analysis Services optimize the building and processing of the dimension. In the case of the time dimension, Member Keys Unique is set to False, because the member keys are not unique throughout the dimension. The member key for the Time dimension is the date field itself. There are multiple days per month (Day 1 exists for all 12 months), hence this property is set to False (by default when using the Dimension Wizard).
Member Names Unique *Boolean*	Also known as AreMemberNamesUnique property within DSO, this property is similar to the Member Keys Unique property except that it is specific to the dimension member name. This particular property is especially important in the context of changing dimensions because it is necessary to preserve the identity of members.
Allow Duplicate Names *Boolean*	This property is set to True or False determining whether multiple dimension member children under one parent are allowed having the same name. In the case of Time, this value is set to False; after all, you would not want more than one day within a month to have the Day value of 1.
Source Table Filter *Text*	This filter is basically putting a WHERE clause on your source dimension table. If there is some data in your dimension table that you do not want to include within the dimension itself, adding SQL statements to this property will allow you to exclude them without actually creating a new view or dimension table.
Storage Mode *MOLAP/ROLAP*	The storage mode can be set to MOLAP and ROLAP (ROLAP is an option only if you are using the Enterprise Edition of SQL Server). ROLAP dimensions allow you to take into account any changes to the source dimension table immediately, but have slower query performance. This can only be done for regular dimensions, and not for parent-child dimensions.
Virtual *Boolean*	By flipping this switch, it is possible to create a virtual dimension. Although this property exists to indicate whether the dimension is virtual or not, creating a virtual dimension also requires the activation of other properties including: Depends on Dimension (and references to its member properties), Changing is set to TRUE, and the Storage Mode to MOLAP.

Table continued on following page

Property	Description
Members with Data *Multi*	This option is available for a parent-child dimension. It allows you to specify what members can be associated with data within an associated fact table: leaf members only, non-leaf data hidden, and non-leaf data visible. In general, leaf members contain data from the underlying data source, while non-leaf members contain aggregations performed on child members. For parent-child dimensions, non-leaf members may also contain underlying data as well. By specifying non-leaf hidden or visible, you are specifying that a non-leaf member can contain data and that it overrides the normal aggregation behavior within a hierarchy.
All Member Formula *Text*	This property allows the user to specify an MDX query for the All Member member. Instead of rolling up the dimension members, the All Member will use the inputted MDX formula. It will override the calculation set up by the measure and instead use this MDX formula. More information can be found below referring to Custom Rollup Formula.

Dimension Level Properties

The basic properties are as follows:

Property	Description
Name *Text*	As opposed to the dimension, this particular value can be more easily changed in that you do not need to drop and recreate the dimension level if you want to rename it. Unfortunately, the same OLAP naming rules apply; you will have to fully reprocess the dimension and any dependent cubes once this change has been performed.
Description *Text*	Allows the user to specify a description for the dimension. This property is readily available for reading from the Analysis Manager meta data or from DSO if requested.
Member Key Column *Text*	The member key column is the column within the dimension table that describes the key for that member. In the case of the time dimension, the key column for the day dimension level is: Format("time_by_day"."the_date", 'yyyy-mm-dd') As noted in the case of time, the member key for a particular day is the entire date; that is the key of a particular day is the yyyy-mm-dd. But in many other cases, this member key is synonymous with the dimension ID of a dimension table.
Member Name Column *Text*	The member name column is the column in the dimension table that describes the member name. In the case of the time dimension, the name column for the day dimension level is: Format("time_by_day"."the_date", 'd')

The advanced properties are as follows; again, please note that some properties will reference MDX, which can be found in the next chapter.

Property	Description
Member Count *Integer*	This property contains the number of members within that dimension level. For the `Foodmart 2000` example, the day level contains 730 members, the 730 days that exist for the years 1997 and 1998. By clicking on an option box located in the property field, the Analysis Manager can determine the member count on its own. This property is important in that it will optimize the building of aggregations during processing based on the number of members that exist within a dimension.
Member Keys Unique *Boolean*	Similar to its dimension counterpart, this property indicates whether the level actually contains unique keys. All of the dimension levels must have a value of True in order for the dimension itself to be set to True. As noted previously, the keys of the time dimension cannot have unique member keys.
Member Names Unique *Boolean*	Similar to its dimension counter part, this property indicates whether the level contains unique names. The time dimension does not have unique member names; Day 1 exists across multiple months in multiple years.
Level Type *Multi*	This property informs client applications the type of level it is querying. This property is handy when it comes to time hierarchies; informing the application whether it is dealing with years, quarters, months, or days.
Key Data Size *Integer*	The size of the column in bytes; if the column was an Integer field , such as `DimID`, then the key data size would be 4. But, in the case of day level, the key data size is set to 20 (for `Char`). This value is determined based on the member key column property above.
Key Data Type *Multi*	The data type of column; if the column was representing an Integer field, such as a SQL Server `int` data type, then the key data type would be integer. Due to the way Analysis Manager builds the time dimension, the day level has a data type of `char`. This value is determined by the member key column property above.
Hide Member If *Multi*	These define different scenarios when you would like to hide a particular member. For example, if you had a hierarchy dimension that contained the type of products within a grocery store (produce, meats, desserts), and there was a store item (a node within that hierarchy) that had no name, this property would allow you to hide this member if you chose the Only child with no name option. In the case of a time dimension, the hierarchy is static and all of the data is predetermined so you would typically stick with the default of Never Hidden.
Visible *Boolean*	By default, for the time dimension, the value of this property is False. But, there are some cases where you do not want a particular level to be shown. The most common occurrence is the case of a grouping level (refer to Grouping below).
Order By *Key/Name*	When client applications query a dimension, the sort order of the dimension data is determined by the setting of this property. Barring queries that override the natural order of a dimension, such as `topcount` or `bottomsum`, this property will sort the dimension members by the key or by the name during processing time. When querying, the dimensions will be in the correct order when the data is returned. In the case that you have built a member property, you also have the option to organize your data by its member property.

Table continued on following page

Property	Description
Custom Rollup Formula *Text*	This property allows you to overwrite the default rollup of the values for that level. In the case of the day level of the time dimension, instead of rolling up all of the days (from 1997 to 1998), you can specify some MDX formula to replace it instead (for example last year of data).
	This concept is similar calculated members, in that there is an MDX formula that is used to calculate some particular value. The difference is that the values of a custom rollup formula are stored directly into dimension table.
	Because of this requirement, this option is only provided if you have SQL Server 2000 Enterprise Edition and have enabled writeback for the dimension. Note, this property cannot be used against a cube that contains a distinct count measure.
Custom Members *Boolean/Task*	Similar to custom rollup formula (which applies to all members of the dimension level), custom members can be created for individual members. The calculation of gross sales (based on the store and specified time frame) is an example of a custom member formula that is created within an account dimension that takes into account of expenses, assets, and liabilities.
Custom Member Options *Boolean/Task*	Though you may have set up custom members, you may want to set up calculation options for these custom members and subsequent unary operators (refer to Unary Operators below) to be active for specific levels.
Skipped Levels Column *Selection*	This option is available only for parent-child dimensions.
	Indicates the column that contains the number of levels between the parent and child node, excluding the parent and child nodes themselves. Using the above employee example, the number of levels between Sheri Nowmer and Rebecca Kanagaki is 0, while the number of levels between Sheri Nowmer and Joseph Thomsen is 3. If these positive integer values exist within your dimension table, you can use this option.
	This option is useful when you have a un-balanced hierarchy. For example, altering the example, let's have Joseph Thomsen report directly to Sheri Nowmer, but his level is equivalent to Harold Bauer and everyone working under Leda Witte. This additional column indicating the number of skipped levels between Joseph Thomsen and Sheri Nowmer will allow you to keep your hierarchy without filling in all the levels between the two.
Root Member If *Multi*	This property is only applicable to parent-child dimensions.
	Indicates the criteria by which members of the highest level are determined. Using the above employee example, Sheri Nowmer is the highest level because she has a NULL parent ID.
Grouping *None/ Automatic*	A limitation with Analysis Services is that it has a limit of 64,000 children members per parent node within a dimension. In the case of a time dimension, this is not a problem because you have at most 31 days per month – as in 31 children nodes per parent (month) node. But in the cases where some dimension members have no pre-defined hierarchy (for example zip codes), the dimension can only hold 64,000 members.
	To avoid this issue, one can build a grouping level above the dimension level that will hit this issue. It will automatically group the data of the level below it into distinct groups – the number of groups it will create is the square root of the number of members. So if you have 40,000 members at the time, it will create 200 groups. By creating these groups, now your dimension can potentially hold up to 12.8 million members.

Property	Description
Unary Operators *Boolean/Task*	Unary operators act only on one operand such as *, &, etc. These operators are used to create custom rollup operators. They are simpler than their custom member formulas counterpart, but utilize only unary operators or mathematical formulae for definition instead of MDX statements. The rules for a custom rollup formula apply as well.

Summary

This chapter has provided a general overview of building and administering OLAP cubes within Analysis Manager, and familiarizing you with the tools available to perform such tasks. To lay the foundations needed for OLAP deployments utilizing the Analysis Manager, we covered these topics:

❑ Creating an OLAP database and its data source

❑ Using the dimension and cube wizards to create OLAP dimensions and cubes (and all of their properties)

❑ Using the storage design wizard and processing cubes (and all of their options)

❑ Viewing the dimension and cube meta data, browsing dimensions and cubes

❑ Utilizing more advanced OLAP features, including calculated member formulas, partitions, usage-based optimization, calculated cells, calculated members, actions, and drillthrough

Data Warehouse

10

Introduction to MDX

With the introduction of the OLE DB Provider for OLAP (which enables access to multidimensional and tabular data) came **Multidimensional Expressions** (**MDX**). MDX is a multidimensional query language unique to Microsoft Analysis Services. MDX is installed when you install Microsoft Analysis Services and provides a powerful syntax and semantics for querying and manipulating data stored both in remote, server-based cubes, and in local cubes (local files with the .cub extension).

Analysis Services' functions provide the ability to query cube data, define calculated members, and build local cubes. These functions allows for interaction with the PivotTable service and other OLE DB providers to query the cube data and return meaningful result sets. MDX also allows you to develop your own functions that you can register and operate on multidimensional data accepting arguments and returning values in MDX syntax.

This chapter introduces you to the syntax and semantics of this language and to the powerful features it provides. The areas that we will cover in this chapter include:

- ❏ Using SQL when handling multidimensional data
- ❏ MDX and Schema
- ❏ MDX construction
- ❏ Calculated members
- ❏ Named sets
- ❏ MDX query syntax

Let's begin by taking a look at SQL.

How Good is SQL?

In the same way that the Structured Query Language (SQL) can be used to query data in relational databases and perform several types of operations on the data in these databases, Multidimensional Expressions (MDX), described in the specification for OLE DB for OLAP, can be used to provide similar functionality on multidimensional data. SQL queries always return two-dimensional result sets (that is, rows and columns), whether the data comes from SQL Server, Analysis Services, or some other SQL-supported data source. If you need to return multidimensional result sets using SQL, you need to play a number of tricks using views and the like. Even then, the job is anything but easy. It involves several steps of building temporary tables and views before you can reach your destined solution, which would still be returned as rows and columns. If you want to easily return multidimensional result sets, you have to use MDX.

Please don't conclude from this that you cannot use regular SQL to query multidimensional data. You can not only query data with regular SQL, but also execute some Data Definition Language (DDL) statements to create dimension tables or fact tables used in creating cubes. Actually, Microsoft added support for SQL in its data abstraction technologies (such as ActiveX Data Objects) to allow access to multidimensional data through these technologies by passing regular SQL statements. One thing worth noting in this regard is the introduction of the OLE DB provider for OLAP and ADO Multidimensional or ADO MD. The OLE DB for OLAP reference, along with the documentation for Analysis Services, discusses these issues in detail. Therefore, we will not cover them here, and if you want further information about them, you may refer to the documentation for Analysis Services.

Could SQL Tricks Do the Job?

As we just discovered, you can use regular SQL queries against the multidimensional database that holds the cubes and their data to return result sets for your reports. The question is "how useful are these result sets?" Moreover, if they are not in an optimal form, how can you make them as useful as possible? To illustrate this concept, consider the following example on using regular SQL queries with multidimensional data (stored in relational table structures). In the example, a query is required to return the total store sales by region and by product category. The schema we are using is shown in the following figure:

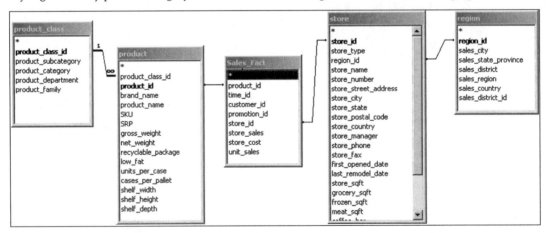

The query would look like this:

```
SELECT r.sales_region,
    pc.product_category,
    Sum(sf.store_sales) AS Total_Sales
```

```
FROM    Sales_fact sf
INNER JOIN store s ON sf.store_id = s.store_id
INNER JOIN  region r ON s.region_id = r.region_id
INNER JOIN product p ON sf.product_id = p.product_id
INNER JOIN product_class pc ON p.product_class_id = pc.product_class_id
GROUP BY r.sales_region,
    pc.product_category
```

The table below represents a partial result set of this query:

sales_region	product_category	Total_Sales
BC	Baking Goods	$2,965.62
CA	Baking Goods	$4,400.84
DF	Baking Goods	$2,592.14
Guerrero	Baking Goods	$1,319.59
Jalisco	Baking Goods	$99.87
OR	Baking Goods	$3,624.91
Zacatecas	Baking Goods	$4,466.08
BC	Bathroom Products	$2,478.10
CA	Bathroom Products	$3,761.57
DF	Bathroom Products	$2,408.50
Guerrero	Bathroom Products	$1,297.05
WA	Bathroom Products	$6,247.63
Yucatan	Bathroom Products	$1,916.51
Zacatecas	Bathroom Products	$3,591.43
BC	Beer and Wine	$2,575.52
CA	Beer and Wine	$4,016.16
DF	Beer and Wine	$2,245.23
Guerrero	Beer and Wine	$1,415.64
Jalisco	Beer and Wine	$101.47
Yucatan	Beer and Wine	$2,036.28
Zacatecas	Beer and Wine	$3,554.12
BC	Bread	$2,826.24
CA	Bread	$4,499.86
DF	Bread	$2,601.79

In the example above, the data returned from the query is represented in tabular form. A more useful form that would be even more readable and multidimensional would look like the next table. To reach this representation using SQL, we need to play some tricks in addition to applying some limiting assumptions as shown below.

The tricks start with building a working storage table from which the desired multidimensional representation will be built:

```
CREATE TABLE Total_Sales
         (Sale_Region          · Varchar(8000) NOT NULL,
          Baking_Goods           Money,
          Bathroom_Products      Money,
          Beer_Wine              Money,
          Bread                  Money)
GO
```

Notice that this working table does not have a primary key, and the product columns allow NULL. Notice also we have to know in advance the number of different products that we need to represent in the table. Adding a new product in the future will require this solution to be re-designed:

Total_Sales	product_category			
sales_region	Baking Goods	Bathroom Products	Beer and Wine	Bread
BC	$2,965.62	$2,478.10	$2,575.52	$2,826.24
CA	$4,400.84	$3,761.57	$4,016.16	$4,499.86
DF	$2,592.14	$2,408.50	$2,245.23	$2,601.79
Guerrero	$1,319.59	$1,297.05	$1,415.64	$3,432.00
Jalisco	$99.87	$12,452.00	$101.47	$2,344.00
OR	$3,624.91	$14,234.60	$231.45	$3,452.00
WA	$2,245.60	$6,247.63	$643.22	$2,321.00
Yucatan	$3,556.87	$1,916.51	$2,036.28	$3,443.25
Zacatecas	$4,466.08	$3,591.43	$3,554.12	$2,312.12

The next step is to fill the table we have just created with data relating to the different products using the following SQL statements. The first column, Baking Goods, will be calculated and stored in our Total_Sales table.

```
INSERT INTO Total_Sales (sales_region, Baking_Goods)
    SELECT   r.sales_region,
             Sum(sf.store_sales) as Baking_Goods
    FROM     sales_fact sf
    INNER JOIN   store s ON sf.store_id = s.store_id
    INNER JOIN   region r ON s.region_id = r.region_id
    INNER JOIN   product p ON sf.product_id = p.product_id
    INNER JOIN   product_class pc ON p.product_class_id = pc.product_class_id
    WHERE    pc.product_category = "Baking Goods"
    GROUP BY r.sales_region
GO
```

The second column, `Bathroom Products`, needs to be calculated and stored in the `Total Sales` summary table:

```
INSERT INTO Total_Sales (Sale_State_Province, Bathroom_Products)
    SELECT    r.sales_region,
              SUM(sf.store_sales) AS Bathroom_Products
    FROM      sales_fact sf
    INNER JOIN    store s ON sf.store_id = s.store_id
    INNER JOIN    region r ON s.region_id = r.region_id
    INNER JOIN    product p ON sf.product_id = p.product_id
    INNER JOIN    product_class pc ON p.product_class_id = pc.product_class_id
    WHERE         pc.product_category = "Bathroom Products"
    GROUP BY      r.sales_region
GO
```

The third column, `Beer Wine`, needs to be calculated and stored in the `Total Sales` summary table as well:

```
INSERT INTO Total_Sales (Sale_State_Province, Beer_Wine)
    SELECT    r.sales_region,
              SUM(sf.store_sales) AS Beer_Wine
    FROM      sales_fact sf
    INNER JOIN    store s ON sf.store_id = s.store_id
    INNER JOIN    region r ON s.region_id = r.region_id
    INNER JOIN    product p ON sf.product_id = p.product_id
    INNER JOIN    product_class pc ON p.product_class_id = pc.product_class_id
    WHERE         pc.product_category = "Beer and Wine"
    GROUP BY      r.sales_region
GO
```

And finally, the fourth column, `Bread`, needs to be calculated and stored in the summary table, `Total Sales`. As you can see, these types of calculations cannot be done simply in a View, but must be individually calculated and stored before they can be presented to the user:

```
INSERT INTO Total_Sales (Sale_State_Province, Bread)
    SELECT    r.sales_region,
              SUM(sf.store_sales) AS Bread
    FROM      sales_fact sf
    INNER JOIN    store s ON sf.store_id = s.store_id
    INNER JOIN    region r ON s.region_id = r.region_id
    INNER JOIN    product p ON sf.product_id = p.product_id
    INNER JOIN    product_class pc ON p.product_class_id = pc.product_class_id
    WHERE         pc.product_category = "Bread"
    GROUP BY      r.sales_region
GO
```

Of course, you might ask "What if one of the columns relating to the product categories includes NULL values?" In this case, we need to change the way we are building the summary table by using a query that selects all states/provinces with the help of outer joins, and using this query to populate the left column of the working table. The next step would be to use the same query in our statements that will populate the product category columns, to ensure that values are inserted properly.

In summary, it can be increasingly difficult and tricky to accomplish a simple task like the goal we were trying to accomplish, using only traditional SQL. Therefore, Microsoft introduced MDX as a powerful alternative that allows you to build, and work with, views like the one discussed above. In contrast to the previous SQL example, by the time you finish reading this chapter and the next chapter, you will see how the same problem can be solved with ease using MDX.

Basic MDX Definitions

The basic form of a simple MDX query is:

```
SELECT <axis_specification> [, <axis_specification>...]
FROM <cube_specification>
WHERE <slicer_specification>
```

The following is a brief explanation of each part of this statement.

The **axis specification** includes the number of axes included in the statement and the members of each axis. This information is defined after the SELECT keyword in the MDX statement. Each one of the `<axis_specification>` parts specifies one axis. The number of the `<axis_specification>` clauses included in the MDX statement defines the number of axes.

The following are definitions of terms used in this chapter. These definitions identify what is referred to as the MDX object model. This model is very rich and is based on the Analysis Services' schema. These definitions also are touched upon in several locations later in the chapter. A basic understanding of these concepts is very important. Therefore, unless you are already familiar with MDX grammar, you will need to study these definitions before proceeding to the next sections.

These definitions have to be considered in light of Chapters 3 and 4. In these chapters, the basics of multidimensional databases are discussed. The diagram opposite can be used to help understand these definitions. In this figure, part (a) represents a cube with three dimensions, product, time, and geography. A query against this cube yields a subset shown in part (b) of the figure. The subset includes only a few members of these three dimensions. The resulting cube is formed by the intersection of these dimensions.

Tuple

A **tuple** is a collection of members from different dimensions. For example, {Michigan, Q2} is a tuple formed by members of two dimensions: geography and time. The tuple {Michigan, Q2, food items} is formed by members of three dimensions: geography, time, and product. A tuple can have a single member, in which case it is called a degenerated tuple. For instance, {Michigan} is a degenerated tuple representing a member in the state level of the geography dimension. A tuple is the basic unit for forming an axis, as you will see in the next definition.

Axis

An **axis** is a collection of members from one or more dimensions organized as tuples. The axis is used to locate or filter specific values in a cube along the dimension members they represent. As an example, in a query returning sales by state and quarter for a product family, you may say a maximum of three axes can be used as a result of the query with each axis representing one of the three dimensions: geography, time, and product. If some of these dimensions are nested, the number of axes can be reduced, for example, nesting the geography and product dimensions results in an axis with tuples, consisting of a member of each dimension projected on the axis. On the other hand, the time dimension, in this case, is projected on the other axis (y-axis). This axis holds tuples representing time values such as first quarter of 1998, second quarter of 1998, and so on.

> Analysis Services supports a maximum number of dimensions in a cube of 128 in addition to one measure dimension. Therefore, the maximum number of axes possible in an MDX query is 129 axes, assuming no nesting of dimensions is taking place. However, in cellsets resulting from MDX queries, it is rare to have more than four axes at any one time.

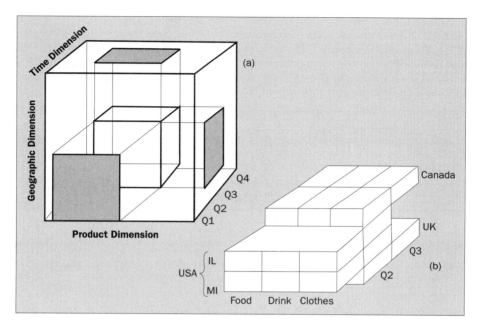

Cellset

A **cellset** is the result of an MDX query on multidimensional data. It identifies a resulting cube that is a subset of the original cube. In the above figure, the smaller cube shown in part (b) is a cellset representing the results of a MDX query. A cellset consists of a collection of axes, usually no more than four axes and typically only two or three, though these are not physical limitations (the limitation is 129 axes), merely recommendations. The figure shows that the resulting cellset can have up to three axes corresponding to the three dimensions of the set.

Cell

A cell is an object positioned at the intersection of axis coordinates. Each cell has multiple pieces of information associated with it, including the data itself, a formatted string (the displayable form of cell data), and the cell ordinal value. Each cell has a unique ordinal value in the cellset. The ordinal value of the first cell in the cellset is zero, while the bottom rightmost cell in the cellset would have an ordinal value of 15 as shown in the following diagram:

| 0 | 1 | 2 | 3 | 4 | 5 | 6 | 7 |
| 8 | 9 | 10 | 11 | 12 | 13 | 14 | 15 |

Slicer

Slicer dimensions filter multidimensional data. Dimensions that are not explicitly assigned to an axis are considered slicer dimensions and will filter with their default members. This dimension appears in the WHERE clause of the MDX statement. In the following figures, the slicer dimension is the geography dimension where a slice containing US data only is taken at the country level.

To make these concepts even clearer, let's look at the example below. The following table shows the results of an MDX query returning sales information for companies in the USA region over the quarters of 1997 and for several product families. This table represents the US slice shown in the figure shown previously. Don't worry for now if you don't understand the query and its specific parts yet, since this will be explained a bit further into the chapter. Also, note that the slicer in the query is represented in a bold font. The slicer shows that we only picked the USA country level member from the `Store` dimension.

```
SELECT
    {[Product].[Product Family].Members} on columns,
    {[Time].[1997].Children} on rows
FROM Sales
WHERE ([Store].[All Stores].[USA], [Measures].[Store Sales])
```

Total Sales in the USA			
Product Families			
1997 Quarters	**Drink**	**Food**	**Non-Consumable**
Q1/1997	$11,585.80	$101,261.32	$26,781.23
Q2/1997	$11,914.58	$95,436.00	$25,315.69
Q3/1997	**$11,994.00**	$101,807.60	$26,470.29
Q4/1997	$13,341.83	$110,530.67	$28,799.12

In this example, the measure dimension is the total sales figure. Two axes represent the time, and product dimensions. Additionally, only one member, USA, represents the geographical `Store` dimension. Therefore, the two dimensions, product and time, are axis dimensions, while the `Store` dimension is a slicer dimension. An example of a cell is the intersection of the x-axis (products) and the y-axis (time) for the members: Drink, Q3/1997. The data value of this cell (shown in bold face) is $11,994.00. The ordinal value of this cell in the resulting cellset is 6. The ordinal value is calculated by considering the first cell in the first row as number 0, and adding one to this number as we move to the right and to the bottom of the cellset.

MDX Basics

As we saw in previous chapters, a sales and inventory solution can be better represented using a multidimensional schema. The schema is composed of a set of cubes with each cube having measures and dimensions. You also saw that members of a dimension might be consolidated or aggregated along a hierarchy. Some dimensions, such as the time dimension, can have more than one hierarchy, allowing members to roll up in multiple ways. Each hierarchy has levels, and each level is made up of a set of members. Understanding these hierarchies is essential to understanding MDX, because MDX is built to deal with these hierarchies.

Notes on the Syntax

The MDX syntax, developed specifically for Analysis Services, is fully described in the OLEDB for OLAP specification. Originally developed for Plato (Analysis Services before Microsoft acquired it), MDX was the only "described" language for multidimensional databases. Due to the effort early in the product's life, MDX was further refined into a formal specification for querying multidimensional databases. Having such a specification gives developers a higher degree of comfort in using the language in their products and services. This comfort translates into more products, and of a higher quality, produced for the end-user marketplace.

On MDX Functions

Functions and their operators are largely optional in MDX. You may choose to include the whole function call and its operators if you want, but this will create long code lines, which, in turn, will make debugging and long-term support more difficult. Therefore, it is a good idea to leave out some of the unused operators (as defined by the function's specifications) when possible. Two representations are used for functions: the standard VB-style format of calling a function as `Function(arguments)`, and the object-oriented representation in which the function is called as a method of an object using the dot notation (`.Function()`). There are no standard rules for using these two representations, you just have to know which to use with which function.

An example on the first representation is the `Hierarchize(set)` function, which returns the given set after putting the members of its dimensions into hierarchical order. An example on using object notation for MDX functions is the `member.Children` method. This method returns a set of members from the next level down within a dimensional hierarchy.

One final note on MDX functions is that you do not have to provide parentheses for functions that do not take any arguments. For example, if a function does not have any arguments, it can be called as: `Call FunctionName` or `Call object.FunctionName`, and not as: `Call FunctionName()` or `Call object.FunctionName()`.

On Language Syntax

Let's take the simple query that retrieves the total sales for stores in the USA for the second and third quarter of 1998 (all products are included). Don't worry now about the syntax and knowing what everything is in the query. The remainder of the chapter covers all of these areas.

```
SELECT
    {[Measures].[StoreSales] } on columns,
    {[Time].[1998].[Q2], [Time].[1998].[Q3]} on rows
FROM SalesCube
WHERE ([Store].[States].[USA])
```

The different parts of this query are explained in the following diagram. Note that the diagram corresponds only to this sample query. Other queries could very well have additional parts, or miss some of the parts shown in the diagram.

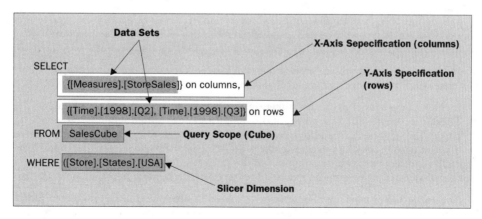

The following may be concluded from the syntax of the query above:

❑ You notice that MDX uses curly brackets { } to represent a set of members of a dimension or group of dimensions. In the query above, only the `time` dimension and the `measure` dimension are referenced.

❑ You also may conclude that axes are defined in the query by mapping dimensions onto the different axes. The first three axes of an MDX query are called rows, columns, and pages. If more than one dimension is mapped onto an axis, the axis will consist of tuples (elements) that include members of each of the mapped dimensions.

❑ The order of numbering of axes is columns, then rows, then pages. We will see what axes are in more detail in just a little bit.

❑ The `FROM` clause includes the name of the cube on which the query is based. Only one cube per query is supported in SQL Server 2000 Analysis Services.

❑ The `WHERE` clause includes slicer dimensions (see previous definition of a "slicer") by specifying the one member included in these dimensions in the query. In our example, the slicer dimension is the geographic location dimension. The only member included on the country level is "USA".

❑ Finally, notice some similarity between the general syntax of MDX queries and regular SQL queries. After all, the two kinds of queries use the clauses: `SELECT...FROM...WHERE`. However, as you learn more about MDX, you will also learn that it diverges significantly from regular SQL in many ways to allow it to support multidimensional data.

A Simple MDX Query

Just as the purpose of a regular SQL `SELECT` query is to specify a dataset (also referred to as result set or recordset), the general MDX statement also specifies a dataset (referred to as a cellset). However, in order for the MDX statement to do so, it must contain information about the following:

❑ **Scope (cube):** Each MDX query has a scope that is defined by one or more cubes. A cube is the basic component of the MDX statement and determines what kind of data the query is expected to return. A query that includes the `Sales` cube, for instance, is expected to return a dataset about the sales facts, such as profit, revenue, and cost, in terms of the sales cube dimensions (such as `Time`, `Store`, `Customer`, and `Product`).

❑ **Axes:** The number of axes is another part of the MDX statement that has to be defined. Each axis defines one or more dimensions along which data is to be aggregated. For instance, an axis that includes the `Time` and `Product` dimensions will result in aggregations along these dimensions with each tuple including members of the two dimensions.

❑ **Dimensions:** Dimensions are projected on the axes with the possibility of nesting them, which makes such dimensions and the level of their nesting another essential part of the MDX statement.

❑ **Included members of projected dimensions:** The whole dimension isn't included all the time. Therefore, the included members of the dimension or included member tuples are another part of the statement, in addition to the sort order of such dimensions. As an example, the time dimension may have year members for 1997 and 1998. If we only include 1998, then 1998 represents an included member of the projected time dimension. The member 1997, on the other hand, represents an excluded member of the same dimension.

❑ **Non-projected dimensions:** Sometimes you need to filter members of projected dimensions based on non-projected dimensions. This also makes such members from a non-projected dimension part of the MDX statement. This will become clearer when you read about filtering members, which is explained later in the chapter.

To better understand the concept of the axis specification, consider expanding the example illustrated in the previous table, to include another dimension nested with the product dimension, that is the customer dimension:

```
SELECT
    CROSSJOIN(
        {[Customers].[All Customers].[USA].[CA].[Altadena],
        [Customers].[All Customers].[OR].[Albany]},
        {[Product].[Product Family].Members}) on columns,
    {[Time].[Year].[1997].Children} on rows
FROM
    Sales
WHERE
    ([Store].[All Stores].[USA], [Measures].[Store Sales])
```

In the query above, we are using a function and two methods, specifically: CROSSJOIN, Members, and Children. MDX functions and methods are explained later in this chapter and in more detail in the next chapter.

The expanded example is illustrated in the following table:

Total Store Sales in the USA						
	Altadena			**Albany**		
	Product Families			**Product Families**		
1997 Quarters	**Drink**	**Food**	**Non-Consumable**	**Drink**	**Food**	**Non-Consumable**
Q1/1997	$96.00	$863.91	$229.06	$347.76	$3,149.80	$993.70
Q2/1997	$109.37	$1020.03	$264.27	$220.21	$1,854.00	$434.98
Q3/1997	$47.45	$1005.03	$266.03	$268.13	$2,957.79	$861.18
Q4/1997	$114.42	$1265.43	$304.59	$274.22	$2,144.47	$603.57

In this table, you can see that the horizontal axis (x-axis) includes two nested dimensions, customer and product families. The sales figures in the cells of the table show that the axis defines 6 tuples with each tuple having a member of each of these two dimensions. The tuples, therefore, look like this:

```
(Altadena, Food)
(Altadena, Drinks)
(Altadena, Clothes)
(Albany, Foods)
(Albany, Drinks)
(Albany, Clothes)
```

Therefore, you may think of an axis as a set of tuples set in a linear form. If the axis has one dimension, each tuple will include a member of the dimension. If the axis has multiple dimensions then each tuple includes a member of each of the nested dimensions. To represent the tuples illustrated in this paragraph in the MDX statement, you need to use the unique names of the members included within these tuples. Thus, they become:

```
([Customer].[All Customers].[USA].[CA].[Altadena], [Products].[Food]),
([Customer].[All Customers].[USA].[OR].[Albany], [Products].[Food])
```

and so on. If the tuple is composed of members of more than one dimension, you should enclose the tuple in parentheses. However, if a tuple is composed of members of only one dimension, you don't need to use the parentheses.

Let's now look at the vertical axis (y-axis). There is only one dimension included in the y-axis – the time dimension at the quarter level. The tuples of this axis include the members of the dimension included in the table:

```
Q1/1997
Q2/1997
Q3/1997
Q4/1997
```

Dimensions available in a cube are typically divided into two sets: axis dimensions, and slicer dimensions. Axis dimensions are dimensions for which data is retrieved for multiple members. Slicer dimensions filter multidimensional data, usually in the WHERE clause of the MDX query. The example illustrated in the table in the previous section explains this concept very well. Besides the measures, the Store dimension is the slicer dimension because only one member, USA, is included from it. As you can see, the components of the WHERE clause are surrounded by parentheses, even if only one element is defined in this clause.

The query discussed in this section is just the general form of a simple MDX query that is meant to familiarize you with the syntax of this language. MDX queries have many variations that add to their complexity. Some of these variations are discussed later in the chapter when more than one dimension and more than two axes are involved. Hence, before we discuss more complex forms of the MDX query, let's look at how OLAP schema is represented in MDX. Knowing this will help us to gain a greater understanding of the syntax of the more complicated MDX queries discussed later in the chapter, and in the next chapter.

MDX Representation of OLAP Schema

OLAP schema (commonly referred to simply as **schema**) includes information on cubes, measures, dimensions, levels, members, hierarchies, and member properties. All of these items are represented in some way or another in MDX queries. Therefore, it is important to study the relationship between OLAP schema and MDX queries, because this study will help us better navigate our multidimensional data.

Using Square Brackets

In MDX, you can refer to names of schema items in one of two ways, delimited and non-delimited. The delimiting character is the square brackets []. As you probably know, the naming of dimensions, cubes, measures, and member properties follows some rules, such as starting with an alphabetic character. Naming dimension level members, however, does not follow any such rules. If you choose not to delimit the names referring to schema in your MDX queries, additional rules may have to be fulfilled, even for member names. One important rule to remember is that you cannot have spaces in the name unless the name is contained in square brackets ([]).

It is good practice to always use square brackets to delimit member and other schema names. Name-specific rules still apply for cubes, dimensions, measures, and member properties. If the name of the member includes a square bracket, the escape sequence `[[` or `]]` should be used. For example, if the member name is `Chocolate Milk with [Marshmallows]` then the representation of this member in MDX queries is: `[Chocolate Milk with [[Marshmallows]]]`. A member could also be empty which is represented simply as `[ ]`.

Using the Period in Schema Representation

If an identifier has more than one name part, MDX uses periods to separate these parts. For example, to refer to the cheese level of the product dimension, you may write:

`[Products].[Food].[Dairy].[Cheese]`

This identifies cheese as a food product of the dairy category. The periods are placed between the brackets, and not within. Hence, `[Products].[Food].[Dairy].[Cheese]` is not equal to `[Products].[Food].[Dairy.Cheese]`. The latter represents a food product category named `Dairy.Cheese`, and not the cheese subcategory of the dairy category of the food product family.

Establishing Unique Names

When referring to schema names, it is very helpful to use unique names. For example, if you have a dimension called `Time`, you can refer to it directly by its name if the name is unique. Otherwise, you will have to identify it by the cube name, then its dimension name, with a period in between, such as `[SalesCube].[Time]`. For an even better example, when you refer to a level of the `Time` dimension, let's say the year level, specifically 1997, you need to write: `[Time].[Year].[1997]`. Generally speaking, the following rules can be used to establish unique names in MDX. These rules apply within the context of the cube. If you are building unique names outside the context of a certain cube, you need to prefix all these names defined below by the cube name in square brackets followed by a period. An example of this would be referencing one cube from within the definition of a calculated measure of another cube.

Dimensions and Measures

Dimension and measure names are unique within the same cube, so you can uniquely identify a dimension or a measure simply by using its name within the context of the cube. For example, the name `[Time]` or `[Store Sales]` uniquely identify the `Time` dimension and the `Store Sales` measure in the current cube.

Hierarchies

A hierarchy can be defined by prefixing its name, which is enclosed in square brackets, by the name of the dimension it belongs to (enclosed in square brackets) and followed by a period. For example, to refer to the fiscal hierarchy in the time dimension, you may write:

`[Time].[Fiscal]`

If only one hierarchy exists in a dimension, there is no need to represent its name. The name of the dimension will be the same as that of the hierarchy. For example, if there is no fiscal hierarchy in the time dimension, the implicit time hierarchy can be simply represented as `[Time]` instead of `[Time].[Time]`.

Levels

Continuing along the same path as the above two sections, the name of the level is identified by the name of the dimension in square brackets followed also by the name of the hierarchy in square brackets, then by the name of the level. Periods separate the names of the dimension, hierarchy, and level. For example, to identify the `Year` level in the `Fiscal` hierarchy, you can write:

```
[Time].[Fiscal].[Year]
```

To identify the State level of the Region dimension, you can write:

```
[Region].[State]
```

This assumes there is only one hierarchy in this dimension.

Members

Identifying member names is a little trickier than the previous names we have identified so far. The difference here is that you will have to literally go through the hierarchy adding the names of the members at all levels above the level of the member of interest. For example, to identify the first month of the third fiscal quarter of 1997, you may write:

```
[Time].[Fiscal].[All Time].[1997].[Quarter 3].[April]
```

This assumes that the fiscal year 1997 starts on the first day of October 1996. As another example, to identify the Detroit member of City level of the Region dimension, you can write:

```
[Region].[All Regions].[USA].[Michigan].[Detroit]
```

Member Properties

To uniquely identify a member property, you need to add the name of the member property following the name of its level with a period between the two names. For example, to get the population of Detroit, you would write:

```
[Region].[All Regions].[USA].[Michigan].[Detroit].Properties("Population")
```

More on MDX Queries

As promised, I will discuss the construction of MDX queries more comprehensively at the end of the simple MDX query section. In this section, we will see how punctuation, operators, and functions are used in the MDX query. We will also cover the special keyword, WITH, which is used to define Calculated Measures in MDX queries.

Constructing MDX Sets

MDX cellsets (or sets) are an important part of the MDX statement. They are often seen in the SELECT part where they reflect the cells of the cube that are to be returned from the query. Sets are usually surrounded by braces { and }. Like any programming language, MDX has a number of operators that it uses to manipulate these sets. You may, for instance use the comma and colon to separate members in cellsets. You may also use the period and the .Members operator to return the members in a dimension, level, or hierarchy. This section examines the basic operators, including the comma, colon, .Members, in addition to some of the basic functions used in the MDX queries to identify data sets, such as Crossjoin(), Order(), and Filter().

Separation of Set Elements (Comma)

The comma (,) is one of the most widely used operators, and is present in almost every MDX query because it is an essential part of the set construction. The comma is the operator that separates the elements of such sets (tuples and subsets). For example, you can see how the comma is used to identify a set composed of the first three quarters of 1997:

```
{[Time].[Q1/1997], [Time].[Q2/1997], [Time].[Q3/1997]}
```

Another example is the set that holds three states, Michigan, Ohio, and Illinois, in addition to Canada along the Store dimension. In this example, the set is actually composed of two members at the country level, USA and Canada. The USA member is also composed of the three states mentioned above. The set, therefore, identifies members of two levels of the geographical dimension (Store).

```
{{[Store].[USA].[MI], [Store].[USA].[OH], [Store].[IL]}, [Store].[Canada]}
```

Identifying Ranges (Colon)

Sets may include ranges of members of a dimension, dimension level, or hierarchy. As you have already seen, Analysis Services organizes dimension data, in different levels and, accordingly, certain hierarchies. The data may be ordered in a logical way to reflect a certain order of the members of the dimension level, or hierarchy. For example, in a time dimension, the members of the month level are usually ordered according to the months of the year beginning with January, and ending with December for a calendar hierarchy.

To express such ranges in MDX sets, you can use the colon operator (:). This is similar to how ranges of cells are defined in Microsoft Excel. Hence, to construct a set that includes all the calendar quarters of 1997, you can write:

```
{[Time].[Calendar].[Quarter1] : [Time].[Calendar].[Quarter4]}
```

And to identify the months of fiscal 1997, assuming that the fiscal year starts on the first day of October, you can write:

```
{[Time].[Fiscal].[October 1996] : [Time].[Fiscal].[September 1997]}
```

Notice that the 1997 fiscal year actually starts with October 1996 in the example.

> **You need to be aware that Analysis Services handles ranges in one direction. That is a range given by: {[Time].[Calendar].[July 1998] : [Time].[Calendar].[February 1998]} will not return the expected range between February 1998 and July 1998. Instead, it will return the range starting with July 1998 and ending with the last member of the hierarchy at that year level.**

Also note that we are including the hierarchy definition in constructing the set when the dimension has more than one hierarchy. This is because Analysis Services will not find the dimension and will return an error if the hierarchies are not supplied in this case. If the dimension has one hierarchy that does not have a name, the name of the dimension will be enough to express the members of the set.

A range of one member will return a set with only that member. For instance, the set shown below includes only one member, [July 1998].

```
{[Time].[Calendar].[July 1998] : [Time].[Calendar].[July 1998]}
```

You can mix the comma and colon in constructing sets. For instance, if a cell is composed of the range July 1998 to October 1998 in addition to the month of February 1998, you can write the set as:

```
{[Time].[Calendar].[February 1998], [Time].[Calendar].[July 1998] :
[Time].[Calendar].[October 1998]}
```

Identifying the Set Members with the .Members Operator

We have so far seen how the comma and colon can be used to help construct a set. However, how can one refer to all members of a dimension, level, or hierarchy without including ranges and individual elements? This question arises when there are many members in a dimension level without a clear logical order. In a situation like this, it makes sense to refer to members of the dimension level altogether with one operator. The answer to this question is to use the .Members operator. This operator returns the members of the dimension, level, or hierarchy. For example, to return all the product categories in the category level of the product dimension, you can write:

```
{[Product].[Product Category].Members}
```

To build a query in which the members of the product categories level are laid across the columns of the cellset, you can write:

```
SELECT
    {[Product].[Product Family].Members} on Columns,
    {[Time].[Year].[1997].Children} on rows
FROM Sales
```

Again, you notice that if a dimension has more than one hierarchy, you need to append the hierarchy name to that of the dimension; otherwise, Analysis Services will not be able to recognize the dimension. Finally, you need to keep in mind that when the .Members operator is used, it does not return calculated members of the dimension, level, or hierarchy. The solution to this is referring to these members by their names in the set, or using the MDX function AddCalculatedMembers(), which is explained later in the chapter.

CrossJoin()

More often than not, your cells will include members of more than one dimension. How would your MDX query look like to make this happen? The answer lies in the CrossJoin() function. The general syntax for this function is:

```
CrossJoin({Set1}, {Set2})
```

This function returns the cross product of the members of two different sets ({Set1} and {Set2}). A Cross, or Cartesian, product means all possible combinations of these members. For example, to return the results shown in the table earlier, where both the customer and product families are laid across the x-axis, we can write:

```
SELECT
    CROSSJOIN(
        {[Customers].[All Customers].[USA].[CA].[Altadena],
         [Customers].[All Customers].[USA].[OR].[Albany]},
        {[Product].[Product Family].Members}) on columns,
    {[Time].[Year].[1997].Children} on rows
FROM
    Sales
WHERE
    ([Store].[All Stores].[USA], [Measures].[Store Sales])
```

Just as a reminder, here are the results it produces:

1997 Quarters	Total Store Sales in the USA					
	Altadena			Albany		
	Product Families			Product Families		
	Drink	Food	Non-Consumable	Drink	Food	Non-Consumable
Q1/1997	$96.00	$863.91	$229.06	$347.76	$3,149.80	$993.70
Q2/1997	$109.37	$1020.03	$264.27	$220.21	$1,854.00	$434.98
Q3/1997	$47.45	$1005.03	$266.03	$268.13	$2,957.79	$861.18
Q4/1997	$114.42	$1265.43	$304.59	$274.22	$2,144.47	$603.57

The query construction above assumes that the product family level of the product dimension only includes the three members shown in the table: Drink, Food, and Non-Consumable. However, if there are other members and we only want to show these three members, the query has to be changed as follows:

```
SELECT
    CrossJoin(
        { [Customers].[All Customers].[USA].[CA].[Altadena],
          [Customers].[All Customers].[USA].[OR].[Albany] },
        { [Product].[Product Family].[Drink],
          [Product].[Product Family].[Food],
          [Product].[Product Family].[Non-Consumable]}) on Columns,
    {[Time].[Year].[1997].Children} on rows
FROM
    Sales
Where
    ([Store].[All Stores].[USA])
```

This syntax goes in line with the discussion earlier regarding using the comma to include separate members of a dimension, level, or a hierarchy into a set.

It is worth noting here that it does not matter which order the sets are placed in the CrossJoin function. We could have written the query in the following form without affecting the results (this will affect the primary and secondary column headers):

```
SELECT
    CrossJoin(
        { [Products].[ Product Family].[Drink],
          [Products].[ Product Family].[Food],
          [Products].[ Product Family].[Non-Consumable]},
        { [Customers].[All Customers].[USA].[CA].[Altadena],
          [Customers].[All Customers].[USA].[OR].[Albany] }) on Columns,
    {[Time].[Year].[1997].Children} on rows
FROM Sales
Where ( [Store].[All Stores].[USA] )
```

The CrossJoin() function handles only two dimensions at a time. If you want to evaluate the cross product of more than two dimensions, you need to nest the call to this function. For example, if you want to nest the customer, product, and store dimensions and lay them all on the x-axis, you can use the CrossJoin() function like the example below:

```
CrossJoin(
    CrossJoin( {[Customers].[All Customers].[USA].[CA].[Altadena],
        [Customers].[All Customers].[USA].[OR].[Albany] },
        { [Product].[Product Family].Members }),
        { [Stores].[All Stores].Members })
```

This would be the same as writing:

```
CrossJoin(
    {[Customers].[All Customers].[USA].[CA].[Altadena],
        [Customers].[All Customers].[USA].[OR].[Albany] },
        CrossJoin(
            { [Product].[Product Family].Members },
            { [Stores].[Countries].Members }))
```

Another point to consider here is that the CrossJoin() function takes two sets as arguments. If one of the sets includes only one tuple, it would be a good practice to surround it by braces to convert it to a set, even though not doing so will not produce any errors.

The * (asterisk) Operator

The asterisk operator * is an alternative to the CrossJoin() function. It also finds all possible combinations of the sets joined. The general syntax for using this operator is illustrated in the example below, which is identical to the example in the CrossJoin() function section:

```
SELECT
    {{[Product].[Product Family].[Drink],
    [Product].[Product Family].[Food],
    [Product].[Product Family].[Non-Consumable]}
    *
    {[Customers].[All Customers].[USA].[CA].[Altadena],
    [Customers].[All Customers].[USA].[OR].[Albany] }} on Columns,
    {[Time].[Year].[1997].Children} on rows
FROM Sales
Where ( [Store].[Store Country].[USA] )
```

If there are more than two sets, this operator can still be used as illustrated in the example below:

```
{   { {[Customers].[All Customers].[USA].[CA].[Altadena],
        [Customers].[All Customers].[USA].[OR].[Albany] }
    *
    {[Product].[Product Family].Members}  }
    *
    {[Stores].[Store Country].[USA]}  }
```

The advantages of using the * operator is ease of typing and combining more than two sets, but the disadvantage of using this operator is that it could be easily confused with the numerical multiplier operator.

Filter() Function

The `Filter()` function is another function that helps define the set and its members. As the name implies, this function allows you to filter some values out of a set, excluding them based on certain criteria. The function takes as parameters a set and a `Boolean` expression. The `Boolean` expression determines the values to include or exclude from the passed set.

```
Filter ({Set}, Boolean Expression)
```

Boolean Operators Used in MDX

MDX allows several Boolean operators as part in the Boolean expression. These operators are listed in the table below:

Boolean Operator	Description
=	Equal
<	Less than
<=	Less than or equal
>	Greater than
>=	Greater than or equal
<>	Not equal
IsEmpty(Expression)	Checks to see if the `Expression`, which is any valid MDX expression, returns an empty set
AND	Logical AND; the Boolean expression evaluates to TRUE if both sides of the AND operator are TRUE
OR	Logical OR; the Boolean expression evaluates to TRUE if either side of the OR operator is TRUE (or both)
NOT	Logical NOT; the Boolean expression evaluates to TRUE if the expression to the right of the NOT operator evaluates to FALSE

As an example on using the `Filter()` function, let's return all the product families for Altadena and Albany whose sales exceeded $1,000 in the USA in 1997. The Boolean expression for this example is in bold:

```
SELECT
Filter(
    {  {  [Customers].[All Customers].[USA].[OR].[Albany],
          [Customers].[All Customers].[USA].[CA].[Altadena]}
        *
    {  [Product].[Product Family].Members}
    },
    ([Measures].[Store Sales], [Time].[Year].[1997] ) > 1000) on columns,
    {[Time].[Year].[1997].Children} on rows
FROM
    Sales
Where
    ( [Store].[Store Country].[USA],   [Measures].[Store Sales] )
```

The results from a query containing the `Filter` function above would look similar to the results shown in the previous table, except that only annual sales totals greater than $1,000 will show up:

1997 Quarters	Total Store Sales in the USA				
	Albany			Altadena	
	Product Families			Product Families	
	Drink	Food	Non-Consumable	Food	Non-Consumable
Q1/1997	$347.76	$3,149.80	$993.70	$863.91	$229.06
Q2/1997	$220.21	$1,854.00	$434.98	$1,020.03	$264.27
Q3/1997	$268.13	$2,957.79	$861.18	$1,005.03	$266.03
Q4/1997	$274.22	$2,144.47	$603.57	$1,265.43	$304.59

This function, like most MDX functions, can be nested with other functions, which provides greater flexibility in expressing and constructing the sets we are interested in retrieving. The above example shows how tuples are defined in the set by nesting the `Filter()` and `CrossJoin()` functions.

The Order() Function

Another function used in the construction of sets is the `Order()` function. This function helps to put the tuples in the set in a specific order. The function takes as arguments a set to order, a criterion for ordering, and an optional parameter that serves as a flag to whether the order will be ascending or descending. The syntax of this function is presented below:

```
Order ({Set}, Criterion for Ordering, Flag (DESC, ASC, BASC, BDESC))
```

The function above returns a cellset ordered according to the criterion provided and based on the value of the optional flag, the set could be ordered in ascending or descending order. The ASC and DESC operators keep the ordering within the hierarchy, whereas the BASC and BDESC operators break the hierarchy boundaries and order the results as one unit. To understand the difference between ASC and BASC, the following example shows the results of the function when ordering the members of the following set:

```
Order(
    {[USA], [France], [California], [New York],
     [Italy], [Paris], [Los Angeles],
     [New York City], [Albany], [Rome], [Naples]},
    ([Time].[1997], [Store Sales]),
  DESC))
```

Set Member			Store Sales (x $1000)
Country	**State**	**City**	
USA			1200
	California		240
		Los Angeles	81
	New York		210
		New York City	121
		Albany	36
Italy			280
		Rome	110
		Naples	87
France			94
		Paris	88

As you can see from the table above, using the DESC flag causes OLAP Services to sort the results in a hierarchy in terms of geographic location and sort the sales for each hierarchical category alone. The same function as above would return the following results when using BDESC instead of DESC:

```
ORDER(
    {[USA], [France], [California], [New York],
        [Italy], [Paris], [Los Angeles],
        [New York City], [Albany], [Rome], [Naples]},
    ([Time].[1997], [Store Sales]),
    BDESC)
```

Set Member	Store Sales (x $1000)
USA	1200
Italy	280
California	240
New York	210
New York City	121
Rome	110
France	94
Paris	88
Naples	87
Los Angeles	81
Albany	36

Clearly, from the table above, the BDESC flag caused OLAP Services not to categorize the set and to treat it all as one unit when it sorted the results.

Again, this function can be nested with other functions to provide maximum flexibility in the resulting cellset. For example, let's write a query that does the same function as the last query, except that the returned cellset members correspond to store sales greater than $50,000. This condition is done using the Filter function:

```
ORDER(
FILTER(
    {[USA], [France], [California], [New York],
        [Italy], [Paris], [Los Angeles],
        [New York City], [Albany], [Rome], [Naples]},
    ([Measures].[Store Sales] ) > 100000),
    ([Time].[1997], [Store Sales]),
    DESC)
```

The results of the query above are shown in the table below. Compare these results to the results of the same query without the Filter function, which we saw earlier.

Set Member			Store Sales (x $1000)
Country	State	City	
USA			1200
	California		240
	New York		210
		New York City	121
Italy			280
		Rome	110

It is worth noting that the default sort order flag is ASC if no order flag is assigned.

Ordering sets in MDX is not a simple issue. We will revisit this topic in the next chapter when we discuss ordering sets. The complexity comes when you don't elect to break the orders of the hierarchies, which causes Analysis Services to sort the results within each hierarchy level as you have seen in the example above.

Dimensional Calculations in MDX

Multidimensional calculations in MDX carry a great deal of resemblance to two- and three- dimensional spreadsheet calculations. If you are familiar with such calculations in a spreadsheet program, like Microsoft Excel, you will find MDX calculations to be an easy topic. On the other hand, compared to SQL, MDX calculations are much easier to perform and understand. One aspect of multidimensional calculations is that you can perform these calculations on ranges of cells, which spares you from repeating the calculations for each cell.

In SQL, if you were to perform any calculations, the calculations have to be embedded in the queries with the fields of the different tables that participate in the calculation explicitly or implicitly selected as well. As an example, to calculate the employment duration of all employees in a company, you may issue the query:

```
SELECT  emp_name AS EmployeeName,
            emp_start_date AS StartDate,
            emp_end_date AS EndDate,
            DateDiff(month, ISNULL(emp_end_date, GetDate())
                    , emp_start_date) AS MonthsEmployed
FROM    EmployeeTable
```

Notice in the query above that we used three built-in SQL Server T-SQL functions, `DateDiff`, which takes the parameters `date part` (`month` in our case), and the two dates we want to subtract one from the other; `ISNULL()`, which checks the value of the end data field, and replaces NULLs with the result of the third function we used, `GetDate()`, which retrieves the current system date. The calculation will be performed on each row of the result set yielding the number of months of employment of the employees of the company. If you were to store this calculation in SQL, you might need to add a field to store its result. The added field value could then be calculated when a record is updated with a new end-date value. This can be achieved in several different ways, such as an update trigger, or through the application that set the end-date value. The other way to "pseudo" store the calculation in SQL is by creating a view based on the query presented above.

In MDX, calculations are placed in the axes of the query as new members of the dimensions, which fill in the cells with the calculation results. The keyword `Member` is used to indicate adding a new member to the dimension. The syntax generally looks like this:

```
Member: member_name AS calculation_formula
```

The `member_name` parameter in the general syntax formula above follows the same rules for defining unique members of a dimension. The dimension name (and possibly the hierarchy) along with the level name should be part of the `member_name`. In MDX, calculated members are handled in one of two ways: they can be calculated privately to the query using the `WITH` operator, in which case, they are only available for the duration of the query run time; or they can be evaluated and made available for more than one query with the `CREATE MEMBER` statement. These two methods will be explained later in the chapter.

Query-Defined Calculated Members (WITH Operator)

The `WITH` operator can be used in MDX queries to specify a calculated member. It can also be used to define named sets (discussed later in the chapter). The `WITH` operator comes before the `SELECT` clause of the MDX statement and defines a section in which the calculated member along with any named sets can be defined. The example below illustrates how this operator can be used to make accessing data and calculations very simple. In the example, we find out the duration of employment for the employees defined as a new member in the `WITH` section:

```
WITH
    MEMBER  [Measures].[Days Employed] AS
    '[Measures].[EmpEndDate] - [Measures].[EmpStartDate]'
SELECT
    { [Measures].[EmpStartDate],
      [Measures].[EmpEndDate],
      [Measures].[Days Employed] } on columns,
    { [Employee].[City].[Troy - Michigan].[EmpName] } on rows
FROM EmployeeCube
```

Notice that in this example the member was added to the `Measures` dimension. Also, notice the syntax for the formula and how it is surrounded by single quotes. A sample of the results of the query is represented in the following table:

	Start Date	End Date	Days Employed
John Doe	1/1/1997	---	1703
Janet Smith	7/15/1998	---	1143
Mike Smith	1/1/1992	2/15/1998	2237
Susan Davis	12/15/1988	1/15/1989	31
Yvonne Michaels	1/15/1990	---	4260

The member added with this query to the measures dimension (Days Employed) is only available for the duration of this query and cannot be accessed or used by other queries.

Let's now go back to the sales and inventory examples. A query that retrieves the profits for the months of October and November of the 1998 calendar year for stores located in Troy, Michigan, along with the percent change in sales, cost, and profit between the two months may look like:

```
WITH
    MEMBER  [Measures].[Profit] AS
    '[Measures].[Sales] - [Measures].[Cost]'
    MEMBER  [Time].[Percent Change] AS
    '((([TIME].[November-1998], [Measures].Currentmember) - ([Time].[October-1998],
[Measures].Currentmember))/([TIME].[November-1998],[Measures].Currentmember)',
    FORMAT_STRING = 'Percent'
SELECT
    { [Measures].[Sales],
      [Measures].[Cost],
      [Measures].[Profit] } on columns,
    { [Time].[October-1998],
      [Time].[November-1998],
      [Time].[Percent Change] } on rows
FROM EmployeeCube
WHERE ( [Stores].[City].[ Troy, Michigan ] )
```

> Note the use of the .CurrentMember function in the Percent Change calculated measure. As the Percent Change calculation is done across the columns, the current Measure (Sales, Cost, or Profit) needs to be used to ensure proper results.

The results of this query are presented in the following table:

	Sales	Cost	Profit
October-1998	$120,000	$59,000	$51,000
November-1998	$150,000	$71,000	$79,000
Percent Change	25%	3%	**55% or 22%?**

You notice from the previous example that we added two members in the WITH section: the Profit member and the Percent Change member. We projected the Profit member on the x-axis making it a column; and the Percent Change member projected on the y-axis, making it a row in the table. You may be wondering which calculation took place first – the profit or the change? If you were calculating Percentage Change, then the value would be 22%, but if you calculate Profit, the value would be 55%.

The reason this is a good question is the corner cell at the right and bottom of the table. This cell should represent the change in profit between the two months. The value of this cell is expected to be the same when calculated from the columns or from the rows. Surprisingly enough, these two values are not the same (55%) and (22%). So, which calculation takes precedence?

MDX solves this problem with what is called the Member Solve Order property, which is specified when the member is created. The member with the higher number is calculated based on the results of the calculation of the members with the lower number. This number can only be zero or higher. The number actually specifies precedence of calculation among the calculated members, and it is up to us to decide that precedence in the query. However, if no value is specified for this property, the value defaults to zero.

In our example, we need to find the change in profit between October 1998 and November 1998 rather than the difference of the sales and cost change. Therefore, we give a higher value to the Percent Change member than the Profit member to have the profits calculated first. With this the query becomes:

```
WITH
      MEMBER   [Measures].[Profit] AS
      '[Measures].[Sales] - [Measures].[Cost]',
      SOLVE_ORDER = 1
      MEMBER   [Time].[Percent Change] AS
    '(([TIME].[November-1998], [Measures].Currentmember) - ([Time].[October-1998],
[Measures].Currentmember))/([TIME].[November-1998],[Measures].Currentmember)',
    FORMAT_STRING = 'Percent',
      SOLVE_ORDER = 2
SELECT
      { [Measures].[Sales],
        [Measures].[Cost],
        [Measures].[Profit] } on columns,
      { [Time].[October-1998],
        [Time].[November-1998],
        [Time].[Percent Change] } on rows
FROM EmployeeCube
WHERE ( [Stores].[City].[ Troy, Michigan ] )
```

The results of this query are presented in the following table:

	Sales	Cost	Profit
October - 1998	$120,000	$69,000	$51,000
November - 1998	$150,000	$71,000	$79,000
Percent Change	25%	3%	55%

It is worth noting the following things about the syntax of the WITH block when more than one member are specified:

- ❏ Members are not separated by any punctuation; the keyword MEMBER is the separator.

- ❏ The formula used to evaluate the calculated member is quoted in single quotes

- ❏ FORMAT_STRING defines the presentation of the calculated member

- ❏ SOLVE_ORDER values can be either zero or positive integers

- ❏ The SOLVE_ORDER property is separated from the definition of the member by a comma

Non Query-Defined Calculated Members (CREATE MEMBER)

So far, you have seen how you can define a calculated member in an MDX query. Such members will be visible only to the query they are created in. MDX also allows for defining calculated members on both the server and client levels. Server-level calculated members are visible to all clients that can access the cube on which the member is defined. The syntax that allows this to happen is the CREATE MEMBER function. This function has to be used with the cube name and dimension name. The CREATE MEMBER command is not part of the query in which the member is used. Instead, it is a separate statement, which is executed separately from the SELECT query. The statement follows the same syntax as the definition of the calculated member in the WITH clause. The only difference is the addition of the cube and dimension names. The following statement created the two calculated members used in the last two examples above:

```
    CREATE MEMBER   [EmployeeCube].[Measures].[Profit] AS
 '[Measures].[Sales] - [measures].[Cost]',
    SOLVE_ORDER = 5
    CREATE MEMBER   [EmployeeCube].[Time].[Percent Change] AS
 '(([TIME].[November-1998], [Measures].Currentmember) -
([Time].[October-1998], [Measures].Currentmember)) /
([TIME].[November-1998],[Measures].Currentmember)',
FORMAT_STRING = 'Percent',
    SOLVE_ORDER = 10
```

Using the CREATE MEMBER command adds the calculated member to the schema, allowing it to be used via OLE DB for OLAP or Decision Support Objects (DSO). Calculated members can also be defined using the Analysis Manager. These members are also visible to all clients that have access to the cube on the server.

Named Sets

One powerful feature of MDX is allowing for the definition of named sets. These are regular sets you define using the rules and techniques we went through so far. This ability provides great benefits, such as holding certain values in sets of their own and giving the sets descriptive names, thus making them easier to reference. Additionally, named sets make programming and writing SELECT statements easier, since, you only use the name of the set rather than the whole definition.

Just like calculated members, named sets are defined in the WITH block. The syntax for defining them is similar to that of calculated members, except that you use the SET keyword instead of MEMBER, and there is no need to specify the name of a cube or dimension. As an example on named sets, the following two queries produce identical results. The second one uses a named set of My Products:

```
SELECT
    { [Product].[Bread], [Product].[Cookies], [Product].[Cake] } on columns,
    { [Measures].Members } on rows
```

```
FROM InventoryCube

WITH
    SET  [My Products] AS
        '{ [Product].[Bread], [Product].[Cookies], [Product].[Cake] }'

SELECT
    { [My Products] } on columns,
    { { [Measures].Members } on rows
FROM InventoryCube
```

Just like calculated members, named sets are also sensitive to the scope in which they are defined. Named sets defined in the WITH block of the SELECT query are local to the query and end with the execution of the query. However, you can use the command CREATE SET to create sets on the server or client. Sets created on the server will be available to clients accessing and querying the cube on which the sets were defined. Sets created by a client will only be available to the client and will go out of scope as soon as the client connection to the server is terminated or they are dropped.

An example of creating the same set in the example above with the CREATE SET command is shown below:

```
CREATE SET  [InventoryCube].[My Products] AS
    '{ [Product].[Bread], [Product].[Cookies], [Product].[Cake] }'
```

You notice here that the cube on which the set is defined has to be part of the name of the set. The dimension, however, does not have to be part of the set's name.

Unlike calculated members, named sets don't show up in the cube's schema, and OLE DB cannot be used to manipulate them (at least for this release of Analysis Services). You can, however, still use them programmatically using Decision Support Objects (DSO).

Named sets are evaluated the first time they are encountered and saved for subsequent use thereafter, until they go out of scope. This results in significant improvement in query processing, which is yet another benefit of named sets.

Axis Numbering and Ordering

One major part of the MDX SELECT statement is the axis definition. Axes are numbered from 0 to 128. If you choose 0 axes in the statement, then the chances are you have a slicer dimension in the WHERE clause. If you don't, the global aggregate for the cube will be returned as a result, because your query will look like this:

```
SELECT
FROM [SalesCube]
```

You have to be extremely careful when using numbered axes in your queries. The axes should be laid in the query according to their order and you cannot skip numbers. For instance, a statement like:

```
SELECT
    ... ON Axis(0),
    ... ON Axis(1),
    ... ON Pages,
    ... ON Chapters
```

is OK because it maintains the order of the axes. It is worth mentioning here that the first five axes are given the names `Columns`, `Rows`, `Pages`, `Chapters`, and `Sections` to look like a printed report. Continuing our example, the following two statements will generate errors because the first one does not maintain the order of the axes, and the second one skips axis numbers:

```
SELECT
    ... ON Axis(1),
    ... ON Pages,
    ... ON columns

SELECT
    ... ON Axis(0),
    ... ON Pages,
    ... ON Chapters
```

The first ill-formed example has the axes in the wrong order: 1, 2, 0 for rows, pages, and columns respectively; whereas the second ill-formed example has the order of the axes as: 0, 2, 3 for columns, pages, and chapters axes respectively, skipping the rows axis (1).

In summary, if you are defining n axes in your query, you must number these axes from 0 to n-1 in an ascending order.

Selecting Member Properties

MDX queries allow you to select member properties defined on individual dimension levels or on the dimensions themselves. The properties are included on the statement axes. The keyword DIMENSION PROPERTIES is used to specify that member properties are to be retrieved. For example, the following code retrieves the birth date and gender member properties of the employees from the employee cube:

```
SELECT
    { { [Employee].[Michigan].[Troy].Members },
      DIMENSION PROPERTIES
      [Employee].[BirthDate],
      [Employee].[Gender] } on columns,
    { [Product].[Product Family].Members } on rows,
    { [Measure].[Store Sales]} on pages
FROM
    SalesCube
WHERE
    ( [Measures].[Sales], [Time].[July, 1998] )
```

The results of the query above would look like this:

	Employee Sales in Troy, Michigan				
	Birth Date	Gender	Food	Drinks	Clothes
John Doe	1/23/1959	M	$13,400	$15,005	$18,019
Janet Smith	11/5/1968	F	$10,300	$11,204	$13,112

The example above will retrieve the employees with their birth dates and gender and their sales in July, 1998 in Troy, Michigan.

Summary

In summary, this chapter introduced you to MDX. You can clearly see that MDX is a powerful language that allows you to query multidimensional cubes in an efficient and powerful manner. Like SQL, MDX can be used in combination with other programming languages, which adds to its power and benefits. The next chapter discusses the more advanced features and issues with MDX in more detail, and presents the sample VB application that ships with Analysis Services, which allows for easy writing of MDX queries.

Data Warehouse

11

Advanced MDX Topics

In the previous chapter we talked through the basics of MDX. It is essential that these basics are understood so that you can use MDX confidently within your Microsoft Analysis Services projects. You will find that this chapter will be expanding on the topics we met in the last chapter, and adding new elements to the discussion that describe common use scenarios, special cases, and alternative actions. There will also be a host of new topics that we will meet specifically for advanced use of MDX.

Topics covered in this chapter include:

❑   The Format String

❑   Empty Sets

❑   MDX Expressions: Set Value Expressions and Conditional Expressions

❑   An MDX Sample Application

The last thing we tackled in Chapter 10 was retrieving member properties. In this chapter, we will start with a more detailed presentation of the MDX statement, defining data and context for the different parts of the statement.

Advanced MDX Statement Topics

Retrieving Cell Properties

Microsoft OLE DB Provider for Analysis Services supports several advanced properties for cells in multi-dimensional cubes. Besides the value property, a cell can have properties that help customize its formatting and coloring. The table overleaf lists cell properties supported by Microsoft OLE DB provider for OLAP, given that OLE DB providers may add their own properties that fit their systems.

Property Name	Mandatory/ Optional	Data Type	Description
value	Mandatory	DBTYPE_VARIANT	Actual un-formatted value of the cell
formatted_value	Mandatory	DBTYPE_WSTR	Character string representing the formatted display of the value
cell_ordinal	Mandatory	DBTYPE_UI4	Ordinal number of the cell in the cellset
format_string	Optional	DBTYPE_WSTR	The format string used to create formatted_value (see next section)
fore_color	Optional	DBTYPE_UI4	Foreground color of the cell for displaying the value or formatted_value
back_color	Optional	DBTYPE_UI4	Background color used for displaying the value formatted_value
font_name	Optional	DBTYPE_WSTR	Font used to display the value or formatted_value
font_size	Optional	DBTYPE_UI4	Font size used to display the value or formatted_value
font_flags	Optional	DBTYPE_I4	Bitmask detailing the effects on the font, such as bold (1), italic (2), underline (4), or strikeout (8)
cell_evaluation _list	Optional	DBTYPE_WSTR	A semicolon-delimited list of evaluated formulas related to the cell, in order from lowest to highest solve_order
Solve_order	Optional	DBTYPE_I4	Defines the order in which calculated measures are computed during a query

The data types used in the table above are the types used by the OLE DB specification. To understand these types better, let's map the ones used in the table above to the equivalent types in ADO, as shown in the following table:

OLE DB Type	ADO Type	Description
DBTYP_VARIANT	AdVariant	Indicates an automation variant
DBTYPE_WSTR	AdWChar	Indicates a NULL-terminated Unicode character string
DBTYPE_UI4	AdUnsigned Int	Indicates an unsigned integer (4 bytes)
DBTYPE_UI2	adUnsigned SmallInt	Indicates an unsigned small integer (2 bytes)
DBTYPE_I2	AdSmallInt	Indicates a 2-byte signed integer

As you might expect, a provider must support the mandatory cell properties listed in the first table – optional properties do not have to be supported. However, providers may also add their own specific cell properties. Your application can be written to query what properties a provider supports by returning a PROPERTIES rowset, with the data type column restricted to MDPROP_CELL. Your application may also limit the properties returned by using the CELL PROPERTIES keyword in the WHERE clause of the query. As an example, the following query returns a dataset in which each cell has the properties, VALUE, FORMATTED_VALUE, FORE_COLOR, and BACK_COLOR:

```
SELECT NON EMPTY Products DIMENSION PROPERTIES Products.ID, Products.Name
    ON ROWS,
CROSSJOIN (Years, (Sales, ActualSales)) ON COLUMNS
FROM SalesCube
WHERE ([March-1998], SalesPerson.[All], Store.USA)
CELL PROPERTIES VALUE, FORMATTED_VALUE, FORE_COLOR, BACK_COLOR
```

Each provider has a default set of properties that includes the mandatory ones. For example, the default Microsoft Analysis Services cell properties are: VALUE, FORMATTED_VALUE, and CELL_ORDINAL. If a provider has other mandatory cell properties, these properties will be part of the default set. Optional properties, on the other hand, are not returned unless the CELL PROPERTIES keyword is used to specify what properties to include in the WHERE clause. The latter case can include any properties, and may also exclude the mandatory ones. If the mandatory properties are not specified in the CELL PROPERTIES specification, they are not returned. Any properties requested that do not exist will return an error by Analysis Services.

The Format String

As you have already seen in the table of Analysis Services cell properties, the format string is used to generate the FORMATTED_VALUE cell property. The format string varies based on the data type of the cell value. The following is a description of this string for three data type categories, character, numeric, and date/time data types.

Format String in Character Values

The format string can have one or two sections separated by a semi colon ";". The first section of the format string applies to non-NULL, non-zero-length string values. The second section applies to NULL and zero-length string values. If there is only one section in the format string, then that format applies to all string values. The format string may include the characters listed in the following table:

Character	Description
@	A character placeholder that either displays the character or a space character. The default is right justified. If the string has a character corresponding to the position of the @ character, the character is displayed; otherwise a space is added. For example, when expressing the word "book" using the format string "@@@@@", we get "book" with a space at the beginning.
&	A character placeholder that displays either the character or nothing. If the string has a character corresponding to the position of the & character, the character is displayed. Otherwise, nothing is displayed. For example, when expressing the word "book" using the format string "@@&&&", we get "book" with **no** space at the end.
<	Displays all characters in lowercase format. For example, when expressing the word "BoOk" using the format string "<", we get "book".

Table continued on following page

Character	Description
>	Displays all characters in uppercase format. For example, when expressing the word "BoOk" using the format string ">", we get "BOOK".
!	Forces filling placeholder left-to-right instead of the default, right-to-left filling. For example, if "!" is used with the first example in the table: "!@@@@@" then the result would not be " book", instead, it would be "book ", with the additional space to the right of the word.

Format String in Numeric Values

The format string may include between one and four sections separated by semi colons. Depending on the number of sections, the format string will be interpreted differently according to the following table:

Number of Sections in the format string	Interpretation
One	The format expression applies to all values
Two	The first section applies to positive values and zeros, the second to negative values
Three	The first section applies to positive values, the second to negative values, and the third to zeros
Four	The first section applies to positive values, the second to negative values, the third to zeros, and the fourth to NULL values

For example, the format string "%##.#0;;\Z\E\R\O" has three sections, the first section applies to positive values, the second section is left blank, therefore, negative values will also use the first section for their display. The third section will display the word "ZERO" when a "0" is encountered. The following table specifies the characters that can appear in the format string for numeric values:

Character	Description
none	The numeric value has no formatting.
0	This character is a digit placeholder. If a numeric expression has a digit at the location corresponding to this character, the digit is displayed. Otherwise, a zero is displayed. If the number of zeros specified exceeds the length of the expression to the left or right of the decimal point, leading and trailing zeros are added. For example, using a format string of "0.0000" will express 7.345 as 7.3450, and using the format string "#.#00#" will express the same number as 7.345.
#	Similar to the 0 character, except that it either displays the digit or nothing (no zeros are displayed).
.	Decimal placeholder, and based on local settings of your system, it could be a comma ",". This character determines the number of digits to the right and left of the decimal point. If an expression evaluates to less than 1, and the # character is used for a placeholder, no digits will be displayed to the left of the decimal point. To display a leading zero, you need to use the "0" placeholder.

Character	Description
%	Percentage placeholder. The expression is multiplied by 100 and the % character is displayed. For example, using the format string "%###.####" to express the number 0.3453 will yield %34.53.
,	Thousand separator. Other characters may be used based on your machine locale setting.
:	Time separator used to separate hours, minutes, and seconds in time values. Other characters may be used based on your machine locale setting.
/	Date separator used to separate years, months and days in data values. Other characters may be used based on your machine locale setting.
E-, E+, e-, e+	Scientific format used to display exponential values. For example, 2.3×10^{13} would be expressed as 2.3E+13 when using the format string "###.###E##"
- + $ ( )	Displays a literal character. For example, the format string "$#,##0.00" used with a value of "34.6" would display as "$34.60".
\	Displays the next character in the format string. For example,the format string "\z\e\r\o" can be used to display the word "zero". If you want to display a back slash, you need to double it in the string: For example, "\\\z" will display "\z".
"ABC"	Displays the characters in quotation marks as a string within your expression.

Format String in Date/Time Values

Only one section exists in this string and the following table specifies the characters that can appear in the format string for date/time values.

Character	Description
:	Time separator used to separate hours, minutes, and seconds. When specified, time values will be formatted. For example, the time value "10.5" will be expressed as "10:30:00". However, the actual character appearing in the time value will depend on the locale system settings.
/	Date separator used to separate days, months, and years.
c	Displays date and time in the format ddddd and ttttt respectively. See examples of these formats later in the table.
d	Displays a date format as the day of the month with no leading zeros: 1 - 31
dd	Displays a date format as the day of the month with leading zeros: 01 - 31
ddd	Displays the day name as three letters, Mon through Sun.
dddd	Displays the whole name of the day: Monday through Sunday.

Table continued on following page

Character	Description
ddddd	Displays the date as the system's short date format, depending on how your system setting defines short format. For instance, if the system setting for short format is "dd/mm/yy" then the date will be displayed as "13/1/01"; and if the system setting for short data is "dd/mm/yyyy" then the date will be displayed as "13/1/2001". The system setting for short dates can be set using the Regional Settings applet in the Windows Control Panel. (See figure below:)

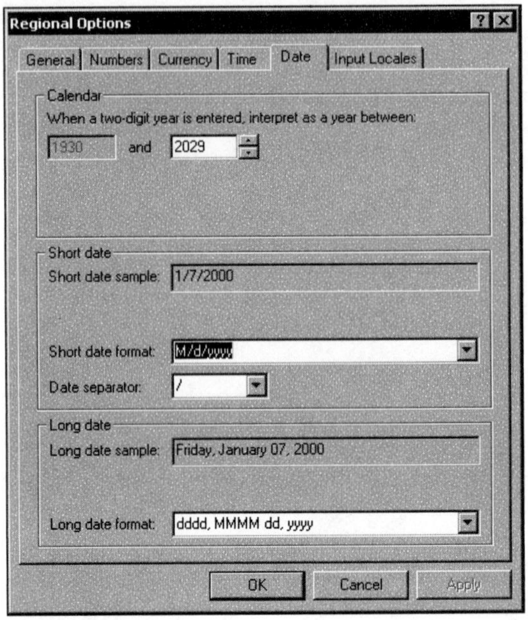

Regional Options ? X

General | Numbers | Currency | Time | Date | Input Locales |

Calendar
When a two-digit year is entered, interpret as a year between:

1930   and   2029

Short date
Short date sample: 1/7/2000

Short date format: M/d/yyyy
Date separator: /

Long date
Long date sample: Friday, January 07, 2000

Long date format: dddd, MMMM dd, yyyy

OK   Cancel   Apply

Character	Description
dddddd	Displays the date as long format (mmmm dd, yyyy). Long date format can also be set using the Regional Settings applet in the Windows Control Panel as shown in the figure above. An example of long date format is: January 1, 2001.
w	Displays the number of the day in the week (1 for Sunday and 7 for Saturday).
ww	Displays the number of the week in the year (1 to 52).
m	If this character does not follow the h/hh characters, it displays the month as a number without leading zeros from 1 to 12. 1 for January, and 12 for December.
mm	Displays the month number with leading zero if needed: 01 – 12. January being represented by 01 and December by 12.
mmm	Displays the month name as a three characters, Jan – Dec.
mmmm	Displays the full name of the month: January – December.
q	Displays the quarter of the year as a number: 1 – 4.
y	Displays the day of the year as a number from 1 to 366.
yy	Displays the year as two digits (00 to 99).

Character	Description
yyyy	Displays the year as four digits (0000 to 9999).
h, hh	Displays the hour of the day with or without leading zero (0 – 23) or (00 – 23).
n, nn	Displays the minute with or without leading zero (0 – 59) or (00 – 59).
s, ss	Displays the seconds with or without leading zero (0 – 59) or (00 – 59).
ttttt	Displays time according to the settings in the Regional Settings applet in the Windows Control Panel. An example is: 12:34:32
AM/PM, am/pm	Displays upper or lower case AM or PM based on 12 hour cycles.
A/P, a/p	Displays A or P for AM and PM respectively in upper or lower case based on a 12-hour cycle.
AMPM	Uses the 12-hour clock. Displays the AM or PM string literal as defined by your system. AMPM can be either uppercase or lowercase, but the case of the string displayed matches the string as defined by your system settings. For Microsoft Windows, the default format is AM/PM.

MDX Cube Slicers

As we saw in Chapter 10, slicers are defined in the WHERE clause of the MDX statement. Slicers and axes are similar in many ways. Actually, if you choose to eliminate slicers in your statements, you can do so and still limit your returned dataset to the values it would have if the slicer were used. For example, the following two queries return the exact same datasets:

```
SELECT
    {[Measures].Members} ON COLUMNS
    {[TIME].Members ON ROWS
FROM SalesCube
WHERE ([ProductCategory].[Dairy Products], [Store].[Detroit, Michigan])
```

and

```
SELECT
    {[Measures].Members} ON COLUMNS
    {[TIME].Members ON ROWS
{[ProductCategory].[Dairy Products], [Store].[Detroit, Michigan]} ON PAGES
FROM SalesCube
```

The first one of the two queries above uses a slicer in the WHERE clause to limit the resulting dataset to dairy products and the location to Detroit, Michigan. The second statement does not use the slicer, but adds a third axis that, by intersecting the other two axes, defines the resulting dataset to be the same as in the first query.

You might ask then why do we even bother with slicers, and why don't we just specify everything in the statement using axes? The answer is that you can do that, but slicers make it more intuitive and easier to construct the statement and understand it. The calling clients will also be able to interpret the statement's dataset better and faster if slicers are used. Clients will interpret the first query as a two-dimensional array, but the second one as a three-dimensional array. For clarity, and future support issues, using the WHERE clause is the best bet.

Beefing up MDX Cube Slicers

Just as slicers may include simple members from the cube, they can also include calculated members from different dimensions, including Measures. For example, it is safe to write:

```
WHERE ([Measures].[Average Sales Per Product Category], [Time].[Sum YTD])
```

Or even include MDX expressions and functions (see MDX Expressions later in the chapter):

```
WHERE (Descendants([Dairy Products], [Brands]),
BottomPercent([Geography].[States].Members, 25, Sales))
```

The seemingly complex slicer above limits the returned dataset in the query it is used in to the descendant brands of the dairy products category, and to the states corresponding to the bottom 25% sales. To make this clearer, the descendants of the Dairy Products will include members such as: cheese, milk, etc. As for the states, to get the states that contributed the bottom 25% sales volume, some sorting of the states according to their sales figures will take place. The sales for the sorted states will be added from the bottom up until we hit the 25% of total sales. The states included in the count are the ones included in the slicer.

In the examples above, you notice that the slicer defines sets of multiple tuples. Although you can write your slicer to include such sets, Analysis Services will aggregate the result and return one tuple. In other words, the sets participating in the slicer above are {Dairy, Cheese, Milk,...} and {California, Michigan, New York,...}.

Joining Cubes in the FROM Clause

Although the current release of MDX supports only one cube in the FROM clause, some OLE DB for OLAP providers may support joining multiple cubes together in the future. This could be done by simply listing the names of the cubes in the FROM clause separated by commas. Unlike relational databases, where joins on tables have to be explicitly defined in the SQL statement either in the WHERE clause, or in the FROM clause using the Join operators, MDX should not require such joins to be explicit. The fact that two cubes have shared dimensions should allow implicit joins between them if listed together in the FROM clause. It is also possible to create a virtual cube then submit MDX queries against it.

> Note: Two cubes are said to have shared dimensions if and only if the dimensions have the same DIMENSION_UNIQUE_NAME property.

The following are notes on joining cubes along their common dimensions:

❑   If two cubes have a common dimension, but do not have any common members in this dimension, the two cubes cannot be joined. For instance, if the first cube has a geographic dimension, just as the second cube, but the members of that dimension for the first cube are countries and cities in Europe, while the members of the dimension in the second cube are countries and cities in South America, then the two cubes cannot be joined.

❑   If two cubes with a common dimension have identical sets of members of that dimension, the two cubes can be joined and the resulting cube will have the total number of dimensions from both minus the common dimension. To clarify this further, take the example of the previous bullet. If the geographic dimension in both cubes had the same countries and cities in Europe, then these two cubes can be joined along this dimension. If the first cube had 3 dimensions and the second had 4, then the resulting cube from the join operation will have 3 + 4 −1 = 6 dimensions.

To better understand the last point, consider the example of cube A and cube C with dimensions (X, Y, Z) and (Z, W) respectively. Dimension Z is the common dimension between the two cubes. Assuming that members of the common dimension are identical for both cubes, the resulting cube AB will have the dimensions (X, Y, Z, W), and the following statements apply:

```
SELECT AB.X ON COLUMNS, AB.Y ON ROWS, AB.Z ON PAGES
WHERE (W.[ALL])
```

is the same as the cube A(X, Y, Z).

And the dataset:

```
SELECT AB.Z ON COLUMNS, AB.W ON ROWS
WHERE (X.[ALL], Y.[ALL])
```

Is the same as the cube B(Z, W).

This type of join is referred to as the **natural join**. Providers have the freedom to expand it in the future to make it as sophisticated as they wish.

Working with cubes that have common (shared) dimensions allows them to be joined together as a virtual cube, which provides the greatest flexibility within Analysis Services. No additional space is used, and calculated measures can still be created.

Empty FROM Clause

OLE DB for OLAP allows for derivation of a cube name from the MDX statement. This is considered an optional feature that providers can take advantage of. If a provider chooses to support this feature, then a cube name can be derived from the specified axis and slicer dimensions without having to explicitly name the cube in the FROM clause. For example, with support for this feature, you will be able to write a statement like the query below:

```
SELECT
   {Product.Members}, {[Measures].[Costs]} on columns
   [Store].[Michigan].[Cities].Members on rows
WHERE ([1998])
```

If the OLE DB for OLAP provider supports this feature, then it will derive the cube name from the axis dimensions: Product and Store, and from the slicer dimensions: Time and the cost measure, even though no FROM clause is included.

Checking the MDPROP_MDX_JOINCUBES property of the data source helps determine if the provider supports this feature. The MDPROPVAL_MJC_IMPLICITCUBE bit will be set if the provider supports this feature.

Using Outer References in an MDX Query

In many cases, data you want to retrieve in your MDX query is segmented in different cubes. For example, a cube may hold actual costs data, whereas budgeted costs may reside in another cube. Your query may need to reference tuples or members in a cube that does not appear in the FROM clause. For instance, you may want to retrieve the actual costs of products that exceeded their budgeted costs. The query would look like:

```
SELECT
FILTER (Product.Members, [Measures].[Costs] >
```

```
            [Budgeted Costs Cube].[Measures].[Cost]) on columns
            [Store].[Michigan].[Cities].Members on rows
   FROM   [Actual Costs Cube]
   WHERE  ([1998])
```

The query above will filter the resulting set retrieving only tuples where costs exceeded their budgeted values grouping the results by city in the state of Michigan for the year 1998. The `Filter` function will be explained later in the chapter.

Using Property Values in MDX Queries

Frequently you'll want to make a query based on a property value, rather than the dimension member itself. For instance, assume that you have a cube containing vehicle information for an auto manufacturer and you want to limit your query only to cars that have automatic transmission, are convertibles, and have V6 engines, which are member properties of the Model Year level of the Product dimension as shown in the figure below.

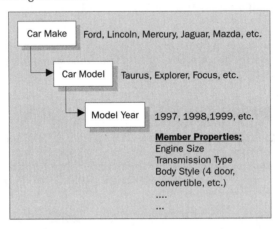

The MDX query would look like this:

```
   SELECT [Measures].[Sales] ON COLUMNS,
       Filter(Product.MEMBERS, ([Model Year].[Engine Size] = "V6" AND
                                [Model Year].[Transmission] = "Automatic" AND
                                [Model Year].[Body Style] = "Convertible")) ON ROWS
   FROM [Vehicle Cube]
   WHERE ([1998])
```

The query will retrieve all sales in 1998 for all models and model years where the engine size is V6, the transmission is automatic, and the body style is convertible.

A query like this would be very helpful when used in a search engine. This search engine could be used as the basis to search inventory in a data warehouse directly from a web page.

Overriding the WHERE Clause

In MDX expressions, individual sets, members, tuples, or numeric functions execute in the larger context of the entire statement. In some cases, a coordinate is specified in both the WHERE clause and another part of the MDX statement, such as a filter. In this case, coordinates obtained in the WHERE clause are overridden by any coordinates obtained in axis specification. As an example, consider the following MDX statement:

```
SELECT
    FILTER({USA.Children}, ([1997], ActualSales) > 10000) ON COLUMNS
    Quarters.Members on ROWS
FROM SalesCube
WHERE ([1998], ActualSales, [Products].ALL, [Salespersons].ALL)
```

The statement returns actual sales in 1998 where the actual sales exceeded a certain value in 1997 as determined by the filter. The WHERE clause already includes all the actual sales for 1998. In this case the filter overrides the WHERE clause specification and only 1998 sales where the 1997 sales exceeded the 10000 threshold are returned.

In other words, the WHERE clause in the statement above includes all the sales of 1998 as [1998] as part of the clause. However, the FILTER function overrides this by only including the 1998 sales where the actual sales for the previous year were greater than 10000. By allowing Analysis Services to execute the filter, no additional work is required by the client.

For example, if the first quarter sales were $12,000 in 1998, and only $9,000 in 1997, then the $12,000 contributed in the first quarter of 1998 will not be tallied as the 1998-year sales in the query because the 1997 sales are less than the filter criteria ($10,000).

Default Hierarchy and Member

As we have seen in previous chapters, each dimension has a default hierarchy. Each hierarchy has a default member as well. These defaults become significant in the following situations:

❑   If your query specifies that a dimension, such as the Time dimension, will be positioned on one of the axes, such as the x-axis, but does not choose any members from that dimension to occur along the specified axis. In this case, the provider chooses a hierarchy and member as the defaults and places them on the axis (for example [Time].[All Time]).

❑   If your query indicates that a dimension, such as the Time dimension, must be a slicer dimension but does not choose a member as the slicer. In this case, the provider uses a default slicer (such as year), which yields the default member (such as current year).

❑   If the OLE DB interface, IMDFind::FindCell, does not specify a member for one of the constituent dimensions of an axis, the provider uses the default member for that dimension.

❑   If the OLE DB interface, IMDFind::FindTuple, does not specify a member for a constituent dimension on the axis, the provider uses the default member for that dimension.

Note: IMDFind is an OLE DB interface. This interface is an optional interface on the dataset object, and has methods to find the ordinal number of a cell in the dataset and the ordinal number of a tuple on the axis. It is no surprise that these two methods are: FindCell and FindTuple respectively. To find a cell with the FindCell method, you need to specify an array of members and a starting ordinal position. To find a tuple using the FindTuple method, you need to specify the array of members and a starting ordinal and axis identifier.

You can explicitly select the default member and default hierarchy by using the expressions Dimension.DefaultMember, and Hierarchy.DefaultMember. It is also safe to assume that the default member of a dimension is the default member of the default hierarchy of the dimension.

Empty Cells

MDX queries can sometimes return sets that might have empty cells. For instance, if you are trying to find out the sales of vehicles per dealer per model for a two-month period, chances are one particular model is not sold at a particular dealership, which results in an empty cell. The following sections discuss some of the issues associated with empty cells beginning with how they can be formed, NULL and invalid members, and how empty cells can be handled and how they can be counted.

NULLs, Invalid Members, and Invalid Results

When performing MDX queries, you need to be aware of situations where invalid results can be returned from calculations. You also need to be aware of NULL members and NULLS in your calculations that may result in empty cells.

> **Microsoft Analysis Services does not treat errors, like division by zero, as an empty value; instead, it may return a bogus value.**

Some external function libraries, if used in your queries, may detect such errors and raise an ActiveX error that you can trap. However, it is best if you test for conditions of floating-point overflow and the like when building your expressions to avoid these bogus results.

NULL values usually lead to empty cells in the resulting cubes from the MDX queries. If you think of cross joining several dimension tables in your query, and each table includes several NULL values, the resulting cube will have far more empty cells than the dimension tables' NULL values, which leads to data sparsity problems in OLAP systems in general. Sparsity does not always result from NULL values in dimension tables. Empty cells can actually result from absence of rows corresponding to other dimension values.

For example, if we are cross joining the geography and time dimensions on one axis, selecting all cities in the state of Michigan to return the sales of a certain product (the other axis) will result in empty cells when the product is not sold in a certain city. So, if brand XYZ of cheese is not sold in Grand Rapids during the period specified on the Time dimension, an empty cell corresponding to the intersection of the two axes will result at this city and for this brand of cheese. This empty cell results from the lack of a row in the sales fact table corresponding to this situation. Clarifying the value of the data prior to processing it into the cube will greatly improve the reliability of the information queried from the cube.

MDX provides a function, IsEmpty() to check whether a cell is empty, and Microsoft Analysis Services provides the NULL keyword to express missing values. The OLE DB for OLAP specification states that empty cells are treated in a similar fashion to zeros in numerical expressions, and a zero length string in string expressions.

> **Boolean types are not allowed for cell values in Analysis Services, and if you try to insert a Boolean value using a function to return it, the value will not parse. In Analysis Services, the contents of a cell are either numeric or string.**

Unlike other programming languages, in OLAP services two variables that are NULL in value are considered equal (Null = Null), and the expression (Null <> Null) is always false (This is unlike other programming languages such as Visual Basic; if variables A and B are both NULL then we cannot say that A = B. We have to say that A <> B). To further discuss NULLS in MDX and Analysis Services, let's discuss the following example. If you are trying to find the percentage difference between the sale price and cost, you may write:

```
100 * ([measures].[sales] - [measures].[cost]) / [measures].[cost].
```

If the sales value is NULL, but the cost is not NULL, then the expression evaluates to:

```
100 * (0 - [measures].[cost]) / [measures].[cost]
```

which is –100%. However, if the cost is NULL and the sales are not, then the expression results in an overflow due to the division by zero. Analysis Services returns a bogus value in the string "-1.INF". If both the cost and sales were NULL, then Analysis Services will result in an empty value. This example gives you an idea of how you may get incorrect results (even though the calculation was correct) when dealing with NULLs and that you always have to guard against such situations.

Another way you can get empty values for your cells is when you reference invalid members or tuples. Invalid members can occur in several ways. For instance referencing the children of a leaf-level member will yield an empty value because there are no children of leaf levels in Analysis Services' hierarchies. Thus, assuming that the leaf level for the geography dimension is City, the expression:

```
[Seattle - Washington].Children
```

will yield an empty cell, and using this expression as part of a tuple or set will also yield an invalid tuple or set. Thus the set:

```
{[Seattle - Washington].Children, [1998]}
```

includes only empty tuples.

It is particularly important to check for invalid members when using the range operator, the colon. The reason this is important is because if a range is specified, and one of the two values specifying its boundaries is invalid, Analysis Services returns a range that extends to the edge of the database, with the ordering of members on the same level as the valid member.

For example, if we take the range: [December].NextMember:[July], the second member (July) will be valid. However, December.NextMember will be invalid. Analysis Services, in this case returns the range: {[January]:[July]}.

On the other hand, if you were to specify the range, [July]:[January].PrevMember, with the invalid member on the right, the resulting set would be: {[July]:[December]}. If both sides of the range specify invalid members, the resulting set will be empty.

To test and guard against these situations, you can either use the IsEmpty() function, or you can be more creative in using the IIF() function. For example, if you are calculating a three-month total sales moving average, you need to make sure at least three months exist for the period over which you are calculating your results. To do this, you can write:

```
IIf(
     COUNT( LastPeriods(3, [Time]), INCLUDEEMPTY) >= 3,
     Avg(LastPeriods(3, [Time]), [Measures].[TotalSales]),
     Null
     )
```

In the example above, we are checking the count of periods to make sure we have at least three going backward before we do the calculation. If we don't have three or more periods, we return a NULL for the moving average. As another example, if you want to find the sum of total sales for a particular range of time and you suspect that the left side of the range could be empty or invalid, you can check for this conditions using the IsEmpty() function:

```
IIf(
  NOT IsEmpty( [Time].CurrentMember.Lag(12)),
  SUM([Time].CurrentMember.Lag(12):[Time].CurrentMember, [Measures].[TotalSales]),
  Null
  )
```

One last note is that the colon is not the only way you can construct ranges. You can build your ranges using functions like ParallelPeriod() and Cousin(). The same principle also applies to dealing with invalid members to these ranges.

The COALESCEEMPTY Function

Another way to find out about empty cells and handle them is by using the COALESCEEMPTY function. As the name implies, this function coalesces the value of an empty set to a number or a string. Support for this function is mandatory and all OLE DB providers for OLAP should support it. The structure for this function is:

```
COALESCEEMPTY(value_expression, value_expression [, value_expression] ...)
```

As a result, an empty cell will end up with some non-empty values. For example, COALESCEEMPTY(Value1, Value2) returns Value1 if Value1 is not empty, and Value2 if Value1 is empty. The function COALESCEEMPTY(Value1, Value2, Value3, ...Valuen) returns the first non-empty values of the arguments passed to it.

The COALESCEEMPTY function is similar to using a CASE expression. Thus COALSECEEMPTY(Value1, Value2) is similar to saying:

```
CASE
WHEN NOT ISEMPTY(Value1) THEN Value1
ELSE Value2
END
```

Which means that if Value1 is not empty, the CASE statement will return Value1, otherwise, it will return Value2.

Taking this even further, COALESCEEMPTY(Value1, Value2, Value3, ...Valuen) is the same as saying:

```
CASE
WHEN NOT ISEMPTY(Value1) THEN Value1
ELSE  COALESCEEMPTY(Value2, Value3, ..., Valuen)
```

Which can be expanded further to read:

```
CASE
WHEN NOT ISEMPTY(Value1) THEN Value1
ELSE
     CASE
     WHEN NOT ISEMPTY(Value2) THEN Value2
     ELSE COALESCEEMPTY(Value3, Value4, ..., Valuen)
```

Counting Empty Cells

Many MDX functions, such as COUNT and AVERAGE, evaluate the count of cells. All MDX functions, except for the COUNT function, ignore empty cells. The COUNT function has an optional parameter, INCLUDEEMPTY, which, if provided, results in including empty cells in the count process. In general, counting empty cells is a little tricky and has to be done with caution. For example, if you are presenting the sales of automobile models at dealerships across a certain region, you may want to show all the dealerships in that region, even if the sale of a particular model was nil in that dealership (which corresponds with empty cells). On the other hand, if you are calculating average sales of automobile models per dealer per region, you may not want to include the dealerships that did not sell the model of interest because including it would decrease the average.

Empty Cells in a Cellset and the NON EMPTY Keyword

As we saw at the beginning of the *Empty Cells* section above, MDX queries might result in empty cells as part of the returned set. Just like any other cell, an empty cell is associated with a set of tuples. Sometimes the tuple itself is said to be empty when every cell is empty at the intersection of this tuple and any other tuple in all of the other axes.

End-user applications may choose to show or hide empty cells from the cellset. MDX provides the keyword NON EMPTY to provide for this capability. This keyword is usually provided at the axis level. If provided, NON EMPTY forces the result to exclude empty tuples along an axis from the dataset. The NON EMPTY keyword fits in the MDX statement as follows:

```
MDX_Statement ::= SELECT axis_specification
                        [, axis_specification...]
                  FROM cube_specification
                  WHERE slicer_specification
axis_specification ::= [NON EMPTY] set_expression ON axis_name
```

As you can see, NON EMPTY is an optional keyword. The default is not to provide it, which means returning all cells including empty tuples.

If you think about it, you can still get empty cells even if NON EMPTY is specified in the MDX statement for all axes. As an example, let's say that the dealer named Jackson Cars did not sell any Ford or Lincoln cars in the first and second quarter of 1998. Let's say that in the third and fourth quarter they sold specifically Lincoln cars, but still no Ford cars. Now, consider the following query:

```
SELECT
    NON EMPTY CROSSJOIN({Jackson Cars, Anderson Vehicles}, {[Ford], [Lincoln]})
        ON COLUMNS,
    NON EMPTY {[1998], [1999]} ON ROWS
FROM Sales
WHERE (Sales)
```

This results in the following dataset:

	Jackson Cars		Anderson Vehicles	
	Ford	**Lincoln**	**Ford**	**Lincoln**
1998		$250,000	$1,023,900	$567,450
1999	$350,940	$780,000	$1,125,000	$612,900

You notice in this example that the cell corresponding to Jackson Cars/Ford/1998 is empty because this dealer did not sell any Ford cars in 1998. The reason this cell was still empty in the cellset despite the NON EMPTY operator is that it does not represent an empty tuple, and the NON EMPTY operator filters out only completely empty tuples.

More on Named Sets and Calculated Members

As you might recall from the previous chapter, you can define named sets and calculated members using the WITH operator. Let's take a look at the example you saw in Chapter 10:

```
WITH
     MEMBER  [Measures].[Profit] AS
     '[Measures].[Sales] - [Measures].[Cost]',
     SOLVE_ORDER = 1
     MEMBER  [Time].[Percent Change] AS
     '((([TIME].[November-1998], [Measures].Currentmember) - ([Time].[October-1998],
[Measures].Currentmember))/([TIME].[November-1998],[Measures].Currentmember)',
     FORMAT_STRING = 'Percent',
     SOLVE_ORDER = 2
SELECT
     { [Measures].[Sales],
       [Measures].[Cost],
       [Measures].[Profit] } on columns,
     { [Time].[October-1998],
       [Time].[November-1998],
       [Time].[Percent Change] } on rows
FROM EmployeeCube
WHERE ( [Stores].[City].[ Troy, Michigan ] )
```

You notice here that we have multiple formulae to evaluate. It matters which formula is evaluated first on the resulting set. The table below results from the evaluation of the members according to the provided SOLVE_ORDER.

	Sales	Cost	Profit
October, 1998	$120,000	$69,000	$51,000
November, 1998	$150,000	$71,000	$79,000
Percent Change	25%	3%	*55%*

As we saw in Chapter 10, the hilighted value in the table above, is particularly sensitive to this solve order. The following rules define the semantics of SOLVE_ORDER:

❑   Evaluation of expressions with solve order values specified is always done before the evaluation of expressions and members that don't have a solve order. The evaluation among members with solve orders takes place from the lower SOLVE_ORDER to the higher SOLVE_ORDER.

❑   Solve orders must always be greater than or equal to 0.

❑   The default solve order of an expression is 0.

Let's revisit, for a moment, a topic we met in the last chapter – lifetime and scope of named sets and calculated members. If the scope of these values is not identified in their formula, the scope defaults to the formula itself, and the values don't exist outside the formula. Named sets provide a powerful mechanism to preserve state during a session and for all sessions as well. To define a custom scope for a named set or calculated member, you may write:

```
Create-Formula_Statement := [Scope]  formula_specification
```

The `formula_specification` is the same as the formulae used to create the set and/or member. The `[Scope]` operator, can be used to extend the lifetime and scope of the set or member. The value of this operator can be set to either:

❑ `GLOBAL`: The entity created with this specification will be visible to all sessions and queries from all of these sessions can use it.

❑ `SESSION`: The entity created with this specification will only be visible to queries in the session in which it is created. The session is started by connecting to Analysis Services, and ends by disconnecting from it.

If the scope value is not defined, it defaults to the session value.

The name of the entity, named set or calculated member has to be qualified with the cube name to which it belongs. You can also have two named sets or calculated members with the same name qualified by the same cube name as long as each exists in a different session from the other.

An example of creating a named set with session scope is:

```
CREATE SET SESSION SalesCube.RowsAxisSet AS {Qtr1.CHILDREN, Qtr2, Qtr3,
Qtr4.CHILDREN}
```

or:

```
CREATE SET SalesCube.RowsAxisSet AS {Qtr1.CHILDREN, Qtr2, Qtr3, Qtr4.CHILDREN}
```

and, as an example of creating a named set with a global scope:

```
CREATE SET GLOBAL SalesCube.RowsAxisSet AS {Qtr1.CHILDREN, Qtr2, Qtr3,
Qtr4.CHILDREN}
```

MDX Expressions

An MDX statement contains expressions that operate on different items of the Analysis Services schema. These expressions deal with sets, tuples, members, numbers, and strings. This section, therefore, will present certain issues that have to do with particular expressions, which warrant more explanation beyond the definitions and examples provided in the appendix.

Set Value Expressions

As we discovered previously, a **set** is a collection of tuples, which are in turn a collection of members from different dimensions. Set expressions operate on the different levels of the set elements starting with the set as a whole, and continuing to the individual members of its tuples. Drill-down and drill-up operations are some of the most common operations in applications with graphical user interfaces that present multi-dimensional data in a hierarchical fashion. Drilling operations can be conducted on the member or the level basis. For example, take the set {1998, 1999}. You might want to obtain a set that contains 1998, 1999, and all the children of 1998. This is a sample of drilling down by member. On the other hand, consider the set {1998, 1999} again and let's try to get a set that contains 1998, 1999, and all the quarters in 1998, which is an example of a drill-down operation by level. MDX allows you to combine any of these drilling operations with a top or a bottom condition. For example, consider the set {1998, 1999} and return a set that includes 1998, 1999, and the top two quarters of 1998 based on Sales.

> Please note that MDX functions that perform drill-up and drill-down operations require a set that is formed from a single dimension. In other words, the set used as an argument to these functions cannot be the result of a CROSSJOIN operation. Functions that have this restriction include: DRILLDOWNMEMBER, DRILLUPMEMBER, DRILLDOWNMEMBERTOP, DRILLDOWNLEVEL, DRILLDOWNMEMBERBOTTOM, DRILLDOWNLEVELTOP, DRILLUPLEVEL, DRILLDOWNLEVELBOTTOM, and TOGGLEDRILLSTATE.

To better understand the following functions, let's take a look at the hierarchy of the product dimension presented in the following figure:

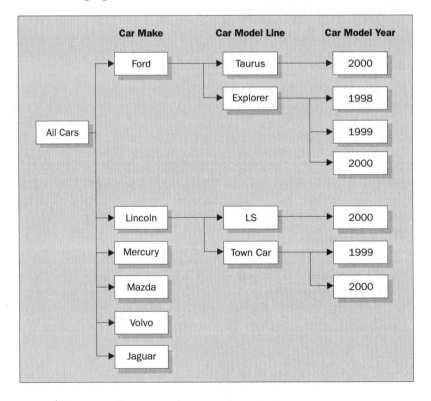

Drilling by Member

The first function to discuss is the DRILLDOWNMEMBER() function, which is used to drill down by a member. The syntax for this function is:

```
DRILLDOWNMEMBER(Set1, Set2 [, RECURSIVE])
```

This function drills down the members of the set Set1 that are present in Set2. If the word RECURSIVE is provided, then the drilling continues beyond the first next level of these members. Since Analysis Services only accepts complete hierarchies, the RECURSIVE keyword will cause the drill down to go all the way to the leaf level of the dimension hierarchy.

For example, the function:

```
DRILLDOWNMEMBER({Ford, Lincoln}, {Ford, Honda})
```

will yield the result {Ford, Taurus, Explorer, Lincoln}.

Providing the optional RECURSIVE flag will yield the set:

```
{Ford, Taurus, [Taurus-2000], Explorer, [Explorer-1998], [Explorer-
1999], [Explorer-2000], Lincoln}
```

The way this function works is as follows:

❑ The member "Ford" from Set2 is inspected to see whether it is present in Set1. The inspection yields a positive result; therefore, it is drilled down to yield the set that has Ford, all models in Ford (in this example), and Lincoln as the result set.

❑ The second member of Set2, Honda, is inspected to see whether it is present in Set1. It is not; therefore, Honda is not drilled down any further, and the set result is still the same. If Honda were to be part of Set1, then it would have also been drilled and the resulting set would have been joined in a union operation to the first result.

This process is sensitive to the order of the members in Set2. This becomes clearer if we were to have another member in Set2 that is also present in Set1.

This function is typically used in applications with a graphical user interface that allows users to click on a "+" sign, for instance, to expand the contents of a branch. In this case, the function is called with the parameters: DRILLDOWNMEMBER(Set1, {m}), where {m} is the member that was clicked. More sophisticated applications allow for drilldown of multiple members and for recursive drilldowns as well.

The DRILLDOWNMEMBERTOP function is a variation of DRILLDOWNMEMBER. Instead of including all children (or descendants) of a member, it includes only the top n children (or descendants) based on the evaluation of a numeric expression. The syntax of this function is as follows:

```
DRILLDOWNMEMBERTOP(Set1, Set2, Index [, [numeric_expression][,
RECURSIVE]])
```

The desired number of children (or descendants) is specified by Index, and <numeric_ expression> gives the criterion. For example, the call

```
DRILLDOWNMEMBERTOP ({[Lincoln LS], [Ford Explorer], [Ford Taurus]}, {[Ford
Explorer], [Honda Accord], [Lincoln LS]}, 2, [Unit Sales])
```

335

returns the following set:

```
{[Ford Explorer], [Ford Explorer - 1998], [Ford Explorer - 1999],
[Lincoln LS], [Lincoln LS - 2000], [Ford Taurus]}
```

In this case, the top two model years of the Ford Explorer and Lincoln LS in sales were included in the result set. For Lincoln LS, since only the 2000 model year is available in our example, only this model year was returned.

Use of the RECURSIVE flag has an effect similar to its effect in DRILLDOWNMEMBER.

The function DRILLDOWNMEMBERBOTTOM is similar, except that the bottom condition is applied instead of the top condition.

To drill up by a member, use the DRILLUPMEMBER function. The syntax is as follows:

```
DRILLUPMEMBER(Set1, Set2)
```

Drills up the members in Set1 that are present in Set2. To understand this function, let's take a look at the following example:

```
DRILLUPMEMBER({Ford, Taurus, [Taurus-2000], Explorer, [Explorer-1998],
[Explorer-1999], [Explorer-2000], Lincoln}, {Taurus, Explorer, [Honda
Accord]})
```

The result is the set:

```
{Ford, Lincoln, Taurus, Explorer}
```

In this example, the car model line-level was rolled up (drilled up) for the model lines in Set2 that exist in Set1.

> Note that there is no RECURSIVE flag for the DRILLUPMEMBER function. This is because when a member is drilled up, all the descendants (not just the immediate children) are removed. In other words, drilling up is usually recursive in nature and does not need to be explicitly specified to be so.

Finally, a useful function that combines both the DRILLDOWNMEMBER and DRILLUPMEMBER is the TOGGLEDRILLSTATE function. The syntax for this function is:

```
TOGGLEDRILLSTATE(Set1, Set2[, RECURSIVE])
```

This toggles the drill state for each member of Set2 that is present in Set1. If a member m of Set2 that is present in Set1 is drilled down (that is, has a child or descendant in Set1), then Analysis Services applies the function DRILLUPMEMBER(Set1, {m}). On the other hand, if the member m is already drilled up (there is no descendant of m that immediately follows m in Set1), then Analysis Services applies the function DRILLDOWNMEMBER(Set1, {m}[, RECURSIVE]) to Set1. If the TOGGLEDRILLSTATE function were called with the optional RECURSIVE flag, the DRILLDOWNMEMBER is also called with that flag.

For example, the function:

```
TOGGLEDRILLSTATE({Ford, Taurus, [Taurus-2000], Explorer, [Explorer-
1998], [Explorer-1999], [Explorer-2000], Lincoln}, {Taurus})
```

will be the same as running the function:

```
DRILLUPMEMBER({Ford, Taurus, [Taurus-2000], Explorer, [Explorer-1998],
[Explorer-1999], [Explorer-2000], Lincoln}, {Taurus, Explorer, [Honda
Accord]})
```

This is because m, which corresponds to {Taurus}, is already drilled down in the first set (it has the child: [Taurus-2000]).

Drilling by Level

The first function to discuss here is the DRILLDOWNLEVEL function. The syntax for this function is:

```
DRILLDOWNLEVEL(Set [,Level])
```

The function drills down the members in Set to one level below Level, if it is specified. If Level is not specified, it defaults to the lowest level in Set. Using the same product hierarchy presented in the figure we saw previously, we can build the following example on this function:

```
DRILLDOWNLEVEL({Ford, Lincoln}, [Car Make])
```

will yield the set:

```
{Ford, Taurus, Explorer, Lincoln, LS, Town Car}
```

In this example, the level below the car make level is the car model. Therefore, OLAP services drills down the members in the set to that level. In real-life applications, the application allows the user to select a level to which they want to drill down the set members to from something like a drop-down list.

A number of functions similar to the drilling by member functions are also available to allow for drilling by level while only including the top or bottom m number of members in the resulting set. These functions include DRILLDOWNLEVELTOP and DRILLDOWNLEVELBOTTOM. Similar to their member drilling counterparts, these functions take an index that determines the number of members to return after the drilling operation, and a numeric expression the result of which is used to order members in a level in an ascending or descending order.

> *Notice that there is no RECURSIVE flag with these functions, that is because we specify the exact level we want to drill to (or it is specified by default) and the RECURSIVE flag makes no sense in this situation, since the function does not go beyond the specified level.*

Just like there is a DRILLUPMEMBER function, there is a parallel one for the level case. The function is called, DRILLUPLEVEL, and has the syntax:

```
DRILLUPLEVEL(Set [, Level])
```

A practical example use of this function may explain what it means and does. Imagine having a graphical user interface that shows an expanded hierarchy of products, similar to the figure overleaf. Clicking the "-" sign at any level will drill-up the members of the hierarchy immediately below the "-" sign to the level at which the sign is located. However, to drill up all the members to the level of your interest, you may want to select a level from a drop-down list.

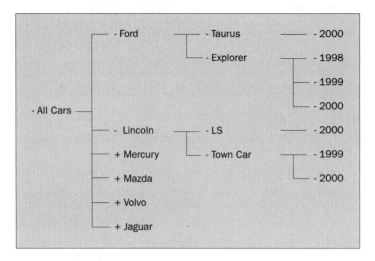

For example, to roll up the set to the Ford car make level, click the "-" next to the Ford make. The result will be similar to the figure shown below:

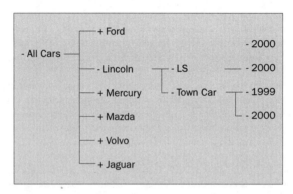

This is equivalent to using the DRILLUPMEMBER function as follows:

```
DRILLUPMEMBER({Ford, [All Ford Models and Model Years], Lincoln, [All Lincoln
Models and Model Years], Mercury, Mazda, Volvo, Jaguar}, {[Ford]})
```

On the other hand, the following figure shows the difference between this result and the result of applying the DRILLUPLEVEL function as follows:

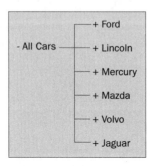

```
DRILLUPLEVEL({Ford, [All Ford Models and Model Years], Lincoln, [All Lincoln
Models and Model Years], Mercury, Mazda, Volvo, Jaguar}, [Ford Models])
```

Preserving State During UI Operations

Many multi-dimensional applications allow users to drill up and down data sets to view the data. In order to avoid re-writing the query to perform drill operations, MDX provides a powerful way to preserve state of these queries using the DRILLUP and DRILLDOWN functions. The way this works is by representing each axis expression by a named set. The named sets can then be represented in the drill functions, such as DRILLDOWNMEMBER, DRILLDOWNLEVEL, and so on.

For example, as you saw earlier, we can create a set with global scope with a statement like:

```
CREATE SET GLOBAL SalesCube.RowsAxisSet AS {Qtr1.CHILDREN, Qtr2, Qtr3,
Qtr4.CHILDREN}
```

or:

```
CREATE SET GLOBAL SalesCube.Q1Childern AS {Qtr1.CHILDREN}
```

This named set can then be used in the DRILLUP and DRILLDOWN functions, which will make these functions have the same scope as the set. For example, using the two named sets above in the following function will cause the function to persist:

```
DRILLUPLEVEL(SalesCube.RowsAxisSet, SalesCube.Q1Childern)
```

Finally, when you use the function above in the MDX query below, you persist the query:

```
SELECT DRILLUPLEVEL(SalesCube.RowsAxisSet, SalesCube.Q1Childern) on rows
FROM SalesCube
```

Of course this is a simple query, and if it were more complex, you might end up using many named sets and Drill functions along the different axes of the query.

Conditional Expressions

MDX includes some conditional expressions that enrich it and make even more powerful. These expressions include:

❑   If Statements

❑   Simple Case Expressions

❑   Searched Case Expressions

Before we start explaining these expressions and bring up some samples of how they can be used, let's look at the comparison, logical, and conditional operators provided by MDX:

Operator	Description
<	Less than (a < b)
>	Greater than (a > b)

Table continued on following page

Operator	Description
<=	Less or equal (a <= b)
>=	Greater or equal (a >= b)
=	Equal (a = b)
<>	Not equal (a <> b)
IsEmpty(Exp)	Returns True if Exp is NULL

MDX also provides some logical operators, such as the AND, OR, NOT, and XOR operators.

XOR is called Exclusive OR (or logical exclusion). The syntax for it is: A XOR B. *In simple terms it means either A or B can be true, but not both or neither. The following table summarizes the results it can return based on the values of A and B:*

A	B	A AND B	A OR B	A XOR B
True	True	True	True	False
True	False	False	True	True
False	True	False	True	True
False	False	False	False	False

If Clause

The If clause is used in MDX in the form IIF. This clause allows you to search on a certain condition and returns one of two value expressions based on the search result. The general syntax for the IIF clause is:

```
IIF(Search Condition, True_Value_Expression, False_Value_Expression)
```

If the search condition is true, the True_Value_Expression is returned. Conversely, if the search condition is false, the False_Value_Expression is returned. The two value expressions, True_Value_Expression and False_Value_Expression must be of the same data type, for example, they can either both be strings or both be numeric.

The following is an example on how the IIF clause can be used in MDX queries. The query in the example returns the sales, the goals and the difference between the actual sales and the goal of automobiles for two car dealerships. The IIF statement ensures that no negative values are returned:

```
WITH MEMBER [Measures].[Diff] AS
     'IIF ((Sales > Goal), (Sales - Goal), (Goal - Sales))'
SELECT
   {Sales, Goal, Diff} ON COLUMNS,
   CROSSJOIN(  {[Jackson Cars], [Anderson Vehicles]},
              {[Q1-1998], [Q2-1998], [Q3-1998], [Q4-1998]}) ON ROWS
FROM Sales
WHERE ([1998], [Cars].[Ford])
```

This results in the following dataset (sales in thousands of dollars):

1998	Jackson Cars			Anderson Vehicles		
	Sales	Goal	Diff	Sales	Goal	Diff
Q1	125	100	25	207	150	57
Q2	131	110	21	143	150	7
Q3	119	120	1	181	145	36
Q4	123	115	8	190	145	45

Simple Case Expression

The CASE expression comes handy in many situations when writing MDX queries. The general syntax for this expression is:

```
CASE Case_Value_Expression
    WHEN  When_Value_Expression  THEN Then_Value_Expression
    ...
    ...
    ...
    ELSE  Else_Value_Expression
END
```

The dots in the code above indicate that the WHEN clause can be repeated several times. This expression returns the Then_Value_Expression corresponding to the first When_Value_Expression that evaluates to True. In other words, even if more than one of the When_Value_Expressions is True, the statement will return the first one of these True expressions in the list. If none of the When_Value_Expressions evaluates to True, the Else_Value_Expression is returned. It is important to note that the data type of the When_Value_Expression, Then_Value_Expression and the Else_Value_Expression is VARIANT. The ELSE part of the statement can be left out. In this case, if none of the WHEN expressions evaluates to True, the statement returns an empty cell value (basically does nothing). The following example demonstrates the use of this function:

```
WITH MEMBER [Measures].[Rating] AS
    'CASE ([Measures].[PerformanceRating)
            WHEN   5  THEN  "Excellent"
            WHEN   4  THEN  "Very Good"
            WHEN   3  THEN  "Good"
            WHEN   2  THEN  "Poor"
            WHEN   1  THEN  "Very Poor"
            ELSE   "NA"
    END'
SELECT {[Measures].[Sales], [Measures].[Rating]} ON COLUMNS,
    Dealerships.MEMBERS ON ROWS
FROM Sales
WHERE ([1998], [Geography].[States].[MI], [Products].[All])
```

The MDX query above returns the sales amount together with a performance rating for car dealerships in Michigan. The rating value is decided based on the value of [Measures].[PerformanceRating]. A CASE expression is used for this purpose to return the appropriate value for the performance rating.

Searched Case Expression

The Searched Case Expression takes the simple case expression a step further by making the WHEN operands search conditions themselves. In the example presented in the previous section, a performance rating is evaluated based on a rating value from 1 to 5. What if the evaluation is based on the percentage of sales above target sales? For example, if the salesperson exceeds their target sale (the value of the named member in the query below is higher than 100%), then the rating is 5. To express this logic in the MDX statement, you can write:

```
WITH MEMBER [Measures].[PerformanceTemp] AS
    ([Measures].[Sales] - [Measures].[TargetSales])/
    [Measures].[TargetSales]*100
MEMBER [Measures].[Rating] AS
    CASE
        WHEN [Measures].[PerformanceTemp] > 100 THEN 5
        WHEN [Measures].[PerformanceTemp] > 50  THEN 4
        WHEN [Measures].[PerformanceTemp] > 0   THEN 3
        WHEN [Measures].[PerformanceTemp] > -25 THEN 2
        ELSE 1
    END
SELECT {[Measures].[Sales], [Measures].[Rating]}
    ON COLUMNS,
    Dealerships.MEMBERS ON ROWS
FROM Sales
WHERE ([1998], [Geography].[States].[MI], [Products].[All])
```

The example above shows the same results as the simple case expression example, except that the performance rating is evaluated based on ranges of values of the percentage gain of targeted sales for Michigan dealerships in 1998.

Note that the WHEN clauses have to be in the order presented above in order for this case expression to work (same is true for the simple case example too). This is because we are using the ">" operator rather than bracketing the values between "<" and ">" operators. In other words, if we were to express the WHEN clauses as:

```
WHEN [Measures].[PerformanceTemp] > 100 THEN 5
WHEN ([Measures].[PerformanceTemp] > 50  AND
[Measures].[PerformanceTemp] <100) THEN 4
WHEN ([Measures].[PerformanceTemp] > 0   AND
[Measures].[PerformanceTemp] < 50) THEN 3
WHEN ([Measures].[PerformanceTemp] > -25 AND
[Measures].[PerformanceTemp] < 0) THEN 2
```

Then we would not have to keep these WHEN clauses in the same order.

MDX provides a rich set of built-in functions and operators to handle all situations from specifying cells and tuples, to performing numerical calculations and aggregations, to filtering operators, ordering functions, and hierarchy-preserving functions, to name but a few.

The MDX Sample Application

To make writing MDX statements easier and avoid syntax problems, Microsoft shipped a sample MDX application to help write such statements. The application is installed with the Analysis Services installation. The application is written in Visual Basic and its code is provided in the folder located at "`<Drive Letter>:\Program Files\Microsoft Analysis Services\Samples\MDXSample`". If you are a seasoned VB programmer, you may want to consider looking closely at the code, or even modifying it to fit you needs. The MDX sample application can be launched from the Analysis Services group in the Start menu. Once launched, you are prompted to enter an Analysis Services server name to connect to, and an OLE DB Provider for OLAP to use. The defaults are your local Analysis Services Server, and the OLE DB Provider for Microsoft OLAP (MSOLAP). Although the application is anything but as sophisticated as the query-by-example (QBE) tools provided in MS Access and MS Visual Studio, it still serves as a good start to get familiar with the MDX syntax and avoid such errors when building your expressions.

The main application screen after passing the connection dialog box is shown in the following screenshot. In this screen, you can select an Analysis Services database from the Database (DB) drop-down menu (located on the toolbar), select a previously saved query to work with, and select one of many views provided to make building the MDX statement and testing it easy:

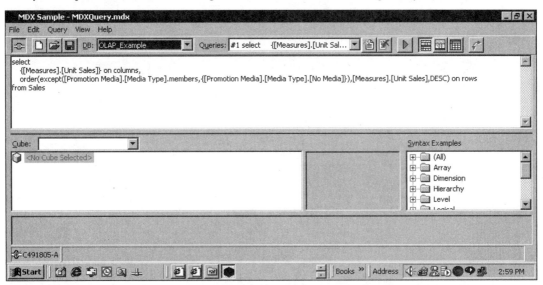

The main screen is composed of a number of ActiveX controls that allow you to view the multi-dimensional database cubes and the cube schema, write your query against the Analysis Services database, view and select from a list of available functions, and view the results after running the query. We will not go into the details of the VB applications and the individual user controls that comprise the application; instead, we will simply look at how you can write a sample OLAP query with this tool.

In the example, we will be using the Sales cube in the `FoodMart 2000` database that ships with Analysis Services and build a query that retrieves the percentage store profits for the different departments, ordering the results based on the profit rate in descending order. The query that accomplishes this is shown below:

```
WITH member [Measures].[Store Profit Rate] as
        '([Measures].[Store Sales]-[Measures].[Store Cost])/
         [Measures].[Store Cost]', format = '#.00%'
```

```
SELECT
    {[Measures].[Store Cost],[Measures].[Store Sales],
        [Measures].[Store Profit Rate]} on columns,
    Order([Product].[Product Department].members,
        [Measures].[Store Profit Rate], BDESC) on rows
FROM Sales
where ([Time].[1997])
```

You can either type the query in the query section of the MDX Sample Application screen, or you can build it using the functions and tools available to you. Let's see how you can build it making sure the syntax is correct.

❑ First define your calculated member using the WITH clause. Type "WITH MEMBER " and double-click the **Measures** dimension in the cubes' schema tree.

❑ Name the calculated member as [Store Profit Rate] and type AS

❑ As a definition of the calculated member, type the formula shown in single quotes dragging and dropping the measure dimension members from the tree view whenever possible.

❑ Use the FORMAT operator to format the string resulting from the calculation of the specified member as format = '#.00%'. This will format the member as a percentage with two decimal digits. So far, the screen should look as shown below:

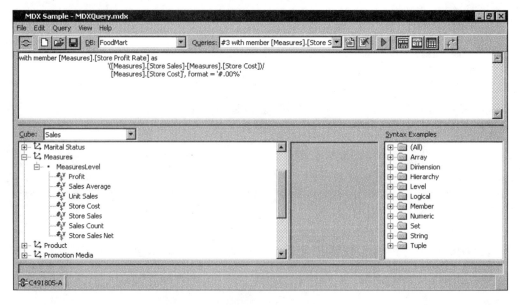

❑ Next, you can type the SELECT statement, or type the keywords and drag and drop the members and dimensions from the cubes' schema tree view onto the query section.

❑ What is worth mentioning here is that when adding the Order function, select it from the function list found under the **Syntax Examples**, then drag and drop it onto the query pane. The function provides you with guidance as to what arguments it needs. Replace the different sections showed in the figure above with measures, dimensions, etc. that you drag and drop from the cubes' schema tree view.

❑ After you finish building the rest of the query, you can run it to view the results:

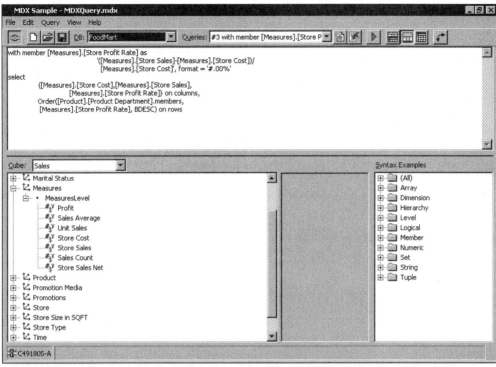

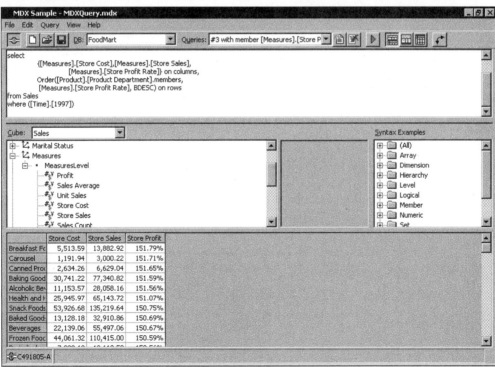

Summary

Unfortunately, the release of Microsoft Analysis Services did not include the comprehensive documentation of MDX, with samples, that one would like to see. This chapter built on what we learned in Chapter 10 to include some of the powerful concepts and features of MDX. Together, these two chapters should have you well on your way to using this language to build queries that you can use in your OLAP applications. Finally, the sample MDX application provided with Analysis Services can be of great help to familiarize you with the language syntax. The next chapter marks the end line of the OLAP solution design and implementation. The chapter discusses the end-user part of this solution – the reporting tools that deliver the data to the user in the form that benefits them most.

Data Warehouse

Using the PivotTable Service

Throughout this book we've explored the means by which the SQL Server 2000 Analysis Services provide a powerful OLAP server engine that facilitates data mining and OLAP. While the earlier chapters focused on the server side tools and services of Data Warehousing and OLAP Services in SQL Server 2000, this chapter will discuss the robust client tool found in the SQL Server 2000 Analysis Services architecture: the PivotTable Service.

In this chapter, we'll be covering the following areas:

- ❑ What the PivotTable Service is
- ❑ How the PivotTable Service can be used
- ❑ Multidimensional expressions
- ❑ The PivotTable View
- ❑ Creating and using a PivotTable in Microsoft Excel 2002

The example spreadsheets and code covered in this chapter are available as a download from http://www.wrox.com. Let's begin this chapter by taking a look at the PivotTable Service.

Introducing the PivotTable Service

The SQL Server Analysis Services were architected for client-server systems. The two main parts of the Analysis Services are the Analysis Services server and the client PivotTable Service that allows client manipulation of OLAP data.

The PivotTable Service is a set of tools that enable the transfer of OLAP cubes to client applications from the OLAP server. To achieve its goals practically, the PivotTable Service provides the developer with two programming interfaces for querying OLAP Data sources:

❑ OLE DB for OLAP

❑ ActiveX Data Objects Multidimensional (ADO MD)

To harness the full power of these interfaces, tools such as those within the Visual Studio .Net are used to create applications that can query multi-dimensional data sources. The relationship scenario is illustrated in the Figure below. There is an observable performance problem with ADO MD when used in C++. For this reason, developers tend to favor using OLE DB for OLAP in their C++ applications and ADO MD in Visual Basic, and ASP applications.

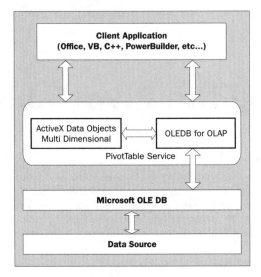

Quick Primer on Data Access Technologies

Microsoft specifies quite a lot of data access interfaces that developers can use. It can be quite confusing to fully understand the purpose of all these interfaces. Here is a summary of the major data access standards that you need to know of before diving into the core concepts of the PivotTable Service.

OLE DB is a COM-based data access interface for manipulating data from any kind of data storage. It provides set of rich, high-performance, low-level API that developers can use to query and manipulate data sources. The OLE DB API is a very broad and subtle topic that is out of the scope of this chapter. A full reference to OLEDB can be found on MSDN at http://www.msdn.microsoft.com/library/default.asp?url=/library/en- us/oledb/htm/oledbpart1 _introduction_to_ole_db.asp.

ActiveX Data Objects (ADO) is yet another COM-based data-access interface that is one layer on top of OLE DB. It provides an elegant object model for data access that is preferred by VBScript and Visual Basic programmers. Keep in mind that ADO is in effect a simpler form of OLE DB, which means that when you are calling ADO methods and assigning properties, you are using OLE DB. The ADO object model encapsulates the complexity of the core OLE DB API. To query a SQL Server relational database with ADO, T-SQL statements are used as command strings. For a complete reference on ADO refer to *ADO 2.6 Programmer's Reference*, written by David Sussman, and published by Wrox Press, ISBN 1-861004-63-X.

Usage of the PivotTable Service

The PivotTable Service architecture is engineered to reduce the workload of the OLAP server while providing flexibility for the developer to query the OLAP data source. The service is capable of achieving some great results apart from simply retrieving data from OLAP cubes.

The PivotTable Service can temporarily cache slices of OLAP cubes or entire OLAP cubes in the primary storage (more commonly referred to as either RAM or memory) on the client machine. In this case, it doesn't have to re-query the OLAP server repeatedly to obtain the same cube or slice of a cube it retrieved earlier. Let's say that, an hour ago, you queried the OLAP data source for cubic data on the details of orders that were shipped to Mexico during the year 2000. Right now, you want an analysis report that compares the 2000 figures with the 2001 figures. The statistics for 2000 could have not been amended, so the PivotTable Service instantly queries the OLAP data source for the 2001 data cube, using the cached 2000 data to provide you with an analysis. This reduces network traffic and server-side processing while generating a faster result at the same time.

The PivotTable Service can also save entire OLAP cubes on a secondary storage device on a client machine. One cube is saved as a cube (*.cub) file. This way, it provides for the availability of the data even when the client is disconnected from the network. In a mobile computing environment, you have the flexibility of retrieving data cubes from the OLAP server, storing them on your own machine, and having them available for analysis even when you are disconnected from the network. A cube that is saved on the client machine is referred to as an **offline cube**. The service can also work with Microsoft Internet Information Server to import data from an internet source.

The luxury of the PivotTable Service comes at a considerable cost to client resources. In spite of the points above, The PivotTable Service needs a constant connection to the network server providing the OLAP data. According to the MSDN documentation, it is required that the PivotTable Service be installed on every client machine connected to the OLAP data source and that it be provided with at least 500KB of memory and 5MB of disk space on each machine where it resides to effectively operate in a Client/Server environment. Added to that, each client workstation must have installed Microsoft Data Access Components (MDAC) 2.6 or later. This means that after the installation of an application that uses the analysis services, you will discover that you used a large amount of disk space on each client workstation running the PivotTable Service. Of course, these are merely the minimum requirements, and it would make sense to take advantage of the relatively huge memory and hard drive sizes available with new computers.

OLE DB For OLAP

In order to harness the full power of the OLE DB standard API, an OLE DB provider must be used as an interface. There are several OLE DB providers on the market today. For example, the OLE DB provider for SQL Server allows you to access SQL Server data through the OLE DB interface. The OLE DB for OLAP provider, which is part of the PivotTable Service, enables you to manipulate both relational and multidimensional data from an OLAP Data source.

It is advisable to use the OLE DB for OLAP provider only with applications accessing multidimensional data. OLE DB for OLAP provides the developer with an extended OLE DB API for accessing OLAP data sources, and processing data mining tasks. It enables the developer to create multidimensional queries that returns cubic data.

Operating in a COM environment, the client application uses the core OLE DB standards to connect to an OLAP provider. Making extensive usage of OLE DB for OLAP's three main interfaces; `IMDDataset`, `IMDRangeRowset`, and `IMDFind`, the application is engineered into an elegant transactional structure that can manipulate multidimensional data more efficiently. The interfaces are covered in more detail in Chapter 4.

Multidimensional Expressions

The Multidimensional Expressions (MDX) standard is the subset of T-SQL used to query multidimensional data sources. The MDX syntax is a lot like the standard T-SQL you are used to. Unlike T-SQL, however, MDX allows you to manipulate data the multidimensional way.

While it is possible to query an OLAP data source with T-SQL and SQL, an attempt to format a query that does this is a daunting task. Furthermore, there are a many performance issues that come up when the T-SQL query is being parsed and executed by the server. SQL and T-SQL were structurally designed to query relational data sources, not multidimensional data – MDX is the multidimensional language.

The MDX syntax can be used to query OLAP data, and alter OLAP structures. This chapter provides you with a quick walk through MDX by focusing on some basics that you need to understand in order to get up and run with programming the `PivotTable Service` in the subsequent chapters. Before jumping into MDX, be sure that you fully understand the concepts of cubic data and how it is stored. You can read about cube concepts in Chapter 4,6 and 9. For a complete overview of MDX syntax refer to Chapters 10 and 11.

Data Retrieval

When called, an MDX query retrieves a chunk of multidimensional data referred to as a **dataset**. This dataset is a slice of a cube as defined by the member(s) of an axis or axes of the dimension(s) that are specified in the query.

To better understand the concepts of data retrieval in MDX, let's take a good look at the syntax of its `SELECT` statement:

```
SELECT [<axis [, <axis>...]]
    FROM [<cube >]
[WHERE [<slicer>]]
```

This statement reads: **Select** the specified **axis** dimension from the specified **cube**, **where** the specified **slicing criterion** exists on that specified cube.

`axis` represents the axis that you want to retrieve. In this context, an axis refers to one dimension of a cube. An axis that you specify in the `SELECT` clause of an MDX query is analogous to the columns or fields that you write in the same clause of a SQL query statement.

The `cube` or cubes from which axes are to be retrieved are specified in the `FROM` clause of the statement. A purpose of a cube in this statement is analogous to that of the tables or views in SQL.

The filter for the retrieval of the axes is specified in the `WHERE` clause. An MDX filter is very different from that of SQL. MDX allows you to virtually slice a cube by the criteria that you specify in the `WHERE` clause. The criteria are made up of the names of the members of each axis. To specify a correct slice, each member that you define in the `WHERE` clause must be pointing to one unique data element from a dimension of the cube. This is to ensure that you never format a query to return a slice for more than one member of one dimension.

ActiveX Data Objects, Multi-Dimensional

The ActiveX Data Object Multi-Dimensional (ADO MD) is simply an extended ADO API on top of OLE DB for OLAP. It is the flavor of ADO that is used to query multidimensional data sources. While T-SQL is used for querying relational data sources through ADO, a different, new standard called MDX is used to query SQL Server OLAP Data sources from within ADO MD.

While the ADO object model is best suited to the format of relational data, ADO MD's object model is very simple and aims to cater for the manipulation of multidimensional data.

The ADO MD Object Model

The ADO MD object model provides for two views of a multidimensional database that it connects to: the Database Structural View and the Dimensional View. While the structural view objects visually interpret the structure of the database, the dimensional view objects are what you use to retrieve the actual data.

The Database Structural View

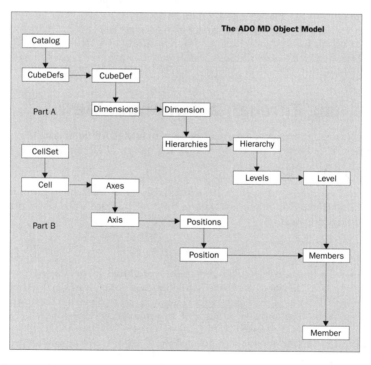

The Database Structural View of ADO MD is illustrated in the above figure. This view provides you with a hierarchy of objects and collections that represent the entire structure of the database. This section is an overview of the objects and collections you need to get accustomed to.

The `Catalog` object defines the identity of the server and database to which you are connected. The functionality present in that object allows us to connect to OLAP services. In the example `FoodMart 2000` database structure, `Catalog` represents the `FoodMart 2000` database.

`CubeRef` defines any individual cube. Notice that the `Catalog` object has a `CubeRefs` collection that contains all the `CubeRef` objects within that catalog, thus all the cubes in the database. A `CubeRef` object can legally represent the Budget cube in FoodMart 2000.

`Dimension` stands for any dimension of a `CubeRef` object. The available dimensions for any `CubeRef` object are stored within its `Dimensions` collection. The `Dimensions` collection of a `CubeRef` object representing the `Budget` cube contains the `Account`, `Store`, `Category`, and `Time` dimensions.

The `Hierarchy` object defines each hierarchy of a dimension. A list of hierarchies for a given dimension object can be found in its `Hierarchies` collection. In the `Budget` cube, `Account` and `Category` have one `Hierarchy` each while `Store` has four and `Time` has three.

The `Level` object provides information about the level of a hierarchy. The `Levels` collection holds the available levels for its parent `Hierarchy` object. It is important to get one thing clear when it comes to levels. We can see in the `FoodMart 2000` database structure that the `Quarter` hierarchy is a child of the `Year` hierarchy of the `Time` dimension of the `Budget` cube. This is not the case in the ADO MD object model. One `Level` object is never the child of another `Level` object. Instead, the two exist at the same level, but their actual levels are maintained by their properties.

The `Member` object stands for any individual `Member` property of a `Level` object. The `Members` collection of a particular `Level` object holds a list of member properties for the parent hierarchy object of its parent `Level` object.

Example Working Through a Structural View

This is a sample of working through the structural view of an OLAP database. All we do here is attempt a connection to the OLAP Server, and try to display the names of all the `Catalog`, `Cube`, and `Dimension` objects in a hierarchical way.

Load Excel 2002 and open the `StructuralViewDisplay.xls` worksheet. From the **Tools Macro** Menu, load the **Visual Basic Editor** and navigate to the **frmStructuralView UserForm** object. The code is very straightforward.

How It Is Done

The code module for the `UserForm` holds five variables at global scope. `Catalog` represents the connection to a valid OLAP Services database, while the two collections declared beneath it reference cubes and dimensions within a cube respectively. The `Cube` and `Dimension` variables in the code module represent single a `Cube` and `Dimension` of an actual cube respectively.

Take a closer look at the `Click` event procedure for the `cmdConnect` button control:

```
Private Sub cmdConnect_Click()
    cmdConnect.Caption = "Connecting..."
    Dim i As Long 'loop counter

    'Create an instance of the catalog object
    Set Catalog = CreateObject("ADO MD.Catalog")
```

```
    Catalog.ActiveConnection = _
            "Data Source=LOCALHOST;Provider=MSOLAP;" _
        & "Database=FoodMart 2000;" _
        & "UserId=<user>;Password=<password>;"
    txtCatalog.Text = Catalog.Name

    'get the list of cubes
    Set Cubes = Catalog.CubeDefs

    'Populate the available cubes into the Cube(s)
    For Each Cube In Cubes
        lstCubes.AddItem Cube.Name
    Next

    'Disable further attempts to connect
    cmdConnect.Enabled = False
    cmdConnect.Caption = "Connected"
End Sub
```

This event handler does three things:

❑   Connect to the FoodMart 2000 data source by assigning a valid connection string to the ActiveConnection property of the Catalog object. For the code to work, you will need to replace the DataSource parameter with the name of your OLAP server. In this case we've used LOCALHOST. UserID, the Password must also be specified if your data source requires them.

❑   Display the name of the data source inside the txtCatalog edit control.

❑   Populate the lstCubes ListBox control with the names of all the cubes in the data source by looping through the Catalog's Cubes collection.

Run the example VBA solution and click the Connect button. The Cube(s) list box is populated. Now, click any one of the cubes listed in the box, and notice that the Dimension(s) list box is populated with the name(s) of the available dimension(s) for the clicked cube. This action is performed in the code that handles lstCubes's Change event:

```
Private Sub lstCubes_Change()
    Dim strName 'Name of cube

    'Get the name of the selected cube
    strName = lstCubes.Value
    lstDimensions.Clear   'Empty the dimensions List

    'Load a list of dimensions
    For Each Dimension In _
        Catalog.CubeDefs(strName).Dimensions
        lstDimensions.AddItem Dimension.Name
    Next
End Sub
```

In the following section we take a look at the more useful PivotTable View of the ADO MD object model.

The PivotTable View

Not surprisingly, the Database Structural View is only good for what its name says. A developer cannot access data through the Database Structural View method. The PivotTable View offers a solution. With it, one can connect to the OLAP data source, get some cubes, and obtain real data to work with. The part of ADO MD's object model that does this was illustrated in Part B of the diagram shown earlier.

A summary of the Objects in this model is as follows:

❑ The CellSet object allows the developer to express a query and provide a connection to one cube. Its functionality is analogous to ADO's Connection object.

❑ A Cell object refers to a single cell in the cube (multi dimensional structure) generated by the query. It is used to review data returned by the MDX query that generated its CellSet object.

❑ An Axis object collects the members of one or more dimensions in a cube that represent one axis of the cube. All the available axes for a cube represented by a CellSet object are stored inside the object's Axes collection property.

❑ The Position object refers to one position or coordinate (x,y,z) along the axis represented by its parent Axis object. One Axis object can have several Position objects stored inside its Positions collection property.

❑ An Axis object can contain data from more than one dimension. In such a scenario, each Position object for that particular Axis will be storing data from more than a single source. The Member object helps in simplifying the process of referencing a cell's data by representing one source of data at each Position.

PivotTable Service and Excel

Microsoft Excel uses the core OLE DB for OLAP API extensively to provide support for analyzing and presenting OLAP data to the user. Although any Office application can make use of OLAP data, Microsoft Excel is always the favored candidate for data analysis because of its information analysis-centric architecture. The best aspect of it all is that Microsoft Office provides the developer the ease of implementing ADO MD solutions in VBA, and therefore anywhere in Microsoft Office that can automate Excel tasks.

Implementing OLAP-Centric PivotTables in Excel

This section takes you through the steps necessary to implement an Excel PivotTable that uses an OLAP cube to analyze data. It is assumed that you already know the basic PivotTable terminologies.

Our example does not have a commercial application; it is simply for the demonstration of the conceptual bases of the PivotTable Service in Excel 2002. We use the FoodMart 2000 database to know what the sales totals were for different genders per country.

Visually we want to end up with something looking like this:

Countries	Male Total (M)	Female Total (F)	Country GrandTotal
Country1 (C1)	Sum M for C1	Sum F for C1	Sum all for C1
Country2 (C2)	Sum M for C2	Sum F for C2	Sum all for C2
Country3 (C3)	Sum M for C3	Sum F for C3	Sum all for C3
Country4 (C4)	Sum M for C4	Sum F for C4	Sum all for C4
Gender Grand Total	Sum M for All	Sum F for All	Sum all Sales

A `PivotTable` can become more complex than this. You can drill down to know the sum for states and cities in the particular states. This is out of our context here because we are simply learning how to use cubes to make a `PivotTable`.

In the `FoodMart 2000` database, the `Sales` cube provides us with all the information that we need. To implement a `PivotTable` in Excel that will give us the information retrieved from the `Sales` cube, follow these simple steps:

❑ Open Microsoft Excel. To start the PivotTable and PivotChart Wizard, click PivotTable and PivotChart Report from the Data menu.

❑ In Step 1 of the wizard, specify that you want to use an External Data Source and that you want to create a PivotTable:

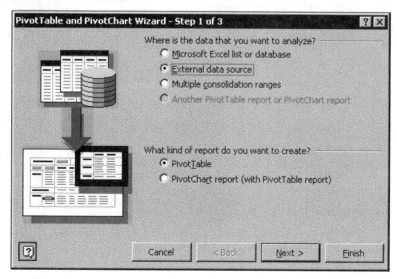

❑ Be sure that the Step 1 dialog looks like the one illustrated in the above screenshot, and then click the Next button.

❑ In Step 2; click the **Get Data** button to specify a data source for retrieval. Excel automates Microsoft Query and pops up the **Choose Data** dialog. Note that Microsoft Query must be installed as part of your Office setup before you can use this option.

❑ Select the **OLAP Cubes** tab. You are presented with the list of any cubes that you may have defined earlier. You can click on any cube that you want to use as your data source and then click the **OK** button. When a new cube is defined here, it is saved as a cube file on the client hard disk. In our case, we want to define a new cube.

❑ Click to highlight the **<New Data Source >** option in the list. Click the **OK** button. In the **Create New Data Source** dialog, specify a name for the new cube definition by typing ExampSalesCube in the field labeled 1.

❑ In field 2, click the **Microsoft OLE DB Provider for OLAP Services 8.0** option. This tells Microsoft Query that our new cube will be using the version of OLE DB for OLAP that ships with SQL Server 2000 Analysis Services.

❑ Click the **Connect** button. The **Multi-Dimensional Connection** dialog allows you to connect to either an OLAP services server or an existing cube file (*.cub) on your hard disk. For our example, specify the name of your OLAP server. As illustrated in the screenshot below, mine is TERRENCE. Click **Next**, and select the FoodMart 2000 database as the one that we will be using. Click the **Finish** button.

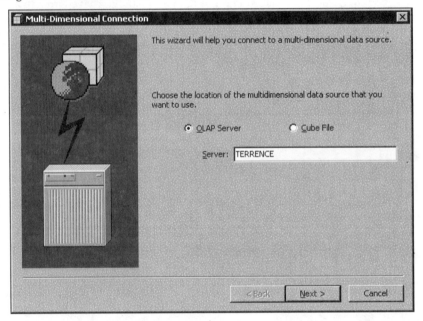

❑ We are now back to the **New Data Source** dialog. Field 4 allows you to select the cube that you will be using for the PivotTable data. Select the **Sales** cube and, before clicking the **OK** button, make sure the dialog looks like the illustration in the screenshot opposite:

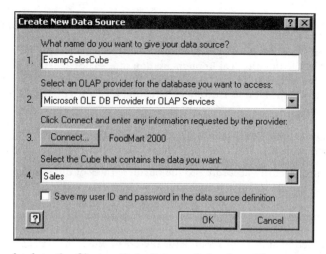

❑ We are now back to the **Choose Data Source** dialog box. Notice our newly added cube **ExampSalesCube** in the list. Make sure that it is selected and click the **OK** button to get back to the **PivotTable and PivotChart Wizard** in Excel.

❑ Click the **Next** button. In Step 3 of the Wizard, you are prompted for a location to put the `PivotTable`. Select the **Existing worksheet** option and click cell A3 in Sheet1.

❑ Click the finish button and Excel embeds a new, empty `PivotTable` object into the worksheet. You are also presented with the **PivotTable** toolbar and the **PivotTable Field** list which gives you a list of items to drop onto the **PivotTable**.

❑ Inside the **Item List Tree** in the **PivotTable Field** list dialog, click the **Customers** node. Select the **Row Area** option from the drop down list of `PivotTable` sections below the **List Tree**. Now, click the **Add To** button to add the **Customers** dimension as a member of the **Row Area** of the `PivotTable`. Notice the available countries for the customers are generated as rows.

❑ Inside the **Item List Tree** in the **PivotTable Field** list dialog, click the **Gender** node. Select the **Column Area** option from the drop down list of **PivotTable** sections below the **List Tree**. Now, click the **Add To** button to add the **Gender** dimension as a member of the **Column Area** of the **PivotTable**. Notice the available genders are generated as columns.

❑ Scroll down the **List Tree** and click to select the **Sales Count** measure. This is the measure that provides us with the amount of sales that were made to each item in the column group in relation to items in the row group. Select the **Data Area** option from the drop-down list of **PivotTable** sections below the **List Tree**. Now, click the **Add To** button to add the **Sales Count** measure as a member of the **Data Area** of the PivotTable. Notice the **PivotTable** refreshes itself with all the data available. The final **PivotTable** looks like the one shown below.

Sales Count	Gender ▼		
Country ▼	Female	Male	**Grand Total**
USA	42831	44006	86837
Grand Total	42831	44006	86837

This section taught you how to implement a `PivotTable` that uses a cube as its data source. Cubes and `PivotTables` work seamlessly together when it comes to analyzing data. The best of all is that the `PivotTable` data is already in multidimensional form before it reaches the client.

Implementing OLAP-Centric PivotTables in Excel VBA

In this section, we walk through the implementation of the above example in Visual Basic for Applications (VBA). While the physical implementation of a `PivotTable` is always possible as demonstrated in our last example, if you are a Microsoft Excel developer, it is not the most efficient way to create a `PivotTable` and sell it to customers. Creating a `PivotTable` programmatically provides you with several advantages:

- ❏ You have more control over the data that is presented to the user. An example of this is when you want to disable drilldown for some users while allowing others to use it.

- ❏ You can control security according to the business rules of different customers.

- ❏ You can dynamically manipulate the data.

- ❏ You can communicate to other COM-based applications right from within the `PivotTable`.

Our example in this section aims to programmatically create the same `PivotTable` that we created in the last section. The only extension in this example is that you interact with Outlook to send an e-mail message to your supervisor when the `PivotTable` is created. The purpose of extending the example is simply to demonstrate the impressive things you can achieve when things are done programmatically.

Load Microsoft Excel and open the `CreatePivotTable.xls` workbook, which is available as part of the code download from http://www.wrox.com. The file contains all the source code we need for our example. Be sure that your macro security settings allow us to run macros and VBA code.

Open the VB Editor from the Tools Macro menu. In the Project Explorer window click the Sheet1 node under the Microsoft Excel Objects node. The code window for Sheet1 appears. We'll have to edit some parts of the code in order for the sample to run.

There is a list of constants in the declaration area of the code window. Look for CONNECTIONSTR. This defines the connection string to the OLAP Services server. Change the DataSource section to the name of your own OLAP server. Change the TOADDRESS constant to your email address.

Exit the VB Editor and go to the Sheet1 worksheet. There is a button labeled Create PivotTable at the top left corner of the worksheet. Click this button. A `PivotTable` is created in Sheet1 and an e-mail detailing its specs is sent to the address you specified in the TOADDRESS constant.

The Code

The code that does all the work is inside the code window of the Sheet1 object. The button that you clicked above is named cmdCreatePivotTable. Look for its click event handler procedure called cmdCreatePivotTable_Click. This procedure calls the MakeAPivotTable procedure.

Inside the MakeAPivotTable procedure, we do the following:

Create the PivotTable

We create the `PivotTable` with this code:

```
With ActiveWorkbook.PivotCaches.Add(xlExternal)

    'Attempt a connection to the OLAP server
```

```
        .CONNECTION = CONNECTIONSTR

        'Set the type of data connection
        .CommandType = xlCmdCube

        'Define the cube that we will be using
        .CommandText = Array(CUBE)

        'Create the PivotTable object
        .CreatePivotTable _
            TableDestination:=Range(PVTRANGE), _
            TableName:=PIVOTTABLE
    End With
```

Set PivotTable Properties

PivotTable properties – row fields, data fields, and column fields – are set using this chunk of code:

```
    With ActiveSheet.PivotTables(PIVOTTABLE)

        'Set the Row fields
        With .CubeFields("[Customers]")
            .Orientation = xlRowField
            .Position = 1
        End With

        'Set the Column fields
        With .CubeFields("[Gender]")
            .Orientation = xlColumnField
            .Position = 1
        End With

        'Set the Data fields
        With .CubeFields("[Measures].[Sales Count]")
            .Orientation = xlDataField
            .Position = 1
        End With
    End With
    Send Email
```

This is the most interesting part of the code because here, you discover the robust capabilities of programmatic control. In our example, we simply send an e-mail to John Doe, our supervisor. We provide Mr. Doe with a detailed description of the PivotTable that we create. The string that represents the body of the e-mail is built inside the CreateBody procedure:

```
    Sub CreateBody()
        Dim objPvtTable
        Dim objPvtItem

        'Get a reference to the PivotTable
        Set objPvtTable = _
        ThisWorkbook.Sheets(1).PivotTables(PIVOTTABLE)

        'Build the string for the body of the email
```

```
        strBody = ""

        'Letter header
        strBody = "Dear Mr. John Doe." & _
            vbCrLf & vbCrLf
        strBody = strBody & "Below is the " _
            & "specification for the " _
            & "PivotTable that I just created." _
            & vbCrLf & vbCrLf

        'Information about the Data Fields
        strBody = strBody _
            & "The Data Fields are as follows:" _
            & vbCrLf

        For Each objPvtItem In _
            objPvtTable.DataFields
                strBody = strBody _
                & objPvtItem.Name _
                & vbCrLf
        Next objPvtItem
        strBody = strBody & vbCrLf

        'Information about the Column Fields
        strBody = strBody _
            & "The Column Fields are as follows:" _
            & vbCrLf

        For Each objPvtItem In _
            objPvtTable.ColumnFields
                strBody = strBody _
                & objPvtItem.Name & vbCrLf
        Next objPvtItem
        strBody = strBody & vbCrLf

        'Information about the Row Fields
        strBody = strBody _
            & "The Row Fields are as follows:" _
            & vbCrLf
        For Each objPvtItem In _
            objPvtTable.RowFields
                strBody = strBody _
                & objPvtItem.Name & vbCrLf
        Next objPvtItem
        strBody = strBody & vbCrLf

        'Footer
        strBody = strBody _
            & "I do hope that you like it Sir." _
            & vbCrLf & vbCrLf
        strBody = strBody & "Yours" _
            & vbCrLf
        strBody = strBody & "Mr. Johny Dhoe" _
            & vbCrLf
        strBody = strBody & "The Nerdy Excel Guru" _
```

```
                & vbCrLf

        'Free memory
        Set objPvtTable = Nothing
        Set objPvtItem = Nothing
    End Sub
```

The `SendEmail` procedure automates Outlook and sends the e-mail to John Doe:

```
Sub SendEmail()
    Dim OutlookApp, MailItem

    'Automates an outlook application object
    Set OutlookApp = _
        CreateObject("Outlook.Application")
    'Creates a mail item
    Set MailItem = _
        OutlookApp.CreateItem(olMailItem)

    'Set mail properties
    With MailItem
        .To = TOADDRESS
        .Body = strBody
        .Send
    End With

    'Free memory
    Set OutlookApp = Nothing
    Set MailItem = Nothing
End Sub
```

Summary

This chapter prepared you for programming client applications that use SQL Server OLAP Services. It took a conceptual approach to introducing client data access methods using the PivotTable Service and VBA in Microsoft Office.

The PivotTable Service is the client part of the SQL Server OLAP Services architecture. It provides two interfaces for data access: the OLE DB Provider for OLAP and ADO MD.

The OLE DB provider for OLAP provides an extended OLE DB API for accessing multidimensional data, while ADO MD is the consumer that sits one layer on top of OLE DB for OLAP to provide a more elegant interface to access OLAP data. ADO MD is an extension of ADO. While SQL is used to query relational data sources through ADO, MDX is used for multidimensional queries in ADO MD.

Data Warehouse

13

OLAP Services Project Wizard in English Query

The other night my wife asked me a question. She said, *"Now, what's this book about again?"* Considering that I've been hiding in my office, staying up late writing, this was more than a reasonable query. She's an intelligent person and takes a casual interest in my work but is not immersed in the Information Technology industry. Without a whole lot of thought I answered, *"It's about OLAP and Data Warehousing."* *"Uh, huh"*, she said, *"What's that?"* *"You know how relational databases are designed to minimize redundant data entry and help keep your data reliable and accurate by enforcing rules of normalization?"* She said, *"Yea, I think so. I've heard you talk about that."* *"Well, when it comes to reporting on and analyzing all the information, looking for trends and trying to figure out what is relevant to business, it makes sense to create a completely separate copy of the database that breaks the normalization rules so it's easier and faster to get important information back out."* At that point she told me that she didn't want to know any more about it. She was quite content to know that the book had something to do with database reporting.

In a later conversation, my wife said, *"With all the sophisticated software out there, why can't you just ask the computer for the information you want?"* This is a very good question and until just a few years ago the answer may have been, *"Because you have to speak to computers using computer language."* Of course, the term *computer language* means many things at different levels. In the world of databases, this might be SQL and multidimensional expressions (MDX). Though not real complicated for programmers and database professionals, for most folks it's still pretty cryptic, technical stuff.

English Query is a comprehensive approach to bridging the gap between computers and normal human beings (if there is such a thing). It lets people talk to computers in a natural language instead of a programming language. English Query (EQ) translates English phrases into database query language, either Transact SQL or MDX, depending on the type of database. At the core, English Query is a set of components and object models that provide adaptable translation services for OLTP and OLAP data sources. On the surface, simple user interface tools allow users to type questions in plain English and then see the results of their query. An English Query Application is a project created in Microsoft Visual InterDev in a highly customized development environment. Even if you don't plan to deploy a web solution using English Query, the Application Wizard runs in an Active Server Page environment. If you plan to develop a Windows application for your users, you may elect to use the web application only for maintenance and administration. Creating custom projects and programming for EQ will be discussed in Chapter 15.

In this chapter we will work with the Project Wizard in Visual InterDev and discuss the following:

❑ Development Requirements – What you need and what you need to know

❑ Application Installation Requirements – what your users will need to use the application

❑ Creating models, relationships, and language elements for your application

❑ Specifying follow-up questions to reduce redundant questions

❑ Building and deploying an application

Throughout this chapter we will be using an example, the FoodMart Sales project, to illustrate the main building blocks used to create a web based English Query project.

What is the Project Wizard?

"It's the slickest thing since sliced bread," my father would say. It really is an impressive tool that combines easy-to-use tools for power users and some advanced programming features if you need to take it to the next level.

With little effort and no custom programming, the Project Wizard may be used to create a complete web query front-end for your OLAP database. Here is a simple example of the query web page created when a solution is deployed:

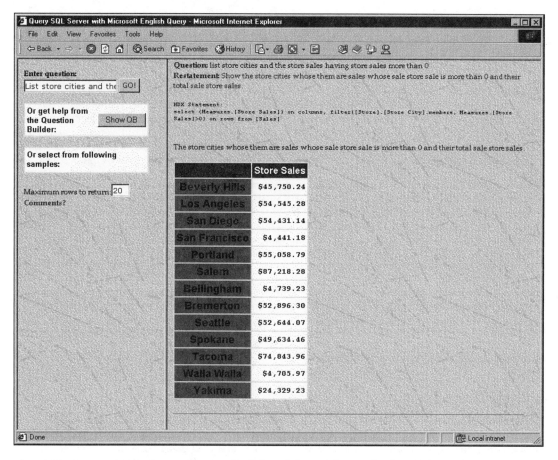

A question is typed into the text box on the left and the results are displayed in a table on the right. In between, we see a restatement of the question for clarification and the multidimensional query expression that is actually passed to the database.

Behind the scenes, an English Query model is created that manages user sessions and the context of entities and semantic relationships. The elements of a model are compiled to a domain file that defines the solution. English Query is integrated with the Office Spell check and language tools. For example, if the English Query engine doesn't understand a question, it may go to the thesaurus to suggest alternative words for clarification. Advanced users may use more sophisticated tools in the solution to model entity relationships and build questions. We'll play with these features in a later demonstration.

Development and User Installation Requirements

The following components and applications should be installed on the developer computer:

- ❏ English Query
- ❏ Visual InterDev 6.0
- ❏ Internet Information Server 4.0 or greater

- ❑ FrontPage 98 or 2000 Server Extensions

- ❑ SQL Server Analysis Services

- ❑ Analysis Services Service Pack One or greater if you are running Office XP or Windows XP

The Project Wizard runs in the Visual InterDev 6.0 development environment. To develop a model, it is necessary to have Visual Studio or Visual InterDev 6.0 installed on your development computer. Your development machine will also need to have the SQL Server Analysis Services installed. It is not necessary to have your OLAP database or SQL Server installed locally. For Visual InterDev to run, you will need to install Internet Information Server 4.0 or greater and the FrontPage 98 or 2000 Server Extensions. Windows 2000 and Windows XP install IIS automatically. For Windows NT, IIS is part of the Windows NT Option Pack.

Due to compatibility issues with some newer components, if you are running Office XP or Windows XP, you will need to install SQL Server Analysis Services Service Pack One or greater. I recommend you install the latest service pack in any case. If you are using any newer applications or components, you should check the MSDN knowledge base for any compatibility issues with Visual Studio, Windows, SQL Server Analysis Services, Office Web Components, and the Microsoft Data Access Components. This information may be obtained from http://msdn.microsoft.com.

Because Active Server Pages (ASP) performs all of the processing on the web server, users can access the wizard-built web application using any web browser that supports frames. It may run in an Internet or intranet environment. Of course, security may be applied to your site to restrict user access.

If you do not have these resources installed on your development computer, make sure you have access to a server running SQL Server 2000 Analysis Services and Internet Information Server 4.0 or greater with permission to publish files to the web server.

Before You Begin

Like any other form of solution development, it is imperative to create a proper design and functional specification prior to development. Begin with documented business requirements, a statement of vision and scope, formalize a plan and stand your ground as enhancement requests creep up. Add new features in subsequent versions only after you have thoroughly tested and released a version with the designated features.

For many projects, even though we make every effort to plan ahead and formulate a complete design prior to building the project, we simply cannot envision every requirement or fully appreciate the opportunity to include certain features. Building a prototype can let you experiment with ideas and demonstrate functionality to your users and sponsors. Just make sure that you don't use the prototype project for the release version. Start over once you have completed this important design phase.

This is the information you will need before creating your production model:

- ❑ The business need – what information do users need to solve business problems?

- ❑ What specific questions will be asked to obtain results?

- ❑ The OLAP server name

- ❑ The OLAP database name

- ❑ Security credentials and connection information appropriate for your data sources and network environment

- ❑ The cube(s) that contain the facts, dimensions, members, and measures necessary to answer the questions

Keep It Simple

An EQ model can contain any number of entities and can include multiple cubes. However, more entities can mean more opportunity for confusion as different cubes may have entities with duplicate or similar names. Duplication can also occur between different dimensions within a cube as well. If your model must contain a larger number of entities, it is important to plan ahead and design your OLAP database and cubes with clear and distinctive names.

Creating a Model

We will create a new project that will allow us to query sales information in the FoodMart 2000 OLAP database using English Query, and then deploy the solution to our local IIS web server. Of course, Visual InterDev can deploy to any IIS server, public or local, to which you have access. To begin, select English Query from the Microsoft SQL Server start menu group, and then Microsoft English Query.

When you create a new project, Visual InterDev opens to New Project dialog showing English Query Projects. To create a new OLAP project, select OLAP Project Wizard and then provide a name and path for your new project files:

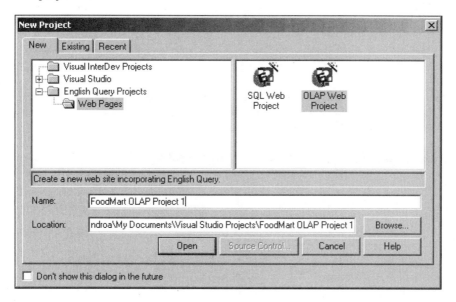

You are prompted for a server name and database. Enter your Analysis server name and select the OLAP database for this project. If you are working with a test Analysis Server on a development computer, you may enter localhost to use the local OLAP server. If your web server and OLAP server reside on separate computers, you will use the network name of your web server. It's a good idea to use the specific server name in a production environment even if it is on the same computer.

In the next dialog, you are prompted to select one or more cubes provided by your database. In the Available column, select the Sales cube and use the arrow to move it to the Selected column:

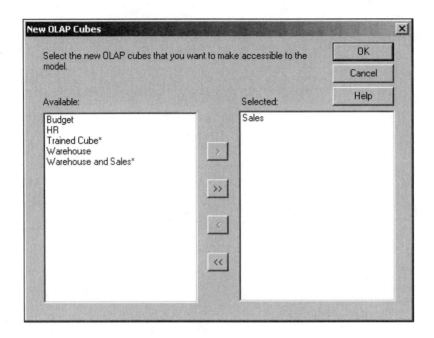

Entities

The next dialog enables the inclusion of cube entities in the model. Entities for all selected cubes will be listed and selected by default. You can use this dialog to deselect any entities that you wish to exclude from your model. We will leave all entities selected for this project.

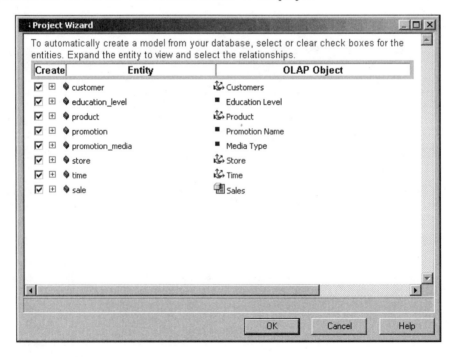

The Project Wizard creates entities and analyzes entity relationships based on member levels, measures, and other associations in the source cube(s). After this process is completed, you will be looking at the Integrated Development Environment (IDE) in Visual InterDev. If you have worked in this environment, you will recognize the Project Explorer, Data View, Property Sheet, and Task List windows docked along the right side and bottom of the window. The tree view and center panes are unique to the English Query model. Semantic Objects include Entities and Relationships. You can expand entities to view related members.

Integrated Development Environment Features

The following are elements of the Visual InterDev Integrated Development Environment (IDE) English Query. Each of these panes and windows may be hidden or displayed from the View menu. Windows may be docked to nearly any position within the main IDE window or can float freely. Alternative UI layouts may be selected using the right-most drop-down list on the standard toolbar and may be customized using the Window UI toolbar. All of the windows in this project are displayed in their default position:

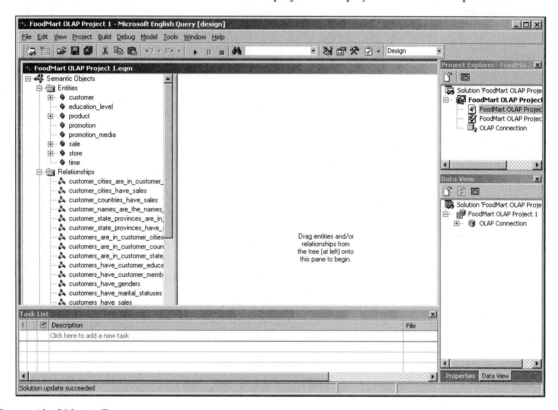

Semantic Objects Tree

The left hand pane shows a tree view that lists all of the entities and relationships in the English Query model. Expand entities to view subordinate members. Drag from this list to diagram and modify relationships in the Relationships Diagram Pane.

Relationships Diagram Pane

The middle pane is a graphic modeling tool for maintaining relationships. Adding entities will immediately display any relationships that exist between them. Drop an entity onto another to create a relationship. Double-click an entity or relationship to edit or view the detail. Clearing or removing items from this pane does not delete any relationships or entities.

Project Explorer

The right-hand pane is the Project Explorer, a standard feature in Visual Studio. All objects and files for a project and projects that belong to a solution are displayed in this tree view. Right-click to add, edit or rename an item.

Data View (tab page)

Below the Project Explorer is the Data View tree allows a developer to maintain data source connections. For a connection, you may expand and view data source objects such as tables, views, stored procedures, fields, cubes, dimensions,and related members.

Properties (tab page)

The Property Sheet shares the same screen space as the Data View Tree. Select this tab to view and modify properties for the selected object. Properties and values are listed in a tabular view in alphabetic or categorical order.

Task List Pane

This tabular list displays items that should be completed prior to project deployment. Items may be added explicitly by the developer or may be added automatically by the development environment based on keywords in the source code. When a task is completed, place a check in the box to remove it from the active task list.

Relationships

Based on existing elements in the OLAP cube(s), the Project Wizard creates initial relationships that describe the semantic associations between all relevant entities. Additional relationships may be added by dragging and dropping entities into the Relationship Diagram pane. Relationships may then be modified and customized. Relationships may also be created, deleted and modified by double-clicking relationships in the tree list or the diagram pane.

Synonyms

In the Advanced dialog for an entity, you may define Name Synonyms for entity values. Synonyms are used to translate abbreviated or cryptic names and values into more common terms. Synonyms also provide redundant coverage for similar words or phrases that user may use in a question.

Semantics

Remember back in school when you learned all about sentence structure. You couldn't imagine how this information could possibly be relevant in business. You may have thought, "What am I going to do with *prepositions, subjects, verbs,* and *adjectives*?" The answer lies right before you. You are finally going to be able to put those old English lessons to work for you!

In order to translate common English into relevant expressions, semantic phrasing elements relate to the entities (*dimensions, levels,* and *members*) of your OLAP cube. Essentially, semantics serve as connectors to bridge the gap between related entities.

The following are the semantic phrasing types supported in English Query relationships:

Name/ID Phrasing

This provides verbose clarification for an entity. A Name/ID phrase will enable an entity to be referred to using common terms like *Product Number* or *Identifier* in place of ProductID.

For example:

Titles are the Names of Books

Trait Phrasing

Describes the relationship between two related entities using possessive terms. This often describes the relationship between an object and one of its attributes:

Customers Have Phone Numbers
Cities (Customers) Have Sales
Genders (Customers) Have Sales
Sales Have Product Names

Preposition Phrasing

Describes the nature of a relationship between two entities. A preposition phrase describes a relationship between the subject (s) and object (o) entities:

Regions (s) are In Countries (o)
Cities (s) are In States (o)
Products (s) are In Brand Names (o)

Adjective Phrasing

These are phrases that describe an entity's characteristics. An adjective can quantitatively compare one entity to another:

Some Employees are **Older** than others
Some Products are More **Expensive** than others
A Store may be More **Profitable** than another store
Unit Sales indicate how **Popular** Products are

Subset Phrasing

Some entities belong in the class of another entity. A subset entity is a member of another entity group but the second entity might not be a member of the first entity group:

Some Products are Food
Some Cities are in Canada

Verb Phrasing

Verbs simply describe what an entity can do:

Customers Buy
Stores Sell

Command Phrasing

A command phrase is a special type of statement that will allow the model to call some type of process to perform an action. This allows the modeling tool to actively participate in the business process rather than to just display static data. Commands may also be used to extend reporting functionality by automating the reporting tool:

Print a Customer Report
Order a Product
Archive the Sales Records for Customer 'John Smith'

FoodMart Sales Project

Now that we have a basic understanding about how a model is constructed, let's return to the FoodMart Sales project and create a new relationship:

What are the five most successful promotions?

In order for the model to deal with this question, we will have to define the adjective *successful*. The easiest way to create a new relationship is to drag entities into the relationships modeling pane.

❏   Expand Sale and drag sale_profit into the modeling pane.

❏   Drag the promotion entity onto sale_profit.

❏   The New Relationship dialog opens. To add a phrase for this relationship, click the Add button next to the Phrasings box.

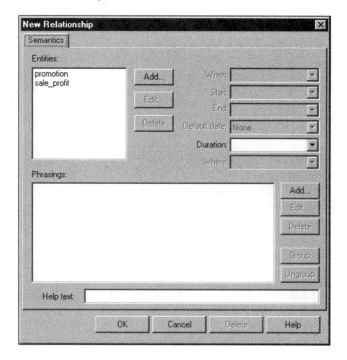

To define the adjective "Successful" highlight the **Adjective Phrasing** option and click **OK**:

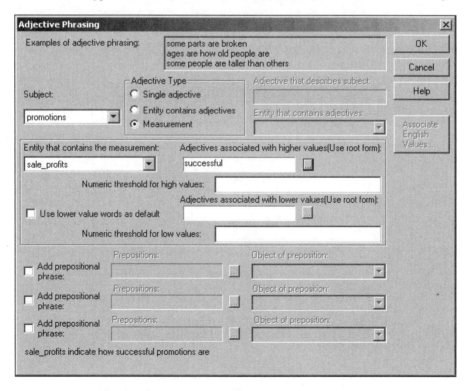

Adjective phrasing allows you to create a phrase to describe one or more adjective(s), a relative subject and other related elements. The term successful describes how profitable a given promotion is (the sum of related sales profits).

In the Adjective Phrasing dialog, select **Promotions** from the **Subject** drop-down list and enable the **Measurement** button in the **Adjective Type** option group. Sales profits are the total dollars and the measurement of promotion success. Select **sales_profits** from the drop-down list titled **Entity that contains the measurement** and type "successful" in the text box labeled **Adjective associated with higher values**:

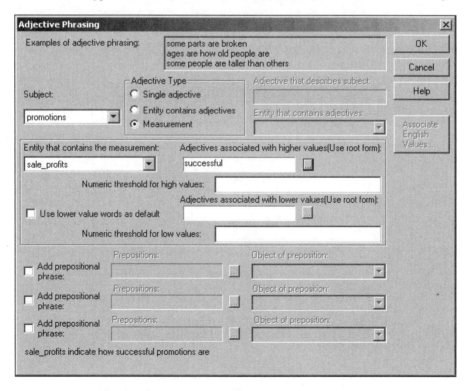

The builder button, labeled with an ellipsis (...), to the right of the adjective box will look-up the word in the thesaurus and populate a drop-down listbox with synonyms. Select any of the suggested words to add them to the adjective list. In addition to using the term *successful* to describe profitable sales, we can also ask questions like *What are the 10 most lucrative products* or *What product sales are doing well?*

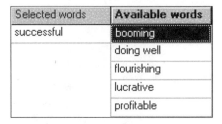

Selecting multiple adjective synonyms will produce a comma-delimited list. You may add high and low threshold values or EQ will prompt for relevant values when a question is submitted:

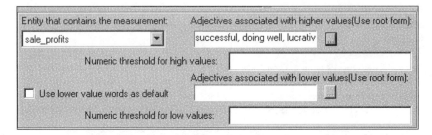

Click **OK** to close the **Adjective Phrase** dialog and return to the **New Relationship** window. The phrase sale_profits indicate how successful promotions are describes this new relationship between promotions and sales profits:

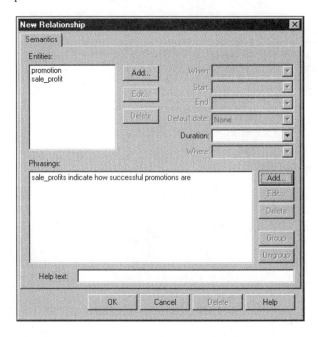

Click OK to accept the new relationship. You should see the relationship diagrammed like below:

Entities are diagrammed using blocks. The relationship appears and a circle with lines connecting the associated entities. Let's now look at how we can test this relationship using the Model Test Window.

The Model Test Window

The Model Test Window is at the heart of the Project Wizard. This dialog is very similar to the HTML version that users will see in the deployed solution. Let's take a look at the features of this dialog. To call up the Model Test Window click Start from the Debug menu. Once the window appears, you can enter queries and run the project by clicking the Start button on the toolbar (the one that looks like the *play* button on a VCR.).

Let's test the new relationship we just created with a simple query/question:

❑   Run the model to open the Model Test Window (Debug | Start).

❑   Type in, "What are the five most successful promotions?" In the Query box and press Enter.

❑   To see the results, make sure the View Results button is depressed in the toolbar.

This is the result of our query:

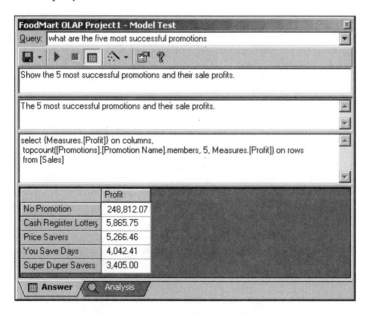

English Query will refine the question in two stages, eliminating noise words and simplifying syntax. Note the word "five" is expressed using the numeral "5" in the first stage with more explicit syntax for the values to be returned in the query. In the second stage, the word Show is dropped, as it is unnecessary.

Finally, the question is translated into a multidimensional expression (MDX) and executed against the cube.

Note that the highest-ranking return value is for sales profits that do not have an associated promotion.

Model Test Window Features

The features on this screen are categorized as either Toolbar Buttons or Dialog Controls. All of the controls except the Query/Question box are contained in two tab pages, Answer and Analysis. The above diagram shows all of the controls on the Answer tab page.

Toolbar Buttons

The following table shows the functions of all the buttons that appear in the toolbar of the Model Test Window:

Toolbar Button	Function
Save Query Button	Saves the question, restatement, answer and MDX query to the current regression test file (eqr.). This information may be used to compare the result with other regression tests.
Submit Query Button	Click this button to process the question and submit the resulting query to the database. If English Query is unable to parse and restate the question appropriately, feedback will be provided that may be helpful to restate the question or debug the model.
Cancel Query Button	Use this button to suspend processing.
View Results Button	This is a toggle button that will enable the query results grid.
Suggestion Wizard Button	After submitting a question, click this button to view suggested relationships or modifications that may be helpful to enhance or debug the model.
Test Properties Button	Use this dialog to set the query time-out and maximum row values for a query.
Help Button	Displays context-sensitive help in SQL Server Books Online

Dialog Controls

The following table shows the function of all the dialog controls of the Model Test Window:

Dialog Control	Function
Query (Question) Box	This box is used to enter the question that English Query will use to create the query. The caption for this box is a little confusing. We use the term Query to describe the expression that is executed against the database and the term Question to describe the text that should be entered into this box.

Dialog Control	Function
Restatement Pane	This is a read-only text pane that is used to display a restatement of the submitted question to verify that your question was understood by the EQ engine. Resize this pane vertically to view the entire text or to make room for other panes in the dialog.
Answer Pane	This is a read-only text pane that is used to display the answer statement based on the question. Resize this pane vertically to view the entire text or to make room for other panes in the dialog.
MDX/SQL Query Pane	In an OLAP project, this read-only pane displays the multidimensional expression (MDX) that will be sent to the OLAP database for execution. Likewise, in a SQL project, this pane is used to display a SQL expression. This pane may also be resized.
Results Pane	This pane hosts a grid with the results of the query. To see the results of a query, click the View Results button.

Regression Tests

When the model is tested, a question is processed, restated, and an answer phrase is derived. The English Query engine uses this information to build a multidimensional expression (MDX) that will be executed against the OLAP database. All of the information for this process may be written to a Regression Test (.eqr) file. Multiple files may be saved with the project to capture multiple regression tests. The regression test details are stored as an XML structure. Note the following example:

```
<?xml version="1.0"?>

  <QUESTION>show stores and their sales only for stores with sales over 0
    <RESTATEMENT>Show the stores that have sales whose sale unit sale is more
    than 0 and their sales.
    </RESTATEMENT>
    <ANSWER>The stores that have sales whose sale unit sale is more than 0 and
    their sales.
      <QUERY>
        <![CDATA[select {Measures.[Unit Sales]} on columns,
        filter([Store].[Store Name].members, Measures.[Unit Sales]>0) on rows
        from [Sales]
        ]]>
      </QUERY>
    </ANSWER>
  </QUESTION>
  <QUESTION>List the store managers in British Columbia
    <RESTATEMENT>Which store managers are in British Columbia?</RESTATEMENT>
    <ANSWER>The store managers that are in British Columbia are:
      <QUERY>
        <![CDATA[with
        member Measures.[Store Manager] as
        '[Store].currentmember.properties("Store Manager")'
        select {Measures.[Store Manager]} on columns,
        generate(nametoset("[Store].[Store State].[BC]"),
        descendants([Store].currentmember, [Store].[Store Name])) on rows
        from [Sales]
        ]]>
      </QUERY>
    </ANSWER>
  </QUESTION>
```

You may save individual results into different regression test files to compare results with other tests. This iterative regression process may be helpful as you debug the model and add functionality.

Analysis Page

After a question has been submitted, you can use the Analysis tab page to display the entities (green brick icons) and relationships (red balloon icons) that were used to create the query:

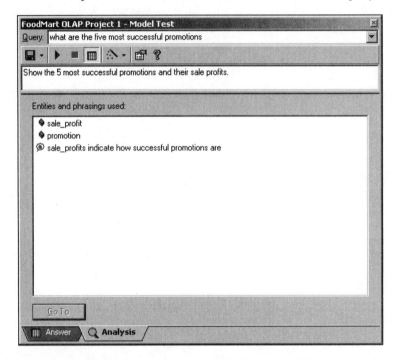

Other tab pages may be displayed for certain types of SQL projects. These are mentioned in the online help but are not applicable to OLAP projects.

Suggestion Wizard

This dialog lists suggested relationships that may clarify a query or enable a question to be processed. Click the Suggestion Wizard toolbar button on the Model Test dialog to open the Suggestion Wizard. If the appropriate relationship is suggested, check the corresponding check. This will create the relationship and display it in the relationship diagram pane:

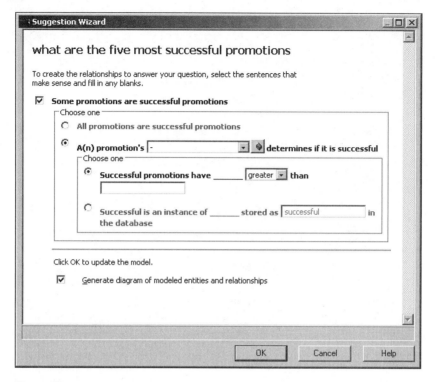

Follow-up Questions

English Query has the capability to maintain a conversational context for follow-up. After a question has been asked and processed, subsequent fragmented questions or requests will be applied as modifiers to the original question. For example, after asking for the top sales, an appropriate follow-up request would be either in Washington or sort by Unit Sales.

To verify that support for follow-up questions is enabled, select the project in the Project Explorer and then select (project name) Properties from the Project menu. This will open the Project Properties dialog. Select the English tab. Follow-up questions are enabled if the checkbox titled Enable user context is checked:

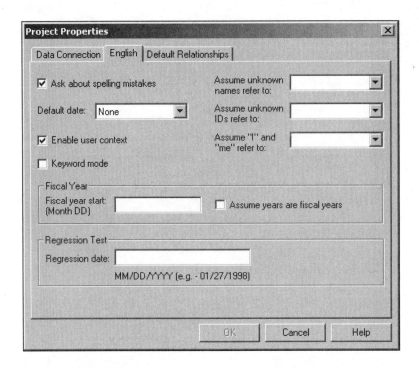

Note: You may also right-click the project in the Project Explorer and select (project name) Properties to open this dialog.

Adding and Modifying Phrases

A relationship is represented by a phrase that typically describes the association between the entities. However, there may be more to the relationship than a simple statement. Additional settings and alternative phrases may also belong to a relationship. After creating the initial relationship, additional phrases may be added to support additional functionality such as adjective synonyms and threshold values. For example, for the relationship "products have sales_profits", we could define threshold values for a product's sales profit. We may indicate that a sales profit value of **200** ($200.00) or more is considered **high** and that a value of **100** ($100.00) or less is considered **low**.

Now we'll add synonym values for an entity to make it easier to specify a value. If we ask for a list of store states and cities, we will see that the database contains states and provinces in Canada, Mexico, and the US.

Enter the following phrase into the Query box in the Model Test dialog:

List the store cities and their store states

Make sure the View Results button is depressed and click the Submit button:

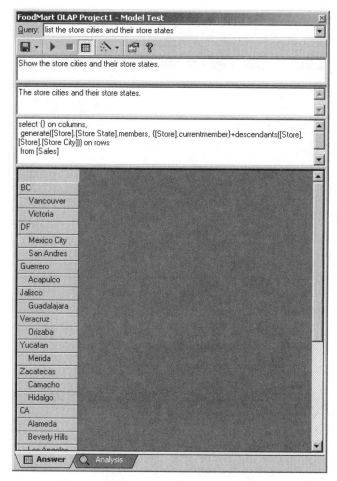

For some states, the full name has been entered and others have only a two-letter abbreviation. To accommodate a consistent form, we will specify a list of synonyms for translation. Close the Model Test dialog and expand the store entity and then double-click on the store_state entity:

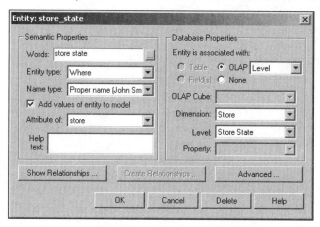

In the Entity dialog, click Advanced.

On the Advanced Entity Properties dialog, select the Name Synonyms tab and enter the following information:

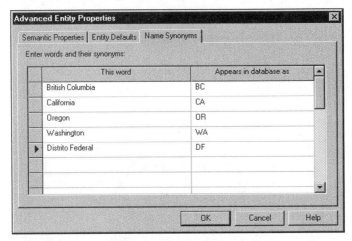

Note: The tab key doesn't work as you might expect in this dialog. You must use the mouse to move from cell to cell, or the arrow keys.

Click OK on both dialog boxes. To test for the use of a state synonym, ask a question using one of the new values. This example will produce a scalar (single value) result:

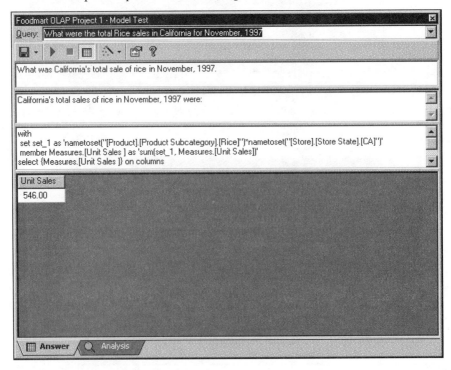

Here is another test using a state and time that returns a list of products and their sales. As you see, the value California is translated to equate to values stored as CA in the database.

Enter: **What were product sales in Oregon for November, 1997?** in the Query box and click **Submit**:

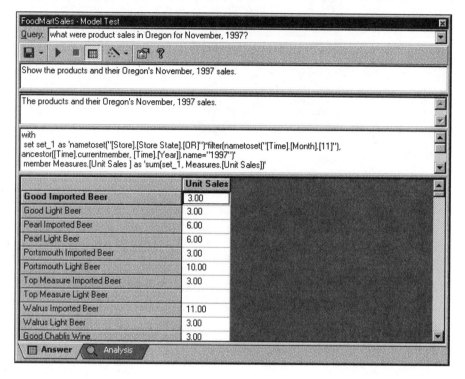

Test the Query

Now we'll put our two examples together and ask a question using our promotions profit adjective and use the state name synonym.

Enter: **What were the five most successful promotions for sales in Washington during 1997?** into the Query box and click **Submit**:

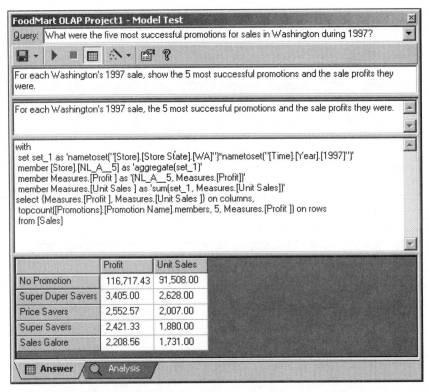

Switch to the Analysis tab to view the entities and relationships that were used to create this query:

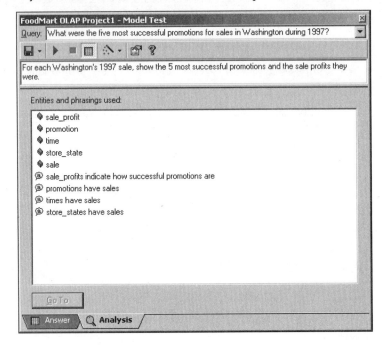

Now that we have a working model, let's build and deploy to the local web server on the development computer. Before we do that, let's make sure that the appropriate server extensions have been installed and are working. If you are deploying to a production or properly configured test server, you may not need to perform this step.

Check IIS Server Extensions

Under Windows 2000 and Windows XP Server editions (Server, Advanced Server, or Data Center Server) IIS is installed by default. If you are developing on a computer running Windows 2000 Professional or Windows XP Professional, you will need to install IIS as an optional component. To install IIS, open Control Panel|Add/remove Programs and then Add/Remove Windows Components.

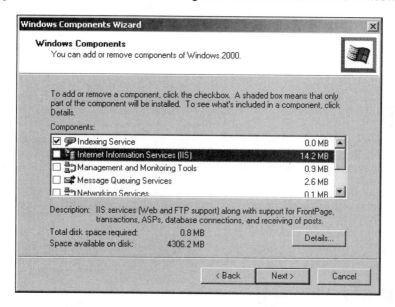

FrontPage Server Extensions are installed with IIS by default but may need to be configured. To do this, open the Internet Services Manager. In Windows 2000 and Windows XP, this may be found in Control Panel, under Administrative Tools. Right-click the web server in the tree and select All Tasks | Check Server Extensions.

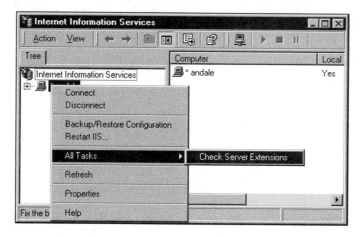

After you have ensured that the server extensions are working and that IIS is running, we are ready to deploy the application to the web server.

Building the Application

Before a model may be tested or deployed, a solution must be built. As we have been testing the model, the project has already been rebuilt with each new relationship and feature. However, projects are automatically built in Debug mode when testing, and for deployment the project needs to be built in Release mode instead.

On the Build menu, select Build Configuration and then Release. This sets the build mode. Now rebuild the project by selecting Build from the Build menu.

Deployment

Since the English Query Project Wizard creates a web-based project in Visual InterDev, you may simply run the project in the development environment to maintain your model. However, if you plan to make the web solution available to your users, you will need to deploy it to a production web server.

The Project Wizard creates an Active Server Pages solution that may be deployed to a web server running Internet Information server 4.0 or higher with FrontPage Server Extensions. Any user running a browser that supports frames may use your web solution. To deploy your solution to a web server, select Deploy to Web from the Project menu. A series of four wizard dialogs are displayed:

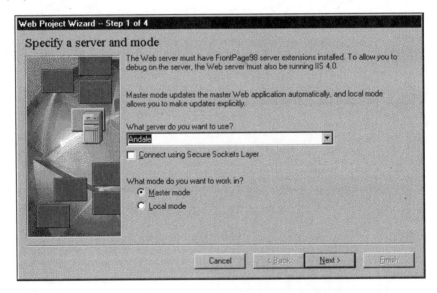

The first screen is used to select the server name and related options. If the destination server doesn't appear in this list, you may type a valid URL for your server (http://domain.com). You must have permissions to publish to this location. If you are unable to publish, check your server permissions, network connectivity of the form, and the server extensions on the web server.

The working mode determines whether you are working with a local, off-line copy of the web project, or directly against the server. If you are publishing to an active web site on a production server, you may consider using Local mode to isolate your test files from the server. If you are working in a test environment with a new or test web server, you may select Master mode. You may change this setting later. Right-click the web project in the Project Explorer and select Working Mode from the pop-up menu.

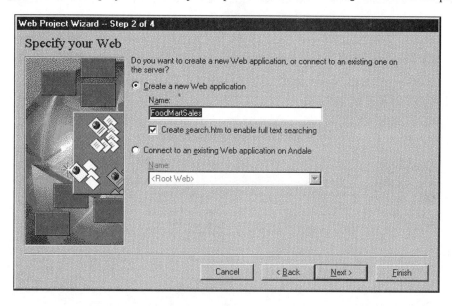

Enter a name for the web application. A folder with this name will be created under the root folder of your web server (usually C:\INetPub\WWWRoot\...). Additional settings and maintenance options are available through the Internet Information Services Manager console accessible through Control Panel | Administrative Tools.

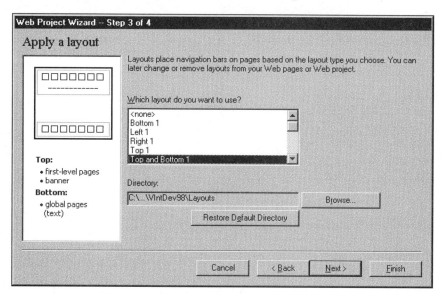

Specify a layout style for the web pages in the application. Keep in mind that these styles use generic templates that contain some elements that are not utilized in an English Query project unless you add custom pages.

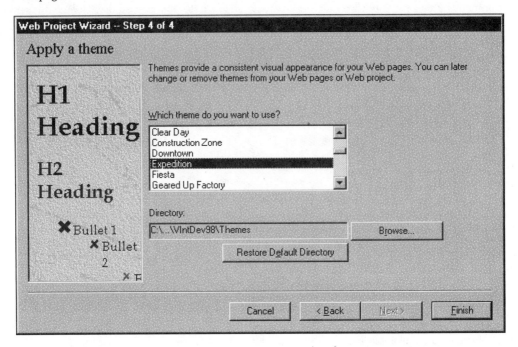

Finally, you may apply a FrontPage-style theme to your web application. This uses a style sheet to specify cosmetic elements to all of the pages and includes fonts, colors, backgrounds, graphics and effects.

The new web project can be expanded in the Project Explorer to reveal all of the files in the project:

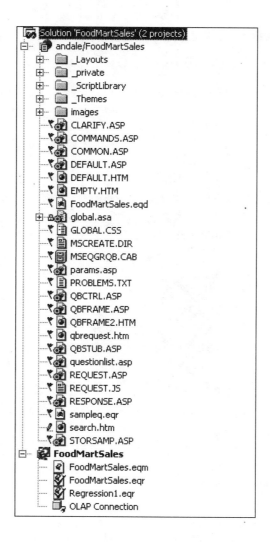

Test the Solution

To test the solution from Visual InterDev, right-click the new web project in the Project Explorer and choose **View in Browser**. This opens Internet Explorer to a URL for the local web server on the development computer (if you are working in **Local** mode). The query page has two frames. Type a test question into the textbox titled **Enter question** and click **GO!** Try something simple like "List the products and their sales" or "Show the ten most successful products". The question will appear at the top of the right frame with the restatement and MDX statement. The answer text appears above a table with the query results:

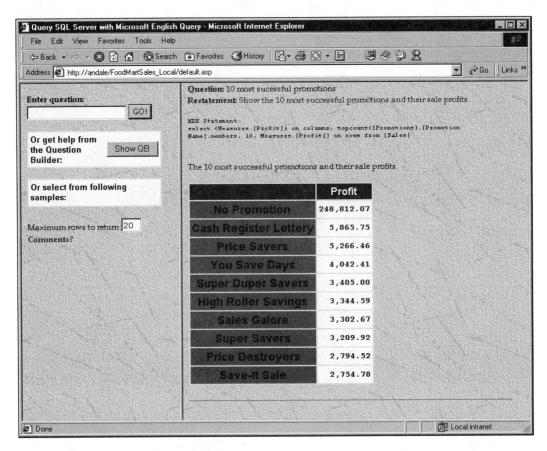

Click the button captioned Show QB to change the page view to a multi-frame set that may be used to build a query and suggest questions for adhoc relationships. The left-most frame displays a tree view of the entities and existing relationships. Drill down into the tree and drag items into the center frame to diagram a relationship. Similar to the Model Test window, entities may be dropped onto one another to expose relationships. Suggested questions are displayed in the right-most frame. Click on the hyperlink text for a question to place this text into the question textbox or click the corresponding question mark icon to execute the question. The lower frame displays the question, restatement, MDX statement, and results in a table.

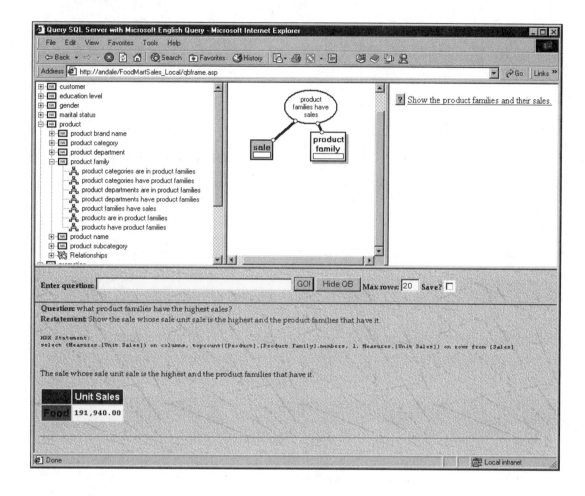

Summary

The power and flexibility of this tool is truly impressive; just imagine how much work it would take to build a custom project with the same features from the ground up! You may want to drag and drop different entities into the diagram frame to model relationships and produce suggested questions. Again, it's important to understand the business requirements for your solution before you begin any serious work. If you can anticipate the types of questions your users will be asking, you can design the database and cubes accordingly. With this foundation, build the relationships in your model and add synonyms and phrases to enable your users to obtain the information they need.

The best way to learn the capabilities of the English Query Project Wizard is to create a prototype project and take it to its limits. Use this to validate users' requests and to get feedback from project sponsors. This will help to incorporate appropriate design into the production model. Above all, make this an enjoyable and educational experience; both for you, the solution builder, and for those who will use the finished product to more effectively do their jobs.

Data Warehouse

Programming Analysis Services

Although there are several resources available to easily query and present OLAP data using simple user tools, custom-developed solutions can be constructed to include both simple and advanced OLAP reporting features. In this chapter we will cover the following topics in the context of custom programming:

- ❏ Introduce ADO MD and multidimensional extensions to the ADO object model
- ❏ Present a case study that will be used for code examples
- ❏ Use Multidimensional Expressions (MDX) to retrieve cube data in code
- ❏ Use the Office Web Components to display and interact with OLAP data obtained in code
- ❏ Introduce Decision Support Objects (DSO) and demonstrate programmatic cube management

In addition to the case study scenario, sample code will be provided for the sample `FoodMart 2000` database that installs with SQL Server Analysis Services.

ADO: The History and Future of Data Access

As you probably know, ActiveX Data Objects (ADO) and OLE DB are the products of an important directive at Microsoft called Universal Data Access. This was a major paradigm shift in reaction to a number of older data access programming standards that included Data Access Objects for JET databases and Remote Data Objects for early versions of SQL Server. With lessons learned from these early efforts, the goal of Universal Data Access was to define a data access architecture flexible enough to work with a variety of unique data sources. These efforts have proven to be very successful. Over the past few years, we have witnessed a new generation of database solutions that use scalable, modular components. They run on web servers and in browsers, exchanging data over the Internet and across distributed component servers.

One of the chief goals of this directive was to provide painless access to non-traditional data sources such as hierarchal and multidimensional data stores. This goal has been realized through several specialized object models that extend the capabilities of ADO. The ADO MD object library is the extension to ADO to support multidimensional data sources such as Microsoft SQL Server Analysis Services. We will explore the fine points of ADO MD later in this chapter but first, we'll take a look at using Multidimensional Expressions and programming the Office Web Components – PivotTable and Chart controls that install with Office 2000 and Office XP.

Case Study

The following case study will be used to exemplify realistic scenarios in this chapter. The information is fictitious for purposes of confidentiality but it is based on a real scenario.

QueryWare is a training and consulting services provider based in the Pacific Northwest. They offer a variety of training classes to IT industry professionals and primarily work with industry leaders and government agencies. Training courses include programming, database design and administration, project management, networking, and related subjects from a number of software companies including Microsoft. The company has had extensive experience with a variety of products and technologies through consulting, custom development, and education services. In this very competitive business, customers tend to give their business to training providers who offer the most convenient scheduling and packaged services. It has found that with specific information about the history and needs of its customers, account representatives are more effective in culturing relationships and building customer loyalty. By proactively anticipating customer needs, customers are less likely to go to competitors.

During the past twelve years, it has maintained a database of sales leads, customers, class schedules, and student attendance that has been mostly unutilized. Last year, QueryWare implemented a sophisticated Customer Relations Management package from a leading vendor, and began gathering a wealth of additional information about its customers and related sales activity. With more complete customer information, it is able to make better use of related historical data.

User Audience

Many people within the organization will access the data warehouse from various locations. Sales Associates spend a little over half of their time in their respective home sales offices. They also spend a good portion of their time either working from home or on-site with customers. They will need to obtain current and historical customer, product, and scheduling summaries from all of these locations. Although they currently have the ability to dial in or connect to the office network over the Internet, it often isn't feasible to use desktop applications over remote connections.

The training managers, sales managers, scheduling coordinators, and executives will need to access summary data over the corporate intranet and occasionally from remote locations.

Business Requirements and Vision

Queryware's leadership and sales staff realize that they are missing valuable opportunities. They believe that solving the following problems will enable them reach their sales goals:

❑ When a customer calls or is contacted, their complete training history is difficult to obtain.

❑ Training needs are often tied to a customer's long-term objectives and certification goals. This information is only recently being recorded but is difficult to find.

❑ The goals and history for employees who work for a company is too time-consuming to research.

- ❑ If the preceding problems were resolved, sales staff would be able to propose long-term and on-going packaged services. This would encourage relationships and repeat business.

- ❑ Currently, programmers create reports as needed. This process can take weeks and report projects are often not completed on-time, if at all. Programmers often create elaborate reports when all the users need are figures and answers to their questions. Some reports are only used once or occasionally.

The company needs a solution right away to report and analyze customer interests and sales trends. This industry is highly competitive and dynamic. It is imperative that it is able to learn from its data and invest appropriately into advertising and sales opportunities. In order to do this, it must be able to obtain the right information quickly and easily.

According to Mike Smith, Vice President of Information Systems, the company has an immediate need for a simple solution.

> "Right now, all we need are simple tools that will enable us to track trends and inefficiencies in our main and remote offices. We should be able to use our past experience to determine the likely outcome of our sales and scheduling efforts with a particular product or customer. Training is a seasonal business and our sales efforts may yield different results at different times of the year. We just need to get a handle on the details."

Scott Bergmeier, President of QueryWare says,

> "If we can have more sophisticated functionality later on, that would be great. Right now, we just need to analyze the data collected over the past 10 years to gain a better understanding about how to focus our efforts. It would be ideal to give our people access to a secure web site and a tool that would help them forecast trends and problem areas, but this can come later. Right now, we need to put tools in front to them so we know where we are and where we've been."

Development Tools and Environment

QueryWare employs about 25 consultants and trainers who possess software development skills with several products that include Visual Basic, Web Development, Java, C#, and Visual C++. However all of these employees have full-time commitments to consulting customers and training classes. The only people who have time to focus on developing a solution and managing a project are less-experienced interns and administrative assistants who have limited technical skills.

Proposed Solution

Queryware needs a solution rather than a temporary fix, but it needs something right away. All of the data exists in their newer customer relations management system and historical client-server database, but these data structures are optimized for transactions – not for reporting. The data warehouse will provide the source for a multidimensional data structure to contain pre-aggregated values and data points optimized for retrieval.

A project team was organized consisting of the CIO, who will serve as the Product Manager; a senior developer, who will be the Program Manager for the first phase of the project; a delegation of the sales staff and other users; a software developer and database administrator. Others who will fill supporting roles include a technical writer and the hardware/network administrator. This team was charged with analyzing users needs and business requirements, and proposing a solution. They interviewed business leaders to obtain the business perspective. They spend time with users in a variety of settings including shadowing, individual interviews and group discussions. The team also analyzed the current and former systems to better understand the data and reporting requirements. Their analysis and initial proposal follows:

❑ Create a data warehouse to store data in a simplified, read-only form.

❑ Design replication and export routines to populate the warehouse with pertinent data each weekend.

❑ Based on current reporting requirements, build multidimensional cubes for each reporting area such as customers, sales, location, technology, etc.

❑ Create a desktop application using Office Web Components and standard Windows controls that allows users to analyze the cube data. Results may be presented using PivotTables, Charts, and Data grids.

❑ Deliver the above application for internal network users in two months.

After the successful deployment of this first solution, the team will go back to the drawing board to propose a long-term solution to address additional needs such as remote user support. The tasks identified for the second solution are as follows:

❑ Research additional reporting requirements, Internet security, and remote access possibilities

❑ Create an English Query model and propose a desktop and/or secure Internet solution with these advanced features

❑ Seek user and sponsor approval

❑ Develop, test, and deploy version two according to plan

Data Storage and Structure

To get the most from the investment in the new CRM system, the CIO has already organized an effort to capture sales, scheduling, and revenue data into a data warehouse for reporting and decision support. A scheduled job runs every night to replicate new data from the transactional system to the data warehouse. A subset of this database is diagrammed here:

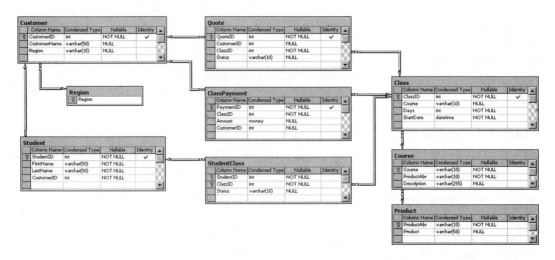

Based on this data warehouse, cubes have been created in Analysis Services from views in this SQL Server 2000 database. Let's take a look at one simple cube that was created in Analysis Services and is stored in a multidimensional OLAP database (MOLAP.):

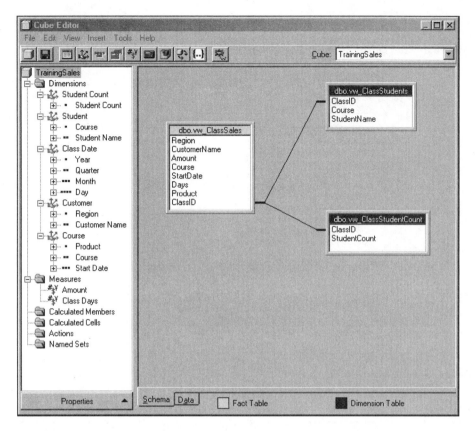

A cube is a multidimensional data structure consisting of a fact table and related dimensions and measures. The TrainingSales cube is based on a fact table, actually a view in the source warehouse database called vw_ClassSales. This view is joined with two other views in order to provide level and member detail. After the cube has been processed, a rolled-up subset of the data is stored in the MOLAP cube with aggregated values. In this cube, the Amount and Class Days measures contain the SUM and COUNT of related fields in the warehouse database. A variety of functions may be specified for aggregation including SUM, AVERAGE, COUNT, MEAN, MIN, and MAX.

We will now take a look at some techniques for displaying data stored in cubes.

Programming Office Web Components

Two sets of sample code are included in this first exercise. The first set is for our Training Center case study and the second is for the FoodMart 2000 database that installs with SQL Server 2000 Analysis Services. Use the FoodMart 2000 examples for your own testing.

With little or no modification, the following code should work on a form in Visual Basic, Access, or on a User Form in Excel, Power Point, or Word. I am using Visual Basic 6.0 and components installed with Office XP. The example code will demonstrate the use of the PivotTable and Chart controls. The Office web Components were introduced with Office 2000 and enhancements were made in Office XP. Although we are using Office XP, the Office 2000 versions may be used as well. Note that a number of compatibility issues and bugs were rectified in the Office XP versions.

399

To begin, we will create a new EXE project in Visual Basic 6.0. This project will be used for the next two examples to program the PivotTable and Chart controls. Open the Components dialog from the Project menu and enable the Office XP Web Components library:

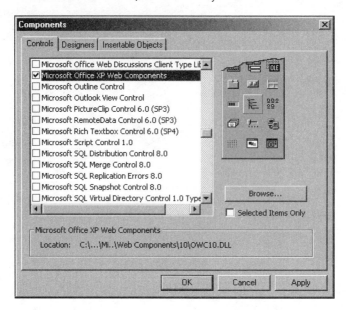

This library contains five ActiveX controls:

Control		Description
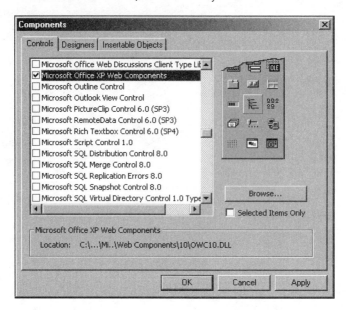	Chart	In code, the Chart control is referred to as the ChartSpace object. This control displays pivot and summary data in a simple graphic chart. Data may be obtained from the Spreadsheet, PivotTable List, or Data Source control or may be populated programmatically.
	Spreadsheet	Provides simple Excel-like functionality in a lightweight user interface for web page solutions.
	Data Source	Provides an ADO connection for data consumer controls such as the Chart and PivotTable control. This control was designed for data Access pages in Access to bind controls to an ADO data source. It is not necessary to use this control if you plan to set a control's data source using code.
	Record Navigation	Also designed to support data binding in Access Data Access Pages.
	PivotTable	Similar to the PivotTable Report in Excel, displays aggregated totals at row and column intersections. Dimensional data points may be pivoted by dragging field names to the row header, column header, or filter areas.

Let's now see how we can use these ActiveX controls to display cube data.

Programming the PivotTable Control

In our first example, we'll build a simple VB form and populate a PivotTable control in code. The PivotTable is an appropriate user interface for a cube because it allows the user to "flatten" multidimensional data based on a selected dimension. Other dimensions are used for filter criteria. The PivotTable will get data from the cube using an MDX (Multidimensional Expression).

> *In the following exercises we will be using MDX to present the cube data in a variety of interfaces and applications. If you are new to MDX, I recommend that you use the MDX Sample Application that gets installed with SQL Server Analysis Services to help write and test your expressions. For learning purposes, several queries have been provided that you can use to query the sample* FoodMart 2000 *database. Sample queries are contained in the file* mdxquery.mdx *located at* <install drive>:\Program Files\Microsoft Analysis Services\Bin. *You can try copying and pasting the sample query expressions into the examples provided in this chapter to gain more experience with these tools.*

Open up a new form then add a PivotTable control and a button to run the code that populates the PivotTable control:

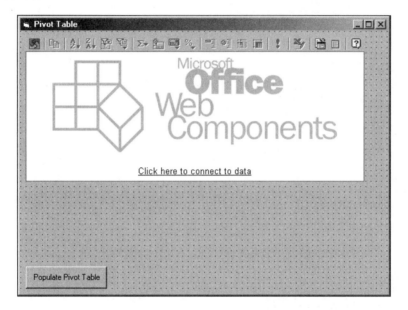

One of the first things you'll notice is that the control cannot be resized at design time. A simple remedy is to include code to handle this in the form's `resize` event.

In the `click` event of the button, enter the following Visual Basic code or download it from **www.wrox.com**. The `ConnectionString` property contains the name of the Analysis server, OLEDB provider, and the name of the database. The name `LocalHost` is one way to refer to a server running on the local machine. In production, change this to the name of your server. `MSOLAP` is the name of the OLEDB provider for SQL Server Analysis Services.

```
    Dim strSource As String

    ' -- Store MDX expression in variable"""""
    strSource = "SELECT [Customer].Members ON COLUMNS, " _
            & "[Course].Members ON ROWS " _
```

```
                & "FROM TrainingSales"

    With Me.PivotTable1
        ' -- Set the PT connection string using the OLAP OLEDB provider
        .ConnectionString = "Data Source=LocalHost;Provider=MSOLAP;" _
                        & "Initial Catalog=TrainingSales"

        ' -- Set the PT data source to the MDX expression
        .CommandText = strSource

        ' -- Format the totals as local currency
        .ActiveData.DataAxis.Totals("Amount").NumberFormat = "Currency"
    End With
```

When we run the application and click the button, the PivotTable displays data from our TrainingSales cube:

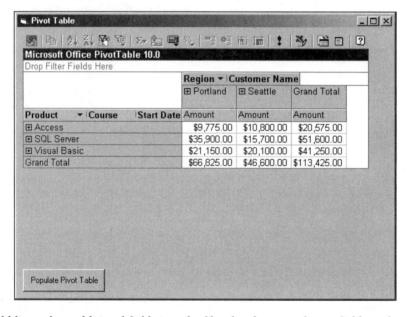

Use the field list to drag additional fields into the filter header or exchange fields in the row and column headers. Open the File List dialog from the built-in toolbar on the control to add additional members to the grid or header area to provide filter criteria. Drill-down into more detail using the level expand boxes (+) or hide the detail using the collapse boxes (-).

This screen shows the same dialog with filtering by date (Quarter 2) and drill-down details on the class data. It also shows the three axes and toolbar:

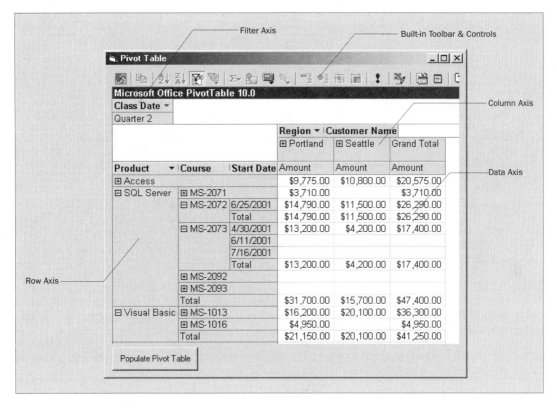

Here is another example for the `FoodMart 2000` database that installs with SQL Server Analysis Services:

```
Dim strSource As String

' -- Store MDX expression in variable
strSource = "SELECT [Measures].[Unit Sales] ON COLUMNS, " _
        & "[Promotion Media].[Media Type].Members " _
        & "ON ROWS FROM Sales"""""""

With Me.PivotTable1
    ' -- Set the PT connection string using the OLAP OLEDB provider
    .ConnectionString = "Data Source=LocalHost;Provider=MSOLAP;" _
                & "Initial Catalog=FoodMart 2000"

    ' -- Set the PT data source to the MDX expression
    .CommandText = strSource

    ' -- Format the totals as local currency
    .ActiveData.DataAxis.Totals("Unit Sales").NumberFormat = "Currency"
End With
```

Let's now take a look at another tool that we can use to display data, the Chart control.

Programming the Chart Control

The Chart control is very similar to the PivotTable for programming, since it possesses some of the same properties. Our PivotTable sample code can be applied with few modifications:

```
    Dim strSource As String

    ' -- Store MDX expression in variable
    strSource = "SELECT [Course].Members ON ROWS, " _
            & "[Customer].Members ON COLUMNS " _
            & "FROM TrainingSales"

With Me.ChartSpace1
    ' -- Set the PivotTable connection string using the OLAP OLEDB provider
    .ConnectionString = "Data Source=LocalHost;Provider=MSOLAP;" _
                    & "Initial Catalog=TrainingSales"

    ' -- Set the PivotTable data source to the MDX expression
    .CommandText = strSource

    ' -- Format the totals as local currency and set the chart type
    .Charts(0).Axes(1).NumberFormat = "Currency"
    .Charts(0).Type = chChartTypeColumnClustered3D
    .ChartSpaceTitle.Caption = "Training Center Revenue by Product"
    .ChartSpaceTitle.Font.Bold = True
End With
```

Note the `Charts` collection reference. The `ChartSpace` control can include more than one chart. Therefore, the `Charts` collection is used to manage each `Chart` object. Many significant properties belong to members of the `Charts` collection rather than the control itself. Since we are only using one `Chart`, we can reference it as `Charts(0)`.

The `Axes` collection contains `Axis` objects. In the code, `Axes(1)` refers to the vertical axis that displays sales amount values, which are formatted for currency.

To generate the chart run this code and click the **Populate Chart** button:

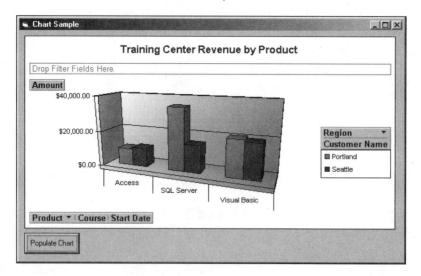

Using ActiveX controls of any type is usually a fairly simple matter. The PivotTable and Chart controls contain advanced features that are hidden from the solution developer. For simple interfaces, using these controls can add value and useful features with little programming effort. In the next section, we'll talk about a more advanced technique requiring a little more work, but with more flexible functionality.

Programming with ADO MD

ADO MD provides programmatic access to the PivotTable Service, the foundation of the analysis components in Office and SQL Server. ADO MD has a standard COM interface and is programmable from many tools such as Visual C++, C#, Visual Basic, VBA. and Visual Basic Scripting Edition. In this section, we will explore the capabilities of the Microsoft ActiveX Data Objects (Multi-Dimensional) object library and the OLE DB Multidimensional Data Provider, and provide samples in Visual Basic 6.0.

The first order of business is to set a reference to the ADO MD object library. Open the References dialog from the Project menu and set a reference to the ADO MD object library. As you can see, it is titled Microsoft ActiveX Objects (Multi-dimensional).

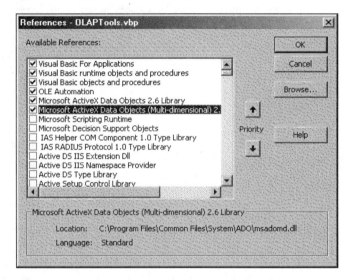

Programming for multidimensional data sources is relatively straightforward. If you understand how to work with recordsets in ADO, you are well on your way. You will notice several functional similarities between the methods and properties exposed by the ADO and ADO MD object libraries.

Cellset Object

The `Cellset` object in ADO MD is the OLAP equivalent of the `Recordset` object in ADO. The query language of OLAP is MDX, similar in many ways to SQL. Like the `Source` property of the ADO `Recordset` object that accepts a SQL expression, an MDX string is passed to the ADO MD `Cellset`'s `Source` property in order to populate it with cube data.

Cellset Methods

Methods	Description
Close	Closes the connection but doesn't destroy the object
Open	Opens the connection and populates the Cellset

Cellset Properties

Property	Description
ActiveConnection	An ADO Connection object. This property may be set to a connection string or an existing ADO Connection.
FilterAxis	Returns information about the dimensions used to slice the data in a cube.
Source	A string that sets the data source of the Cellset. This property becomes read-only after the Cellset is open.
State	The connection state such as open, closed, executing, or connecting.
Item	Returns a Cellset object using cell coordinates.

Cellset Collections

Collection	Description
Cells	Each Cell object represents the data at the intersection of axis coordinates
Axes	Each Axis object represents a data point and can be associated with an MDX Level or Member
Properties	Members include standard properties and may be used to return provider-specific properties

To open a Cellset begin by opening an ADO connection using the OLAP data provider, MSOLAP. In order to be flexible, there are a few different ways to set properties and instantiate objects. This has some advantages but it can be a little confusing. For example, the Connection object has a Provider property that is optional if this value is provided in the ConnectionString property. The Cellset object has an ActiveConnection property, which may be set to an ADO Connection object, or it may be set to a string value specifying a valid ConnectionString. As you look at example code, take note of these various techniques.

In the following code, we will instantiate an ADO Connection and use it to set the ActiveConnection property of the Cellset object:

```
Dim Conn As ADODB.Connection
Dim TheCellset As ADOMD.Cellset

Set Conn = New ADOMD.Connection
Conn.Provider = "MSOLAP"
Conn.DataSource = "...enter your data source here.."

Set TheCellset  = New ADOMD.Cellset
Set TheCellset.ActiveConnection = Conn
TheCellset.Source = "SELECT ... (enter the MDX Statement here).."
TheCellset.Open
```

Let's work with the objects we've covered so far. Again, we will use our TrainingSales cube in the TrainingSales OLAP database. You can substitute the database name and the MDX expression from the previous exercise if you would like to use the FoodMart 2000 sample database.

We will populate an unbound `FlexGrid` control with code behind a command button. This control is fairly easy to program and has some nice features. Once you get the knack of iterating through cells in a `Cellset` to populate the grid, you should be able to apply the same technique to a variety of controls or output methods.

First, from the Projects I Components dialog, select the Microsoft FlexGrid Control and click OK, thus adding the `FlexGrid` control to your Controls Toolbox. On a new form, add this `FlexGrid` control and a command button with the caption Add Cellset to Grid.

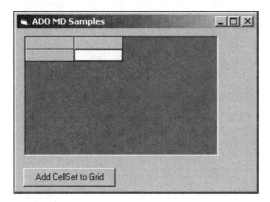

This code, entered into the click event of the command button, should work without modifying any of the grid properties at design time:

```
Dim adomdCat As ADOMD.Catalog
Dim adomdCS As ADOMD.Cellset
Dim iCol As Integer
Dim iCellCol As Integer
Dim iCellRow As Integer
Dim strSource As String
Dim strRowData As String

Const ColumnAxis As Integer = 0
Const RowAxis As Integer = 1



' -- Stored MDX expression for data source
strSource = "Customer.[Customer Name].Members ON COLUMNS " _
        & "SELECT Course.Course.Members ON ROWS, " _""
        & "FROM TrainingSales"

' -- Create ADOMD objects
Set adomdCat = New ADOMD.Catalog
Set adomdCS = New ADOMD.Cellset

' -- Create connection and source. Open Cellset
adomdCat.ActiveConnection = "Data Source=LocalHost;" _
                & "Initial Catalog=TrainingSales; " _
                & "Provider=MSOLAP;"
adomdCS.Source = strSource

Set adomdCS.ActiveConnection = adomdCat.ActiveConnection
adomdCS.Open

' -- Get column count and setup grid (Add 1 for row header)
```

```
    Me.MSFlexGrid1.Cols = adomdCS.Axes(ColumnAxis).Positions.Count + 1

    For iCol = 0 To adomdCS.Axes(ColumnAxis).Positions.Count - 1
        Me.MSFlexGrid1.TextMatrix(0, iCol + 1) = adomdCS.Axes(ColumnAxis) _
            .Positions(iCol).Members(0).Caption
    Next iCol

""      ' -- Get row data and add tab-delimited cells to new row
    For iCellRow = 0 To adomdCS.Axes(RowAxis).Positions.Count - 1
        strRowData = strRowData _
                & adomdCS.Axes(RowAxis).Positions(iCellRow) _
                .Members(0).Caption & vbTab

        For iCellCol = 0 To adomdCS.Axes(ColumnAxis) _
            .Positions.Count - 1
            strRowData = strRowData & adomdCS(iCellCol, iCellRow) _
                .FormattedValue & vbTab
        Next iCellCol

        Me.MSFlexGrid1.AddItem strRowData
        strRowData = ""
    Next iCellRow

    ' -- Remove blank row at top of the grid
    Me.MSFlexGrid1.RemoveItem (1)

    ' -- Clean up - destroy objects to avoid memory leaks
    Set adomdCat = Nothing
    Set adomdCS = Nothing
```

By default, the `FlexGrid` has two columns and two rows including a fixed column and fixed row for header captions. We have to count up the required columns and change the `Cols` property to make room for column data. An anomaly of programming the `FlexGrid` in this way is that we end up with a blank row before the first row of inserted data. We'll remove this row after the grid has been populated.

The populated grid looks like this:

	City of Portland	Dept Of Trans	Niker	Outel	King County	Micros
MS-1300	$3,000.00			$4,900.00		$10,8(
MS-1539				$1,875.00		
MS-2071			$1,500.00	$2,210.00		
MS-2072	$6,890.00		$4,200.00	$3,700.00	$3,600.00	$7,90(
MS-2073		$2,500.00		$14,900.00	$4,200.00	
MS-2092						
MS-2093						
MS-1013	$16,200.00					$20,1(
MS-1016			$1,450.00	$3,500.00		

Let's take a look at the Row axis definition:

```
strSource = "SELECT Course.Course.Members ON ROWS, "...
```

Course.Course.Members refers to the Course member of the Course dimension. This is why we only see Course names in the first column. This behavior can be modified by simply removing the member name. If the code were instead to read:

```
strSource = "SELECT Course.Members ON ROWS, "...
```

the column would contain all levels of the Course dimension including All Course, product, course number, and class date.

Now that you know how to work with the Cellset object, you should be able to use it to suit your needs. Whether populating a spreadsheet, tables or files for reporting or formatting an ASP response page, DHTML or static web page, the technique is just about the same. We're not going to go into detail on web solution design. The example below is an ASP page that will run under Internet Information Server. Microsoft Visual InterDev is a development tool designed to create an Active Server Page solution.

We'll use some code similar to the previous ADO MD example to build a web page. To get the right format tags a simple web page was created in FrontPage, copied, and then pasted to the source. HTML tag strings are concatenated with the cell values as we iterate through the cell values. We will create an Active Server Page named CellSetDemo.asp and deploy this to our local web server root folder (typically C:\InetPub\WWWRoot). With IIS running on the development computer, the page is accessible in the browser by entering the path \\ ComputerName/CellsetDemo.asp in the address box.

In the code below, we first begin to create the table in pure HTML, and blank out the top-left cell of the table. We use the ASP Response.Write method to fill these cells with our column heading values: after the empty cell at position 1,1, we fill the rest of the top row using the Caption property of the Cellset.Axes().Positions().Members. Look at the code under the comment '—...Column Headers. The Response.Write method is used to populate the table, and then we finish the table in pure HTML.

```
<!-- CellSetdemo.asp -->

<html>
<!-- Write the Page Header -->
```

```
<head><title>Training Center Revenue</title></head>
<body>
<p><h1 align=center>Training Center Revenue </h1><p>
<div align=center><center>
<table border=2 cellspacing=1 cellpadding=1 width=50%
       id=AutoNumber1 bgcolor=#FFFFCC>
<tr>
<!-- Blank out the top left hand cell of the table -->
<tr><td bgcolor=#00FFFF></td>

<!-- Now we populate the table from the ASP code -->

<%
    Dim adomdCat
    Dim adomdCS
    Dim iCol
    Dim iCellCol
    Dim iCellRow
    Dim strSource
    Dim CR

    Const QUOTE = """"
    Const COLUMNAXIS = 0
    Const ROWAXIS = 1

    CR = Chr(13) & Chr(10)

    ' -- Stored MDX expression for data source
    strSource = "SELECT Course.members ON ROWS, " _
          & "Customer.[Customer Name].members ON COLUMNS " _
          & "FROM TrainingSales"

    ' -- Create ADOMD objects
    Set adomdCat = CreateObject("ADOMD.Catalog")
    Set adomdCS = CreateObject("ADOMD.Cellset")

    ' -- Create connection and source. Open Cellset
    adomdCat.ActiveConnection = "Data Source=LocalHost;" _
             & "Initial Catalog=TrainingSales;Provider=MSOLAP;"
    adomdCS.Source = strSource

    Set adomdCS.ActiveConnection = adomdCat.ActiveConnection
    adomdCS.Open


    ' -- Fill in the column headersColumn Headers
    For iCol = 0 To adomdCS.Axes(COLUMNAXIS).Positions.Count - 1
      Response.Write "       <td bgcolor=" & QUOTE & "#00FFFF" & QUOTE & ">" _
          & adomdCS.Axes(COLUMNAXIS).Positions(iCol).Members(0).Caption _
          & "</td>"
    Next

    ' -- Next Row
    Response.Write "     </tr>" & CR & "<tr>"

    ' -- Create the body of the table with values
    For iCellRow = 0 To adomdCS.Axes(ROWAXIS).Positions.Count - 1
      ' -- Row Header
      Response.Write "<tr>" & CR & "<td bgcolor=" & QUOTE & "#00FFFF" _
            & QUOTE & ">" _
            & adomdCS.Axes(ROWAXIS).Positions(iCellRow) _
            .Members(0).Caption & "</td>"
```

```
    ' -- Column Values
    For iCellCol = 0 To adomdCS.Axes(COLUMNAXIS).Positions.Count - 1
        Response.Write "        <td><p align=" & QUOTE & "right" _
        & QUOTE & ">" _
        & adomdCS(iCellCol, iCellRow).FormattedValue & "</td>"
    Next
  Next

    ' -- Clean up
    Set adomdCat = Nothing
    Set adomdCS = Nothing
%>

<!-- Now finish the page -->

</tr></table></center>
</div></body>
</html>
```

Concatenating strings to programmatically form HTML can get a bit convoluted. With a little trial and error, the result is a nicely formatted table on a simple web page. As you see below, the first row contains member captions. For each row, the first column contains the member caption for the row and then each column cell contains a formatted value.

Training Center Revenue

	City of Portland	Dept Of Trans	Niker	Outel	King County	Microswift
All Course	$26,090.00	$2,500.00	$7,150.00	$31,085.00	$7,800.00	$38,800.00
Access	$3,000.00			$6,775.00		$10,800.00
MS-1300	$3,000.00			$4,900.00		$10,800.00
5/28/2001						
5/7/2001	$3,000.00			$4,900.00		$10,800.00
MS-1539				$1,875.00		
5/21/2001				$1,875.00		
SQL Server	$6,890.00	$2,500.00	$5,700.00	$20,810.00	$7,800.00	$7,900.00
MS-2071			$1,500.00	$2,210.00		
5/21/2001			$1,500.00	$2,210.00		
MS-2072	$6,890.00		$4,200.00	$3,700.00	$3,600.00	$7,900.00
6/25/2001	$6,890.00		$4,200.00	$3,700.00	$3,600.00	$7,900.00
MS-2073		$2,500.00		$14,900.00	$4,200.00	
4/30/2001		$2,500.00		$10,700.00	$4,200.00	
6/11/2001						
7/16/2001				$4,200.00		
MS-2092						
7/16/2001						
MS-2093						
7/9/2001						
Visual Basic	$16,200.00		$1,450.00	$3,500.00		$20,100.00
MS-1013	$16,200.00					$20,100.00
4/16/2001	$16,200.00					$20,100.00
6/18/2001						
6/4/2001						
8/6/2001						
MS-1016			$1,450.00	$3,500.00		
4/30/2001			$1,450.00	$3,500.00		
7/9/2001						

As we continue to look at the details of the ADO MD object model, the next main object is `CubeDef`.

CubeDef Object

Schema information is exposed through the `CubeDef` object. The `CubeDef` may be used to retrieve dimension information through the `Dimensions`, `Hierarchies`, and `Levels` collections. The `CubeDefs` collection belongs to the top-level `Catalog` object

Properties Collection

Property	Description
CatalogName	Name of the parent catalog
CreatedOn	Date and time of creation
CubeGUID	Cube ID, a 32 char Globally Unique Identifier
CubeName	Name of the cube
CubeType	Type of the cube
DataUpdatedBy	User ID of the person who did the last update
Description	Description of the cube
LastSchemaUpdate	Date and time of last schema update
SchemaName	Name of the parent schema
SchemaUpdatedBy	User ID of the person who did the last schema update

Methods

❑   `GetSchemaObject`: Returns objects using their unique names, using the `UniqueName` property

This example will document the properties and members of a cube. The following code sample for the **Process** command button uses a Visual Basic form to return properties and hierarchal object member information for a cube using the `CubeDef` object. After setting the connection from values supplied in textbox controls (containing the server name, database, and cube names) we iterate through each property and add the name to a listbox. We then iterate through each member of the `Dimensions` collection. For each `Dimension`, we iterate through the related `Hierarchy` and `Level` objects in subordinate collections. The `Name` property values for the `Dimension` and `Level` objects are added to a listbox. You may set a breakpoint and step through the following code to observe this process.

```
        Dim adomdCat As ADOMD.Catalog
        Dim adomdCD As ADOMD.CubeDef
        Dim intProp As Integer
        Dim intDim As Integer
        Dim iIntHier As Integer
        Dim intLev As Integer
        Dim strConnect As String

        ' -- Create ADOMD objects
        Set adomdCat = New ADOMD.Catalog

        ' -- Now we create the connection and source from information supplied in
```

```
' -- the text boxes. Open CubeDef

strConnect = "Data Source=" _
        & Me.txtOLAPServerName & ";" _
        & "Initial Catalog=" _
        & Me.txtOLAPDatabaseName & ";" _
        & "Provider=MSOLAP;"
adomdCat.ActiveConnection = strConnect

Set adomdCD = adomdCat.CubeDefs(Me.txtCubeName)

' -- List Properties
For intProp = 0 To adomdCD.Properties.Count - 1
' -- Format the output by adding extra spaces to Name, and then take
' -- the first 25 characters to create a fixed column width.

    Me.lstProperties.AddItem Left(adomdCD.Properties(intProp).Name _
    & Space(25), 25) _
    & adomdCD.Properties(intProp).Value

Next intProp

' -- List Dimensions
For intDim = 0 To adomdCD.Dimensions.Count - 1
    Me.lstDimensions.AddItem adomdCD.Dimensions(intDim).Name
    For intHier = 0 To adomdCD.Dimensions(intDim).Hierarchies.Count - 1
        For intLev = 0 To _
            adomdCD.Dimensions(intDim).Hierarchies(intHier).Levels.Count - 1
            Me.lstDimensions.AddItem "    " _
            & adomdCD.Dimensions(intDim).Hierarchies(intHier) _
            .Levels(intLev).Name
        Next intLev
    Next intHier
Next intDim

' -- Clean up
Set adomdCat = Nothing
Set adomdCD = Nothing
```

Here's a summary of what we did in this code. We obtained connection information from the textboxes along the left side of the form and concatenated the connection string using these values. After obtaining a reference to the CubeDef object, we looped through its properties and add these values to the first listbox. We did the same for the members of the dimensions collection, adding values to the listbox on the right. The finished product is a list of properties, dimensions, and levels for the cube.

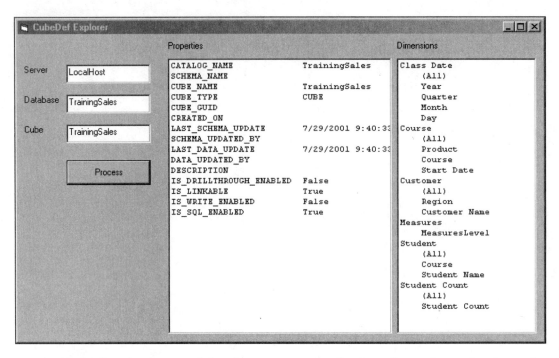

Again, ADO MD is the object model used to programmatically obtain data and meta data for a cube structure and its members. Next, we look at a set of tools to manage these objects.

Managing OLAP Objects with DSO

Decision Support Objects (DSO) is the object model used to programmatically manipulate OLAP objects as an alternative to using the graphic tools in the Analysis Manager. Like ADO MD, DSO exposes objects through COM and can be programmed in any language or tool that can use COM objects. Using DSO objects in your custom application, you may create, interrogate, and modify all of the objects that are exposed through the Analysis Manager, and more. Understanding DSO will help you better understand OLAP objects and their relationship to one another. This may also enable you to perform remote and scheduled maintenance on your OLAP server.

Let's begin by looking at a logical object model. We will start with a simplified view and then go into a little more detail. The DSO model begins with the Server object that owns the Databases collection. A Database object has Datasources, Cubes, and Shared Dimensions.

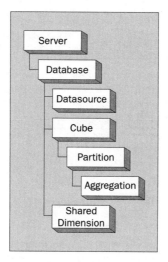

If we take a closer look at the Cube object, we see that a cube owns collections of Members and Dimensions, and Dimensions have Levels.

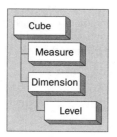

This is a logical view of the object model, and is also quite simplified. The DSO object model is a little different than some other models in that the Server, Database, Cube, and Partition objects each have a collection called MDStores. This collection exists at various levels. The MDStore collection can contain Database, Cube, Partition, and Aggregation objects. The object type is inherited from a base class specified by either specifying a constant indicator or by explicitly declaring the variable as the appropriate object type. Fortunately, it's not quite as complicated as it sounds.

We'll use Visual Basic 6.0 for our first example. Begin by setting a reference to the DSO object library (Microsoft Decision Support Objects) in the Project | References dialog:

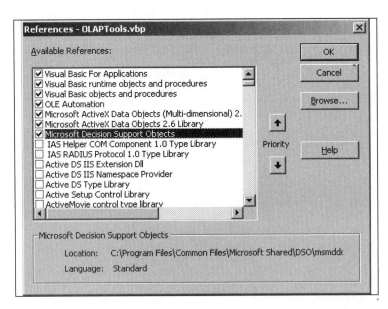

The following sample uses a Visual Basic form containing two list box controls and a command button. The code behind the button will interrogate common objects for a cube in the FoodMart 2000 sample database and display properties in the listboxes. Open up a form, add one command button and two listboxes, calling them lstDimensions and lstCubes. For the command button code enter the following variable declarations:

```
Dim dsoSvr As DSO.Server
Dim dsoDS As DSO.DataSource
Dim dsoDB As DSO.Database
Dim dsoCube As DSO.Cube
Dim dsoDimen As DSO.Dimension
Dim dsoLev As DSO.Level
Dim dsoMeas As DSO.Measure
```

Then add the rest of the code:

```
Private Sub cmdListMembers_Click()
    Set dsoSvr = New DSO.Server
    dsoSvr.Connect "localhost"
    Set dsoDB = dsoSvr.MDStores("FoodMart 2000")

    ' Populate the lstDimensions Listbox with dimension/level data

    Me.lstDimensions.AddItem "Dimensions/Levels:"
    Me.lstDimensions.AddItem "------------------"
    For Each dsoDimen In dsoDB.Dimensions
        Me.lstDimensions.AddItem "  " & dsoDimen.Name

        ' Now display the levels with a further indent

        For Each dsoLev In dsoDimen.Levels
            Me.lstDimensions.AddItem "    " & dsoLev.Name
        Next
```

```
      Next

      ' Populate the lstCubes Listbox with cube/measure data

   Me.lstCubes.AddItem "Cubes/Measures:"
   Me.lstCubes.AddItem "-----------------"
   For Each dsoCube In dsoDB.Cubes
      Me.lstCubes.AddItem "   " & dsoCube.Name
      For Each dsoMeas In dsoCube.Measures

      ' Now display the measures with a further indent

         Me.lstCubes.AddItem "      " & dsoMeas.Name
      Next
   Next
End Sub
```

We are simply walking through the object model in this code. Beginning with the `Server`, a connection is created to the local analysis server and then the `Database` object is used to reference the `FoodMart 2000` database. Using the `Dimensions` collection of the `Database` object, we add the `Dimension` and related `Levels` to the first list box. For the second list box, we iterate through each `Cube` in the `Cubes` collection of the `Database`, through the `Measures` collection for each `Cube`. Here is the result for the `FoodMart 2000` OLAP database:

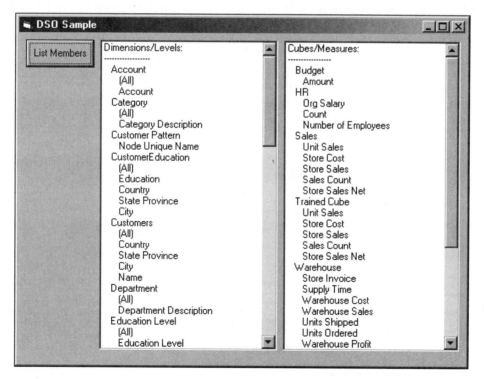

Let's look at some sample VB code to create a new OLAP database. We'll begin by setting a reference to the DSO object library and declaring object variables as specific object classes within the object model. Beginning with same variable declarations as in the previous example, add the following code snippets to a command button. First we add the code that instantiates the `Server` object and sets some properties to reference the local OLAP server:

```
Dim dsoSvr As DSO.Server
Dim dsoDS As DSO.DataSource
Dim dsoDB As DSO.Database
Set dsoSvr = New DSO.Server
    dsoSvr.Connect "LocalHost"
```

The next section of code uses the `MDStores` collection. In this code, we are adding a `Database` object to `MDStores`. After modifying any property values, the `Update` method is called to refresh the server with these changes:

```
Set dsoDB = dsoSvr.MDStores.AddNew("New Database")
dsoDB.Update
```

An anomaly in the DSO model is that several members of the model are not exposed such that the intellisense features in Visual Studio can enumerate them. If an object or property doesn't show in an object's members list while you are writing code, test it before you assume that you have a syntax error.

Finally, the last section of code adds a `DataSource` object and sets its `ConnectionString` property for a SQL Server database. Again, the `Update` method persists changes to the OLAP server. You should substitute the name of your warehouse database and the name of your SQL Server for the `Initial Catalog` and `Data Source` values, respectively. Note that in the next exercise, we will be using a connection string for an ODBC data source name (DSN) rather than an OLEDB data provider.

```
Set dsoDS = dsoDB.DataSources.AddNew("New Datasource")
    dsoDS.ConnectionString = "Provider=SQLOLEDB.1;Integrated Security=SSPI;" _
        & "Persist Security Info=False;" _
        & "Initial Catalog=MySQLDatabase;Data Source=ServerName"
dsoDS.Update
```

If you run this code and browse to your Analysis server, you'll find that a new database and data source have been created.

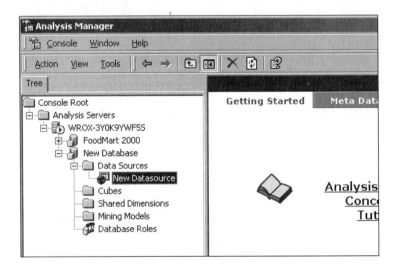

Putting it all together, we can use DSO to create a cube, measure, dimension, and related level objects to construct an entire OLAP database structure. The remaining sample code in this chapter is all from one sub procedure. We will break it up into pieces for discussion. Enter all of this code into the `click()` event of a command button to test the sample. This procedure will create an analysis database using the `FoodMart 2000` warehouse database that installs with Analysis Services. The new analysis database will contain one cube with one dimension that has employee salary information. Levels for the employee are `Education Level`, `Gender`, and `Name`. The code is as brief as possible for the sake of simplicity. You may consider enhancing the sample code to add additional features.

Our example code begins with procedure-level variables that reference classes in the DSO object library. Here, we instantiate the top level objects: `Server`, `Database`, and `DataSource`. Note the use of the `LockObject` method of the `Database` object. This prevents other connections to the database while this code runs and is necessary when creating some subordinate objects. To create the connection, a standard ADO-style connection string is used. We are using the sample `FoodMart 2000` database and an ODBC data source that are installed with Analysis Services. This DSN references an Access database called `FoodMart 2000.mdb`.

```
    Dim dsoServer As DSO.Server
    Dim dsoDatabase As DSO.Database
    Dim dsoDataSource As DSO.DataSource
    Dim dsoCube As DSO.Cube
    Dim dsoDimension As DSO.Dimension
    Dim dsoLevel As DSO.Level
    Dim dsoMeasure As DSO.Measure
    Dim sDBName As String


  ' -- Server
    Set dsoServer = New DSO.Server
    dsoServer.Connect "LocalHost"

  ' -- Database
    sDBName = InputBox("New OLAP Database Name:", "Enter Database Name")
    Set dsoDatabase = dsoServer.MDStores.AddNew(sDBName)
    With dsoDatabase
       .LockObject olaplockWrite, "Building database"
       .Description = sDBName & " database created on " & Date
       .OlapMode = olapmodeMolapIndex
    End With

  ' -- Datasource
    Set dsoDataSource = dsoDatabase.DataSources.AddNew("LocalHost - FoodMart 2000")
    With dsoDataSource
       .ConnectionString = "Provider=MSDASQL.1;Persist Security Info=False;" & _
                    & "Data Source=FoodMart 2000;Connect Timeout=15"
       .Update
    End With
```

A shared dimension is created, base on the `employees` table. Note the `FromClause` property value. Literal quotes are required around the database objects, entities, and attribute references. Doubled-up quote characters are interpreted as a single, literal quote. The entire expression is encapsulated in quotes as well. Thus the expression `"""employee"".""full_name"""` is interpreted as `"employee"."full_name"`. The storage mode for the dimension fact values and aggregations will be multidimensional (MOLAP) rather than relational or heterogeneous.

```
  ' -- Dimension
    Set dsoDimension = dsoDatabase.Dimensions.AddNew("Employees", 0)
    With dsoDimension
```

```
      Set .DataSource = dsoDataSource
      .DimensionType = dimRegular
      '.EnableRealTimeUpdates = EnableRealTimeUpdates
      .FromClause = """employee"""
      .StorageMode = storeasMOLAP
   End With
```

Three levels are added to the dimension. We'll review some of the important properties. `AreMemberNamesUnique` is set to `True` when you are certain that member names at this level will not be duplicated. This is a safe bet at the `All` level. The `EstimatedSize` property is used for the initial member count. Of course, this value may change as the cube is reprocessed with new data. If this property value isn't set, it will be calculated when the cube is processed – as we will see in this example. I have commented this line but left the code so you can see how it would be used. You may use ADO data type constants for the `ColumnType` property. A constant enumeration chart may be found in SQL Server Books Online for the `LevelType` property.

```
' -- Dimension Level
   Set dsoLevel = dsoDimension.Levels.AddNew("(All)", 0)
   With dsoLevel
      .AreMemberNamesUnique = True
      .ColumnType = adInteger
      .EstimatedSize = 3
      .IsVisible = True
      .MemberKeyColumn = "All Employees"
      .MemberNameColumn = "All Employees"
      .LevelType = levAll
   End With

   Set dsoLevel = dsoDimension.Levels.AddNew("Education Level", 0)
   With dsoLevel
      .AreMemberNamesUnique = True
      .ColumnType = adWChar
      .ColumnSize = 50
      .IsVisible = True
      .MemberKeyColumn = """employee"".""education_level"""
      .MemberNameColumn = """employee"".""education_level"""
      .LevelType = levRegular
   End With
   Set dsoLevel = dsoDimension.Levels.AddNew("Gender", 0)
   With dsoLevel
      .AreMemberNamesUnique = False
      .ColumnType = adWChar
      .ColumnSize = 1
      .IsVisible = True
      .MemberKeyColumn = """employee"".""gender"""
      .MemberNameColumn = """employee"".""gender"""
      .LevelType = levRegular
   End With

   Set dsoLevel = dsoDimension.Levels.AddNew("Full Name", 0)
   With dsoLevel
      .AreMemberNamesUnique = False
      .ColumnType = adWChar
      .ColumnSize = 50
      .IsVisible = True
```

```
                .MemberKeyColumn = """employee"".""full_name"""
                .MemberNameColumn = """employee"".""full_name"""
                .LevelType = levRegular
            End With


            dsoDimension.Update
```

The shared dimension is added to the cube object's `Dimensions` collection after its creation. The `EstimatedRows` property is similar to the `EstimatedSize` property of a dimension. If the approximate number of rows is known, this value is used for initial allocation and is recalculated during cube processing.

```
    ' -- Cube
        Set dsoCube = dsoDatabase.MDStores.AddNew("EmployeeSalary", 0)
        With dsoCube
            .DataSources.Add dsoDataSource
            .EstimatedRows = 1155
            .SourceTable = """employee"""
            .SourceTableAlias = """employee"""
            .FromClause = """employee"", ""department"""
            .IsVisible = True
            .JoinClause = "(""employee"".""department_id""" & _
                        "=""department"".""department_id"")"
            .Dimensions.AddNew "Employees"
        End With
```

Next we add a measure object to the `EmployeeSalary` cube, a currency type value. Again, ADO data type constants may be used for the `SourceColumnType` property. This is the final step in this simple example. The cube is updated to refresh the meta data storage, and the database lock is released so others may gain access to the model and data.

```
    ' -- Measure
        Set dsoMeasure = dsoCube.Measures.AddNew("Salary", 0)
        With dsoMeasure
            .FormatString = "currency"
            .IsVisible = True
            .SourceColumn = """employee"".""salary"""
            .SourceColumnType = adCurrency
        End With

        dsoCube.Update
        dsoDatabase.UnlockObject
```

Finally, we release all of the objects and display a message box indicating that the database has been successfully created.

```
        Set dsoServer = Nothing
        Set dsoDatabase = Nothing
        Set dsoDimension = Nothing
        Set dsoMeasure = Nothing
        Set dsoLevel = Nothing
        Set dsoCube = Nothing

        MsgBox sDBName & " database created." & vbCrLf & vbCrLf _
            & "Refresh the server in Analysis Manager to view changes.", _
            vbInformation, "Done"
```

Open the Analysis Manager to see the new database and related objects. To finish the process, you will need to create aggregations and process the cube. Right-click on your newly created EmployeeSalary cube, and select Edit…. In the Cube Editor, select Tools | Process Cube… to begin processing the cube. Click Yes when prompted to calculate the member counts. For this simple cube, this will just take a few seconds.

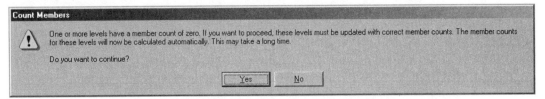

Next, you will be prompted to design aggregations for the cube. Click Yes to continue.

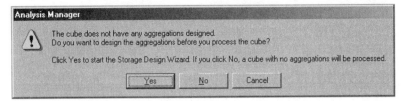

For more information about designing aggregations and processing a cube, please refer to Chapter 9.

You can choose all default responses in the Storage Design Wizard and then process the cube. Click the Close button in the Process dialog when processing has completed. Back in the Cube Editor window, switch to the Data tab to see data values in your new cube.

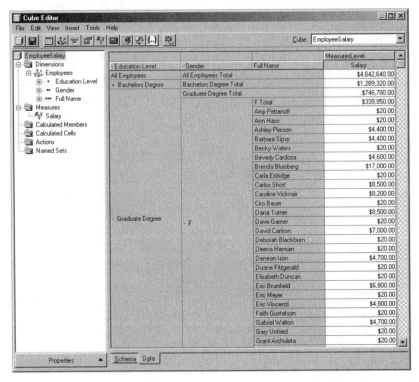

As you know, creating an analysis database doesn't populate the structure with data. Aggregations and storage options must be specified prior to processing the cube. All of this may also be performed using DSO as well; however, defining aggregations in code can be a lot of work.

Meta Data Scripter Utility

The SQL Server 2000 Resource Kit (http://www.microsoft.com/SQL/techinfo/reskit/default.asp) includes a utility called the **Meta Data Scripter** that will take an entire OLAP database or other specific objects and produce DSO code in VBScript to generate all of the objects. The resulting code may be used as a starting point or working sample to learn more about DSO. The Meta Data Scripter is provided as a VB 6.0 project that must be compiled to a DLL prior to use. It runs as a COM add-in for the Analysis Manager. The SQL Server 2000 Resource Kit may be purchased from Microsoft and is also included in the MSDN Universal subscription.

Summary

DSO is a powerful tool that may be used to create a variety of custom solutions from simple automated maintenance procedures to complete database and cube construction. Before digging into the DSO object model and writing code to modify your databases, learn to use the administrative tools to thoroughly understand the concepts of OLAP and data mining. DSO can then be used to take these features to a new level.

We began with a case study to provide some perspective for a custom analysis solution. Though the details were fictitious, the scenario is quite real. Storing gigabytes of data is pointless if it can't be turned into the meaningful information necessary to make informed decisions.

The Office Web Components are ActiveX controls used to add a sophisticated user interface to your applications with minimal supporting code. ADO MD gives you programmatic access to the data exposed by the OLAP database for custom reporting, web-based queries, and more. DSO provides access to the mechanics of the model for administration and maintenance. Using these tools, objects and functionality can be added to an OLAP database through custom programming. DSO gives solution developers the ability to duplicate, replace, or enhance the features found in the Analysis Manager.

All of these tools can be used to add compelling functionality to your solutions. The purpose of Analysis Services is to turn data back into information; giving information workers and business decision makers conclusive, high-level information about the state of important business information. ADO MD, MDX, and the Office Web Components are the puzzle pieces that can be used to create a polished solution that may be used to deliver this information in a concise package. Keep your designs simple and focus on the business need.

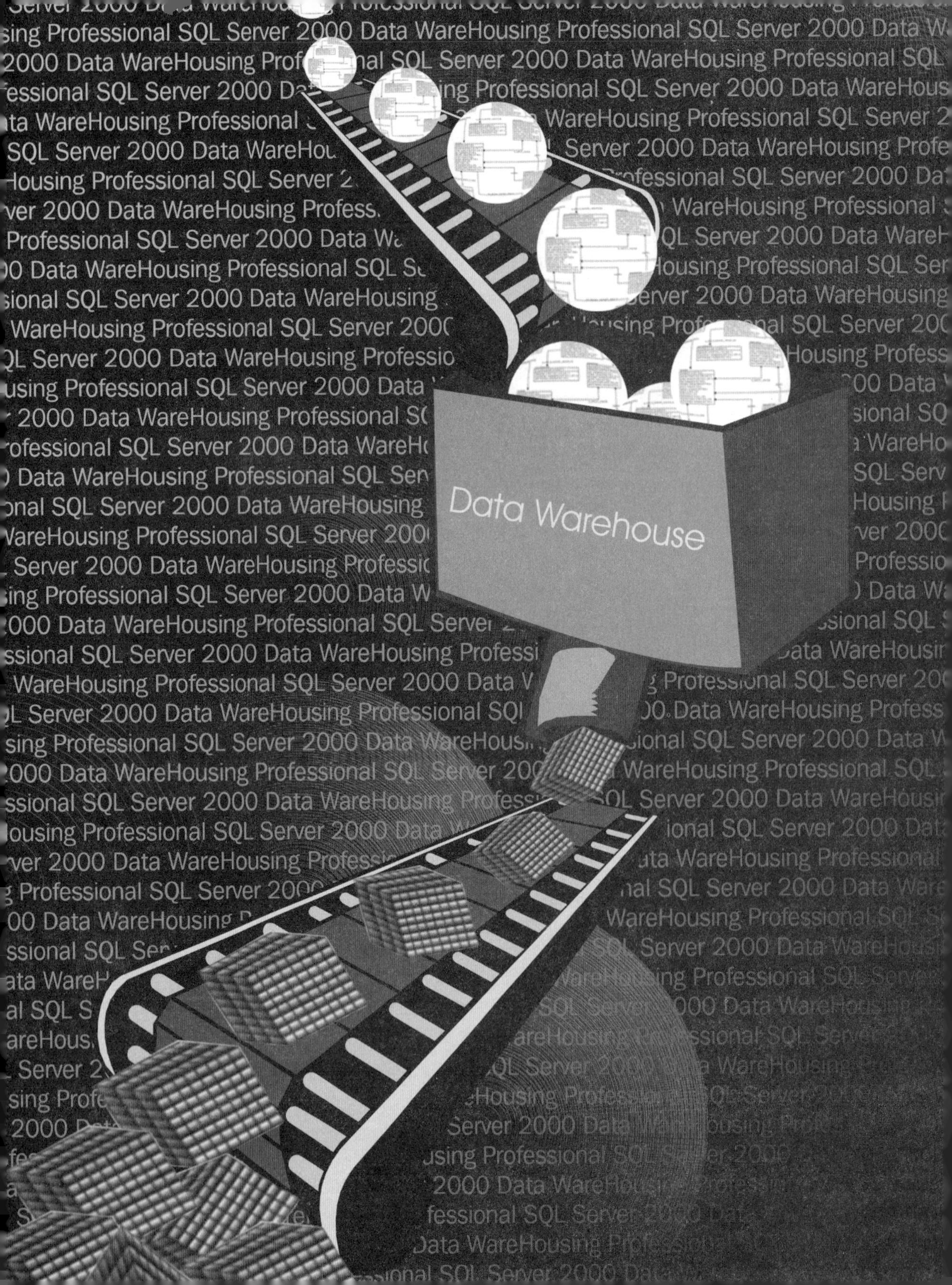
Data Warehouse

15

English Query and Analysis Services

We will get right down to business in this chapter and build a complete, custom English Query solution. First, we'll discuss the fine points of the object models. We will take a brief look at the Question Builder control, and then we will build a sample Visual Basic project from start to finish. To build the sample application in this chapter, it is assumed that the reader has some fundamental programming skills with Visual Basic.

Three object models provide functionality for English Query. These include:

❑   Author Object Model

❑   Engine Object Model

❑   Question Builder Object Model

An important concept to understand is that English Query doesn't return any data. That's the job of the client application using a data source connection and APIs. English Query outputs a query expression – either SQL or MDX, depending on the data source of the model. It's up to the developer to query the database with this query expression.

The foundation of an English Query application is defined by a domain file with an EQD extension. This file contains the entire model with objects and semantic definitions in compiled form. In an English Query Project, this file is created in Visual InterDev when you **Build** the project. Not that the file doesn't show in the Project Explorer but it is written to the local project folder. Refer to Chapter 13 for details about building and deploying projects using the English Query Project Wizard. We will use a domain file to initialize the English Query session in later code examples. Also, in this chapter, we will show simplified code snippets with procedure level object variable declarations so you can see the variables declared and used in the same procedure. Variables that are used by more than one procedure should be declared with appropriate scope – either in the declaration section of the module or in a general module as public variables.

Programming English Query

The **English Query Author Object Model** can be used to build or recompile an English Query model at run time. These objects are used by the English Query Project Wizard to simplify English Query model and project management. If you would like to perform these functions outside of the EQ project environment (which runs in, or is deployed from, Visual InterDev) you can use the objects in this model in a custom application. The friendly name for this library is **Microsoft English Query Authoring Type Library x.x**. In code, the COM library is referred to as MSEQAuthor and is contained in the file mseqsmf.dll.

The functionality of this simple model extends the capabilities of the Document Object Model (DOM) library designed for managing XML documents and offers specific features for managing English Query projects. The authoring model may be used to maintain the following files in an English Query project or application:

File Type	Description	Extension
EQ Project	Contains the definition for the design elements of an English Query application with references to associated modules and test regression files	EQP
EQ Module	An XML document that contains definitions and properties for entities, relationships, and related semantic elements	EQM
EQ Domain	Compiled Application based on a project and one or more models	EQD
Semantic Modeling Format project file	Optional XML-based English Query project file including all module definitions for the project	SMF

Just a note about English Query projects and models for advanced developers: Unless you have a good reason to create and manage your own English Query model manually, I would strongly recommend that you use the English Query project Wizard. In such a case, all of the files are created and maintained within the project. The Project wizard takes one of two possible approaches for defining a model. It creates a project file (with an EQP extension,) and one or more module files (with an EQM extension). Outside of the project wizard, a single Semantic Modeling Format (SMF) file may be used in place of separate project (EQP) and module (EQM) files. In either case, a domain file may be compiled from either an SMF file or separate project and module files. SMF is an XML-based language.

English Query Engine Object Model

The object model is contained in the file MSEQOLE.DLL. The description associated with the library is **Microsoft English Query Type Library x.x**. In code, you will reference the library as **MSEQ**.

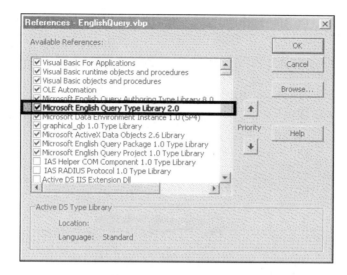

This model is at the core of English Query and includes the functions that are used to submit questions, resolve and clarify user input, and handle any resulting errors. The outputs for this model are user input prompts for clarification and error phrases that are used to guide a user to obtain a translated SQL or MDX expression based on their question.

Mighty PolyMorphin' Objects

Some objects in the model are polymorphic. A polymorphic object inherits an interface (specific properties, methods, and events) from different classes based on certain conditions when it is created. The model uses inheritance to modify the type of some objects to different object classes depending on the state of a request. For example, if a question is translatable, the session will return a `Command Response` object containing the translated query text. If clarification is required, the `Response` object becomes a `UserClarifyResponse` with an entirely different set of properties and methods, but appropriate in context, to support user input used to clarify the question.

Three Polymorphic objects are offered as either a generic object class with a `Type` property (used to determine what specific type the object it is,) or specific object classes that support only appropriate properties and methods:

- ❑ `Response`
- ❑ `Command`
- ❑ `UserInput`

The generic form of the object will support all of the properties and methods of the specific classes, although some of the members will be inappropriate depending on the type.

If you are working in a programming environment that supports early binding, you may want to declare strongly typed variables, that are declared using specific classes, and then instantiate a new object using the appropriate variable after you have determined its type. This is helpful for coding and debugging as the IntelliSense features will be enabled in Visual Basic. IntelliSense provides dynamic code completion, assistance with code syntax, and object member lists. If you are working in a programming environment that only supports late-bound objects such as VBScript or JavaScript, you are probably just as well to use one variable for the generic object class as there would be no gain in performance or efficiency. In our examples, we will use the early-binding method.

This is a high-level diagram showing all of the objects in the English Query Engine object model. A table follows with descriptions and detailed information about the objects and members of the model:

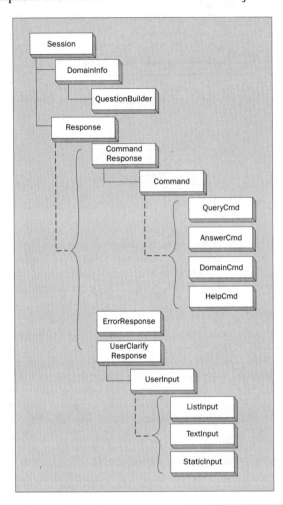

Member	Description
Session Object	Manages the user session for an EQ model using a domain file.
DomainInfo Property/Object	May be used to access session information like the path and name of the domain. Contains the QuestionBuilder model..
QuestionBuilder Object	Provides programmatic access to the features of the Questions Builder control. This subordinate model may be used to automate several features of the engine model, similar to the EQ Project Wizard.
Response Object	A generic object returned by the Session object's ParseRequest method. Returns information about the status of a request and objects to clarify a question, receive an answer, help or error information, or to execute the resulting query expression.

Member	Description
CommandResponse Object	A specific class of Response object returned when the engine successfully parses a request. Contains a collection of Commands used to obtain an answer or execute the translated SQL or MDX expression.
Command Object	A generic object type used to classify all members of the CommandResponse object's Commands collection.
QueryCmd Object	A specific class for a Command object in the CommandResponse object's Commands collection. Returns a string containing the translated query expression.
AnswerCmd Object	A specific class for a Command object in the CommandResponse object's Commands collection. Returns a string containing the answer to the request or question that doesn't need to be executed against the database.
DomainCmd Object	A specific Command object used to execute an action defined by a Command type relationship in the EQ model.
HelpCmd Object	A specific Command object that returns help information based on a request for help.
ErrorResponse Object	A specific class of Response object resulting from a request that couldn't be successfully parsed.
UserClarify Response Object	A request that is successfully parsed but requires clarification or more information before the engine can return an answer or translated expression. This is a specific type of Command object.
UserInputs Collection	This collection is populated with one or more objects containing prompts for user input as a result of a UserClarifyResponse. User Inputs can be in the form of a single string containing a question, multiple choice options, or static feedback. UserInput items are used for output (list item captions and clarification questions) and for input, to return the user's input or selection.
ListInput Object	A specific class of UserInput object. Each object or this type in the UserInput collection represents an option on a single-select list with a caption and a Boolean value.
TextInput Object	This specific UserInput object type is used to prompt for and return a single text value for clarification.
StaticInput Object	This specific type of UserInput object is used to return only feedback in the case of a UserClarification Response. The UserInput collection may contain other members that may be used for input.

Solution Components

Now that we have introduced the objects in the model, let's break down the process into basic steps. The first order of business is to submit a question or request and obtain a response from the engine.

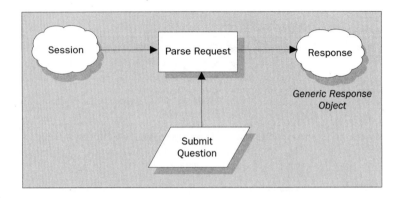

Session Object

This is the top-level object in the Engine model used to maintain the user session with an English Query model. The `Session` object is used to initialize a model using a domain file. This is accomplished using the `InitDomain` method, passing the path to the domain file. This file was created when the English Query project was built in Visual InterDev. For more information on creating and building an English Query project, refer to Chapter 13.

```
Dim ses As Mseq.Session

Set ses = New Mseq.Session
ses.InitDomain "C:\Program Files\...\FoodMart\FoodMart.eqd"

'  Do stuff . . .

'Clean up at end
ses.EndCommands
Set ses = Nothing
```

Questions are submitted and parsed in order to return a `Response` object. The session's `ParseRequest` method accepts the question text as a string argument and returns the `Response` object.

Before terminating the session, you should call the `EndCommands` method to release the domain file and free unneeded resources.

Response Object

The `Response` object is returned by the `ParseRequest` method of the `Session` object and is used to maintain the context of a submitted question. As a polymorphic object, the generic form of a `Response` may represent one of three different object classes:

- ❏   `CommandResponse`
- ❏   `UserClarifyResponse`
- ❏   `ErrorResponse`

The `Type` property the `Response` returns an integer value that is used to determine what type of object it is. The following constant enumeration may be used to test the value:

Constant	Value
nlResponseCommand	0
nlResponseError	2
nlResponseUserClarify	3

Once the `Response` object's type has been determined, either treat the object as the designated type (continue using the `Response` object variable) or set a variable of that type equal to the generic `Response` object. In this Visual Basic example, we are using strongly typed variables:

```
Dim res As Mseq.Response
Dim resCmd As Mseq.CommandResponse
Dim resUserCl As Mseq.UserClarifyResponse
Dim resError As Mseq.ErrorResponse

'Instantiate a session object and submit the user'
'"Me" refers to the current form object
Set res = ses.ParseRequest(Me.txtQuestion)
```

The `ParseRequest` method will return a generic `Response` object. The next step is to determine the specific type of `Response` that it represents.

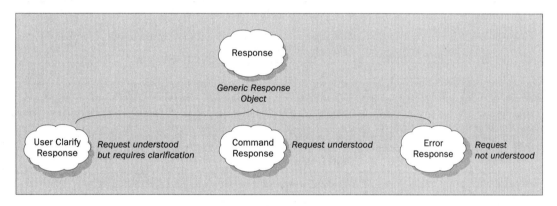

In this simplified example, we use a `Select...Case` decision structure to test the value of the `Type` property. Later we'll use some different logic to deal with user clarification:

```
Select Case res.Type
    Case nlResponseUserClarify      'Prompt for clarification and Reply
        Set resUserCl = res
        ...

    Case nlResponseCommand          'Good to go - execute Command
        Set resCmd = res
        ...

    Case nlResponseError            'Return error and start over
        Set resError = res
        ...

End Select
```

CommandResponse Object

A **Command Response** is returned when a question is successfully parsed. This object has the following members:

Member	Description
Commands Collection	Contains one or more Command objects that are used to obtain the answer or query text
Restatement Property	Returns a string with a rephrased form of the question that was submitted as the request

The generic Command object has only one property, the CmdID, which is used to determine the specific type of Command object. There are three types of Command objects.

Command Object	Description
AnswerCmd	Returns a string with the answer to the submitted question.
DomainCmd	A request that corresponds to a Command type relationship in the EQ model returns this type of Command object. The DomainCmd object is used to execute an action in response to a command type request, rather than a question.
QueryCmd	This type of command is used to execute a query against the database or OLAP cube.

The Command object is also polymorphic and can inherit from any one of these three object types. Instead of using the Type property, like the Response object, a Command object's type is determined using the CmdID property. A constant enumeration may be used to evaluate the command type using the CmdID property as follows:

Constant	Value	Description
NlCmdQuery	1	Query Command – returns translated expression
NlCmdAnswer	2	Answer Command – returns string
NlCmdHelp	3	Response to help request
NlCmdExit	4	Response to request to exit
NlCmdDomain	5	Domain command

UserClarifyResponse Object

If a UserClarify type of response has been returned, we must prompt the user for additional information in order to resolve the ambiguity. If successful, the Response object will be retyped as a **Command Response**.

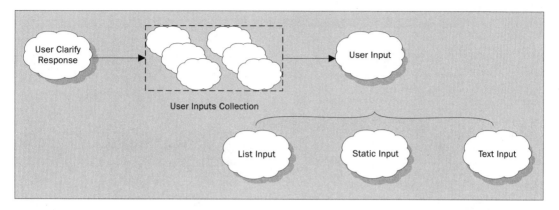

Clarification criteria are provided in the `UserInputs` collection. This collection may contain objects of three different types. Use the following list of constants to interrogate the `Type` property of the `UserInput` object to determine the object type:

Constant	Value	Description	
`nlInputList`	0	List Input	Contains array of `Items`, variant type.
`nlInputText`	1	Text Input	`Caption` property contains a clarification question. `Text` property is used to obtain a clarifying answer.
`nlInputStatic`	2	Static Input	Used only for output. `Caption` property contains user feedback.

ErrorResponse Object

The `ErrorResponse` object is used to return error information. This occurs when a request or question cannot be successfully parsed. The `ErrorResponse` has only one property, the `Description`, which returns a verbose description of the error or problem in resolving the request. English Query will often provide an intuitive error response including a restatement of confusing terms. For example, if a question includes reference to a person (such as *I, my* or *our*) that cannot be resolved with existing semantics in the model, English Query my respond with an error description like ***I don't know about people***.

Question Builder Object Model

This is actually a subset of the Engine object model. The `QuestionBuilder` object is a child of the `Session` object's `DomainInfo` property. This model offers programmatic access to the features of the **Graphical Question Builder control**.

The Question Builder Control

The **Graphical Question Builder** is an ActiveX control used to explore a model's entities and relationships, and to help build questions. The control is contained in the file `Mseqgrqb.ocx`. Some rudimentary documentation about its functionality is available in the help file `Eqqbhlp.chm`.

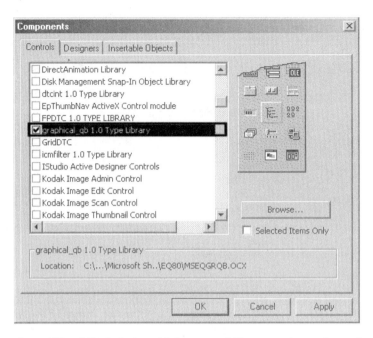

To use the control on a Visual Basic form, add the control library to the project using the Components dialog. This adds the **GraphicalQB** icon to the control Toolbox.

Place the control on form. The **Graphical Question Builder** control consists of three sizable panes. After the control has been associated with a model in code at run-time, entities for the model will appear in the **Entities** Pane. The **Relationships** and **Sample Questions** panes are used to interact with the user and build questions to submit to the model. We will see how each of these features are used in our solution walk-through. See the section titled "Build Questions" towards the end of this chapter.

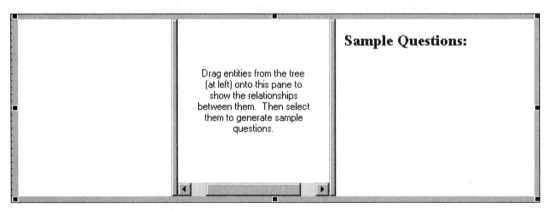

Here is how the Question Builder control looks at run-time:

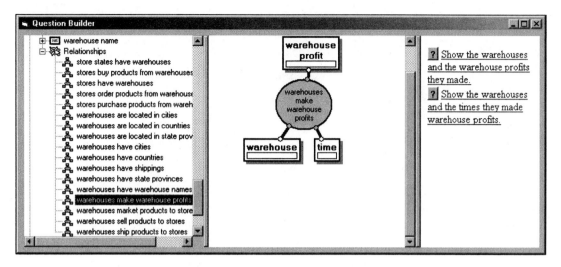

Entities Pane

The left-hand pane contains a tree view that displays entities in a hierarchal form to represent dimensions, members, and measures for the OLAP cube or cubes used to build the model. Relationships for each entity are displayed within the tree. Drag **entities** and **relationships** from this pane onto the **Relationships** pane. The Question Builder constructs questions based on intersecting relationships and related semantic elements. These questions are displayed as hyperlinks in the **Sample Questions** pane.

Note that only relationships and semantics that exist in the model will produce sample questions. If the question you are looking for isn't available, you may need to open the project and enhance the model to support the desired question. For more information about enhancing an English Query model, see Chapter 13.

Relationships Pane

The middle pane is the Relationships pane. A relationship item from the **Entity Pane** dragged into this pane creates a diagram of entities and their relationships. Additional entities and relationships that are added become joined in the diagram to indicate a relational path for the entities. To remove an entity, drag it from the **Relationships Pane** to the **Entities Pane** or right-click and select **Remove** from the pop-up menu.

The pop-up menu may include these additional options (depending on the selected item and other conditions) to control the view and behavior of diagram elements in this pane:

Menu Selection	Behavior
Explode	For an entity, display all relationships and related entities.
Implode	Hide relationships and related entities for the selected entity.
Lock	Prevent the selected item from being automatically repositioned when additional items are added to the diagram.
Unlock	Allow automatic repositioning of items when the relationships diagram is modified.
Remove	Remove the selected item from the diagram.

Table continued on following page

435

Menu Selection	Behavior
Select All	Select all items in the relationships diagram.
Lock All	Lock all items to prevent automatic repositioning.
Unlock All	Unlock all items to allow automatic repositioning.
Zoom In	Zoom in to view fewer diagram items in the relationships pane.
Zoom Out	Zoom out to view more diagram items in the relationships pane.
Full Screen	Zoom the relationship pane to a full screen window. Right-click and deselect Full Screen from the menu to restore the pane.
Clear	Remove all items from the diagram.
Animate Layout	This feature serves no practical purpose. Items progressively move as items are added or removed from the diagram.
Help	Display on-line help in the standard Windows Help dialog.

A value may be selected or entered for an entity in order to provide query selection criteria. To supply a value, click the entity in the diagram. A drop-down list will be displayed.

Sample Questions Pane

The right-hand pane displays questions derived from relationships and selected items in the diagram. Sample questions appear as hyperlink text. A button also appears next to each question. Clicking either of these items will result in events that can be handled in code.

QuestionBuilder Control Events

The Graphical Question Builder control supports a few simple events. At run time, if the question mark button preceding a question is clicked, the ExecuteExample event fires. If the question text is clicked, this fires the SelectExample event. Both of these events pass the question text as a string type argument called szExample. The Validate event fires after a question has been selected, providing the opportunity to cancel question submission or query execution.

Select an entity or relationship in the relationships pane to display sample questions.

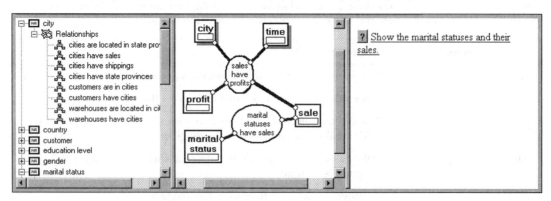

Each entity block in the relationship diagram pane has a box to enter or select a criterion value. Note that this value is used to generate more specific suggested questions in the **Sample Questions Pane**.

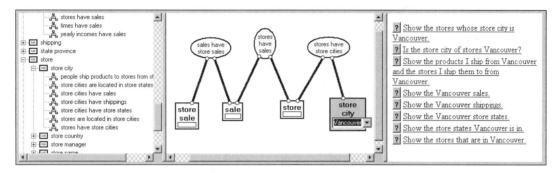

Building the English Query Application

Now that we understand the objects and various steps in the process, let's tie all the pieces together and create a simple English Query application. You may use a variety of programming tools to create the application. We'll use Visual Basic 6.0 for demonstration purposes. This project will use only the **English Query Engine** object model. In program code, this object library is referred to as **MSEQ**.

To build this project, you will need the following software installed on your development computer:

- ❑ Visual Basic 6.0 Professional or Enterprise Edition
- ❑ Visual Studio Service Pack 4 or greater
- ❑ Office XP (for the Office Web Components PivotTable control)
- ❑ SQL Server 2000 Analysis Services

In Visual Basic, create a standard executable project and set a reference to the Microsoft English Query Type Library. If you are working in late-bound programming environment, such as VBScript, you may skip this step and use variant type variables and appropriate object code syntax. For example, use the `CreateObject()` function rather than the `New` key word. We will create three forms in the project: a main query dialog, user clarification, and the form for Question Builder.

The first form will be used to enter questions, view restatements, answers, and the query expression results in a PivotTable control installed with Office XP.

We have experienced mixed success with the Office Web Components for Office 2000. The word from Microsoft is that many improvements were made to these components in Office XP and that they should be much more reliable. In our trials, the Office 2000 (9.0) PivotTable worked reasonably well when properties were set at design time but we had difficulty with many MDX expressions when properties were set at run time. This project is designed to work with the Office XP version.

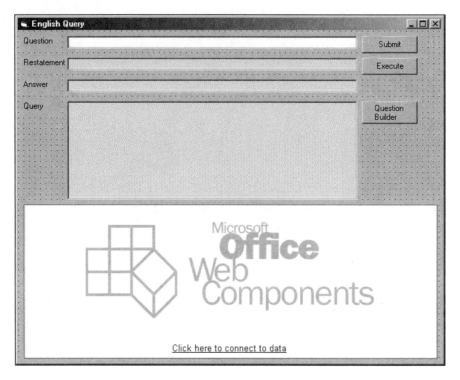

We'll name this form `frmEnglishQuery` and set it as the startup object for the project. Add the following controls to the form:

Control Name	Type	Properties	Description
txtQuestion	Textbox		User enters an English question to submit
txtRestatement	Textbox		Used to display question restatement
txtAnswer	Textbox		Used to display answer type responses
txtQuery	Textbox		Used to display the query expression
cmdSubmit	Command Button		Submits question to EQ engine
cmdExecute	Command Button	Enabled = False	Executes query expression and enables PivotTable
cmdQB	Command Button	Enabled = False	Shows Question Builder form and loads the `QuestionBuilder` object based on session model
PivotTable1	PivotTable	Visible = False	From the Office XP Web Components library; will display multidimensional result set based on MDX query expression

Change the `Enabled` properties for `cmdExecute` and `cmdQB` to `False` and change the `Visible` property for `PivotTable1` to `False`.

The next form is named `frmListInput`. It will be used to display multiple select options for user clarification.

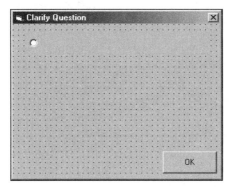

There are only two controls on this form. The Option button will be used to build a control array to list all list options at runtime, and the Command Button will update the user input selection. Add these controls with the following properties:

Control Name	Type	Properties	Description
optListItem	Option Button	Index = 0	First item in a control array used to dynamically add items to a list for selection.
cmdOK	Command Button		Sets the selection value for `ListInput`. This clarifies a question that can be resolved from a list of options.

Set the `BorderStyle` property of the form to `Fixed Dialog`.

The third form will host the Question Builder control. Add this control to the Toolbox using the Components dialog and then add the `GraphicalQB` control to this form. The form name should be changed to `frmQuestionBuilder`. No properties need to be changed other than setting the name of the control to `QB`.

Now, we'll step through the process and take a look at the corresponding code that you will add to each form as indicated. For event procedures, you may either double-click the control with the form in design view or select the control name from the object list and then the event from the procedure list in the code design window header. Either of these techniques will create an event procedure shell ('`Private Sub ...`' and '`End Sub`'.) Type the rest of the code from the samples provided in these directions.

Start by opening the `frmEnglishQuery` form and declare the following variables in the declaration section of the form module:

```
Dim ses As Mseq.Session

Dim res As Mseq.Response
Dim resCmd As Mseq.CommandResponse
Dim resUserCl As Mseq.UserClarifyResponse
```

```
        Dim resError As Mseq.ErrorResponse

        Dim cmd As Mseq.Command
        Dim cmdAns As Mseq.AnswerCmd
        Dim cmdDom As Mseq.DomainCmd
        Dim cmdHelp As Mseq.HelpCmd
        Dim cmdQry As Mseq.QueryCmd

        Dim UserIns As Mseq.UserInputs
        Dim UserIn As Mseq.UserInput

        'Public so it can be changed from frmListInput
        Public ListIn As Mseq.ListInput
        Dim StaticIn As Mseq.StaticInput
        Dim TextIn As Mseq.TextInput

        Dim item As Variant                  'Holds ListInput Items
```

Submitting a Question

In the click event of the Submit button, cmdSubmit, we call SubmitQuestion. This procedure was created as a **public** sub so it can be called from another form and other procedures. The Question Builder form contains code that calls this procedure when our user selects a sample question.

```
Private Sub cmdSubmit_Click()
    SubmitQuestion
End Sub
```

Add the following code to the form module to create the SubmitQuestion public sub procedure. The routine in this project is a bit lengthy. In production, I would break it up into smaller subs and functions. However, in this sample project, it's easier to follow the logic if it is left as one sub procedure. Let's take a look at the entire routine to get the big picture, and then we'll break it down into manageable code fragments. Note that the object "Me" is used to refer to the active form. Although this reference in code is optional, it aids in debugging and automatic code completion.

```
Public Sub SubmitQuestion()
    Dim iListIndex As Integer
    Dim Items As Variant

    If ses Is Nothing Then StartSession

    Set res = ses.ParseRequest(Me.txtQuestion)

    Me.txtAnswer = ""
    Me.txtQuery = ""
    Me.cmdExecute.Enabled = True
    Me.cmdQB.Enabled = True

    Do While res.Type = nlResponseUserclarify
        Set resUserCl = res
        For Each UserIn In resUserCl.UserInputs
            Select Case UserIn.Type
                Case nlInputList
                    Set ListIn = UserIn
                    'Items is an array, not a collection
                    Items = ListIn.Items
                    'Load form to add option buttons
                    Load frmListInput
```

```
                        frmListInput.Caption = ListIn.Caption
                        'For Each item In ListIn.Items
                        For iListIndex = 0 To ListIn.ItemCount - 1
                            If iListIndex > 0 Then
                                'Add option buttons to the form
                                'for each list item
                                Load frmListInput.optListItem(iListIndex)
                                frmListInput.optListItem(iListIndex).Top = _
                                            (iListIndex * 350) + 200
                                frmListInput.optListItem(iListIndex). _
                                            Visible = True
                            End If
                            'Stretch form to fit option buttons
                            If iListIndex > 5 Then frmListInput.Height = _
                                        (iListIndex * 350) + 1500
                            'Set the caption of the option button
                            '  using the List Item text
                            frmListInput.optListItem(iListIndex).Caption = _
                                        Items(iListIndex)
                        Next
                        'Show form as modal to pause code here
                        'If more then 1 ListInput, form will be reloaded
                        '  after it's closed
                        frmListInput.Show vbModal
                    Case nlInputStatic
                        Set StaticIn = UserIn
                        Stop
                    Case nlInputText
                        Set TextIn = UserIn
                        TextIn.Text = InputBox(TextIn.Caption)
                End Select
            Next
            Set res = resUserCl.Reply
        Loop

    Select Case res.Type
        Case nlResponseCommand
            Set resCmd = res
            Me.txtRestatement = resCmd.Restatement
            For Each cmd In resCmd.Commands
                Select Case cmd.CmdID
                    Case nlCmdAnswer
                        Set cmdAns = cmd
                        Me.txtAnswer = cmdAns.Answer
                    Case nlCmdDomain
                        'Used to perform an action based a command
                        '  explicitly added to the model
                        'This feature isn't enabled in this project
                        Set cmdDom = cmd
                        MsgBox cmdDom.CommandName, vbInformation, _
                                "EQ Domain Command"
                    Case nlCmdExit
                        'Request to exit the application
                        If MsgBox("Would you like to exit the " _
                                & "English Query application?" _
                                , vbYesNo, "Exit?") = vbYes Then
                            End
                        End If
                    Case nlCmdHelp
                        'Request for help
                        Set cmdHelp = cmd
                        MsgBox cmdHelp.HelpText, vbInformation, _
```

```
                         "EQ Command Help"
                Case nlCmdQuery
                    Set cmdQry = cmd
                    Me.txtQuery = cmdQry.QueryText
                Case nlCmdUnknown
             End Select
        Next

    Case nlResponseError
        Set resError = res
        MsgBox "Error Number " & resError.ErrorID & vbCrLf & vbCrLf _
            & resError.Description

        Me.cmdExecute.Enabled = False
        Me.cmdQB.Enabled = False

        'Select Question text for resubmit
        Me.txtQuestion.SelStart = 0
        Me.txtQuestion.SelLength = Len(Me.txtQuestion)
        Me.txtQuestion.SetFocus
    End Select
End Sub
```

The two local variables in this procedure, `iListIndex` and `Items`, are used in the code that builds the list for user clarification:

```
Dim iListIndex As Integer
Dim Items As Variant
```

As you can see, we first test to see if a session was previously instantiated. If not, our code will create this object and then submit the question. We will be seeing the code that starts a new session later on. The last five lines in this group clear the contents of the text boxes and then enable the `Execute` and `Question Builder` buttons:

```
If ses Is Nothing Then StartSession

Set res = ses.ParseRequest(Me.txtQuestion)

Me.txtAnswer = ""
Me.txtQuery = ""
Me.cmdExecute.Enabled = True
Me.cmdQB.Enabled = True
```

A `Response` object is returned by the session's `ParseRequest` method. Since we don't yet know what specific type of response this is, the object is held by the generic `Response` object variable, `res`. The `Type` property of the `Response` object is used to determine the type of response (`UserClarify`, `Command`, or `Error`). Rather than using a `Select...Case` decision structure at this point, it makes more sense to test for a `UserClarify` type of response in a loop – since this takes the greatest amount of effort to deal with, we'll deal with it first. If the response is a `Command` or `Error` type, this code is skipped.

As we discussed in the beginning of this chapter, the `Response` object is polymorphic. The object can get retyped and inherit from one of three classes.

Clarifying a Question

If a submitted question requires clarification, the object is typed as `UserClarifyResponse` object. In this case, one or more `UserInput` objects are added to its `UserInputs` collection. After each user input is modified by some type of user interaction, the response object is "refreshed" using its `Reply` method. At this point, there are two possibilities: the updated response object remains a `UserClarify` type because further clarification is required, or the object type changes to a `Command` or `Error` type. In the latter case, the loop terminates and execution continues.

We'll look at the specific logic for dealing with List type input after this code. For simplicity at this stage, these details have been removed from this example. A `Select ... Case` structure is used to test the `UserInput` object type.

In the code in this project, after the object type is determined, we set the generic object equal to a variable of the appropriate class type and then use that object variable. This isn't necessary but it helps with debugging.

A `StaticInput` object is used to provide read-only instructions and typically accompanies other objects in the `UserInputs` collection. We are simply displaying the `Caption` property in a Message Box.

If the question can be resolved with a single text value, a `TextInput` object is used to prompt for, and obtain the value. We're using an `InputBox` function, passing the `TextInput.Caption` property as the message prompt and then returning the value to the `TextInput` object's `Text` property. Here is the `Do ... While` loop of the `SubmitQuestion()` subroutine:

```
Do While res.Type = nlResponseUserclarify
    'use specific response variable (UserClarifyResponse class)
    Set resUserCl = res
    For Each UserIn In resUserCl.UserInputs
        Select Case UserIn.Type
            Case nlInputList
                Set ListIn = UserIn

                '(... List Input code removed for simplicity)

            Case nlInputStatic
                Set StaticIn = UserIn
                MsgBox StaticIn.Caption, vbInformation, _
                                "User Input Information"
            Case nlInputText
                Set TextIn = UserIn
                TextIn.Text = InputBox(TextIn.Caption)
        End Select
    Next
    Set res = resUserCl.Reply
Loop
```

Now for the `ListInput` object. If English Query can't determine what type of entity a word or phrase represents, it will create a list of candidate entities. These text values are used to populate the `Items` array, which is a property of the `ListInput` object. Note that the syntax for working with an `array` property is much different from the collections we use with other objects. `Items` is a variable declared as a variant that holds an array of strings. Each value is an item in the list of options the user should choose from.

The List Input form has one option button so we use this existing control for the first list item. For subsequent items, a new element is added to the control array resulting in an option button for each item. Using the index as a ratio, the top property of each control is set at 350 twips increments, beginning with the second control, 200 twips from the top of the form. The form is also resized vertically to make room for the buttons and an additional 1500 twips for the **OK** button. This code will cause the form's `Resize` event to fire. In the event, the **OK** button is repositioned, relative to the bottom of the form.

```
'Items is an array, not a collection
Items = ListIn.Items
'Load form to add option buttons
Load frmListInput
'set the form's caption to the List Input caption
frmListInput.Caption = ListIn.Caption

For iListIndex = 0 To ListIn.ItemCount - 1
    If iListIndex > 0 Then
        'Add option buttons to the
        'form for each list item
        Load frmListInput.optListItem(iListIndex)
        frmListInput.optListItem(iListIndex).Top = _
                        (iListIndex * 350) + 200
        frmListInput.optListItem(iListIndex). _
                        Visible = True
    End If
    'Stretch form to fit option buttons
    If iListIndex > 5 Then frmListInput.Height = _
                        (iListIndex * 350) + 1500
    'Set the caption of the option button
    '  using the List Item text
    frmListInput.optListItem(iListIndex).Caption = _
                        Items(iListIndex)
Next
'Show form as modal to pause code here
'If more then 1 ListInput, form will be reloaded
'  after it's closed
frmListInput.Show vbModal
```

As you can see, an option button is added to the List Input form for each list item. The form's caption was changed at run time to the List Input caption. This is the question or directive given for item selection.

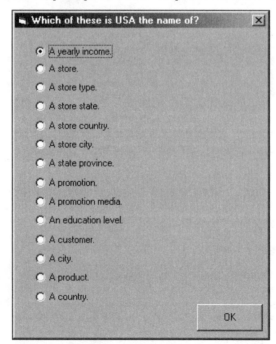

When the List Input form is unloaded, the `SubmitQuestion()` code continues to execute and complete the `UserInput` loop. With the `ListInput` object's `Selection` property set, the engine may have enough information to resolve the User Clarify type `Response` object to a different object type. We update the response object by calling the `Reply` method. This returns a new (and perhaps differently typed) `Response` object back to our generic object variable, `res`.

```
Set res = resUserCl.Reply
```

If a `UserClarifyResponse` object is returned again, the process is repeated until we get a `CommandResponse` or `ErrorResponse`. With the clarification task out of the way, the rest of the process is pretty easy.

Resolving the Response

Using a `Select...Case` structure, test the response object type for every option except `UserClarifiy`, which we have already handled. A `CommandResponse` indicates a successful translation of the question. The appropriate command objects are added to the `Commands` collection to facilitate executing the query. A command type is obtained using the `CmdID` property. Using a `Select...Case` structure, execute appropriate code to return and answer, execute a pre-designed command in the EQ model, exit and terminate the session, obtain help, or execute the translated query expression. Note that we are not going to handle Domain Commands or Help Commands in this project.

```
Select Case res.Type
    Case nlResponseCommand
        Set resCmd = res
        Me.txtRestatement = resCmd.Restatement
        For Each cmd In resCmd.Commands
            Select Case cmd.CmdID
                Case nlCmdAnswer
                    Set cmdAns = cmd
                    Me.txtAnswer = cmdAns.Answer
                Case nlCmdDomain
                    'Used to perform an action based a command
                    ' explicitly added to the model
                    'This feature isn't enabled in this project
                    Set cmdDom = cmd
                    MsgBox cmdDom.CommandName, vbInformation, _
                        "EQ Domain Command"
                Case nlCmdExit
                    'Request to exit the application
                    If MsgBox("Would you like to exit the " _
                            & "English Query application?" _
                            , vbYesNo, "Exit?") = vbYes Then
                        End
                    End If
                Case nlCmdHelp
                    'Request for help
                    Set cmdHelp = cmd
                    MsgBox cmdHelp.HelpText, vbInformation, _
                        "EQ Command Help"
                Case nlCmdQuery
                    Set cmdQry = cmd
                    Me.txtQuery = cmdQry.QueryText
                Case nlCmdUnknown
            End Select
        Next

    Case nlResponseError
        Set resError = res
```

```
        MsgBox "Error Number " & resError.ErrorID & vbCrLf & vbCrLf _
            & resError.Description

        Me.cmdExecute.Enabled = False
        Me.cmdQB.Enabled = False

        'Select Question text for resubmit
        Me.txtQuestion.SelStart = 0
        Me.txtQuestion.SelLength = Len(Me.txtQuestion)
        Me.txtQuestion.SetFocus
    End Select
```

Let's now look at the other functions we need in order to run the application.

Starting a New Session

Enter the following code into the form module as a standalone procedure. This routine initiates a new session. In production, you may want to provide an alternative to a hard coded path to the domain file. For example, you could open a common dialog, allowing the user to select the domain file; or read a previously saved setting written to a registry key. The ClarifySpellingErrors property of the Session object is used to determine whether spelling errors are corrected with or without prompting. If this property is True, a spelling error in the question text will result in a UserClarificationResponse, and the user may be prompted to select a correctly spelled word from a list. We'll demonstrate this behavior using this application.

```
Sub StartSession()
    Dim sDomainPath as String

    sDomainPath = "C:\Program Files\Microsoft English Query" _
        & "\SAMPLES\Models\FoodMart\FoodMart.eqd"

    Set ses = New Mseq.Session
    ses.InitDomain sDomainPath
    ses.ClarifySpellingErrors = True
End Sub
```

List Item Form

The following code runs in the click event of the **OK** button on the List Item form. The selected item is obtained from the option button control array and passed back to the public object variable, ListIn, on the main form using the Selection property.

```
Private Sub cmdOK_Click()
    Dim iItem As Integer

    For iItem = 0 To Me.optListItem.Count - 1
        If Me.optListItem(iItem).Value = True Then
            frmEnglishQuery.ListIn.Selection = iItem
        End If
    Next
    Unload Me
End Sub
```

Since this form was opened modally in the SubmitQuestion() routine using the Show method, the calling code was suspended.

Executing a Query

After the `QueryCmd` object returns the query expression in the `QueryText` property, the expression must be executed against a data source. This is outside the scope of English Query but is easy enough to do in our application using the Office Web Components available in Office XP, or a later version. Enter this code into the Click event of the `cmdExecute` button:

```
Private Sub cmdExecute_Click()
    'Connect the Pivot Table control to the OLAP database
    ' using an OLEDB connection string
    With Me.PivotTable1
        .ConnectionString = "Provider=MSOLAP.2;Integrated Security=SSPI;" & _
                            "Persist Security Info=False;" & _
                            "Data Source=localhost;" & _
                            "Initial Catalog=FoodMart 2000"
        .CommandText = Me.txtQuery
        .Visible = True
    End With
End Sub
```

Once you have a query expression, you can do many things such as create a `Recordset` using ADO to return data in a custom interface or use a specialized control or third-party tool.

Using the Question Builder

The Question Builder command button, cmdQB, opens frmQuestionBuilder and sets the `QBEngine` property of the `GraphicQB` control to the session's `QuestionBuilder` context.

```
Private Sub cmdQB_Click()

    frmQuestionBuilder.Show
    'Sync the QB control to the session EQ model
    frmQuestionBuilder.QB.QBEngine = ses.DomainInfo.QuestionBuilder
End Sub
```

In the Question Builder form, there are only two simple event procedures. The resize event for the form resizes the `GraphicQB` control to match the size of the form. Note that you may need to adjust these values on your form. We tolerate a run-time error in case the user makes the form too small for the control:

```
Private Sub Form_Resize()

    On Error Resume Next
    Me.QB.Height = Me.Height - 615
    Me.QB.Width = Me.Width - 315
End Sub
```

Finally, the `SelectExample` event fires when the user clicks a hyperlinked question in the Sample Question pane of the control. This code places the question text in the Question textbox on the main form and calls the `SubmitQuestion` procedure:

```
Private Sub QB_SelectExample(ByVal szExample As String)

    frmEnglishQuery.txtQuestion = szExample
    frmEnglishQuery.SubmitQuestion
End Sub
```

Tying up Loose Ends

The only remaining code to write in this project is just for form navigation and a little cleanup. In the `Resize` event of the main form, we can automatically resize the PivotTable. You'll need to adjust these values to match your form dimensions.

```
Private Sub Form_Resize()
    On Error Resume Next
    Me.PivotTable1.Height = Me.Height - 4320
    Me.PivotTable1.Width = Me.Width - 555
End Sub
```

In the form's `Unload` event, close the domain, end all of the commands and clean up all of the object variables' memory allocation by setting each object to `Nothing`. This releases resources used by objects and helps prevent application memory leaks.

```
Private Sub Form_Unload(Cancel As Integer)
    'Garbage collection
    ses.DomainInfo.Close
    ses.EndCommands
    Set ses = Nothing
    Set res = Nothing
    Set resCmd = Nothing
    Set resUserC1 = Nothing
    Set resError = Nothing
    Set cmd = Nothing
    Set cmdAns = Nothing
    Set cmdDom = Nothing
    Set cmdHelp = Nothing
    Set cmdQry = Nothing
    Set UserIn = Nothing
End Sub
```

The `Resize` event will fire for the List Input form, `frmListInput`, when the height is changed in the list building code in the `Submit` procedure. This code positions the **OK** button relative to the lower-right corner:

```
Private Sub Form_Resize()
    'Move the OK button if form is resized to fit option buttons
    Me.cmdOK.Top = Me.Height - 975
End Sub
```

Test the Solution

Finally, let's fire up the application and test it. In the Question textbox, enter a question or request that applies to the `FoodMart 2000 Sales` cube such as **List the store states that have sales greater than 25000**. Click the **Submit** button.

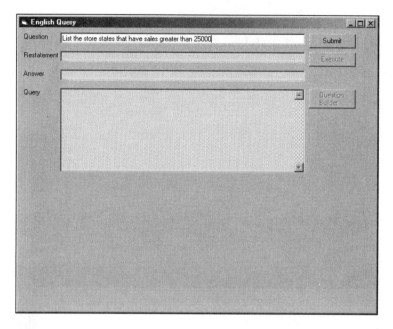

Submit a Question

The purpose of the restatement phrase is to make sure that English Query correctly understood the question. If the request is valid, a restatement phrase will be entered into the restatement textbox and the query expression will appear in the larger Query textbox:

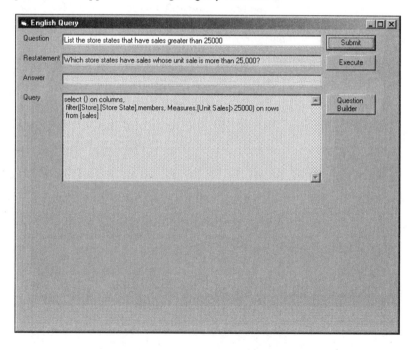

Execute the Query

To view the query output in the PivotTable, click the Execute button:

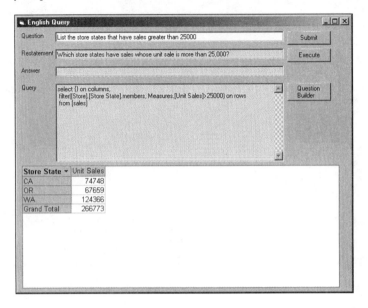

Clarify a Request

Next, let's test the spelling clarification feature. Enter a new request or question in the Question textbox. You may want to Submit and Execute the request to verify that it is correct. Now, modify the spelling of a word so it is incorrect. In this example, we'll enter List the stoers that have sales greater than 2000. Note that the word *stores* and been purposely misspelled as *stoers*.

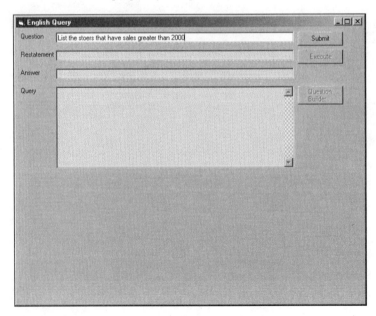

Click **Submit**. You should see the List Input form open up requesting clarification of the misspelled word.

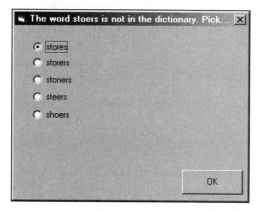

Select the correctly spelled form of the word stores and click **OK**. On the main English Query form, click the Execute button. The query results should be listed in the PivotTable based on a syntactically correct query.

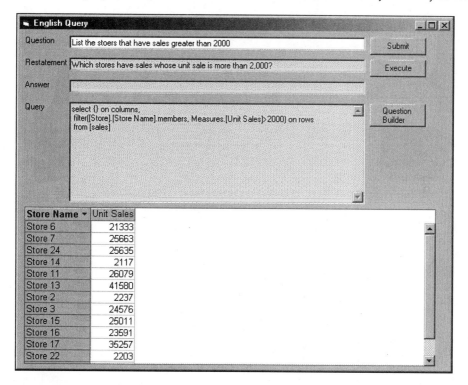

Build Questions

The last test will be for the Question Builder. You may recall that in Chapter 13 we built this model based on the `FoodMart 2000 Sales` cube. All of the relationships we will see in the Question Builder were created for entities (dimensions, levels, and measures) that exist in the cube. We also added and enhanced a few relationships as well.

Click the Question Builder button on the main form. After the Question Builder form opens, expand the Warehouse entity node on the Entities Pane tree and expand the Relationships node. Drag the relationship Warehouses make warehouse profits onto the Relationships Diagram Pane in the center of the form. Two questions should appear in the Sample Questions Pane on the right side. Click on the hyperlink text for the question Show the warehouses and the times they made warehouse profits.

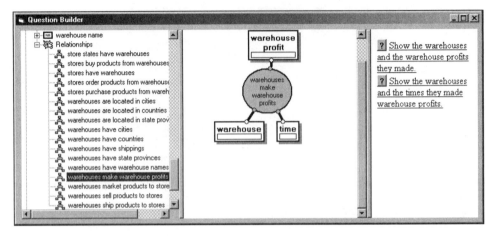

The question on the main form will be updated with this text. Switch to the main English Query form and click Execute. One useful feature of the Query Builder is that you can easily discover combinations of entities that don't have relationships in the model. This is a great tool for finding these associations so you can add appropriate relationships using an English Query Project or custom code using the Authoring object model.

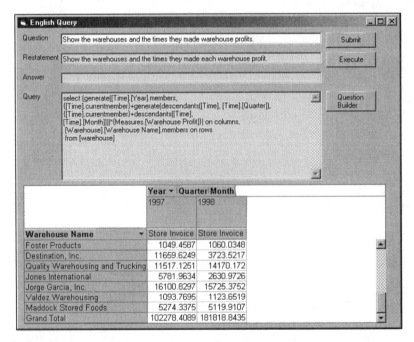

You should see the results of the question built by the Question Builder.

Summary

English Query is one of the most powerful, yet underutilized tools in the Microsoft development suite. If you own SQL Server, you own English Query. The **Question Builder control** is an easy tool to add to an interface with very little code. Three object models compose the English Query functionality. The **Engine model** is at the core, exposing features to submit, clarify, and execute English language requests and questions. The **Question Builder model** extends these features by providing programmatic access to the features of the Query Builder control. The **Authoring model** provides programmatic access to the features we have seen in English Query Projects created by the Project Wizard. For most applications, the Project Wizard and Engine model should provide all of the functionality needed to build a very capable solution without writing code for the Authoring model.

A few years ago, when most people envisioned a data report, they pictured a long list of tabular values, printed on paper with some totals and summary information. Today, reporting can be a dynamic (and multidimensional) interactive process that gives people information, not just data. We have finally arrived at a stage where people can ask for information in normal, natural language rather than cryptic commands – or depend on software developers to make programming changes when they need these reports to group or aggregate values.

With little effort and some creativity, this can be an incredibly useful tool for your users and business decision makers. Compared to designing custom, static reports for each business unit with special needs, English Query is a far more flexible tool. I expect to see compelling solutions evolve quickly using these tools. Speech technology is a natural extension of natural language queries. The Microsoft Speech SDK, the Microsoft Agent or other speech technologies can be used to enhance an English Query solution for convenience or for visually-impaired users. We expect to see voice support in future generations of web browsers to support the VoiceXML standard.

What ever the application or data, whoever the user build custom, ad hoc reporting features into your database and warehouse solutions that allow non-technical people to more easily ask for and get real information about their business.

Data Warehouse

16

Data Mining: An Overview

So far we have worked on creating a data warehouse designed and tuned for reporting and decision support. The analytical data store is structured differently from transactional systems since the users of the data warehouse are interested in generating broad reports on the contents of the information.

In this chapter we begin to look at the process of knowledge discovery, also known as data mining. This emerging technology and its techniques are quickly becoming critical processes by which large growing companies and small companies who want to be close to their customers can remain competitive. Using automated processes of analysis, hidden relationships and trends can be identified and used to determine how to improve profits.

This chapter provides a background and an overview of data mining. We will introduce the concept of data mining, what it is, where it came from, and its use in helping companies to succeed in competitive markets. We will look at approaches for how data mining and the tools that are available to the analyst enable them to complete their task. Specifically, this chapter will cover the following topics:

- ❑ What is data mining and why it is a critical emerging technology
- ❑ How data mining is used
- ❑ How data mining works
- ❑ Descriptions of various data mining techniques and methodologies, including Decision Trees and Clustering

Data Mining

Generally speaking, we are all to some greater or lesser extent, creatures of habit. In college I would stop every morning at a local bagel shop on my way to classes. I would walk into the store, and get in line. By the time I made my way to the counter, the girl behind the counter (who worked there 4 days a week) had my order ready for me, the coffee made right, and would ask me about my day. She knew my needs and preferences, and was able to anticipate what I would ask for.

A few years later another bagel shop opened up, a little closer to where I lived. It was part of a big chain, with twice as many varieties of bagels, and a dozen different coffee choices. I stopped in a couple times, but generally I would go to my old haunt. The new place may know a lot about bagels, but they didn't know me.

Books on marketing and sales tell us that the way to be competitive in today's market is to know thy customer. We return to places that are familiar and do business with those who know our needs and preferences and consistently meet them. In the small boutique type business, providing one-to-one service is simply a matter of learning about your customers. Larger businesses, especially during high growth periods tend to loose contact with those they serve. With the mountains of data collected about customers, products, and sales, a rapidly growing business needs some way to make sense of this data.

Enter Data Mining, an automated process by which an algorithm is applied to a set of data to identify patterns and relationships that help predict future behavior. With its automated mechanisms by which the computer searches through large amounts of data identifying hidden relationships and trends, businesses are able to take advantage of what they know about their customers to be more competitive. They can use these analysis techniques to determine the next course of action that is most likely to succeed and understand the reasons why. Often selling new products to receptive existing customers is far less expensive than acquiring new customers.

Historical Perspective

Computers have changed the way that businesses work. With the introduction of business computers in the late 1950s and 60s records about what people buy and the services they use has been stored to track the progress of a transaction. Because processing power was expensive, and storage was limited, the information was available online only for short periods of time, to serve the purpose of processing the transaction. Storage was generally structured for efficient use of space by creatively defining bit fields to represent larger values, and only large mainframe computers had the processing power required to make use of it.

In 1961 the first generalized database management system was introduced: GE's Integrated Data Store. The wide distribution of this technology popularized data structure diagrams with record types and set types. This terminology formed the basis of the Network Data Model developed by the Conference on Data Systems and Language Database Task Group (CODASYL DBTG). In the mid 60's IBM, GM, TRW and other companies expanded the popularity of database systems for such things as credit reporting, airline reservations, and other systems.

In 1970 E.F. Codd developed the theory of relational databases. The problems of previous database systems of insertion, deletion, and update of data were addressed, as well as theories for designing data models. Codd's rules of data normalization form the core of present data modeling and design work. In the late 70's commercial application of these theories began to be converted into real products.

Oracle Corporation introduced the first truly relational database system in 1979. Several other companies have followed suit, and today there is a plethora of relational database technologies available, including offerings from IBM (DB2), Microsoft (SQL Server), Informix (recently acquired by IBM), Sybase (SQL Anywhere), and others. With the explosion in processing power available on desktop computers, single user databases, such as Microsoft Access, have evolved as well.

In the mid 1980's with the explosion in Database Management Systems (DBMS) technology, massive amounts of information began to become more available to the analyst. As the price of storage decreased and processing power increased, the price of entrance into the world of data mining became more attractive. For the last decade the processor speeds have doubled every 1.5 years, resulting in very powerful corporate computing systems that are capable of processing information that until then were only possible using expensive mainframe and super-computer systems.

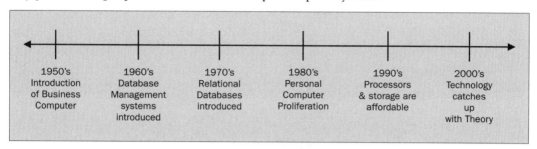

Two applications of databases have evolved, transactional systems designed for efficient capture and management of transactional systems (sometimes called Online Transactional Systems or OLTP), and analytical systems tuned to be able to generate complex reports based on aggregated and summarized data (On-Line Analytical Processing or OLAP). The major difference between them is that the transactional system is tuned for writing and updating information in the data store while the analytical system is designed for efficient reading.

The data warehouse is tuned for reading often, but writing once only. Accordingly, the design and construction of a data warehouse differs from a transactional database. While the performance of a transactional system is tuned for adding information, analytical systems are tuned for reporting.

Why is Data Mining Important?

As computers have become more powerful, and data collected in businesses has become available online as the price of storage becomes more affordable, data mining has entered the mainstream of the corporate world. Because business is competitive, and market share can be tough to get and hold onto but easy to lose, the ability to make smart business decisions is a critical success factor for most companies.

Data mining helps companies notice customer needs, remember their preferences, and learn from past experiences in order to provide better services and products. Understanding our customers and providing ways to make it easier for them to do business with us helps to build customer loyalty.

This is important for the following reason:

> **Even if you aren't using data mining, you can be certain that your competition is.**

With automated data mining tools readily available, gathering intelligence from the information captured is now, more than ever before, becoming a critical success factor to remaining competitive.

It allows a company to notice patterns. A pattern is a series of events or characteristics that happen regularly enough to be predictable. Once a pattern has been identified we devise rules to explain and predict the pattern. For example, if it is noticed that people who buy popcorn also buy apples, a relationship between the two can be made. Once the correlation between the sales has been established, based on these rules, we can create new ideas to try such as running a promotion on apples to see the affect on popcorn or vice-versa.

Why Now?

Until recently data mining activities were limited by computer capabilities and were very expensive. Recently, several factors have come together to make the investment in data mining an attractive one to ordinary businesses. To be competitive, businesses need to leverage the power they already own, through the use of the following:

- ❏ Inexpensive Data Storage
- ❏ Affordable Processing Power
- ❏ Data Availability
- ❏ Off-the-shelf data mining tools and utilities

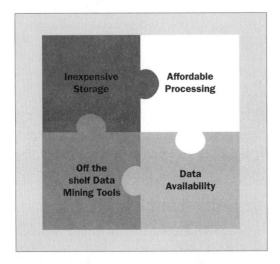

Inexpensive Data Storage

When the first computers were brought online, they physically took up entire rooms, but had less data storage capacity than some of today's digital watches. Because the technology was limited, much, if not all, long-term data storage was kept offline – either as punched cards or on magnetic tapes. When disk storage became an option, more information was available, but early 10 MB disks still took up almost as much space as a washing machine.

In the 1990's the capacity of disk drives sky-rocketed as the prices plummeted. As recently as 1994 databases were limited to 2 GB of storage due to 32 bit addressing and lack of higher capacity disks. Today it is not uncommon to have 40 or 60 GB of disk on a home computer. Current business computers have more capacity than mini-computers did 5 years ago.

Because more information can be kept online, we are able to more easily include it in our analysis, resulting in better results and more accurate predictions. The advances in storage technology have been complemented by corresponding increases in the advances in the CPU.

Affordable Processing Power

Early in the 1990s, the standard desktop CPU ran at 33 MHz, and this was considered fast. In 1995 Digital Equipment Corporation (DEC) introduced an Alpha chip that was capable of running at 150 MHz and 200 MHz. The race for faster chips was on. Intel introduced its Pentium and Pentium II. Other manufacturers followed suit, taking advantage of new techniques for squeezing more processing power of out of a small square chip of silicon.

Over the last 5 years the speed of the CPU has increased to over 1 GHz and promises to go faster still. At the same time that the CPU is faster, parallel processing systems have arrived outside the mini-computer world, resulting in n-tier solutions that help distribute the processing among multiple machines. At the same time, new versions of Windows have been released that take advantage of the multiple processors and are better able to leverage the available processing power. These advances in performance decrease the amount of time it takes to analyze large databases, allowing for more analysis to be run and for a quicker turnaround time from the point the questions are asked to the point at which you can apply what you've learned to the marketplace.

Data Availability

Information is being captured at a greater rate than ever before. Strategically using this information to learn about the customers and the market in which a business competes means that this information's potential value has never been greater.

When I go online to order say, a computer, from an online retailer, information is collected at unprecedented rates. The phone company creates records about the phone call to connect to the Internet. The retailer collects information about the pages I visit, how long I am there, and the route I take to add items to my basket. When I am ready to check out it asks for billing and delivery information. Next the system generates an order to the fulfillment center, which then picks, packs, and ships the item. I receive a tracking number from the shipping company identifying their record of my purchase, and the credit card company adds a detail item to my bill. When the computer arrives, I set it up and it registers my ownership information with the manufacturer so that I can receive future updates and register for product support.

Not only is this information being captured, it is being loaded into data warehouses designed for this type of analysis. Decision Support and OLAP data stores are used to track sales performance, customer information, and more.

Off-the-Shelf Data Mining Tools

As processing power and availability of information have increased, techniques that had once been primarily in the domain of academic research have evolved into cost-effective, real-world solutions. Companies like DigiMine, NetPerceptions, Cognos, Epiphany, Microsoft, Oracle and others have begun to offer a vast array of tools to organize, sort, cluster, and trend the corporate data mountain.

Definition

Data mining is a form of knowledge discovery in which we rely on the computer to exhaustively search through the data looking for patterns and trends. While OLAP tools allow the user to browse for and look for relationships and trends, data mining automates this process allowing a more complete analysis than a user might achieve. It uncovers unexpected patterns and trends and makes visible the associations between various factors that influence your customers' behavior.

The algorithms used in data mining originated as techniques used in statistics, computer science, and artificial intelligence. The different models may be used at different times during the course of a data mining project to explain various things. The goal of data mining is to come up with some good ideas that can be put into practice to help businesses succeed.

Some discussion may be helpful in understanding how data mining differs from data warehousing and operational systems.

Operational Data Store vs. Data Warehousing

An Operational Data Store (ODS) contains the information that is necessary to do business. Generally speaking, it is designed for speed of capturing transactional information and managing it efficiently. Normalization is a process that is used to reduce redundancy of information, and increase the likelihood of consistency of the data stored. This type of a database is used to support Online Transactional Processing (OLTP).

An example of this is a cash register at a retail store. It is designed to record transaction information about customer purchases. If a corporate marketing report were run against the database on the register, it could on impact the performance and affect the ability of the register to do its job. To get company wide results, these reports would need to be run against all registers in all stores. This is not practical.

A data warehouse is a data store structured for performance on generating reports about an organization. It is designed to contained aggregated and summarized information that is useful in generating reports in support of On-Line Analytical Processing (OLAP). While the operational system is designed for efficient gathering of information, the data warehouse is tuned for reporting on **read-only** copies of the data. Because the types of reports generated can be processor intensive, and the risk of bogging down the operational database is very real, it is not uncommon for the data warehouse to exist on its own server. Data from various sources is consolidated, cleansed, and transformed in order to be consistent when it is loaded into the data warehouse. The loading process runs on a periodic basis instead of in real time.

OLAP vs. Data Mining

Aren't these two things the same? While they are both part of SQL Server 2000 Analysis Services, and both are used in decision support, OLAP is an efficient structure for storage of multidimensional information and Data Mining is a process for understanding and learning from it. The OLAP data store contains information about the business, its history with customers and vendors, summarized and aggregated into an easy-to-navigate form. Like applying intelligence to knowledge to get wisdom, when data mining is applied to an OLAP data store it can lead to better business strategies.

Data Mining Models

The data mining model describes where the source of data is that is used to train the model (that is, to run the algorithm against) is stored. This source can be an OLAP cube in which the model is called Multidimensional OLAP or MOLAP for short, or it can be a set of relational tables in a traditional database such as SQL Server or Oracle. This second type is called ROLAP or Relational OLAP. A third option which attempts to take the best of each is called a Hybrid OLAP or HOLAP. The sections that follow provide more detail about each.

ROLAP

As the name implies, Relational OLAP uses relational structures to store the information being analyzed. This approach stores calculated summaries of information according to the various dimensional (hierarchical) attributes described in the mining algorithm's columns. Using special views of the information contained in these tables, the OLAP engine provides access to the data. The ROLAP engine takes multidimensional queries and converts them to SQL, which is then run against the relational database. The result set is then converted into a format consistent with an OLAP cube when returned to the calling program.

Because OLAP is primarily used for generating reports, the relational tables are heavily indexed to provide fast access. The additional calculations required when aggregating data, in addition to the additional indexes, requires additional processing, resulting in slower performance than using MOLAP (see the next section). On the other hand, ROLAP is able to handle large amounts of data and legacy information and is well suited when a large amount of historical information is required to get good results.

MOLAP

Multidimensional storage for OLAP pre-calculates and summarizes information according to hierarchies called dimensions and then stores it in a structure that uses various indexes to allow the user to view the information in different ways. Each possible combination of the various dimensions needs to be processed, which impacts on the time to load new data. What if the information in the OLAP model changes frequently? Because the summarized results are stored in highly indexed cells, the performance of updating the information can become very expensive.

HOLAP

HOLAP (Hybrid OLAP) combines the strengths of MOLAP with those of ROLAP to provide a nice compromise between the two. Basically the non-aggregated data is stored in a relational database, while the summarized, aggregated pieces of information are stored in MOLAP. The two refer to each other with structures that have indexes to the relational records.

The advantage of HOLAP is that it can handle very large data sets, without compromising performance. The disadvantage is that the HOLAP solution needs to coordinate changes and updates between the two models.

Data Mining Model Algorithms

Microsoft includes two algorithm choices "out of the box" to the user – clustering and decision trees, and also provides an interface by which third parties can integrate their solutions. These algorithms may fall into more than one category, depending on their intent. These categories include:

- ❑ Classification Models
- ❑ Clustering Models
- ❑ Descriptive Models
- ❑ Predictive Models

Classification Models

Classification models group cases together based on various metrics and attributes. An example of a classification model is "Baby-Boomers", people born between 1946 and 1964. Anyone with this classification is presumed to be facing similar life challenges at predictable times. The use of classification models is good for demographic type research.

Classification uses predefined categories to describe the cases contained in the data. These might be type of service provided, male or female, which state or region the customer resides in, or a store concept type. Cases fit into classes that describe the data in concrete, yes or no, true or false categories.

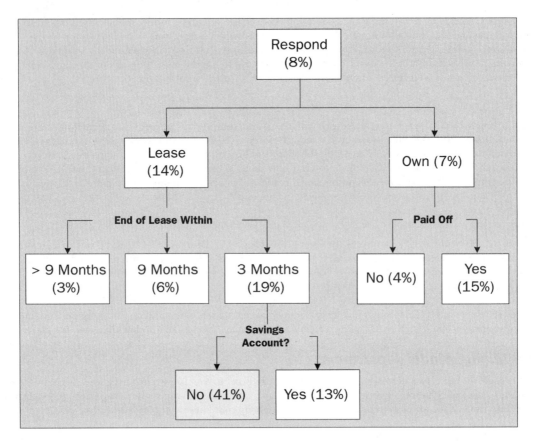

Clustering Models

Clustering models group cases together that have similar characteristics. Because these similarities are often not obvious, they apply an iterative technique of repeatedly passing through the data to identify characteristics of cases that are similar. The algorithm makes several passes through the case set redefining the boundaries of the groupings. The result is groupings of characteristics that describe the cluster of similar cases.

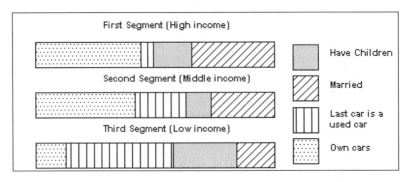

Descriptive Models

Sometimes the goal of data mining is to describe the data being looked at. By using descriptive models such as Market Basket analysis, the analyst can gain insight into what drives the observed behavior. Sometimes by simply understanding the situation better, explanations can be developed that will help to drive future data mining activities such as clustering or decision tree analysis.

Predictive Models

Predictive models are used to identify market segments that would most likely be receptive to a new product or promotion. For example movie houses may preview their movies to sample audiences and gather their impressions of the movie and then compare their demographics to their response. This allows them to focus their advertising to that segment of the population who would most likely enjoy the show. A popular predictive model that is included with SQL Server 2000 Analysis Services is Decision Trees.

Hypothesis Testing vs. Knowledge Discovery

Data mining activities can be described as one of two ways – either to prove or disprove a theory or hypothesis, or to discover relationships and trends. The first is sometimes called directed learning or hypothesis testing, while the second is considered to be more data-directed, as an automatic or semi-automatic process in which the outcome is not known. In the course of a data mining exercise the use of one may lead to use of the other.

Directed vs. Undirected Learning

Sometimes hunches are made about the affect of a particular variable on a pattern, other times there is no obvious link. Using directed learning, the analyst specifies which variables to watch. Undirected learning is used when there are no preconceptions of what the results may be. Using machines to run algorithms that are unconcerned with how a human may put relative value on particular things, undirected learning is performed to see if patterns or trends can be found.

How is Data Mining Used?

When you log onto a web site to order a book and it suggests other books you may be interested in, this could well be an example of data mining in action. The online book-seller may track your purchases, and based on your buying habits, be able to make intelligent and often accurate guesses about books you could be interested in.

Our focus has primarily been on the commercial uses of data mining. The same techniques that help determine which products should be paired in promotions and which services to cross sell, are also used in vastly different fields. Criminologists use link analysis from field cases to create profiles of the likely perpetrator. Meteorologists look at predictive models to tell us whether we will need a raincoat, a pair of shorts, or a snow shovel for the next day. Stock market analysis, city growth, and even casinos, use data mining to predict the next big thing.

> *As information makes itself available to the analyst, and opportunities are found for using the information to grow, data mining is becoming a core component of the analyst's tool belt for doing their job.*

For example, the consumer electronics industry is a highly competitive one. Every day new products are announced that promise to change the world. New computer models are released multiple times a year in order to take advantage of advances in the underlying technologies. A new personal digital assistant promises to make our lives better. New DVD technologies provide faster performance and better fidelity. As the new products line up, retailers are eager to get their piece of the pie.

463

In order to be competitive, customer habits are tracked to determine what predictive factors will improve loyalty and repeat business. Using data mining techniques, it is determined that two factors drive the business – pricing strategy, and customer service.

How Data Mining Works

This process of knowledge discovery begins with an assessment of the situation. The analyst gathers information about the problem into a consolidated data store and then selects a technique that is likely to provide answers. An algorithm is selected, and a representative sample of data is processed against it, during which process the mining model is trained or loaded with a set of statistical and probability information. The results of this analysis can then be used to support a course of action that will likely succeed based on what has been learned.

The basic process results in the discovery of relationships, hidden patterns, and trends that lead to future good ideas that can then be applied. These ideas are put into practice and the results are measured. Then, the cycle begins again, with an assessment of the new situation that takes into account what has been learned last time through.

The Cycle of Data Mining

To be of true value to an organization, the outcome of data mining needs to be measurable, actionable items. This means that not only is the analysis performed, but something is learned from it and it is applied in practice. The basic cycle of data mining is not unlike that of most organic processes:

- ❏ Understand the situation
- ❏ Build the model
- ❏ Run the analysis
- ❏ Take action
- ❏ Measure results
- ❏ Repeat

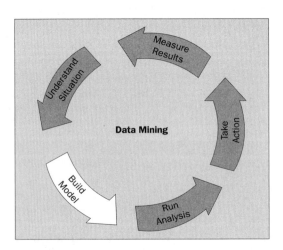

Understand the Situation

Understanding the situation is where opportunities are identified and questions are asked. Very often questions are raised asking why one region's sales are better than another, or why one product sells better than another, or whether offering a new service would improve customer loyalty. These questions are good candidates for using data mining. Is the price sensitivity a more important consideration among profitable customers than selection?

Select and Build a Model

Based on the opportunity found, determine what information will be needed. Do we already have a data warehouse built that contains what we need or do we need to bring together additional information to run the analysis? During this part of the process an OLAP solution is designed and the data is loaded into the various structures. A mining model is trained against the data store and validated.

To get the analysis started, a type of model is selected. A clustering or classification type of model might be used to get an idea of what to look for, and then a decision tree or some other model might be run to get additional information.

Run the Analysis

After validating that the information is complete, the model is trained and the data mining engine runs the analysis against the complete set of data. The results are used to look for trends, patterns, and behaviors that stand out from the rest. Data mining should lead to actions taken because of it, so plans based on what has been learned can be put together.

Take Action

This is the part of the process where the results from data mining are put to use and the results of the actions are fed into the measurement phase. It is important to take an assessment before changing things so you have a benchmark to compare the results against.

Measure the Results

Was the action taken correct? Did the actual results meet our expectations and did our predictions hold true? This part of the cycle feeds the learning curve to improve the accuracy of future data mining efforts.

Repeat

We review the new situation and repeat the process again. This renewal of ideas and spirit feeds the organization to grow and become better than it was before.

Tools for Data Mining

Microsoft and other vendors provide several tools with SQL Server 2000 Analysis Services that provide a quick way to make use of data mining techniques. These include:

- ❑ Decision Trees
- ❑ Clustering Analysis
- ❑ OLE DB for Data Mining
- ❑ Third-party tools

Decision Trees

Decision trees are a form of classification in which a series of binary or yes/no questions are answered until a case can be described as belonging to a particular class. The decision tree algorithm repeatedly passes through the data splitting it into smaller groups that provide a set of rules that describe what something is. This process continues until it reaches a set point at which further division of the groups doesn't make sense according to preset parameters. These rules are readily expressible in clear language, such as income greater than $25,000 but less than $50,000, or the respondent is Male vs. Female.

This technique can be useful for explaining why someone was denied coverage, or turned down for a loan. Its strength lies in that it doesn't require much computing, it generates understandable rules about the pattern, and it provides clear evidence of which factors are most important in making a classification (by listing the number of cases at each decision point).

Clustering Analysis

The process of bringing order to a heterogeneous population of objects by grouping like objects together into classes of similar objects is called clustering. This is generally an undirected data mining approach that is helpful in visualizing relationships between various cases. Because it makes no assumptions about the data, it can highlight anomalies in the data and be useful in identifying strategies for future data mining efforts. While classification uses predefined categories for cases, clustering works along a continuum of values, visually presenting like values close to each other.

Unlike decision trees, no rules are implied from the identified clusters that can be readily applied to prediction models. Because of this, the results can be more challenging to interpret.

OLE DB for Data Mining

Microsoft continually makes new technologies available to the developer in ways that they can be plugged into other applications and systems. Just as OLE DB provides access to corporate data stores from various applications, OLE DB for Data Mining exposes the data mining classes and tools that can then be integrated into user applications, providing visibility to data mining from standard business applications.

Third-Party Tools

Some of the main contributors of data mining are presented in the table below along with their flagship product in the field.

Company	Tool	Web Address
SPSS		http://www.spss.com/products/products/families/clementine/
	Clementine Data Mining Systems	
Knowledge Discovery, Inc.	KD Data Mining Suite	http://www.datamining.com/dmsuite.htm
SAS Institute	Enterprise Miner	http://www.sas.com/products/miner/index.html

Table continued on following page

Company	Tool	Web Address
IBM	Intelligent Miner	http://www-4.ibm.com/software/data/iminer
Cognos	4Thought Scenario	http://www.cognos.com/products/scenario/index.html
Silicon Graphics Inc. (SGI)	MineSet	http://www.sgi.com/software/mineset/overview.html
Alta Analytics	NETMAP for Claims	http://www.altaanalytics.com/
Data Mining Technologies	Nuggets	http://www.data-mine.com/
WizSoft	WizWhy	http://www.wizsoft.com
PilotSoft	Discovery Server	http://www.pilotsw.com
Oracle Corporation	Darwin	http://www.think.com

Success Factors for Data Mining Projects

As if running a software project weren't already filled with opportunities to loose track of requirements, scope, and resources, Data Mining presents a whole new minefield full of obstacles that needs to be traversed. Unlike other types of software projects, like building cash register software or an application security system or a data replication scheme, the results of data mining are far less tangible and much easier to loose track of. The goal of data mining is to learn something by applying various techniques to the analysis of a set of data. How do you quantify learning?

Good project management skills are necessary in any project, but one of this type requires that you also be a good observer, a fair judge, and a reasonable taskmaster. In other projects we are primarily focused on the goal or deliverable such as a working application. In data mining the path we take to get there is just as important because of what we learn on the way. Data Mining is an iterative process in which we pick a direction, take a shot, evaluate the results, and then pick another direction. In the course of trying different approaches we try to learn the nature of the system.

Any serious effort, whether it is giving a speech, writing a book, or building software, can be evaluated by looking at and understanding three things: the intent of the project; the content or plan to accomplish this, and the delivery of how the plan was carried out. If these three factors don't line up, you risk exerting yourself on a technical adventure that may end up as simply a learning experience. Like the boats that find the rocks in the surf you can find your project scuttled by management in favor of spending their attention elsewhere. Therefore we need to do three things:

- ❑ **Intent.** Understand the situation
- ❑ **Content.** Create a plan
- ❑ **Delivery.** Communicate where we are at as we execute the plan

The Situation

When we start a project we need to understand what it is we are trying to accomplish. Why are we working on this and what can we use to measure our success? Who are we providing our results to, and what is their role in the process? The person who is directing the research may not be the same as that who is funding it, so we need to take the various interests into account. What is our timeframe and do we have an idea of what is it that our audience will be looking for us to provide them when we are done? We need to ask these questions as we begin to understand why we are undertaking the project.

In addition to the project motives, we need to understand enough about the business to be able to speak the same language. The pillars of retail are product (also called SKU), inventory, pricing, employees, and customers. In the insurance industry it is claimant, provider, benefits, renewals, and rates. What are the main objects and the language of the business that you are working with and what does their data look like? Where is it stored and how can we access it?

There is usually an operational data store or transaction-oriented database that contains the information that is used to conduct day-to-day business. Sometimes there is a data warehouse that is used for decision support and reporting purposes. Perhaps they already have a data mining group that has already started down the path you are on that you could interview to see what they've already learned. Sometimes the information is in one database, other times it is spread across many servers as well as platforms. You need to take inventory of where the information that is the focus of the investigation can be found and how you can access it.

The most important part of understanding the situation is finding where the information your investigation is about can be found so that you can bring it together to be processed. While explaining how to do this is outside the scope of this book (there are several others out there that do an excellent job of explaining the tool and all its bells and whistles including *Professional SQL Server 2000 DTS (Data Transformation Services)* ISBN 1-861004-41-9), you can use DTS to bring information from disparate sources such as DB2, Oracle, SQL Server, Access, and/or Excel, and transform them into a consistent format for use during data mining. Simply put, for data mining to be successful you need data.

Understanding the intent of the project will act as our compass. This directs us towards the goal of what we want to learn. It will help us evaluate whether we are on course or if we need to change directions as the result of something we learn.

Create a Plan

Once we know "the what" of the project we need to determine "the how". We need to create a plan for approaching the problem and allocate the resources to do it. This may include creating a common location for the information we are using. Who will build and process the mining models, and who will interpret the results? What machines or servers can we use for this?

We can use SQL Server or some other data store, but we need to keep in mind that the way we structure the data store should follow a consistent approach. By that I mean that if you have product types that are numeric in one data source, and descriptive in another, that you use DTS or some similar tool to transform or change the non-consistent values to follow a single standard.

Other key pieces to the plan that should be part of any methodology include determining a timeframe for the project, and determining how we will report our progress. We need to keep the other stakeholders informed of where we are at and what has been learned so far. Failure to communicate and thereby manage our client's expectations is one of the big reasons that software projects fail.

The plan we are creating is our map for this project and it should include enough information to help us when we get stuck. But just as a map is a point in time picture of reality, our plan is based on what we know when we create it. We need to use our compass to confirm that the landmarks we see make sense and fit with what we expect.

Delivering on the Plan

It would be nice if all we had to do was execute the plan and by magic we were given the answer. Unfortunately, this is not likely the case. There is no free ride, you can't get something for nothing, and good results in data mining come from attention to the task. Data Mining is an art that is learned from practice. The tools we use apply complex algorithms to large amounts of information and attempt to find patterns and trends.

Of course it depends on the circumstances, but the results are not always clear and easy to interpret. It may take looking at the output from different angles before the patterns you look for are found. While patience is important, another key success factor is persistence. If the first approach you took failed to generate results, try another. Alter the model a little, change mining algorithms, or use a different sample of data. Try to look at the problem from more than one perspective. If you find the plan is outdated, then change it, but be sure to inform the other stakeholders.

Finally, we need to communicate where we are at in the process. Don't just give the good news, if you run into problems or delays that will affect our ability to generate results, tell people. We need to set the expectations of others involved with the project that learning is not something that can be scheduled, and that we may not find the answer we are looking for. It is better to under-promise and over deliver than the other way around.

Summary

This chapter provided a background and overview of data mining, its emergence as a critical technology in today's economy, and how you can use it as part of your repertoire of techniques for analysis. In the course of the discussion in this chapter we covered:

- ❑   What Data Mining is
- ❑   Why it is important
- ❑   Some data mining techniques
- ❑   The different data mining models
- ❑   What SQL Server 2000 Analysis Services provide
- ❑   Some considerations to think about in running a data mining project

In the next chapter we will look at some practical examples of data mining. We will see how to use the various tools that are included with SQL Server 2000 and Analysis Services.

Data Warehouse

17

Data Mining: Tools and Techniques

We understand what data mining is, and why it is important. We've looked at factors that help make projects like these successful. These include understanding our objective, developing a plan for approaching the questions to be answered, and then executing the process to get results. Now we will focus on what SQL Server 2000 Analysis Services have to offer to the data mining analyst. We will use these techniques as we go through examples using the FoodMart 2000 database of how to create predictive and descriptive Data Mining models and then we will analyze the results.

For this chapter, we will use the FoodMart 2000 sample database that comes with SQL Server Analysis Services. We will open the hood of the database and look inside to see what we can learn about the sample company. Then we will ask some questions that can be answered using data mining techniques. Over the course of this chapter, we will use the various tools to see how they work and what they can tell us.

In the first part of the chapter, we will cover the following:

- ❑ Introduce the FoodMart business model and some likely challenges is faces
- ❑ What we want to learn from the project of data mining
- ❑ How we use the cluster model to answer some of these questions
- ❑ How decision trees fit into the mix
- ❑ Other tools and techniques that are available

The sample database installed with SQL Server Analysis Services is used in a variety of examples throughout this book. From the standpoint of a data miner, we need to understand some basic information about the business in order to come up with pertinent questions and create a focus for our investigations. From that perspective we ask, what do we know about FoodMart, and what types of things can we learn?

We will use Decision Support Objects to manage the process of creating a data mining model. We will then look at how the object can be used from a client application using PivotTable services that expose the language of predictive queries.

In the second part of this chapter, we will look at advanced data mining concepts, including the object models, what they are, and how and when to use them. We will also look at how DSO and PivotTable Service expose the data mining models making them available to the developer. We will also look at the language of Predictive Queries and then DTS's data mining tasks.

Let's start this chapter with a look at approaches to data mining.

Data Mining Approaches

One of the critical success factors of any project is to understand what we are trying to accomplish with our efforts. Defining what is in and out of scope will help us to not get caught on a technical adventure that, while it may be fun and educational, doesn't meet the objectives for which we got funding. Our role as a data miner is to understand the business enough, or at least work with our business partners, so that we are able to ask relevant questions.

FoodMart 2000

This chapter will use the example database that comes with SQL Server 2000 Analysis Services. It is a Microsoft Access database that contains corporate information from a hypothetical retail grocer. This database contains a good deal of information that we can use to illustrate various techniques. For the purposes of this section, I used DTS to import the tables into a SQL Server database and then I ran Query Analyzer to process the queries below. You can also run most of them from Microsoft Access by using the SQL View in the query designer tool, but you can only run one query at a time and you will need to remove the comments (they start with two dashes).

FoodMart is a mid-sized retail grocer founded in 1951. Since then it has grown to 25 stores employing over 1,150 people on a full or part time basis, serving over 10,000 customers. In our database, we have sales records for the years 1997/1998, which provide information about the customer, product, store, and promotions involved.

With standard SQL queries we can look at the information contained in the database to give us some idea of the table sizes and value ranges that we are working with. Using some simple scalar functions we can retrieve some interesting facts about the nature of this company. The sample queries below are fundamentally table counts with summaries grouped by specific columns to get some interesting facts.

Employees

The employees in our stores are the face we give our customers. What defining characteristics do we know about our employees that might be worth pursuing?

```
-- How many active employees do we have?
SELECT count (*) AS 'ACTIVE',
    (SELECT count(*) FROM employee
    WHERE end_date is NOT NULL) AS 'INACTIVE'
FROM employee
WHERE end_date is null
```

```
-- How many employees work at a typical store?
SELECT store_id, COUNT(*) AS 'EMPLOYEES'
FROM    employee
GROUP BY store_id
ORDER BY 2 DESC, STORE_ID
-- Note: the 2 in ORDER BY above is the 2nd selection column

-- What is the tenure of our staff?
SELECT hire_date, COUNT(*) AS 'COUNT'
FROM    employee
GROUP BY hire_date ORDER BY hire_date
```

If you run the queries, you'll see that we have over 1,100 employees working in our 25 stores and that we only have information on active employees. It appears that there are probably about 6 types of stores in that the employee count per store falls neatly into that many groupings. Our staff is fairly new, which raises questions about whether a staff retention program would help boost sales.

Customers

Who shops at FoodMart? What do the demographics look like? In our example database, we are very good at capturing profile information on our customers, in that there are no missing values in many of the columns that contain characteristic information about the customer:

```
-- How many distinct customers do we have on record?
SELECT count(*) FROM customer

-- Cars owned
SELECT num_cars_owned AS 'Cars',COUNT(*) FROM customer GROUP BY num_cars_owned

-- Customer city
SELECT city AS 'City', COUNT(*) AS 'Count'
FROM customer GROUP BY city ORDER BY 2 desc

-- Customer occupation
SELECT occupation AS 'Occupation', COUNT(*)
FROM customer GROUP BY occupation

-- Customer children
SELECT total_children AS 'Kids', COUNT(*)
FROM customer GROUP BY  total_children

-- Zip codes…is this any different than BY city?
SELECT COUNT(distinct postal_code) FROM customer
```

There are over 10,000 customers, with 5 different occupations, wholive in more than 100 cities. We have information on many attributes including annual income, number of children, age, occupation and more.

Product

Next, we look at product information. To speak the language of the business, we need to understand how FoodMart organizes what it sells. The term **taxonomy** refers to the hierarchical relationship between products and the departments that they belong to. The queries below give us some insight into this as well as some idea of brand information:

```
-- Let's take a quick look at our taxonomy
SELECT COUNT (distinct x.product_id) AS 'Count', p.product_class_id,
    CONVERT(varchar(25),product_family) AS 'product_family',
```

473

```
            CONVERT(varchar(25),product_department) AS 'product_department',
            CONVERT(varchar(25),product_category) AS 'product_category',
            CONVERT(varchar(25),product_subcategory) AS 'product_subcategory'
FROM product_class p, product x
WHERE p.product_class_id = x.product_class_id
GROUP BY p.product_class_id, product_family, product_department, product_category,
product_subcategory
ORDER BY 'Count' desc, product_family, product_department, product_category,
product_subcategory

-- More taxonomy stuff
SELECT COUNT(distinct product_family) AS 'Family' FROM product_class

SELECT COUNT(distinct product_department) AS 'Department' FROM product_class

SELECT COUNT(distinct product_category) AS 'Category' FROM product_class

SELECT COUNT(distinct product_subcategory) AS 'Subcategory' FROM product_class

-- How many brands do we carry?
SELECT CONVERT(varchar(25),brand_name), COUNT(*) AS 'Count'
FROM product
GROUP BY brand_name
ORDER BY 'COUNT' desc, brand_name
```

FoodMart sells 1,560 products that are categorized into 3 families (food, drink, and non-consumable). These are further broken down into 23 departments, 47 categories, and 107 subcategories.

Sales

The sales fact tables contain information about the product sold (also called a SKU or stock keeping unit), the suggested retail price (SRP), and whether a promotion was active for the transaction. We will need to keep in mind that the sales tables in this database have been denormalized in that there isn't a separate transaction header table from the item detail:

```
-- What products do we sell the most of and what is that distribution?
SELECT CONVERT(varchar(50),product_name) AS 'Item', SKU,
       COUNT(*) AS 'Count'
FROM    product p, sales_fact_1998 s
WHERE p.product_id = s.Product_id
GROUP BY p.Product_id, product_name, sku
ORDER BY 'Count' desc

-- What information do we have in the sales fact tables that might be of
-- interest?
SELECT TOP 100 CONVERT(varchar(30),p.product_name) AS 'Item',
               s.*, p.SRP
FROM           sales_fact_1998 s, product p
WHERE s.product_id = p.product_id
ORDER BY time_id, customer_id, promotion_id, p.product_id, store_id

-- Some sales info about a typical brand
SELECT p.product_id, CONVERT(varchar(30),p.product_name),
       COUNT(*) AS 'Count'
FROM product p, sales_fact_1998 s
WHERE p.product_id = s.product_id and brand_name LIKE 'Ebony%'
GROUP BY p.product_id, p.product_name
ORDER BY 'COUNT' desc
```

From a cursory review of the sales fact table from 1998 (running a query that counts the records grouped by product), we see that all the products have fairly uniform distribution of sales. What we don't know is how promotions affect product sales.

Promotions

From looking at the structure of the promotion table, we can see that promotions are store-specific. In FoodMart during 1998 there were 240 promotions across all stores associated with approximately 25% of the sales transactions. No promotion lasted more than 4 days:

```
-- Promotional info
SELECT promotion_id, promotion_district_id,
       CONVERT(varchar(30),promotion_name) AS 'promotion_name',
       CONVERT(varchar(20),media_type) AS 'media_type',
       CONVERT(money, cost) AS 'cost',
       CONVERT(varchar(18),start_date), CONVERT(varchar(18),end_date )
FROM promotion ORDER BY start_date
```

Stores

The 25 stores accounted for just over $1 Million in sales, with a profit margin of about 60%. The profit margin varies between stores by less than 1%, which implies that the product mix for FoodMart sells fairly consistently at all locations:

```
SELECT  sum(store_sales) 'sales',
        sum(store_cost) 'cost',
        sum(store_sales)-sum(store_cost) 'profit',
        ((sum(store_sales)-sum(store_cost))/sum(store_sales))*100 'margin'
FROM sales_fact_1998

SELECT  f.store_id,
        convert (varchar(20),store_city) 'city',
        convert(int,store_sqft) 'sqft',
        convert(varchar(12),first_opened_date,110) 'open',
        convert (money, sum(store_sales)) 'sales',
        convert (money, sum(store_cost)) 'cost',
        convert (money, sum(store_sales)-sum(store_cost)) 'profit',
        convert (money, (sum(store_sales)-sum(store_cost))/store_sqft) 'ppsf',
        ((sum(store_sales)-sum(store_cost))/sum(store_sales))*100 'margin'
FROM sales_fact_1998 f, store s
WHERE f.store_id = s.store_id
GROUP BY f.store_id, store_sqft, store_city, store_sqft, first_opened_date
ORDER BY 'profit' DESC
```

This gives us a sense of what FoodMart is and a good idea of the type of information we are working with. We have investigated customers, products, promotions, and basic sales information. We could have done the same thing with OLAP cubes, but for the basic facts like these SQL can be faster.

What Can We Learn?

In any project we need to know what our objective is. What is the point of this activity? In our analysis of who and what FoodMart is, several questions may come to mind when projecting performance and looking for opportunities for future growth. What are the characteristics of the customers that we make the most profit on? What sets the best performing stores apart from the others? What products tend to sell well together? Does employee experience play a factor in the success of store? Do promotions have the expected affect of increasing sales at the store for the duration of the sale?

We can focus our investigation down several avenues. In a retail organization, the questions fall into several categories, some of which are listed below.

❑　Customer Sales Focus

❑　Store Performance Focus

❑　Price Performance Focus

Let's take a look at each of these in more detail.

Customer Sales Focus

What defines profitable customers that we want to keep as opposed to those that cost us money to keep? We can look at customer purchases over the 2 years to determine who are the most active. Does the number of children make a difference? How about number of cars? Home ownership? To answer these questions, we could look at the sales per customer over time and then analyze which variables make a significant difference. We can use data mining to see if we can find groupings of customers that have similar characteristics and look at the profitability of those groups.

Store Performance Focus

Which stores are most profitable? By profitable we could look at gross profit, or we could be a little trickier and look at the profitability per square foot. Do new stores tend to outperform older stores? Do amenities such as a coffee bar or expanded meat market tend to improve sales performance? Do the characteristics of the employees who work in and manage the stores may make a difference? What factors differentiate the profitability of one store from another?

Our sample database provides us with 25 different store attributes that could be used in our data mining efforts. Included among these are the total square footage of the store and the various departments, when it opened and when it was last remodeled, and whether there is a coffee bar or a video store. A store-focused data mining effort may take some or all these attributes into account when looking at employee retention or sales performance, in order to create predictive models that help us decide which to include in new stores.

Price Performance Focus

If there is no margin, there is no mission. The benefits from running a promotion need to outweigh the cost. There are two variables associated with promotions, the type and the duration. Questions related to price performance tend to center on understanding when to have sales, and the type to run. What items should be promoted together, and which should not? For example, if it is found that people who buy diapers also tend to buy beer and not the other way around, will a promotion for diapers increase beer sales?

The other end of promotions is choosing the selling price. According to the basic laws of economics, supply drives demand, and by increasing resistance, the flow of goods goes down. Data mining can be used to identify products that sell huge volumes at low prices, but may have less profitability than selling less volume at a greater margin.

Practical Data Mining

Data Mining is the process of probing a set of information for descriptive and predictive purposes. The idea behind the entire process is to identify patterns and trends that allow us to better understand and to focus our efforts to achieve a desired outcome. With the release of SQL Server 2000 and Analysis Services, Microsoft provides the analyst with powerful data mining capabilities right out of the box, including data mining algorithms for Clustering and for Decision Trees.

The term for what is being analyzed is a **case**, and all the cases that make up the population of the data being studied is called the **case set**. Like relational tables have indexes, primary and foreign keys, there is a unique identifier to each data mining case called the **key**. There also may be several descriptive pieces of information called **attributes** or **measures** that tell us something about the case. A case may consist of information from a single table or from multiple tables. If there is more than one we describe the case as containing **nested tables**. The hierarchical attributes of the case that allow for convenient groupings such as region, district, and location, or department, class, and subclass, are called **dimensions** of the case.

In the course of the data mining analysis, there are three distinct sets of data that we will need. After the data mining model has been created and is first processed, the results created by the algorithm are saved for future purposes. The initial set of records that is processed by the model is called **training set** data in that it is used to "teach" the model about the population being analyzed.

A second set of data, with different cases from the first, should be used to give us confidence in our new model. Processing the model with a sample of **test cases** in which we omit some known attributes helps us confirm that the model correctly predicts the missing values.

The final set of data is the **evaluation set**. These cases are the focus of our investigation. If we are looking at customer behavior, then the training data might be a subset of our current customers. The test cases would also come from our existing data, except that we look at various aspects of our model where we have removed some attributes in order to confirm the model's behavior. A final set of cases we process is the situational data, or evaluation set. The evaluation set would include new customers and future customers. We can use the model to identify or predict behavior based on what the mining activities have learned and to drive sound business strategy.

Clustering

As human beings we have always tried to make sense of things, to at least gain an understanding of our surroundings even if we can't explain them. By confronting the unknown, exploring and learning about our world we deal with our fears and meet a basic need to comprehend.

Clustering attempts to make sense of the "Big Picture" by helping us break something large down into smaller, more manageable groupings that share similar traits. The old saying of keeping it simple is often easier said than done. We find that we are confronted not with too few patterns, but rather with too many, and that what we are trying to understand is clouded with too much noise to be seen clearly. This question of how we can identify the combination of the most significant traits is what Microsoft has attempted to answer with the clustering data mining tool.

Clustering is a great way to start analysis of data, particularly if you are faced with a large and complex set of data that tends to have a lot of internal structure. By applying this approach, the analyst can break down a large problem into a number of groups with common traits. These clusters provide a description of the members in each. By providing a way to classify these clusters, we gain a certain bit of understanding of the nature of the problem. While it may be the first technique used in the project, it probably isn't the last. Clustering is often used as a source of future mining efforts by illuminating other promising areas to investigate.

As the analyst, you may need to do some experimenting with the model's parameters in order to get the best outcome. Because the algorithm takes into account many different attributes some of the groupings may be somewhat surprising. It is these unexpected diamonds in the rough that will often yield the most value in the long run for the project.

> The process of data mining can be described as almost an art. Analyzing the results from clustering may require patience, but the results are well worth it.

How Clustering Analysis Works

Unlike some algorithms for clustering that measure the distance between points in a model and require multiple passes through the entire population of cases, Microsoft implemented what is called a Scalable Expectation Maximization algorithm that creates clusters based on population density. You can read the details of the algorithm on Microsoft's web site at ftp://ftp.research.microsoft.com/pub/tr/tr-98-35.pdf, but the key thing to know is that this approach works really well for a commercial product. The processing can be stopped and restarted (if new data becomes available). It requires at most a single pass through the source data and provides reasonable results at any point during its computation. Best of all it works within a limited amount of memory.

What does that mean? Basically, as the algorithm processes records it creates a number of clusters. The centers of these clusters are adjusted as more data is processed. This results in finding the set of characteristics that best describe cases that have similar qualities. The entire process runs relatively fast and doesn't kill your machine by eating up all the available memory.

Suppose we are investigating new car purchases, comparing the age of the customer and the type of vehicle purchased. Using sales data from a typical day at a car dealership, we can categorize 12 new car purchases by 3 vehicle types: sedan, truck, and mini-van. For purposes of illustration, the table below captures sales and lists only two obvious attributes of the buyer. A third attribute that could also be analyzed from the dataset is gender:

Name	Age	Car type
John Smith	25	Sedan
Mike Stevens	34	Truck
Joyce Bingham	55	Sedan
Dan Gains	37	Truck
Sara Thompson	29	Minivan
Matt Roberts	44	Truck
Richard Walsh	61	Sedan
Eric Clark	23	Sedan
Jim Franchett	63	Sedan
Steve Adams	32	Minivan
Linda Johnson	28	Minivan
Michael Miller	19	Sedan

We can create a chart of the data using the age and car type as the two axes.

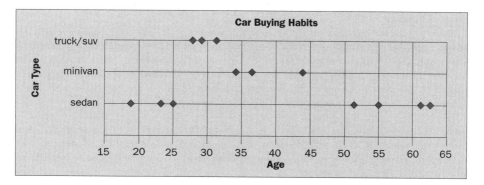

There appear to be 4 groupings or of people who purchase the different types of vehicles. People between the ages of 25 and 30 tend to buy trucks, people aged 35 to 40 tend to buy minivans, and those older than 50 and younger than 25 tend to buy sedans. Another cluster that is not readily apparent is that those older than 65 and younger than 19 don't tend to buy new cars.

Strengths

The strengths of clustering include:

❑ **Undirected:** The clustering technique will analyze the complete set of data to find similarities and patterns that may be missed by a directed technique.

❑ **Not limited by type of analysis:** Clustering analysis will work on any type of data being investigated, from meteorology to insurance to retail to manufacturing. Its ability to identify patterns is not limited by the type of attributes being analyzed.

❑ **Handles large case sets:** Earlier version of the clustering algorithm that were easy to implement required multiple passes through the data to identify groupings. Microsoft's version only passes through the data set once, which provides significant performance gains in the amount of time it takes to process large sets of data. This means that clustering can be used on large sets of data within a reasonable amount of time.

❑ **Memory:** Only a subset of the cases is kept in memory during processing, which means that this algorithm doesn't eat up all your available memory.

Weaknesses

The weaknesses of clustering include:

❑ **Measurements need to be carefully chosen:** The weight of one attribute may not relate directly to that of another. One attribute may be measured in miles, another in pounds, and a third in square feet.

❑ **Results may be difficult to interpret:** Clustering is an undirected activity. You are not necessarily starting with an idea of what you expect to find, hence you may not recognize it when you find it.

❑ **No guaranteed value:** As with anything else, there is no sure way to know that the clusters that are found will have anything more than a descriptive value to the analysis.

Decision Trees

Decision trees are used to solve prediction problems, such as whether someone will like a movie or purchase a particular product. An example such as predicting if a student will enroll in a particular class can be analyzed using a database that contains demographic information from a test segment of the population. The decision tree algorithm identifies the most relevant characteristics and then creates a set of rules that give percentages of probability that new cases will follow the pattern.

The results can be expressed in clear language. Analysis Manager includes a graphical representation that provides the analyst with the statistics for each decision. Because our sometimes-litigious society demands reasons, these numbers can then be used to explain why someone was turned down for a loan or was given special attention in school.

How Decision Trees Work

The process of creating a decision tree is called recursive partitioning. The algorithm determines which attribute is most relevant and splits the population of cases by that attribute. Each partitioned group of cases is called a **node**. This process is repeated for each subgroup over and over until a good stopping point is found (because either all cases in the node meet the criteria, there aren't any more attributes to split on, or there isn't enough data to provide statistically reliable results). The last group of cases forming the final division is called a **leaf node.**

For purposes of illustration, we will demonstrates the recursive partitioning algorithm on a sample of cases that has two attributes (P1 and P2), each of which has four values. At the intersection of these is our prediction attribute of O or X:

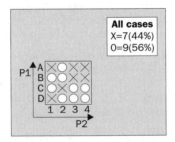

The algorithm begins by scanning all the possible splits of the input variables P1 and P2 to find the best split based on purity of the resulting clusters. We see that the first split should be on P1, with the first cluster contains all records where P1 is either A or B, and the second cluster where P1 is C or D:

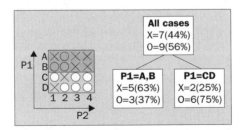

At this point the process is repeated. Each cluster is scanned individually to identify the next partition. The first cluster is split on P2 between the values of 2 and 3, and the second cluster happens to split on the same variable P2 between the values of 1 and 2:

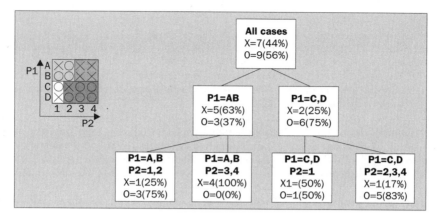

We need to stop partitioning the resulting clusters at some point before the model becomes what is called **over fitted**. An over fitted model is one in which the leaf nodes contain only one value, as our tree does for the top left cluster. All cases in this cluster have a prediction attribute of X. The danger is that the model is too pure, and looses its ability to provide a realistic prediction. In practice, the algorithm will stop itself before it gets to this point.

Strengths

The strengths of decision trees include:

- ❏ **Visual results:** Sometimes a picture is worth a thousand words. The results of this technique can be viewed in a straightforward tree, visually showing the splits and distribution of the results.

- ❏ **Understandable rules:** The resulting distributions of cases that fit the various attributes forming the nodes can be expressed in simple language. This results in a fairly easy-to-follow train of logic to end in a particular leaf node.

- ❏ **Predictive:** If the training set of data is properly chosen, decision trees provide rules that will predict the likelihood of new cases fitting into the model.

- ❏ **Performance for prediction:** Since we have a set of rules found from the training data, new cases can be quickly classified resulting in good performance for prediction.

- ❏ **Shows what is important:** The decision tree algorithm determines which attribute will provide the best splits by comparing the various inputs. This allows the analyst to see where to put priority and emphasis when acting on the results of the analysis.

Weaknesses

The weaknesses of decision trees include:

- ❏ **Can get spread too thin:** Generating a tree with too many classifications leads to the potential of too few cases fitting the final category. This can lead to false conclusions about the viability of the predictions made with such a model.

- ❏ **Performance of training:** Because each split requires analysis to determine the best attribute to use, the cases in the node are sorted multiple times. This can be computationally expensive and require patience on the part of the analyst.

The Setup

FoodMart has decided to evaluate customer loyalty. The questions are who shops at FoodMart, and does the FoodMart Club Card influence purchasing behavior? As the data analyst, our job will be to look at who carries the card, and analyze their purchasing behavior. To begin with, we need to devise some way to categorize the customer base. We will use clustering to look at the defining characteristics of the people who have the FoodMart Club Card.

We have the option of basing our mining model on either an OLAP or a Relational data store. Using OLAP allows us to take advantage of the predetermined aggregations and dimensional information from the source cube. If we choose the other we need to provide information on what describes a complete case. If this requires more than one table then we need to define how the tables are joined.

For the purposes of our investigation, we will start with the Sales Cube from our OLAP FoodMart data warehouse.

Building An OLAP Clustering Data Mining Model

To create a cluster model for this, lets look at the characteristics of the most profitable stores. We start by running the Analysis Manager and performing the following steps:

- ❑ Select the source of data for our analysis
- ❑ Select the cube to analyze
- ❑ Choose the algorithm for this mining model
- ❑ Define the case's key
- ❑ Select the training data
- ❑ Save the model
- ❑ Process the model

Open Analysis Services Manager

Begin by opening Analysis Services and opening the FoodMart 2000 database. Expand the navigation tree to show the data mining models. From Analysis Manager, right-click on Mining Models and select New mining model…:

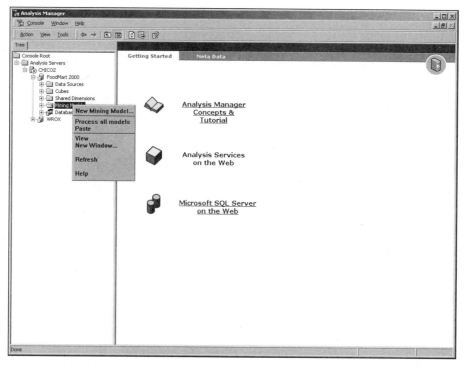

This opens up the Data Mining Wizard screen with which we will create our cluster mining model:

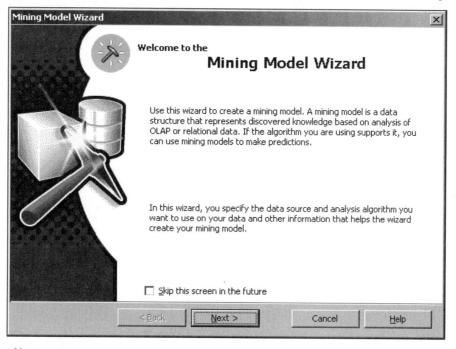

Click on Next to continue.

Select the Source of Data for Our Analysis

The user is presented with a choice of Relational or OLAP data stores for the cases being analyzed. Since we are looking at customer's behavior from a sales focus, we can use the existing cube in the FoodMart 2000 database for Sales. Consequently, we will choose the OLAP path. In our next example, we will demonstrate creation of a relational-based model, but at this point select OLAP Data and then click on Next to continue:

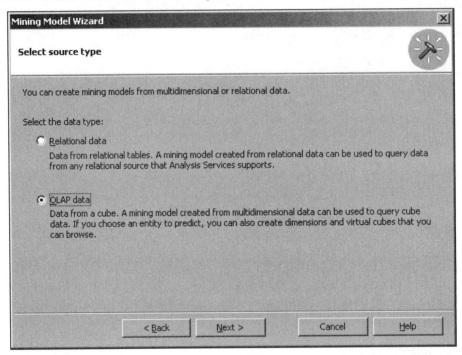

Select the Source Cube

Next, we select the source of our data. We will be looking at our sales data with the customer as the focus of our clustering. When you click on the Sales cube, the available dimensions that can be used in our analysis are listed. Only dimensions that have at least one visible level can be used:

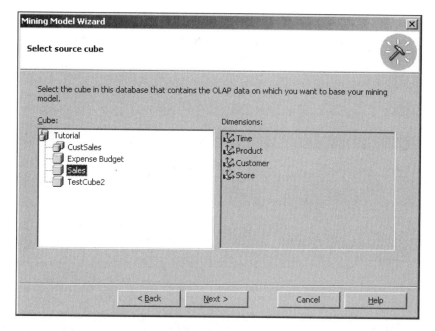

Choose the Algorithm for this Mining Model

There are two choices: clustering, and decision trees. The purpose of this initial analysis is to identify general patterns and groupings in our data, so we will be using Microsoft Clustering. Select this technique and then click on Next to continue:

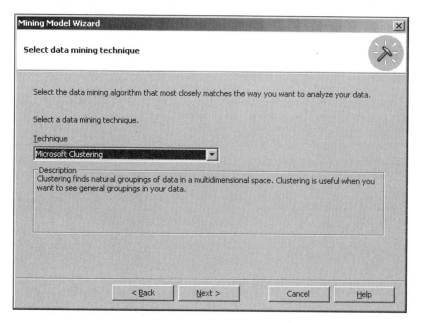

Define the Key to Our Case

In the cube being analyzed there are several dimensions that can be used to uniquely identify our case, including customer, product, store, etc. By default, the lowest level is set, although you can select other levels from this screen. For example, if we were interested in looking at how different cities behaved, we could choose customer as our dimension and city as our level.

Select Customer as the dimension, with LName as the level and click Next to continue:

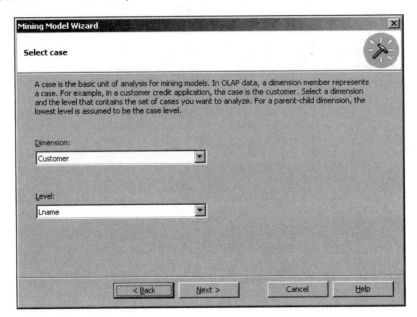

Select Training Data

After the case has been defined, we are presented with the option to further specify the set of training data. The OLAP cube contains more information than just the dimension that we are studying, so the wizard defaults to the dimensions previously selected as the source of the training data. You can specify which levels to include for each of the dimensions, as well as any other attributes that should be included.

For our analysis, we will include the Customer dimension. Click on Next to continue:

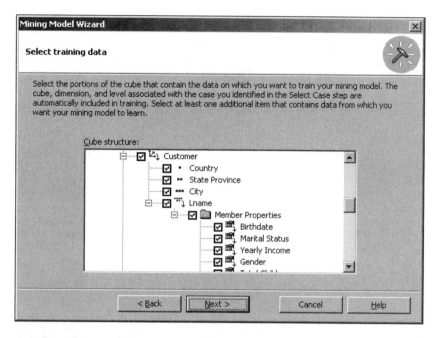

Save the Model

Next, we save and process the model. The data mining engine uses the parameters we entered and trains the data mining object with the information from the sales cube. Processing the model populates the training data and generates the resulting cluster model:

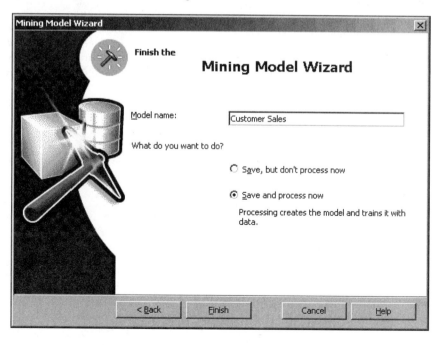

Process the Model

The progress dialog provides real-time information about where the mining algorithm is in its processing. You can stop the build at any time and it will halt and await further input as to whether you want to reprocess or simply exit to the OLAP Data Mining Editor:

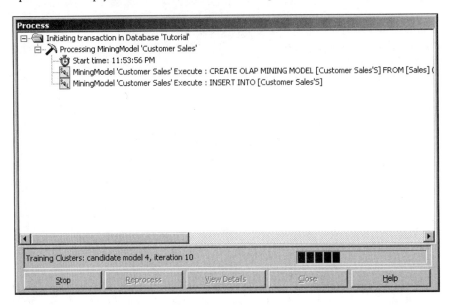

Analyze the Results

When the process has completed the OLAP Data Mining Model Editor screen is opened. If you had saved but not processed the model from the wizard or if you had interrupted processing after the model had been saved, you would see a similar screen except that only the structural pane on the left side of the screen would be visible and you would be directed to process the model before you could browse it. Both the toolbar and menu can be used to process the model:

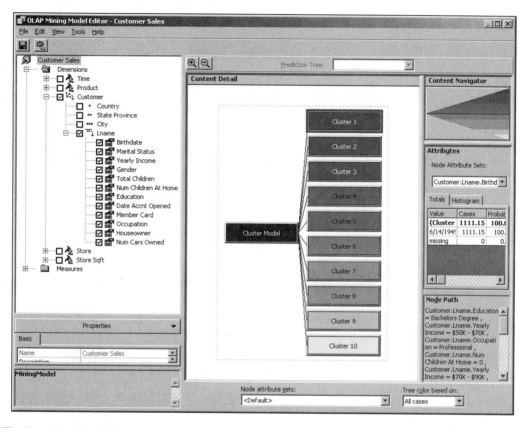

The Data Mining Model Editor displays the results of our analysis. The left-hand pane contains the parameters that were used to create the cluster. The middle pane is a graphical representation where the colors of the panes show the concentration of the distribution of cases. The right-hand pane shows the attributes of the results.

By clicking on a cluster, the node path describes what defines the cluster. You can change to other node attribute sets to see other pieces of information about our model. By default, the displayed attribute set is the first one in the dimension definition.

The most interesting clusters are those that contain the most cases. Likewise those with a smaller population provide less meaning because of their probably coincidental nature. Some clusters can be disregarded because the specific combination of various attributes doesn't give us enough information to make generalized distinctions.

The number of clusters generated defaults to 10. Sometimes, changing the number of clusters to a larger or smaller value is helpful in simplifying results. To do this, click on the top node in the left-hand pane. The Properties window will show the number of clusters to generate. Changing this number will require reprocessing of the model.

The more attributes that are included in the analysis, the more complicated the resulting cluster model is. It is easier to understand the results after pruning out excessive properties that confuse the results.

What We Learned

A cursory review of the clusters gives us a starting point to look for interesting patterns. One approach is to look at the rules for each cluster. Unfortunately, these descriptions are not the clearest and it can be difficult to make heads or tails of what each cluster contains.

A better way is to look at the histogram, or bar graph in the attributes pane, for each of the attributes we measured. We can click through the clusters to see which values dominate for each. I created a quick table that summarizes some of the attributes below (remember that these are the dominant values, not the only ones):

Cluster	Cases	Income	Occupation	Education	Member Card	Marital Status	Cars Owned
1	14.5%	$50-90K	Mgmt & Professional	Bachelors	Bronze	Single	2.5
2	13.2%	$70K +	Mgmt & Professional	Mix	Bronze	Single	2.5
3	13.2%	$10-30K	Manual & Skilled Man.	Partial H.S.	Normal	Single	1
4	11.3%	$30-50K	Manual & Skilled Man.	H.S.	Bronze	Single	2.5
5	10.7%	$30-50K	Manual & Skilled Man.	Mix	Bronze	Single	2.5
6	9.2%	$70K +	Professional & Mgmt	H.S. & Bachelors	Bronze	Married	2.5
7	8.1%	$30-50K	Manual & Skilled Man.	H.S.	Bronze	Married	2.5
8	8.0%	$10-30K	Manual & Skilled Man.	Partial H.S.	Normal	Married	1
9	6.2%	$50K +	Professional & Mgmt	Bachelors	Gold	Married	3
10	5.6%	$30-50	Manual & skilled man	H.S.	Gold	Married	3

From this table we can see that the attributes that tend to drive the groupings in our model include Income, Occupation, and Education. We will use this information to do some further analysis on club card membership. FoodMart wants to be able to predict who to focus efforts on broadening membership of the Gold Card. We will use decision trees to analyze the information from the customer and sales fact tables to identify predictive factors.

Building a Relational Decision Tree Model

We will create our Decision Tree data mining model from the relational data contained in the `FoodMart 2000` Access database. The process for using a relational model is similar to that of OLAP, but there are some differences we will highlight as we proceed. These steps include the following:

- ❏ Select the type of data for our analysis
- ❏ Select the source table(s)
- ❏ Choose the algorithm for this mining model
- ❏ Select the source table(s)
- ❏ Define how the tables are related
- ❏ Define the key
- ❏ Identify input and prediction columns
- ❏ Save the model but don't process it

Select the Type of Data for Our Analysis

As in the last example, the user is presented with a choice of relational or OLAP data stores for the cases being analyzed. For this example, we will be using the relational FoodMart 2000 database. Select Relational Data and then click on Next to continue:

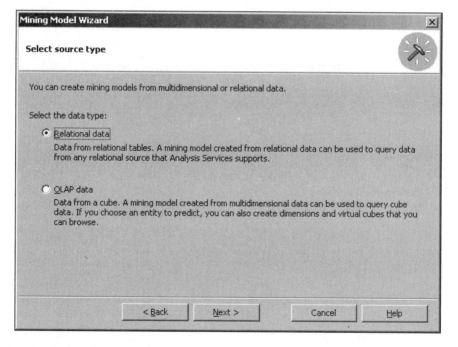

Select the Source Table(s)

On this screen, we define our data source. The window will list the data sources defined in the database you are creating this model in. You have the option of adding a new data source by clicking on the button on the screen. We are building a decision tree that uses two tables, customer and sales_fact_1998. Select the radio button for Multiple tables. We add the tables from the list of those available by highlighting the name and either double-clicking or using the arrows to move the table to the selected list:

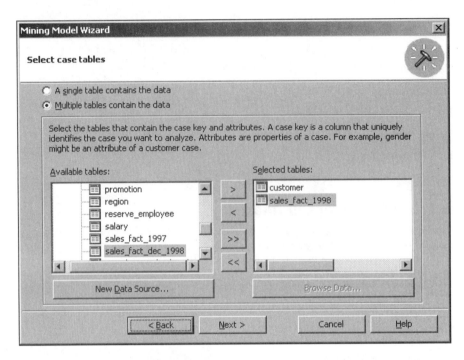

Choose the Algorithm for this Mining Model

Next, we will specify that this model will be created with Microsoft Decision Trees. Make sure that this option is selected and click Next to continue:

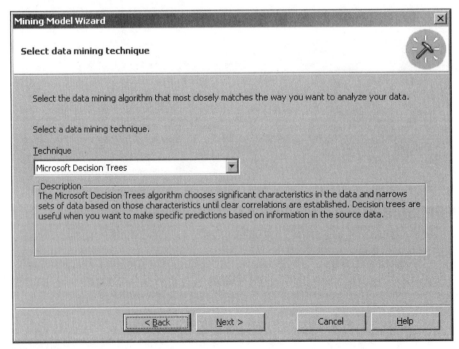

Define How the Tables are Related

Next, we define how the tables are joined. By default, the wizard will assume that the key relationship defines how the joins are made and will use this as the default; however, you could change this if needed. Click on Next to continue:

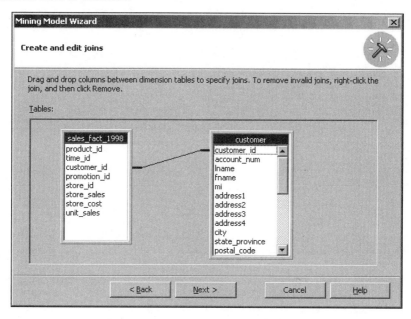

Define The Key

Next, we select the table and key column that uniquely identifies our case. If you have multiple cases, you need to decide which one is driving your analysis. Since our focus is on the customer, select the Customer table and the Customer ID column as the key for this analysis:

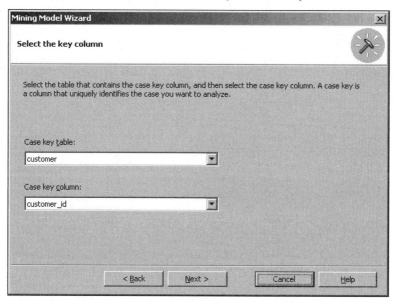

Identify Input and Prediction Columns

Input columns are considered during the partitioning process to determine the best split. Prediction columns are those attributes that we would like to ask questions about. We are interested in learning how the various demographic factors for a customer drive their card membership and sales behavior. Add member_card from the Customer table, and unit_sales from the sales fact table. Add the all the columns from birthdate on from the Customer table to the input list.

If you wanted to edit the model before it is saved, you have that option by selecting the checkbox to finish the model in the editor. Otherwise clicking Next will take you to the last step of the wizard:

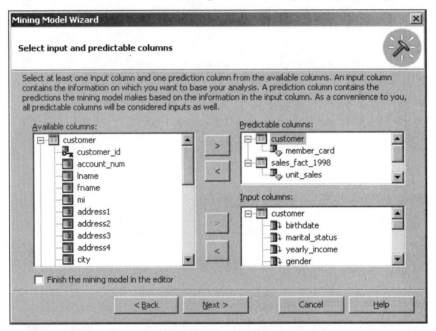

Save the Model but Don't Process It – Yet

The last step of the wizard names it and saves the model definition. You have the choice to process the model immediately or you can edit it in the Relational Data Mining Model Editor first. We have some work to do before we process the model. Save the model, but don't process it:

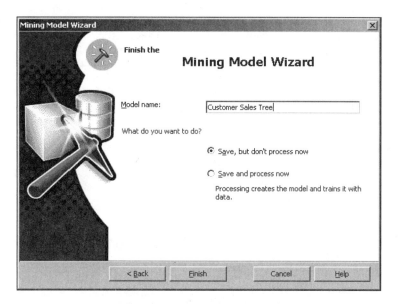

Edit the Model in the Relational Mining Model Editor

The relational editor is similar to the OLAP Mining Model Editor, except that the parameter pane on the left hand side of the screen displays table and column information instead of cube dimensions and measures. The right-hand pane contains two tabs for browsing the schema information and the contents of the model:

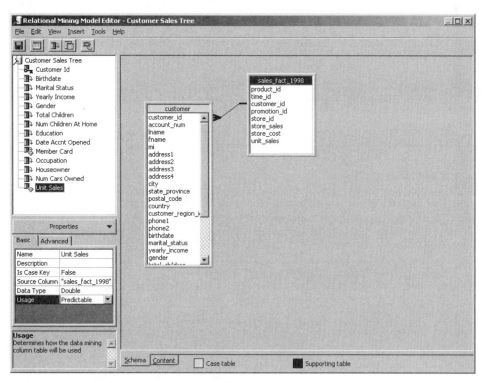

We need to change the sales fact column from both input and predictable to just predictable. Select the column from the tree of columns available, and the properties for that column are listed. Basic properties are self-explanatory and include the name of the column, a place where you can add a description, whether or not the column is part of the case key, the table that is the source of the data, the column's data type, and the usage. The advanced properties are less obvious. We will cover the meaning of these in more depth in the next chapter. Change the usage property of the Unit Sales column and set it to Predictable. Then we process the model by clicking on the process icon on the tool bar, or if you click on the Content tab you are prompted to save and process the model.

Progress Window

The progress window is displayed and shows the status of each step in building the model. The SQL items contain the statement that is being executed. The first statement creates the mining model with the columns and options defined by the wizard, and the second trains the model with the source data by executing the INSERT command:

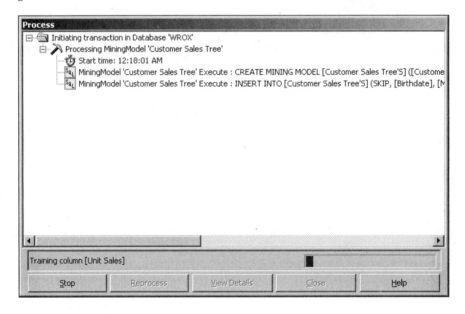

Analyze the Results

We used a relational data source with nested tables, so processing the model may take some time to complete (mine completed in about 9 minutes). If you need to cancel the process, you can click on the Stop button and close the processing window or restart it by clicking on Reprocess. When the model has complete processing, the contents tab displays the results:

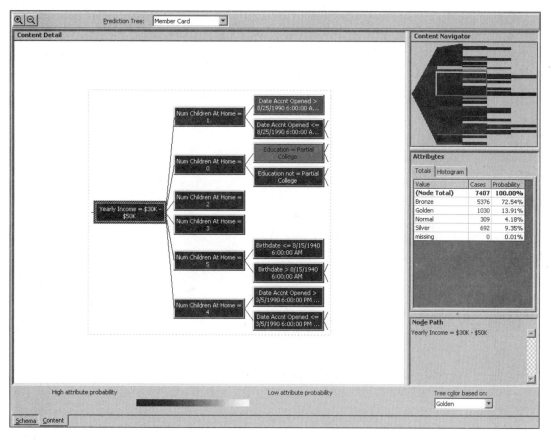

Selecting the color based on the type of card we are interested in issuing we can see that some nodes have a much higher concentration of cases than the others. Selecting one of them shows that if the person who has the card has a Partial High School education, more than 1.25 cars and more than 2.25 children, there is a 73% likelihood that they will own the Golden Card.

You can modify the attributes that are used to categorize the tree. Pruning the tree is to take attributes out of the model to clarify the results. If you make changes, the editor will prompt you to reprocess the model in order to display the changes.

When you are finished editing the model, save and close the editor to return to Analysis Manager. In order to see the weight that the various attributes play in the resulting tree, Microsoft has included a tool that will graphically display the weight of each attribute and it's strength in predicting other attributes. This is called Browsing the Dependency Network Browser.

Browse the Dependency Network

Decision trees are a predictive model we can use to determine the likelihood that similar cases will have similar behavior. Microsoft has included a tool for browsing the attributes of a tree to see which have the greatest impact on the prediction. This is called the Dependency Network Browser, and you can open it by right-clicking on a decision tree data mining model in Analysis Services explorer tree control.

Select the data mining model you just created and right-click on it to open the menu. Select **Browse Dependency Network** and the browser opens:

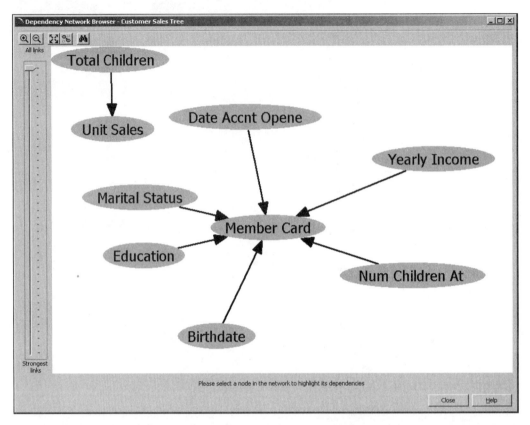

As you move down the slider on the left-handside of the screen, the weaker links are shaded gray and the stronger links remain. The node that is predicted as well as that which it predicts are shown in colors to help you understand which attribute is playing the strongest role in driving the decision tree. You can use the dependency network browser to identify which factor makes the biggest difference in predicting the outcome of new cases.

By moving the slider to the bottom of the control to show the strongest links we find that the greatest predictor of card membership is yearly income. Next is the number of children (both at home and total), and then marital status, and so on. This information can help us understand the target segment for us to focus our efforts on in developing a business strategy.

Let's now move on to take a look at some more advanced data mining techniques.

Advanced Data Mining Techniques

The Analysis Services manager snap-in provides a means for building and managing data mining models. Its interface is fairly straightforward and follows standard Windows interface guidelines that makes it easy to learn. With such a tool at your disposal, why would you want a way to incorporate data mining into your own applications?

Suppose you work for a large company that supports multiple locations. It is likely that a centrally located group of people would be tasked with analyzing information and providing reports to other departments. For example, the Marketing department might be interested to see trends of customer buying behavior. While the personnel in that department may be able to identify key questions to ask, they may not be as interested in getting down and dirty with the data to find the answers.

The Analysis Manager snap-in is defined for the Database Administrator, providing the tools and interfaces necessary to build and use an OLAP data store. This works well for the DBA, but it is probably overkill to expect it to fit all usage scenarios. For this reason, the object models that Microsoft used to create the snap-in are available to the developer to allow them to build applications that are as complex or simple as the situation requires.

These interfaces address two types of uses: administrative tasks including the definition of a data mining model, its data sources, and so on; and client applications that use the results from the data mining algorithm to make predictions. The question to ask about which technology to use when you are putting together an application is what its scope is. While DSO runs on the Analysis Server, PivotTable Service runs in the context of the client workstation.

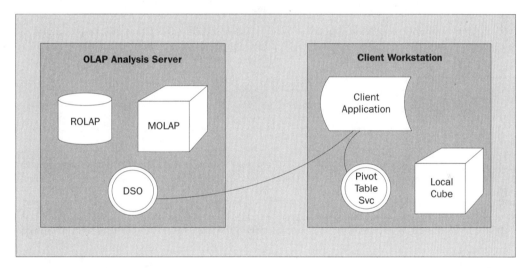

Administrative Tasks

With Analysis Manager, the database designer can create data sources, cubes, measures, dimensions, and various other objects to support an application. This may include archiving and restoring a database, managing roles, migrating the meta data repository, and so on. These administrative tasks define the structure of the analysis server. It is like designing a bucket to hold information; you don't necessarily care how the bucket gets filled or who uses it, you want to make sure that the bucket is designed correctly to hold the expected amount of information and allows the end user to access it as needed.

Although these tasks can be accomplished several ways, developing an application designed to an end user's needs can provide simplified and protected access. The process for creating a data mining model can be quite complex. While the Analysis Manager tool provides wizards to assist you, there are some tasks such as defining predictability of input and output columns that can be completed more easily and with more control if done programmatically.

Client Applications

While the structural administrative tasks of data mining define how the information is stored on the server, the predictive use of the results derived from the data mining algorithm works better from within a client-based application. For example, if you were an automobile dealer who is interested in determining the best mix of inventory to stock, you might use the data mining results against historic data to predict buying trends and patterns.

The application would probably reside on the dealership buyer's workstation. The buyer could connect to the corporate Analysis Server using PivotTable Service to retrieve the data mining model, then store it locally for their own use. Using information about their customer demographics the buyer could then run situational analysis against their local copy to determine type and color of inventory to order.

Developer Options

Two technologies used to perform these tasks are Decision Support Objects (DSO) and PivotTable Service. DSO is used to perform administrative tasks that run on the Analysis Server Engine, while PivotTable Services is the primary interface for client based applications.

Both are Component Object Model (COM)-based classes and interfaces that can be leveraged to build applications using VB, APS, C++, or C#. Both allow a great deal of flexibility for the developer in designing and using data mining models. While DSO is designed like DB-Library for use on managing the Analysis Server objects, however, PivotTable Service is accessed from ADO and treats the cube or data mining model data in a way similar to recordsets.

Decision Support Objects

Decision Support Objects (DSO) is the collection of interface classes that define and expose the objects managed by Analysis Services using COM. Using these objects, we can administer and manage the data mining models.

Analysis Manager uses Decision Support Objects (DSO) to manage the objects and collections stored on the OLAP server. DSO is also available to the application developer to interface with the functionality of the Analysis Server engine. It allows us to programmatically build applications to perform administrative tasks.

DSO Architecture

When you open the Analysis Services Manager, the tree of objects that are viewable follows closely to the class architecture exposed by DSO (see below). The root of the tree is a folder that contains registered servers. Each server contains one or more databases that in turn comprise a collection of objects. These objects include data sources, cubes, dimensions, mining models, and roles.

The classes that compose the hierarchy of DSO follow the tree control in the Analysis Manager. At the root of the tree is the collection of Servers, each of which contains one or more databases complete with a set of objects.

DSO Object Model

Access to the Analysis Server is exposed through DSO using a hierarchy of classes that define the internal structure of the objects. There are three main objects that we are concerned with from a data mining perspective: the `Server` object, which contains information about a server that is running the Analysis Services engine; the special `MDStores` collection which exposes a common interface used by both databases and cubes; and the `MiningModels` object.

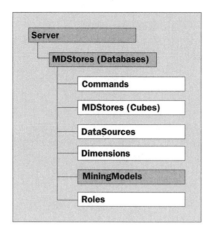

The Server Object

The object at the top of the tree, the Server, contains databases that are accessed via the MDStores collection. Each database contains collections of objects of specific types, including data sources, cubes, dimensions, roles, and mining models.

The table below lists the properties, collections, and methods of the Server object:

Properties	Collections	Methods
ClassType	CustomProperties	CloseServer
ConnectTimeout	MDStores	Connect
Description		CreateObject
Edition		LockObject
Parent		Refresh
ProcessingLogFileName		UnlockAllObjects
ServiceState		UnlockObject
State		Update
Timeout		
Version		

The Server object allows you to connect to the server and manage the Analysis Server Service. You can also create databases via the MDStores collection and lock the service to control the read/write state while you are performing updates.

The MDStores Collection

The MDStores is a special type of collection containing objects that expose what are called an MDStore interface. These include Databases, Cubes, Partitions, and Aggregations. What this means is that the objects have an interface defined by MDStore in addition to their class-specific interface. The object defined by the MDStore and clsDatabase interfaces is the primary means for working with the databases that have been registered with the server. Objects in this collection have the following properties, collections, and methods:

Properties	Collections	Methods
AggregationPrefix	Commands	BeginTrans
ClassType	CustomProperties	Clone
Description	DataSources	CommitTrans
EstimatedSize	Dimensions	LockObject
IsReadWrite	MDStores	Process
IsValid	MiningModels	Rollback
LastProcessed	Roles	UnlockObject
LastUpdated		Update
Name		
OlapMode		
Parent		
Server		
State		
SubClassType		

The MiningModel Object

A MiningModel is a specific type of object that is contained in the database collection MDStores and is of class type clsMiningModel. It defines the structure of the data mining model and contains a collection of columns that describe how the model is processed.

The most important determinant for the use of the object is setting the model's subclass type to either OLAP (sbclsOLAP) or Relational (sbclsRelational) because this drives which of the rest of the objects properties are required for processing. If the model subclass type is relational then you define columns, otherwise you need to set the case dimensions, which automatically include the corresponding column definitions from that dimension's level.

The table below shows the properties, collections, and methods that make up the clsMiningModel structure:

Properties	Collections	Methods
AreKeysUnique	Columns	Clone
CaseDimension	CustomProperties	LockObject
CaseLevel	DataSources	Process
Classtype	Parameters	UnlockObject
Description	Roles	Update
Filter		ValidateStructure
FromClause		
IsVisible		

Properties	Collections	Methods
JoinClause		
LastProcessed		
LastUpdated		
MiningAlorithm		
Name		
Parent		
SourceCube		
State		
Subclasstype		
TrainingQuery		
XML		

After setting the `MiningModel` object's properties, you add column definitions to complete the model design. The column defines the structure of the case set being analyzed. The column can either be a regular column, similar to that in a relational table, or it can be multidimensional in which case it stores information defining a nested table.

Example: Browsing Mining Model Information

For our example we will create an application build the OLAP Data Mining Model using the clustering algorithm. This model uses the HR cube defined in the FoodMart database to create clusters of their employees. Whether you are creating a relational or an OLAP model, with either the decision tree algorithm or the clustering one, the process for using DSO to build data mining models follows a basic set of steps. These steps include:

- ❑ Connect to target Analysis Server
- ❑ Create a data mining model
    - ❑ Select database from the `MDStores` collection
    - ❑ With the `MiningModels` collection of the Database object add a new model
    - ❑ Create and assign roles for the mining model
    - ❑ Set properties for the model
    - ❑ Add column definitions and set their properties
    - ❑ Save the model in the repository
- ❑ Process the model
    - ❑ Lock the mining model object
    - ❑ Process the model
    - ❑ Unlock the model

Getting Started

We will use VB 6.0 for this example. Create a new project and then add a reference to Microsoft Decision Support Objects in the Project References dialog the same way we did in Chapter 16. We will create a new form and add some controls to allow us to change the name of the server, database, and model name as we test it:

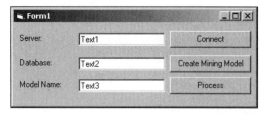

We will be writing code for the three buttons to connect to the server specified in Text1, and then create the mining model specified in Text2 and Text3. Finally, we will add code to process the model. For clarity and for brevity, I've kept the code as simple as possible.

Housekeeping Chores

Before we get too far we need to take care of some preliminary business. We will start by declaring some global variables and coding the form load and unload functions. We also add some code to the Form_Load to set up our default values, and then in the Form_Unload event we clean them up before we exit:

```
'-------------------------------------------------------------------
' Global declarations for server and mining model
'-------------------------------------------------------------------
Dim dsoSvr As DSO.Server
Dim dsoDMM As DSO.MiningModel


'-------------------------------------------------------------------
' Form_Load ()
'    Setup the defaults for our example
'    Create persistent objects for Server and Mining model
'-------------------------------------------------------------------
Private Sub Form_Load()
    Text1.Text = "localhost"       '' OLAP Server
    Text2.Text = "FoodMart 2000"   '' Database Name
    Text3.Text = "WROX Example"    '' Mining Model Name
    Set dsoSvr = CreateObject("DSO.Server")
    Set dsoDMM = CreateObject("DSO.MiningModel")
End Sub


'-------------------------------------------------------------------
' Form_UnLoad ()
'    Cleanup after ourselves
'-------------------------------------------------------------------
Private Sub Form_Unload(Cancel As Integer)
    Set dsoDMM = Nothing
    Set dsoSvr = Nothing
End Sub
```

Connect to the Server

Connection to the server is pretty straightforward. We've already created an instance of the DSO Server object in the form load function, so we don't need to worry about that in here. If an error occurs during this function it will drop processing control to the error message explaining what happened. The error collection contains enough description to give a message that explains the problem without having to write lots of code:

```
'------------------------------------------------------------------
' cmdConnect_Click ()
'    Connect to the server specified in Text1 .text box
'    If connect is successful then enable other buttons on form
'------------------------------------------------------------------
Private Sub cmdConnect_Click()
    '-- text1 contains the name of the server we are using

    On Error GoTo ErrConnect
    Me.MousePointer = vbHourglass

    dsoSvr.Connect Text1.Text

    Me.MousePointer = vbDefault
    Exit Sub

ErrConnect:
    MsgBox "Error connecting to " & Text1.Text & " - " & Err.Description
    Me.MousePointer = vbDefault
End Sub
```

Create the Mining Model

Next we will add the logic for adding a new mining model. This process can be broken into two parts, one for model-specific code, and a second that manages the columns. The code for the button calls two corresponding subroutines:

```
'------------------------------------------------------------------
' cmdCreateMiningModel_Click ()
'    Call CreateMiningModel function
'    Call AddColumns function
'------------------------------------------------------------------
Private Sub cmdCreateMiningModel_Click()

    Me.MousePointer = vbHourglass

    CreateMiningModel
    AddColumns

    Me.MousePointer = vbDefault

End Sub
```

CreateMiningModel

This subroutine handles the model-specific code including setting the type of model, the source, the training query, and the algorithm. We are creating our model from the HR cube in FoodMart 2000 and looking at the Employee dimension for our clusters:

```
'------------------------------------------------------------------
' CreateMiningModel ()
'    Connect to the server specified in Text1 text box
'    If connect is successful then enable other buttons on form
'------------------------------------------------------------------
Public Sub CreateMiningModel()

    Dim dsoRole As DSO.Role
    Dim dsoCol As DSO.Column
```

```
            ' Text2 contains database name
            Set dsoDB = dsoSvr.MDStores(Me.Text2.Text)

            ' Text3 contains model name...if it exists then delete it
            If Not dsoDB.MiningModels(Me.Text3.Text) Is Nothing Then
                dsoDB.MiningModels.Remove Me.Text3.Text
            End If

            ' Add new OLAP mining model using text3 as the name
            Set dsoDMM = dsoDB.MiningModels.AddNew(Text3.Text, sbclsOlap)

            ' Create role for mining model
            Set dsoRole = dsoDMM.Roles.AddNew("All Users")

            ' Set mining model properties...Note that DSO will define training query

            With dsoDMM
                .Description = "Example OLAP Mining Model"
                .MiningAlgorithm = "Microsoft_Clustering"
                .SourceCube = "HR"
                .CaseDimension = "Employees"
                .TrainingQuery = ""
                .Update
            End With

    End Sub
```

AddColumns

After we've created the model, we will set up the columns that define the structure of our model. The subroutine `AddColumns` adds the 6 columns that are part of the `Employees` dimension in the `FoodMart 2000` database. After we've defined the structure the last thing we do is to save the model in the repository:

```
Public Sub AddColumns()

        ' Set column properties...for the case dimension "Customers" columns are
        ' automatically added but are disabled. We need to enable them and set
        ' the case key

        Set dsoCol = dsoDMM.Columns("Marital Status")
        dsoCol.IsInput = True
        dsoCol.IsDisabled = False

        Set dsoCol = dsoDMM.Columns("Position Title")
        dsoCol.IsInput = True
        dsoCol.IsDisabled = False

        Set dsoCol = dsoDMM.Columns("Gender")
        dsoCol.IsInput = True
        dsoCol.IsDisabled = False

        Set dsoCol = dsoDMM.Columns("Salary")
        dsoCol.IsInput = True
        dsoCol.IsDisabled = False

        Set dsoCol = dsoDMM.Columns("Education Level")
        dsoCol.IsInput = True
        dsoCol.IsDisabled = False

        Set dsoCol = dsoDMM.Columns("Management Role")
        dsoCol.IsInput = True
```

```
      dsoCol.IsDisabled = False

      dsoDMM.LastUpdated = Now     '' Mark the model as updated
      dsoDMM.Update               '' Save our changes

      Exit Sub

  End Sub
```

Process the Model

Before we can process the model we first need to lock it so that no one updates it while we are in the middle of training it. There are three types of locks we can apply:

❑ **OlapLockRead**: Other processes can also issue read locks, but the data does not change until the read locks have been released.

❑ **OlapLockProcess**: Other processes can lock for reading, but only one process lock is allowed at a time. Write locks are disallowed while a process lock is in place.

❑ **OlapLockWrite**: The locking process has exclusive rights to the object and no other locks are allowed.

Once we have a lock we call the process method to run the algorithm against the source data. We have two options for processing as well, either full or refresh. A full processing gets rid of any previous information that might have come from previous processing of the model, while a refresh runs the algorithm against the new information adding the results to those that the model already processes:

```
  '-----------------------------------------------------------------
  ' cmdProcess_Click ()
  '    Lock the model
  '    Process the model
  '    Unlock the model
  '-----------------------------------------------------------------
  Private Sub cmdProcess_Click()

      Me.MousePointer = vbHourglass

      With dsoDMM
          .LockObject olapLockProcess, "Processing Mining Model"
          .Process processFull
          .UnlockObject
      End With

      Me.MousePointer = vbDefault

  End Sub
```

Local Data Mining Models

The fundamental use for Data Mining is to allow the end user to make predictions based on what has been learned from training the data mining model. For example, we could create an application for use at car dealerships to help them predict what inventory is most likely to sell during the next month. A dealership may want to create a local model based on their customers' behavior and then use dealer-specific scenarios to determine the best mix of vehicles to stock. Using a central repository that contains nationwide sales information a local data-mining model can be created based on the analysis run on the central server that contains the basic trends and patterns.

This model can then be stored locally and used to make predictions about the inventory patterns of the dealership. The client application leverages the processing power of the local machine and uses a service called PivotTable as the bridge to interface with the analysis engine on the central server. This interface provides the full functionality for analysis of multi-dimensional data (OLAP) and for predictive models.

PivotTable Service

As introduced earlier, PivotTable Service allows the developer to build client-side applications that can browse OLAP data. Microsoft has extended this service to allow the developer to interact with data mining models using a language that extends SQL to support multidimensional data. As the OLAP interface, PivotTable Service creates and maintains local data mining models, allowing the client application to provide the benefits of data mining to the end user.

The local model doesn't store the data used to train it, instead it stores the results of the algorithm for each of the different cases. The application can then query this information in much the same way as other OLEDB providers. Using a language that extends the familiar SQL statements the developer can create a mining model, train it, and then run predictions based on it. This language is called Multidimensional Expressions (MDX) and it is covered in Chapter 10 and 11.

Data Mining Structures

The information in the mining model is represented in a table-like format similar to the ADO `recordset` model. The column types that support this model include additional information to describe the normalized data in what are called nested tables. Information is stored on a case-by-case basis, where there are key columns that uniquely identify a case.

For example, consider a retail example of data mining sales transactions. Suppose we are investigating the likelihood of products being sold in common with one another. The focus of our analysis is the sales transaction, with a unique identifier being the Transaction ID. The table below defines a sales transaction, the customer, and the items sold:

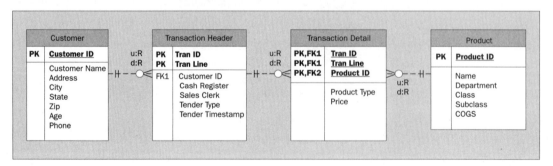

The attributes our mining model is interested in are stored the denormalized table below:

TranID	Customer Name	Cash Register	Sales Clerk	Tender Type	Work Shift	Cust Age	Product Name	Product Type	COGS
10214	Bob Doe	12	Sue	Visa	Night	27	Clock Radio	Electronics	12.72

TranID	Customer Name	Cash Register	Sales Clerk	Tender Type	Work Shift	Cust Age	Product Name	Product Type	COGS
							Music CD	Music	3.46
							Copier Paper	Home Office	1.17

A single traditional normalized table structure doesn't easily define all the various aspects of a single multidimensional case. We need to describe the additional detail information about the products sold. Using the data mining model we have available to us a column type of `nested table`, which contains a reference to the expanded structure's content.

In addition to the `nested table` column type, OLE DB for Data Mining specification includes a number of other types that define discreteness, order, relations and other key pieces of information that are used by the data mining algorithm to process the analysis. These column types include:

- ❑ **KEY**: These are the columns that uniquely identify a case for our analysis. The example above uses the transaction as the focus and as such uses the Transaction ID as the key for the case. We could have easily chosen to focus on product type instead, perhaps to predict which clerks are most productive selling particular types of products.

- ❑ **ATTRIBUTE**: Descriptors of the case, such as the cash register or sales clerk. An attribute describes additional information that may be of interest to our analysis as an input or an output of our results.

- ❑ **RELATION**: A relation is used to classify attributes, such as Tender Type or Product Type. All attributes that have the relations defined for them must be consistent in their use. For example, in all cases where a clock radio is sold, the product type is always Electronics. A column that is a relation describes the discrete types of values that the column can contain.

- ❑ **DISCRETE**: The attribute values contained in the column have distinct values that can be used for grouping like cases together. Examples of discrete attributes include gender or zip code.

- ❑ **ORDERED**: These are discrete attributes that have an implied order to values. Grade level is an example in which the case subject progresses from one grade to the next. One consideration with this type is that the magnitude of difference between values is not necessarily consistent. The belt rating system in martial arts doesn't necessarily mean that a brown belt is twice the skill level of a green belt.

- ❑ **CYCLICAL**: The values of this type are ordered discrete attributes that have a repeating pattern. An example of cyclical attributes is the shift during which the sale was made (Morning, Afternoon, or Night). Date/Time values can be cyclical in that the day or the month follows a cyclical pattern.

- ❑ **CONTINUOUS**: The values of the attributes are not discrete, but have values that follow some distribution. The cost of the goods sold (COGS) can be stored at various precisions which don't provide convenient groupings if the column is to be used as input. Another example might be customer gender or the clerk's salary or the time of sale. Sometimes we can define artificial break points for the values in order to use the attribute for analysis purposes. A continuous column will have an associated distribution that may follow some sort of a bell curve or have a more uniform tendency.

509

❑ **QUALIFIER**: A qualifier has special meaning about an attribute in that the data mining algorithm uses these predefined values in its processing. Examples of qualifiers include probability, variance, or support.

❑ **TABLE**: An instance of a column of this type contains the entire contents of a nested table, where the table is associated via a foreign key reference to the key value of the case. The transaction detail information in the example above would be stored in a nested table in a column of this type.

Using these types of columns to define the case focus, we can define the columns for our example on sales transaction information as follows:

Source Table	Column Name	Column Type	
Sales Tran	Tran ID	KEY	
Customer	Customer Name	Attribute	
Sales Tran	Cash Register	Discrete Attribute	
Sales Tran	Sales Clerk	Discrete Attribute	
Sales Tran	Tender Type	Relation of Tender	
Sales Tran	Work Shift	Cyclical Attribute	
Customer	Customer Age	Continuous Attribute	
Sales Tran Detail	Product Name	Discrete Attribute	} Product Info in a nested table
Product	Product Type	Relation of Product	
Product	COGS	Continuous Attribute	

Building And Using A Local Data Mining Model

Local data mining models can be created with PivotTable Service using a variant of the SQL standard Data Definition Language (DDL) CREATE statement. Running a Data Manipulation (DML) command like INSERT or UPDATE doesn't store the data in the model, rather it engages the data mining algorithm to perform its magic and the results from that processing are stored for future use. Finally, we can use the trained model by SELECTing based on case data using a PREDICTION JOIN clause.

Create Mining Model

The DDL for data mining provides some options on how we create our model that depend on whether we are building it from relational or an OLAP data store. We can also create a new model by copying an existing one.

If we want to store the model locally we need to set the "Mining Location" property of the connection before we open it up. For example, if you use an ADO connection to work with PivotTable Services on a workstation called MyMachine and you have a directory for your analysis called C:\MyData, you add the following code before opening the connection and executing the CREATE MINING MODEL statement. After creating the model you will find a file with the extension .dmm in the specified directory:

```
Dim cn
Dim strDDL
Set cn = CreateObject ("ADODB.Connection")
cn.ConnectionString = "provider=MSOLAP.2; Data Source=MyMachine;
Initial Catalog=FoodMart"
cn.Properties.Item("Mining Location") = "C:\MyData"
cn.Open
strDDL = "CREATE OLAP MINING MODEL..etc.." ' substitute the appropriate
                                          ' statement here
cn.Execute(strDDL)
```

Creating RELATIONAL Models

Because the mining engine doesn't know anything about the source of the data being processed, you need to specify the columns, their type, their predictability, and their relations when you create the model. The basic syntax for creating a relational model is below:

```
CREATE MINING MODEL < model name>
(
    <comma separated list of column definitions>
)
USING <algorithm name> [<optional parameter list>]
```

where the column definition follows the form below:

```
<column name> <type> [<content flags>] [<relation>] [<predictability>]
```

or if we had a nested table:

```
<column name> TABLE [<predictability>]
(
    <comma separated list of column definitions>
)
```

Our sales transaction example above would be coded as follows:

```
CREATE MINING MODEL [SalesTranAnalysis]
(
    [Tran ID]            LONG KEY,
    [Customer Name]      TEXT,
    [Cash Register]      TEXT DISCRETE,
    [Sales Clerk]        TEXT DISCRETE,
    [Tender Type]        TEXT DISCRETE,
    [Work Shift]         TEXT DISCRETE CYCLICAL,
    [Customer Age]       DOUBLE DISCRETIZED () PREDICT,
    [Products]           TABLE
    (
        [Product Name]     TEXT KEY,
        [Product Type]     TEXT DISCRETE RELATION TO [Product Name],
        [COGS]             DOUBLE NORMAL CONTINUOUS
    )
) USING Microsoft_Decision_Trees
```

Creating OLAP Models

Creating a mining model from an OLAP data store allows us to leverage the information we have about the cube. The syntax for creating the model would be as follows:

```
CREATE OLAP MINING MODEL <model name>
FROM <cube name> <olap definition>
USING <algorithm name> [<optional parameter list>]
```

When you connect to the OLAP data store to execute the model creation statement, you can specify the mining location to be a local file by setting the `Mining Location` property. For example if we have defined a cube for sales transactions, with a product dimension, we could a create decision tree data mining model by running a script similar to the one below:

```
CREATE OLAP MINING MODEL [SalesTranAnalysis] from [Sales]
(
    CASE
        DIMENSION      [PRODUCT]
        LEVEL          [Product Name]
            PROPERTY   [Net_Weight],
            PROPERTY   [COGS] PREDICT

)
USING Microsoft_Decision_Trees
```

Copy an Existing Model

Similar to the way that a new table can be created by selecting from an existing table into a new one, creating the table structure on the fly, we can do the same thing with Mining Models. This is useful if you plan to run different algorithms against the same basic structure. The resulting new model will contain the same definitions as the original except for algorithm specific parameters:

```
SELECT * FROM <new model> USING <mining algorithm> FROM <source model>
```

For example, if we wanted to create a copy of the `SalesTranAnalysis` model into a new model called `SalesTranCopy`, we would run the following command:

```
SELECT * INTO [SalesTranCopy] USING Microsoft_Decision_Trees
FROM [SalesTranAnalysis]
```

Unfortunately, there doesn't appear to be a way to alter an existing model by adding additional column specifications. If you want to use the same name you will need to drop the model and then create the new version. To drop a model use the following command:

```
DROP MINING MODEL [SalesTranCopy]
```

Create Mining Model Using PMML

Local data mining models can also be creating using a variant of XML called Predictive Model Markup Language (PMML). The syntax for creating a mining model from a PMML file is below:

```
CREATE MINING MODEL <new model> FROM PMML <XML String>
```

Training the Model

Now that we have a defined mining model structure, we can train it by issuing statements to process the data. This causes the mining algorithm to process the new case information and then stores the results of the algorithm instead of the training values. In this way, the mining model is prepared for use with situational test cases.

If our data mining model is based on an OLAP cube, it can be trained by simply running an `INSERT INTO` statement specifying the model name. Since the OLAP cube has already defined the source and structure of the case information, no additional specifications are required. The syntax of the command is:

```
INSERT INTO <model name>
```

For our example of the OLAP model `SalesTranAnalysis`, the command would read:

```
INSERT INTO [SalesTranAnalysis]
```

Relational mining models require that we specify where the source of the training data comes from, as well as the columns that we require. The source of the information can either be our `INSERT` statement, in which we specify the columns and the values to load, or we can source the information from another data store using a direct SQL select statement specifying the cases we are interested in. The basic syntax is below:

```
INSERT INTO <model name> (<column names>) <source data>
```

The options for specifying the source data are listed below:

❑ **Singleton Constant**: Constant values are included as values in the statement, following the order of the column name list. The difference between this and relational SQL is that the key word `VALUES` is omitted in this case.

```
INSERT INTO [SalesTranAnalysis]
([Tran ID], [Customer Name], [Cash Register], [Sales Clerk])
('10214', 'BOB DOE', '12', 'SUE')
```

❑ **Singleton Select**: The values used are from a SQL Statement that returns only a single row. This can be used to select constant values into named columns, as shown below:

```
INSERT INTO [SalesTranAnalysis]
    ([Tran ID], [Customer Name], [Cash Register], [Sales Clerk])
    (SELECT '10214' as [Tran ID], 'BOB DOE' as [CustomerName],
            '12' as [Cash Register], 'SUE' as [Sales Clerk])
```

❑ **OPENROWSET**: This function connects to a remote data store other than that on which the data mining model resides, queries a set of rows, and returns the values to the calling agent. It is designed to provide cross-server functionality for situations in which not all the required data resides on a single database instance. Besides supporting SQL Server, it can connect to and use data from any OLE DB-compliant provider.

To use this function, you need to specify connection information in addition to the query. After the connection is made, the query is executed and the results are returned to the calling application.

```
OPENROWSET  (<provider name>,
    { <datasource>;<user id>;<password> | <provider string> }
    { <object> | <query> }
)
```

For example, if our data was coming from the central sales server called CORPSALES, and the database was SQL Server, and we wanted to select data from the SALESTRAN table for transactions that occurred during the day shift, we would structure the OPENROWSET function as follows:

```
INSERT INTO [SalesTranAnalysis]
   ([Tran ID], [Customer Name], [Cash Register], [Sales Clerk])
OPENROWSET ('SQLOLEDB', 'CORPSALES'; 'sa'; 'isapass',
   'SELECT * from SALESDB.dbo.SALESTRAN
   WHERE work_shift = 'DAY' ')
```

Alternatively if we were interested in the entire SALESTRAN table we could omit the SQL query and substitute the table name as follows:

```
INSERT INTO [SalesTranAnalysis]
   ([Tran ID], [Customer Name], [Cash Register], [Sales Clerk])
OPENROWSET ('SQLOLEDB', 'CORPSALES'; 'sa'; 'isapass', 'SALESTRAN')
```

❑   **SHAPE**: When using nested tables in the data mining model, the SHAPE function is used to define the hierarchical relationship in the training data. The source data is stored using a snowflake schema that includes a fact table and one or more detail tables. The MDAC Data Shaping Service can be used from an OPENROWSET function call. The basic syntax is below:

```
SHAPE {<master query>}
    APPEND ({<child table query> }
    RELATE <master column> to <child column>)
    AS <column table name>
[
    APPEND ({<child table query> }
    RELATE <master column> to <child column>)
    AS <column table name>
...
]
```

If the source data for our mining model requires a query of the CORPSALES server and additional customer information on a server called CORPCUST, we could use the following statement to define the training data:

```
INSERT INTO [SalesTranAnalysis]
   ([Tran ID],[Cash Register],[Sales Clerk],[Customer Name],[Cust Age])
SHAPE
{
    OPENROWSET ('SQLOLEDB', 'CORPSALES'; 'sa'; 'isapass',
       'SELECT TranID, RegID, EmpID, CustID from SALESDB..SALESTRAN
       WHERE work_shift = 'DAY' ')
}
APPEND (
    {
        OPENROWSET ('SQLOLEDB', 'CORPCUST'; 'sa'; 'isapass',
           'SELECT CustomerID, Name, Age from CRMDB.dbo.CUSTOMER')
    } RELATE CustID to CustomerID
) AS [Customer Info]
```

❑   **SELECT**: You can also use a standard SQL select statement that queries a data store for a set of records that match the case column definitions. This is very useful when the source of the training data resides on the same server as the data mining model:

```
INSERT INTO [SalesTranAnalysis]
   ([Tran ID], [Customer Name], [Cash Register], [Sales Clerk])
   (SELECT A.[Tran ID], [Customer Name], [Cash Register], [Sales Clerk]
   FROM [Transaction Header] A, [Customer] B
   WHERE A.[CUSTOMER ID] = B.[CUSTOMER ID]
```

Browsing the Model – What Have We Learned?

At this point, we have created a data mining model and trained it with a sample of records for which we know the outcome. We can browse the resulting structure of the mining model by querying it for various characteristics. Using scalar functions in normal SELECT statements we can learn much about the nature of the model.

What are the defining characteristics of our model? What is the range of values that were found? What pieces of information were not available in our training set of data? As an analyst this is the time to confirm that what you have built looks like reality, that the distribution of values processed reflect the actual universe of the data being mined. It is better to poke holes in your model now before you make predictions based on the results of the analysis only to find that you should have broadened or narrowed your sample.

You can query the content of the model by issuing the command:

```
SELECT * FROM <mining model>.CONTENT
```

Querying the Model – Prediction Join

Making predictions on a set of cases based on the data mining model is done using the SELECT statement extended by some new qualifiers and key words. The prediction query requires that you specify how the model is related to the case data using the PREDICTION JOIN qualifier. The query takes the form below:

```
SELECT *
FROM <data mining model> as A PREDICTION JOIN <cases table> as B
ON A.KeyCol = B.KeyCol
```

DTS and Data Mining Tasks

SQL Server's DTS tool contains a task for data mining that can be used to process prediction queries and save the results in SQL Tables. This interface is straightforward, and can be used to make predictions based on what the mining model has learned.

The caveat is that DTS will only work with Relation models, and then the only algorithm that is predictive is decision trees:

Use DTS to Create Prediction Queries

Open a new DTS package from Enterprise Manager. On the toolbar is an icon that looks like a small pick. This is the data mining task. Click and drag the icon onto the DTS canvas and then open its properties window:

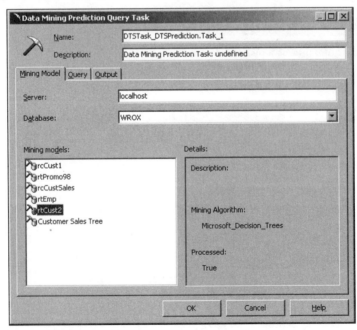

Entering your server name and selecting a database lists the relational mining models that you can use to process your query against. Models that use the mining algorithm of Microsoft's decision trees can be used to make predictions, while the clustering algorithm does not support this. Select a mining model and click on the **Query** tab.

Click on the browse button next to the select data source prompt to define where the data used for the query will come from. A window with the list of drivers defined on your machine will be listed. After selecting a driver, the click on the provider tab to get the list of data sources:

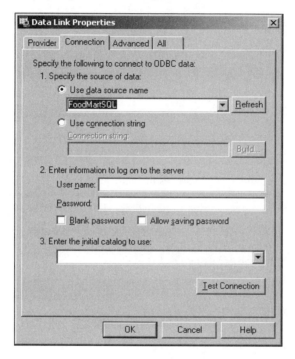

You can set the other options if you need, but when you are ready click the **OK** button to close the window. On the data mining task property sheet, click on the button to add a new query:

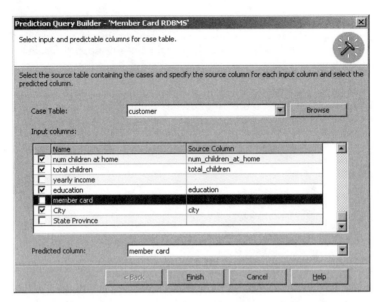

Choose the table that contains the data you are testing with, and specify the column mappings between the table and the mining model. If you don't have information on some of the columns it is OK to uncheck the box next to the column name. When you are done defining the columns click on finish to close this window.

The resulting prediction query is put into the input tab of the property sheet. Selecting the Output tab allows you to specify the destination of the results to be a table on the same or another server. When you are done close the window by clicking OK:

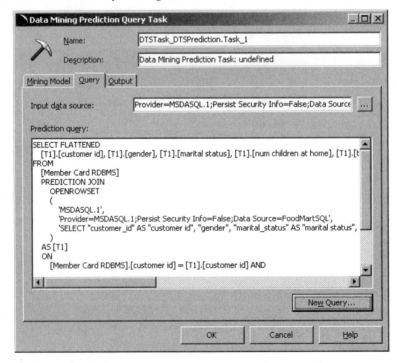

The DTS Canvas should have an icon for the data mining task. You can save the DTS package to either Microsoft's Repository, a structured file, SQL Server, or a Visual Basic file. You can run the package from the **Execute package** command on the menu or by clicking the green arrow icon on the toolbar. When the package executes, it sends the output to the location you specified:

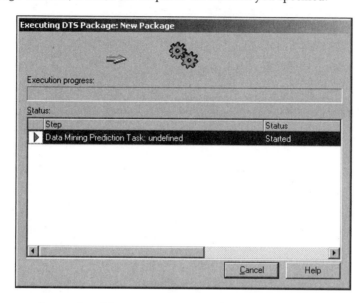

You can then browse the results of the query using your favorite data browsing tool.

Summary

The cycle of data mining involves starting with a question, then performing some analysis. At this point, the results that we have found are used to generate some ideas for addressing the original concern. Actionable items, such as sending credit applications to a target market segment is turned into a plan and acted upon. The results from this plan should be used to feed back into our cycle to help us ask smarter questions.

In this chapter we looked at approaches to data mining. We evaluated the two models included with SQL Server 2000 Analysis Services, and we have built examples of each. Specifically we reviewed what we knew about FoodMart, and asked some questions about the nature of its business. From these questions we developed inquiries that used the data mining techniques.

We covered:

- ❑ How to create Cluster Data Mining models
- ❑ How to create a Decision Tree model
- ❑ The Network Dependency Browser

Data Mining analysis is not limited to using SQL Server's Analysis Services to create, edit, and browse the objects. Microsoft has exposed the object model to the developer using COM and OLE DB. These objects run on the server and/or the client to provide a means for incorporating the benefits of Data Mining techniques in user applications.

In this chapter we have covered a lot of ground. There are starting to be more resources that can help you with specific details on using these tools, but one of the more useful ones comes with SQL Server 2000 – Books Online. This contains a very complete listing of the various functions and statements that are used to build applications.

Other useful places to find information about data mining are on the Internet. I've listed some links that have some great information and if they don't answer all your questions, they may help point you in the right direction:

- ❏ http://www.sys.uea.ac.uk/kdd – Home page for the Data Mining Research Group
- ❏ http://www.acm.org/sigkdd – ACM's Special Interest Group on Data Mining
- ❏ http://www.microsoft.com/data/oledb/dm.htm – Microsoft's intro to OLE DB for Data Mining
- ❏ http://research.microsoft.com/dmx/datamining – Information about Microsoft Research

Professional SQL Server 2000 Data WareHousing
Data Warehouse

18

Web Analytics

The goal of **Web Analytics** is to transform data from different sources in order to obtain meaningful intelligence about your web-based business. It involves the process of collecting, storing, filtering, and analyzing click-stream, commerce, and third-party data, known as **web housing**. We will take a closer look at this data and determine the type of reports and information it can provide (**business intelligence**). Note that business intelligence should not be confused with the term **Business Internet Analytics** (or **BIA**), which is specifically an offering from Microsoft and its partners in order to gain business intelligence about their e-commerce businesses. It is a set of tools, database schemas, and methodologies for the rapid deployment of highly scalable web analytics data warehouses.

The combination of web housing and business intelligence provides the basis for Web Analytics. As we go through these ideas, the reader will understand why Web Analytics has become the latest trend in data warehousing.

In this chapter we will look at:

❑ What constitutes Web Analytics, and the infrastructure it requires

❑ The business questions that can be answered by web housing

❑ How to optimize the performance of a web analytics data warehouse (or any web to OLAP data warehouse)

What is Web Analytics?

Web Analytics is the analysis of web data. More specifically, it is business intelligence that allows analysts to gain insight into their web-based businesses (such as e-commerce, customer support, and so on). Web Analytics allows you to understand customer behavior and identify common sales trends enabling you to personalize services for your customers and increase customer satisfaction. It allows you to understand how well your products, content, and online processes are working.

The difficulty of Web Analytics is that it requires you to combine different sources of data and correlate the data in order to resolve these issues. With the complexity of web sites, multiple locations, and promotions, it is difficult to answer even the most basic questions concerning these online businesses. For example, in order to answer the question "How well did our web promotion work?", you will need to:

❑ Transform web log data to determine the number of users who visited the site due to the promotion

❑ Transform commerce data to determine the number of users who made purchases due to the promotion itself

❑ Associate the commerce data with the web log data, in order to include only purchases that were made due to those promotions

❑ Transform banner ads and e-mail marketing campaign data to determine the number of users who actually received the promotion

❑ Finally, correlate this data against all of the data above

As you can see, there are a number of steps required in order to finally deliver reports that can actually answer the above mentioned question.

Web Analytics Components

As with any other business intelligence endeavor Web Analytics requires the building of a data warehouse. The process of web housing (taking web data and building a data warehouse around it) involves:

❑ **Collecting Data:** Obtaining data from web logs, commerce data, and third-party data sources

❑ **Transforming Data:** Transforming existing web log data into something meaningful and relating this data to your commerce and third-party data sources

❑ **Reporting Data:** Storing and publishing this data in a meaningful manner so that analysts, directors, and VPs can understand what they are reading

The purpose of creating a data warehouse is to store information so that it can be used to answer questions. A well designed OLAP solution or data mart depends on these questions being known and well defined. Therefore, before proceeding with the process of web housing, it is important that you know the types of question that can or cannot be answered. In the next section we will consider the different types of data sources and what questions they can answer.

Collecting Data

In most Web Analytics endeavors, there are three types of data sources:

❑ Web log data

❑ Commerce data

❑ Third-party data, such as banner ads, or customer support logs

Most of the data that you will be analyzing is actually based on the web log data, since it describes the actions and patterns of your customers. The commerce data identifies what purchases were made, but the web log data enables you to identify the actions that customers performed in making those purchases. This may well allow you to simplify the flow from viewing to buying. As an example of this, while banner ad data (an example of third-party data) allows you to know which customers visited your web site, web log data will allow you to determine how effective these banner ads were. Customers that click on banner ads and only see the first page hardly indicate a successful banner ad campaign, while customers that click on banner ads and make purchases (based on the clicked banner ads) reveal that your ads were successful.

Web Log Data

The primary source for web analytics is the web server log files. Depending on how the web server is configured, each time it has been accessed, the web server records each instance to a log file. This information is also known as **click-stream data**, since each click of the mouse produces data. These log files contain valuable information including the visiting patterns, pages viewed, browser and operating system information, and the length of time your customers spent online.

Issues with click-stream data center around the fact that web log data is asynchronous in nature. While each web click that your customers make gets recorded into these log files, the information stored in the web log is organized by date time, so it is not a simple task to monitor an individual user's clicks since users click on web pages at different times. So how do you know if the user actually stayed on this page or was redirected to another page? How do you identify which web instance or page view belongs to which customer?

To answer these questions we need to transform the web server log data, but before we do that, we need to consider what this data provides and what this data lacks. Below is a sample from a Microsoft Internet Information Services (IIS) 5.0 web server log (typically found in the %WindowsDirectory%\System32\LogFiles directory on your Windows NT server) in the World Wide Web Consortium (W3C) Extended Log File format.

The W3C is an organization which sets standards for web-based technologies – more information can be found at http://www.w3c.org/.

```
#Software: Microsoft Internet Information Services 5.0
#Version: 1.0
#Date: 2001-08-03 00:52:45
#Fields: date time c-ip cs-username s-ip s-port cs-method cs-uri-stem cs-uri-query
sc-bytes cs-bytes time-taken cs(User-Agent) cs(Cookie) cs(Referer)

2001-08-03 06:50:47 192.168.0.1 WORKGROUP\me W3SVC1 WEB01 192.168.0.2 80 GET
/shop/WebPage.asp lid=20&vID=1000&cat=books 0 4549 1141
Mozilla/4.0+(compatible;+MSIE+5.5;+Windows+NT+5.0)
58C673C195B84D249FE0FB9DCCF02E9E -

2001-08-03 06:50:47 192.168.0.1 WORKGROUP\me W3SVC1 WEB01 192.168.0.2 80 GET
/images/ico_A.gif - 0 141 641 Mozilla/4.0+(compatible;+MSIE+5.5;+Windows+NT+5.0)
58C673C195B84D249FE0FB9DCCF02E9E
http://www.wrox.com/shop/WebPage.asp?lid=20&vID=1000&cat=books

2001-08-03 06:50:47 204.148.170.161  - W3SVC1 WEB01 192.168.0.2 80 POST
/doc/OLAP.asp - 0 2345 98 Mozilla/4.0+(compatible;+MSIE+5.5;+Windows+98)
JKU198FB898D004758DE27FF9ED239C6 -
```

```
2001-08-03 06:50:47 192.168.0.1 WORKGROUP\me W3SVC1 WEB01 192.168.0.2 80 GET
/images/ico_B.gif - 0 140 640 Mozilla/4.0+(compatible;+MSIE+5.5;+Windows+NT+5.0)
58C673C195B84D249FE0FB9DCCF02E9E
http://www.wrox.com/shop/WebPage.asp?lid=20&vID=1000&cat=books

2001-08-03 06:51:25 192.168.0.1 WORKGROUP\me W3SVC1 WEB01 192.168.0.2 80 GET
/shop/WebPage2.asp lid=38&cat=books 0 4549 1141
Mozilla/4.0+(compatible;+MSIE+5.5;+Windows+NT+5.0)
58C673C195B84D249FE0FB9DCCF02E9E
http://www.wrox.com/shop/WebPage.asp?lid=20&vID=1000&cat=books
```

The following table shows that there is much information that can be extracted from your web logs. What type of analytics or business intelligence you obtain depends on how well you organize this data.

Field	Example from above web log sample	Description
date time	2001-08-03 06:50:47	The date and time the customer clicked on the web page
c-ip	192.168.0.1	The IP address of the client
cs-username	WORKGROUP\me	The username (if this information is available and is authenticated)
s-sitename	W3SVC1	The web site the customer is accessing (if there are multiple web services operational on the same server)
s-computername	WEB01	The web server the customer is accessing
s-ip	192.168.0.2	The web server IP address
s-port	80	The web server port utilized
cs-method	GET	The web page's form methods (either GET or POST)

Field	Example from above web log sample	Description
cs-uri-stem	/shop/WebPage.asp	The web page the customer is accessing
cs-uri-query	lid=20&vID=1000&cat=books	The query string information of the web page being accessed
sc-bytes	0	The number of bytes received by the server
cs-bytes	4549	The number of bytes sent by the server
time-taken	1141	Amount of time taken for the web server to process the page, in milliseconds, from request time to when results were returned to the client
cs (User-Agent)	Mozilla/4.0+(compatible;+MSIE+5.5;+Windows+NT+5.0)	The user agent information that allows you to identify browser, operating system, robot, etc. information
cs (Cookie)	58C673C195B84D249FE0FB9DCCF02E9E	The cookie that is assigned to each customer
Cs (Referer)	http://www.wrox.com/shop/WebPage.asp?lid=20&vID=1000&cat=books	The page that redirected to this page

As noted above, web log data can provide you with a vast amount of information that will allow you to identify the behavior of your customers on your web site. The trick is to be able to decipher this information. To this end, we will break down the web log data into page view, user agent, and customer information.

Page View Information

Page view information describes the page that has been viewed when a user performs the click of a mouse. The page view information that can be easily identified includes:

- ❑ Date/time information regarding when the customer accessed the web page (via the date time field).

- ❑ The web site/server the user is accessing (via the s-computername, s-sitename, s-ip, and s-port fields).

- ❑ The web page the customer is accessing (via the cs-uri-stem field).

❑   The time taken for the web page to be processed on the web server (via the `time-taken` field). This information is important to help you determine if a web page is too slow to render).

❑   The previous web page that linked to the current web page (via the `cs-referrer`, and `cs-method` fields).

❑   The bytes sent and received by the web server to the client (via the `cs-bytes`, and `sc-bytes` fields).

❑   The query string the customer is accessing via this web page (via the `cs-uri-query` field).

As an illustration of the information that can be extracted from a query string, let's consider the following sample query string in connection with an online shopping store:

```
lid=20&vID=1000&cat=books
```

The following table gives an idea of the 'meaning' such a query string can have, though clearly the meanings of such query strings are at the discretion of the web developers.

Query String Part	Example Meaning
`&cat=books`	Category Information: Query strings can contain information about what category and/or subcategories the customer is accessing, in this case the store category of books.
`&vID=1000`	Event information: Query strings can contain information about what event has recently occurred on the web site. For example, this particular identifier could indicate that the user has added an item to their shopping basket.
`lid=20`	Identification Information: Query strings can contain information about a particular subject or object that requires identification. For example, this particular local identifier could be describing a particular book (*Hiking in Western Washington*)

To summarize then, the above query string has enabled us to determine that the customer added the book *Hiking in Western Washington* to their shopping cart when looking in the category books of the store.

The above is just an example of how web data can be organized so that its web logs can provide you with information concerning your customer browsing and shopping habits.

User Agent Information

User Agent information (obtained from the `cs (UserAgent)` field) enables you to identify information such as the browser and operating system the user is using to access your particular web sites. In addition, it allows you to identify what search engines or robots (programs that automatically fetch web pages in order to index a web site, also known as spiders or crawlers) are keeping tabs on your web site.

Following the W3C Extended Format, you can take the user agent string below, and obtain interesting information about who is accessing your web site.

```
Mozilla/4.0+(compatible;+MSIE+5.5;+Windows+NT+5.0)
Googlebot/2.1 (+http://googlebot.com/bot.html)
```

The first user agent string indicates that the person accessing this site is using Microsoft Internet Explorer 5.5 on a Windows 2000 computer. The second user agent string indicates that the search engine Google has requested pages from your web site.

By knowing what browser and operating system information is accessing your web site, you will be able to design your site based for a particular browser or operating system configuration. For example, if you were to find out that many of your customers were Microsoft Internet Explorer 3.0 users, designing a web site that uses the latest IE 5 DHTML techniques could render your site difficult to use for these customers.

By knowing which search engines, robots, spiders, or crawlers are accessing your web site you can determine if your campaign to be included in the top search engines was successful.

Customer Information

Web Analytics on customer information allows you to identify and personalize information for your customer. Though many would suggest that web analytics on customer information is for the purpose of spamming, the primary purpose of web analytics of customer information is in fact **personalization**. Each customer has his or her own preferences and performing web analytics on these preferences will allow you to design a service that caters for their needs. For example, if a user is viewing football information from a sports web site, knowing this will allow you to tailor the site to the football preferences (instead of wrestling, badminton, or some other sport).

Saying this, the customer information that can be obtained directly by the web logs is not able to provide you with the whole picture. The client IP (c-ip field) can give you an approximate geographical location of where the customer is logging in but is extremely unreliable, while it is generally difficult to get username information (via the cs-username field), since most e-commerce web sites ask users to login as "anonymous" and their credentials are then validated against a database. Not only that but the utilization of cookies is limited by the type of browsers the client is using, its browser settings, and the type of web server you are using. As a result, while it is generally possible to set up a web site so that it utilizes cookies, the information you might obtain (via the cs (Cookie) field) regarding the page views a particular user has requested may be limited.

In general, web logs are not able to record accurate information about the customer that is logging into your web site. However, having a methodology of associating the cookie with the customer will greatly enhance your ability to perform web analytics on customer information. This is because you will no longer just be analyzing a customer's session but their entire history. This enhanced history will allow you to be more accurate when tailoring and catering for your customer's needs.

Commerce Data

Commerce data includes the product transactions that have occurred on an e-commerce site as well as the identification and classification of the customers. For product transactions, there are records that contain sale and return transactions, and dimensions such as date, time, and products. For customer information, there are tables containing customer information including geographic location, gender, income group, and any other customer data that the customer is willing to volunteer and the site is able to record.

By itself, this information allows you to look at sales and return transaction data by the type of customers (for example customers living in the Pacific Northwest purchase a lot of outdoor gear). This data in combination with web log data will allow you to add customer patterns and trends (for example customers living in the Pacific Northwest purchase a lot of outdoor gear by visiting the "Outdoor" section of the site instead of the "Clothing" section).

Third-Party Data

Third-party data ranges from information such as banner ads through e-mail campaigns to customer support data. Each of these types of data have their own format and storage mechanisms. Even saying this, the data is typically transactional in nature.

Banner ad data indicates when and how often a user clicks on the banner. This data typically has a transactional format and contains data about the user, the time the user clicked on the banner, and the type of banner the user clicked on. By itself, this data can only tell you when a customer has clicked on a particular type of banner ad. In combination with web log data, it can tell you whether a customer browsed a site based on the banner ad. Adding commerce data, this can now tell you the type of customer that clicked on a particular type of banner ad who made a purchase (for example, a banner ad offering 40% off of school supplies resulted in a 10% increase in school supply purchases by students).

E-mail campaign data is transactional as well; it typically contains e-mail addresses of the users, the type of e-mail campaign message sent, and the time it was sent. By itself, this information can only tell you that an e-mail campaign message of a particular type was sent to a user at some date or time, but in combination with web log and commerce data, this information can now tell you how effective a targeted e-mail campaign is on the bottom line. For example, a targeted e-mail offering free shipping to users who are frequent computer purchasers resulted in a 10% increase in computer purchases.

Customer support data allows you to know how well you are supporting your customers when they do contact you. Information such as which page the user is coming from, what method they are using (e-mail, fax, call), what type of questions they are asking, and the answers they receive is recorded. By themselves, they serve value to ensure quality customer support. By combining this data with your web logs, you may be able to gain further insight. For example, the web logs may indicate to you that customers are typically clicking on the FAQ pages, or that the online customer support documentation is rarely being used. In turn, this information will help you redesign the site so that customers can get immediate answers for their frequently asked questions right from the site.

Banner ads, e-mail campaigns, and customer support data are a small variety of the types of third-party data that can be included in e-commerce data. The general idea is that most of this data is transactional in nature and in combination with Commerce data and web logs, it can provide you with more insight regarding your customers.

Transforming Data

There are many methods to transform the collected data into your SQL and OLAP data warehouse. Common methods include utilizing DTS or developing your own parsing process to go through the data. In general, the difficulty is not in transforming your transactional data (either commerce or third-party), but in making sense of the web log data. This discussion in this section will not be so much on parsing technologies but the issues involved with transforming data.

Transforming Web Log Data

As noted in the previous section, web logs record every single request to the web page. What this implies is that there is a lot of data that needs to be filtered out, leaving the actual data that describes customer actions and patterns.

Filtering

Note, when a user has clicked on a web page, there actually is more than one hit recorded in the web log. The instances recorded include images, style sheets, JavaScript, ASP `include` files, and other files that are called upon by the web page and are integral for the web site, but not for the purposes of analysis. Referring back to the web log we looked at in previous sections, below is a table showing specifically the URI stem and referer.

URI stem	Referer
/shop/WebPage.asp	–
/images/ico_A.gif	http://www.wrox.com/shop/WebPage.asp?lid=20&vID=1000&cat=books
/doc/OLAP.asp	–
/images/ico_B.gif	http://www.wrox.com/shop/WebPage.asp?lid=20&vID=1000&cat=books
/shop/WebPage2.asp	http://www.wrox.com/shop/WebPage.asp?lid=20&vID=1000&cat=books

As you can see, the only pieces of information that really interest you are that users had clicked on the /shop/WebPage.asp, /doc/OLAP.asp pages, and /shop/WebPage2.asp.

In addition to filtering out these files, you may also want to filter out search engine or crawler, robot, or spider activity. As noted previously, these are programs that automatically fetch web pages in order to index your web site. It may be interesting to note the activities of these programs (hence recording this information), but they have nothing to do with customer activity. Determining whether to filter this information out, or how to organize it, is dependent on the questions you want to answer.

Page Views

Once your data is filtered, all that remains is the data indicating the web pages that users have hit. However, determining the number of page views is not the only interesting information that can be derived. As noted in the *Page View Information* section above, you can decipher category and/or event information by assigning values to the query string. The parser application will then perform the task of going through each page view in order to determine which page, category and/or event has occurred for that particular page view.

From this information, it is also possible to determine the number of visits and decipher from this data the distinct number of users.

Visits

There are many ways to determine what constitutes a visit within page views. The simplest definition is that one visit constitutes a set of sequential page views of a particular web site. Referring to the previous section's web log, below is a table containing the URI stem, date/time, and cookie data.

URI stem	Date/Time	Cookie
/shop/WebPage.asp	2001-08-03 06:50:47	58C673C195B84D249FE0FB9DCCF02 E9E
/doc/OLAP.asp	2001-08-03 06:50:47	JKU198FB898D004758DE27FF9ED23 9C6
/shop/WebPage2.asp	2001-08-03 06:51:25	58C673C195B84D249FE0FB9DCCF0 2E9E

As you can see, the cookie can allow you to identify a user and their sequential visits; one user has visited /shop/WebPage.asp and then visited /shop/WebPage2.asp thirty-eight (38) seconds later, while another user visited /doc/OLAP.asp at 6:50:47 in the morning.

However, as noted before, web log data is asynchronous in nature and has its own set of problems. For example, when does a visit start or end? If a user with the same cookie has hit the web site throughout the day, when does one visit end and another begin? A standard practice considers that if there is a time span of thirty minutes between user-clicks then these are taken as two different visits. However, what if this particular page has a lot of content and it took thirty minutes for the person to read it? Is this still two visits? (A standard practice is to say "no" in this situation). What if a user visits a site at 11:55pm and continues to click well until after midnight. Is this a visit for the previous day or are these two different visits on two different days? A standard practice, by the way, is to simply have visits spanning two days constitute two visits.

How about if your site does not require users to register? If users do not register, they typically do not have any cookies associated with them. Then how do you identify users without using cookies? Do you use a combination of IP address and browser? If the user happens to be using a public library computer, the IP address and browser for that public computer would be the same for a large number of visits and users. How do you separate one visit from another?

One can use other methods such as cookies, IP address/browser combinations, user IDs within a web page form, utilizing session variables, or databases to help decipher web log data to determine visits. But, how you decide what constitutes a visit and which issues you tackle, and which you abandon, is purely a business function, rather than a technological one; web logs provide only so much information. Some information, such as browser and operating system information, is only beneficial for analysis from the visit level. After all, there is no point knowing the browser for every request, but it is important to know what browser each visitor is using to view your site.

Users

As implied in the previous section, there are two types of users for your web site: identifiable (users with cookies) and unidentifiable (users without cookies). It may be tempting just to count users that have cookies. However, there are plenty of users who browse sites to read content, view products, and comparison-shop before making a purchase. If you were to force them to register before doing these simple tasks, you may risk irritating the customers you hope to attract.

Non-Identifiable Users

Although these users may not have registered, you still want to know their patterns and habits. This segment of your population makes up a large portion of your web traffic and failing to understand them will result in missed opportunities and poor customer service. After all, if the dominant browser for these non-identifiable users differs from your identifiable ones, you may want to optimize your site for the browser used by these non-identifiable users as well. The time these non-identifiable users visit the site, what categories they peruse, and what events or actions they take are still important in understanding the customer patterns and habits within your site. By understanding these non-registered users, it may be possible for you to build incentives to make them into loyal registered users.

A common technique to "identify" a non-identifiable user is to use the combination of their IP address and user agent string. Referring to the previous web log data, below is a table that contains the web page, client IP address, and user agent string data only.

Page	Client IP	User Agent string
/shop/WebPage.asp	192.168.0.1	Mozilla/4.0+(compatible;+MSIE+5.5;+Windows+NT+5.0)
/doc/OLAP.asp	204.148.170.161	Mozilla/4.0+(compatible;+MSIE+5.5;+Windows+98)
/shop/WebPage2.asp	192.168.0.1	Mozilla/4.0+(compatible;+MSIE+5.5;+Windows+NT+5.0)

As you can see, even without the cookie information, you are able to identify the fact that the same user has hit the /shop/WebPage.asp and the /shop/WebPage2.asp. This technique is not foolproof (due to issues with both how ISPs often provide client IP addresses, and User Agent strings) but it does allow you to estimate the count of non-identifiable users.

Identifiable Users

As noted in the previous section, you can identify users of the web site by utilizing the cookie, but how do you uniquely identify each user? Just because a user has a different cookie does not mean it is a different person – it simply means that there is a new visit. How do you identify who the user is? For that matter, why are you concerned about each user?

In most e-commerce environments, customers can make purchases after registering with the web site. The action of registering saves key customer properties (such as age, geography, income, and so on) and allows one to create an association between a cookie and the specific user and store this in a database. Thus, it is possible to associate the page view actions within the web log to a single user. Though we may not be interested in analyzing the habits of a single user, being able to identify which transactions belong to which user will allow us to classify this data by customer properties (such as, for example, which age group of users visited the site at 12am). Furthermore, this association allows you to associate web log data and all of its information to commerce and third-party data.

What this means is that with identifiable users, you are able to obtain business intelligence for your e-commerce site by associating web log data (browser, operating system, events, categories, and so on) to your commerce data (products, transactions, customer properties) and third-party data sources (e-mail, banner ads, customer support).

Dimensions

In the process of building and organizing your fact information (such as page views for your web log data, sales transactions for your commerce data, and click-through for your banner ad data), you will need to remember to update your dimension tables as well. Examples of dimension data from the web logs include web pages, categories, events, browser, operating system, and crawler (if so desired) information. Recall, the advantage of OLAP is that it allows end users to quickly view the fact data by dimension data (also known as slicing). For example to get a count of page views correlated against browser information over a span of time an OLAP cube would need to contain a fact table of page views and dimensions of browser and time. Neglecting to populate the dimension data may result in an important piece of information being missed (for example, Microsoft has introduced Internet Explorer 6.0, but because the dimension table holding browser information was not updated, the page view information shows only IE 5.5 hitting the site and not IE 6).

In this whole section on data transformation we have considered some standard techniques used to identify users, such as cookies for identifiable users, and user-agent and client IP for non-identifiable users. However, it should be noted that these – are not the only available techniques. How you perform this task will depend on many factors ranging from how much control you have over the web site (adding query strings, session variables, cookies, and so on) to the type of environment. The questions that were raised show how the analysis process is iterative (for example, first classify users with cookies, then user session variables to identify non-cookie users, then use client IP and user-agent strings,…). As you go through the data, you will have to re-define your identification scheme in order to classify more of the data. There may be a point when you will no longer be able to identify these users – for that matter, it may simply not be worth the effort. How much of this data you leave unidentified eventually becomes a business decision rather than a technological one.

Transforming Transactional Data

As noted in previous sections, commerce data encompasses customer property data (such as geographic location, gender, and income group) and customer purchases. Also, third-party data sources include banner ads, e-mail campaigns, and customer support data. What they all have in common is that their data is essentially transactional in nature.

What this means is that the data is typically set up with obvious facts and dimensions. For example, with customer properties, the fact is the customer, and the dimensions include geographic information, gender, and income group. Transforming this data is a relatively straightforward task and tools such as DTS or SQL scripts can often perform these tasks. For more information concerning transactional transformation, refer back to Chapters 7 and 8.

Optimizing the SQL Data Warehouse

The design of your SQL data warehouse should generally consider the convergence of the type of data that you are transforming, discussed in the previous section, and the type of data you want to report on, discussed in the next section. That is, you need to get your web log data, commerce data, and third-party data into a SQL data warehouse so that it will be possible to build your OLAP solution on top.

> Note that, while OLAP can work against many different data sources, the preferred data source is SQL Server 2000.

The planning, design, and implementation of an SQL solution is not what will be discussed in this section. Like the sections throughout this chapter, it is assumed that the reader already has knowledge of how to build these systems. Instead, we will be reviewing various optimization techniques specific to Web Analytics – our focus will be on the web log data because that is where most of the optimization will occur.

Organizing Your Data

Due to the nature of web logs, web log data has a tendency to be reprocessed, and is typically organized by day because each web server will produce a web log for each day in operation. As a result of this, it often makes sense to partition the data within the SQL Server in days as well. That is, create tables with the same schema (for example the `PageView_yyyymmdd` tables below) but with different days of data stored within different tables (for example data from 08/13/2001 goes into `PageView_20010813`, data from 08/14/2001 goes into `PageView_20010814`, and so on). This way, if you need to reprocess a particular day, it is simply a matter of adding information to that particular partition (in other words adding data to `PageView_20010814`) or deleting and recreating that daily partition (in other words dropping and recreating the `PageView_20010814` table).

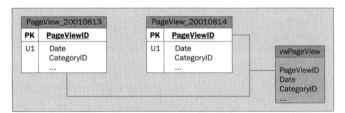

As will be noted in the *'Optimizing your OLAP Data Warehouse'* section of this chapter, cube data should be organized into daily cube partitions as well. This makes reprocessing easier for both the SQL Server and OLAP systems. When a daily cube partition is processing, it will then only access one daily SQL fact table (for example instead of getting all PageView data, it will only process data from the `PageView_20010814` partition) shortening processing time. For example, when processing an OLAP cube partition based on the `PageView` fact table for the date 08/13/2001, the SQL query submitted to the SQL Server (from Analysis Server) will specifically only query the dbo. `PageView_20010813` table.

Visits

Though it is important to know how many page views your web site has served, one of your primary interests is the number of visits that have actually occured. The point from which a person will first enter the web site to where they no longer use the web site any more is described as a visit to the web site. This information will allow you to know the number of distinct visitors (as opposed to the number of distinct users) that have visited your web site.

There is some data that should be associated to the visit, as opposed to the user or the page view. For example, the type of operating system or the browser type is something that will stay identical throughout the visit. Therefore, it may be beneficial to build these additional base aggregations so you can perform your OLAP aggregations on a smaller set of data. For example, instead of trying to aggregate page view information by browsers, you can build a Visit table (aggregate the page view data by cookie/IP address and user agent to get a table of individual visits) and aggregate visit information by browsers. Using the assumption that each visit has at least ten page views, Analysis Server will now query ten times less data from the SQL Server tables to process visit, browser, and operating system information.

Events

As mentioned earlier, it is possible to add query string information to the URL in order to ascertain if a particular event has occurred (for example "Add to Shopping Basket", or "Make a Purchase"). However, not every page view results in some event – it is highly doubtful that customers will click "Add to Shopping Basket" for every single click made within the web site.

Saying this, it may make sense to build base aggregation tables for these types of events (similar to the visits above) so that final cubes built against this fact data will be smaller and can process faster (having less data to process).

This is not to say that event information is not important within a page view context. For example, an analyst may want to know the ratio of clicks a user hits before performing the event of "Adding to Shopping Basket", or know what category the user was in before this event. Note that this data is not page-view-centric (for example, the number of page views for each category) but event-centric. Therefore, your event base aggregations can roll up the number of requests before this event has occurred and indicate the last category the user viewed for each event occurrence.

Referential Integrity

By insisting upon referential integrity between the fact tables and the dimension tables in your SQL database, you are ensuring data integrity by maintaining data in the fact tables that is pointing only to existing rows within the dimension tables. For example, if a visit is indicating that its operating system is Windows XP, if Windows XP is not within the operating system dimension table, SQL Server will raise an error and prevent the addition of this fact. In this case of using primary key/foreign key relationships, the SQL database itself performs the task of ensuring data integrity. The problem with this is that it slows down SQL Server's ability to insert data into your fact tables.

Note that SQL Server will validate any data being added, deleted, or modified within the fact table against the constraints, defaults, and keys.

If you are dealing with eighty million page views a day, conservative estimates would still result in at least ten million page views, two million visits, and two million events all going into their own respective fact tables. Even a few milliseconds for SQL Server to validate the data can add up, causing an issue of how much data you can transform and store each night. This is not to say that you should not use database referential integrity, but if your environment allows you only a short amount of time to scrub and insert data (such as if you receive your web logs at midnight and you need to ensure that your reports are ready by 8 am, giving you an 8 hour window to process the data), you may want to consider a different mechanism to ensure referential integrity.

A common technique is to have your transformation mechanism perform the task of keeping your data clean. If you have a fast parsing application, it can perform the task of both updating dimension information and adding data to the fact tables. The drawback, of course, is that now you are depending on an external system to ensure data integrity within a database. Not only that, but to build a parsing application sophisticated enough to perform these tasks without compromising data quality requires a very strong team of software developers. However, it may also make the difference that allows you to perform transformation and processing tasks within a small window of time.

Optimizing Your OLAP Data Warehouse

In the earlier chapters, you will be able to review the planning, design, and implementation of an OLAP solution. The purpose of this section is not to re-iterate what these chapters have already provided, but instead to provide you with information about the construction of an OLAP solution for Web Analytics.

The design of your OLAP objects (ranging from your cubes to your data source to your dimension) depends on the type of data that you have. Web data (the core component of Web Analytics) is asynchronous in nature and brings on a unique set of issues that will affect the design of your OLAP data warehouse. For example, in a typical Web Analytics OLAP data warehouse, you do not have to worry about write-backs (the ability to write back to your OLAP database) because the users are simply analyzing the data, rather than performing any updates to this data (such as may be required in a financial situation). In a data web house, you will need to worry about having the ability to reprocess previous days' data on a regular basis. It is common to see people forget to include different web logs, resulting in the need to reprocess the data to include the new web logs.

In the next few sections, we will go over the various design considerations and optimizations in order to implement and support an OLAP data warehouse for Web Analytics data. Please note that the recommended aggregation setting is MOLAP. In general this design was chosen in order to perform faster querying, and because the OLAP objects are no longer dependent on the SQL data source once the object has been processed.

Optimizing OLAP Dimensions

As noted in previous chapters, the three major types of dimensions are regular, virtual, and parent-child dimensions. There is also the data mining dimension, but please refer to Chapters 16 and 17 for more information on data mining. Each of these dimensions has its own set of issues and properties, such as hierarchies. In the next few sections, we will consider each of these dimension types and review how to optimize their design in relation to Web Analytics.

Regular Dimensions

In most cases with Web Analytics, the best practice with regular dimensions is to have them shared, balanced hierarchy, and non-changing. Examples of regular dimensions include the date, time, and browser information for your web data logs; gender, education, geographical information from your customer properties; and product, warehouse, and promotion data from your transaction data.

Shared Dimensions

It is best practice to utilize shared dimensions to allow us to relate different data. This is not to say that a private dimension cannot be used. For example, when looking at your page view data (all the web pages that were clicked on by users), you may want to determine whether a GET or POST method was used. This information is not necessary for business analysts per se, but it may be useful to an IT manager, in order to determine which set of pages can be bookmarked (web pages using GET) and which cannot. Since this information is only applicable to page views (as opposed to categories, and events) then a private regular dimension (a dimension that is created for an individual cube as opposed to be shared with other cubes) is all that is necessary to decipher this data. Shared dimensions are the most useful in that this data can be shared across multiple cubes and it allows you to bind multiple cubes together to create your virtual cubes. This latter step is important in allowing you to relate supposedly different sets of data together.

Balanced Hierarchy

A dimension with a **balanced hierarchy** is one where all of the branches of the hierarchy descend to the same level and each child node within the hierarchy is connected to only one parent node above it. A major reason why most regular dimensions are balanced hierarchies is because a parent-child dimension can better handle the idea of a ragged or unbalanced hierarchy. Again, this is not to say that regular dimensions cannot handle ragged or unbalanced hierarchies well. It is just that web log, customer, and transaction data do not have many organizational hierarchies (where ragged or unbalanced hierarchies are more prevalent). For example, let's consider the following browser information:

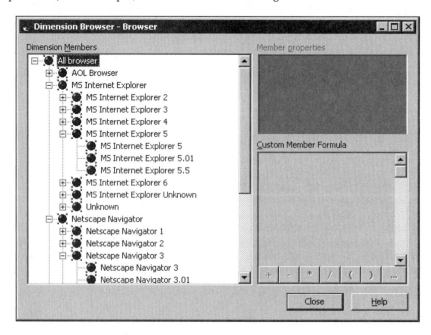

As you can see, this dimension contain three levels and each branch of this dimension goes down three levels deep:

> MS Internet Explorer | MS Internet Explorer 5 | MS Internet Explorer 5.5
> Netscape Navigator | Netscape Navigator 3 | Netscape Navigator 3.01

In addition, each child node (such as MS Internet Explorer 5.5) is associated with only one parent node (MS Internet Explorer 5) above it.

Non-Changing Dimension

A **non-changing dimension** within the Analysis Services context is a dimension that is designed for few changes of its data. The primary reason for this is because virtual and parent-child dimensions are better designed for data that is frequently changed and does not require historical context. In the case where data changes often and you need to keep track of history, this is not a changing dimension per se, because you will use an additional field such as a date time or a version number thus only adding rows of data instead of actually modifying existing data.

An example of this is geographical information from customer property data. Occasionally your customers move, so you will need to record the change in geographic locations for these customers. This way all old commerce transactions for these customers remain associated with their previous geographic location, while new commerce transactions become associated with the new geographic location. Though the customer geographic dimension is "changing", because you are recording all of this information this is actually a non-changing dimension as well. Note, a regular changing dimension requires that the dimension makes use of ROLAP storage mode (this is a requirement by Analysis Services). Although this allows changes to be immediately seen by end users of this data, the resultant queries are much slower.

Not all regular dimensions you will be building for a Web Analytics OLAP data warehouse will necessarily be shared, balanced or non-changing. In general, these are the standard practices because there are other methods or tools that will allow you to handle further types of data and this is the optimal design for your regular dimensions.

Virtual Dimensions

Virtual dimensions come in handy when you are dealing with member properties that change all the time and do not require any historical context. More specifically, virtual dimensions are changing dimensions within an OLAP context, in other words, dimensions that contain members that can be frequently updated and rewrite history in the process.

Examples of virtual dimensions in a Web Analytics environment include events from web logs. Using the earlier example of "Adding an item to your Shopping Basket", if you wanted to alter the event to "Add to your Shopping Basket", you would need to alter the UI output in the web page (a simple VBScript replace statement will do) or you would need to reprocess the dimension and the entire cube. If this type of alteration occurs a lot, you may want to consider setting this dimension as a virtual dimension instead. This way, you can alter the names without worrying about reprocessing the dimension and affected cubes, or making constant UI alterations.

Parent-Child Dimensions

Parent-child dimensions come in handy when you are dealing with ragged or unbalanced hierarchy situations. An **unbalanced hierarchy** is a hierarchy where the branches of different hierarchies descend to different levels. A **ragged hierarchy** is one where a child node has a parent node that is not immediately above it. Either way, the hierarchy is not uniform and parent-child dimensions deal with these concepts rather easily.

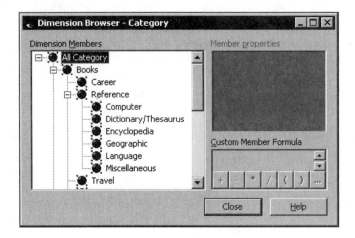

A common Web Analytics problem where parent-child dimensions are useful is for categories. Using the book category example from earlier this chapter, you can see from the above Category Dimension Browser that the dimensions are unbalanced.

```
Books -> Career
Books -> Reference -> Computer
Books -> Reference -> Dictionary/Thesaurus
Books -> Reference -> ...
Books -> Travel
```

Designing a dimension that is parent-child will allow you to keep track of the hierarchy of categories you are dealing with, while avoiding the constraints of a balanced hierarchy.

Optimizing OLAP Cubes

The meaning, design, and implementation of regular, linked, or virtual cubes can be found in Chapters 5 and 6 of this book. As noted in those chapters, the design of OLAP cubes depends on the type of analytics that you are trying to perform. There are some general guidelines on how to design these cubes in relation to Web Analytics. Here we will concentrate mostly on web log data as opposed to transactional or customer data. This is because the biggest complications, complexity and size, come from the web logs.

MOLAP vs. HOLAP vs. ROLAP

OLAP data can be stored in three modes: ROLAP, HOLAP, and MOLAP. As noted previously, MOLAP is the chosen design storage mode due to its faster querying performance and the fact that users can query OLAP data without the underlying data source being resident.

The two main disadvantages of using MOLAP are that it takes a longer time to process the cubes and that you cannot perform real-time updates to the data. However, Web Analytics does not have either requirement. Web logs can only be processed once the data has been collected, and business analysts typically only perform analysis once the data has been transformed and processed. It is for these reasons that it is optimal, in Web Analytics, to design your cubes using MOLAP.

Usage-Based Optimization

When designing the storage for your cubes, it is tempting to set the aggregation percentage to a very high value (such as 90%). The problem with doing this is that a high valued aggregation percentage will result in a very large OLAP database and, in some cases, slower performance. When setting aggregations to a high value, you are asking Analysis Services to calculate almost every possible aggregation that can be calculated with the data that exists.

In Web Analytics, and in most other business intelligence solutions, you are not trying to find out every possible answer – you just want specific answers to some specific questions. In an OLAP context, you are trying to build aggregations for the few queries that the business analysts are performing. By setting the initial aggregations to a small value (such as 5-10%), you can allow the analysts to query the OLAP cube, and then use the Usage-Based Optimization tool in order to optimize the performance of the cube for the user queries.

Organizing Your Data

It may be tempting to simply put all of your Page View or Visit data directly into an OLAP cube and start processing. However, it is possible to carry out similar optimization techniques to those we used for the data source (such as creating tables to hold only one day of data) within Analysis Services. Below, we discuss partitioning, distinct count measures, and the problem of too much data in general.

Partitioning

Web log data has a tendency not to come in regular time intervals, and when it does come, sometimes the data is incomplete. This lack of regularity often forces the OLAP systems reporting on this data to be reprocessed for those days. For example, if your IT department forgot to send you some of the web logs from last Saturday, you will need to process the day again once you receive and transform the missing web logs. Since this has a tendency to occur frequently, the easiest way to organize your data is to partition your web log data by days. That is, build your OLAP cubes using daily cube partitions. This way, when a set of days requireds to be processed, you need to reprocess only the days affected. For more information about cube partitions, please refer to Chapter 9.

The two disadvantages of partitioning by day though, are that it degrades query performance (as opposed to processing performance) and that it becomes a bit of an administrative nightmare.

> *Note that, if you are running SQL Server 2000 Analysis Services pre-SP1, OLAP cubes become corrupt once there are too many partitions and merging those partitions fails for cubes that contain distinct count measures. With the release of SP1, both bugs have been resolved.*

If you have a year's worth of data, this means that now you have 365 partitions in each cube – just think how this looks through the Analysis Manager. However, after a particular time frame, such as a few months, you know that you are no longer receiving any new or replacement web log data. For those daily partitions, the data can be merged up to a week, month, quarter, half, or year.

Since business users are usually viewing data per month, over a range of months, weekly, or daily – the optimal design appears to be that of merging these daily partitions into months. So instead of OLAP querying across 365 partitions it now only needs to query across 12 monthly partitions. For both query performance and administration, merging partitions is necessary when using daily partition cube data.

Distinct Count Measures

Web log data is organized so that every single click by a user is recorded into the web log. Saying this, if you are concerned about the number of visits within page views, or the distinct number of users within your visit data, you will need to perform distinct count measurements against this data.

To ensure optimal performance for your distinct count measures and the cube in general, distinct count measures should be placed into their own cubes. You can only place one distinct count measure per cube because all OLAP cube data is organized by that one distinct count measure. If you have a lot of measures, what this means is that your sum, count, max, and min aggregations are now organized in lieu of the distinct count measure that you have created. This slows down the processing of the cube and slows query performance. Separating distinct count measures from non-distinct count measures, will allow for the cube schemas to be optimized for their measures accordingly. A virtual cube can bind together the different set of cubes so users can still query just one cube.

Too Much Data in a Cube

A temptation to many in Web Analytics is to cross correlate every single dimension with every other one. For example, one might be tempted to be able to look at browser data sliced against operating systems, geography, gender, income level, promotion, product, and transactions. On top of the fact that it would take quite a while to process this data, you can only place so many dimensions in a cube before it becomes too big, and there are limits to the number of measures, members, and other objects that you can have within a cube.

For example, it may make sense to understand browser information, sliced by operating system information, so it is possible for you to optimize your web site for a particular environment. Then again, what does gender have to do with browser information? Does one's gender affect what browser the person uses? Does one's income level affect what operating system one uses? Even if they do, does this really matter? After all, one cares about income level or gender in order to know what they are wanting to and willing to purchase, but this has very little to do with browser information. However, it does have everything to do with promotion, product, and transaction information. Hence, it may make sense to combine gender, income level, product, promotion, and transaction information into one cube making it possible to easily slice and dice the data to analyze customer-purchasing habits.

One must remember that the whole purpose of OLAP solutions is to help provide answers to questions using summary statistics. In Web Analytics, there are sets of questions that can be asked and the purpose of the cubes is to provide suitable answers. Your data should be organized so it can do exactly that.

Processing

Web log data, like any other large data source, places unique challenges on OLAP solutions. A heavily visited web site has tens to hundreds of millions of page views per day per server. This translates to hundreds of gigabytes of data per year. This affects your ability to process data in an efficient manner. How processing Web Analytics based OLAP data differs from any other data source is that web log data has a tendency to be quite large.

Cube Partitions and Updating Dimensions

As noted above, with a large amount of web log data, you may want to design your cube so that it utilizes daily partitions. This not only aids cube reprocessing but in general, means that you are dealing with smaller sets of data (by processing daily partitions) making it a lot easier for the OLAP and SQL Server to resolve.

However, you will still want to merge these daily partitions after the usefulness of processing daily partitions has past. This is because when you perform the task of incrementally updating dimensions (in SQL Server 2000 Analysis Services), its completion will immediately trigger automatic cube refreshes for all cubes connected to these dimensions. Merging daily partitions will help improve the efficiency of the cube refreshes (as well as the query performance and the processing performance).

But why incrementally update dimensions? This is because if you choose to reprocess a dimension using the 'rebuild the dimension structure' option, you will be forced to process any cube utilizing these dimensions. How long would it take for you to reprocess a year's worth of data where you are performing Web Analytics on a web site that has hundreds of millions of page views per day per server? A pretty daunting task to say the least, hence why you would normally incrementally update your dimensions.

One thing to note is that you should design your warehouse so that it will only perform the incremental update (IU) of dimensions as necessary. As stated before, each IU causes an automatic refresh of affiliated cubes. If you have a lot of dimensions and a lot of data in your cubes, this automatic refresh may take a lot longer than you like.

Issues

One key issue is that it is easier to process each dimension or cube separately, since attempting to process all dimensions or cubes in one transaction has a tendency to fail. Related to this is the fact that DSO has a tendency to lose focus when performing a processing function under heavy loads. For example, the code below at times will only process the first few dimensions, instead of all of the dimensions of that particular database.

```
' Initialize variables
Dim objDSODim, objDSOdB

' Loop through each dimension and process it
For Each objDSODim In objDSOdB.Dimensions
    ' Lock object
    objDSODim.LockObject OLAPLockProcess, "Locked for dimension processing"

    ' Process dimension incrementally
    objDSODim.Process processRefreshData

    ' Unlock object
    objDSODim.UnlockObject

Next

' Set the object to Nothing
Set objDSODim = Nothing
```

Instead, if you can dump this information to an array first and then perform your processing, you will be able to avoid this particular issue.

```
' Initialize the variables
Dim objDSODim, objDSOdB, dimArr(), i, dimCount
dimCount = objDSOdB.Dimensions.Count - 1
```

```
    ReDim dimArr(dimCount)

    ' Loop through the dimensions and dump into dimArr()
    i = 0
    For Each objDSODim In objDSOdB.Dimensions
        dimArr(i) = objDSODim.Name
    Next

    ' Loop through dimArr() and process each dimension
    i = 0
    do
        ' Set dimension object
        Set objDSODim = objDSOdB.Dimensions.Item(i)

        ' Lock object
        objDSODim.LockObject OLAPLockProcess, "Locked for dimension processing"

        ' Process dimension incrementally
        objDSODim.Process processRefreshData

        ' Unlock object
        objDSODim.UnlockObject
    Loop Until i = dimCount

    ' Set the object to Nothing
    Set objDSODim = Nothing
```

Reporting Data

Once you have your OLTP and OLAP data warehouse designed and implemented, you need to provide your users with the ability to access this information. For developers who specialize in web analytics, the natural delivery mechanism would be that of the web. Rather than review the security mechanisms or web-specific issues this entails, we will instead consider web-to-OLAP infrastructure, and how to optimize the delivery of OLAP-based reports to the web. Finally, we will review the business Internet analytics or business intelligence component. The key to reporting any Web Analytics data (for that matter, any business intelligence data) is to know what questions the users are asking; these reports will provide the answers.

It is presumed that the reader has familiarized themselves with the topics presented below:

❏   Chapter 10: *Introduction to MDX* and Chapter 11: *Advanced MDX Topics*

❏   Chapter 12: *Using PivotTable Service*

❏   Chapter 14: *Programming Analysis Services*

Web-to-OLAP Infrastructure

The chosen method of presenting the data, in terms of delivering Web Analytics to the users, is through the web. Any IT group or company that is interested in obtaining business intelligence from its web infrastructure will also have web-centric developers. There are many third-party vendors and client application solutions that will allow users to traverse through this information. But, in addition, the Web allows users to traverse through the data using a familiar tool (the browser) that is easy to implement quickly.

There are three methods by which you can have your web page interact with Analysis Server 2000. Two are related and utilize the OLE DB for OLAP Provider, and the third is built utilizing SOAP.

ADO MD Model

The standard methodology, within a Microsoft framework, to have your web server connect to an Analysis Server is through ADO MD. Described in detail in Chapter 14, ADO MD is the multidimensional version of Microsoft's ActiveX Data Objects, which allows you to connect to multidimensional data (OLAP data). This is the preferred method for most situations because it is faster; more information concerning performance optimization for web-to-OLAP transactions can be found later in this chapter.

Connecting Using HTTP

Connecting via HTTP utilizes the above ADO MD model except that instead of specifying a data source as a particular server you can now specify it as an URL. To use this feature:

❑ Copy the `msolap.asp` file from the `\Program Files\Microsoft Analysis Services\bin` folder to the `\Inetpub\wwwroot` folder (or its subfolders)

❑ Alter your web page that connects to the OLAP Server so it now utilizes a connection string in the format below

```
Provider=msolap;data source=http://AnalysisServerName;Initial Catalog=Foodmart
2000
```

With an IIS Server installed on your Analysis server box, your client application (another web server or any client that has PivotTable Service installed) can communicate with the Analysis server using HTTP instead. In cases where you have external users or partners (who build within a Microsoft framework) who need access to your OLAP data, you can provide them with access to your data through this mechanism.

XML for Analysis

Briefly, XML for Analysis standardizes how a client application interacts with a multidimensional data source. As you will note in the *'Reporting the Data* with *ADO MD'* section below, your client application (web server) interacts with the Analysis server database through the OLE DB for OLAP provider, which must exist on the client application. It is a SOAP (Simple Object Access Protocol)-based XML API that allows you to call methods and transfer data using XML HTTP messages. This has the benefit that it decouples the requirement that your client applications must have dependent components in order to interact with the Analysis server. It is extremely beneficial when you are dealing with multi-platform, multi-language environments.

Discussion

Remember, Web Analytics is about the reporting of business intelligence to your users. It serves a small group of users (marketing, directors, business analysts) where it is usually possible to control the platform and environments. This is not to say that XML for Analysis is not beneficial in the field of Web Analytics. If you are sharing data between different groups or different companies, XML for Analysis allows you to share this information without having all the groups involved tied to one type of environment. In addition to the fact that ADO MD is an extension of ADO thereby allowing current web and database resources to ramp up to ADO MD relatively quickly, ADO MD offers better performance than XML for Analysis. Based on this latter reason, the recommended design of Web Analytics systems within a Microsoft framework utilizes ADO MD.

Reporting the Data with ADO MD

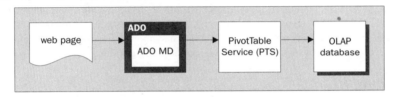

The diagram above shows the basic flow of how a web page interacts with an OLAP database through the OLE DB for OLAP Provider. The web page will perform its interactions with an OLAP database via ADO MD. Before ADO MD communicates with the OLAP database, it will connect through PivotTable Service (PTS).

Expanded on in Chapter 12, PTS is the negotiator between ADO MD and Analysis Services and is a requirement for any client application (for example, a web server) to communicate with the Analysis server (the notable exception is XML for Analysis via SOAP). A benefit of this service is that it caches the MDX queries (from ADO MD) and the multidimensional results (from the Analysis server). Stored in memory, any duplicate queries or similar subsequent queries will utilize the data stored in memory instead of accessing the Analysis server. Improving performance and scalability, it allows the frequently viewed data to be rendered at a client application (like the web server) and infrequent queries to be rendered at the Analysis server.

Listed below are various optimizations you perform in order to improve web-to-OLAP performance.

Connection Object

An example of the ADO connection object connection to an OLAP server is listed below.

```
Dim cnn
Set cnn = Server.CreateObject("ADODB.Connection")
cnn.Open "provider=msolap;Data Source=server;Initial Catalog=OLAPDB;"
```

As noted, the ADO MD connection object connects to an Analysis Services server through PTS. By modifying various PTS properties, you will be able to improve performance between the web services to the Analysis server (and back). We will be discussing the following properties: auto synch period, client cache size, execution location, and large level threshold. Following is an example of rewriting the above connection using these properties.

```
cnn.Open "provider=msolap;Data Source=server;Initial Catalog=OLAPDB;" & _
         "Auto Synch Period=8000;Client Cache Size=50;" & _
         "Execution Location=2;Large Level Threshold=500;"
```

Auto Synch Period

With every query to the Analysis Server, this property controls the frequency of synchronization of meta data between the web server (client) and the Analysis Server. With frequent duplicate or similar queries, these queries often depend only on the client cache, and increasing this property ensures synchronization occurs less often. By the same token, keeping the value too high may result in data consistency issues if the data source is updated often. That is, if a query is commonly resolved through the client cache, such as if the web server resolves the MDX query instead of Analysis Services, then if the OLAP cube is updated with new data, a high auto synch period will prevent the client cache from integrating this new data.

The default value is 10000 (10000ms or 10s), while setting the property to NULL or 0 will shut off automatic synchronization. The lowest non-zero value is 250.

Client Cache Size

This property controls the amount of memory used by the PivotTable Service located on the client (in other words the client cache). By default, 25% of physical and virtual memory (therefore altering the paging file will alter the amount PTS can hold) is utilized, and altering this value will result in an increase (or decrease) in the amount of data that can be cached by PivotTable service. Too small a cache will result in less data cached thus slower performance, while too large a cache will result in poorer performance for the web server. How you choose the amount depends on your environment – that is, empirical testing will need to be done in order to determine what size will benefit your situation.

The default value is 25 (25% of total virtual memory), while setting the property to 0 tells PTS to allow the client cache to use unlimited memory (with the risk of PTS pegging out the server). A value greater than 100 indicates the set amount of memory in kilobytes the client cache can utilize.

Execution Location

This property determines the location of the query resolution, which can either be the web server (client), Analysis server, or both. By default, PTS determines which server will provide optimal performance.

The default value is 1, where PTS determines the query execution location based on the best performance. A value of 2 will force it to the client (for example, in situations where you have a thick-layered client such as Excel or many web servers this will reduce the load against the OLAP server), while a value of 3 will force it to the server (for example in situations where you want the OLAP server to resolve it at all times because you do not want to hang the web servers or cause harm to other clients).

Large Level Threshold

This property sets the number of members that can be sent to the web server (client) in one piece. This particular setting helps with the web server application memory usage. Increasing this value forces the web server to use more of its memory to store members before sending this information to the web page, possibly slowing down web page performance. By the same token, having a smaller value will result in more round trips between the web page and the web service itself.

The default value is 1000, and this default is set by right-clicking on the Analysis Server instance and selecting the Properties | Environment menu. The value can be changed by entering a number in the Large Level defined as textbox.

Altering these PivotTable Service properties will help optimize the performance between the web server (client) and the Analysis Server. Keep in mind though that the settings of your connection are dependent on the type of reporting system you are building, as outlined below:

- **Static Report (similar data):** These reports are consistently providing you with less than 30 rows of the same data. Increasing the client cache size will ensure that the data stays in cache and increasing the auto synch period will ensure that synchronization occurs between the web server's PivotTable Service and the Analysis server.

- **Static Reports (complex data):** These reports are providing you with similar data with many rows of data. You may want to perform similar connection string alterations to those above. In addition, you may want to increase the Large Level Threshold in order to have your data incrementally sent from the server to the client.

- **Ad hoc/dynamic reports:** These reports are dynamic in nature and the majority of the queries differ in complexity and size; often these are one-time queries. Set the auto synch period to a low value since synchronization is not as necessary. Setting the Large Level Threshold to a higher value will allow you to have a larger number of members updated between the Analysis server and the web server. You may want to decrease the client cache size (one-time queries do not need to be cached). If you have a scenario where you have many web servers that are not being fully utilized and queries that take a long time to resolve, then you may want to set the execution location to the client.

Connection Pooling

Connection pooling allows you to develop a client that does not need to re-establish connection to the Analysis server for every query. Instead, the client can utilize an already existing resource from a pool of connections. Users with the same credentials can utilize the same set of connections instead of creating new ones just because they are different users. For the purposes of scalability, this will allow you to have more control over the resources connecting to your Analysis servers.

> Note, connection pooling does have its own caveats – for example, if the number of users exceeds the number of connections you support, it is possible to "starve" a user request. More information concerning this latter issue can be found in *'Professional ASP Data Access'* (Wrox Press, ISBN 1-861003-92-7).

Connection pooling with Analysis server 2000 is a component of XML for Analysis and requires the Microsoft OLE DB Provider for OLAP Services 8.0 (MSOLAP.2) OLE DB provider included within Analysis server 2000 Service Pack 1

For your web applications, you need to be careful about utilizing this within ASP pages due to the way in which IIS works. By default IIS 5.0 or later will interact with connection pooling so that the pool object uses the default IIS user instead of the rights of the currently connected user. You will need to alter the `ASPTrackThreadingModel` property to `True` to rectify this situation, though this will result in a slight performance degradation, so you will need to make this change to the IIS Metabase specific to the web directory, or to the virtual directory that contains the web pages you want to use connection pooling.

> Note, the IIS metabase is a repository similar to that of the Windows NT registry that
> contains the IIS configuration settings. Many of these properties and methods are
> accessible through the Internet Information Service Manager – but this specific
> property (ASPTrackThreadingModel) is not.

Altering the ASPTrackThreadingModel Property

The code below describes how to alter the ASPTrackThreadingModel property using VBScript:

```
'   Initialize variable
Dim ServiceObj

'   This will allow you to connect to the IIS metabase for your
'   specific web directory. Localhost represents the web server;
'   W3SVC is the World Wide Web Publishing Service; 1 is the primary
'   web service. If you have a virtual directory or multiple web services
'   on the box, then this number will change. Typically you will not want
'   to alter the root because this will affect every web page, hence
'   you will want to only alter the directory with web-to-OLAP files
Set ServiceObj = GetObject("IIS://Localhost/W3SVC/1/Root/WebDirectory")

' Set ASPTrackThreadingModel property to True
ServiceObj.Put "ASPTrackThreadingModel", True

' Update the IIS metabase with your changes
ServiceObj.SetInfo

' Close the object created
Set ServiceObj = Nothing
```

Getting your Connection Pooling Object

Once the IIS metabase is altered, so that the authentication mechanism will work with the connection
pooling object, you will need to establish your connection pooling object. Again the code shown below
is written as VBScript:

```
' Initialize variables
Dim cnnPool, strCnn, cnn, cat

' Set the connection pooling object
Set cnnPool = Server.CreateObject("MSXMLAnalysisSC.ADOConPool")

' cnnPool Properties
' Used to set the number of free and used ADO connection objects
cnnPool.MaxSessions = 32

' Used to set the timeout of each ADO connection object
cnnPool.Timeout = 300

' Establishing the connection
```

```
strCnn = "provider=msolap.2;data source=OLAPServer;initial catalog=OLAPDB;"

' Getting the connection string into the cnn object
'   which will be utilized by your OLAP queries.
Set cnn = cnnPool.GetConnection(strCnn)

' Establish your web page to OLAP connections
'   Declare your catalog object
Set cat = Server.CreateObject("ADOMD.Catalog")

'   Set your catalog active connection
Set cat.ActiveConnection = cnn

' Continue with your ADOMD ASP code
...
```

Returning and Maintaining your Connection Pooling Object

Once you have your connection object, before IIS finishes processing the web page, you will need to return the connection back to the pool so it can be utilized again.

```
' Returning your connection back to the pool
cnnPool.ReturnConnection cnn

' Maintain the connections
'   cnnPool.Sessions provides you with the number of active ADO connections
If cnnPool.Sessions > 30 Then
      ' Below will expire and remove free ADO connection objects
      ' from the connection pool
      cnnPool.Shrink

End If
```

You will need to be careful about the settings for the connection pooling properties – each of them can affect the scalability of both your web and OLAP servers. For example, if you set too many MaxSessions then your web and OLAP server may be inundated with too many users. By utilizing this feature, you will be able to maintain the number of resources that are connecting to your Analysis servers, which will increase web-to-OLAP performance (our overall goal).

Middle-Tier Optimizations

There are a couple of other optimizations that will allow you to improve the performance of web-to-OLAP interactions.

Response.Write Instead of String Concatenation

In many web architectures, the Recordset object streams data obtained from a SQL database. Since this data is flat (as opposed to multi-dimensional), a relatively fast way to obtain this data is to concatenate the data into one string variable and then performing a Response.Write of that one variable. Of course, as the number of rows increase, so this string concatenation method may lead to performance degradation.

This performance degradation is a lot more obvious when working with OLAP data. As OLAP data is multidimensional in nature, there is more effort required on the part of the web server itself to perform the task of storing OLAP data in the PivotTable Service client cache and the string variable. For example, when reporting 365 rows of data (representing 365 days), the string concatenation method resulted in the HTML rendering in 8 seconds. Instead, by using the `Response.Write` method, the HTML was rendered in 1 second.

PreQuerying the Data for your Static Reports

As discussed earlier, the initial query to the Analysis Server is where most of the work is done. Once this OLAP data is presented to the web server (client), this information and its query are stored in the PivotTable Service client cache. Therefore, any duplicate or subsequent similar query can utilize the data stored within the client cache instead.

If you have static reports (where there is a limited number of alterations to those queries), you can perform the task of pre-querying these reports so that when your users are viewing these reports the web server is delivering data already stored in its client cache (instead of accessing the Analysis server). A simple way to do this is to have a web server monitoring program that will hit the web pages that access OLAP data every morning. Just as long as the end users logging on to your web site have the same credentials as the web server monitoring program, this process will preload the OLAP data for your reports and store it in its own cache.

The issue with this method is that you become dependent on the web server to "hold" data, and any bouncing of the web server would result in the cache being cleared out. Not only that but if you have too many users performing too many different queries, then the client cache would lose earlier queries and the benefits of pre-querying will be lost.

Saying this, the important thing to note is that since ADO MD goes through PTS in order to get to the OLAP data, and PTS performs client caching, you may want to set up an infrastructure that can make use of these facts. Options range from adding more memory to your web server and increasing the page file on your web server, through controlling the client cache size, to increasing the number of web servers. There are many options that will allow you to utilize the client cache efficiently or inefficiently, but since you have it, you might as well utilize it to improve the performance of user queries.

Mini Case Study

In conclusion, we will now look at a high-level overview of what Web Analytics provides in the case of a fictional online store.

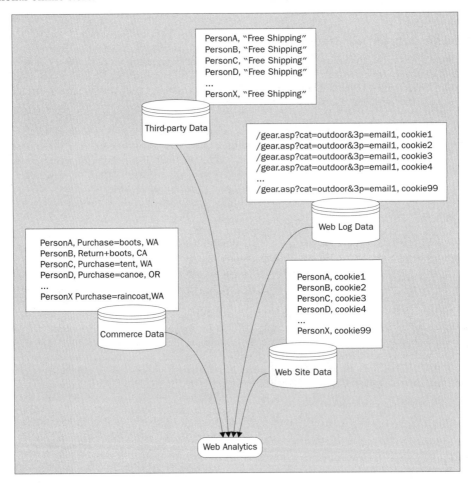

1. A targeted e-mail campaign (third-party data) to customers of the e-commerce site offers free shipping to customers who have purchased in the past. The e-mail campaign data stores contain records of which customers have received the e-mails.

2. The web log data from the e-commerce site records an increase in identifiable users (cookie1, cookie2... cookie99) browsing the site via this e-mail promotion. Many of the customers are perusing the site through the "Outdoor" section of the site instead of the "Clothes" section.

3. Commerce data has recorded an increase in outdoor gear purchases (boots, tents, canoes, raincoats) during this timeframe. It records the location where each of these customers have their orders shipped. Analysis indicates that many of these people are from the Pacific Northwest region.

4. The users who have registered through the site (cookie1, cookie2... cookie99) can be identified allowing us to correlate the purchaser (PersonA, PersonB,... PersonX) with the cookie. This allows us to know the categories and events these customers acted on before making their purchases.

The purpose of combining all of this data is to obtain business intelligence. Using the example of this particular data flow, you can deduce that an e-mail campaign has caused a domino effect where there is an increase in web site viewing. Specifically, there are many people who browse through the "Outdoor" section of the web site, who in the end make outdoor gear purchases. Further investigation indicates that a majority of these purchases are residents of the Pacific Northwest. Thus allowing us to conclude that: A targeted e-mail promotion of free shipping to customers resulted in a 10% increase in outdoor gear sales (though the Outdoor section of the site) to residents of the Pacific Northwest.

Summary

In this chapter we have reviewed the concept of Web Analytics, the infrastructure it requires and the business questions it can answer. The nature of web log, commerce, and third party data has been described, as well as ways in which these can be combined to maximize the business intelligence acquired. In particular we gave an overview of how to transform web log data in order to provide useful data to incorporate into business reports. We have also reviewed the various procedures that will help you run your web analytics data warehouse efficiently.

Being able to maximize the information gathered from web site data in order to draw up business patterns, and building strategies to act on these patterns, is the purpose of Web Analytics.

Data Warehouse

19

Securing Analysis Services Cubes

Analysis Services cubes often contain the most useful, and potentially compromising, information about your organization's activities and progress. In this chapter, you will discover how to secure that information. You will learn how to make subsets of the cube data specific dimensions, data mining models, and even individual cells, available to different users. You will also see how to make cube access secure from the Internet. This chapter includes:

- ❑ Establishing Basic Cube Security
- ❑ Securing Databases
- ❑ Securing Cubes
- ❑ Securing Dimensions
- ❑ Securing Cells
- ❑ Securing Data Mining Models
- ❑ Virtual Security

Establishing Basic Cube Security

Analysis Services security is based on Windows Integrated Authentication. Users gain access to the cube data based on permissions granted through their Windows logons. The process for developing security involves creating users, placing those users in groups, then assigning those groups to roles that grant privileges to access the cube data. The figure overleaf shows the basic model.

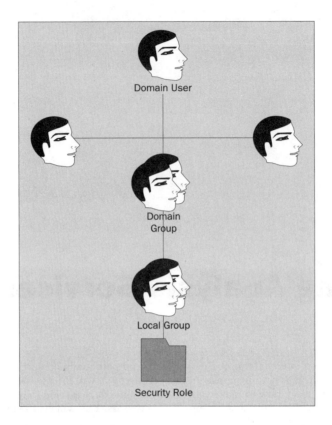

Domain User

Domain Group

Local Group

Security Role

Creating Users and Groups

The first step in giving a user access to the cube is establishing their user account. This should be a domain account that is in the same domain as the Analysis Services server. The account can also be in a domain trusted by the domain in which the Analysis Service server is a member.

The next step is to create domain groups to organize the users. For each distinct role, you should create a domain group. For instance, if your system has three cubes, one for analyzing sales, one for production and one for marketing, you wouldn't want data shared outside of these specific departments. You would create a domain group for each cube; sales, production, and marketing. Place members of the sales team in the sales group, members of the production team in the production group, and members of the marketing team in the marketing group.

The next step is to create local groups on the Analysis Services server. While not strictly required, this simplifies maintaining security (see *Planning Security Groups* for more detail). Create a local group to mirror each of the domain groups and add the domain group as the only member of the local group.

The final step is to map the local group to a database role on the Analysis Services server. You can access the Database Role Manager by clicking the server icon in the Analysis Manager, then the database, then right-clicking **Database Roles**. Clicking **Manage Roles** from the pop-up menu brings up the Database Role Manager. On the Database Role Manager, you can add a new role by clicking the **New** Button. A dialog pops up in which you can name the new role and add users or security groups to the role. The screenshot opposite shows this dialog:

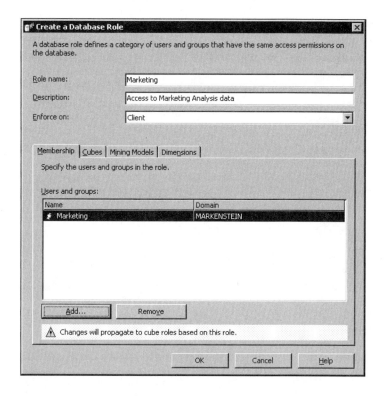

Planning Security Groups

Security groups should be created for each distinct set of security requirements. For instance, if there is a group of managers that need access to the sales and marketing cubes, they can be placed in the same group. The group can map to a single role in the database and you can grant it access to data in both cubes. Conversely, if there is sensitive information in the production database that the marketing group should not see, there should be a distinct group set up that allows access to the production database.

While you can map domain users, domain groups and local users directly into roles within Analysis Services, using local groups can simplify managing users. Once the local groups are created and mapped to internal security roles, network administrators can manage cube access by adding and removing people from domain security groups. Administrators do not need permissions on the Analysis Services computer to administer security. Also, should the Analysis Services computer be moved from one domain to another, you do not have roles mapped to users that the computer no longer trusts. You map permissions to local groups, which remain part of the server.

During installation, Analysis Services automatically creates a local security group on the server named OLAP Administrators. Members of this group have full rights on the server on all databases. OLAP Administrators can perform administrative functions on the cubes, such as loading data or processing cubes, through the Manager interface or programmatically through the Decision Support Objects (DSO). They can also modify security settings. Because members of this group can access, modify and delete any data on any cube, membership to this group should be carefully restricted.

If you install under Windows NT security (NTLM), the domain of the account under which you install Analysis Services is used to gain access to basic security information. Only accounts within that initial domain, or domains that the initial domain trusts, can gain access to the databases.

Assigning Rights to Roles

Once you create the database role, you must assign rights within the database. You can control which cubes and data mining model members of the role can access. You can also restrict access to dimensions and individual cells. Later in this chapter, you will learn how to set security at each of these levels.

Enforcing Security

Analysis Services security can be enforced either on the server or the client. To set where security is enforced, in the Analysis Manager, right-click the Database Roles icon, and click Manage Roles on the pop-up menu. In the Database Roles Manager, click on the button (with the ellipsis ...) in the Enforce On column to bring up the Edit a Database Role dialog. You can set server -or client, side enforcement for each distinct role on the server, as illustrated in the following screenshot:

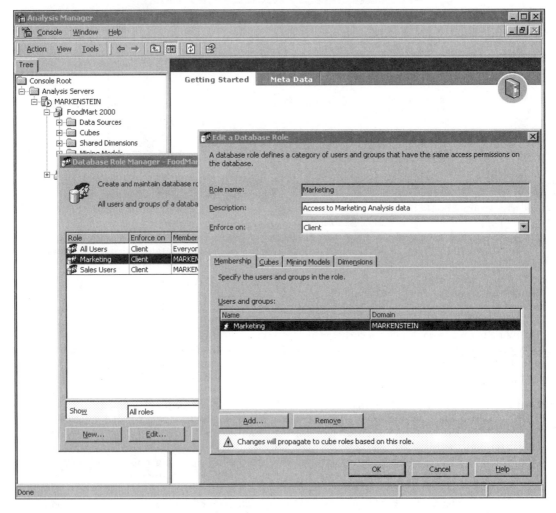

Each type of enforcement offers advantages and disadvantages.

Server-side Enforcement

Enforcing security on the server provides the highest level of security. Queries are completely resolved on the server, including calculated members. Since none of the workload can be delegated to the clients, server-side enforcement increases the workload on the server.

The amount of work to perform the additional calculations depends on the design of the cubes, the number of concurrent connected users, the queries submitted, and other factors. When using server-side security, you should monitor performance. You may wish to use System Monitor to proactively notify administrators when resources such as CPU utilization and memory page faults increase to excessive levels.

Client-side Enforcement

Client-side enforcement is the default. The PivotTable Service .DLL running on the client takes responsibility of handling security. PivotTable Service can also take responsibility for calculated members. This helps reduce load on the server.

The danger is that all the data is sent to the client and filtered there. This incurs more network traffic. Also, if you have set restrictions on dimensions or individual cells, that data is sent to the client. This provides heightened potential for security breaches.

Managing Permissions through Roles

To share the wealth of data within your data warehouse, you need to control who can get to which part of your treasure. Analysis Services provides control of access to cube data through three levels of roles: database, cube, and data mining roles. Additionally, access to dimensions and individual cells can be restricted.

Database Roles

Database roles are the primary mechanism for defining Analysis Services access. Database roles serve a purpose similar to SQL Server logins. They do not have inherited rights. They provide a bridge for mapping Windows authenticated users and groups to specific permissions within the cubes and mining models.

The database role allows default permissions to be set for use of cubes and data mining models. These permissions can be overridden with the setting in the individual cube and data mining roles. You can also restrict dimensional levels and specific cells within the cube.

Building Database Roles with Analysis Manager

The Create (or Edit) a Database Role screen provides the primary tool for building a database role. You can access this dialog by right-clicking the Database Roles icon, then clicking Manage Roles. This displays the Database Role Manager. Click the New button to create a new database role. You can also click on an existing role and click the Edit button to edit an existing role. The Database Role Manager is illustrated in the screenshot overleaf.

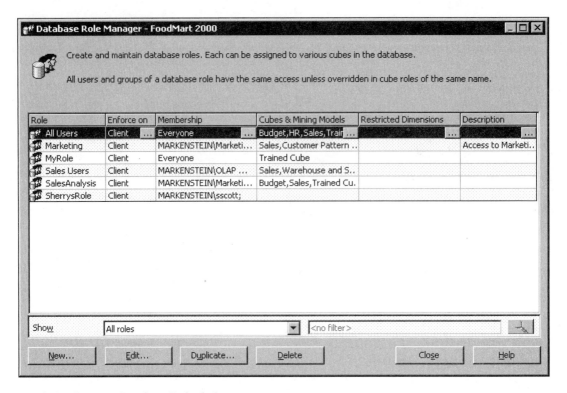

With the Create a Database Role dialog you can:

- ❑ Define a name and, optionally, a description for the role
- ❑ Set where security is enforced (client or server)
- ❑ Add Windows authenticated users and groups to the role
- ❑ Specify specific permissions that you can assign to the role (which will be discussed later in this chapter)

To grant a database role permission to a specific cube (or group of cubes), click the **Cubes** tab on the Create (or Edit) a Database Role dialog. Click in the checkbox for each cube to which you want to grant access. The only way to gain access is to have it expressly granted. If the box is not checked, the role does not have access to the database. This is illustrated in the following screenshot:

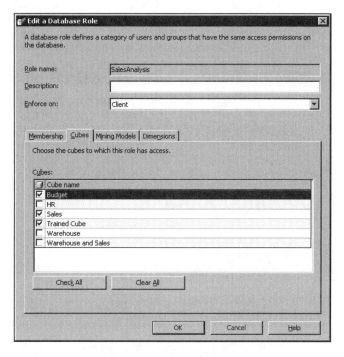

Mining models permission are granted in a manner similar to the cubes. You can use the Create (or Edit) a Database Role dialog to restrict permissions on dimensions as well. Clicking on the Dimensions tab brings up the dialog illustrated below:

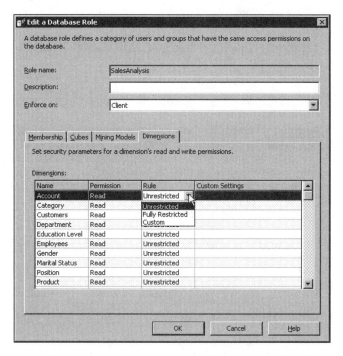

Clicking on the **Permission** cell for any dimension allows you to choose whether the role has read or write permissions on the dimension, provided the cube is write-enabled. You then determine the rule for setting security by clicking the **Rule** cell. You will learn more about dimensional restrictions later in this chapter.

Building Database Roles Programmatically using Decision Support Objects

You can also use the Decision Support Objects (DSO) to create database roles on the server. This code must be run in the security context of a member of the OLAP Adminstrators group, thus preventing anyone from using this method to grant themselves access. The Microsoft Decision Support Objects must be referenced within the project. The following code, written in Visual Basic 6, illustrates this process.

```
Public Sub AddRole(ServerName as String, DatabaseName As String, _
                   RoleName As String, UserList As String)
    'Create object variables
    Dim dsoServer As Object
    Dim dsoDatabase As Object
    Dim dsoNewRole As Object

    'Instantiate objects
    Set dsoServer = CreateObject("DSO.Server")
    Set dsoDatabase = CreateObject("DSO.Database")

    'Connect to the server and database
    dsoServer.Connect ServerName""
    Set dsoDatabase = dsoServer.MDStores(DatabaseName)

    'Add the role to the Roles collection of the database
    Set dsoNewRole = dsoDatabase.Roles.AddNew(RoleName)

    'Set the UsersList property of the role
    dsoNewRole.UsersList = UserList

    'Update the repository with the role's users list
    dsoNewRole.Update

    'Clean up
    Set dsoNewRole = Nothing
    Set dsoDatabase = Nothing
    Set dsoServer = Nothing
End Sub
```

The list of users is a semi-colon delimited list. Ensure the string listing is formatted as Domain\UsersName or Domain\GroupName. For instance, if you intend to add Marketing group and Sales group from the Corp domain, the string would appear as "CORP\Marketing;CORP\Sales". The Update method of the role object saves the role and users list to the Repository, thus saving the role. Also, note that in the documentation, Microsoft recommends not referencing the specific object interface (for example, clsServer or clsDatabase) but rather dimensioning them as generic objects and instantiating them using the CreateObject method.

The database roles can similarly be retrieved from the database. The following code is an example of collecting the roles and their associated users in an array:

```
Public Function ListRoles(ServerName as String, _
                          DatabaseName As String) As String()
    'Create object variables
    Dim dsoServer As Object
    Dim dsoDatabase As Object
```

```
        Dim dsoRole As Object
        Dim aryRoles() As String
        Dim intRoleCount As Integer
        Dim intCnt As Integer

        'Connect to the server and database
        Set Server = CreateObject("DSO.Server")
        dsoServer.Connect ServerName""
        Set dsoDatabase = dsoServer.MDStores(DatabaseName)

        'Prepare array to store the role names
        intRoleCount = dsoDatabase.Roles.Count
        ReDim aryRoles(intRoleCount - 1)

        'Loop through role collection and capture the names
        For intCnt = 1 To intRoleCount
           Set dsoRole = dsoDatabase.Roles(intCnt)
           aryRoles(intCnt - 1) = dsoRole.Name & " : " & dsoRole.UsersList
           Set dsoRole = Nothing
        Next
         'Clean up
        Set dsoDatabase = Nothing
        Set dsoServer = Nothing

        'Return results
        ListRoles = aryRoles

   End Function
```

Cube Roles

Each database can contain multiple cubes. Access to each cube can be defined independently for each database role. When initial access to a cube is defined with the database role, a cube role with the same name is automatically created within the cube. These roles can be used to restrict access to dimensions. You can also control access to cells and drillthrough. These permissions are not available at the database-role level. Permissions set at the cube-role level override the database role permissions.

There is no DENY permission for cube access. If a database role is enabled for a cube, then the users have access. If a person is a member of two roles, one of which has permission and one of which does not, the user will be granted permission to access the cube.

Building Cube Roles with Analysis Manager

In the Analysis Manager, expand the cube for which you want to apply security. Right-click the Cube Roles icon, and then click Manage Roles on the pop-up menu. The following screenshot illustrates the basic interface. To allow a database role access to the cube, click the checkbox in front of the role name. Clearing the checkbox removes that group's access to the cube.

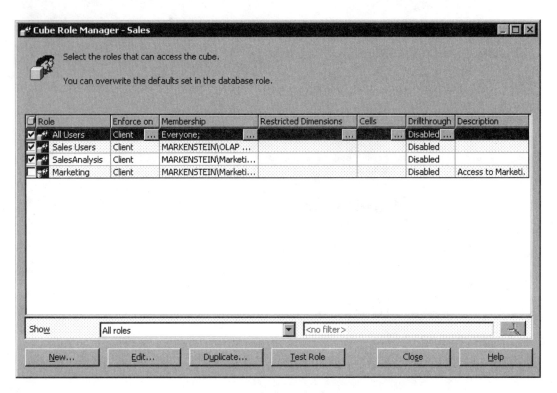

Using the New button to create a cube role will also create a database role with the same name. Using the Duplicate button allows you create a new cube (and database role) with the same permissions as the currently selected role. All you need to do is provide a distinct name. Test Role allows you to test restrictions on a specific role by activating the Cube Browser in the security context of the selected role (except for write-back, but more on that later in the chapter).

Clicking the Edit button, or any builder button in any of the individual columns in the grid, brings up the Edit Cube Role dialog. This dialog allows you to set the specific permissions for the cube role. The dialog is illustrated opposite:

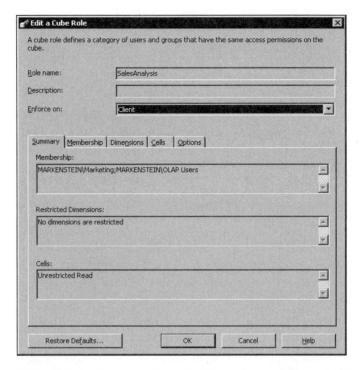

Note that clicking **Restore Defaults** returns the role to the settings stored in the database role definition. The membership of the database role and cube roles is always the same. Thus, modifying membership with this dialog will modify the membership of the database role as well. Setting dimension and cell security will be covered later in this chapter. On the **Options** tab of the dialog, as illustrated in the following screenshot, you can set three options:

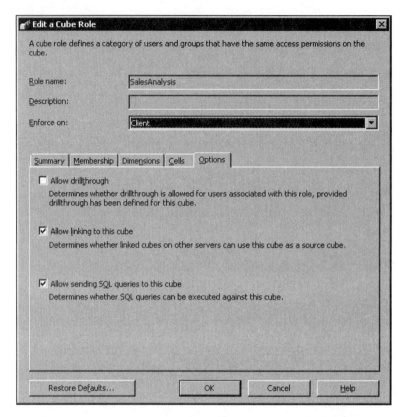

❑ **Allow drillthrough:** Allows a user to drill through the cube to the base data from which the cube was aggregated. This allows the user to access additional information about the source data. Only clients that support retrieving the additional data can make use of drillthrough.

❑ **Allow linking to this cube:** Allows this cube to be linked as a source to another cube. Linked cubes are very useful in distributing data, particularly with Internet applications. Use of linked cubes for security purposes will be discussed later in this chapter.

❑ **Allow sending SQL queries to this cube:** Allows an OLE DB provider or ActiveX Data Object to query the cube. The cube returns a tabular, "flattened" result set rather than a multidimensional cellset as the result. Analysis Services determines what type of result to return by parsing the syntax and determining whether it conforms to SQL or Multidimensional Expressions (MDX) standard. If drillthrough is enabled, SQL queries can return data from the base star (or snowflake) schema.

Building Cube Roles Programmatically using Decision Support Objects

As with database roles, cube roles can be built programmatically. The following code illustrates how to create a new cube role.

```
Public Sub AddCubeRole(ServerName As String, DatabaseName As String, _
                       CubeName As String, RoleName As String, _
                       Access As String, Drillthrough As String, _
                       Linking As String, SQLQuery As String, _
```

```
                    Enforcement As String)
        'Create object variables
        Dim dsoServer As Object
        Dim dsoDatabase As Object
        Dim dsoCube As Object
        Dim dsoNewRole As Object

        'Connect to the server and database
        Set dsoServer = CreateObject("DSO.Server")
        dsoServer.Connect ServerName
        Set dsoDatabase = dsoServer.MDStores(DatabaseName)
        Set dsoCube = dsoDatabase.Cubes(CubeName)

        'Add the role to the Roles collection of the database
        Set dsoNewRole = dsoCube.Roles.AddNew(RoleName)
        dsoCube.Update

        'Set Permissions
        With dsoNewRole
            .SetPermissions "Access", Access
            .SetPermissions "AllowDrillThrough", Drillthrough
            .SetPermissions "AllowLinking", Linking
            .SetPermissions "AllowSQLQueries", SQLQuery
            .SetPermissions "EnforcementLocation", Enforcement
        End With
        dsoCube.Update

        'Clean up
        Set dsoNewRole = Nothing
        Set dsoCube = Nothing
        Set dsoDatabase = Nothing
        Set dsoServer = Nothing
    End Sub
```

The permissions for the cube are set with the `SetPermissions` method. This accepts the name of the permission and the value as strings. The following table enumerates the permissions and their values.

Permission	Value	Description
Access	R	Allows read access to the cube (default)
	RW	Allows read-write access to the cube, if write-back has been enabled
AllowDrillthrough	True	Allows drillthrough
	False	Disallows drillthrough (default)
AllowLinking	True	Allows this cube to serve as a source for linking (default)
	False	Disallows linking to this cube

Table continued on following page

Permission	Value	Description
AllowSQLQuery	True	Allows processing of SQL queries (default)
	False	Disallows processing of SQL queries
EnforcementLocation	Client	Enforces security on the client (default)
	Server	Enforces security server-side

Mining Model Roles

Mining model roles closely mimic cube roles. The basic function of the mining model role is to grant access to data mining models. As with cube roles, there is no DENY permission. If a user is a member of any group that grants the user permission to view the mining model, they can view it. Mining model roles have matching database roles. Membership in the database role grants access to the data mining role.

Building Mining Model Roles with Analysis Manager

To build a data mining model role, right-click the Mining Model icon under the model to which you wish to add a role, then click Manage Roles. The screenshot below illustrates the interface that appears:

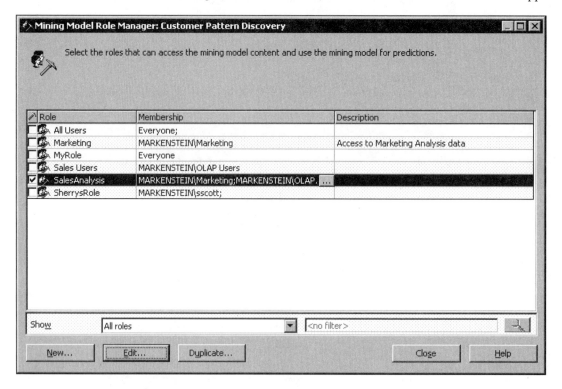

Setting the checkbox in front of a database role grants the members of that role permission to use the model. Clearing the checkbox removes permission from that group. Changing membership in the mining group will also change the membership in the database group.

Building Mining Model Roles Programmatically Using Decision Support Objects

The code for building mining models roles is very similar to the code used to build cube roles. Each database has a collection of mining models. The following code shows how to loop through the mining model roles collection and build an array of mining model names.

```
Public Function GetMiningModelRoles(ServerName As String, _
                                    DatabaseName As String, _
                                    MiningModelName As String) As String()
    'Create object variables
    Dim dsoServer As Object
    Dim dsoDatabase As Object
    Dim dsoMiningModel As Object
    Dim intRoleCnt As Integer
    Dim intCnt As Integer
    Dim aryRoles() As String

    'Connect to the server and database
    Set dsoServer = CreateObject("DSO.Server")
    dsoServer.Connect ServerName
    Set dsoDatabase = dsoServer.MDStores(DatabaseName)
    Set dsoMiningModel = dsoDatabase.MiningModels(MiningModelName)

    'Gather the roles associated with the mining model
    intRoleCnt = dsoMiningModel.Roles.Count
    ReDim aryRoles(intRoleCnt - 1)
    For intCnt = 0 To intRoleCnt - 1
        aryRoles(intCnt) = dsoMiningModel.Roles(intCnt + 1).Name
    Next

    'Clean up
    Set dsoMiningModel = Nothing
    Set dsoDatabase = Nothing
    Set dsoServer = Nothing

    'Return the results
    GetMiningModelRoles = aryRoles

End Function
```

To grant a database role permission to view the mining model, simply add the name of the role to the roles collection of the mining model object, similar to the way roles are added to the cube object. Unlike cube roles, there are no options for these roles. If the role is present in the collection, its users can access the mining model. If the role is removed, they cannot access the mining model.

Dimensional Security

Analysis Services allows you to set which dimensions users can access, and allows you to expose only specified levels within each dimension. Dimensional security can be set at either the database-role or cube-role level. If the dimension is write enabled, you can grant the role read-only permission (the default) or read-write permission. You can then set permissions for the access to the dimensional members. There are three basic settings for accessing dimensional members:

Setting	Description
Unrestricted	Allows full access to all levels of the dimension
Fully Restricted	The dimension is fixed at the All level
Custom	Members or entire levels can be hidden from the role

The system allows you to adjust the aggregations to automatically show totals only for exposed facts. Thus, the aggregate does not inadvertently reveal to the user the fact that some data has been hidden.

Building Dimensional Security with Analysis Manager

Dimension security can be set through either the database role or the cube role. From the cube, right-click the Cube Role icon and click Manage Roles on the pop-up menu. Click the builder button on the Cube Role Manager dialog box, under the Restrict Dimensions tab. You can set the security for any dimension to Unrestricted, Fully Restricted, or Custom:

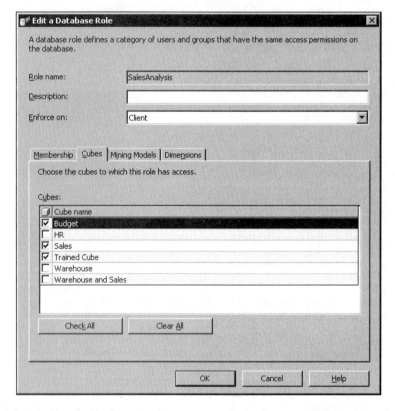

To customize the settings, choose Custom, then set custom rules. Basic customization involves setting the top level and bottom level of the dimension. These are set using the dialog illustrated opposite, which you access by clicking the builder button in the Custom Setting column of the Cube Role Manager dialog box.

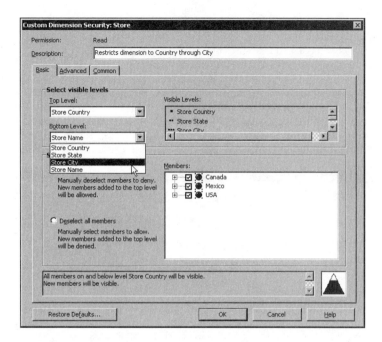

The **Basic** tab of the Custom Dimension Security dialog also allows you to include or exclude individual dimensional members. In the **Members** control, you can click the checkbox to include or exclude members from the dimension. The builder button automatically builds the correct syntax in the dialog.

The **Advanced** tab allows you to specify the top level, bottom level, included, and excluded members using Multidimensional Expressions. Clicking the **Advanced** tab allows access to these settings, as illustrated below.

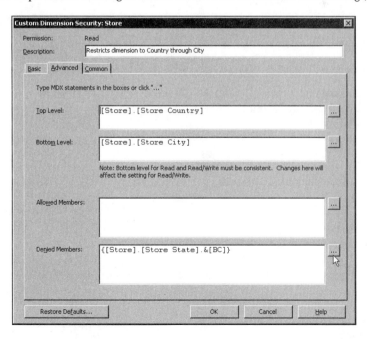

The Common tab allows you to customize several other settings. By default, the cube returns totals from the cube, including all dimensions in the cube. By clicking Enable - Show visual totals you can hide the fact that some dimensions have been masked from the role. It also helps the displayed totals make better sense to the users. You can also set a custom level and display visual totals only from a minimum level and above.

By default, if no member of a dimension is named for any axis or in the slicer specification, the default member is used. Typically, the default member is the ALL member. You can name a different member as the default member. For instance, you could name [STORE].[USA] as the default member of the Store dimension for users in the United States role. You can set the default member using an MDX expression in the Default Member portion of the Custom Dimension Security dialog.

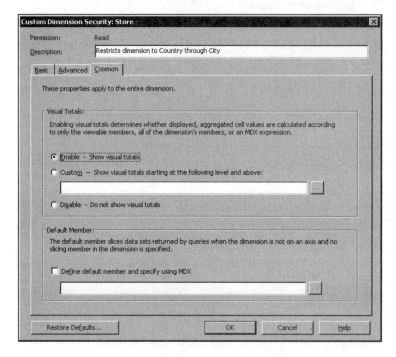

Whenever Multidimensional Expressions can be used to set a custom property, a builder button appears on the interface. You can click the button to bring up the MDX Builder dialog to help craft the Multidimensional Expression:

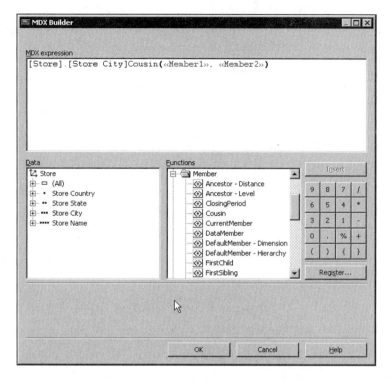

Building Dimensional Security Programmatically using Decision Support Objects

Dimensional security is set programmatically using the SetPermissions method of the cube or database role. The permissions are set as an XML document. The document begins with a parent node named MEMBERSECURITY. It includes three attributes:

Attribute	Value
IsVisible	Boolean text (TRUE or FALSE)
DefaultMember	Multidimensional expression that returns a single member (for example, [STORE].[STORE COUNTRY].[USA])
VisualTotalLowestLevel	Multidimensional expression that returns a level (for example, [STORE].[STORE CITY])

Next come Permission nodes. You can have one node that defines permissions for read-only dimension members, and another for read-write dimension members, if the dimension is write-enabled. The attributes of the Permission node are as follows:

Attribute	Value
Access	Text value, READ or WRITE

Table continued on following page

Attribute	Value
UpperLevel	Multidimensional expression that returns a level (for example, [STORE].[STORE COUNTRY])
LowerLevel	Multidimensional expression that returns a level (for example, [STORE].[STORE CITY])
AllowedSet	Multidimensional expression that returns a set of members that the role is allowed to access (for example, {[STORE].[STORE CITY].members})
DeniedSet	Multidimensional expression that returns a set of members that the role is not allowed to access (for example, {[STORE].[CUSTOMERS].members})
Description	Text description of the dimensional restriction

The syntax for the XML strings is as follows:

```
<MEMBERSECURITY
    [ IsVisible="<Boolean_string>"]
    [ DefaultMember="<allowed_member>"]
    [ VisualTotalsLowestLevel="<level_expression>"
>
    <PERMISSION Access="Read"
        [ UpperLevel="<level_expression>"]
        [ LowerLevel="<level_expression>"]
        [ AllowedSet="<set_expression>"]
        [ DeniedSet="<set_expression>"]
        [ Description="<description>"]
    />
    <PERMISSION Access="Write"
        [ UpperLevel="<level_expression>"]
        [ AllowedSet="<set_expression>"]
        [ Description="<description>"]
    />
</MEMBERSECURITY>
```

The following is an example of building the XML string using Visual Basic. It sets the default member of the Store dimension to [STORE].[STORE COUNTRY].[USA]. It sets the upper limit of the dimension to the Country level, and the lower level to the City level.

```
'Build the XML String
StrXML = "<MEMBERSECURITY IsVisible='True' DefaultMember="
StrXML = StrXML & "'[STORE].[STORE COUNTRY].{USA]'> <PERMISSION "
StrXML = StrXML & "Access='Read' _ UpperLevel='[STORE].{STORE COUNTRY]' "
StrXML = StrXML & "LowerLevel='[STORE].[STORE CITY]' "
StrXML = StrXML & "Description='Hide customer detail' /> </MEMBERSECURITY>"

'Set the permission. This assumes dsoRole is set to the appropriate role
'and dsoCube is set to the appropriate cube
dsoRole.SetPermissions "Dimension:Store", strXML
dsoCube.Update
```

Considerations for Custom Dimensional Access

Allowing and denying members can create conflicts that cannot be resolved, and create conditions that you may not expect. Consider the `Store` dimension of `FoodMart 2000`. If you deny access to `Canada`, you cannot see any of the stores in any Canadian cities or provinces. If, however, you allow access to `Store 19`, `Vancouver`, `BC` and `Canada` become available to complete the hierarchy and reach `Store 19`. `Victoria` and `Store 20` would remain inaccessible.

If you set the bottom level of the dimension to `Store City`, however, `Store 19` is below that level. Since it is below the bottom level, neither it nor its ancestors are available. Similar conditions exist through setting top levels. You must carefully plan the exact members you intend to expose. Then carefully use `ALLOW` and `DENY` to produce that set of dimensional members. Remember that denying a member also denies its descendants. Allowing a member allows its ancestors and descendants (unless the descendants are below the bottom level).

Cell Level Security

You can control security at the individual cell level. Cell-level security is set within the cube role. If the cube is write enabled, you can grant permission for users to update **atomic cells**. An atomic cell is not an aggregate of cells – it is at the base level of each dimension and the same as it appeared in the source fact table.

There are three basic policy settings:

Policy	Description
Unrestricted Read	All cells can be read (default)
Unrestricted Write	All cells can be updated
Advanced	Role can read or update only specified cells

If the `Advanced` policy is chosen, rules determine access to individual cells. Three rules can be applied to the cells within a cube.

1. Read: Cells to which the role has read access.

2. Read Contingent: Cells the role can read if the cells used to derive them are also readable or included expressly in the permission. For instance, assume Net Operating Income is a calculated member derived with the following equation:

```
[Net Operating Income] = [Measures].[Income] - [Measures].[Expenses]
```

If either `Income` or `Expenses` is not accessible through read permissions, the `Net Operating Income` would not be available either. Read contingent cells that are not accessible, by default return #N/A in place of the value. A different return value can be set in the `Secured Cell Value` Property.

3. Read/Write: Cells that the role can update. If a role can update a cell, it can also read it.

There are three settings for each of the rule types. The following chart summarizes them.

Rule Type	Setting	Description
Read	Unrestricted	Role can read all cells (default).
	Fully Restricted	Role can only read cells to which the role has been granted permission in the Read Contingent or Read/Write rules.
	Custom	Permission to read cells is determined by evaluating a Multidimensional Expression.
Read Contingent	Unrestricted	User can view all cells not derived from other cells. For derived cells to be viewed, the role must be granted access to the source cells in either the Read or Read/Write rules.
	Fully Restricted	Role can only view cells to which express permission has been granted in Read or Read/Write rule (default).
	Custom	A Multidimensional Expression is used to determine if an individual cell is viewable (assuming the role has access to read the source cells).
Read/Write	Unrestricted	Role can update all cells.
	Fully restricted	Role cannot update any cells.
	Custom	A Multidimensional Expression is used to evaluate whether a cell can be updated.

The Multidimensional Expressions should evaluate as a BOOLEAN value. If the result is TRUE, the cell is included; if the result is FALSE, the cell is ignored. For instance, if you want to include all the cells that were derived from store sales in the United States within FoodMart 2000, you could use the following expression:

```
Ancestor(Store.CurrentMember, [Store Country]).Name = "USA"
```

The Multidimensional Expression resolves the Store dimension of the current member. If the Name property of store dimension is "USA", the statement resolves TRUE and the cell is accessible. If the Name property of the store dimension is "Canada", the expression returns FALSE and the cell is inaccessible. You can learn more about Multidimensional Expressions and MDX functions (such as Ancestor) in Chapters 10 and 11.

Building Cell Security with Analysis Manager

To set cell-level security, access the Cube Role from the Analysis Manager by right-clicking the Cube Role icon under the cube and selecting Manage Roles from the pop-up menu. Clicking the builder button in the Cell column brings up the Edit a Cube Role dialog with the Cells tab selected, as illustrated opposite.

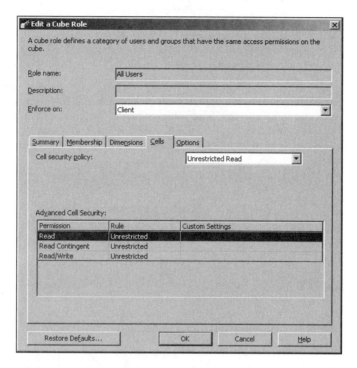

If the cell security policy is set to **Advanced**, you must define rules in the **Advanced Cell Security** grid. Each of the three types of rules is specified in the grid. Clicking the **Rule** cell allows you to choose **Unrestricted, Fully Restricted**, or **Custom**. If **Custom** is chosen, you must then create a Multidimensional Expression to determine which cells will be accessible. A dialog, illustrated below, pops up.

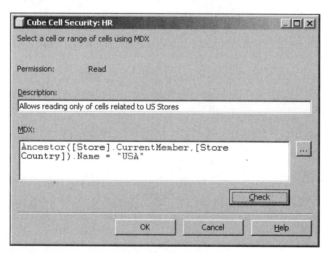

You can enter the Multidimensional Expression and check the syntax within the dialog by clicking the **Check** button. You can also click the builder button to bring up the MDX Builder to help you craft the Multidimensional Expression.

Once the security for the cells is set, you can use the Cube Role Manager to test the cell security for a selected role. The Test Role button brings up the Cube Browser in the role selected in the grid.

Building Cell Security Programmatically using Decision Support Objects

Cell security is implemented programmatically by using the SetPermissions method of the clsCubeRole object. There are three keys that affect cell security permissions: CellRead, CellReadContingent, and CellWrite. The value you enter programmatically with the key is the Multidimensional Expression used to evaluate the accessibility of the cell. To restrict a role to seeing cells related only to United States stores, you could use the following code.

```
'Assumes dsoCubeRole is instantiated to the appropriate role
'Assumes dsoCube is instantiated to the appropriate cube
dsoCubeRole.SetPermissions "CellRead", _
"Ancestor([STORE].CurrentMember, [STORE COUNTRY]).Name=""'USA'"""
dsoCube.Update
```

Virtual Security

Virtual cubes allow you to combine diverse cubes into a single entity. You can also present a subset of the full cube as a virtual cube, showing only select dimensions, and dimensional members. Similar to a view in SQL Server, virtual cubes can be used as a security mechanism.

Linked cubes can also be used to help maintain security. A linked cube draws data from a cube on another Analysis Services server. This can allow you to place Analysis Services in an unsecured area. Web servers are placed between two firewalls, one that faces the public Internet, and one that faces your internal corporate intranet. This area of your network is called the demilitarized zone or DMZ. The web server can host Analysis Services, but that server need not directly host any data. It can connect to a server inside the secure intranet through a linked cube. This way, your cube data is protected.

Virtual Cubes

When processing and storing a virtual cube, the only thing saved is the cube definition. The actual data is stored in other cubes. A virtual cube can combine data from multiple cubes that share one or more dimensions. They can also use a subset of the data from an existing cube, allowing you to hide data that you do not want users to see.

Uses for Virtual Cubes

There are many ways to use virtual cubes in a security role. Examples include:

❑ Several branches can each maintain their own cubes to analyze sales activity. A virtual cube can be used to combine the cubes into a master cube that includes sales from all branches. Access to the master cube can be limited to corporate executives.

❑ A virtual cube can be created that leaves out sensitive facts, such as labor costs or net profit. The data can be distributed through the virtual cube without exposing classified information.

❑ A cube could be created that shows sales of products of all distributors. Virtual cubes could be created that show only the items supplied by each distributor. The distributor could access the virtual cube to improve service to the customer without gaining access to competitive information.

Building Virtual Cubes

You can use the Virtual Cube wizard to build a virtual cube. To initiate the wizard in the Analysis Manager, open a database and right-click the Cubes icon. Select New Virtual Cube from the popup menu. The next step is to choose the source cube or cubes as illustrated below:

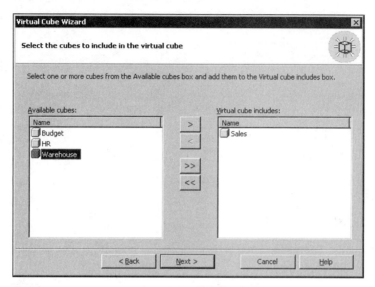

Next, choose the facts to include in the virtual cube.

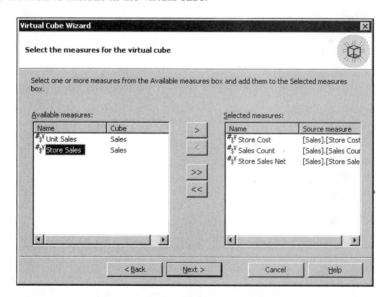

Next, choose the dimensions to include in the new cube. If you chose multiple source cubes, you must include at least one dimension that is shared by all the source cubes.

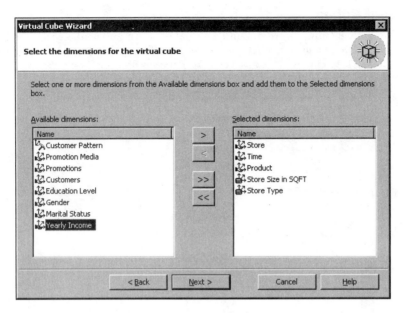

Finally, name the cube. Once the virtual cube is defined, it must be processed before it can be used. Processing creates the meta data for the cube, but does not import data or consume much space.

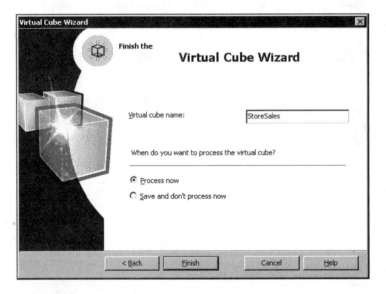

Security for Virtual Cubes

You build virtual cubes with the Virtual Cube Wizard, or with the Virtual Cube Editor. The virtual cube uses one or more existing cubes (including linked cubes) as the source. You define a new cube from the measures and dimensions within the source cubes. If more than one cube is included in the definition, they must share a dimension, and you must include the shared dimension in the cube definition. Once the cube is defined, it must be processed to build the meta data for the structure and the security definitions.

Defining security for a virtual cube is identical to defining security for a regular cube. You grant access to the cube, and restrict access to dimensions and cells using the same process as for regular cubes.

Linked Cubes

Linked cubes allow one server to present data from another server. Similar to a linked server in SQL Server, the data resides on a source server. The subscribing server queries the publishing server for data and presents it to the client when queried. To create linked cubes, you must install Analysis Services for Microsoft SQL Server 2000 Enterprise Edition.

From a security standpoint, a linked cube allows an Analysis Services server to provide data to a client without actually housing that data. The publishing server can be placed safely behind a firewall. A subscribing Analysis Services server is placed in the DMZ and linked to the publishing server through the firewall on an encrypted connection (such as PPTP or L2TP virtual private network channels). If the subscribing server is compromised, the publishing server, which contains the actual data, remains safe behind the inner firewall. This is illustrated in figure below.

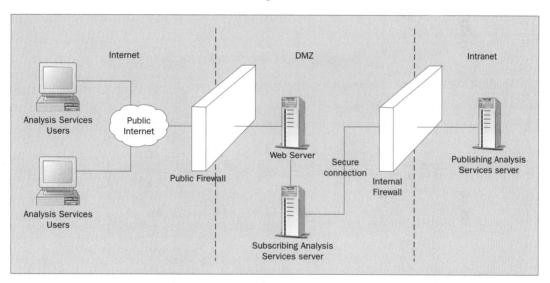

Linked cubes can also be used to control write-back access. The source cube can be write-enabled and permission to access it can be granted to a small number of users. Users who need to read the data but should not be allowed to modify it can be given access to the linked cube, but not the source cube.

Linked Cubes Considerations

Linked cubes can be built with the Linked Servers Wizard. It allows you to connect to the publishing server and build the link. The linked cube always uses ROLAP storage mode, but does not consume space because the data is stored on the source cube. A linked cube can use regular or virtual cubes as the source cubes.

To build a linked cube, keep the following security requirements in mind:

❑ Your Windows user account must have access to the source cube in order to use it as a data source.

❑ You can access the source cube through HTTP or HTTPS if the account has sufficient rights.

❏ The MSSQLServerMSOLAPServices account must have access to the source cube. If cell-level security is in place on the source cube, the linked cube will fail to process, unless the MSSQLServerMSOLAPServices account on the linked cube server is a member of the OLAP Administrators group on the source cube's server.

Linked cubes do not support write-back. If the source cubes use ROLAP for storing dimensions, private or shared, the linked cube will not be processed. Whenever the structure of the source cube is changed and the source cube is processed, the linked cube must also be re-processed to synchronize with the changes. If the source cube includes custom rollups or functions that refer to other servers, the subscribing server must also have access to these additional cubes. If the source cube contains a user-defined function in a DLL, that DLL must also be defined on the linked cube's server. You can create linked cubes to the additional source cubes to provide this access.

Building Linked Cubes

To build a linked cube in the Analysis Manager, open a database under the linked server. Right click the **Cubes** icon, then select **Create Linked Cube** from the pop-up menu. The **Linked Cube** dialog will appear. You must choose an existing cube from the **Multidimensional Data Sources**. The source cube can be a standard cube or a virtual cube. Once chosen, the cube must be processed before it can be used. The Linked Cube dialog is shown below.

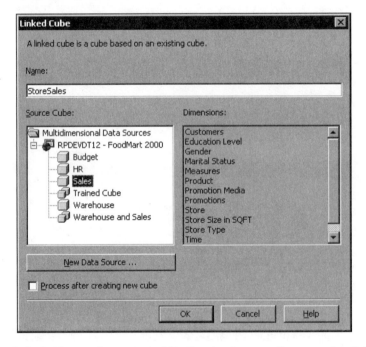

If this is the first linked cube you have created for this database, or if you need to link to a new Analysis Services server, you will need to create a new multidimensional data source. Click the **New Data Source** button to bring up the Multidimensional Data Source dialog shown opposite. Give a unique name to the data source and choose the appropriate server the from the drop-down list. The **Advanced** button brings up the full Data Link dialog, which is seldom required for creating this link.

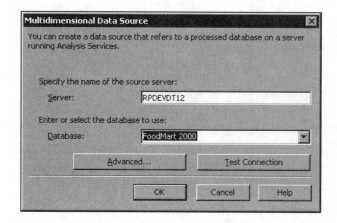

Securing Linked Cubes

As with regular and virtual cubes, linked cubes are secured through roles. Right-clicking the Cube Roles icon under the linked cube and selecting Manage Roles brings up the Cube Role Manager interface. Database roles can be granted permission to access the cube as they are for other types of cubes.

Summary

Analysis Services often provides sensitive, confidential enterprise data that must be protected. The service uses Windows Integrated Security to provide protection to that data. Windows domain and local users and groups can be mapped to database roles. The roles lend permissions to the members of those users and groups.

The database role provides basic access to cubes and data mining models. Additional cube security can be added at the cube-role level. Settings at the cube role override the database-role permissions. Similarly, the mining roles can override permissions set at the database-role level.

Dimension and cell-level restrictions are set as part of the cube role. Dimensions can be hidden, and the member that users access can be restricted. Cells can be hidden as well. If the cube is write-enabled, permission to modify dimensions and cells can be granted on a role-by-role basis.

Virtual cubes can be used to combine several cubes into a single cube, or expose only a subset of dimensions and measures. Linked cubes allow data housed in one server to appear to be housed on another server.

The Analysis Services security model allows you to reveal critical data without endangering the security of your information. Careful planning, proper application of role security, and thorough testing will allow you to deploy Analysis Services data with minimal risk.

Data Warehouse
Professional SQL Server 2000 Data WareHousing

20

Tuning for Performance

At the risk of sounding tacky, we could very call this chapter "Zen and the Art of Performance Enhancement". The analogy is neither perfect nor complete, but casts a little light on the process. Like the monk churning rocks in a garden, SQL DBAs seek balance and understanding in a continual, cyclical pursuit of refinement. They are not discouraged by their infinite ignorance in the face of overwhelming complexity; they recognize they will not soon attain perfection but persist on their path nonetheless.

In this exploration of performance enhancement, we begin with a look at design issues, followed by monitoring, indexes, storage design factor, server tuning, and finally offer some hardware recommendations. Where applicable, we will also walk through some of settings.

The most important topics are Indexing, followed by Analysis Services, Hardware, and finally Query Improvement. While the preceding topics give you the most "bang for the buck", be careful in your haste not to ignore fundamental issues covered throughout.

Performance Tuning Overview

With performance, balance is very important. Efficient SQL queries will run slow on a poorly indexed database. An 8-processor machine with the highest quality hard drives will choke on a bloated and fat database that is non-sequential. Tuning SQL Server is a balanced pursuit.

The best performance derives from understanding. Get to know your server; the hardware in which it dwells, the network through which it communicates and listens, the operating system that provides it continual company and the whimsy of the people whom it serves. This context should be considered for every decision you make.

Finally, appreciate that the journey is one great continuous circle. It is better to conduct performance tuning in concert with your many daily tasks instead of all at once.

Developers often find considerable difficulty with performance. Unlike a programming language, there are few absolutes. You must weigh the consequences of every decision against a myriad of considerations often transcending your databases. The programming precision of IF ... THEN contradicts the muddled world of performance enhancement where system intimacy and understanding have greater meaning. Herein lies the art of performance enhancement. Performance improvements more often result from elegant artful solutions, rather than complicated ones.

Elegant design and implementation conflict squarely with competing interests. Management needs conformance to a delivery schedule, as well as budget. Their schedules typically focus on the immediate fiscal year, for which they are assessed, at the cost of the future. Sloppy database implementation meets that need quite well, with timely and cheap delivery, but is clearly at the cost of scalability and future performance. Similarly, hardware is often specified for this year's bandwidth requirements without thought to next year's growth. Even after years of examples, this is very difficult to convince management of, or shareholders for that matter. In their mind, why introduce the cost of quarters yet to come into this quarter' infrastructure.

There is also an emotional investment required when designing for performance. It takes little effort to "code and fix". On the other hand, it is far more difficult to arrive at an elegant solution, and such solutions often require great contemplation. Take comfort, however, that racking your brain now is far better than trying to fix the nightmare of a horribly slow system that is intertwined into the company after 2 years of abuse.

Common culprits for poor performance are:

- ❑ Poorly authored queries
- ❑ Haphazard design and implementation
- ❑ Errors (consuming threads and resources)
- ❑ Inadequate hardware

While performance is an art form, this chapter will provide some rules to follow, as well as some direction.

Evaluate and Refine the Design

The most common approach to address performance shortfalls is to throw hardware at the symptoms. This is not a good practice, since it often fails to address the underlying disease, unrefined or faulty design. Disciplined design and design refinement deserve as much, if not more, consideration than hardware enhancement.

Some performance improvements should be investigated regardless of usage, while others are dependent upon how the database will be employed. Although the latter performance improvements of the chapter are typically more important than the former, for the sake of simplicity we will move through some of the more generic issues first.

Keep It Clean

In the era when programs will gracefully handle sloppy data types, and perform a myriad of extraneous features out-of-the-box, it is difficult to remember that nativity saves resources. Specifically, the less SQL Server and associated applications have to handle the better they will perform. This includes the operations they have to perform, the data with which they work, and how much SQL Server stores.

Simple, Appropriate Data types

Data type selection seldom receives appropriate attention. While not as important as indexing or other measures, poor data type selection does slow SQL Server down and consume valuable disk space and most importantly, reduces disk input/output. This is especially true in data warehouses, where the sheer volume of data magnifies data type impact.

> **Select data types with as small a format as possible.**

In the simplest terms, where possible, use int instead of varchar, smallint instead of int, and bit instead of smallint. Of course, this statement oversimplifies the decision-making required, but provides a conceptual framework. Let us take a look at some more specific examples.

Varchar, Char, nVarchar

Data types handling characters are perhaps the most common. SQL Server 2000 offers several data types each for specific employment. Unfortunately, most designers seem to select their character data types at random. Without delving into the definitions, here are some considerations and examples.

Avoid text

Unless you have a particularly large amount of characters to store, do not use text. Most people acquire text data type accidentally after a DTS conversion wherein SQL Server converts a memo or similar field into text. Remember, char and varchar each are capable of 8,000 characters. If your field does not require more than 8,000 characters, use char or varchar instead. Text employs a pointer to the larger collection of data, negating many of the powerful capabilities offered by a database. Char and varchar provide more efficient storage and more complete access to aggregate features in SQL Server 2000 as well.

To char or not to char

Char is fixed length whereas varchar has a default 2-byte overhead specifying actual size of a particular cell. When the data in a varchar cell does not occupy all of the allotted space, SQL Server releases the remainder for storage. Because of the volume of data consumed in a data warehouse, the distinction between these gains new importance. 2-bytes a million times over is not insignificant; nor is the space lost using char to store text with a large standard deviation. So, if you are storing US social security numbers, credit card numbers, initials, states, or provinces, all with predictable lengths, char is your choice. If you are storing names, descriptions, narrative or content the length of which has an average standard deviation of more than 2 from maximum, varchar is your choice.

The figure below illustrates a field that should continue to be of the type char(13), since the average length of each record typically deviates by less than 2 bytes from the allocated space.

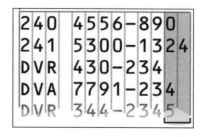

varchar has an additional advantage, when the above conditions are not met (average standard deviation from max < 2). Since SQL Server moves data around in pages, a dynamically sizeable field like varchar can shove more data into a single page, thus reducing disk input/output.

If in Doubt, Leave "n" Out

nChar and nVarchar are often employed by default with DTS or by habit with designers who are throwing a table together quickly. The fact that many examples display nChar or nVarchar does not help matters. If you do not specifically need the Unicode feature, which extends your available ASCII set to international characters, then you should not employ it. First, nChar and nVarchar literally consume twice as many resources, since for each character, there is a second identifier. Additionally, Unicode is not always backwards compatible, which could cause problems in a data warehouse with different types of databases. Of course, if you must store anything beyond the basic ASCII 255 characters, you will need to use a Unicode data type.

An int by Any Other Name can be Slow

When you have reasonable assurance that data will be numeric, you should use a numeric field instead of a character field. Computers prefer numbers, indeed, they convert characters into numbers every time before playing with them. Foreign keys benefit from being an integer, especially considering each field is duplicated, by definition, at least once, and at least three times when indexing is accounted for. Since SQL Server uses foreign keys in a programmatic fashion, the more native format also improves processing time in joins. The decision to use int for foreign keys, however, must take into account data integrity. Sometimes, a Globally Unique Identifier (GUID) will be required to preserve integrity, in which case the performance gain of an int would be not be warranted at such risk.

tinyint is a Big Help

Many foreign keys are for lookup tables that will never have more than a few dozen entries, let alone 255 rows (the limit of tinyint). When these situations arise, tinyint can be a big help, since it only consumes one measly byte, compared to its big brother's 4 bytes. Considering a relational database's love for foreign keys as well as the proclivity for cross reference tables, using tinyint can trim a lot of bloat and improve processing time.

bit is Best.

There is nothing, not even NULL, that a computer loves more than a one or a zero. This is the heart and sole of software, and SQL Server is no exception. Bits fly and fly fast. Do not use y or n in a char(1) field, or 1 and 0 in an int(1) field when you could use bit. The overhead savings in this can really multiply in a data warehouse, especially if you require a slew of flags.

smalldatetime vs. datetime

The advantage of smalldatetime is that it only consumes 4 bytes, compared to the 8 bytes of datetime. smalldatetime has accuracy to minutes, not to seconds. Thus, if the data has to keep seconds, use datetime. When you have a date field that does not require precise time, which is quite often, use smalldatetime.

Table, a Large Data type That We Like.

There are some exceptions to obsessing about keeping the data type small. With SQL Server 2000, one of them is the new table data type. Essentially, the table data type allows us to pull query results into memory for further querying. This strategy is most appropriate for a subset of data from which you wish to perform multiple queries. For example, when running complicated statistics for a specific workgroup in a department, you could select the workgroup into a table data type, and then execute further queries from this table you have placed in memory. This would alleviate disk input-output issues considerably, although it would require commensurate RAM for the task.

Parting Shots

We have just spent considerable ink inspecting data types. Typically data type selection is not the most important step towards improving performance, but in data warehousing, the volume of data involved warrants additional attention to data types. Additionally, the philosophy of keeping as small and close to the native format as possible will be revisited in any discussion about performance enhancement and software, and SQL Server is no exception.

Evaluate Usage Patterns

Before we can make meaningful improvements to performance, we must evaluate the business use and management of the data. The process of tuning in a large sense is a modification of SQL Server's out-of-the-box setup to a subset of requirements more tailored to our usage patterns. SQL Server 2000 must accommodate a myriad of different mutations, from small efficient web databases to bloated legacy repositories and to our own special pain, data warehouses. Additionally, some DBAs do not have a separate server for their database while others have farms of rack servers each dedicated to a SQL Server database. Microsoft has to accommodate all of these scenarios, and we have to refocus the software for our needs.

Patterns

Typically, data warehouses experience far more query operations than input operations. Knowing this simplifies many decisions, especially concerning indexing, which we will cover shortly. We still could benefit from knowing more detail about how the data will be analyzed. For example, a business that requires intricate decision making models will benefit more from processor upgrades; a business that requires extensive but simple aggregation from its data will benefit more from RAM upgrades.

Also look at who is using the data. If your regional offices require frequent data analysis of very specific subsets of data, then data marts are worth the effort. Data marts offer a subset of a parent database on a server collocated with its principal consumer. The advantage is reduced network latency and an offloading of processing from the data warehouse. The cost is greater effort on the part of DBAs in synchronizing the data and setting up independent databases.

Similarly, inspect the environment through which results will travel. Some enterprises have fantastic server farms but poor networks, or overburdened infrastructures. These require more aggressive server-side processing to ensure the thinnest client response. If users connect to the database through intranet servers, you may find an opportunity to offload some decision processing to other technologies. Specifically, you may find opportunities in the client tier to short-circuit database calls by answering queries with data cached on the application server. The strategies for this are very specific to the technologies used, but keep in mind that there may be chances to offload work to other technologies.

Assess peak usage trends throughout your enterprise. Peak usage is the performance metric that perhaps matters the most, since it is when the greatest number of users are connected, and presents the greatest vulnerability to instability. Remember, increased usage seldom engenders a linear decrease in performance, but rather causes a disproportional response under heavy load. Consider when your consumers require data, and what kind of data they require at peak intervals. Will they require data throughout the day at regular intervals, or in large spurts? Will they access similar queries sequentially?

When tuning your database, your decisions to speed one query may negatively affect another query. Always take into consideration the various permutations by which your data will be accessed. Many times, we focus excessively on the most troublesome queries, but would better serve users by optimizing the most common queries. This is especially true in data warehousing, where even common queries can tax a system. Track what your most popular queries are and ensure they receive adequate attention. Also, do not forget that uploading transactions deserve equal attention as query transactions in a data warehouse.

Find out about other environmental usage patterns as well. Ensure that your scheduled events are not conflicting with other major network activity. A courtesy call to the network administrator or server administrators often uncovers unknown activities that negatively affect your scheduled events and peak usage patterns. Your SQL Servers reside on the network and are subject to its problems. A little coordination to remove conflicts can be a cheap performance enhancement.

Monitoring and Assessment

SQL Server offers great tools to monitor various performance parameters. These tools will allow you to identify bottlenecks that are compromising your server's performance. First we will investigate everyone's favorite analysis tool, Windows 2000 System Monitor, followed by SQL Server Profiler and ending with SQL Server Query Analyzer.

System Monitor

The ubiquitous Performance Monitor is quite familiar to most people working with databases on Microsoft operating systems. With Windows 2000, Microsoft has further enhanced this tool and given it a new name: System Monitor.

> **Prior to moving into production, collect a baseline of measurements for your server during beta testing. This will help you identify problems later.**

The Cost of Monitoring

Dr. Werner Heisenberg's Uncertainty Principle informs us that the closer we measure something, the more we modify it (of course, this is a very loose summary of his principle). While SQL Server runs on something more tangible than quantum mechanics, Heisenberg's Uncertainty Principle does correlate to our effort to monitor the system. Performance measurements consume resources from the system. They are not particularly taxing, but the performance cost is worth mitigating.

The first step to lessening the impact of performance monitoring is to offload the monitoring onto a client workstation on the network. This does not completely eliminate the overhead, but does mitigate it. System monitor is available on Windows 2000 Professional, if that is your workstation, under Start | Settings | Control Panel | Administrative Tools | Performance. The + sign allows you to add counters to your monitoring. To monitor SQL Server remotely, enter your server's name in the Select counters from computer drop-down box as you add your counters.

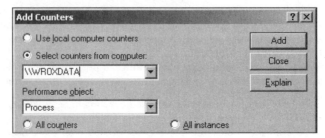

Be careful to type the correct server name in, since on some slower networks an error can take a while for the system to resolve, wasting your time in the process.

> **Do not run System Monitor from a terminal services box!**

Terminal services are real performance killers and should never interface with your SQL Server. After you have assembled your counters, you can save the profile (using the **Save As** in the MMC) on your desktop or another easy location. You will want to create profiles for each of your servers, as we will discuss shortly. By saving them on your desktop, you can quickly access them to peek at a specific server's condition.

When monitoring a system, generate a log instead of a graph. Adding counters to the logs is identical to the process for the chart, except that you begin from **Counter Logs** under **Performance Logs and Alerts**.

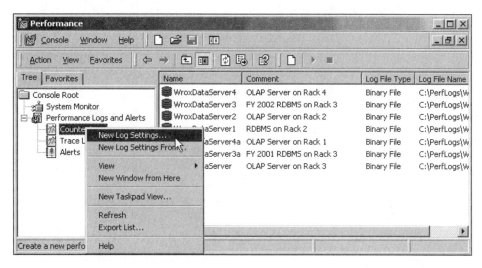

Logs may be stored on a separate drive on the server you are monitoring, since the latency of transmitting the log entries over the network may negate the gains of remote monitoring. For the times that you do want to view the graph, be sure to close the console after you are finished, or the monitor will continue to tax resources. Regularly "clean up" the logs by archiving them, and replacing them with an empty log file for System Monitor to build upon. While smaller log files consume less space on the drive, the more important advantage is that System Monitor will have an easier time working with trim log files than bloated ones.

You can Peek, but Don't Stare

SQL Server 2000 and Windows 2000 offer a large number of metrics for measuring server performance. We only require a subset of these to measure the pulse of our servers. Similarly, we do not need to monitor a large number of these measurements continuously. A preferred approach is to look at definitive subsets of metrics in "bursts" of time targeting a specific area. Peek at intervals that correlate to your business usage patterns, collecting weekly or daily samples to cover the typical usages that your server experiences.

We can describe these assessments with four flavors: low impact, mid impact, high impact, and hybrid. Low impact typically runs in the background at a low sampling frequency, and simply monitors very important stats for long term trending. Mid impact is run in long samples based on business cycle rules as a "system checkup". Employ high impact during development and prototyping, and to resolve specific problems. Hybrids are high or mid impact assessments of very specific counters (one or two at a time, but at a high frequency).

For example, if we have three servers, we could set up a mid impact CPU/Memory monitor on one server for a week, and set up a disk I/O set of counters the following week. This would give us a good, reliable snapshot of this server's health. On one of these days, you may want to intensify the inspection by running a high impact measurement with a more complete set of counters for a 24-hour period. In the background, you could maintain a low impact persistent logging of performance, with a very low sampling frequency, perhaps at a 13-minute interval. When choosing long frequencies, be sure to select a low prime number, otherwise you may often be sampling in synch with another Windows 2000 or SQL Server cyclical process (which tend to run on whole minute intervals).

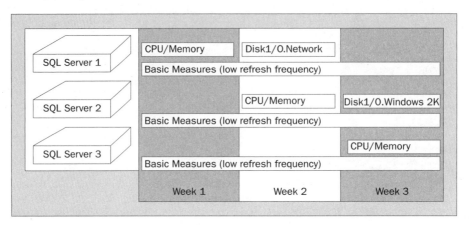

Common Counters

As stated earlier, there are hundreds of counters available in Windows 2000 and SQL Server 2000. The majority of these are only required for very specific diagnoses. We will group the following counters into assessment categories. You may want to mix and match based on your needs, but ensure that for every counter you add you have a specific reason to do so. Remember, every counter contributes to Dr. Heisenberg's estate!

Without belaboring how to add a counter to System Monitor from the Add Counters dialog, we will clarify the 3-part name notation that we shall use to reference the counters in the following section. The first name refers to the Performance Object, the second name to the counter, selected from the list of counters, and the third refers to the Instance, when there is one, which we choose from the Select instances from list box.

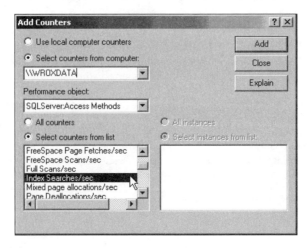

Basic Monitoring

Processor | % Processor Time | Instances 0,1,2,3 (select each processor)
System | Processor Queue Length
Memory | Pages/Sec
SQLServer: Buffer Manager | Page Reads/sec

These counters will form the basis of your Low Impact monitoring. Set these up for each server, and ensure that you have a low sample rate. Sample rate is set by right-clicking the log, and modifying the Interval at the bottom of the General tab. This can be done while creating a new log. If you are using multiple processors, note whether the processors are sharing work equally. The first processor will usually absorb more threads, but the other processors should be close behind, especially when under load. A processor queue length that is 2 times the number of processors on your server is an acceptable measure. A very small queue may not be all together bad, since it indicates overall resource balance. A high Pages/Sec count, around 16, will indicate that you need more memory. The Buffer Manager counter indicates read activity in SQL Server, and will help you determine load.

RAM Health

Memory | Available Bytes
Memory | Committed Bytes
Memory | Pages/sec

A low value for Available Bytes indicates your server is low in memory. Committed Bytes indicates how much memory is actually being used by the system. A value close to your total memory indicates a need to add more memory. Use RAM Health in concert with either Disk System Health or a CPU check to determine the most effective hardware upgrades. When Pages/Sec rises above zero, this indicates that Windows 2000 is using the disk drives for memory, suggesting inadequate RAM.

Disk System Health

Physical Disk | % Disk Time
Physical Disk | Avg Disk Queue Length
Physical Disk | Avg Disk sec/Transfer

To enable disk counters, you will need to execute `diskperf -y` *from the command line or* Run *under* Start.

Avg Disk Queue Length may indicate either a need for faster hard drives (15k rpm versus 10k rpm), or a parallelism strategy for disk I/O, which we will describe later. In concert with RAM health, this counter may additionally indicate inadequate RAM for proper caching. % Disk Time indicates how much time your disks spend spinning. As well as indicating inadequate RAM or disk speed, this measure may also alert you to a looming hard drive failure due to excessive use. Consider adding more hard drives to your array to alleviate some of the disk load. Avg Disk sec/Transfer will help confirm whether or not you need a faster hard drive. If you have baseline data, compare its numbers to a healthy server.

Bandwidth Health

Network Interface | Bytes Total/sec
Network Segment | % Network Utilization

The first counter requires installation of Network Monitor Agent in Windows 2000. The % Network Utilization should remain below 30%, and Bytes Total/Sec should be proportional to your card's capacity. These counters will indicate whether you are experiencing a network bottleneck. Such a bottleneck will tax memory, as the queue is not able to release from SQL Server. Coordinate this investigation with your Network Engineers.

Index Health

SQL Server Access Methods | Full Scans/sec
SQL Server Access Methods | Index Searches/sec

These will measure SQL Server's utilization of indexing. You essentially want very high numbers for Index Searches and low numbers for Full Scans (a 90% to 10% mix is optimal).

Other Counters

When you identify a particular weakness or potential bottleneck, you will want to investigate further with a more complete set of counters pertaining to that problem. Microsoft maintains a complete list of counters with associated descriptions at http://msdn.microsoft.com.

Alerts

System Monitor can also act upon performance counters that exceed a specification. With Alerts, you can log the events, execute a program or even contact a DBA when an event occurs. There are some important Performance Alerts that you can set in order to catch a failing database before it is too late. Additionally, you can use alerts to log troublesome occurrences. These are especially important for those servers that have historically had some issues (and we all have had servers like this).

To set up an alert profile, from the same System Monitor MMC, select Performance Logs and Alerts. Right-click on Alerts and select New Alert Settings. After providing a name for the alert, System Monitor will then display a dialog box in which you can administer the alerts. First, you must add a counter prior to manipulating the other settings. To do so, select Add. The familiar Select Counters dialog appears.

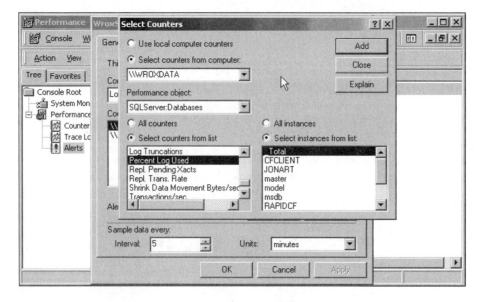

From this, select your desired counter. Again, you may administer this remotely, so that it consumes fewer resources. Your alert profile should only require a small number of counters, based on your requirements.

Some important alerts are:

Alert	Description
SQLServer Databases | Percent Log Used | All Instances	Set the threshold to 75. This will warn you when your transaction logs are about to become fully loaded, at which point your system will grind to a halt. 75% should give you adequate time to take corrective measures.
Memory | Pages/sec	Set the threshold to between 16 and 24. This will tell you if your server requires more memory.
Physical Disk | Avg Disk Queue	Set the threshold to either 3 or 4 (over). This is helpful on newly fielded systems, but if you continue to use it, spread the interval out since it consumes resources.

SQL Server Error Logs

Since this chapter is on performance tuning, we will not delve too deeply into the error logs. Errors do affect performance, however, and can sap considerable resources. SQL Server 2000 offers an easy interface in MMC with which to view error logs. These logs should be reviewed regularly to ensure that recurrent errors are addressed.

To view the logs, open SQL Server 2000 Enterprise Manager. From the Management Folder of the database, select SQL Server Logs.

By default, SQL Server maintains the last 6 archived logs as well as the current log. When the service is cycled with a restart, a new error log is created, and the current one is rotated into the archives. The log files are ASCII text, so they can be offloaded on a scheduled basis to a workstation for analysis.

Pouring through these files not only identifies troublesome errors, but also may provide insight into other events occurring with your server that you were unaware of. It is not uncommon to find something of interest within the entries.

Deadlocks are a particularly interesting error that your logs will expose. Deadlocks occur when a transaction is orphaned due to a lock from another resource. SQL Server 2000 offers better handling of locking than predecessors, but deadlocks are still possible. Most likely, a third-party resource will be the culprit.

SQL Server Query Analyzer

SQL Server 2000 provides the most feature-rich version of Query Analyzer to date. This valuable tool allows you to mould queries into more efficient shapes, and helps identify faulty queries. The tool can provide a graphical representation of a query, deconstructing its major components and providing a cost analysis for each step it takes.

To see how this functions, let us step through a quick example. To open the tool, go to Start | Programs | Microsoft SQL Server | Query Analyzer. Select a database and enter appropriate authentication. When the Analyzer opens, go to Query on the navigation bar, and in the pull-down menu, select Current Connections Properties. Alternatively, you can access this dialog box from an icon on the far right of the navigation bar. In the dialog window that appears, add Set statistics time and Set statistics IO to the selected components. This allows us to view CPU and Disk Input/Output measurements for the queries, very important measurements in the world of SQL Server 2000. From the same drop-down menu, select Show Execution Plan. This will provide us with a graphical representation of the query execution plan.

Next, place a query, or stored procedure into the upper window of an open query pane. Press the green Execute arrow on the navigation bar, and SQL Server will generate the execution plan. Press Show Execution Plan again and the table in the bottom window will reveal the execution plan for the query.

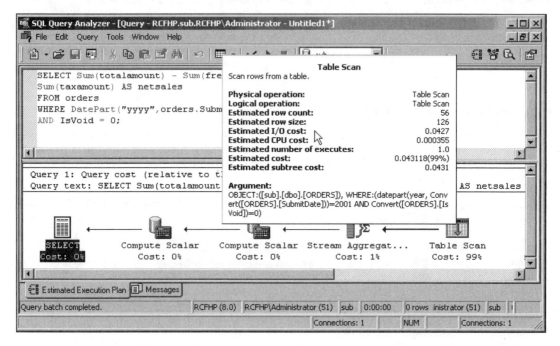

Hovering your mouse over an object in the lower window will reveal detailed statistics about that event. Concern yourself primarily with the two middle measurements, Estimated I/O costs and Estimated CPU costs. In the simple example provided in the figure, you can note that my disk input output significantly exceeded the costs from the CPU execution for this query. You will also note that SQL Server performed a table scan for this query, and did not use an index. This will be a target for improvement later.

The great advantage of SQL Query Analyzer is that it provides a detailed breakdown of performance, instead of a simple total aggregate statistic such as query execution time. Use SQL Query Analyzer in concert with your tuning activities to validate each move's impact. This will become particularly important with the Index Tuning Wizard, to be introduced later, as well as when we are modifying queries for improved performance.

SQL Query Analyzer is a rich environment that provides developers a great platform on which to create queries, with a meaningful color-coded SQL text editor, strong validation routines and quick performance feedback. The interface is highly customizable, and includes a great deal of quick tools to speed development. Fonts can be adjusted, color codes modified and environmental settings can be manipulated to more closely simulate realistic usage. From the Tools menu, select Options. This will bring up a dialog box with seven tabs. In Connection Properties, select Set statistics IO and Set statistics Time so that these are defaulted the next time you open the tool. Also, you may want to customize the Results entries and Connections entries depending on how you employ the tool. Microsoft even provides an interface in which you can add your own custom keystrokes to execute stored procedures. This can be a real time saver for developers. To open the tool, select Tools from the menu, and Customize from the drop-down box.

SQL Server Profiler

Microsoft revamped and improved SQL Server Profiler for SQL Server 2000, adding functionality and improving performance of this utility. SQL Server Profiler is a tracing utility that allows you to observe what transpires on your SQL Server. This system is highly customizable and provides you a great utility with which to develop baseline measurements and test against those measurements.

SQL Server Profiler tracks "events". You define what events it will track, selecting them from a menu when you set your profile up. SQL Server Profiler also can track these events when they meet a specific condition, such as a percentage threshold. This functionality lends itself to multiple purposes, including pre-rollout bench testing and database monitoring. The best application of this tool, however, is to performance enhancement. SQL Server Profiler provides an easy, flexible means to frame our testing and validate our decisions. Unlike System Monitor, which centers on server processes, SQL Server Profiler is event-centric.

When you are ready to update a server, run SQL Server Profiler three times for an hour each time during normal business hours. If you have a scheduled overnight event on your server, run that one independently as a fourth run. The number of runs or length is not terribly important, but we want to collect good statistical sampling without overly burdening the system. The SQL Server Profiler will trace all user activity against the database, based on events that you have identified for collection.

To start the process, launch SQL Server Profiler from Start | Programs | Microsoft SQL Server | Profiler. Click the far left icon to start a new trace. Enter your server in the first dialog box and appropriate login credentials. The Trace Properties dialog box will appear. Beyond the obvious notes such as providing a meaningful Trace Name, on the first tab you may want to select Save to table, since this will store the data in a database that facilitates analysis. Once selected, a Connect to SQL Server window spawns, hauntingly similar to the one that started this process. In this window, enter the SQL Server that will store the trace collection. Another window will appear upon pressing OK, in which you will select a database and a table, as seen overleaf.

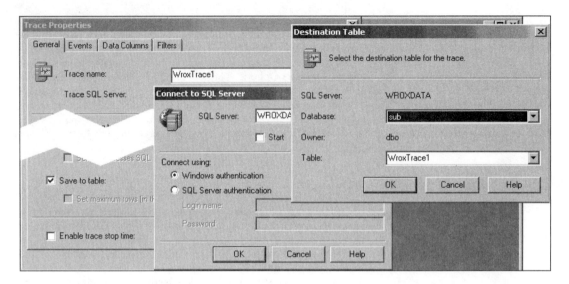

In yet another violation of the earlier advice to monitor from the client side, we will specify that SQL Server 2000 will manage the process to ensure the highest degree of accuracy, since the client connection may not capture all of our events. After having set the table up, the last step in this tab is to select **SQL Profiler Tuning** from the **Trace Template** drop-down box. You can develop your own trace, but the default **Profiler Tuning** trace is clean, simple, and fits our requirements.

Our next step is to set up the events we want to track. Selecting the **Events** tab brings up a screen with more than 100 event classes grouped on the left pane and a set of event classes on the right pane. We want to keep the **Selected event classes** set small during performance analysis, but you certainly may add more meaningful events if you feel the need to track them. For each of the events that it offers, SQL Server 2000 provides you a brief description in a pane below the two event panes.

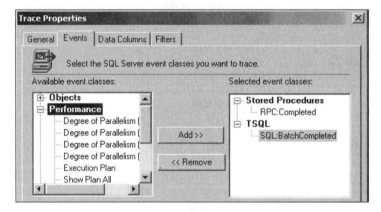

The **Data Columns** dialog tab allows you to specify custom columns in your table. Again, we will maintain the default collection for our purposes, although when tracking down a specific problem or error, you would request a more complete set of fields based on your needs.

As with the previous tabs, in Filters we will maintain the default settings, to include the choice to exclude the SQL Server Profiler database activity, since tracking that would distort our data. While you are here, however, do note the extensive flexibility these filters offer you for error tracking and troubleshooting. This is definitely a tool to turn to when you have a sick database.

The product of the trace is visible from the profiler by selecting Open a Trace Table from the navigation bar then selecting the server and database. The table will be pre-populated for you in a drop-down.

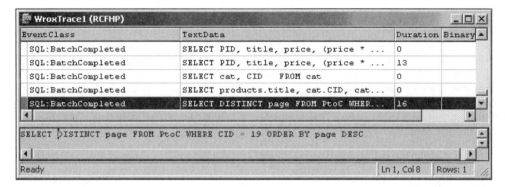

For the simple performance profile, the SQL that executes will be a field along with the query time for the execution. Selecting a row will display the complete SQL statement in a pane below the table. The table, of course, is also accessible through T-SQL or directly through SQL Server Enterprise Manager.

After you have completed your assessment and have applied corrective measures to your database, measures we will introduce shortly, you will want to run SQL Profiler to validate your measures. From SQL Profiler, open one of the trace tables you produced earlier. Next, press Start Replay, the yellow arrow icon in the middle of the navigation bar. This will open the familiar SQL Server connection dialog, followed by a dialog prompting you to specify the server again. Press Start to run the profile, and monitor the System Monitor.

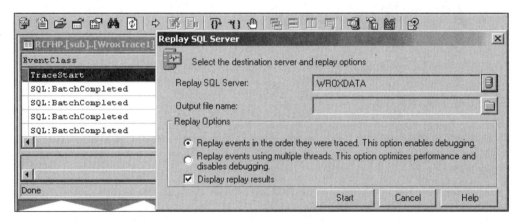

If you specify detailed events in your profile, such as CPU | Greater Than or Equal To, you can derive some meaningful performance assessments from T-SQL through aggregating queries that sum events up. For example, you can COUNT(*) and AVG() fields in the table to uncover the frequency of long CPU processes or high impact events.

There literally are thousands of ways to exploit the SQL Server Profiler, and hundreds of ways to use it to optimize your database. Over time, you should develop very strategic traces that you can execute to test your databases with. The great advantage is that these can be run during low load hours, such as early Saturday morning, to achieve minimal impact testing.

Most importantly, SQL Server Profiler is a key component in the Index Tuning Wizard, which we will look at next.

Indexes

In addition to being a core tool for the Index Tuning Wizard, what SQL Profiler undoubtedly will reveal is the true importance of indexes in data warehouses. Unlike some other iterations of SQL Server, such as web transaction servers and commerce instances, data warehouses almost always benefit from indexes. Whereas the former databases have considerable writing activity and limited query activity (sometimes the ratio can be 1:1, where an entry will only be read one more time ever), data warehouses exist primarily for high-read analysis, and hold considerable amounts of data. This affair actually simplifies your decision process considerably, and allows you to rely more on the tools SQL Server provides.

The tools that Microsoft has bundled with SQL Server keep improving. Indeed, the current set of Indexing tools can probably out-guess many of us when it comes to indexing. In the past, complete understanding of the flavors of indexes and how they work for which situations was vital to a successful database implementation. Now, the understanding of indexes takes a more academic flavor, but is still important.

In case there is any doubt, there is the following suggestion.

> **The most important performance enhancement you can make is a well-implemented indexing strategy.**

Before we introduce the tools for indexing, let us arrive at some communal understanding of indexes. As anyone working with data warehouses probably already knows, indexes come in a couple of primary flavors, **clustered** and **non-clustered**, as well as a few variations. With data warehouses, we will use all of them at some time, and often in concert with each other. This type of index arrangement, with multiple indexes binding the table, is referred to as compound. Its antithesis is a simple index, which typically is a sole primary key on a table. SQL Server stores its indexes in a binary-tree structure (often called a B-tree), which looks similar to an upside-down tree, hierarchically arranged.

Clustered Indexes

Clustered indexes reorder the data they index. The rows of a table with a clustered index are physically maintained in the same order as the index. As a consequence, only one clustered index may be applied to a table, and applying one after the populating the table can be a resource intensive event as the table is reorganized.

An analogy for clustered indexes would be a file warehouse. A clipboard, analogous to the `sysindex`, would identify a root node clipboard. This root node clipboard contains the index information for the data table, identifying the intermediate clipboards that will help us drill down to our data. These clipboards are sequentially ordered, and each one identifies the previous and next clipboard. In a clustered index, a header contains a pointer identifying the location of the page just prior and the page immediately following. Once our row is discovered in an intermediate clipboard, we are directed to the leaf node, which actually contains the data we are looking for. In this case our file folder is referenced by a unique number, and contains the data we were seeking. The folder is analogous to the leaf level of a clustered index, and is the location of our target record.

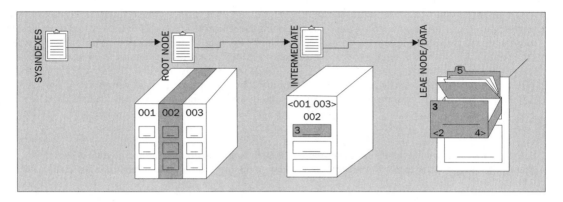

Clustered indexes are great when searching for ranges of data, since everything is sequentially ordered in the table. They are better for columns of low selectivity, where low selectivity is defined as high duplication. Numeric columns with non-NULL entries are preferred by clustered indexes. Primary keys are clustered by default; however, they can be created as non-clustered.

Non-Clustered Index

A non-clustered index is separate from the data and is analogous to the index in this book. Any entry can be indexed multiple times, and referenced by the Table of Contents, the index, or even in a quick search directory in a book. The index does not force any order onto the book, however. It simply refers to the location of the target information, without reordering it. Non-clustered indexes can be used in conjunction with clustered indexes or other non-clustered indexes in a compound index. Non-clustered indexes are also best for queries returning single or few rows.

Non-clustered indexes also begin from the sysindex. The sysindex identifies a root for the table being queried. The root in turn identifies an intermediate level, which refers to either additional intermediate levels or the final Leaf. The Leaf has a collection of rows that identify the row where the data is stored in the table.

Since non-clustered indexes are separate from their target field and table, they can be segregated onto a separate drive. This will allow for more efficient queries, since the disk activity against the index will be independent from that of the target table.

> Both clustered and non-clustered indexes produce overhead for **INSERT** and **UPDATE** queries, since an index entry must be created with the new data.

This is important to note, since this is the reason that most common advice is a bit ambiguous on the value of indexes. In data warehouses, we are selecting considerably more often than we are writing data. In some instances, we will never write data to a database. Thus, with data warehouses, this consideration is significantly less important.

In data warehouses, you must index your dimension tables with a clustered index across the primary key. You must do the same for each of your fact tables as well, to include a non-clustered index across the column that serves as the foreign key. In most situations, foreign keys are important targets for indexing. Slow entry into a dimension a couple of steps removed from the fact table will slow down the remainder of the query.

Any column in your database that is frequently referenced by a WHERE clause should be indexed, with only a couple of exceptions. An example of one such exception is a male/female column, in which there are only two possible entries. Similarly, if a field references a foreign key that only has a small number of keys, such as a large geographic region identifier, this will not benefit from an index.

When creating a new index, you will want to employ a high fill factor in data warehouses. The fill factor is primarily a tradeoff between disk space management and updatability. In a low transactional database, such as a data warehouse, high fill factors will save you valuable disk space and improve performance. Frequent monitoring of statistics will assist you in making this decision.

If, for some reason, you have to run UPDATE and DELETE clauses against your indexed data tables, do so en masse. This way, SQL Server will not continually redefine the index after incremental changes to the database.

Also, after updating any indexes, ensure that you recompile any stored procedures associated with the table. Stored procedures will need to calculate a new query execution plan based on the revised index. If you do not recompile your stored procedure, you will be forfeiting two great performance enhancements.

Index Tuning Wizard

The good news with SQL Server 2000 is that Microsoft has produced a really strong Index Tuning Wizard that lessens the importance of knowing everything about indexes.

Before you can run the Index Tuning Wizard, you first must develop a trace in SQL Server Profiler as we have described earlier. This trace will provide the basis for SQL Server's decisions, so should be a relatively representative trace. With trace in hand, we can begin the process.

From SQL Server Profiler, open Tools | Index Tuning Wizard. A friendly opening page provides a basic introduction to the process. Press Next.

The next screen (assuming you are logged into SQL Server, otherwise you will have to log in) displayed allows us to select our database and provides us our first choices. For data warehouses, we will typically want to keep both Add indexed views and Keep all existing indexes checked. If you are fairly confident that your Profile has captured all scenarios your database will experience, then you may benefit by removing the Keep all existing indexes option, since unused indexes can become an encumbrance in certain circumstances. Move the Tuning mode to Thorough and press Next.

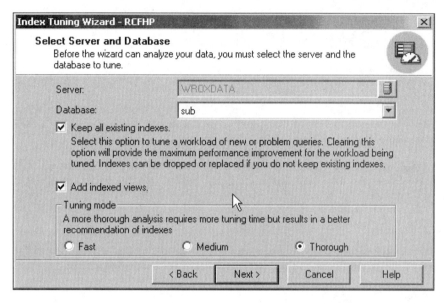

The next screen prompts you for the workload SQL Server will use to derive its indexing decisions.

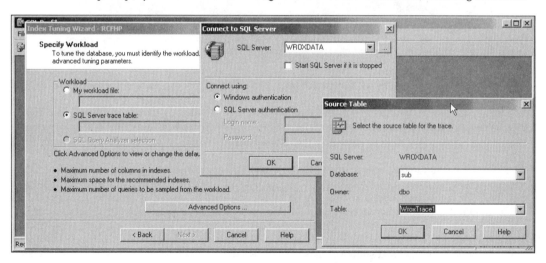

To open our trace that we ran earlier, we select SQL Server trace table. This brings up the ubiquitous Connect to SQL Server dialog from which we select our server. From the next dialog box we select our trace table. The advanced options of the Specify Workload step offers us an opportunity to conform this wizard towards the needs of a data warehouse.

```
Index tuning parameters:
  ☑ Limit number of workload queries          200
     to sample:

  Maximum space for the recommended            20
  indexes (MB):

  Maximum columns per index:               16 ↕
```

First, you may want to remove the default query limitation. This will allow a greater sampling of the test workload. If you have a solid profile that you are confident is representative of standard usage, you will want to improve the indexing across the complete profile. This will, however, take longer to calculate. The second setting you will probably need to change is the **Maximum space for the recommended indexes (MB)**. The default setting of 1 is quite low, and does not take into account the size of a data warehouse database. Bump this up to above what you expect for an index size.

The next screen offers us the various tables that we can tune. Although the screen advice is to take it easy on these choices, for data warehouses, the more appropriate advice is to run the wizard for all of the heavily used tables. The screen advice pertains to databases that experience far more writing activity than a data warehouse would. If this is a considerable task, you may want to do this in multiple steps, and for each of these iterations, select a handful of tables.

Pressing **Next** launches the wizard, and provides a "waiting" dialog box as SQL Server 2000 crunches through your data. When finished, it will produce a list of recommended indexes, or will state that there are no recommended changes. The recommendation also specifies whether the recommended index is clustered or not.

Clustered	Index Name	Table/View Name	Column Na...
☑	[PK_SortOrd]	[dbo].[SortOrd]	[SortID] ASC

Recommended indexes:

The **Analysis** button will provide more detailed information about the tables and columns that have been identified as candidates for improvement.

The final page allows you to execute the recommendations. If you have a few clustered indexes applied over very large tables, you may want to schedule the update instead of running it during business hours. Remember, clustered indexes reorder the data, and that could take some time on a large table.

The wizard does not make recommendations for system tables, primary keys, columns with unique indexes already in place, and inter-database queries between multiple databases. The last is the biggest drawback for data warehouses, which thrive on inter-database queries. You can, to some extent, simulate the load on target databases, and run a profiler from there to at least gain some benefit from tuning.

Run this wizard on a regular basis. Indexes are vital to a data warehouse's performance, since most of the activity is data selection. There are times to remove an index, although this occurs far less frequently in a data warehouse. Candidates for index removal are fields that seldom if ever appear in WHERE clauses, and which reside in tables with frequent writing activity. Indexes consume hard drive space, and slow down writing activity.

Analysis Services Tuning

Attention to Analysis Services tuning is second in importance only to indexes, and like indexes, substantive discussion on the subject would consume an entire book. For most situations, SQL Server 2000's Analysis Services will be the most common interaction your server will experience. Throughout this chapter, we have introduced Analysis Services specific advice with a few exceptions. What we will cover here are those tuning steps that relate solely to Analysis Service.

The good news, once again, is that in SQL Server 2000, Microsoft has done an outstanding job of dynamically tuning the service so that you do not have to. However, there are still some choices to make, and pitfalls to consume you.

Your attention in Analysis Services tuning should focus first on storage mode selection, then on aggregation, and next on indexes. After these big players are addressed, be sure to inspect the relational databases that populate the cubes, and ensure that the cubes are not too sparse. The other issues will contribute to improving performance, but pale in comparison to the three primary considerations.

Storage Mode Selection

As discussed in Chapter 2, there are three possible storage modes available: ROLAP, HOLAP, and MOLAP. You should carefully consider you selection of storage mode.

> **Your selection hierarchy should be MOLAP, HOLAP, and finally ROLAP.**

Go with MOLAP

The most preferred storage mode is MOLAP. The multi-dimensional structure of MOLAP, along with the data's physical co-location with the Analysis Services, typically makes it the fastest of the three. MOLAP's compression may actually speed up queries in some instances, since it lessens the impact of disk input/output costs. Compression's expense is felt in writing, which is performed rarely in Analysis Services. An additional benefit of MOLAP is that the cubes may be detached from the SQL tables, allowing offline processing in some scenarios.

HOLAP Sometimes

HOLAP, the hybrid cross between MOLAP and ROLAP, is best when the data is simply too large to be stored on the same server as the Analysis Services. HOLAP can take advantage of MOLAP's pre-aggregations stored in a multi-dimensional file, and preserve the size capacity of the RDBMS. HOLAP does posses unpredictable performance for different queries, however, since it must query the RDBMS under certain circumstances, yet can operate without the data in other situations.

ROLAP Only When You Must

ROLAP does not have a high-speed data access mechanism, and creates additional tables to manage pre-aggregations. ROLAP also does not exploit multi-dimensional files, and relies on the RDBMS for its data. ROLAP is useful when the data is simply too large for HOLAP to handle, or when real-time processing is vital.

Aggregation

Aggregation selection is an art within itself, but there are some generic observations that will land you at least reasonably close to the correct answer. First of all, 100% and 0% aggregation are seldom, if ever, the correct choice. There is a "sweet spot" for aggregation that lies somewhere between 30% and 60%. Making an initial guess on the small side of this range is a good starting point. As aggregations reach towards 90% they begin consuming considerable space and cube processing resources.

Query usage over time will be your best indicator for modifying aggregation. You will want to nudge it up until you have maximized performance. The process will most likely take awhile, as both usage patterns and data settle into a steady-state.

MDX vs. SQL Queries

MDX will almost always outperform SQL Queries. The boost can be quite significant at times. MDX pre-calculates and stores aggregations in the cube, which gives it a head start when analyzing data. As covered in Chapter 10, MDX offers a powerful means with which to analyze your data, and has been tuned by Microsoft.

Other Considerations

Here are further considerations:

Usage Analysis Wizard

The Usage Analysis Wizard can help you refine your storage mode selection and aggregation choices, although the former rarely requires attention. This wizard should be used in conjunction with the Usage-Based Optimization Wizard. To start the wizard, right-click on your cube and select Usage Analysis. Select Query Run Time Table from the list of report types, and press Next. If you need to exclude dates due to non-standard events, do so in the screen that follows. Selecting Next generates a report. Press Finish.

Right-click on your target cube, and select Usage-Based Optimization. After leaving the welcome screen, set a range in the criteria screen. The range will depend entirely on how long you have employed the current cube. Click Next on the Review Results screen and in the following screen select Replace the existing aggregations. Select your storage option and click Next. On the following screen you can set your aggregation options. Modifying the performance gain percentage will reveal the best-balanced aggregation strategy considering the queries that SQL Server is analyzing.

Inspect your Stars, Snowflakes, and Dimensions

Your data will start at some point from a star or snowflake design. These should be inspected prior to building a cube. Ensure that the leaf level of a dimension has unique key values. While on the subject of dimensions, take into consideration that virtual dimensions can prevent multiplicative growth of your cube. When a dimension comes from the same dimension table as a dimension already existing, the new dimension can "ride" off of the first as a virtual dimension. If you need to aggregate this new dimension, then it will not benefit from this arrangement.

Calculated Measures and Distinct Count

If you must go to HOLAP or ROLAP, calculated measures may be important. Defined in the cube, calculated measures are stored in the target table of a ROLAP implementation, and in a compressed format in HOLAP. Right-clicking the Calculated Members folder of the cube tree creates calculated measures. Build the value expression in the dialog pane and press OK. The calculated measure will then be accessible from the data pane of the cube editor. One note on calculated measures is that distinct counts may yield better performance in some circumstances. This may be true even though MDX experiences some degradation with distinct count. When there are multiple calculated members, setting the correct solve order will improve performance and accuracy.

Partitions

Partitions are valuable for particularly large cubes, but their complexity and overhead may be a liability for most implementations. Partitions may also impart an artificial limit to data design and queries. If you need to employ partitions, research the subject at length from Microsoft's online documentation at http://www.microsoft.com/TechNet/.

Linked Cubes

Analysis Services can run across multiple servers employing linked cubes. While this may appear to be an interesting strategy, the processing complexity and difficulty in implementing lessen its effectiveness. A better alternative to linked cubes is to use additional processors.

Cache

A cold cache, namely running without data in the cache, least affects MOLAP. Since data analysis typically occurs in finite, distinct requests, it can seldom exploit cache anyway. ROLAP and HOLAP can better exploit warm caches, but their overall performance still lags behind MOLAP even with heavy caching.

Query Enhancement

For the analysis not run through OLAP, query refinement will be an important contribution to your system's overall performance. Improving your system's queries should be a continual process, in which slow queries identified by SQL Server Query Analyzer are revised and improved. Some of the following suggestions will have negligible impact on your query's performance in development, but nonetheless may offer measurable improvement to your system in production under certain circumstances.

Our goal in query enhancement will be to reduce the amount of data we are transmitting, reduce the amount of effort SQL Server will have to exert to get that data, and reduce the amount of time it takes to transmit the data.

Stored Procedures

One of the better enhancements you can make is with stored procedures, since the query plan is compiled rather than interpreted. This results in less effort on the part of the server. Additionally, the powerful ability to massage data inside of a stored procedure can prevent the need to transmit excessive data over the network. You can "crunch" the numbers on the machine, and send out a smaller set of results as a consequence.

The place where stored procedures may offer the greatest advantage, in both performance and return on developer time, is in the repetitive one-time queries that are run daily. These queries cannot take advantage of ad hoc caching, which we will discuss shortly, but are frequently executed and are thus worthy of extra attention. Admittedly, we find these less frequently in the data warehouse world, but they do exist.

One word of caution, for those developers from the "old school" SQL Server 6.5 era; temporary stored procedures are no longer beneficial, and indeed, negate the value of stored procedures.

Your SELECT Statement

SELECT statements are the most common interaction with data warehouses, even when OLAP is the analysis method of choice for your system. The goal of your SELECT statement is to pull as little data as you possibly can. Be as descriptive as you can, and carefully select your fields.

Use wildcards only when necessary. Instead of SELECT *, list out the fields you need. There are two advantages to this practice. The first is that SELECT * requires SQL Server 2000 to perform an extra step to determine what fields are available in the target table. The second is that when a developer spells out the fields of a table, invariably several unnecessary fields can be ferreted out.

The other wildcard to watch for is the % and other LIKE operator wildcards. Often, developers employ these wildcards indiscriminately. Avoid them if possible, but if you must use one, try not to use it at the beginning of the string. Using a wildcard at the start of a string negates the use of an index for that column, a very costly mistake in a data warehouse.

Be sure to use TOP x and DISTINCT to further limit the results returned. With TOP x, you may also need to use an ORDER BY clause.

When making comparisons in your WHERE clause, you want to reduce "non-sargable" comparisons, or comparisons which cannot limit a search. A non-sargable expression compromises the effectiveness of an index. Measures of inequality are perhaps the most common culprits. For example, when you use a non-sargable expression such as NOT, <>, !> or !< , SQL Server 2000 may have to execute a table scan instead of an index scan. Using OR in a WHERE clause can lead to the same effect as well. Additionally, using WHERE EXISTS instead of WHERE IN can provide a significant performance boost. The Index Tuning Wizard can assist you in fixing these types of comparisons, and the Query Analyzer will usually reveal these with a "Table Scan" as the first operation.

Do not ask SQL Server to SORT unless it is necessary. Sort operations, especially on non-clustered indexed fields, are costly events. If a field is sorted every time it is queried, then a clustered index should be applied to that field.

Joins and Unions

When you have multipart primary keys on a table that is heavily joined with other tables, consider creating a surrogate key for each record, thereby allowing a single field for the joins. SQL Server 2000 can resolve the relationship to a single field substantially faster than with two. For example, let us assume in a cross-reference table you are using a composite key created by two foreign keys, such as year and model. Creating an additional, unique key and using that as the index will be easier for SQL Server 2000 to handle in queries, at the cost of an additional operation on insertion.

If you have to perform a large JOIN, place each of the components of the JOIN into a view, and JOIN the views. In addition to providing a compiled execution plan, as mentioned earlier you may be able to exploit some ad hoc caching with artful use of views.

When you know your queries will employ joins, employ the most native data types possible for the foreign keys. As discussed at the beginning of this chapter, a foreign key will particularly benefit from being an integer, since SQL Server has an easier time working with numbers versus text.

Hints

Hints can assist SQL Server 2000 in its decision making process. They come in three flavors, Table, Join, and Query. Table hints primarily involve locking behavior, which is not as important with data warehouses. Table hints do include an INDEX hint, which can force indexed scans. The JOIN hints have four types: LOOP, HASH, MERGE, and REMOTE. The REMOTE hint is useful when joining between two separate SQL Servers, and can dictate on which server to perform the join. By dictating the server with the larger dataset, you can send the smaller one over the wire to minimize the impact of network latency as well as network interface bottlenecks. The Query hints include ten different hints and involve GROUPs and UNIONs as well as dictating the query plan.

Ad Hoc Caching

When you run a query, SQL Server 2000 aggressively stores data as well as schema information pertaining to that event in buffer cache. For SQL Server to take full advantage of the cache, a new query must match that in cache. While this may seem to be an unlikely scenario, it actually may occur more often than you think. One way to take advantage of this is with views, which can select a similar subset of data for multiple processes. Thus, if you intend to "work a table", you may want to encapsulate a subset of data in a view, to take advantage of ad hoc caching.

Schedule Events at Usage Trough

When running scheduled procedures, remove any conflict with other processes on your network. Since, in a data warehouse, some of your scheduled procedures may involve multiple servers and communication over the network, your procedures may experience latency even when no users are on the system. A good example of this is scheduled events at midnight. In larger enterprises, there typically are quite a few events that are scheduled at that time. Schedule the procedures to execute at odd, prime minutes, such as 2:13 or 4:07, since you are less likely to hit scheduled processes from the OS or software connected to your data warehouse.

Keep the Application Servers Honest

If your data warehouse is connected to application servers, or if a second tier performs your analytical processing, monitor their activity. Poor coding on them will negatively impact on your servers. For example, if they are executing sloppy queries and pulling unnecessary data across the network, that will negatively impact on your data warehouse. Make sure they are exploiting stored procedures to limit the size of their requests, and to facilitate greater control over their requests. You may be able to exploit caching on the second tier for some queries, which would benefit both technologies. Likewise, share data validation responsibilities with the second tier and the client side. Preventing faulty queries from executing saves everyone some pain. Remember, you want to receive as little and send as little as you possibly can.

Triggers

Inspect your triggers. The first thing you will want to know is if they are doing something "stupid". Perhaps a trigger originally used to assist developers prior to production is still operating. You may be executing some repetitive task that serves no purpose in production and slows activity down. Most triggers are connected to INSERT and UPDATE queries, so in data warehousing, these triggers may not be too difficult to inspect. While you are inspecting, make sure the triggers are not nested unless absolutely required. At the very least, if a trigger is not reused in more than a couple of situations, there is no reason to nest it. The corollary to this thought is also to inspect the level of nesting. SQL Server allows 32 levels of nesting, but performance suffers after just the first level. In such scenarios, investigate the possibility of accidental trigger recursion, wherein a trigger is called by one of its own nested triggers. This can get ugly when a trigger is updated.

SQL Server/OS Tuning

Although this is a chapter on performance tuning data warehouses, it would be remiss not to introduce some of the important environmental settings in both SQL Server 2000 and Windows 2000. The great news is that unlike a Linux box, or even older versions of SQL Server, Microsoft has done a fairly good job with its default settings. SQL Server 2000 comes out of the box ready for war and only needs a few tweaks to improve it.

Windows 2000

Before hitting SQL Server 2000, the first improvement to make to your server is a careful assessment of services currently running on the server. Right-click on My Computer and select Manage. Next, expand Services and Applications and select Services. Often you can find a slew of unnecessary services in there chewing up resources on your server. For running a data warehouse, you want as few services as possible. Coordinate with your network administrator or whoever is responsible for setting your servers up to safely strip as many of these out as you are allowed to.

While there you will want to tune Windows 2000 Server to make a friendlier environment.

❑   First, optimize Windows 2000 throughput, by selecting Start | Settings | Network and Dial-up Conections. Right click on Local Area Connections, select Properties and then click on Properties of File and Printer Sharing. From the Server Optimization tab choose Maximize data throughput for network applications.

❑   Disable the performance boost for foreground applications. To do this, select the Control Panel | System | Advanced tab, and choose the Performance Options button. Change the default setting of Application Response from Applications to Background Services.

❑   When possible, select a different drive for virtual memory from the one holding your OS and SQL Server. As we will introduce in the hardware discussion later, a good solution is to add a drive independent of the primary RAID array for this and other tasks. To make the change, go to Control Panel | System and select the Performance Options button under the Advanced tab. Under the Virtual Memory option, select Change and make the adjustment.

❑   Increase the receive buffers of the Network Interface Card. Open the Computer Management MMC and select Device Manager. Select your Network Card, and the Advanced tab. Select the property: Receive Buffers and set the value to 1024 or the highest value available. This is more important for the OLAP server which may receive more packets from the RDBMS servers.

SQL Server 2000 Settings

While SQL Server 2000 comes with a much better default setup, as alluded to in this chapter's introduction, it still must accommodate a wide variety of implementations out of the box. We, of course, only want a data warehouse for our SQL Servers. There are a few tweaks we can make. Before doing so, however, ensure you have a solid understanding of your usage patterns for each database. Most servers in your organization will have distinct requirements. Keep these in mind as you make your changes.

The first changes we will look at are from the properties dialog box of SQL Server. From Enterprise Manager, right-click on the server instance and select Properties.

We will take a look at two of these tabs:

❏ **Memory** tab. At the bottom, the default setting for **Minimum memory for query** is fairly low at 1024. Advance this to a higher number [up to 2Gb] within the limits of your non-committed RAM (see your System Monitor). This is important with large sorts and hashes. The **Max Server Memory** option default is max, which is good (2147483647). In Data warehousing, it is rare that a SQL Server box is not dedicated.

❏ **Database Settings** tab. The **Recovery Interval** default is 1 minute. This is good for the development environment, but should be moved to 8-16 minutes in production. The impact is that your server will be delayed during recovery for that amount of time. The advantage is that SQL Server 2000 will have to perform its integrity checks less often.

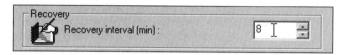

The following settings are available only with stored procedures. The syntax for the stored procedure is:

```
EXEC sp_configure 'min memory per query (KB)',512000
```

As you may have noticed with the example, the settings we made in the **Properties** dialog are also available with the `sp_configure` stored procedure. Before we can access the advanced options, we have to run the following procedure:

```
EXEC sp_configure 'show advanced options', 1
GO
RECONFIGURE WITH OVERRIDE
GO
```

Be careful what you reconfigure, because some of the settings are in their optimal state by default. To see all of the settings available for modification, you can run the following in SQL Query Analyzer:

```
SELECT value, config, comment, status FROM master.dbo.sysconfigures
```

Configurations you will want to investigate include:

❏ Set `'Priority boost'` to 1 on dedicated server. Most, if not all of your data warehouse servers should have this setting.

❏ Tune your `'Network packet size'`. The default is 4096. Depending on the average network packet, you may want to open this up. If you are transmitting multiple packets for every request, and seldom transmit single packets, this will indicate a need to expand the packet size. Do not get too aggressive with this, however, since you can compromise your data transmission if the packets are too large. Use 1024 byte increments.

❏ When using more than 4Gb of memory, set `'AWE enabled in the server'` to 1. This allows SQL Server 2000 to use Windows 2000 Address Windowing Extensions (AWE), to support very large address spaces. There are a few circumstances wherein you will not want to set this when you have 4Gb or more of memory, but typically, in a data warehouse environment, this setting should be made.

Hard Drive Management

Hard drives can easily become the critical bottleneck of your system if not properly managed. There are quite a few strategies to more effectively manage disk input/output. We will shortly investigate RAID and physical hard drive issues in the *Hardware and Environment* section that follows.

Segregate your database across hard drives. Your RAID should do this if you are using RAID 0 or RAID 10. If you are not, then you will have to do this manually. The concept is to allow multiple points of entry to your data with different hardware, so that the system does not have to wait on a single hard drive for its requests, and can access data in parallel. Store any non-clustered indexes on separate hard drives for the same reason.

Additional candidates for segregation are `tempdb` and log files (as mentioned earlier). `tempdb` is used by SQL Server for aggregation in `GROUP BY`, `ORDER BY` and `DISTINCT` operations, whenever a temp table is used in queries or stored procedures, and in cursors and Hash joins. As its name suggests, `tempdb` is not permanent.

Hard drive Nirvana is when SQL Server simultaneously accesses four different hard drives at the perfect harmonious frequency, faster than the CPU can queue up the next request for data.

Binary Sort Order

Binary Sort Order definitely provides a performance advantage. Unfortunately, it can only be set upon installation. If you can enforce case sensitivity adherence in your databases, and most of your sorting is date or ID based, this is an important setting to choose for future installations. Ensure all developers are aware of this decision, so they can likewise enforce conformity. There are functions you can create to massage your data into case conformance, although this may be a dangerous practice if not carefully investigated.

Hardware and Environment

Balance is very important for hardware, even more so than for software. Hardware is indentured to its slowest or worst performing component. To make matters more complicated, decisions in hardware must be balanced against cost effectiveness. In data warehousing, where decisions span multiple servers, the decisions are even more difficult.

Solutions will vary for many of the SQL Servers in your data warehouse. Each type of implementation has varying degrees of requirements. Your OLAP boxes, for example, will have different processor and RAM requirements from your pure storage servers. The decisions on hardware setups should be derived from the usage patterns you discerned earlier.

The ultimate setup has all components working in concert quickly delivering requests. The CPU does not wait for hard drive information, the RAM does not wait for the network card to clear, and the internal bus delivers content to a component at the precise moment when that component has released its last request. This balance also has to arrive at a cost proportional to the other investments into the whole system. Of course, this balance is only achieved in the dreams of IT personnel who have just approved the $50,000 purchase of servers. The reality is that one component will always be a system bottleneck for an event, upon which all the other components wait.

As introduced earlier, System Monitor and SQL Profiler will help identify these bottlenecks. Do note that the bottlenecks are typically associated with events, and are not necessarily the same bottlenecks for every event in a system. The same SQL Server box may experience a disk I/O bottleneck for one query and a CPU bottleneck for another. Be sure to run SQL Profiler to identify the biggest culprits. If you rely on System Monitor alone, and run a handful of queries, you may not uncover the bottleneck deserving the most attention.

So, in no particular order (because, remember, we want balance!), here is a breakdown of hardware considerations.

Hard Drives

Even though I said there are no absolutes, there are some absolutes in hard drives. The first is that your hard drives must be high quality and with a SCSI, Fiber Channel, or similar fast interface. Additionally, they should be fast, spinning at either 10k or 15k rpm. A slow hard drive can absolutely grind SQL Server to a snail's pace. These higher-end models also offer an important reliability advantage, which will save you many a headache.

The other absolute is RAID, or Redundant Array of Independent Drives (used to be Inexpensive Drives, but the RAID convention has since changed its mind on this). RAID can offer important data redundancy to guard against hard drive failure, and may improve disk access performance. While RAID comes in many different configurations, we will simplify the decision by narrowing the choices down to three for data warehousing: RAID 0, RAID 1 and RAID 10.

Before diving into the specifics of each type of RAID, a bit of universal advice should be provided. First, avoid the temptation of software "RAID", such as Windows 2000 Mirroring. This particular solution can "cost" up to 50% extra I/O activity, and indeed increase the probability of failure, even though it was intended to do quite the opposite. Hardware RAID controllers are the only choice for data warehousing. In addition to superior I/O management, independent of the CPU, they offer some extras that are particularly important to SQL Server. The most important of these extras is an onboard caching mechanism, which can optimize the input/output interaction. This particular feature takes best advantage of careful data typing, in which data is already manipulated in efficient packets with minimal padding.

RAID 0

RAID 0 is only for development servers or bench testing servers, where fault tolerance is not important, but performance is. **Do not use RAID 0 in production**. RAID 0, also known as striping, spreads data across multiple drives in the array, allowing multiple points of entry for data. Allegorically, it is similar to taking three of the platters off of a drive and spreading them to three other drives, so that all four drives can be employed during a disk interaction. The solution is relatively low cost, without requiring redundant hard drives. The one area in production where RAID 0 may be appropriate is for the temporary file folder of Analysis Services, which would greatly benefit from the added performance, but does not require a high degree of fault tolerance.

RAID 1

RAID 1 is known as mirroring, and provides the highest level of fault tolerance. Essentially, RAID 1 "mirrors" or replicates all of the data onto a redundant hard drive. This solution is not cheap, since it requires twice as many hard drives to store the same amount of data. When you compare the cost to the consequences of inadequate fault tolerance, RAID 1 is a bargain. A failed hard drive can bring your entire server down for hours, and in some cases days. With RAID 1, when a hard drive fails, you can hot swap it with only marginal degradation of performance, and without shutting the system down. RAID 1 can be used in production, but does not offer the performance of its bigger brother, RAID 10.

RAID 10

RAID 10, or RAID 1+0 (or RAID 1/0, it has many names), is also known as mirroring and striping, and offers the best combination of fault tolerance and high performance. As the name suggests, RAID 10 is a hybrid of RAID 1 with its mirroring and RAID 0 with its striping. Similar to RAID 1, RAID 10 is relatively expensive, since it requires two disks for one disk worth of storage. When coupled to a competent RAID controller, however, RAID 10 offers a significant performance advantage, especially when the controller has a solid onboard caching. Ensure that the RAID controller has both read and write caching.

RAID 10 is a must for production servers.

The following diagram provides a simplified view of how RAID 10 behaves logically and virtually.

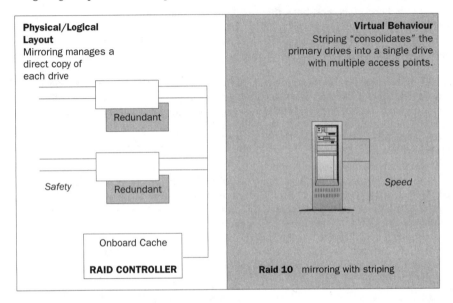

There is one alternative to the three RAID formats discussed above, and that is RAID 5. RAID 5 offers a compromise between the fault tolerance of RAID 10 and the cost to implement that solution. RAID 5 maintains a backup of parity, and only uses a single redundant drive in an array. In an array of four drives, therefore, RAID 5 will provide you with 3 disks of space, whereas RAID 10 would provide you 2 disks of space for the same investment. RAID 5, however, does not offer the fault tolerance of RAID 10.

Other Hard Drive Issues

There are some hard drives that you may not need to maintain in your RAID array. For example, it is a good strategy to segregate log files from your SQL Server drives. This includes log files from other software on your server, such as Windows 2000. You can similarly employ this drive for your SQL Profiler and other system operations that you establish.

Large hard drives are not necessarily good. The more interaction you have with your hard drives, the smaller you will want them to be. Smaller drives can take greater advantage of striping and similar parallel strategies. Of course, smaller drives are also more expensive per unit of storage. For a database in your warehouse that is mostly archival in nature, with limited analysis running against it, you would select slightly larger hard drives, since the performance is not such an issue. For the databases that form the backbone of your data warehouse, you would want to select smaller hard drives, such as 18Gb drives. Considerations for rotational speed should follow similar logic.

CPUs

While it may seem logical that hard drives are a major bottleneck, many people fail to realize the importance of the CPU. Databases love to consume CPU resources. Performance monitoring will bear this out. SQL Server 2000 and Windows 2000 both have improved their ability to exploit multiple processors; systems used for data warehousing should support multiple processors, if not starting with them by default. For most situations, begin with a quad-capable motherboard supporting two CPUs. There are diminishing returns with multiple processors, and these are especially conspicuous beyond four processors. Additionally, Analysis servers hosting HOLAP or ROLAP will benefit less from multiple processors than the RDBMS servers or MOLAP storage solutions will.

There are other factors that complicate processor selection. Perhaps the most important is licensing. Most of Microsoft's SQL Server 2000 licenses are per processor, meaning that instead of $1000 for an additional processor, you could be paying several thousand dollars. To compound matters, server companies typically charge a significant premium for their processors, which cleverly have unusual form factors, stepping or voltage to make alternatives difficult to select. While writing this, a quick survey of three prominent server manufacturers revealed as much as a 3-fold mark up for their proprietary processors.

While this should not dissuade consideration of adding processors, it definitely complicates the decision. These circumstances actually may justify purchasing a high-end processor for the server. Normally, the highest clocking processors charge a disproportional premium for the performance gain (which is never one for one with clock speed anyway), but because your licensing is independent of this benchmark, the cost is diminished versus the alternative.

CPU queue is the standard determinant for replacing a CPU. As mentioned earlier, when the queue consistently reaches twice the number of processors that you have (so when the queue is 4 on a 2 processor system), then it is time to upgrade. Low queue numbers (1 or 2) are not bad, however, and indicate that your system is probably relatively balanced.

RAM

RAM has become a cheap and easy investment for performance enhancement. When purchasing a new server, ensure that the box will accommodate a good amount of growth. While there is no upper limit for how much RAM you can use, apart from server hardware limitations, there certainly is a lower limit. Even though Microsoft claims 64 Mb is the minimum requirement, realistically you should start at around 512 Mb, and quickly target more. At 256 Mb and less of RAM, there is a real exponential slowdown of data warehouses on SQL Server 2000. Data warehouses may not benefit from additional RAM as much as transactional databases, since queries are more infrequent, and caching occurs less often. The Analysis Services servers, however, do consume RAM.

If you perform large table aggregations, such as summing revenue numbers for thousands of records, RAM can assist the CPU by maintaining the data in cache as it performs its task. Enhancements such as the `table` data type also benefit from RAM. By reducing disk I/O, RAM preserves your investment in hard drives as an added advantage.

Network Interface Cards

Network Interface Cards (NICs) are often overlooked, but are relatively important in data warehouses that share information between boxes quite fluidly. The advice is simple here, though. Do not go cheap with network cards. They already are inexpensive, and the cost for the highest quality cards pales in comparison to the cost of the server and its components. Ensure the NIC you choose has quality fault tolerance. Most servers from the large companies ship with very good network cards. On an annual basis, audit your card drivers to ensure you have the latest from the manufacturer. These are periodically updated, and some of the updates can improve performance.

Summary

Performance enhancement is an artform. Even servers within a server cluster will have distinct enhancements unique to that server's requirements. Enhancements that benefit one implementation may handicap another.

Since the answer "it depends" is frustrating to hear, here is an over simplified priority list of enhancements:

- ❑   Index your data warehouse tables
- ❑   Select an intelligent analysis storage strategy, preferably MOLAP
- ❑   Select a considered aggregation level for your Analysis Services
- ❑   Buy high quality hard drives and RAID controllers
- ❑   Extract only what you need
- ❑   Trim out excess, in SQL, data types, and your server

The process is continuous, and as soon as you have completed enhancing all of your servers, you will most likely have to start again with the first one. It will become a regular part of your scheduled routine. Consequently, document the behavior of your server farm continually, building a repertoire of information to help guide future decisions and resolve problems as they arise.

When discouraged, remember the old Zen master's advice of persistence:

"Seven times knocked down. Eight times get up"

Data Warehouse

21

Maintaining the Data Warehouse

Your job as a data warehouse professional does not end with creating and populating the data warehouse. The data warehouse must be maintained and taken care of on a daily basis if it is to continue to receive new data and continue to perform to users' expectations. It will probably take a few months after you roll out your data warehouse to get it to a stable state where regular maintenance and administration is needed. This chapter addresses the following points:

- ❏ Developing backup and recovery strategies for the data warehouse
- ❏ Automating the data warehouse administration tasks (SQL Agent)
- ❏ Responding to events
- ❏ Creating a maintenance plan
- ❏ Archiving and restoring Analysis databases

Let's begin this chapter by taking a look at backup and recovery.

Backup and Recovery

One of the most important maintenance operations of the data warehouse is backup and recovery. No matter how well you design your data warehouse, it is almost certain that at some stage throughout its lifecycle it will be necessary to restore the database from a backup. By designing a rock-solid backup strategy for your data warehouse, you can be confident that this will be possible when needed.

Data warehouses are characteristically large. A SQL Server 2000 database can theoretically be as large as 1,048,516 terabytes (TB) (there is no way we can verify this Microsoft claim at this time, although multi terabyte databases are becoming increasingly common). Given that a terabyte is 1,099,511,627,776 bytes, you can imagine how big such storage is. If a data warehouse database is 1 TB in size it might take days, if not weeks, to reconstruct and repopulate it – assuming, of course, that the operational data that fed the original data warehouse is still available in some way, shape, or form.

With an available backup of the data warehouse, recovery is much faster. It can be reduced to a matter of hours instead of days or weeks, depending on the hardware used for backup and the size of the database. In addition, an organization cannot afford to keep a data warehouse down for an extended period, especially if many decisions are made based on its data. A good backup strategy will balance the amount of downtime users experience with costs that are acceptable to implement such a process.

Before you decide on the appropriate backup strategy, you should be aware of the issues that will influence the procedures you decide to use. These issues include:

❑ How critical is the database? If it is a test database or can be easily recreated from source data there is probably little point spending a lot of time developing a complex backup strategy. If the database is considered mission critical to your organization, you need to plan the backup strategy accordingly.

❑ How frequently is the data within the database modified? For example, if your data is only modified by nightly batch operations then there is little reason to perform backups every 15 minutes during the day. By understanding how the data is modified you will minimize the resources consumed by unnecessary backup operations.

❑ How much data loss is acceptable? When first asked this question, most organizations reply that no data loss is acceptable. However, when presented with the actual cost of a backup strategy that will deliver zero data loss, most organizations rethink their decision and come up with 'real' acceptable data loss requirements. You should ensure that the backup strategy you implement will not lose more data than that which is acceptable.

❑ When can backups be created? While online backups in SQL Server have a low system impact, understanding the time and duration of periods of low system activity will assist in planning a backup strategy that will not inadvertently cause unacceptable performance degradation to users of the data warehouse.

❑ If failure occurs, how long can the data warehouse be down? Your backup strategy should allow the data warehouse to be recovered within a period of down time that is acceptable to your organization. The backup strategy focuses only on the time it takes to backup and restore the database, not issues that may affect the underlying platform such as repairing faulty hardware, or drying out the servers after a flood has occurred. However these are important issues and should be considered in detail when developing a disaster recovery plan for an organization.

A data warehouse is not a static system, the amount of data and utilization of the warehouse constantly changes over time. Therefore, it is important that you regularly review your backup strategy to determine if all the objectives are being met. This should involve review of the business requirements and also review the ability of the backup strategy to successful meet these requirements – in other words don't wait until a failure happens to discover that your backup strategy is inadequate.

SQL Server Database Backup

Before you can restore a SQL Server database, you must first explicitly back it up. Backup of the physical disk files in which a database resides is not recommended, because restoration may not be possible from these files. Instead, you should backup your database from within SQL Server or by using a third-party backup utility that has a SQL Server-specific agent.

You have three decisions to make when planning to implement SQL Server backups:

❑   Which backup method are you going to use? The backup method determines the operations you will need to perform as part of you strategy.

❑   What recovery model are you going to use? A recovery model affects the way in which database transactions are logged and what level of recoverability is available.

❑   What media will you use to store your database backup?

We will look at the first two of these considerations now, and will have a brief look at backup media later in this chapter.

Choosing the Backup Method

SQL Server has a number of methods of performing database backups. Each method has its advantages and disadvantages that you should be aware of when designing your database backup strategy.

Full database Backups

A full database backup takes a complete copy of a database. A full database backup is the most common and mostly easily managed form of backup.

For all but the smallest of databases it is not practical to take full database backups constantly during periods of high usage due to the performance impact. Usually full database backups are scheduled for periods of low usage when a suitable window is available, such as on a nightly or weekly basis. As a week's, or even a day's, worth of data can be a large amount of information for an organization to lose, a full backup is often companioned with more frequent, less impacting backup methods such as transaction log and differential backups.

Transaction Log Backups

A backup of the database transaction log is usually conducted on a much more regular basis than a full database backup. The transaction log is a serial record of changes made to the database and which transactions caused these changes. Using the transaction log SQL Server can roll forward committed transactions or roll back uncommitted transactions for recovery purposes. Transaction log backups may be taken every few minutes for a highly active database, or maybe made only a couple of times a day for low activity databases.

Increasing the frequency of the transaction log backup does not significantly increase the amount of disk space that the transaction log backups will require as only the transactions that have occurred since the last transaction log back up will be included. For example if we had a database that generates 100 transactions per minute, and we backup up the transaction log every 30 minutes, in each 30 minute period we would create a backup containing 3000 transactions. If we increased the frequency of the transaction log backup to every 15 minutes, over the same period we would create two backups that each contain 1500 transactions. However increasing the frequency of the transaction log backup will reduce the amount of space the transaction log itself will require. As we said earlier transactions that have been committed are retained in the transaction log until a log backup is performed. The less frequent the log backups the more transactions that will be retained in the transaction log increasing the amount of space required.

In an Online Transaction Processing (OLTP) system, where database modifications occur frequently, it is important to take the transaction log into account when backing up the database. In a data warehouse or data mart scenario where modifications to data are rare, you still need to worry about backing up the transaction logs. This is because most backups take place during the night when the usage of the data warehouse is minimal. It is usually during this time that data is fed into the data warehouse through tools such as Data Transformation Services (DTS). Such feeds can take a long time because they bring data from several data sources and perform data cleansing and scrubbing before dumping it in the warehouse. These operations can generate a large number of database transactions that will be written to the log where they will remain until they are backed up.

Differential Backups

A differential backup only backs up the data pages that have been modified since the last full database backup. This can allow for restorations that are more efficient than using only full and transaction log backups. There are two reasons for this:

- ❏ Firstly, if a data page has received a large number of updates since the last full database backup the transaction log will contain a record of all the updates that have occurred so these transactions can be reapplied. However, a differential backup will contain only a single record for that data page, a copy of the data page as it was when the differential backup was initiated.

- ❏ Secondly, to restore a database that has been backed up using the full and differential methods you only need to restore the last full database backup and the last differential backup. Restoration using transaction log backups requires restoration of a full database backup and all the transaction log backups that occurred since the full backup.

A differential backup may be preferable if you are only modifying data in batch jobs at specified times, and recovery to a point within the period that these modifications were running is not required. For example, it is common for data warehouses to be read-only to users and only be modified by imports that occur on a nightly basis from other systems. While a large number of transactions occur during the import, if the database becomes corrupted during the day you are only interested in restoring the database as it was after all the imports had completed. Taking a full database backup each day after the importing is finished is an option, but in our example it would be very inefficient as only 5% of the data changes daily. A better solution would be to back up the full database once a week, and then perform a differential backup every day after the data load has completed. If corruption occurs we would simply need to restore the last full database backup and also restore our last differential backup. The equivalent strategy using transaction log backups would require restoration of the full database backup, as well as every transaction log backup made after this.

Filegroup and File Backups

The data contained within a SQL Server database is physically stored in files located on the server's disk drives. By default a database consists of a single data file, but additional files can be added to a database to allow the data within it to be distributed across multiple disks. When creating database objects, such as tables and indexes, you cannot specify which disk files are used to store these objects. Instead, you specify a Filegroup. A Filegroup is a logical collection of database disk files and the storage of the database object is proportionally distributed between the files that form the filegroup. By default, a database has only one Filegroup, called `Primary`, but more can be added.

SQL Server also allows you to backup filegroups individually, which can be useful for dividing the backup of very large databases into units that can be backed up during your available backup window. Filegroup backups will increase the complexity of your backup regime and will require more management to ensure that your recovery requirements are met. For this reason you should use full database backups instead of file and filegroup backups unless you have a specific reason not to. One such situation may be if your database is so large that a full backup cannot be completed during the hours of low database usage. You may consider distributing the data across multiple filegroups, keeping these filegroups small enough that they can each be backed up during the non-peak period. For example, if you split you database into seven filegroups and backup a different filegroup each day over the cause of a week you will obtain a full backup of this database.

Filegroup backups are only possible if you are using Full or Bulk-Logged recovery models and you are also taking transaction log backups. To restore a database to an accessible and consistent state restoration of the transaction log backup is required after a filegroup backup restoration. The reason for this can be demonstrated in the following example:

❑ FILEGROUP A contains a table called CUSTOMERS. This table contains information on customers who have placed orders and the Primary Key for this table is a column named CUSTID.

❑ FILEGROUP B contains a table called ORDERS. This table contains the details of the orders placed by customers. The orders table has a foreign key that references the CUSTID column in the customers table.

❑ The Customers table has five customer records with CUSTID's of 001 to 005. The ORDERS table also contains five records, an order for each customer.

❑ A Filegroup backup of FILEGROUP B is taken.

❑ A scheduled task has been defined that deletes customers who have not purchased within the last 12 months and their orders. This evening when the task runs the customer with the CUSTID of #002 is deleted.

❑ A transaction log backup is taken.

❑ At 7:00 am a developer runs an incorrect SQL statement which deletes all the records in the ORDERS table.

❑ The DBA restores the FILEGROUP B backup. As this backup was taken before customer #002 was deleted the ORDERS table still contains orders for customer #002. However, as the CUSTOMERS table is not affected by the filegroup restoration, customer #002 remains deleted from the CUSTOMERS table. At this point, the database is in an inconsistent state, because a record in the orders table references a non-existent record in the CUSTOMERS table.

❑ The DBA restores the transaction log backup taken before the developer ran the faulty code. Restoring the log reapplies the delete that happened as part of the scheduled task – the delete that removed the order record for CUSTID #002 from the ORDERS table. The database is now back to a consistent state and is once again accessible.

File backups are similar to filegroup backups in that they require the transaction log to be restored after the file backup has been restored. File backups also have the advantage that you can perform differential file backups. If you use differential file backups, you only need to restore the last file backup, the last differential file backup, and the transaction log backups made after this differential file backup.

SQL Server allows for several backup methods: full backup, differential backup, transaction log backup, and file and filegroup backup. With a full backup, the whole database is backed up to the backup media. With differential backup, only changes that occurred since the last full backup will be written to the backup media. With a transaction log backup, committed transactions in the log will be written to the backup media. Finally, with a file and filegroup backup, you can elect to backup only certain tables that are located on certain data files or data filegroups.

Choosing the Recovery Model

SQL Server 2000 introduces the concept of database recovery models which specify how transactions are logged and how backups of the log can be used in database restoration. A recovery model is set per database and the three recovery models are:

❑   **Simple**: The simple recovery model allows a database to be recovered from the last full database backup, or differential backup.

❑   **Bulk-Logged**: The bulk-logged recovery model allows a database to be recovered from a full, differential or transaction log backup. This also optimizes bulk data operations.

❑   **Full**: The full recovery model allows a database to be recovered from the last full and differential database backups and also to a specified point in time from transaction log backups.

When a database is using the Simple recovery model, the transactions are removed from the log after they have successfully completed and the changes they made have been written to the database. Transaction log backups are not required or even possible using this model. While the Simple recovery model is easier to implement and has a lower administrative overhead in the event of database failure you will only be able to restore from your last full or differential backup. This may be entirely appropriate for your data warehouse if it is updated by batch imports and users are making no online updates.

Both Full and Bulk-Logged recovery models require the transaction log to be backed up to clear committed transactions. If the transaction log isn't backed up, completed transactions remain in the log indefinitely and it will continue to grow with each new transaction until it eventually consumes all the available space on the disk(s). It is important to be aware of log space requirements, especially during high transaction periods such as bulk-inserts and updates so you can schedule appropriate log backups. Unlike the Full recovery model, operations such as BULK INSERT and index creation are minimally logged in the Bulk-Logged recovery model, which reduces both the overhead and log space requirements but does restrict the ability to roll the log forward to a specified point in time.

In earlier versions of SQL Server it was possible for a log backup sequence to be invalidated by performing a "non-logged" operation such as a bulk data insert. To improve performance these operations bypassed recording in the transaction log what data changes were being made. Once such an operation had occurred all further transaction log backups would fail until after a full database backup had been made. In SQL Server 2000 it is now not possible to break a log backup sequence as there are no longer any "non-logged" operations, instead SQL Server 2000 uses a minimal logging technique for these bulk-data operations, which still provides the performance needed by these tasks while also recording information about the changes being made in the transaction log.

Setting the Recovery Model Using Enterprise Manager

To set the recovery model using SQL Server Enterprise Manager, right-click the database you wish to set the recovery model for and click on Properties. In the Database Properties window select the Options tab. In the middle of this window is a dropdown from which you can select the recovery model used for this database:

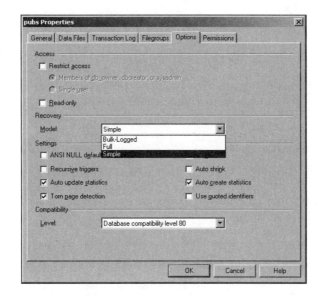

Setting the Recovery Model using T-SQL

You can also set the Recovery Model that a database uses from T-SQL. To do this we use the ALTER DATABASE command with the following parameters:

```
ALTER DATABASE database SET RECOVERY {FULL | BULK_LOGGED | SIMPLE}
```

For example to change the pubs database to use the Simple recovery model execute:

```
ALTER DATABASE pubs SET RECOVERY SIMPLE
```

What to Backup?

Now that we have determined to implement a backup and recovery strategy for the data warehouse, we need to find out exactly what we need to backup. Do we only backup the database that hosts the data warehouse? Or do we also need to backup some system databases with it, too?

When we install SQL Server, several databases are created by default. These databases are the master, tempdb, msdb, model, pubs, and Northwind databases. As the figure overleaf shows, some of these databases are system databases (master, tempdb, msdb, and model), and others are example user databases (pubs and Northwind). Another system database that is created when the server participates in replication is the Distribution database. System databases must be backed up periodically (except for tempdb for reasons that you will see in the following sections):

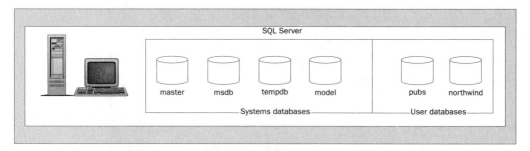

Actually, it would be a good idea to include backing up these databases as part of the backup and recovery strategy of the data warehouse, although they don't contain data stored in user databases they do contain important information needed to support your data warehouse such as logins. Bearing this in mind, your backup strategy should include:

❑   The user databases of concern (the data warehouse database)

❑   Database logs (if you think is necessary)

❑   The system databases indicated in the following sections

Let's take a look at each of the databases in turn.

The master Database

The master database records system information for SQL Server, including:

❑   All login accounts

❑   All system configuration settings

❑   The existence of all other databases

❑   The location of the primary files that contain the initialization information for the user databases

❑   The initialization information for SQL Server

As changes to this information usually doesn't occur on a highly frequent basis daily or weekly master database backups are usually suitable. If you do not backup your master database and it becomes corrupted, you will still be able to restore your user databases that have been backed up but any login or configuration information will be lost.

> **The master database must be backed up periodically to maintain the system information when database recovery is needed.**

The tempdb Database

The tempdb database is created when the SQL Server starts, and is reconstructed the next time the server is restarted. This database plays an important role because:

❑   It holds all temporary tables and temporary stored procedures

❑   It fills any other temporary storage needs such as work tables generated by SQL Server

❑   It is a global resource; the temporary tables and stored procedures for all users connected to the system are stored there

tempdb is recreated when the server starts, so there is no need to include it in the backup plan for the user and system databases.

> **tempdb** grows automatically in size by default since its initial size is very small (default is 8 MB for the data file and 0.5 for the log file). Each time the system is started, **tempdb** is reset to its default size. You can avoid the overhead of having **tempdb** autogrow by using **ALTER DATABASE** to increase the size of **tempdb**, for example:
>
> **ALTER DATABASE tempdb MODIFY FILE (Name=TEMPDEV, SIZE=20MB)**
>
> To find the optimal size of your **tempdb** database simply check its size after your SQL Server has been running under normal load for a period of time.

The model Database

The model database serves as a template for creating other databases on the system. Each time you create a database, a copy of the model database is created and used as a starting point. The model database has to exist on the SQL Server system if you want to successfully create new databases.

The msdb Database

The msdb database is used by the SQL Server agent to store scheduled jobs, alerts and recorded operators. It can also be used to store DTS packages (as we have seen in Chapter 7)when we choose to store them in the SQL Server or the Repository.

> The **msdb** database also needs to be backed up when we build our backup and recovery plan to avoid loss of saved alerts, scheduled jobs, and any DTS packages that have been saved in SQL Server.

The Pubs and Northwind Databases

These two databases are sample user databases that are shipped with SQL Server. These two databases do not need to be included in our backup and recovery plan, because losing them will not affect server functionality or adversely affect other user databases. If you decide to remove these sample databases you can later get these back by executing the recreation scripts in Query Analyzer. You can find the script files to do this under the \Program Files\Microsoft SQL Server\mssql\install directory on the drive that you installed SQL Server; use instpubs.sql to recreate the PUBS database and instnwnd.sql to recreate the Northwind database.

Defining the Backup Device

When backing up a database in SQL Server you must specify a backup device for the backup to be written to. SQL Server uses three types of backup devices: disk, tape, and named pipes. Disk and tape backup devices are usually created using the Enterprise Manager. The tape backup device should be physically attached to the SQL Server; it is not possible to perform backups to remotely located tape drives unless you are using a third-party backup tool. Named pipes devices are usually created with third-party tools, allowing vendors to use specialized backup and recovery software. An example of third-party backup tools that can create such devices is the Seagate Backup Exec or Computer Associates Arcserve backup.

Named pipes are the default network libraries that ship with SQL Server allowing clients to communicate with the server on a one-to-one basis. The named pipe library uses inter-process remote procedure calls (RPC) in Windows NT to establish the communication between the client and the server. With named pipe backups, the data is backed up over the network using this library to a remote storage location.

To add a backup device in Enterprise Manager, you need to expand the Management folder on the tree pane and right-click the Backup item underneath it. From the pop-up menu, you can then select New Backup Device. This will open the dialog shown below:

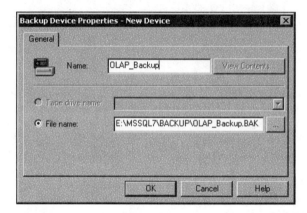

In the dialog above, you can select a name for the backup device and a path if you want to define it as a disk device. If you want to specify the backup device as a tape device, you need to select the Tape Drive Name from the appropriate drop-down list. In the figure above, this option and the associated drop down list are disabled because the computer used to generate the dialog is not physically linked to a tape drive.

When you choose the backup device to be a disk device, make sure the device is not physically on the same disk as the database files. If they were both on the same disk, any disk failure would kill both the database and the backups preventing you from recovering the database later on.

You can use T-SQL script to define the backup device. We use the sp_addumpdevice system stored procedure, which has the following syntax:

```
sp_addumpdevice [Device Type], [Logical Name], [Physical Name]
```

and the arguments of this procedure have the following definitions:

❑   Device Type: As we described above, a backup device can be defined for a disk file, or a tape drive.

❑   Logical Name: The logical name is the name we will use when referring to the backup device from SQL Server, for example when using the BACKUP DATABASE command

❑   Physical Name: This is where the backup device is physically located, for example c:\mydevice.bak for a disk device or \\.\TAPE0 for a tape device

For example, the following script specifies the tape as the backup media for the `OLAP_Example` database, and chooses "OLAP_Backup" as the name for the backup.

```
use OLAP_Example
exec sp_addumpdevice {'tape', 'OLAP_Backup', '\\.\tape0'}
```

Had we wanted to use disk backup instead of the tape backup used in the script above, we would have replaced the keyword `tape` with `disk`. We also would have replaced the tape name `\\.\tape0` with the path of the backup device. For example, for disk backup, the script would become:

```
use OLAP_Example
exec sp_addumpdevice {'disk', 'OLAP_Backup',
    'D:\Backups\December30.bak'}
```

Backup devices can contain more than one backup of a database; this depends on your usage of the `INIT` and `FORMAT` parameters of the backup command which we will look at next. To view the contents of a backup device execute the following command:

```
Restore HeaderOnly from MyBackupDevice
```

How to Perform a Backup

You can conduct a database backup using Transact-SQL commands or using the SQL Server Enterprise Manager (EM). With Transact-SQL, you use the BACKUP DATABASE command. This command is explained in detail below. With EM, you can use the **Backup Database** dialog or the **Backup** wizard. You can also use SQL DMO to backup a database from within an external application written in a different language, such as Visual Basic or Visual C++. Using SQL DMO to backup the database will, however, not be discussed in this book. You can read more about it in the SQL Server Books-Online, or in *Professional SQL Server 2000 Programming,* ISBN 1-861004-48-6, published by Wrox Press.

Backup using T-SQL

The BACKUP DATABASE Transact-SQL command allows you to create a backup copy of the specified database to a disk or tape location. The BACKUP DATABASE command has the following syntax:

```
BACKUP DATABASE database_name
TO backup_device
WITH backup_option
```

Some of the more common backup arguments are:

❑ INIT | NOINIT: If you are backing up to a media device, such as a disk file or tape, that has previously been used for SQL Server backups the INIT argument will cause any existing backups on the device to be overwritten. INIT however will not overwrite any backup media description information such as the media set name. NOINIT on the other hand does not overwrite existing backups, the backup will simply be appended.

❑ FORMAT | NOFORMAT: This has the same effect as INIT and NOINIT respectively except specifying the FORMAT argument will also overwrite any media description information.

❑ UNLOAD | NOUNLOAD: These options are really only valid for backups to tapes; the UNLOAD argument causes the tape to be rewound and unloaded from the tape drive after the backup completes. On the other hand, specifying NOUNLOAD will not rewind the tape and it will still be available for subsequent backups.

❑ STATS: When backing up a database, especially large databases, it is useful to be able to track the progress of the backup. If you specify the STAT S argument with a percentage value, each time the database restoration progress reaches a multiple of this percentage SQL Server will output a message indicating the backup progress.

> You need to use extreme caution when using the FORMAT or INIT clauses of the BACKUP statement. This is because they will result in permanently loosing any backups previously stored on the backup media.

As an example, the following command will perform full backup of the OLAP_Example database to the backup device called OLAP_Device, with append (not overwriting any existing data on the backup media):

```
BACKUP DATABASE OLAP_Example
    TO Olap_Backup
    WITH NOINIT,
    NOUNLOAD,
    NAME = 'Full Backup of OLAP_Example'
GO
```

Backup with the Enterprise Manager

With the Enterprise Manager, you can create backups by selecting the Backup Database menu command. This command is available from All Tasks submenu of the context-sensitive menu that pops-up when you right-click the database name in the tree view of the Enterprise Manager. The command is also available from the Tools menu on the menu bar. Once the command is selected, the SQL Server Backup dialog appears as shown in the screenshots below:

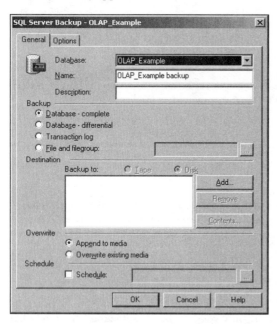
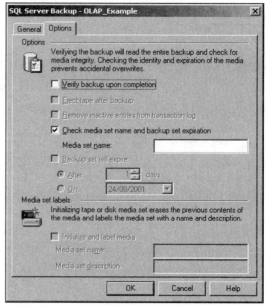

As you see in the figure above, you can specify the database you want to back up from the Database drop-down menu. You can also specify a name for the backup and add a description that would remind you of certain things you need to remember about this backup. Backup options available through this dialog include:

❑ Type of backup (full, differential, transaction, or filegroup backup).

❑ Destination: disk or tape. This is where you can add the backup devices you need to use in the backup.

❑ Options on whether you want to append the data to the backup media, or overwrite whatever is on the media.

❑ An option to set a schedule for the backup. Scheduling and automating tasks will be discussed later in the SQL Agent section of the chapter.

❑ An option to have SQL Server verify the backup, which checks for media integrity to prevent accidental loss of data.

❑ An option to set the media set name. The media set name is a logical media grouping that the tape belongs to and typically the tapes that participate in a rotation for a database or server will use the same media set name. When the first backup is created on a tape, a media set name can be specified. The media set name used for all subsequent backups must match the tape's existing media set name otherwise the backup will not run. This can help prevent database backups being written to the wrong tapes.

❑ An option to specify the number of days to retain the backup, or to specify an explicit expiration date for the backup. This prevents the backups on the media being overwritten if a backup command is issued with the INIT parameter.

❑ An option to initialize the backup media, which is equivalent to using the FORMAT clause in the BACKUP DATABASE T-SQL command.

Enterprise Manager also provides a wizard that leads you through performing most of these tasks listed above and this wizard can be started by clicking the Tools menu, selecting Wizards and choosing the Backup Wizard from under the Management node. However, the backup wizard will not allow you to perform filegroup backup. I will not discuss the backup wizard because it is very straightforward, and if one knows how to use the Backup Database dialog shown above, it would be easy to use the wizard.

Now that we have seen how to perform the a database backup using SQL Server Enterprise Manager let's take a look at how this can be achieved in code using Transact SQL.

Database Restoration

Database restoration will return the database to its condition at the time the backup was created. When restoring a database from backup, the data is copied from the backup media to the database, and committed transactions in the transaction log backup are also copied and stored in the database. Uncommitted transactions are rolled back to maintain database consistency.

Database restoration from backups can be used in a variety of different situations. These include:

❑ Migrating the database to a new server; you can use backups to restore the database after you create it from scripts on the new server.

❑ Disk failure caused complete loss of the databases on the server. Backups come to the rescue in this crisis situation.

❑ Natural disasters may strike, such as a flood, fire, or tornado, causing permanent damage to the server and making us rebuild the server after emotional recovery from the natural disaster.

These are only a few examples of possible situations – you may encounter many others that require restoration from backups.

Rebuilding System Databases

System databases (`master`, `msdb`, and `model`) can be restored from a backup if you have one, or can be rebuilt if you don't have a backup. To rebuild the system databases, you need to run the command-line utility `rebuildm.exe`, located in the `binn` directory under the SQL Server installation or on the SQL Server CD. Before you run this utility, you need to make sure that the SQL Server services are stopped.

> **Caution: Rebuilding the system databases causes all information about your system configuration and user databases to be lost. To regain access to your user databases you should restore these from backup; alternatively if valid copies of the data files still reside on your server you can reattach the database by executing `sp_attach_db`. For more information regarding this command see SQL Server Books Online, Rebuild Master utility. These can be found at http://www.microsoft.com/sql/techinfo/productdoc/2000/books.asp.**

Restore using T-SQL

T-SQL provides a command, `RESTORE DATABASE`, which allows for database restoration. The syntax of this command is:

```
RESTORE DATABASE database_name
FROM backup_device
WITH restore argument
```

The command takes several arguments; some of the common ones are:

❑ `RECOVERY | NORECOVERY`: When you restore a database these options controls what happens to transactions that were still in progress when the backup was taken. If `RECOVERY` is specified these transactions are rolled back and the database is restored to a consistent state for general use, however no subsequent transaction log backups can be restored. Specifying `NORECOVERY` leaves uncommitted transactions in the restored database and allows transaction logs to be restored, however, the database is in an inconsistent state until any additional backups have been restored and the database recovered. To recover a database without restoring additional backups use `RESTORE DATABASE database_name WITH RECOVERY`.

❑ `MOVE`: When a backup is created information about where the database data files are located is also held within the backup. When restoring a database the data files will be recreated at the same file path where as they were when the backup was created. However if you specify the `MOVE` argument you can specify new file locations for each data file.

❑ `REPLACE`: When restoring a database with the same name as an existing database the `REPLACE` option must be specified for the existing database to be overwritten. If this is not specified the restoration will fail.

❑ `STATS`: If is often useful to track the progress of a database restoration, especially when dealing with large databases that may take many hours to restore. Every time the restoration progress reaches a multiple of the supplied percentage argument, SQL Server will output a message indicating the restoration progress.

A host of other optional arguments can also be specified. These arguments are explained in detail in SQL Server Books Online under the Restore command.

Restoring a full database might look like this:

```
RESTORE DATABASE OLAP_Example
    FROM OLAP_Backup
```

Restoring full and differential backups could look like this:

```
RESTORE DATABASE OLAP_Example
    FROM OLAP_Backup
    WITH NORECOVERY
RESTORE DATABASE OLAP_Example
    FROM OLAP_Backup
    WITH FILE = 2
```

In the example above, the OLAP_Example full backup is recovered with the NORECOVERY option. This option causes uncommitted transactions not to be rolled back. The full restore is followed by differential restore. The backup set #2 on the storage media is used during the recovery of the differential backup.

The following example backs up and restores the OLAP_Example database, virtually making a copy of it:

```
BACKUP DATABASE OLAP_Example
    TO DISK = 'c:\OLAP_Example.bak'
RESTORE FILELISTONLY
    FROM DISK = 'c:\OLAP_Example.bak'
RESTORE DATABASE TestDB
    FROM DISK = 'c:\OLAP_Example.bak'
    WITH MOVE 'OLAP_Example' TO 'c:\test\testdb.mdf',
    MOVE 'OLAP_Example_log' TO 'c:\test\testdb.ldf'
```

In the example above, the BACKUP DATABASE command created the OLAP_Example.bak file. The RESTORE FILELISTONLY returns a list of the database and log files contained in the backup set. The following commands create a new database, testdb, by creating a copy of the OLAP_Example database.

Finally, the following example shows how to restore certain files or filegroups:

```
RESTORE DATABASE OLAP_Example
    FILE = 'OLAP_Example_data_1',
    FILE = 'OLAP_Example _data_2',
    FILEGROUP = 'new_customers'
    FROM 'OLAP_Example _Backup
    WITH NORECOVERY
-- Restore the log backup.
RESTORE LOG 'OLAP_Example
    FROM 'OLAP_ExampleLog1
```

To restore the database over the top of another database, only the user performing the restore can have a connection to the database. If other users have open connections the restore will fail. In earlier versions of SQL Server this was a bit of a problem; the only way to restore the database was to look through the list of connected users and try and kill each user process and hope the didn't connect again before you had time to start the restore. Thankfully this has been greatly improved in SQL Server 2000 with the ability to kill connections using the ALTER DATABASE command. The syntax of this command is,

```
ALTER DATABASE database_name SET SINLE_USER WITH ROLLBACK IMMEDIATE
```

This command will halt and undo any transactions that are currently in progress then kill all the user process accessing the database. This command also places the database into single user mode, which means only one connection is allowed to the database. In this case it would be the connection of the user restoring the database.

Restoring with Enterprise Manager

In the Enterprise Manager, you can right-click a database name and select the Restore Database command from the All Tasks submenu of the pop-up menu. The figure below shows the dialog box you get when you do so.

In this dialog, you can specify the database name, the type of restore to perform (database, file, or filegroups, for example) or to restore the database from a device. Each selection will result in slightly different options in the next sections of the dialog. For instance, if you were to specify filegroup or files restore, the First backup to restore drop-down list will disappear:

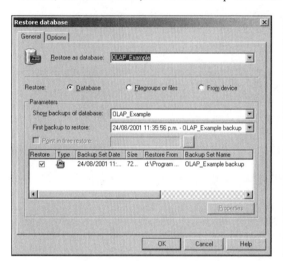
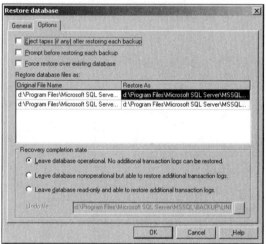

Managing Backup Media

Managing backup media involves selecting the right media for the backup and establishing a plan to accommodate full and differential backups. The plan calls for reuse of the media when it is full in a way that allows full recovery in cases of failure. You should always have one full backup and the last differential backup since that full backup accommodated on the backup media. For example, if you conduct a full backup every Friday night, and you take a differential backup every other night, to restore the database you need to have both the full backup from Friday as well as the last differential backup available.

Backup Media

Although SQL Server allows for backups on disk, it is recommended that backups are performed on removable storage media. In fact, only small backups are warranted on disk. Removable storage media nowadays ranges from 650 MB recordable CD-ROMs to 70 GB digital linear tapes (DLTs). For Datawarehousing, small media is not recommended. You need to use fast, high capacity, and economical media.

The best media that meet the criteria that we are looking for are tape devices. In order for these devices to perform quickly, you need to use tape drives that support Small Computer System Interface (SCSI) interfaces. These interfaces provide a fast way for transferring data (up to 40 Mb per second) and can connect to multiple tape, disk, or CD-ROM devices (up to 14). Some of the most widely used tape drives are listed here:

❑ **Quarter Inch Cassette and Travan Drives**

These are mostly used for system backups such as the Jumbo 250 that can store 250 MB on a single tape. With the Travan technology, the capacity can be increased to 2 GB. However, these drives are slow (around 500 Kb/second) and not very reliable.

❑ **4mm Digital Audiotape (DAT)**

These tapes have been in use for several years. They can store 12 GB of uncompressed data on one tape. The storage capacity doubles when implementing hardware compression of the data. Transfer rate for these drives is around 1 Mbps. This is a good and economical option for smaller databases (around 20 GB) and if you are not too concerned about speed of backup.

❑ **8mm Tape**

These use the same technology as VCR tapes except that they are digital. They are comparable to the 4mm digital audiotapes in storage size, but slightly faster (around 1.2 Mbps). These tapes are not used as much now because the 4mm tapes present a cheaper comparable option.

❑ **Digital Linear Tape (DLT)**

These tapes come with various capacities up to 70 GB of compressed data. Transfer speed can reach 10 Mbps, making this a very fast option for backing up large databases in shorter periods. Tape changers and libraries can be used with this option to increase the storage capacity to the terabyte order of magnitude.

For more information on DLT tapes, visit the web site: http://www.dlttape.com.

❑ **Advanced Intelligent Tape (AIT)**

This is the newest format of tape drives and is based on the 8mm tape technology. These tape drives provide capacities of around 50 GB of compressed data and a transfer speed around 6 Mbps. These devices are perfect for large data warehouse backups where the size of the warehouse is in terabytes because they can implement tape changers and libraries that tremendously increase the storage capacity offered by them.

For more information on AIT tapes, visit the web site: http://www.aittape.com.

Be aware when using hardware compression in your tape backups. Such compression is usually proprietary and one compression format may not be compatible with all brands of tape drives. Therefore, if you use compression with your backup, make sure that the drives you use to recover data understand the compression format of the drive used to create the tape backup.

Rotating Backup Tapes

Cost is usually an important factor to consider when backing up the data warehouse. The number of tapes used in backups will be limited by their cost. Such tapes, therefore, will usually be rotated and used as a set.

Implementing full backups every time is not a good idea because it takes longer and wears down the tape quicker. Besides, let's say all you have is a full backup from last night, and you find out that the database (or parts of it) is corrupted. You need to recover to a backup that does not have the corrupted data. If all you have is last night's backup, you are in trouble.

The ideal solution is to have a mix of a full backup and a number of differential backups since that full backup. One scheme that fits data warehouse backups and allows for even use of the tapes while allowing for fast reliable recovery is the Grandfather/Father/Son rotation scheme. Grandfather stands for monthly backups, Father for weekly backups (usually on Friday night), and Son for daily backups. This system rotates the tapes so that each tape will be used in each of the backup types above and allows access for backups for each day in the previous week, and each week in the previous 10 weeks. The tape rotation according to this system is presented in the table below:

Week	Mon	Tue	Wed	Thu	Fri
0					Tape 10 – Full
1	Tape 1 - Diff	Tape 2 - Diff	Tape 3 - Diff	Tape 4 - Diff	Tape 5 – Full
2	Tape 1 - Diff	Tape 2 - Diff	Tape 3 - Diff	Tape 4 - Diff	Tape 6 – Full
3	Tape 1 - Diff	Tape 2 - Diff	Tape 3 - Diff	Tape 4 - Diff	Tape 7 – Full
4	Tape 1 - Diff	Tape 2 - Diff	Tape 3 - Diff	Tape 4 - Diff	Tape 8 – Full
5	Tape 2 - Diff	Tape 3 - Diff	Tape 4 - Diff	Tape 5 - Diff	Tape 6 – Full
6	Tape 2 - Diff	Tape 3 - Diff	Tape 4 - Diff	Tape 5 - Diff	Tape 7 – Full
7	Tape 2 - Diff	Tape 3 - Diff	Tape 4 - Diff	Tape 5 - Diff	Tape 8 – Full
8	Tape 2 - Diff	Tape 3 - Diff	Tape 4 - Diff	Tape 5 - Diff	Tape 9 – Full
9	Tape 3 - Diff	Tape 4 - Diff	Tape 5 - Diff	Tape 6 - Diff	Tape 10 – Full

Notice in the table above that if the system crashes on Wednesday of week 8, then you can restore the database using the full backup from the previous Friday on Tape 8 and the differential backup on Tape 3. If you fear data corruption during week 8, you can restore all the way from Tape 6 in week 5 and restore the database to the way it was each day of the previous week.

It is recommended that grandfather backups be full backups and the tapes on which they were stored never be reused (or at least not for a year or two). This is because accidental data loss may be unnoticed for several months. Therefore, having the grandfather backup from the period prior to the data loss will help recover the database to a stable state.

With this backup rotation scheme, you end up using 10 tapes with each tape used evenly 17 times in an 11 month period.

Automating the Data Warehouse Administration Tasks with SQL Agent

SQL Server provides powerful tools to automate administrative tasks that are repetitive or tedious in nature. An example of automation of such tasks is the act of backing up the database servers every night. Let us say that Darren the database administrator is responsible for backing up the database servers of the company every night. Darren performs the following tasks so he could still leave work at 17:00 and have the servers backed up on schedule:

- ❑ Darren defines himself and his manager, Lewis, as operators and defines Lewis as the failsafe operator. The failsafe operator is simply a backup for the primary operator.

- ❑ Darren creates a backup job with T-SQL to perform the backup. Jobs and steps will be explained next.

- ❑ Darren schedules the job to start at 9:00 PM every night.

- ❑ Darren remembers that the backup might sometimes not go as scheduled for a variety of reasons, such as the backup tape is sometimes accidentally left write protected. Therefore, he defines the job to notify him by pager, write to the Windows NT event log a message with the problem description, and page the failsafe operator.
- ❑ Finally, Darren starts the SQL Server Agent service, which is the tool that automates administrative tasks.

With this, Darren can leave work at 17:00 confident that the backup will take place according to schedule. If anything goes wrong, the SQL Server Agent will page him letting him know of the problem. If he is not available, the failsafe operator will be also informed via pager of the problem.

Automatic Administration Components

In this section we will see what jobs, operators, and alerts are and how these components can be utilized for automatic server administration.

Jobs

Jobs are used to define administrative tasks once, and then run them one or more times afterwards manually or automatically, according to a defined schedule. These jobs can be executed on the local server or on several remote servers participating in a multi-server administration configuration. Alerts, which are explained a little bit later in the chapter, can be used to trigger the execution of jobs. Each job is made up of one or more steps, each defining a particular task.

Job steps provide a powerful and flexible tool for administrators because they can be any of the following:

- ❑ Executable programs
- ❑ Windows Batch Files
- ❑ T-SQL statements or stored procedures
- ❑ ActiveX Script
- ❑ Replication agents

Job scheduling also provides several options, including scheduling the job to run:

- ❑ When the SQL Server Agent service is started
- ❑ When CPU utilization is at a level defined as idle
- ❑ At one point in time
- ❑ On a recurring schedule
- ❑ When an alert occurs

To define a new job, you need to right-click the Jobs item on the tree view in the Enterprise Manager, and select New Job from the pop-up menu. This will open the New Job Properties dialog shown in the following figure:

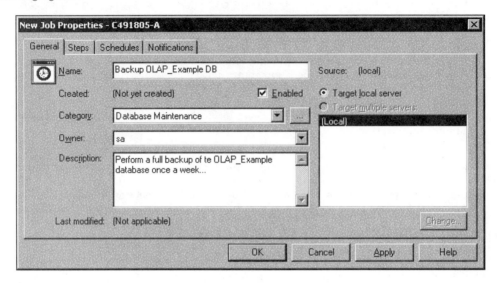

The figure above shows that the job will perform a full backup of the OLAP_Example database. In the Steps tab, we can specify a new step by clicking the New button, which will open the New Step Properties dialog shown below:

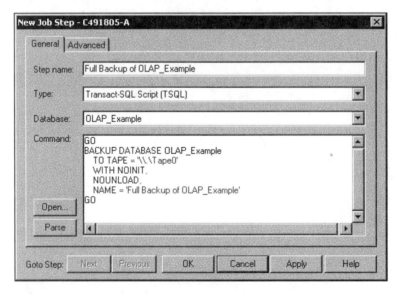

In the New Step Properties dialog, you can specify the name and type of step to be executed. You can also specify the database on which the step will be executed as well as the command to be executed in the step. I selected the step type to be Transact SQL script and the command is the same script we saw earlier in the chapter that performs a full backup of the OLAP_Example database.

The Job Properties dialog we saw earlier allows us to manage steps, editing them, inserting new steps, or prioritizing them to run in a certain order.

The Schedule tab of the New Job Properties dialog allows us to schedule the job to run according to the possibilities mentioned earlier. In the example shown below, the job will run every Friday at 9:00 PM:

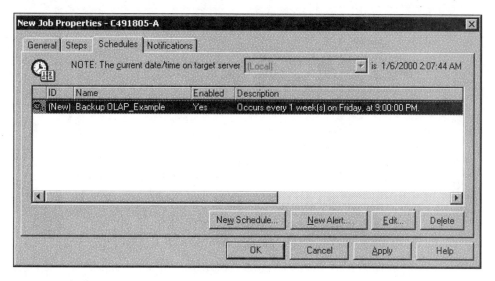

The Notifications tab allows us to send e-mail, pager, or network message notification in case of failure (or success, or completion) to designated operators. It also allows us to send a message to the Windows NT/2000 event log.

Operators

An operator is a person who conducts maintenance tasks for the SQL Server. An operator is usually the Database Administrator (DBA). SQL Server Agent, along with SQL Agent Mail allows us to notify operators when alerts happen via e-mail, pager, or network messages. SQL Server Agent allows us to rotate responsibilities among several operators so that if the database backup fails in the first week of the month, Joe will be notified, if the failure happens in the second week, Darren will be notified, and so on. Failsafe operators can also be assigned so that they too are notified in case notifications to the main operator(s) fail.

The dialog box overleaf shows how you can define operators using SQL Server Agent. To open the dialog, right-click the Operators item on the tree view of the Enterprise Manager and select New Operator from the pop-up menu:

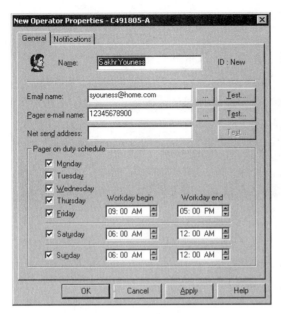
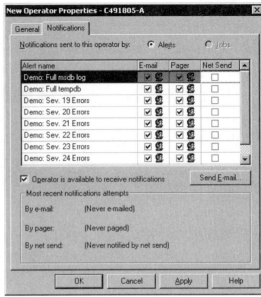

Alerts

An alert is an event that takes place when one or more SQL Server events happen. The alert definition also includes the response that should be taken when the alert occurs, such response is usually a predefined job. The alert definition also includes a list of operators to which the alert should be forwarded.

The following are some of the events that trigger alerts in SQL Server:

❑   Specific error numbers

❑   Severity level of errors

❑   Performance issues with the SQL Server

> **The severity level of an error message provides an indication of the type of problem that Microsoft SQL Server has encountered. Messages with a severity level of 10 are informational messages. Severity levels from 11 through 16 are generated by the user, and can be corrected by the user. Severity levels from 17 through 25 indicate software or hardware errors. System administrators should be informed whenever problems that generate errors with severity levels 17 and higher occur.**

To define an alert, you can use the New Alert Properties dialog shown below. This dialog can be opened by right-clicking the Alerts tree branch in the tree view of the Enterprise Manager and selecting New Alert from the pop-up menu. You can specify the alert name and type, in our example they are: Severe Error: Hardware Failure and SQL Server event alert respectively. The type can be either a SQL Server Event alert or a SQL Server Performance Condition alert. With the SQL Server event alert, you can define the event as a specific error number or a specific severity of the error that took place; we are using the later in the example shown in the figure above. You can also define the database and an error message for the event. In our case, error 24 is not database-specific, thus the All Databases is selected in the Database Name drop-down list. The error message we choose to display when the DBA is informed is shown in the Error message contains this alert textbox.

In the case of a SQL Server performance condition alert, you need to identify the object that caused the alert and the counter, such as free space scans/second for example. You need to also identify a value for the counter at which, under which, or above which the alert occurs. For example, you may specify that an alert will occur if the number of full scans/second exceeds 10.

The response page of the alert dialog allows you to specify the operators who will receive the alert and the way they should be notified (pager, e-mail, or network message). This page also allows you to specify what job to run in response to the alert.

SQL Agent Mail

For the operators to receive e-mail when alert conditions occur, or when a job step fails, SQL Agent Mail needs to be installed and configured on the database server.

Those who have worked with previous versions of SQL Server may know this as SQL Mail which was the name used to define the processes that sent e-mail from the database server. In SQL Server 2000 this term has been spilt into two, SQL Mail is used when referring to the process that sends e-mail from T-SQL code, SQL Agent Mail is used when describing the processes that send e-mail in response to SQL Agent events.

To configure SQL Agent Mail can be very difficult or very easy. It can be very easy if you have the right software, the right mail server, and follow the instructions carefully. It can be very difficult if you don't have these things. E-mail from SQL Server works best when using Outlook 2000 and Microsoft Exchange server. It is possible to use other mail clients and servers, however this often takes additional effort to get everything working correctly. For our example we will assume you are using Microsoft Exchange Server as you mail server and you have access to the Outlook 2000 client software.

Installing SQL Agent Mail

As we discussed earlier the installation can be relatively straightforward if you follow the instructions carefully. The first thing we must do is to ensure the SQL Server and SQL Server Agent services are running under a named account, not the local system account. This can be done in Enterprise Manager on the server properties page, and on the SQL Agent properties page as shown below. Note, the account you choose to use for the service requires a number of permissions be granted to it; search for Setting up Windows Services Accounts in SQL Server Books Online for more information:

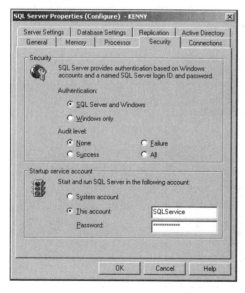
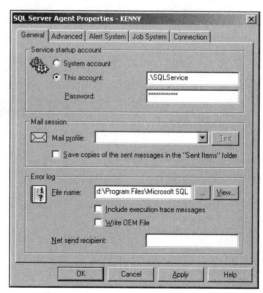

Next, make sure this named account has a valid mail profile created in Microsoft Exchange. This mail profile should not be a member of any distribution lists.

We now need to install Outlook 2000 on your server. Choose all the default option, until you are asked to choose the e-mail service options, as shown in the screen below. You must choose the Corporate or Workgroup option for SQL Agent Mail to function smoothly:

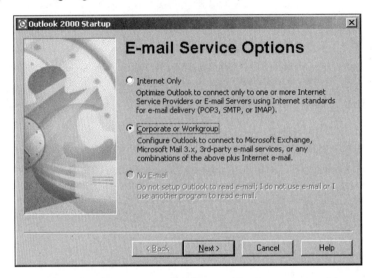

Next, we need to log in locally as the user that we have assigned to the SQL Server services on the SQL Server itself. This is probably the most important step and is often the one that trips people up. If you can't get access to the physical console of the server, using Terminal Services client will also work.

The next step requires us to set up a mail profile on our server. To do this, right-click the Microsoft Outlook icon that should now exist on the desktop. An empty mail profile will be shown and to this we wish to add the Microsoft Exchange Server service that will be in the list shown when you click the Add button. Once you click OK you will be asked to enter the name of you Exchange Server and the mailbox name. Enter this information and click OK, and you will see profile information similar to that shown below:

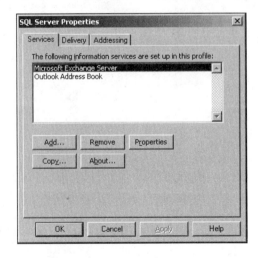

Click OK to close the properties window and start Microsoft Outlook. Once you are in Microsoft Outlook, test the ability to send and receive e-mail, if it doesn't work from here it is not going to work from within SQL Server. If you have any trouble sending or receiving e-mail go back and check your mailbox settings both on the client and on Exchange Server. Don't go any further until these problems are resolved.

Once you are happy with that e-mail is working OK from Outlook we are almost ready for configuring SQL Server to use this e-mail account but there is one more setting that we should check before attempting this. When using Internet Explorer 5.5 we need to make sure that the email program setting in the Internet options is set to Microsoft Outlook. If it isn't SQL Server may not be able to access the mail profile we have set up. To check this, right-click Microsoft Internet Explorer on the desktop and select properties. Click on the Programs tab and make sure the E-mail drop down box is set to Microsoft Outlook. Click OK to close this window:

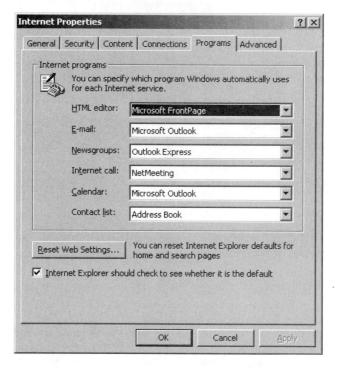

Finally, we are ready to configure SQL Server to use this mail profile. First we must restart SQL Server so it picks up the mail profile we have configured. The easiest way to do this is using the SQL Server Manager, which usually sits in your task bar or can be started from the Microsoft SQL Server program group. Obviously as all users will be disconnected, and transactions in progress will be rolled back this should be done outside normal hours for production servers.

When SQL Server has been restarted we can reconnect to the server in Enterprise Manager. If we drill down to the SQL Server Agent under the Management node, right click and select properties we will once again see the window overleaf. This time however, if we have configured the SQL Server mail profile correctly, in the mail profile drop-down we will see the name of the mail profile that we have just created. Select this profile and choose Test; a message will be displayed telling us that SQL Server could successfully use the mail profile:

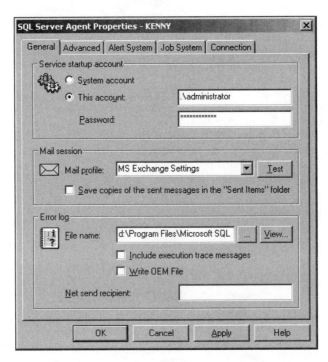

Finally click **OK** to save these settings. This completes the installation of SQL Agent Mail. We can now specify that notifications, such as an alert condition occurring or job outcomes, be sent to our database administrators via e-mail.

Multi-server Administration

Multi-server administration involves automating the administration tasks of more than one SQL server over the network. Besides the ability to manage several servers from a central location simultaneously, this process allows us to schedule information flows between enterprise servers for data warehousing.

Multi-server administration involves having at least one master server and more than one target server. The master server stores a central copy of the job definitions for jobs that need to run on target servers. The master server then distributes the jobs to the enlisted target servers while receiving events from these target servers. The target servers connect periodically to the master server and update their list of jobs to perform. If a new job exists for the target server, it downloads it and disconnects from the master server. The target server will connect again to the master server when it finishes executing the job to upload the job status to the master server. The figure opposite shows the basic architecture of multi-server administration:

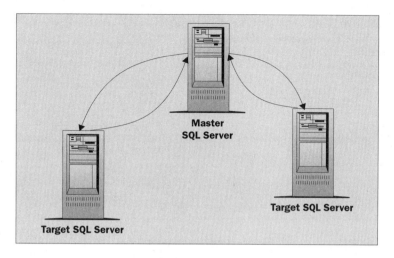

If you need to perform the same automated task for company servers, you can write that task as a job and deploy it on the master server. All servers that need to run the same job are then enlisted as target servers in the multi-server configuration, which will make the job run on all of them.

> Creating and running jobs on the master server in multi-server configurations can be done by the **sysadmin** role of the master server. Users with **sysadmin** roles on the target servers will not be able to change the job or its steps. With this security measure, accidental changes of jobs or their steps or schedules are avoided in this configuration.

Defining Master and Target Servers

Now we know what master and target servers are, let's see how they can be defined in SQL Server. To define the master server, follow these steps:

❑   It is recommended that you choose a SQL Server that is not already heavily utilized for your master server so that you do not affect the performance of applications running on production servers.

❑   Expand the Enterprise Manager's tree view for the server you want to make as the master, making sure the Management item is expanded.

❑   Underneath this item, you will see the SQL Server Agent. Right-click it and select Multi server Administration | Make this a Master... from the pop-up menu. This will launch the Make MSX Wizard, which will help you define a master server operator (called MSXOperator). The first two screens of the wizard are shown below. Follow the steps of the wizard to create the MSXOperator under which the master server will operate.

> Make sure the account under which the SQL Server Agent service runs is a Microsoft Windows NT domain account for each of the master and target servers participating in the multi-server administration. Also, make sure all target servers and the master servers are running SQL Server 2000 or SQL Server 7.0.

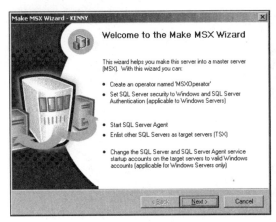
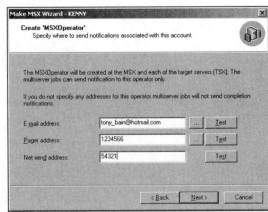

To define target servers, you can do so from the previous wizard, or by expanding the server that will be enlisted as target server in the tree view of the **Enterprise Manager** (given it is registered in the **Enterprise Manager**) and right-clicking the **SQL Server Agent** tree branch. After this, you need to select the **Multi Server Administration | Make this a Target ...** menu item from the pop-up menu. This will launch the **Make TSX** wizard that will allow you to enlist the server as a target server with a master server.

It is worth noting that a target server can be enlisted with only one master server. So if you need to enlist a certain server with another master server, you will need to break its enlistment with the first master server first. Also, if the computer name of the target server changes, you need to first break its enlistment with the master before changing its name, then re-enlist it afterwards. Finally, if the NT domain account under which the SQL Server Agent service on a target server is run is changed, you also need to break the enlistment with the master before you change the domain account for the SQL Server Agent on the target server.

DBCC Commands

Database corruption occurs from time to time, but in reality it is very rare. In almost all cases of serious database corruption the cause can be traced to faulty hardware, but whatever the cause we want to detect signs of this corruption as early as possible. SQL Server 2000 provides a number of Database Consistency Check commands for validating and maintaining our database structure. Below I have listed some of the most useful DBCC commands; for specific information regarding their syntax look in SQL Server Books Online.

❑   DBCC CHECKDB: DBCC CHECKDB will run an allocation and structural consistency check against every table in the specified database. The performance of this command has improved greatly over earlier versions of SQL Server but it still can take a long time for large databases so it should only be run during low usage periods as it impacts heavily on system resources. Although not neccesarily a requirement, most DBA's will run this on a weekly or monthly basis for that extra peace of mind.

❑   DBCC INDEXDEFRAG: If a table receives a lot of updates the indexes created on the table can become fragmented which reduces index-scanning performance. In earlier versions of SQL Server it was nessecary to rebuild the table indexes to remove this fragmentation; in SQL Server 2000 DBCC INDEXDEFRAG will do this in a much more efficient way. Most importantly this command is online which means it won't block users from accessing the table while the de-fragmentation is running.

❑ DBCC SHOWCONTIG: To determine if you need to defragment a tables indexes you need to know how much fragmentation exists within these indexes. DBCC SHOWCONTIG analyses the specified table or index and produces a report detailing the number of pages used by that object, and the amount of fragmentation that exists within the object.

❑ DBCC SHRINKDATABASE: There are times when free space may be made available with a database, such as when historical data is archived and deleted. DBCC SHRINKDATABASE can be used to reduce the amount of disk space used by the database files by releasing the free space. There are two modes that can be used to remove the free space from a database. The first simply truncates the database to remove the free space from the end of the data files; the second mode reorganizes the data contained within a database to remove the free space from throughout the data file. The second mode obviously is a much more intensive process and should only be run during times of low system activity.

Database Maintenance Plan

If all these maintenance procedures just seem like too much bother for you, rest assured that Microsoft has provided a simple solution to managing database administration. A Database Maintenance Plan allows you to schedule some of the most common DBA tasks using a simple wizard interface. Let's step through creating a maintenance plan for the Northwind database.

You can start the Database Maintenance Plan Wizard in Enterprise Manager by connecting to a SQL Server and selecting Tools | Database Maintenance Planner. You will be presented with a welcome screen, on which you'll click Next. The following screen asks you to select which databases this Maintenance Plan will operate for. For this example, we are going to specify just the Northwind database, and click Next:

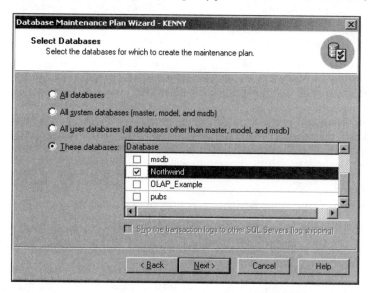

The following screen allows us to start specifying what we want the maintenance plan to actually do. This screen is focused on data organization and we should look at each option in turn. You should exercise some caution when selecting these options as they can take a significant amount of time to complete for large databases:

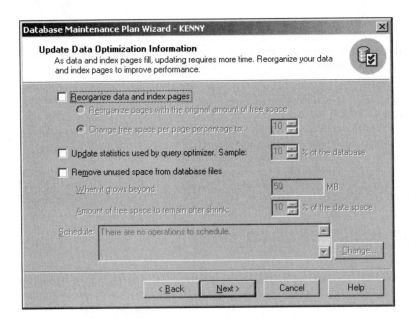

❏ **Reorganize data and Index pages**

If you specify this option, all indexes on all tables within the selected databases will be recreated. If your data warehouse is mostly read-only then it is likely that selecting this option will not result in any performance increase. You can also increase the percentage of free space to leave in the index to allow for more efficient index growth. Once again, if your data warehouse is infrequently updated this should be kept to a minimum.

❏ **Update Statistics**

The Query Optimizer uses table distribution statistics to assist it in choosing the most efficient query execution plans. Unless you explicitly configure a database not to, SQL Server will automatically update the distribution statistics when it determines they have become out of date. If your database is only updated by regular bulk load operations you may find some benefit in turning off automatic statistics updates for a database and scheduling this as part of a maintenance plan that runs after the bulk load has completed. The greater the value of the sampling percentage, the more accurate the statistics will be; however, the larger the value, the longer the update statistics operation will take to complete.

❏ **Remove Unused space**

This option reorganizes the database data files and removes any unused space over the percentage you specify. Unless your data warehouse is shrinking in size, which would be very unusual, there is normally no need to shrink the database as part of a regular maintenance procedure. For one-time shrinking of a database, use the DBCC SHRINKDATABASE command we discussed in the previous section

After selecting the options you require, you will need to schedule these tasks to occur at a specific time. To do this click on the Change button next to the schedule information:

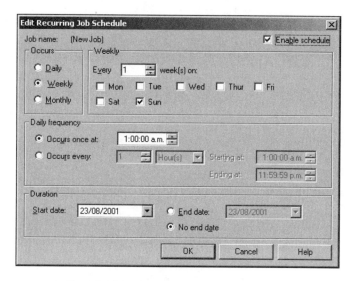

From this window you can select the frequency of the tasks, whether this is daily, weekly, monthly, or even to the level of scheduling the tasks to occur on the 3rd Monday of every 2nd month. Next you can either specify the time the tasks should occur, or a reoccurrence frequency between a start and end time. Finally, you can specify a date when the job should no longer run. The default is No End Date, which means the job will continue to run using the specified schedule until modified otherwise.

Select the schedule you require, click OK, and click Next to take us to the following screen:

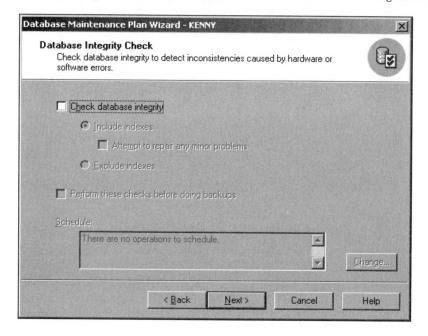

This screen allows us to specify if we want the integrity of the database to be checked. SQL Server 2000 has greatly increased the reliability of it's databases so checking the integrity is not as important as it once was. However hardware errors can cause problems within databases so it is still worthwhile scheduling this to run regularly. There are a couple of options you can select:

❑ Include or Exclude Indexes

If you choose to exclude indexes from the integrity checks SQL Server will not attempt to detect errors contained in non-clustered indexes. For data warehouses this can reduce the amount of time required to perform the integrity check; however, as it is a less thorough check you should only exclude the indexes if you do not have enough time in your maintenance window to perform a full check.

❑ Attempt to repair any minor problems

If you include indexes in your integrity check you can also choose to have SQL Server repair any minor problems it discovers within those indexes. These repairs can occur without risk of data loss; however, SQL Server will not attempt to repair serious errors that affect the data itself.

❑ Perform these checks before doing backups

If you select this option the Database Integrity check will be performed before the databases are backed up (if you include database backups as part of the same maintenance plan). If the integrity checks fail the backups will not be attempted.

Choose the integrity checking options you require and set the schedule in the same way you did for the data organization options. Click Next to go to the Database Backup Plan screen:

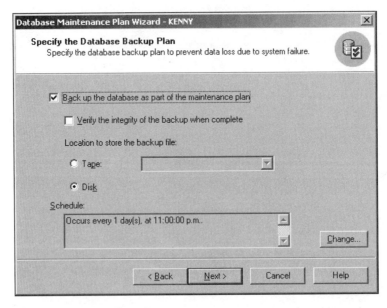

If you choose to back up the database as part of the plan, you can specify if you want the database to be verified as well. If you select this option, SQL Server will simulate a restore to ensure that the backup that has been created is valid once the backup is completed. Obviously, this will affect the duration of the backup procedure, but it is recommended to run it if you have the time and your backup files are not being validated elsewhere (such as being restored regularly on another server).

Secondly, you will need to specify if you wish the backup to be written to a disk file or directly to tape. To backup to a tape natively, the tape drive must be directly connected to the SQL Server. As most organizations centralize their tape backup solution, it is common to backup the SQL Server database to a disk file, and then have the disk file written to the tape drive over the network as part of the enterprise backup. If you are writing the backup to disk file ensure that the directory path where you are creating the backup files is accessible and is being backed up by your tape backup procedure. Also, make sure that the database backup finishes before the tape backup procedure attempts to write the backup files to tape.

Once you have made your selection and scheduled the backup time hit Next. If you have selected backup to tape you will go directly to the transaction log backup screen. If you selected disk backup you will first need to enter some more information about where to store the disk-based backup files:

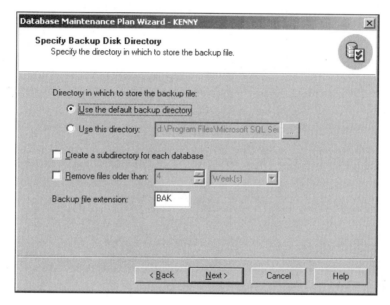

First, you will need to choose where to store the files created by the backup procedure. This can either be the default backup directory (\Program Files\Microsoft SQL Server\Mssql\Backup for the default SQL Server instance) or a directory you specify. Next, you will need to select if SQL Server creates a directory within the backup folder to store each database's backup files. This is recommended if you will be keeping more than one or two backups on disk as it makes locating a particular database backup much easier. Lastly, you specify how many days the backup files should be kept on disk before being deleted. If your tape backup routine only runs Monday to Friday you may want to keep at least 3 days backups on disk so that the weekend backup files will be written to tape on Monday. Of course, this will be dictated by the amount of free disk space that you have.

Clicking Next will take us to the Transaction Log Backup screen:

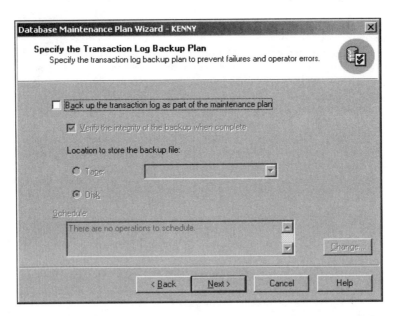

Set the options here as you did for the database backup. However, take care when scheduling the log backup as this will normally happen more often than the full database backup. Depending on when and how your system is updated you may want to perform log backup regularly throughout the day, or maybe only at night if your system is updated only by batch jobs.

Once again if you selected to store the transaction log backups on disk you will need to set a few more options on the next screen:

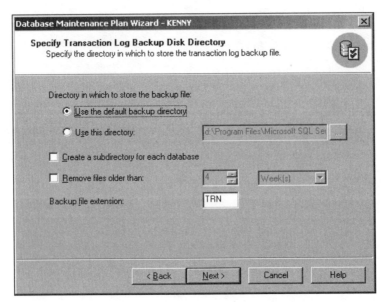

After you have selected the disk options click Next to go to the reporting section of the Maintenance Plan Wizard:

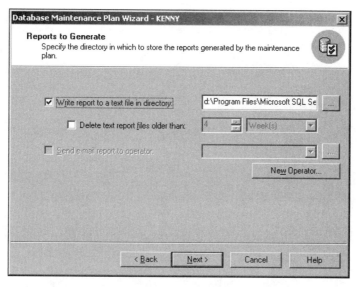

On this screen, you specify if you wish the maintenance plan to keep a log file of its operation. This log file is quite detailed and is invaluable for solving Maintenance Plan failures so I suggest that you always have the maintenance plan create a log. Once again, you may wish to keep at least 3 days worth of log files available on disk so you can diagnose any weekend failures on Monday. You can also instruct the Maintenance Plan to e-mail the log file to a nominated operator. Click Next when you have finished setting options on the Maintenance Plan History screen:

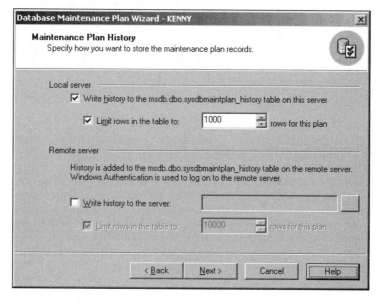

On this screen, we can specify to record the history of this job within a table in msdb. Once again, this is valuable information when diagnosing job failure. It is a good idea to limit the number of rows recorded to prevent excessive growth of the msdb database. To view the history of a Maintenance Plan once it has been created and executed right-click the Maintenance Plan in Enterprise Manager and select Maintenance Plan History...:

Clicking Next one more time will take us to the last screen in the Maintenance Plan Wizard. This screen presents a summary of the Maintenance Plan that we are about to create, and also allows us to name the plan:

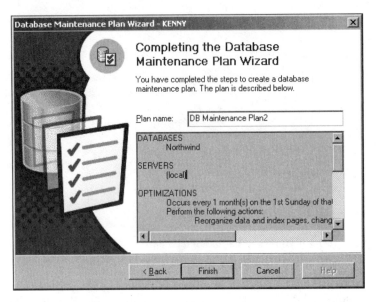

I suggest you give the Maintenance Plan an appropriate name when you first create it as the name specified is used to create jobs in the SQL Server Agent. Even if you go back and rename a plan from the default DB Maintenance PlanX at some point in the future, the jobs are not renamed, and this can lead to confusion.

If all your databases have the same needs you can include these all within one maintenance plan, however, if your databases have different needs, such as the time and frequency of backups, you can create multiple database plans customized for each requirement. That's all there is to it. We have successfully created a regular, hassle-free Maintenance Plan that will take care of some of the more basic day-to-day operations that our database requires.

Archiving Analysis Databases

So far in this chapter we have only been discussing maintenance tasks that relate to SQL Server relational databases, however it is also important to also consider the backup requirements for our Analysis Service databases. As all the data contained in an Analysis database is extracted from an existing data source it is not important to back these up for the purpose of protecting from data loss. Instead, we backup an Analysis database to retain our configuration information as well as allowing for much faster restoration than reprocessing all of our Analysis objects.

Archive Creation

Backup of an Analysis database is not the same as backing up a relational SQL Server database. The Analysis database is simply a collection of files located on disk; the archival process creates a .CAB file that contains the disk files as well as meta data describing the database. We can create these archive files either through Analysis Manager or using the command line.

Archiving using Analysis Manager

From the Analysis Manager find the database we wish to backup, right-click, and select Archive Database:

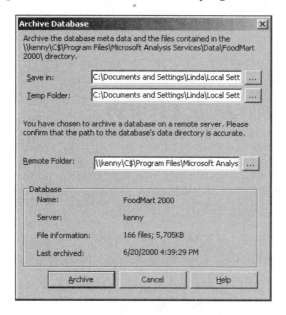

In the Archive Database dialog you can specify two file locations. The first is where the archive .CAB file should be created; the second is where on disk to temporarily build the .CAB file. You should ensure you have enough space available on both the temporary and final locations to store the backup files.

The Remote Folder option will only appear if you are running the backup across the network from a client machine. This option specifies the location of the Analysis database that is accessible from the client you are making the backup from. Unless you have administrative privileges on the Analysis server a specific share that points to the database file path will need to be created with appropriate permissions granted to your user. This is because the source database files will be copied across the network to you client machine where the archive .CAB file will be created locally. Once you click on the Archive button, Analysis will begin creating the backup file.

Archive Creation using the Command Line

As we are likely to want to schedule the backup procedure to run on a regular basis Microsoft has provided a handy command - line utility that we can use create our Analysis database backups. This utility is called msmdarch.exe and can be located in the \Program Files\Microsoft Analysis Services\Binn directory. By default, the location of this executable is not included in your computer's PATH variable, so we must specify the full file path to this executable to use it. It takes the following case-insensitive parameters when used to create an archive file:

```
msmdarch.exe /a [Analysis Server Name] [Path To Analysis Data]
             [Analysis Database Name] [.CAB file name] [Log File Name]
             [Temporary Workspace Path]
```

For example, we can create a backup of the default FoodMart 2000 database by executing the following command:

```
Msmdarch /a SERVER1 "\Program Files\Microsoft Analysis Services\Data\"
          "FoodMart 2000" \FoodMart2000.CAB \FoodMart2000.LOG \temp
```

Archive Restoration

Of course, there is little point in creating a backup if we are unable to restore it. Fortunately, this is a trivial task within Analysis services. You should be aware that to restore an Analysis Services database you need to be in the OLAP Administrations NT group, and you will need write access to the directory where the Analysis Services data files are located.

Archive Restoration from Analysis Services

Open Analysis Services and right-click on the server where you wish to restore the database. Browse and locate the .CAB file that contains the archive you wish to restore. The following dialog box will appear informing you of the restoration you are about to make. If you are restoring over an existing database you will receive a box requesting confirmation before the restore is made. Unlike SQL Server databases it is not possible to restore an Analysis database to a new database with a different name using this method:

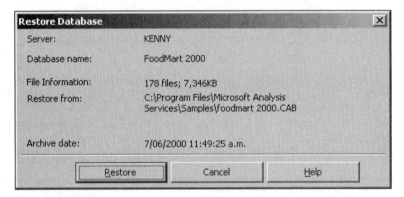

Archive Restoration from the Command Line

Restoration from the command line is very similar to the command we used to create the archive. We use the following command:

```
Msmdarch /R [Analysis Server Name] [Path to Analysis Data]
            [Backup .CAB File Name] [Log File Name]
            [Temporary Workspace Path]
```

If we do not wish to overwrite existing databases, we use a slight variation on this command:

```
Msmdarch /RS [Analysis Server Name] [Path to Analysis Data]
             [Backup .CAB File Name] [Log File Name]
             [Temporary Workspace Path]
```

For example to restore the FoodMart 2000 database and overwrite it if it already exists we would run:

```
Msmdarch /R SERVER1 "\Program Files\Microsoft Analysis Services\Data\"
            \FoodMart2000.CAB \FoodMart2000.LOG \temp
```

Summary

Mundane administration tasks do not require someone sitting at the console running them. These can be scheduled using the SQL Server Agent and the DBA only needs notifying if for some reason the task has failed. This significantly reduces the day-to-day operational tasks that a DBA needs to carry out, freeing them up for more valuable work such as database design, planning, and implementation.

While the database tasks themselves can be scheduled and left to do their own thing, the backup strategy itself should be regularly reviewed to ensure that it is in line with the organization's requirements. Databases are not static, the size and number of users can change regularly, which will affect the backup strategy. Regular review will ensure that with use of the database the ability to recover the database does not become compromised.

Creating reliable backups is the most important task that can be performed for a database. No matter what else you do, all the hard work, not to mention business information, could be lost tomorrow if it is not properly backed up. A good backup strategy should provide everyone with confidence that in the event of database corruption, restoration is possible.

Data Warehouse

Index

A Guide to the Index

The index is arranged hierarchically, in alphabetical order, with symbols preceding the letter A. Most second-level entries and many third-level entries also occur as first-level entries. This is to ensure that users will find the information they require however they choose to search for it.

W

X

p2p.wrox.com
The programmer's resource centre

A unique free service from Wrox Press
with the aim of helping programmers to help each other

Wrox Press aims to provide timely and practical information to today's programmer. P2P is a list server offering a host of targeted mailing lists where you can share knowledge wi your fellow programmers and find solutions to your problems. Whatever the level of your programming knowledge, and whatever technology you use, P2P can provide you with th information you need.

ASP
Support for beginners and professionals, including a resource page with hundreds of links, and a popular ASP+ mailing list.

DATABASES
For database programmers, offering support on SQL Server, mySQL, and Oracle.

MOBILE
Software development for the mobile market is growing rapidly. We provide lists for the several current standards, including WAP, WindowsCE, and Symbian.

JAVA
A complete set of Java lists, covering beginners, professionals,and server-side programmers (including JSP, servlets and EJBs)

.NET
Microsoft's new OS platform, covering topics such as ASP+, C#, and general .Net discussion.

VISUAL BASIC
Covers all aspects of VB programming, from programming Office macro to creating components for the .Net platform.

WEB DESIGN
As web page requirements become more complex, programmer sare taking a more important role in creating web sites. For these programmers, we offer lists covering technologies such as Flash, Coldfusion, and JavaScript.

XML
Covering all aspects of XML, including XSLT and schemas.

OPEN SOURCE
Many Open Source topics covered including PHP, Apache, Perl, Linux, Python and more.

FOREIGN LANGUAGE
Several lists dedicated to Spanish and German speaking programmers categories include .Net, Java, XML, PHP and XML.

How To Subscribe

Simply visit the P2P site, at **http://p2p.wrox.com/**

Select the 'FAQ' option on the side menu bar for more information about the subscript process and our service.